JEWS AND CRIME IN MEDIEVAL EUROPE

Praise for *Jews and Crime in Medieval Europe*

"In *Jews and Crime in Medieval Europe*, Ephraim Shoham-Steiner has painstakingly gathered and incisively analyzed an impressive array of sources to treat the incidence and conceptualization of criminality within Jewish society from a variety of perspectives. Offering a series of suggestive comparisons along geographic, chronological, and societal lines, Shoham-Steiner has produced a strikingly new and fascinating work that will undoubtedly spawn additional discussion and reflection by students and scholars of medieval social and intellectual history."
—Ephraim Kanarfogel, E. Billi Ivry University Professor of Jewish History, Literature and Law, Yeshiva University

"This is an eye-opening study of the largely neglected subject of Jewish crime and criminals in medieval Christian Europe. For too long, apologists have ignored or denied a police blotter of cases—thievery, fencing, assault, and murder, perpetrated by and on Jewish men and women in pre-modern Europe. Shoham-Steiner documents that Jews were more like their Christian neighbors than we thought possible, even while they struggled to rise above the moral chaos of the violent society in which they lived."
—Ivan G. Marcus, Frederick P. Rose Professor of Jewish History, and professor of history and of religious studies, Yale University

"In this meticulously argued book, Shoham-Steiner draws on a range of religious and legal sources to explore a fascinating and almost entirely neglected topic. He reveals that alongside the rabbis and martyrs so revered in Jewish memory, medieval Jewish communities also encompassed thieves, brawlers, murderers, and wife-beaters. In illuminating these darker corners of Jewish life, *Jews and Crime in Medieval Europe* restores medieval Jews to their full humanity, showing them to be subject to the same passions and drives as (and sometimes conspiring with) their Christian neighbors, even as they grappled with unique challenges and restrictions."
—Sara Lipton, professor of history, State University of New York at Stony Brook

"*Jews and Crime in Medieval Europe* is an exceptionally rich work of impeccable scholarship. With his eye on a wide range of crimes that encompassed violence, economic wrongdoings, and sexual transgressions, Ephraim Shoham-Steiner offers an important new perspective on medieval Jewish society. This erudite study of criminal activity, undertaken within the broad context of history, culture, and mentalités, combines methodological sophistication, interdisciplinary scholarship, and highly accessible writing. This work will justly appeal to a wide audience of scholars, general readers, and students."

—Jay R. Berkovitz, Distinguished Professor (Emeritus of) Judaic and Near Eastern Studies, University of Massachusetts Amherst

JEWS AND CRIME IN MEDIEVAL EUROPE

EPHRAIM SHOHAM-STEINER

WAYNE STATE UNIVERSITY PRESS
DETROIT

Copyright © 2021 by Wayne State University Press, Detroit, Michigan 48201. All rights reserved. No part of this book may be reproduced without formal permission.

 ISBN (hardcover): 978-0-8143-4559-7
 ISBN (ebook): 978-0-8143-4560-3

 Library of Congress Control Number: 2020943887

Wayne State University Press
Leonard N. Simons Building
4809 Woodward Avenue
Detroit, Michigan 48201-1309

Visit us online at wsupress.wayne.edu

CONTENTS

Acknowledgments   ix

Introduction   1
What Is Crime?   5
Why Crime?   6
Methodology and Methodological Issues   8
Historical Context   11
The Concepts of Crime and Punishment in Medieval Europe   12
Temporal and Geographical Scope   19
The Scarcity of Historical Information   22
The History of Medieval Crime   25
The History of Jewish Medieval Crime   27
The Sources   28
The Plan of This Book   31

1. "The Thieves That Go from House to House": Jewish Thieves in Medieval Europe   35
   A Time of Great Risk, Opportunity, and Change: The Late Tenth and Early to Mid-Eleventh Century   37
   A Guilty Conscience Needs No Accuser?   71
   For We Can Do No Wrong: Jewish Communal Regulations on Theft   77
   Stealing from Jews   81

CONTENTS

Using Magic to Steal	90
People of the Book: The Rough Waters and the Solemn Banks of the Stolen Hebrew Book Market	92
Battling Theft by Preaching	103
Theft within and from the Community	108

2. "Be Gone Thou Man of Blood": Murder and Murderers in Medieval European Jewish Society — 115

An Israelite and a Levi on the Edge of Tzarfat: A Case from Limoges, Late Tenth Century	120
The Status of a Murderer: What's in a Gaze?	128
"He Who Kills in Our Times": From the Gaonic Period to Fifteenth-Century Europe	131
Lethal Inclinations, Gentiles, and Exile: The Homilies of Rabbi Judah the Pious	136
A Murderer in Our Midst: Addressing Extreme Violence in the Community	149

3. Women and Crime — 191

Methodological Problems	194
Prostitution	197
Violence in the Domestic Sphere	244

Conclusion — 257

Appendix 1: "Lest She Go Astray"	265
Appendix 2: The Plundered Goods Caravan	267
Appendix 3: The Renegade Cleric	269
Appendix 4: Letter of Deliverance	271
Appendix 5: The Case from Poland	275
Appendix 6: The Manual of Penance	277
Appendix 7: A Ḥazan Who Has Killed a Soul	283
Appendix 8: A Responsum by Meir of Rothenburg	285
Appendix 9: The Death of the Wife of Milo	289
Appendix 10: A Responsum by Rabbi Haim Eliezer Or Zaruaʿ	291
Appendix 11: The Case of Isaac and Sara	295

Notes	299
Bibliography	391
Citations Index	427
General Index	431

ACKNOWLEDGMENTS

In putting this project into book form I was aided and supported by many friends and colleagues. I began my work while I was on sabbatical leave at the Tikva Center for Jewish Law and Civilization at New York University's School of Law in 2010–2011. I wish to thank the Center's directors, Joseph H. H. Weiler and Moshe Halbertal for inviting me to be a fellow at the center, as well as for their friendship and wise counsel. During the year at the center, I benefited greatly from conversations with some of the fellows, among them Robert Chazan, Elisheva Carlebach, Maoz Kahana, Perry Dane, and Gary Anderson. During the time I spent conducting this research I greatly benefited from the friendship, wise council and patience of friends with whom I shared some of my observations, and discussed sources, discoveries, thoughts, and ideas. It gives me great pleasure to thank one of my oldest friends in academia, Adiel Schremer, for long hours of discussions, lengthy phone calls, and his shared enthusiasm. I also wish to thank my friends Daniel Abrams, Rainer Joseph Barzen, Simcha Emanuel, Rachel Furst, Yair Furstenberg, Yuval Harari, Eva Haverkamp, Elisabeth Hollender, Ephraim Kanarfogel, Katrin Kogman-Appel, Peter S. Lehnardt, Ora Limor, Sara Lipton, Micha Perry, Dudu Rotman, Elchanan Reiner, Rami Reiner, Pinchas Roth, Haim Weiss, Eli Yassif, and Sara Zfatman. All kindly shared their wisdom and experience with me. My graduate students Chana Rosby Shacham, Ahuvah Liberles-Noiman, and Liat Sivek participated in graduate seminars that focused on some of the material discussed in this book, provided invaluable insight on many sources and helped me refine my argumentation. I owe special thanks to my two "academic running buddies," Kobi Cohen-Hattab, a geographer from Bar-Ilan University, and Josh Goldberg, a neuroscientist at the Hebrew University, who lent patient ears as I held forth, no doubt tediously, about the sources discussed in this book as we gasped our way over Jerusalem's hills three times a week over the past few years. In the words of the prophet: "Each one helps the other, saying to his fellow, 'Take courage!'" (Isaiah 41:6). I would also like to thank the two anonymous lectors appointed by Wayne State University Press who read the manuscript and shared with me their invaluable advice, critique and wisdom.

My department chairs, Motti Zalkin and Amnon Raz-Krakotzkin, as well as the dean of humanities and social sciences at Ben-Gurion University, Haim Hames, staunchly supported my scholarly efforts all along the way.

I would also want to thank the people without whose help this book would never be published: my neighbor and friend Haim Watzman improved this book's manuscript a great deal and Kathy Wildfong and Annie Martin, the editors in chief at Wayne State University Press who encouraged me along the way. Special thanks are owed to Kristin Harpster who accompanied this book through the editorial and production process and to Amy Pattullo who meticulously copyedited the book and gave it its final look.

Finally, I take special pleasure in thanking my family. This book would never have reached fruition if not for their love, support, and encouragement along the way. My mother Ziona Steiner, may she live long and in good health, continually radiates wisdom and kindness. My sons Shahar, Adi, Yuval, Be'eri, and Shaked are a source of constant comfort and pride. Most of all, I am indebted to my soulmate and the love of my youth, Oshrat Shoham-Zidon, who apart from being the accessory to all my crimes and endeavors in life, is a formidable crusader against crime in her capacity as a criminal prosecutor for the Jerusalem district attorney's office.

I dedicate this book to the memory of my beloved father, Ya'akov E. Steiner of blessed memory (1927–2014), a man who was as remote from crime as one can possibly be, but who, along with so many others was the victim of some of the worst crimes perpetrated by mankind in the terrifying years of the Holocaust. My father survived thanks to the intervention of the finest of human beings, those righteous among the nations, among them Raul Wallenberg, Károly Szabó, and Pál Szalai, who could not tolerate the crimes perpetrated against fellow humans and took up the task of saving Jewish lives in the darkest of hours, risking their own lives in doing so. After the war, my father was a member of the generation that rose from the ashes like a phoenix and ascended from the depths of oppression and depression, to build a new family and pursue a brilliant scientific career in Israel. May this book serve as a humble monument to his blessed memory.

INTRODUCTION

> For there are among them [the Jews] those who speak ill of one another
> and those who fornicate with harlots
> and those who thieve
> and those who murder
> and those who swear false oaths uttering the name of the avenging God.
>
> Daniel Goldschmidt, Mahzor le'Yamim Noraim

Such calumny, written in medieval Europe, might look as if it were the work of a blatant anti-Jewish polemist, or a perhaps a Jewish convert to Christianity seeking to paint the Jews as morally degenerate. In fact, it comes from a *piyyut* (a liturgical poem recited as part of synagogue prayers) penned by an eleventh-century Jewish *paytan* (author of *piyyutim*) from northern France, Rabbi Binyamin b. Shmuel. The *paytan* puts this indictment in the mouth of the Attribute of Judgment (*Midat ha-Din*), the personification of the divine attribute of strict justice. He argues that the Jewish people, arraigned before God on Rosh Hashanah (the new year festival and day of judgment), should be given a harsh sentence. The prosecutor in the heavenly court charges that Jews are unworthy of being acquitted. They are not as pious and law-abiding as they claim to be. On the contrary, they are criminals who wallow in sin.

Rabbi Binyamin was neither a chronicler of his time nor a historian writing retrospectively. His *piyyut* is not a historical account of misdeeds perpetrated by members of the Jewish community in northern France to which he belonged. He was a pious liturgical poet bound by the conventions of literary genres characteristic of his time. Nevertheless, many liturgical poets of his era wrote with a specific audience in mind. The list of transgressions he chose to include in this poem is therefore telling. Jewish individuals recited *piyyutim* composed for Rosh Hashanah and Yom Kippur (the Day of Atonement) during their public prayers. While most of the laity was probably not fluent in the flowery Hebrew and Aramaic in which *piyyutim* were written, presumably the congregants understood at least part of what they were reciting. Although Rabbi Binyamin intended the accusations made by the Attribute of Judgment to sound hyperbolic, they were not completely baseless. Indeed, they described a state of affairs not far from the truth. As such, the indictment presented in the *piyyut* is informative. The sins and crimes it ascribes to the Jews may be overstated, but they were not inconceivable to medieval European Jews.

This book had its genesis as I was planning my doctoral project in the late 1990s. I was young and bold enough to suggest a far too ambitious undertaking that would explore social attitudes toward a host of individuals who were deemed marginal in medieval European Jewish society. I was fascinated by the application of social science methodologies to the research of historical societies. Even more, I was intrigued by the growing number of studies that, rather than focusing on the mainstream of medieval society, looked to its margins. In my research proposal I suggested a study of the lives and plights of individuals with physical and mental disabilities, a group I labeled "involuntary marginals." The project was also originally intended to include the lives of and social attitudes toward the criminal margins of Jewish society, whom I termed "voluntarily marginals." The wise counsel of some of my mentors deterred me from such an overambitious undertaking. In the end, my doctoral dissertation considered the lives of Jewish men and women who suffered from leprosy, madness, and physical disabilities. A book based on my dissertation was published in Hebrew in 2008, and in 2014 an updated and slightly abridged version appeared in English. The current book, on Jewish involvement in crime and the social attitudes toward crime and criminals in medieval Jewish society, takes up the material left out of my doctoral dissertation—people who chose to behave contrary to the social norms of their time.

Before we embark on this journey, I want to make it clear that this book is not a history of Jews and crime in medieval Europe. The available sources, both those produced by contemporary Jewish communities and those from the predominantly Christian society in which they were embedded, are not adequate for such an endeavor. We simply do not have the figures and the facts. There is no registry of Jewish involvement in criminal actions, nor are there court records, or even lists of sentences handed down by tribunals, of the kind that have come down to us from other medieval societies. Rather, I here engage in literary archeology to uncover the way crimes of a violent, economic, and sexual nature are depicted in medieval literary works, primarily rabbinic sources, but also other medieval narratives. Examining the way crimes are depicted in these documents, I glean information about what crimes were committed, to what extent the perpetrators were aware that they were breaching norms, and how the transgressors were treated by their respective communities.

The subject of Jewish crime in the Middle Ages cannot be divorced from the libels leveled by Christians at Jews during that era. Christians charged that the Jews killed the Savior, engaged in the ritual murder of Christians, and sought in their greed to defraud and impoverish their Christian neighbors. They were thus, at times, presumptively seen collectively as criminals and murderers. A study such as this one runs the risk of perpetuating such accusations and even being used by modern antisemites to further their agenda. Fear that this would happen has led to self-censorship. Jewish scholars have deliberately disregarded some of the source materials I mine in this book, out of fear of its implications for the image of the Jews, and as part of a long tradition of apologetics. Indeed, I was advised by some colleagues not to pursue the subject.

It is no secret that non-Jews, during the Middle Ages and into the early modern and modern periods, often portrayed Jews as criminals. While these accusations were, for the most part, unfounded, in other cases the accusations were not altogether baseless. For example, in 1279, hundreds of English Jews (some accounts put the number at 680, more than ten percent of that country's entire Jewish population at the time) were accused of debasing and devaluing the currency by coin clipping. They were incarcerated in the notorious dungeon of the Tower of London. Many confessed under torture and were subsequently hanged.[1] Coin clipping was very a serious offense in medieval England and elsewhere in Europe. It was seen as an economic transgression, debasing and devaluing legal currency in the pursuit of personal gain, but beyond that was an act of treason, punishable by death, as it undermined popular trust in the royally sanctioned currency.[2] In the end, King Edward I, who had been outside the realm at the time, intervened and commuted the death sentence, suggesting that, in this case, either the Jews were innocent, or that the accusations were exaggerated, or that, for political reasons, he was not willing to act so harshly against the Jews.[3] But that may not have always been the case. The Lemberg (Lviv) edition of the responsa of the thirteenth-century decisor Rabbi Meir of Rothenburg includes a letter of support for his contemporary, Rabbi Judah Sar ha-Birah, in his campaign against Jews he knew had taken oaths not to engage in coin clipping and yet were, in fact, engaging in this felony: "Their hand should be severed till its middle ... for so much blood has been spilled on the account of these coin embezzlers. They have caused the ruin of our brethren who dwell in France and the Island (England) ... and if the will of the inquirer and the respondent be done, I would stretch them on a pole."[4] In other words, while many Jews jailed and executed for these crimes were innocent, some were not. In some places, as in late thirteenth-century England, economic stress and the deteriorating legal standing of the Jews that led to the expulsion of 1290 were driving forces behind Jews' involvement in such crimes.

European municipal, civic, and criminal records from the later Middle Ages, especially those of a more local nature, offer further indications of significant involvement of Jews in crime.[5] Arguably, the sources from outside the Jewish community are often motivated by anti-Jewish bias and prejudice. Research has shown that Jews were more often indicted and falsely accused of crimes than were their Christian neighbors. When convicted, they were sentenced more severely than gentiles who committed the same offenses.[6] Anti-Jewish biases both fed common notions and reacted to them, creating a vicious circle in which truth and falsehood and real and imagined accusations blended together. The phenomenon became ever more prominent as time progressed, toward the fifteenth century and beyond. This is not necessarily indicative of change, however, as the greater number of references might be attributable to the growing municipal bureaucracies in late medieval and early modern Europe. Whatever the case, Jewish crime was not just a figment of the medieval mind and its anti-Jewish biases. As such, it is a social phenomenon that needs to be addressed by historians.

WHAT IS CRIME?

The English word crime originates from the Latin *crīmen*, from the root *cernō*, meaning "I decide," "I give or pass judgment." The criminal thus acts in defiance of society and its authority to promulgate, implement, and enforce laws. The Hebrew word for crime is *pesha'*; in the Bible the term is used to refer to both sin (*ḥet*), a breach of divine law, and a transgression of human authority. When God speaks in the Bible of transgressors, he calls them "*ha-posh'im bi*," "those who transgress against me." They have defied divine authority and sovereignty.

Today crime is commonly defined as a breach of rules or laws that a governing authority has instituted. The authority, using mechanisms such as regulatory or police power, may in response initiate proceedings which, if they end in conviction, can result in a punishment being imposed on the malefactor, such as internal or external banishment, incarceration, or execution. While every crime violates the law, some violations may rank as lesser in the eyes of society, its lawmakers and enforcers. Breaches of contract and contravention of other civil provisions may rank as offenses or infractions. In traditional, premodern societies, crime was at times more broadly defined. For example, a violation of social norms, such as evasion of or refusal to engage in certain religious practices or to profess certain religious beliefs, could be labeled a crime.[7] Jewish religious leaders termed members of their communities who did not dress in distinctive Jewish apparel or who failed to obey certain commandments "criminals of Israel" (*posh'ei yisra'el*).⁸ Most often, though, only activities seen as injurious to the general population or to society as a whole, including activities that may cause serious loss or damage to individuals, were considered crimes. Furthermore, terming an act or behavior a crime asserts the hegemony of a dominant population, or reflects a social consensus condemning such deeds, thus justifying any sanctions or punishments prescribed by society and its lawmakers or guardians.

WHY CRIME?

The human fascination with crime is evidenced by the pervasiveness of criminals and criminal behavior in the news media, film, and literature. It is nothing new—premodern societies were no less avid about the subject than current ones are. Writing about the Norwich blood libel of the mid-twelfth century, British medievalist Gavin Langmuir notes that "The detective story in which the investigator is an amateur without official standing is a particularly English genre." Thomas of Mommouth's book on the topic, he proposes, was "perhaps the earliest example . . . an investigation that was pursued unofficially by an individual who arrived on the scene after a crime, disagreed with the official stance, pursued his own investigation and reported his results in *The Life and Passion of Saint William the Martyr of Norwich*, which Thomas of Monmouth started in 1149/50 and completed in 1172/73."⁹

But it is not the crime alone that enthralled. In medieval times, public executions, floggings, and other punishments of criminals, gory, gruesome, and often theatrically orchestrated, were popular social events that drew large crowds.¹⁰ Such entertainment moved from the public square into the home during the early modern period, as literacy spread and pamphlets and inexpensive quartos brought crime stories to a growing audience of readers.¹¹ Then as now, criminals could become public figures, simultaneously public enemies and popular heroes.

Crime is another prism through which to view a society. The book before you is the product of a comprehensive research project that collected and analyzed evidence from an array of sources on medieval

Jewish involvement in crime and the medieval Jewish criminal underworld. It is a topic that has hitherto, for the most part, been avoided, overlooked, or deliberately ignored. When scholars eventually acknowledged that medieval Jews did indeed engage in crime, they sometimes insisted that the causes lay not inside the Jewish community but in surrounding non-Jewish society, and could thus not tell us much about Jewish life. The implication was that medieval Jewish society was inherently law-abiding and chaste, if not outright holy. It was only because of the expulsions and persecutions Jews endured as an oppressed minority that they were susceptible to criminal corruption and depravity, which infected Jews through their unavoidable daily dealings with non-Jews. In this, scholars were uncritically accepting the way medieval Jewish communities perceived themselves, as more pious and chaste than their surroundings. Although all scholars of medieval Jewish communities may agree that the notion of the *kehilah kedoshah* or *kehilat kodesh*, the sacred community, is more a literary construct than a depiction of reality, the way medieval European Jewish communities are portrayed by scholars remains to this day heavily laden with apologetics.[12]

Two fundamental assumptions lie at the basis of this study. The first is that a society's attitude toward those of its members who are involved in criminal activity is determined not only by actual criminal actions, but also by a much broader context of culture and mentality. By mentality (*mentalité*) I refer to the inexplicit worldview held in common by a large number of people in a given culture—values, beliefs, positions, and everything else taken for granted by those who share it, an understanding or attitude that changes only very slowly and gradually. Mentality is not identical to a learned worldview or to cultural norms, though these play a part in shaping it.[13] A society's attitude toward individuals identified as criminals by others or themselves can serve as a window into that society's mores, and can provide insight into what kinds of ostensibly forbidden activities the members of that society engaged in. It also provides a way into the mindset that shaped how such transgressors understood themselves. While the study of crime and social attitudes toward criminals is by now firmly established in the social sciences, the history of crime, and of social attitudes toward crime and criminals, is relatively new, especially in the field of medieval studies.

METHODOLOGY AND METHODOLOGICAL ISSUES

The historical study of crime and criminality encounters the same seemingly intractable problems that other sorts of sociohistorical research must overcome. Historians, after all, cannot conduct observations of the society they study, as social scientists can. But the field of medieval Jewish social history faces particular methodological problems, given a dearth of archival material from before the fifteenth century. The problem is even more acute because the Jews, as a society, were geographically dispersed throughout medieval Europe. Fortunately, previous generations of scholars blazed a trail for me by showing that a historian can reconstruct something of the Jewish milieu of the time by combining current knowledge of medieval European history and Jewish history with the use of theoretical and analytical tools borrowed from the social sciences to mine Jewish sources. This book has been influenced by medievalists and historians of medieval and early modern Jewry who have integrated historical and social science methods to lay a general theoretical foundation for the composition of social history. While the trail I follow here is relatively new, it runs within the boundaries of a map whose contours and boundaries have been drawn by others with great expertise. Many scholars are now following the trail to expand knowledge of the social history of medieval Jewry.[14]

To obtain information about the Jewish men and women who were involved in what is generally considered crime, I searched out sources that define a person as criminal either by stating so explicitly or by labeling him or her with another term used to designate criminal activity. These sources were, for the most part, not written by the alleged criminals themselves, but rather by external observers. This presents a further methodological difficulty, as the texts offer the point of view of their authors and their judgment of whether the individuals in question were criminals or not. It is the same issue encountered by the study of women, children, and the poor in medieval society as a whole, and medieval Jewish society in particular.[15] Most of the sources discussed in this book were originated, penned, copied, and consulted on by a small group of either Christian or Jewish men belonging to their societies' scholarly and literary elite. This needs to be kept firmly in mind when reading the sources—it is their worldview that is presented. In the absence of a proper demographic database and the relative lack of archival sources, the scholar must work around the fact that he lacks fundamental information that may be impossible to find, such as the number of crimes that were actually committed, the pervasiveness of crime in medieval Jewish society, and the percentage of criminals who were actually tried by a given tribunal. The reader, too, needs to take care not to draw hasty conclusions about how prevalent the breaching of norms and laws was in medieval Jewish society.

Not all writers on medieval crime are compelled to work with such scarce evidence. Historians of medieval England have a relative abundance of sources at their disposal, enabling them to write a proper history of crime. For example, in her book on rape, abduction, and adultery in medieval England, Caroline Dunn looked at 300 cases recorded in manuscript sources alone.[16] No such wealth of material is available on my subject. While the difficulties limit what may be done, there is a silver lining. They can spark a refreshing change in approach to the available sources. Squeezing all the information they offer out of them requires close reading and attention to fine detail.

Another difficulty is that a vast corpus of texts must be surveyed in order to extract the relevant facts. The temporal scope of this work is a large one, from as early as the tenth century to the late fifteenth. On top of that, because of the scarcity of primary sources in any one locality, I have had to cast my net wide to bring in enough material to enable me to draw significant conclusions. Under these circumstances, the texts adduced here come from as far west as England and range to the eastern Slavic frontiers of Europe and even beyond, into late medieval Poland. This poses yet another problem, as law and legal tradition differed over this vast region.

Today laws and legal systems differ between countries or provinces, but this diversity is dwarfed by the multiplicity of jurisdictions and legal systems of medieval Europe. Throughout this era, many political entities were not only divided into hundreds of geopolitical subunits, but were governed by a multiplicity of legal systems. By and large, more than one system of law was enforced in each geopolitical entity, each one applying, or claiming to apply, to a different class of people. Different agents of power competed for jurisdiction over territories, individuals, and groups. Thus an action sanctioned by one of these sets of laws, for the member of one class or estate, might be criminal under another system, or if committed by a member of another class. Christian clergy were governed by a different legal system than that of the burghers who were their neighbors. The burghers, in turn, were subject to a very different set of duties and prohibitions than were the peasants and serfs who came on occasion to do business in the city's marketplaces. Yet, despite this complexity, it was usually quite clear to contemporaries when someone was operating outside of and in defiance of the law. For example, most societies, regardless of their religious beliefs and legal traditions, saw the taking of a human life as abhorrent and transgressive, even though there were cases in which killing a person could be justified.

The Jewish population was treated more or less the same by the Christian authorities throughout Europe. Generally governed by the legal systems of the jurisdictions in which they lived, Jews for the most part enjoyed a certain amount of legal autonomy codified in charters called "privileges." These privileges sanctioned communal self-government, including some measure of judicial authority based on the community's own laws. Jews could bring grievances against other Jews before the Jewish community leadership and rabbinic courts for resolution in accordance with communal edicts and regulations (*takanot*) or Jewish religious law, *halakhah*, implemented by rabbis. The records that have come down to us, and from which I draw part of the evidence I have gathered on Jewish criminal activity, were written by the latter. It should be noted, however, that judicial ledgers and court records, even if they existed, have not survived from the earlier part of the period under study. (These kinds of documents survive from later periods, such as the invaluable records of the *beit din*—rabbinic court—of Metz.)[17] If and when we hear of court proceedings, it is usually in responsa literature that quotes from or summarizes the record of the proceedings.

This does not mean, however, that Jews did not petition authorities outside their communities, invoking and seeking the protection of the legal systems of the Latin West to settle disputes with other Jews. While the *halakhah* strictly forbade this, the practice was not uncommon. The Jewish communal system operated on a voluntary basis, and was limited in its power both to impose physical sanctions against transgressors, including against those who took their cases to gentile courts, and in exacting severe punishment like capital punishment, banishment, and incarceration. As such, it was not at all easy for communal and halakhic authorities to persuade Jews, especially those who had the means to do so and connections outside the Jewish community, to settle their grievances within the communal framework. In any case, when Jews did business outside their communities, they were subject to the judicial system of the state, where they brought suit when in conflict with non-Jews. The records of such cases are a further source of information about Jewish involvement in crime.

HISTORICAL CONTEXT

After collecting the extant material on crime among Jews in medieval Europe, I scrutinized the social attitudes toward the individuals and groups labeled as criminals, as reflected in the texts. These can be derived from both reports about criminals and the writers' own attitudes toward internal criminals and criminals among the surrounding society. With this critical mass of data, I could weigh the evidence from the Jewish arena and compare it to its closest parallel, contemporary Western European Christian society.

This comparative dimension is of critical importance. First, the Jews of medieval Western Europe were an integral part of the society around them. They shared its climate and living conditions, generally spoke the larger society's language, and interacted with it in myriad economic and social ways. They also constantly reacted to the surrounding society by either adopting or rejecting its prevalent norms and ideas. We might expect, then, to see similarities in their responses to identical human phenomena. Contemporary writers shared this belief, asserting that the Jews were influenced by the society around them, despite cultural differences and religious confrontation. The thirteenth-century author of *Sefer Ḥasidim*, for example, states specifically that the social conduct of the surrounding non-Jewish society greatly influenced the lifestyle and mores of local Jews. "In most places, the Jews in each and every city follow the customs of the non-Jews,"[18] he wrote. I thus devote special attention to the non-Jewish environment. I have made an effort to identify points of tangency, similarities, and differences, as well as to present the implicit and explicit polemics conducted by the two societies over Jewish involvement in crime. These could have serious and even lethal implications for Jews, as in instances when accusations of ritual murder arise. The comparative dimension offers another layer of inquiry and insight, as it offers a way of tracing patterns of continuity and change. For example, the author of *Sefer Ḥasidim*'s position on the punishment that should be meted out to a murderer, and his insistence on the importance of compensating the family of the injured party, cannot be understood without reference to the prevalent notions in medieval German society. Germanic law and conduct, after all, shaped the way these issues were perceived, not just among the Germans, but among the Jews of Germany as well.[19]

THE CONCEPTS OF CRIME AND PUNISHMENT IN MEDIEVAL EUROPE

Medieval Europe had a welter of legal systems, which differed in their concepts of what constitutes a crime and how crimes should be tried and punished. The major distinction usually cited is that between English and Continental law. In England, at least from the time of the Norman conquest of 1066, legal proceedings begin with a presumption of innocence, whereas in mainland Europe suspects in crime had to prove their innocence.[20] The English system is adversarial while the Continental system is inquisitorial. The adversarial model puts its trust in the dialectical process of persuasion in the courtroom, while the inquisitional model trusts the state and its officials to pursue the truth in criminal cases. This distinction, although broadly accepted, has also been contested, as popular participation in judicial proceedings, in the form of a jury, was not limited to England alone. Another important factor in the difference between English common law and Continental law was that, from the twelfth century on, the latter gradually came under the influence of Roman law.[21]

Until the twelfth century, criminal trials were initiated both on the Continent as well as in England mainly by individuals who made an accusation against another person; the two people involved were the parties in the proceedings. The trial took the form of a debate between the two of them—the accuser stated his case and the defendant responded. The court decided on the method of proof—either by ordeal or compurgation. The latter is a procedure under which defendants are acquitted on the basis of witnesses they call, who swear under oath to their innocence. In many European regions, influenced by the different forms of Germanic legislation that underscored the importance of compensation, the settlement between the defendant and the injured party (or the victim's kin) took the form of material compensation, with the amount determined in accordance with the gender, lineage, and social status of the injured party or victim. As the influence of Roman law on both Church and lay courts increased on both sides of the channel, the use of proof by ordeal diminished and was eventually almost abandoned, to be replaced by a procedure based on evidence and argument.[22] A consequence of the appeal to evidence, as opposed to the appeal to God, was an increase in the role played by trained legal experts—lawyers. This was the general framework, but the details varied greatly from one medieval European legal system to another.

Many groups in Europe held immunities to the general rule; royal officials enjoyed immunity from prosecution, under what were called royal safeguards. Other classes that enjoyed special protection were traveling merchants and Jews; certain places were also outside the reach of local authorities, among them marketplaces and universities.

Inquisitional proceedings tended to move very slowly in the German lands.²³ In this region, the absence of a central authority of the type that England and France enjoyed, meant that there was a huge variation in procedures.²⁴ This is important, as many of the examples that appear in this book either come from the German lands or are described by Jewish adjudicators from this realm.

Where do the Jews fit into this picture? From the beginnings of Jewish settlement in Europe north of the Alps and Pyrenees, Jews either sought or were offered privileges from European rulers that would not only protect their lives and limbs, belongings, and occupations, but also grant them communal autonomy.²⁵ An essential part of such autonomy was the ability to use internal mechanisms of adjudication and enforcement. Another was immunity from criminal procedures that were common among their Christian peers. From as early as the Carolingian dynasty, perhaps from the time of Charlemagne himself, Jews were largely exempt from trial by ordeal.²⁶ By the late eleventh century, the *Hehlerrecht*, formulated at the Imperial Chancellery of Emperor Heinrich IV (1084–1105), offered protection to merchants, including Jews, in whose possession stolen goods were found. If the person from whom the goods had been stolen found them in the merchant's inventory and wished to regain possession, the original owner had to compensate the merchant for sometimes half and sometimes the entire value of the goods.²⁷ By this time, Jews were legally protected from being prosecuted for trading in illegally obtained goods and spoils of war, an act mirrored by the Jewish legal construct known as *takanat ha-shuk*. We may assume that during the turbulent first half of the century, as opposed to the more peaceful era that followed, such matters were less of a concern and hardly possible to enforce by law.²⁸

The judicial autonomy that medieval Jewish communities enjoyed in criminal cases was, for the most part, limited in the punitive measures it could enforce. It did not include the power to mete out capital punishment, even for the gravest offenses. In this, the Jewish European milieu did not differ much from that of their coreligionists in the Islamic world. In many parts of medieval Europe, the communal body was seen as a miniature state, so that those who breached its trust and inner legal system were treated harshly. This treatment focused heavily on social ostracism and the communal ban. If a member of the community was suspected of reporting the alleged infractions of a fellow-Jew to state or church authorities, he was termed a *malshin* or *moser*, and treated as a traitor.[29] In Jewish eyes, this could be seen as the ultimate crime; the evidence shows that, at least in theory, it was punishable by death. Understandably, the non-Jewish authorities who by and large mandated Jewish legal autonomy were reluctant to sanction harsh measures against Jewish informers, given that such people gave them tighter control over the Jewish corporative body.[30] The Jewish leadership had sufficient bargaining power to obtain permission to punish informers harshly. In general, however, the Jews of northern Europe enjoyed less authority in this matter than did the Jews of Iberia.[31]

Some of the early privileges granted to Jews provide for a Jewish magistrate to be appointed as synagogue elder or official (*archon*), with powers over the Jews of the town comparable to those of the local bishop; indeed, in some cases, the title granted to this person was *Episcopus Iudaeorum*, Jewish bishop, referring more to this person's bureaucratic and magisterial capacity and less to his religious persona. Nevertheless, the exact function of and judicial authority invested in this official is not all that clear.[32] In his analysis of the Jewish communal leadership in early medieval Europe, Kenneth Stow suggests that, in the eleventh and twelfth centuries, there was an attempt to define the communal body as governed by lay leaders, not by rabbis sitting as a *beit din*, a notion supported by Avraham Grossman's research into communal governance in the early days of Jewish settlement in the region.[33] The rise in the prominence and influence of rabbinic figures inside the community circa 1000 and beyond changed this picture. Stow suggests that rabbis gradually took over judicial and arbitrational authority, while the lay leaders (*parnasim*), who lacked rabbinic knowledge, held on to leadership positions. The *parnasim* did not lose authority altogether but, beginning in the eleventh century, rabbinic authority grew, especially in those communities with a strong rabbinic presence and which were home to a rabbinic academy. The Rhenish communities of Speyer, Worms, and Mainz are prime examples.[34] Growing rabbinic power gave Jewish tribunals more authority to address crime, as they were able to mete out communal sanctions such as the ban (ḥerem) based on legal discussions in the Talmud. Nevertheless, even at the height of their success, these tribunals could not or would not impose corporal and capital punishment. Usually, both lay and rabbinic communal authorities were reluctant to turn a Jewish offender over to the non-Jewish authorities, although this was certainly done in extreme cases, when all communal powers had been exhausted. Jews who sought retribution against fellow Jews had fewer scruples. Seeking justice from non-Jewish authorities was always an option that Jews availed themselves of, despite rabbinic condemnation.

In the absence of one centralized secular government and a single authoritative Jewish legal body north of the Alps, the Jewish communities of northern Europe apparently sought to create, and in some cases managed to establish, a supercommunal mechanism to coordinate Jewish practice on many fronts, including how crime was handled. These bodies generated legislation in the form of rabbinic edicts or regulations (takanot).[35] The takanot sought to curb crime, as well as to discourage Jews from appealing to the legal authorities outside their communities in cases involving other Jews.[36] It is hard to say to what extent Jews actually used the criminal justice systems of their non-Jewish neighbors, whether manorial, baronial, royal, or ecclesiastic courts. For the earlier period, that they did so can be deduced simply from the fact that it was proscribed in an edict attributed to Rabbi Gershom ben Judah of Mainz (d. 1028). Direct evidence appears in the more abundant archival material surviving from the thirteenth century, beginning in England. Jews appeared before non-Jewish courts not only when they petitioned them against non-Jews but also of their own volition in cases against other Jews. When non-Jews accused Jews of crimes, or vice versa, the cases were heard in non-Jewish courts. In some cases a Jew so accused was subjected to extreme enforcement and interrogational measures. Jewish communal authorities attempted at times to intervene on such a person's behalf, demonstrating Jewish solidarity, but not always, and not always successfully. In some cases, Jews received punishments harsher, more gruesome, and more humiliating than those imposed on non-Jews.[37]

Under the terms of many of the privileges granted to Jews in medieval Europe, acts of extreme violence lay outside the purview of autonomous Jewish institutions.[38] Nevertheless, such cases were not always tried outside the legal purview of their respective communities. Nor were the accused invariably arraigned in non-Jewish courts and punished more severely. Sources from the late fourteenth and early fifteenth century document Jewish courts imposing mutilation or amputation on violent offenders. Sometimes these practices were justified by Jewish courts on the grounds that they furthered the offender's penitential process. On the other hand, as royal, noble, and ecclesiastical coffers were in constant need of replenishment, a Jew sentenced to death or corporal punishment for a grave offense in a non-Jewish court often got off with a fine or hefty bribe paid by the convict, their family, or the community. In other cases, grave offenses committed among Jews were able to pass unnoticed by non-Jewish authorities due to a rigorously enforced Jewish community code of silence.

Homicide seems to have been far more common in urban societies than in suburban and rural environments. The city, with its denser and more heterogeneous population, and public institutions where diverse people encountered each other (taverns, inns, brothels, slaughterhouses, and urban industrial plants) offered more occasions for crime, in particular for violent crimes like assault and murder. This is not to say that the suburban and rural areas were crime-free; in particular, travelers on the roads between settlements, including major arteries, risked attack and even loss of life at the hands of highwaymen and robbers. One of the most famous cases of the rape of a Jewish woman by two fellow Jewish wayfarers occurred on the road.[39]

Against this backdrop, it is perhaps surprising that, proportionally, a significantly lower percentage of Jews are documented as both the perpetrators and victims of killings and murders in the medieval city, excluding instances in which Jews were killed or accused as part of ethnoreligious persecutions. Medieval European Jews were, by and large, an integral part of the urban segment of the general population. While later in the era they were slowly segregated, sidelined, and restricted to designated living areas, up until the fourteenth century

Jews enjoyed relative freedom of movement and dwelled without restriction in medieval towns and cities. Even where there was a Jewish quarter or a Jewish street, normally not all the inhabitants were Jews.

The statistical discrepancy due to a number of factors may explain this inconsistency. Most obvious is the incomplete nature of city records. Often, municipal legal documents represent only the cases where a body was found, a complaint lodged, and a suspected perpetrator arrested and tried. In the absence of the equivalent of a modern police force and third-party criminal prosecuting entities, not all cases were discussed or even noted. This began to change only in the fifteenth century.

Furthermore, cases that occurred within the Jewish community may have been kept from the municipal authorities altogether, due to the particulars of the local power structure. In some instances, we know that although Jews were considered members of the city, they owed their livelihood and protection to a regional, regal, or even imperial lord. These allegiances and affinities varied greatly, creating situations in which Jews did not appear in municipal records even if they were part of the town's social and economic fabric. Another factor was that violence committed by a member of one of a city's patrician clans against anyone of inferior socio-legal standing was often not recorded in the municipal records, when such record-keeping became more prevalent in the fourteenth century.[40]

Legal historians, including Guido Kisch and Salo Baron, have argued, furthermore, that as the Jewish population's legal standing declined, from the second half of the fourteenth century, the governing authorities tended to tighten their grip on the Jews. Paradoxically, as Jews lost their rights, it became risky to attack Jewish individuals. Royal and imperial protection and the Jews' position as economic assets of the local nobility or the crown served in many instances as a deterrent. Municipal authorities thus preferred to avoid getting involved in acts of violence in which Jews were involved, whether intra-Jewish or even violent acts by Jews against non-Jews.[41]

TEMPORAL AND GEOGRAPHICAL SCOPE

The literature on crime and criminals in medieval Europe, influenced by the *Annales* and the *Geschichte von Unten* (History from Below) schools, as well as the historical aspects of criminological inquiry, indicates that changes (if and when they occurred) can be discerned and understood more deeply when a study covers a long period of time.[42] The temporal scope of this study is thus broad, encompassing the entire period during which Jewish life in the geocultural space called Ashkenaz was at its acme, from the eleventh century to the beginning of the fifteenth century, though a few examples are dated even earlier.

Geographically, the study focuses on the geocultural sphere of northwestern Europe, from England in the west to the Russian frontier in eastern Poland. Regardless of whether Jews first settled communally in the area north of the Alps in the ninth century or lived in some areas even in earlier times,[43] documentary evidence of the existence of Jewish communal life in these areas appears only after the tenth century.[44] The earliest material I have found relating to Jewish involvement in crime comes from the late tenth century. I have chosen the late fifteenth century as my endpoint because, during that century, most of the Jews still living in Western Europe migrated out of the cities and towns and gradually scattered among small rural communities in the German countryside. Many others moved east to Poland and south, to Italy.[45] This constituted a fundamental change in the form of Jewish existence. The Protestant Reformation and the Catholic Counter-Reformation brought about a change in the medieval state of affairs, and thus it seems fitting to draw a line at the end of the fifteenth century.

While the Ashkenazi Jews migrating south to Italy and east to Poland, Bohemia, and Hungary preserved their unique character and traditions in their new homes, they were exposed to new lifestyles and lived within a different cultural atmosphere. Even though these changes took place over a relatively long period of time, some significant junctures are evident at the close of five centuries of medieval Jewish life in Western Europe. One important change was linguistic. Although Judeo-German was spoken in the communities of the

Ashkenazi diaspora until the modern era, different local mentalities infiltrated and somewhat altered the earlier Ashkenazi mindset that held its ground until the large waves of migration. Another important change in the Late Middle Ages was in legal attitudes toward crime, from a system based on lawsuits to an adversarial inquisitorial system that sought to police and regulate society. By the early sixteenth century this system was firmly in place. When discussing the historiography of medieval European crime, David Napolitano noted "the evolutionary and binary paradigm of a transition from an accusatorial process driven by private interests to a public interest-oriented inquisitorial procedure."[46] With the appearance and eventual growth of city- and state-controlled courts and legal systems, from the thirteenth century but more significantly from the fourteenth century, the role of the community in dispensing justice began to decline. Combined with the great forced expulsions and migrations of European Jews, it led to new attitudes toward crimes and criminals.

The current fashion in studies about crimes and criminals in medieval Western Europe is to look at broader phenomena, treating all of Latin Europe as a single unit. At the basis of the claim that Latin Christendom was a single cultural entity is the similarity between the area's political units and forms of government, its sociopolitical organization, material culture, high culture, and cultural-religious underpinnings.[47] The Jews of medieval Latin Europe were, for the most part, members of the population's urban component; in addition to the characteristics they shared with one another, they had, despite their geographical dispersion, much in common with medieval city dwellers. Yet, while the surrounding urban Christian population knew and appreciated the many common denominators the Jews shared with them, they also perceived Jews as a minority and marginal group. Perhaps precisely because of their awareness that the two groups had much in common, they attempted to differentiate and separate themselves from Jews.[48] Indeed, in the eyes of many medieval Christians, both learned and commoners, all Jews were criminals of sorts, and not just criminals but murderers. Deliberately blind to the gospel of Christ and his salvation, the Jews had plotted the death of God's only begotten son. The indictment appears explicitly in Matthew 27:25:

"And all the people answered, His blood be on us and on our children!" In his book *Christ Killers*, Jeremy Cohen writes: "Even before the Gospels appeared, the apostle Paul (or, more probably, one of his disciples) portrayed the Jews as Christ's killers.... But though the New Testament clearly looks to the Jews as responsible for the death of Jesus, Paul and the evangelists did not yet condemn all Jews, by the very fact of their Jewishness, as murderers of the son of God and his messiah. That condemnation, however, was soon to come." The presumption that all Jews were guilty of Christ's death simply by virtue of their being Jews was well established by the Middle Ages in both theological works aimed at the learned elite and in popular media, such as sermons, passion plays, and visual art.[49] Jews were, of course, well aware of this, as evidenced by the words Solomon bar Simson, the twelfth-century Jewish chronicler of the Crusader rampages of 1096 put in the mouths of the Christian mob as they slaughtered the Jews of northern France and the Rhineland: "They said: 'You are the descendants of those who killed our deity and crucified him... we are his children and it is our responsibility to avenge him upon you.'"[50] While in ordinary times Jewish culpability in Christ's death was not generally used to justify violence against them, when Christian fervor rose or tensions increased, Jews were seen as legitimate targets unprotected by the law.

But killing Christ was not the only crime Jews were accused of collectively. Another heinous offense attributed to them, conceptually linked to the crime of homicide and deicide, was that of ritual murder.[51] Ritual murder, followed later by the desecration of the host—stabbing the consecrated Eucharist until it bled, of which Jews were first accused in Paris in 1290—were understood as distorted reenactments of the crucifixion, black magic aimed at blocking the expiation of sins that Christ's death provided.[52] These purported acts were also imagined to mock the passion of the Christian God and Messiah.[53] The Jews have lived in the shadow of the charges of deicide and ritual murder from first-century Jerusalem through mid-twelfth century Norwich, to the present day in some places.

Beyond seeing them as murderers, Christians believed Jews to be innately carnal and less spiritual than themselves. Enslaved to mammon, they were obsessed with material possessions and the accumulation of wealth. Judas Iscariot's betrayal of Jesus for thirty pieces of silver (Matthew 26:15) was the archetypical example of Jewish perfidy and greed cited in anti-Jewish propaganda. As money-hungry backstabbers, Jews were presumed to be double-crossing their Christian neighbors by commercial deceit in their greed and pursuit of profit.[54] The stereotype was reinforced by mendicant preachers, especially when Jews were increasingly excluded by law from engaging in trade and gradually forced to make their livelihoods from money-lending and other financial occupations.[55]

THE SCARCITY OF HISTORICAL INFORMATION

Finding material for this book was not an easy task. Long centuries of exile and persecution made Jews extremely cautious about publically discussing their own shortcomings, and all the more so the criminal acts of their coreligionists. This changed with the emergence of the *Haskalah* (Jewish Enlightenment movement) of the late eighteenth and nineteenth centuries, when its advocates, the *maskilim*, had no compunctions about mocking their traditional brethren, not only depicting them as uneducated boors but also charging some of them of engaging in economic and sexual transgressions.[56]

Later on in the nineteenth century, with the growth of interest in premodern Judaism, Jewish writers preferred to depict premodern Jewish society as chaste, law-abiding, and spiritually elevated, if not positively holy, in line with popular Jewish self-perceptions from medieval times to the present. Three very powerful historiographical trends adopted this model in the nineteenth and twentieth centuries: the *Wissenschaft das Judentums* (Jewish Studies) movement, Zionist historiography, and Jewish Orthodox historiography. All three narratives shaped the past to fit their present visions, needs, and social agendas. The *Wissenschaft* movement, which operated in western and central Europe in the age of enlightened liberalism, during and after the struggle to legally and socially emancipate the Jews, sought to portray premodern Judaism as more rationalistic and legally regulated than its surrounding medieval non-Jewish counterparts. It promoted the Jewish community as the forerunner of rationalism and a model civil realm. While acknowledging that some Jews had been involved in crime, it largely attempted to downplay the phenomenon and its impact on the Jewish community. These scholars were extremely self-conscious about exposing unfavorable aspects of premodern Jewish society, not just crime but also the belief in magic.

A responsum found in a fourteenth-century copy of an eleventh-century manuscript contains a reference to the ruling of Rabbi Gershom ben Judah of Mainz (d. 1028) that discusses, in considerable and revealing detail, the intricacies of a criminal partnership between two Jews and two local gentile thieves.[57] The two Jews were at odds over the ownership of some coats that one of the Jews had ordered gentile thieves to steal so that he could resell them. The suit eventually reached Rabbi Gershom's court. MS Montefiore 98, where this responsum can be found, was first used by Rabbi Dr. Joel Hacohen Müller (1827–1895) in 1881 as the primary source for a collection of responsa by early Ashkenazi masters that he published in Vienna. The collection, known as *Teshuvot Ḥakhmey Tzarfat ve-Lotair* (*The Responsa of the Sages of France and Lorraine/Lotringen*), is one of the earliest and largest printed collections of halakhic material from pre-Crusade Ashkenaz printed by a *Wissenschaft* scholar. Significantly, Müller omitted the responsum about the Jewish merchant's partnership with gentile thieves.[58] Its omission cannot be attributed to oversight or negligence. Most likely, it was deliberately omitted for apologetic reasons, so as to avoid advertising Jewish involvement in an intricate criminal operation pursued in collaboration with non-Jews. Given the heated debate about the role of "the Jewish language of thieves" in the German press in the 1870s, this was probably prudent at the time.[59] It is just one of many examples of the attempts made by nineteenth-century scholars to draw attention away from, or even conceal, evidence of Jewish involvement in crime in the Middle Ages. Indeed historians and scholars living in an era of antisemitic policies against Jews may have had a legitimate reason not to highlight crime, especially when such reports were (and are still) culled by anti-Jewish writers who collected crimes committed hundreds of years earlier in their advocacy of antisemitic policies.

The second historiographic school that downplayed the role of crime in medieval Jewish life was Zionism. The Zionist political vision was, and in many ways remains, founded on the belief that the Zionist movement and Jewish national aspirations, embodied in a Jewish state, would return the nation from the ahistorical exile to normality and historicity as a nation in its own homeland. In Zionist thought, especially in its early days, normality and materiality, as opposed to a lofty existence, would only be fully realized in the Jewish nation-state.[60] As the famed Hebrew poet and scholar of the national Jewish revival, Chaim Nachman Bialik (1873–1934), reportedly said in the 1920s, "We will know our dream of a nation-state has been fully realized when we have a Jewish state with Jewish thieves, Jewish prostitutes, and a Jewish police force." The implication was that premodern, prenational Jewish life in the Diaspora was lofty, almost spiritual, and hence noncriminal.

The third movement to downplay crime in Jewish history is Jewish Orthodox historiography. Not that Orthodox Jewish writers were alone in the way they had depicted the traditional, preindustrial European world as ideal, pious, and religious—a world that was shattered by modernization, secularization, reformist trends, and globalism. The attempt to idealize it was common also among those non-Orthodox Jews who made Irving Howe's *World of Our Fathers* a bestseller. But this trend was later replaced, in liberal circles, with a more critical view. The Orthodox practice of idealizing the past began in the midst of the large waves of Jewish emigration from Europe in the late nineteenth century.[61] It intensified in the wake of the events of the first half of the twentieth century: the shattering social forces of mass migration, the Holocaust, and the ultrasecularist oppression of the Communist regimes in the Soviet bloc. The surviving Orthodox Jews grew extremely nostalgic about the lost world of their mothers and fathers, attempting to depict it, as well as its historical forerunners, as impeccable.[62] In short, Jewish Orthodox historiography was no less constructed to fit ideological ends than the Zionist mode of writing history.

A fourth, although somewhat different narrative, was what the late Salo Baron called the "lachrymose conception of Jewish history." He was referring to a widespread way of writing Jewish history that paints the medieval Jewish experience in bleak colors, focusing on legal, economic, and social discrimination against the Jews and highlighting the persecution, pogroms, and blood libels they suffered from. Baron argued that the template used by Jewish historians was that of "the history of suffering and scholarship," a phrase coined by his teacher, Heinrich Zvi Grätz. Acknowledging the existence of Jewish crime and a Jewish underworld would undercut the lachrymose agenda. Crime exemplifies empowerment and vitality, contradicting the bleak picture of a subdued and disempowered minority.

THE HISTORY OF MEDIEVAL CRIME

Although the study of crime and the criminal underworld in medieval Europe is not new, it was only in the second half of the twentieth century, with the broadening of the historical perspective of the medieval past, that the subject came to be taken seriously by scholars of the era. As historians turned their attention to the disempowered strata of society, such as women, ethnic minorities, the poor, and the lower social echelons, crime, criminality, and the breach of legal norms came to the forefront. The underlying assumption was that criminals belonged to these strata of society and broke the law in part because they were disempowered, standing outside the circle of social, legal, and religious decision-makers. As part of this new focus, scholars began employing a more varied tool kit to analyze medieval sources, availing themselves of theories and methods from the social sciences, alongside philology and historical inquiry. Such was the work of James Bellamy, who looked at the relationship between crime and social order in medieval England.[63] Another important milestone in this field is the work of James Buchanan Given on homicide in thirteenth-century England.[64] Although it focused on a single century in one country, it is a book of great significance.[65] Given considered more than three thousand homicide cases in twenty eyres in seven different counties, enough for a proper quantitative study of the trends reflected in these court proceedings. Barbara Hanawalt's *Crime and Conflict in Medieval Europe* was another landmark. It broadened the scope of research to crime in general and extended beyond well-documented England.[66] In his book on the medieval underworld, Andrew McCall approached the subject with a different emphasis, discussing the criminal underworld alongside other marginalized and disempowered sectors of medieval European society, an approach I found fruitful and useful in my work.

Another contribution to this discourse was "Historical Trends in Violent Crime: A Critical Review of the Evidence," an influential article by a political scientist, Ted Robert Gurr. Gurr weighed the empirical evidence on secular trends in lethal criminal violence. This study, and several others by Gurr, highlighted, for the first time, what would become a staple of scholarly understanding about crime in medieval Europe: homicide rates declined in Europe over several centuries. The empirical evidence showed that, beginning in the early seventeenth century, fewer and fewer killings were documented, especially in England and Holland, the nations that pioneered modernization. Gurr also showed that the phenomenon slowly spread to other regions.[67] These findings corroborate many of the theses of the "civilizing process" framework proposed by Norbert Elias.[68] Yet, as Manuel Eisner has correctly pointed out, the diffusion of self-control and the ability to withhold anger at agitation was sustained not only by compliance with the state's monopoly of power but by a variety of other disciplining institutional arrangements.[69] The work of Pieter Spierenburg, a particular inspiration for this book's discussion of murder, was greatly influenced by Gurr's analysis and Eisner's modifications.[70]

A more nuanced survey of the state of research into the history of crime, criminals, and law enforcement, by Xavier Rousseaux, appeared in the late 1990s. It presented the main contributions to the field and summarized the scholarly discussion on the subject.[71] Another effort worthy of mention in the field of the historical and social research of crime in medieval Europe is that of Trevor Dean, who focused on medieval Italy. In his recently reprinted monograph (published originally in 2001), he drew some wider conclusions about the trends prevalent in medieval Europe.[72]

THE HISTORY OF JEWISH MEDIEVAL CRIME

While Jewish crime in the medieval period has not received specific attention during the last four decades, it has not been entirely ignored. Some scholars have discussed specific aspects of the medieval Jewish underworld and Jewish involvement in crime in medieval Europe. A number of social and legal historians of medieval Jewry, especially in the last half-century, have discussed cases of crime, violence, and the underworld both in the Jewish milieu in Iberia and in the Western European realm of Jewish existence, Ashkenaz. Avraham Grossman, probing eleventh-century Ashkenazi communal court records preserved in responsa literature, uncovered evidence that parties to adjudicated cases threatened and used violence to intimidate complainants, witnesses, and judges and alter the outcomes of suits.[73] The late Ilana Luria discussed some aspects of organized crime among Jews in fourteenth-century Valencia.[74] In his exhaustive study of what he termed the "Golden Age of Aragonese Jewry" in the thirteenth and early fourteenth centuries, Yom-Tov Assis devoted a chapter to violent crime and Jewish criminals in the *Juderia* (the Aragonese Jewish quarter) as documented in the records of the Aragonese royal court and the responsa literature.[75] Esther Cohen used court records from fourteenth-century Paris to explore some cases involving Jews.[76] Back in the 1960s, Shlomo Simonson researched the life and plight of medieval Italian Jewish vagabonds accused of criminal misdeeds in the later Middle Ages.[77] Similarly, Yaakov Guggenheim and Israel Yuval have both written about Jewish vagabonds in late medieval Germany, highlighting their factual and possible relation to crime mostly from the late fourteenth century to the waning of the medieval period, basing their research on both Jewish and German urban sources.[78] Zefira Entin-Roke'ah, a specialist in medieval England, has investigated the Jewish entries in the rolls of medieval England archived in the Public Record Office in London (now known as the National Archives).[79] One of her articles is about the case of a band of Jewish church robbers who were also accused of host desecration in late thirteenth-century Norwich, just before the Jews were expelled from England in 1290.[80] Maria Boes studied cases relating

28 INTRODUCTION

to Jews that appear in the criminal records of late medieval German towns, specifically from the fifteenth century in Frankfurt am Main. Her comparative analysis exposed the extreme anti-Jewish bias of the city council and magistrates, as reflected in these records and in the penalties imposed on Jews.[81] Jörg Müller revealed the existence of bands of Jewish robbers in the western regions of Germany in the fourteenth century, based on municipal and other German and Latin records.[82]

Note that almost all these researchers have limited their scope to either one region or a specific incident, and usually to one aspect of criminal activity. With the single exception of Assis, none consider the social phenomena, nor do they delve into the criminal's interaction with the larger Jewish community. Furthermore, most writers on the subject have mined mainly archival sources, which are largely not available before the fourteenth century. The large corpus of Jewish material, in particular the legal responsa literature, has barely been touched.

THE SOURCES

As one may imagine, the sources on medieval crime in general and Jewish medieval crime in particular differ from contemporary documentation. Researchers of crime in contemporary society avail themselves of records produced by the police, courts, and the public institutions of incarceration, which are responsible for carrying out the inquiry, justice, and punishment most common in modern society. Medieval Europe was different not only in its record-keeping but in its institutional approaches to crime and punishment. For example, although prisons existed in medieval Europe, they functioned quite differently from our own jails.[83] In general, Jewish communities did not have prisons. In dealing with grave criminal offenders, most communities, if they had the legal option of doing so, imposed a form of voluntary banishment as a punishment. In February 1314, to take one instance, two Jewish thieves were caught red-handed trying to break into the synagogue in the Aragonese town of Daroca in an attempt to steal silver apple ornaments off the wooden cases containing the Torah scrolls. They were apprehended by the communal authorities and held in custody, but apparently the means of doing so were not effective, as the culprits escaped, probably aided by others. The communal authorities decreed a sentence of banishment for five years, severing all business and social ties between the Daroca community and the renegades.[84]

Toward the later Middle Ages, it became more common for a judge or a tribunal, operating as part of a criminal justice system in the general society, to preside over cases and impose penalties. The surviving records document the proceedings or the court's decision and sentence, such as imposing a fine, or corporal or capital punishment. Before this time, however, the records document the accusational processes driven by private claims. Evidence from before the twelfth century is scarce and, when it exists, is generally truncated in the extreme. Even in a relatively well-documented society like that of medieval England, with a centralized system of record-keeping (dating at least from after the Norman conquest) and relatively meticulous court documentation, very little information is available from earlier than the twelfth century.

The earliest European Jewish records date to the late tenth century and early eleventh century, in the Rhineland. They are in the form of legal responsa penned by talmudic scholars for legal and scholarly purposes. Some of these responsa refer to and quote (at times verbatim) court minutes that were kept by Jewish scholars who served as local judges or as courts of appeal. This literature was considered by talmudic and halakhic scholars as among the highest in legal-religious importance. Written in Hebrew, these rabbinic rulings served both as legal precedents and as material for scholarly elaboration and discussion. Thus, although many of the manuscript copies that survive were penned no earlier than the fourteenth century, the prosopography, legal and linguistic markers, and real-life descriptions in the material indicate that many of the attributions of such responsa to actual tenth- and eleventh-century masters may be held to be credible and are accepted as such by most scholars today. They seem to reflect records that were kept, constantly updated, and consulted by Jewish legal authorities over time.

Although the early material in the responsa reflects the autonomy and legal self-government enjoyed by Jews, the records that survive are of civil suits, not criminal trials, heard by local Jewish courts or supercommunal adjudicators, either because they were forwarded by local tribunals or appealed by one of the parties. Given the nature of the material, evidence of criminal activities (such as violence or complicity in violent acts) is conveyed incidentally within the discussion of what is a civil case. The language about the crimes committed is quite clear; for the most part it does not need to be parsed for hidden meanings. The responsa also record the voices of the individuals involved, as they reflect on their actions in a vivid realization that they are breaching norms and conducting themselves in what some around them would consider criminal behavior. This is quite unusual. Today, formal documentation of crime omits the personal viewpoint, which for the historian can be a window onto the surrounding society. The Jewish texts, which quote plaintiffs and their statements in the courts, offer the unmediated voice of tenth-century individuals, a novelty in and of itself. The Jewish records provide a first-hand account of real-life cases where ordinary individuals (not nobles) were involved.

Another methodological problem innate to the material is that of authorship. As traditional rabbinical material originates from the circles of a trained male elite, it requires careful reading, so as to enable the reconstruction of the other voices it contains. Although the texts bring forth the plight of both male and female victims, and offer the voices of the less learned and illiterate as well, these are at times heavily redacted by the rabbinic mediators. It is necessary, when working with this material, to be mindful of this bias.

Criminals generally operate far from the social, religious, and political center, even if some can be found among the powerful and elite. As such, an investigation of criminals differs from one of, for example, the role of intellectuals in a given society. Criminals leave little trace, or hope to: given the clandestine nature of their criminal activities, they seek not to make an appearance in public records, and seldom document their own doings. The sources left to us by those at the center of political, religious, and intellectual life seldom address criminals. Consequently, I had to gather the data piecemeal, and from disparate evidence reconstruct a chronological and geographical whole.

My ultimate aim has been to derive historical data, beyond the anecdotal, from the available documentation. Most of the sources I analyze come from anthologies that have been studied by writers on medieval Jewish legal history. Principal among these are responsa and other types of halakhic literature. Beyond that, I also make use of Jewish ethical and folk literature, Bible commentary, sermons, and commentaries on and interpretations of liturgical poetry (*piyyut*), sources that often bear the strong imprint of the world in which their authors lived and the prevailing mood of commentators, preachers, and their communities. While parts of the material are not new to scholars, they have not yet been examined from the perspective offered here. Likewise, this study required tracking down references to criminal individuals and responses from such individuals themselves, in sources that still exist only in manuscript form.

THE PLAN OF THIS BOOK

This book begins with a historical and philological analysis, after which the sources are addressed by the type of crime they involve. I also differentiate between criminal violations within the Jewish community and those aimed at individuals outside the community (both Jews from other communities and, more interestingly, non-Jews). I do this on the presumption that reactions to crimes whose victims were members of the same community as the criminal would be treated differently than crimes against outsiders.

The next step was to analyze the material using methods borrowed from the social sciences, with the end of offering a theory about the nature of the criminal engagements. Some of the questions I explore are:

> How was criminal behavior defined? Was there a difference between breaking the law and violating longstanding moral or religious codes?
> What caused Jews to become criminals? Was there a criminal "profession"?
> What mechanisms were employed to prevent criminal behavior and to punish perpetrators? How did punishment correspond with Jewish

tradition and talmudic law on the one hand and surrounding legal systems on the other?

How was justice administered, and by whom? When was punishment decreed and enforced by the Jewish authorities?

What was the actual impact of the Jewish penal system on criminals? Were groups of criminals treated differently than individuals? How did the fear of losing group members to the majority Christian society influence social control and law enforcement?

A very common feature of medieval crime policy was the concept of outlawry. Could and did the Jewish community "outlaw" people? Were the legal status of *ḥerem* and *nidui* (excommunication and banishment) the equivalent of outlawry, and if so, in what way?

Was Jewish crime common or rare? How were the criminals, especially those involved in violent crime, viewed by their society? Were there criminals that were heroized, especially when they hurt members of other groups?

Did religious, ethnic, and familial identity matter to the criminals, and if so, in what way?

Were convicted Jewish criminals reported and turned in to state or ecclesiastical authorities, or were such people dealt with only internally? If so, in what manner? Were there regional differences?

How does the Jewish ideal of repentance (*teshuvah*) fit into this picture, if at all? Was there a system of *teshuvah* for those who transgressed? What happened when an individual decided to withdraw from criminal life? Was there a protocol for doing so?

The book is divided into three chapters. For obvious reasons, I could not discuss every aspect of crime, and have chosen three general categories of criminal activity as the main focus. The first section deals with theft and crimes of a financial nature. In it, I explore accounts of Jewish involvement in theft, larceny, fraud, and similar felonies, taking a chronological approach. In the second part of the book, I discuss physical violence and murder, most importantly among Jews but also incidents when Jews attacked others and even cases in which Jews asked non-Jews to commit violence against fellow Jews. In the final section of the book, I look into the role of women in crime and explore the gender differences, surveying the nature of the crimes involving women both as perpetrators and as victims, as well as the reaction to their involvement in criminal activities among medieval European Jews.

Recent advances in scholarship, along with the relatively new scholarly attempts to understand crime in medieval Europe discussed above, have convinced me that I have identified a lacuna that needs to be filled by means of a comprehensive scholarly approach to the involvement of Jews in medieval crime and the underworld, and the manner in which Jews addressed crime within their own communities. Trevor Dean's work serves as a guidepost for my research, touching as it does also on issues previously overlooked by scholars, such as the role of women and gender differences within the context of crime. In turn, this book will complement and complete the picture Dean and others have crafted on medieval European crime in general with new evidence and insight specifically on the role Jews played.

Investigating the lives of those members of the Jewish minority in medieval Europe who engaged in criminal activity or were members of the underworld offers a more nuanced understanding of many larger issues. These include the social stratification of medieval Jewish society and the mechanisms of group cohesion. It also provides a better map of the tension between communal authorities and the individual, and a better understanding of communal relations in premodern societies, especially among ethnoreligious minorities. It serves as another perspective from which to explore Jewish society and its intricate relationship with the surrounding Christian majority society.

1

"THE THIEVES THAT GO FROM HOUSE TO HOUSE"

Jewish Thieves in Medieval Europe

And the thieves that go from one house to another take the hand of the dead with them. [Once they enter a house] they place it in the middle of the room and this way it causes everyone in the house to shiver and to fall asleep. And they take four burning candles and they throw diamond dust on the candles. Then they place the candles in the four corners of the house and it seems to the house dwellers that the house is rolling and moving. And when the thieves wish, they take the hand of the dead and place it on the heart of the owner of the house and they ask him where he has hidden the keys to the gold and the silver hidden in the house and he tells them about all his belongings.[1]

This epigraph, written in Hebrew, appears in a collection of practical potions, spells and amulets copied by an Ashkenazi scribe in the southern Italian city of Trani in the fifteenth century. It describes in great detail not only how a burglar can cast a spell on members of a household so that he can break in and steal their belongings, but also how the burglar can use magic to obtain important information about the household vault, with all its gold and silver valuables.

Theft was by far the most common crime in medieval times.[2] In the urban environment, where most Jews in medieval Europe lived, food, produce, and livestock were stolen as a matter of course. Outside the towns, travelers on the roads between cities were frequently robbed as well, making such trips a risky business, especially if one carried valuables or money.[3] Under the circumstances, theft was severely punished. According to William C. Jordan, "Theft in a society where surpluses were low was not a petty crime unless the coveted article or money was trivial in value, and theft, then as now, was often accompanied by serious physical violence. As a felony, therefore, it merited corporal punishment. Habitual thievery, by this logic, deserved the ultimate sanction, death."[4]

A clear distinction must be made between petty theft and what we still today refer to as grand larceny. Petty theft, such as today's shoplifting, was an everyday event that usually occurred in the marketplace. Throughout the medieval period, many people, at times a vast percentage of the population, lived at the subsistence level, in dire economic need. At a time of rampant poverty, especially during the economic crisis of the late thirteenth century, the indigent commonly filched small items from market stands and pickpocketed other shoppers.[5] Attempts to halt such crime through the imposition of harsher sentences, including the death penalty, often backfired—public hangings, meant to serve as a warning and deterrent to thieves, provided an ideal opportunity for pickpockets to ply their trade.[6]

The burglary of homes or businesses and commercial theft was also common. Such crimes were not always premeditated; the thief might spontaneously exploit an opportunity when chancing upon a house, barn, workshop, warehouse, or store that had been left unattended or unlocked. Such opportunities were the subject of a proverb attributed to the talmudic sage Raba: "A broken fence beckons the thief" (BT Sukkah 26a). Burglaries plotted in advance were much less common. They required choosing potential victims, gathering intelligence, organizing a team, maintaining secrecy and discretion, preparing a getaway plan, and securing potential buyers for the stolen goods.

The last of these, the partnership between the burglar and the dealer, was an essential component of any burglary scheme, especially a large-scale one. Evidence that Jews engaged in trade and commerce sometimes provided this vital service can be found from the beginning of the Jewish presence north of the Alps.

The Latin words *judaious* (Jew) and *mercantor* (merchant) were virtually synonymous in the tenth and early eleventh centuries.[7] According to early eleventh century legal codes, there was a fundamental distinction between the actual perpetrator of a theft and any third party who benefited from the theft, including the dealer who sold the stolen goods. While most thieves in the eleventh century were either condemned to death, maimed, or required to pass a trial by ordeal if they sought to prove their innocence, Jewish thieves were treated differently. Most importantly, they were exempt from trial by ordeal.

A TIME OF GREAT RISK, OPPORTUNITY, AND CHANGE: THE LATE TENTH AND EARLY TO MID-ELEVENTH CENTURY

> Whereas in our times the holy church has been afflicted beyond measure by tribulations through having to join in suffering so many oppressions and dangers, we have so striven to aid it, with God's help, that the peace which we could not make lasting by reason of our sins, we should to some extent make binding by at least exempting certain days. In the year of the Lord's incarnation, 1085, in the eighth *indictio*, it was decreed by God's mediation, the clergy and people unanimously agreeing: that from the first day of the Advent of our Lord . . . until the end of the day of the Epiphany. . . . The purpose of it is that those who travel and those who remain at home may enjoy the greatest possible security, so that no one shall commit murder or arson, robbery or assault, no man shall injure another with a whip or a sword or any kind of weapon, and that no one, no matter on account of what wrong he shall be at feud, shall, from the Advent of our

Lord to the eighth day after Epiphany, and from Septuagesima until the eighth day after Pentecost, presume to bear as weapons a shield, sword, or lance—or, in fact, the burden of any armor... it is unlawful, except for those going a long distance, to carry arms.[8]

With these words, written in 1085 during the reign of Emperor Heinrich IV of the Holy Roman Empire, the armistice that would later come to be known as the Truce (or Peace) of God (*Treuga Dei*) commenced. It marked the beginning of the end of a century and a half of turmoil and instability in the German realm. During this time, in particular prior to 1050, Germany suffered from political, cultural, military, and economic turbulence.[9] Rival local lords fought continually, carrying on age-old feuds, attempting to seize land, livestock, crops, merchandise, and anything else of value from one another, wreaking havoc on their rivals' lands. The loser took the first opportunity to retaliate against the victor. These turbulent times in the Ottonian Empire offered lucrative opportunities for those who were willing to take risks.

In the following pages I consider several local cases recorded in the Jewish legal responsa literature written during the late tenth and early to mid-eleventh century. This literature constitutes some of the earliest documentation from medieval Europe of a world in which Jews and non-Jews partnered for profit. While violent and very risky, it offered not just economic opportunities but also the potential for intimate collaboration between Jews and Christians. The sources I examine here show that the individuals involved in these activities do not fit stereotypes about the criminal underworld.

The geographical area the sources come from was one of the centers of the new and rapidly growing Jewish settlement north of the Alps, the area where many of the traditions now referred to as Ashkenazi were formed. As of the late tenth century, this region produced a steady stream of halakhic and other rabbinic material, including liturgical poetry (*piyyutim*) and exegetical writing. Thanks to these texts, it is possible to trace the outlines of the medieval north European Jewish experience.[10] Through the prism of this literature, the halakhic works in particular, I will portray the times and the people who braved the

TIME OF GREAT RISK, OPPORTUNITY, AND CHANGE 39

treacherous waves of opportunity within the law, on its boundaries, and well outside of it.

Honor among Thieves?

By the early eleventh century, the Jewish presence in northern Europe had become not only slightly more rooted and visible but also better documented.[11] The first families to settle north of the Alps in the ninth and tenth century had grown in size, and the Jewish communities in the Rhineland and Danube basin were bolstered by a constant trickle of new immigrants from southern Europe, especially from Italy and southern France.[12] By the late tenth century, Cologne, Mainz, and Worms, to name just the larger towns, had a visible Jewish presence. Jewish merchants and businessmen were becoming a common sight in the markets, fairs, and trading posts of the Ottonian Empire.

Historiography tends to highlight the Jewish affiliation with trade and commerce. Some have even gone so far as to suggest that non-Jews followed Jews into commerce, and that the entire pre-Crusade beginnings of the commercially driven urban revival in northern Europe should be attributed to the Jews.[13] More recent research has shown that the deep-rooted notion that Jews were at this time engaged in long distance international trade is more of a myth than a fact.[14] Even the critics of the earlier scholarly paradigm agree, however, that intraregional and interregional trade and commerce indeed correlated with a visible Jewish presence during this period.

One of the significant sources of information regarding Jewish involvement in illegal activity during these times is an enlightening case[15] found in responsa[16] from the late tenth or early eleventh-century Rabbi Gershom ben Judah of Mainz (d. 1028), discussing a breach of the inner Jewish laws of *ma'arufiah*.[17]

The laws of *ma'arufiah* (from the Arabic root *'arafa*, "to know") were instituted in early medieval Ashkenazi settlements in an effort to regulate business partnerships between Jews and non-Jews and minimize competition between members of the Jewish communities.[18] In the spirit of medieval European economic logic, which sought to curb and regulate competition rather than encourage it, the laws of *ma'arufiah* stipulated that once a Jew had established a business relationship with a gentile, their relationship would be exclusive. Thus, unless the Jew "owning" this exclusive relationship unequivocally terminated it, no other Jew was allowed to form a parallel relationship with that person, unless the Jew holding the right explicitly authorized it.[19] Breaching the laws of *maʿarufiah* was punishable by a fine or even the imposition of a communal ban, a *ḥerem*, in the more extreme cases.

A suit based on *maʿarufiah* rights came before Rabbi Gershom, probably as an appeal. The dispute described in the query concerned the determination of which Jew possessed the right to an exclusive business relationship with a gentile partner, whom the text refers to as a thief. The plaintiff who brought the suit to a rabbinic court alleged that a fellow Jew had attempted to co-opt his business acquaintances in the hopes of diverting some of the profit they could provide into his own pockets.[20] Both sides went to considerable lengths to prove their case, making extremely revealing statements about the nature of their relationship with the non-Jewish partners, namely the thieves. These statements, reiterated in the question sent to Rabbi Gershom, were designed to show the court how intricate and elaborate the partnership was, how deep the personal acquaintance between the partners, and how intimate their relationship. Given the *maʿarufiah* rule, both sides presented themselves as the legal "owner" of the partnership and the opposing side as the usurper.

The business partnership described in this question was clearly for the purpose of instigating theft and selling the stolen goods thus obtained. From the account in the responsum, it seems that both the thieves and the two Jews—who were neighbors—had a longstanding working relationship. This was no ad hoc partnership but rather a relationship forged by mutual interest, which grew over time. The arrangement between them covered every aspect of the crimes, including planning the theft and extending lines of credit. Evidence of the intimacy of the relationship was that the two parties were able to disclose much information of a personal nature, such as each other's living quarters, the thieves' hideaway, and even the place where the stolen goods were stored. All this would have been highly classified information, inaccessible to anyone outside the partnership.

TIME OF GREAT RISK, OPPORTUNITY, AND CHANGE 41

According to the evidence provided to the court, the bond between the Jews and the gentile thieves was cemented by food and drink supplied by the Jewish partner. This is not surprising considering both that the Jews could not eat food prepared by non-Jews and that the Jews were the senior members in the partnership, with the thieves in their employ.[21] As there is no indication that the food was in fact consumed together, but only that it was provided by the Jews to the gentiles, it may have been part of the payment to the thieves for their services.

The two Jews seem to have had other business connections, enterprises, and sources of income apart from dealing in stolen goods. According to the information the text relates in the name of the plaintiff (who is referred to as Reuven, the standard alias the responsa literature uses for the first party in a dispute or case), during the grape harvest he, his wife, and other members of the household moved to the vine-growing areas outside the town walls.[22] This assertion, when taken together with the fact that the case was brought before Rabbi Gershom of Mainz, suggests that the case came from a Jewish community in the wine country of the middle Rhine and Mosel valley areas, where increasing numbers of Jews lived in the late tenth and early eleventh century. The respondent in the case, alias Shimon, is also described as having other business, involving long-distance interregional trade with the Danube basin area (referred to in the Hebrew text as Donoi). The responsum reports that "his men" were about to set out to that destination when the thieves arrived, offering to sell stolen coats.

The text describes the relationship between the Jews and the non-Jewish thieves, and their usual manner of conducting business. The thieves would scout out places some distance from where they and the Jews lived. Returning to their own town with booty stolen elsewhere seems to have been a way of avoiding suspicion, as they would look no different from legitimate merchants entering town with goods purchased far away. It would thus be easier to sell the merchandise.

On their scouting excursions, the thieves chose targets. They then shared their plans with their Jewish accomplice, including a list of tools that they required for the proposed burglary. So as to demonstrate just how close his relationship was with the thief, Reuven claimed that the tools used in the theft at issue belonged to him, referring specifically to a mallet or a hammer (*kurnas*) that he had given to the thieves to use in breaking a certain lock.[23] The thieves would also provide an assessment of the market value of the goods they proposed to steal. According to the responsum, the Jewish partner would either request in advance that certain items be stolen, or tentatively agree to buy the stolen goods, based on the thief's knowledge and assessment of market value. The Jewish dealer would then pay the thieves an advance, to cover the costs of the operation; the rest of the money was paid to the thieves once the stolen goods were sold. While there are no corroborating texts from this period, presumably the next stage was that the Jew sold the goods and split the proceeds among the partners.

The responsum makes it clear that all the parties involved in the case—not just the plaintiff and respondent, but also the members of the first court and Rabbi Gershom, understood that the activities that formed the basis of the case were not legal. Indeed, the responsum text explicitly uses the terms "thief" and "theft." Furthermore, the conversations reported suggest that it was clear to all parties that Reuven and Shimon were breaking the law. For example, Reuven tells the court that "his" thief was coerced into working for Shimon, who threatened that if he failed to do so, Shimon would turn him over to the authorities. It is a telling bit of information, as is Reuven's admission that when he encountered "his" thief and an accomplice on the way to carry out a threat, he, Reuven, took the precaution of not discussing "business matters," because he was not acquainted with the second thief. The argument that in the Rhineland, during the chaotic and probably lawless early eleventh century, no one was law-abiding is belied by the responsum. While Rabbi Gershom discusses criminal operations freely and candidly, he nevertheless makes it clear that the criminals feared the authorities. Otherwise, they would have had no reason to keep their operations secret.

Shimon's means of intimidating the thief is worthy of some special attention. How could Shimon threaten to turn the thief over to the authorities, if the thief could simply betray him in return? After all, the thief was privy to incriminating information about Shimon. The sword of an informer is almost always double-edged and must be wielded cautiously. Yet, according to the responsum, the thief kept his peace and gave in to Shimon. Perhaps he was the submissive type, but more likely he felt bound to acquiesce because he recognized Shimon's likely immunity in such a case. Apparently, when it came to the law of the land and the long arm of the authorities, the Jewish instigators and the gentile thieves did not stand on equal ground.

Under the privileges granted as early as the Carolingian era and later under the Ottonian empire, Jews, and Jewish merchants in particular, enjoyed a measure of immunity. During this period, and in some cases up until the thirteenth century, many communities in Europe still imposed trial by ordeal on suspected thieves.[24] Rabbi Gershom himself supplies evidence that trial by ordeal and trial by duel were frequently the way accusations of theft and robbery and disputes over property ownership were handled. In another responsum, he writes that "Those suspected, on whom they found nothing, were tried by ordeal—their hands were passed through the fire in accordance with the local [gentile] practice."[25]

Immunity from trial by ordeal was one of the most important privileges obtained by Jews from the Carolingian regime in the ninth century. Although Charlemagne himself had generally sanctioned trial by ordeal, his heirs, such as Louis "the Pious" (reigned 813–40), exempted Jews.[26] As the ordeal was usually imposed when the defendant was not a free man, the exception signified the "elevation of the city Jews above the rank of un-free."[27] Given this difference in the legal procedure, along with the innate inequality before the law that was typical of medieval times, the fact that the gentile thief did not threaten Shimon by exposing him is hardly surprising. Under the law of that time and place, individuals were tried or exempt from trial and granted other privileges based on group affiliation, as well as on their social and economic status.[28] The gentile thief's capitulation to Shimon's intimidation was probably a product of his understanding that Jews with Shimon's affluence and social standing would be favored by authorities and their illegal activity ignored or overlooked, while his illegal actions would cause him harm. A Christian from a rural area would often be subjected to harsher interrogation methods, trial by ordeal, incarceration, and perhaps corporal or even capital punishment. Furthermore, in many cases in medieval local legal traditions, including eleventh-century Rhineland, the actual thief, the one implicated or caught in the act, was prone to much harsher treatment than that accorded to accomplices or business partners.[29]

Rabbi Gershom responds to the long and detailed question put to him (probably by the initial petitioners) concisely and definitively. He stands by the laws of *maʿarufiah* and defends them as binding, not only because they have gained public acceptance, but also because they are sanctioned by *halakhah*. His ruling is probably the reason why this responsum was edited and copied thereafter, until it made its way into the fourteenth-century manuscript that has survived to the present. For the same reason, Avraham Grossman included it in his 1975 article, which was not about crime but rather the earliest medieval European Jewish attitudes to communal rule as reflected in the writings of late tenth- and early eleventh-century halakhists. In his answer, Rabbi Gershom states the following:

> For if this were the case and Shimon came to know about it and seized the opportunity, then he [Shimon] would have been designated a wicked man [*rashaʿ*], as we have learned [BT Kiddushin 59a]: "A poor man who turns a cake [*hararah*, a cake baked by the poor on smoldering coals] and another man comes and takes it from him, the latter is called wicked."[30] And this is in the case of a cake without an owner (*hefker*). In the same fashion, any goods about which one knows that his friend has already struck a deal with the sellers and has fixed a price, and one enters deceitfully [*be-ramaʾut*] and takes the merchandise, it is in these cases that we call him a wicked man.

Notably, Rabbi Gershom discredits Reuven's claim that he is the underdog in this case, that is, the poor man referred to in the talmudic analogy. He further repudiates the argument that Shimon was an evildoer who sought to put Reuven out of business, and rejects Reuven's demand that the coats that he alleges were unlawfully taken from his home be returned to him. Furthermore, Rabbi Gershom rejects any hypothetical claims Reuven might have on the coats, for example, that

TIME OF GREAT RISK, OPPORTUNITY, AND CHANGE   45

the coats belong to him because they were initially in his possession (or on his property—*ḥatzero*).

Rabbi Gershom's attitude toward the two men is also significant. The hint at an ethical statement in his responsum is an allusion to a verse from Genesis. In recounting Reuven's sighting of the two thieves from a distance, Rabbi Gershom uses language that resonates with the biblical passage telling how Judah turned off the road and was tempted by a prostitute (*kedeshah*) he saw at a crossroads (Gen. 38:16). This may have been intended as a play on words for readers of this responsum. We do not know if the phrase was used originally by the unknown individuals who sent the query to Rabbi Gershom, by Rabbi Gershom himself, or whether it was inserted by his scribe or by a later anonymous copyist or compiler of the responsum.[31]

Why did Rabbi Gershom not engage in moral reckoning with the two dealers in stolen goods, given that both of them admitted to engaging in criminal activity? I can only speculate and offer a few possible answers, some of which will not satisfy modern readers. Perhaps Rabbi Gershom was indifferent to the moral aspects of the case. After all, other rabbinic adjudicators do take moral stands in cases that come before them.

Rabbi Gershom's responsum seems to represent his legal reaction to a matter forwarded to him as a court of appeal or as a court of higher consultation. As a legal authority removed from the parties to the case, Rabbi Gershom saw no reason to offer a moral assessment of two men who apparently did not appear before him in person. Responsa written in later periods do contain such judgments. Rashi (Rabbi Shlomo ben Yitzhak), who studied in Germany with the younger peers and disciples of Rabbi Gershom, and whose writing displays many legal features of the eleventh-century Ashkenazi responsa style, explicitly reprimanded transgressors who sought his legal advice. Even in cases where Rashi himself was approached as a court of appeal or a court of higher consultation, he did not hesitate to reproach those seeking his advice directly or indirectly.

Another explanation for Rabbi Gershom's moral silence might be that he sought to bolster his authority and remain relevant to a larger audience. He might well have thought that chastising Jewish criminals would be counterproductive if he wanted to maintain the halakhic system's relevance to the laity. Doing so might have deterred both Jews engaging in similar doubtful activities, and the judicial, religious, and lay leaders who dealt directly with their cases, from consulting with him in the future, not only on criminal cases but on other matters as well.[32]

Another possible explanation for Rabbi Gershom's silence on the moral issue, one that may have been profoundly influential at a later time, relates to the fact that both the perpetrators and the victims of the theft were not Jewish. While it may be jarring to modern readers for whom judicial impartiality is a given, the fact that the thieves were gentile made the ethical issue less pressing from the rabbinic point of view. Despite the clear talmudic injunction to the contrary ("The robbery [*gezel*] of a Canaanite [gentile] is prohibited," BT Baba Kama 113 a-b), Rabbi Gershom clearly acted differently when a Jew was implicated or victimized.

In fact, many of the legal systems of the time made a fundamental distinction between the actual perpetrator of the felony and those who stood to profit from it. This was true also of the Jewish legal system, which followed a similar logic, codified in the *Hehlerrecht* and the "market stipulation" (*takanat ha-shuk*). These two legal codes drew a clear distinction between the person who committed the theft and the person who sold the stolen goods: the former is considered more culpable.

The next case is somewhat different. Also from the responsa of Rabbi Gershom ben Judah of Mainz, it centers on a partnership between a gentile and a Jew that comes to an end at the Jewish partner's death.

Selling Plundered Goods in Tenth-Century Germany

In the "plunder economy" that characterized Germany in the early eleventh century, the line between stolen goods and legitimate merchandise was not all that sharp. Perhaps no one bothered to ask dealers where they had obtained their stock. The imperial *Hehlerrecht* that protected merchants in whose hands stolen goods were found, while promulgated only in the late eleventh century and mentioned explicitly in the privileges granted to Jews, may have simply codified existing

TIME OF GREAT RISK, OPPORTUNITY, AND CHANGE 47

practices and customs. While the facts of the case are not directly relevant to understanding crime in medieval Ashkenaz, the ruling by Rabbi Gershom offers an abundance of information that casts light on the subject. As is the case with many responsa, it is not clear exactly when it was written, but a few historical references in the text indicate that it was probably written in the first years of the eleventh century.[33]

The case centers on a Jewish merchant of stolen goods who disappeared during a business trip, not for the first time. In the past, however, Reuven—the name Rabbi Gershom uses in his responsum—had been kidnapped for ransom, held, and eventually freed when the ransom was paid. Such incidents are said in the text to have happened more than once. We learn that in a previous event Reuven's kin were threatened by his business partners, their rivals, and people whose belongings were plundered and that Reuven had sold. This time, no demand for ransom was forthcoming. Instead, there was a troubling silence.[34]

LEST SHE GO ASTRAY

The matter Rabbi Gershom was asked to rule on in this case involved a fine point of Jewish matrimonial law. A certain Jew, referred to in the responsum as Shimon, wished to seize the opportunity provided by Reuven's prolonged absence to marry his wife. He presumed that Reuven was dead and that his wife was legally widowed. Shimon made a marriage proposal to the wife's kin, one that most probably had to do more with finances than romance, and the would-be groom set a date for the wedding, thus turning this into a matter of some urgency. Shimon was presumably a man of some standing in the community, otherwise Reuven's kin would probably not have considered the proposal.

The problem was that, without proof that Reuven was in fact dead, his wife was not a widow and could thus not remarry. Under Jewish law, a woman cannot divorce her husband unilaterally, so she had the status of an *'agunah* (a bound woman—that is, a woman whose husband has vanished but might still be alive). Rabbi Gershom was asked, probably by the court to whom the case was brought by Reuven's kin, to rule on the validity of testimonies to the effect that Reuven was dead.[35] If Rabbi Gershom was convinced by the testimonies, he could declare Reuven's wife a widow, eligible for remarriage and, more importantly, the heiress to a part of the dead man's fortune, depending on whether there were children or not. The legal ramifications and financial stakes were significant.

Judging from the details offered in the question, the wife seems to have still been rather affluent. Although she had probably spent considerable sums to search for and gain news of her missing husband, she remained wealthy enough to be attractive to a suitor like Shimon. The text mentions no other next of kin—children or siblings of Reuven's—who would also have been heirs to his estate.[36] After deliberating and weighing the evidence, Rabbi Gershom declared Reuven dead and sanctioned Shimon's marriage to the widow, on the condition that the evidence was indeed as solid as possible in these cases. One reason for his ruling was compassion for such bound women:

> My inclination, based on the teachings of my own masters, is that in these matters the Sages were more lenient. They were concerned with the wellbeing of the daughters of Israel, lest they be left 'agunot and lest they go astray. Since death and dying under such circumstances is not uncommon [mita shekhihah] we hold by the presumption[37] that in these matters we allow the woman to marry [by voiding her status as an 'agunah] based even on the testimony of a single witness[38] and even on the basis of hearsay [as opposed to eyewitnesses, required by the letter of the halakhah].

The concern that a woman not be left both alone and unable to remarry, along with awareness that a woman in such a situation might engage in sex outside of marriage, prompted Rabbi Gershom, like many legal authorities in later centuries, to take advantage of every possible legal loophole to release bound women and allow them to remarry. In this particular case, the concerns were probably bolstered by the 'agunah's affluence. The prospect of a financially independent woman with no male supervision was not very appealing to communal and religious authorities and was perhaps another factor in Rabbi Gershom's ruling.

TIME OF GREAT RISK, OPPORTUNITY, AND CHANGE

A Not Uncommon Death

While Rabbi Gershom's ruling is of great interest to students of Jewish matrimonial laws, its importance for the subject of this book comes from the materials and facts the text offers. The first of these is the phrase "death and dying under such circumstances is not uncommon." It offers an observation about the time and place in which Rabbi Gershom lived, as relates that Reuven's way of making his livelihood was highly risky, to the point that it apparently brought about his kidnapping, incarceration, and subsequent violent death. Reuven was neither a thief nor a plundering nobleman. In the Ottonian Empire plunder economy of late tenth and early eleventh century, pillaging raids conducted by local lords and strongmen into neighboring territories were not uncommon. During the long period of civil and political unrest that waned only in the 1030s, after Rabbi Gershom's death, a plundering raid was a common form of retribution exacted by rival feudal lords. It was staged for material gain and as a means by which one feudal lord could demonstrate his superiority to another, as part of an ongoing struggle for power, dominance, and control.

The text also mentions accusations made against Reuven by villagers who were the victims of such raids, as well as by their lords. Their claim was that, by virtue of the fact that he was eager and prepared to buy or serve as an agent for selling plundered goods, Reuven provided an incentive to the feudal lords who were his business acquaintances to launch raids and loot the villagers. A modern equivalent might be victims of car theft claiming that dealers who traded in questionable vehicles and unmarked spare parts were liable for the victims' losses.

We do not know whether these claims were made in a court of a local or regional ruler; perhaps they were part of a legal or semilegal process targeting Reuven or the castle lords mentioned in the text as instigating the raids. The charges against Reuven might have been based on hearsay, market gossip traded by disgruntled victims of raids. Whatever the case, Reuven would have been an easy target, being the weakest link in the power structure of society at the time. It was far easier to accuse a nonnoble city dweller of instigating plunder raids than it was to blame a local or even a rival lord, who were members of the ruling feudal elite and could retaliate violently. The text does not mention that Reuven was targeted because he was Jewish, which is hardly surprising. The responsum mentions that the claims against Reuven were made first by the villagers who were direct victims of plunder raids. They were backed up by the villagers' lords, who were indirectly affected by the raids.[39]

These allegations are significant, as they appear repeatedly with regard to Jews, increasingly so from the late thirteenth century onward, once Jews were reduced to pawnbroking and moneylending.[40] They became part of the larger structure of anti-Jewish sentiments that lasted into early modern times.

In the story at hand, Reuven seems to have made a healthy profit from selling the livestock and goods plundered by marauding lords in areas a bit behind the battle lines. In these probably urban market areas, Reuven could get a good price for the livestock, which was the main object of his trade. Furthermore, his financial situation was good and he had cash in his purse that he could lend, something especially important in a predominantly rural economy based mostly on the barter of commodities. He was thus a valuable business partner. Over time, Reuven expanded his business dealings into other avenues of profit. His transactions were not only connected directly to the plunder raids and the plundered goods. When the castle lords were unable to pay him, Reuven extended a line of credit in the form of small commercial loans, secured by valuables that he held as collateral. Some of the loans were paid, but others expired and the securities were seized by Reuven to cover his losses.

A lot about Reuven's life can be read between the lines in the responsum. Arguments, squabbles, and misunderstandings over the market value of the seized pledged objects, and disputes over payment schedules, frustrated many of his business partners, but did not change the fact that they remained very dependent on him. His commercial game was slipping into a gray area with very high personal stakes. Up to a point the feudal lords who sold Reuven their plundered animals and took out loans from him for pledged objects stood by Reuven. But eventually their grievances built up. Given the violent tenor of society as a whole, Reuven's lower social status as a city dweller made it

TIME OF GREAT RISK, OPPORTUNITY, AND CHANGE 51

increasingly likely that he would come to harm, especially while on the road. Rabbi Gershom's dossier (which we know existed but unfortunately is not copied in the material that made it into the responsa collection) refers to several instances in which not only Reuven himself but also his close family members, perhaps involved in his business, as well as other members of the Jewish community to which Reuven belonged, were apprehended and held captive for ransom by nobles indebted to Reuven.[41] The nobles had no compunctions about employing violence. The toll—financial, physical, and emotional—this took on Reuven and his close associates was heavy. Detention in a late tenth-century castle dungeon or hold, even if only until the ransom payment arrived, could not have been a pleasant experience.[42] The people with whom Reuven had business transactions knew very well that the Jewish community would pay the ransom of any Jew held captive, as the Jewish communities were small and tightly-knit, with many family ties.

Eventually, the text tells us, a larger war broke out involving great lords. During the war the troops of either the French king or the duke of Burgundy laid siege to one of the castles or towns near his home, disrupting Reuven's plans and plunging him into what turned out to be mortal danger. Apparently the large scale of the war between the two noblemen led to a commensurate increase in plunder raids, and thus to the number of people trading in plundered goods. According to Rabbi Gershom's responsum, Reuven, who had once plied his trade almost without competition, suddenly found himself with commercial rivals who were moving looted goods from the front lines to the markets. He had once been probably one of a few dealers in plundered goods who plied the roads in his region; now the region was full of others like him. In response, Reuven altered his accustomed route, changed his plans, prolonged his stay away from home, and went farther than he had originally planned.

The question posed to Rabbi Gershom indicates that the evidence about what had happened to Reuven was unsettling but inconclusive. He was apprehended by enemies who harbored old grudges and whose debt to him had accumulated. This time no ransom demand was delivered, which was not a good sign.

In contrast to the responsum by Rabbi Gershom previously discussed, Reuven's gentile business associates are not here explicitly stated to be thieves. From the plundered villagers' point of view, Reuven was certainly a criminal who was profiting from goods stolen from them. His abductors and eventual murderers also held him responsible for wrongdoings. However, Reuven must have had a unique personality. Balancing his life between his enemies and the people he did business with, who were often far from friendly, required Reuven to be politically savvy and a skilled negotiator. The risks of losing one's freedom and possibly one's life probably deterred other Jews who might have been tempted to join Reuven's profession. The text, unfortunately, offers no hint about what made Reuven's life different from that of other Jews in Central and Western Europe and the German Empire at around the turn of the millennium. It could be that quite a few Jews were involved in such high-risk and dangerous commercial activities, walking a fine line between business and crime.

Nothing Ventured, Nothing Gained

No better illustration of the risks incurred by Jews during the troubled late tenth to mid-eleventh centuries can be found than a third responsum by Rabbi Gershom ben Judah of Mainz. This time Jews were the victims rather than the criminals. The responsum presents a case of a financial dispute over a successful attempt to reclaim plundered goods.[43] The case brought before Rabbi Gershom involves two Jews who suffered losses when their town was raided by a neighboring town's military forces.[44] One of the Jews, again given the alias Reuven, resided in the raided town, while the other, alias Shimon, had assets there but was not present at the time of the raid. The confiscated goods were passed on to local merchants (*tagarin*), who transported the loot to Shimon's hometown to sell it for a profit. Reuven alerted his friend to the possibility that the goods taken from him, Reuven, in the raid could be salvaged if Shimon could quickly assemble a posse to attack the merchants' caravan before it reached its destination.

Reuven's resourcefulness is the most notable thing about the incident. Having lost his possessions to pillagers, he made use of his web of Jewish connections to organize a risky effort to retrieve the lost

TIME OF GREAT RISK, OPPORTUNITY, AND CHANGE

assets.[45] He suggested to Shimon that he recruit armed non-Jewish locals to snatch the goods from the convoy. Shimon replied that he too had suffered losses when the town was raided, and if given the opportunity, he would rather reclaim his own property before that of someone else. In any case, he felt that the proposed operation was very risky and thus rejected the idea. In the end, however, Shimon reconsidered and decided to organize an attack on the convoy after all.

Well aware of the risk involved in attacking a well-armed merchant caravan, Shimon followed Reuven's advice and hired gentile strongmen for the purpose. Their operation was a success; some of the merchants were killed, others fled, while still others surrendered to their assailants. Thus a considerable amount of the goods plundered from Reuven's town was now in the hands of Shimon and his associates.

Once word of the successful raid reached Reuven, he demanded his share of the booty. The raiding party and Shimon initially refused, but Reuven apparently continued to make considerable efforts to receive some sort of compensation. After what appears to be a constant bombardment of appeals, possibly accompanied by physical threats, Shimon capitulated and promised Reuven "a pound" (probably an actual pound) of precious metal from the salvaged goods. Having promised, however, Shimon regretted and retracted his offer. This, apparently, triggered the petition to Rabbi Gershom's court. By alerting his friend to the possibility of retrieving the goods, and having shared with him the destination of the pillaged merchandise, Reuven believed he deserved a share of the revenue derived from the recovered goods.

Rabbi Gershom's ruling is unambiguous. "So I have been instructed from the heavens!" he wrote, a powerful statement in the realm of jurisprudence, testimony to both the decision-maker's sense of authority and the further authority he hoped to gain in the eyes of others who would hear of his ruling.[46] He introduced into the legal discussion the rabbinic concept of a "find," (*metzi'ah*), based on the assumption that once out from the hands of its rightful Jewish and non-Jewish owners, the goods in the convoy were ownerless (*hefker*). That being the case, anyone prepared to run the risk of confronting the armed men who had seized the goods was free to take possession of them. As Rabbi Gershom saw it, the Jew who had assumed the risk earned his profit rightfully; the plaintiff had no right to demand compensation. Furthermore, Rabbi Gershom regarded Shimon's promise to pay Reuven a pound (of silver or other precious metal) not as proof that Reuven's claim had legal foundation, but rather as a gesture of compassion or pity from Shimon, who had taken the risk to secure the goods.

Here, as in other cases from this early period, victims of theft took initiative to recover their losses, rather than resigning themselves to their fate without question. In fact, they exerted considerable energies toward turning the circumstances in their favor. This is also true of the next case.

Theft by Unlawful Taking: The Case of the Sunken River Barge

The next case addresses a concept of importance for the understanding of early Ashkenazi attitudes toward the acquisition of goods from dubious sources. The case of the sunken river barge, also known from the responsa of Rabbi Gershom ben Judah of Mainz, was quoted extensively by later halakhic authorities and by historians of medieval Europe. Rabbi Gershom used this case to reinforce the ground rules of the legal autonomy granted to Jewish communities by the local and regional governments and sovereigns of northwestern Europe. Scholars have cited it to show how halakhic authorities came to endorse the regulations (*takanot*) promulgated by Jewish societies' lay leadership (*kahal*) in the mercantile communities that emerged at this time along the evolving north European trade routes.

The case revolves around a sunken barge that had carried Jews (and possibly others) and their merchandise on a river (most probably the Rhine).[47] Rabbi Gershom's responsum offers many details and obscures others. It does not, for example, recount how the barge sank, although it does say that all the passengers survived. The freight was stowed in large crates in the hold and on deck. Following the accident, the Jewish passengers did all they could to salvage their cargo. One of them (probably Reuven, who had been the owner of much of the merchandise) quickly hired a local gentile for the purpose. The task turned out to be more difficult than it had initially seemed, and the hired hand had no choice but to break open one of the chests in an attempt to salvage its contents. In doing so, he exposed the valuables inside—including money and gemstones (referred to in the Hebrew text as *yohar*, from the Middle-Persian word *gohar*). In the meantime, the sun set, night fell, and the recovery operation could not continue. Under the cover of the dimming light and the chaos that prevailed, a number of local non-Jews purloined some of the man's treasure.[48] He still did not despair of recovering his property, however. First thing the next morning, he appealed to the local authorities, offering them bribes (the text uses the word *shihed*, lit. "bribed") to get them to hunt down the thieves and secure the return of his goods. Probably in response to his demand, the Jewish communities in the area declared that a ban (*herem*) would be issued against any Jew discovered to be in possession of valuables that could be traced back to the cargo belonging to the Jews who had sailed on the sunken barge.

The community response proved not to be precipitous; they may well have had previous experiences with such incidents. At some point during the month that followed the accident, as Reuven continued to try to track down his goods, a gentile approached a Jew (alias Shimon) from one of the communities that had issued the ban, and sold him some of the valuables from the sunken barge. When Reuven learned of this, and apparently identified gemstones from his broken chest, he demanded that the buyer return the goods to him, only to be refused. He petitioned a local court, and the case was subsequently forwarded to Rabbi Gershom in Mainz.

The resulting responsum became a cornerstone of the halakhic sanction of the powers of the lay Jewish communal and supercommunal self-governing bodies of northern medieval Europe. It discusses the force of local non-Jewish government rulings, as well as the authority of the Jewish lay leadership to institute regulations and enforce them by threatening transgressors with a ban. Regardless of who the executive authorities in the community were, Rabbi Gershom ruled, once they had been elected or nominated they represented their community; their decrees had the same force as any rabbinic body. It made no difference if the lay leaders were businessmen with possible conflicts of interest.

Here, however, I want to consider the responsum from a slightly different perspective, not as it bears on judicial authority per se but on the history of crime and lawlessness. Reuven made serious efforts to minimize his loss by immediately approaching the local authorities with an offer to cover their expenses so that they could address the matter. In other words, he offered them bribes, as was the custom at the time. He also asked them to track down the thieves who stole the chest or its valuable contents under cover of darkness. Neither was he so naive as to think that his coreligionists would refuse to buy valuables if offered to them by non-Jews in the aftermath of the barge's sinking. He thus applied to the leaderships of the Jewish communities along the river, some of whose members were heavily involved in trade, to make legal arrangements to guarantee the restoration of his stolen property and ensure that none of their members would attempt to profit off his misfortune. While communal solidarity and unity were important values, Jews nevertheless found it hard to resist the opportunity for financial gain that the accident offered. Eventually, the leaders ruled that Jews were forbidden to buy goods from non-Jews suspected of pillaging the sunken barge, on pain of banishment. As in the cases discussed above, the Jews involved here were not the plunderers themselves, but rather merchants eager to profit from an ostensibly criminal act. Rabbi Gershom accepts the wealthy Jew's suit:

> My inclination on this matter is that Shimon has no claim in this business. For his claim that an object that was lost on a river is anyone's to take has no merit. It should be noted that it was not he who had salvaged the "find" from the river but the Gentile from whom he bought it. And the local city authorities had ruled [at the first Jew's request] that anything recovered from the river must be returned to its rightful owner. And the law of the land is binding and should be followed [dina de-malkhuta dina]. If we examine the laws of the Gentiles, we find that if one salvages someone's property from the river and he admits to have taken it, he may take payment for his trouble, and the object must be returned to the owner. But if he denies that he salvaged it from the river, he is condemned as a thief and is forced to return it to the owner and receives no compensation. The gentile in

question, who has not acknowledged that it came from the sunken barge, is thus a thief, and Shimon is not a "finder" but rather a person, one who bought something from a thief. In this case we invoke the Market Stipulation [takanat ha-shuk]. He should therefore swear as to the sum he paid [for it] and he should deduct his expenses and return the object.... And rule this way also in keeping with the regulations and ordinances instituted by our communities [takanat ha-kehilot]. Shimon must return the object to the other Jew even if the first Jew had despaired of ever retrieving it. For what the court has ruled as forfeited is considered forfeited [hefker beit din hefker] for the scripture reads [Ezra 10:8] "and anyone who did not come in three days would, by decision of the officers and elders, have his property confiscated," and this does not refer solely to the courts of Shamai and Hillel or Rabban Gamliel, for the sages have ruled: "why wasn't the name of each elder [in Num. 11:15–30] given in full?" So that one may not say: "this [elder] is like Eldad and Meidad [who plotted against Moses in Num. 11:24–30] and this [elder] is like Nadav and Avihu [the Aharonite priests who died for their sin in Lev.10:1–7]," (BT Rosh Hashanah 28a) and it is also written [1 Sam. 12:11]: "And the Lord sent Jerubbaal and Bedan and Jephthah, and Samuel" [listing each name in a single verse, as if they are of equal standing]. "All this is to teach us that Jephtah in his generation is as important and authoritative as Samuel was for his generation [Yiftah be-doro ke-Shmuel be-doro]. Thus: anyone appointed as an official [parnas] of the public is like the most important knight [abir she-ba-abirim]. Therefore: Shimon must return the valuables [yohar], since there are several reasons why he had not gained it properly and this is my ruling!"[49]

Rabbi Gershom's responsum is important because the voices and opinions of some of the opponents to his ruling emerge from between its lines. These people defended the Jews who ignored the ban and traded in the goods from the sunken barge a month or so after it sank. Their argument was based on a halakhic principle governing the disposal of items found in or around a river. These are called "river finds," and Shimon's supporters argued that the goods he bought from the gentile belonged to this category. The term refers to a talmudic ruling that, when goods are washed away by a river in an area that is governed by non-Jews, Jews may assume that the original owner of the goods has despaired of reclaiming his property and has thus for all intents and purposes renounced his claim. As such, the goods are regarded as ownerless (*hefker*).[50]

This apparently was the claim made in the court by Shimon, most probably supported by others who may have also purchased goods of the type the community ban prohibited, or whose livelihood depended on such transactions. In the face of resistance from communal and maybe even supercommunal officials, they sought to undermine the officials' authority to prohibit such commerce. They questioned the officials' integrity and charged that they were acting in their personal interest rather than for the good of the community. Accusations of this nature were not uncommon; it was the categorical tenor of Rabbi Gershom's response to such charges that caught the eye of historians of the Jewish communal organization.[51] In his answer, Rabbi Gershom addressed the claims made by Shimon's supporters, both those of a financial nature and those regarding the issue of the community leadership's authority, and rejected them.

It is clear that Rabbi Gershom believed that these people were not only defying the communal leadership's edict but also Jewish law applying to allegedly ownerless goods. Rabbi Gershom believed that the affluent merchant's actions were sufficient proof that he had not despaired of regaining his property and therefore had not lost claim to it. What remains unclear in the responsum, however, is the question of whether Rabbi Gershom considered the Jews who profited from the sale of the pillaged goods to be criminals.

Strange Bedfellows

A fifth case involves several eleventh-century Rhineland Jews who seem to have had shady dealings with a renegade Christian cleric.[52]

The case appears in a responsum attributed to Rabbi Judah ben Meir ha-Kohen (c. 975–c. 1050), also known as Rabbi Judah ha-Zaken (the Elder) or Rabbi Judah Baʻal Sefer ha-Dinim (the author of the *Book of Rulings* or the *Book of Judges*).[53] Rabbi Judah lived in Mainz soon after Rabbi Gershom and was one of his most prominent successors

TIME OF GREAT RISK, OPPORTUNITY, AND CHANGE   59

there. In one of his responsa, he takes up a financial dispute between two Jews.

It is unclear whether the two parties to the dispute were from Mainz, or whether it was one of those cases brought before Rabbi Judah by petitioners from other Jewish communities or forwarded to him as an appellate court. The Hebrew wording of the responsum, "Reuven and Shimon came to the court" suggests the former since Rabbi Judah was the head of the local tribunal in Mainz.[54] As usual, the parties are given the aliases Reuven and Shimon, and are described as having approached the bench to seek justice.[55]

Reuven bought stolen gold articles from a certain Christian cleric, though he claimed that, at the time of the purchase, he was not aware of its illegal source. Only when he overheard a conversation between Shimon and other members of the Jewish community, who were plotting to rob the cleric, did Reuven realize that the gold items he had purchased were of dubious provenance. Aware that he was in a precarious situation, Reuven warned Shimon that, if the matter became known as a result of the scheme Shimon was plotting, causing him financial harm, he would hold Shimon accountable and file suit to be compensated for his losses. In the event, Shimon's robbery scheme took a wrong turn and was found out. Reuven was not only implicated but suffered a double loss, both of the money he paid the cleric in exchange for the gold objects, and of the potential profit he hoped to make by reselling it (apparently the goods were confiscated from him). Reuven therefore sued Shimon before Rabbi Judah's court.[56]

As is often the case in the responsa literature, Rabbi Judah does not provide a systematic account of the facts of the case. These must be reconstructed from the language of the claims made before the court. Most of the narrative included in the text is in the first person, suggesting that a court scribe, or Rabbi Judah himself, took notes when the plaintiff, Reuven, and the respondent, Shimon, presented their claims to the court.[57]

The story began when a *galaḥ* (tonsured cleric) showed up on Reuven's doorstep, offering gold for sale.[58] Given the *ma'arufiah* edict, it stands to reason that Reuven either had previous business dealings with this specific cleric, or with the church, monastery, or priory he represented (or that Reuven thought he represented). It is also possible that this was the first encounter between the two. From Reuven's testimony it is not clear whether he knew, when first approached by the cleric, that the cleric was offering gold fixtures from a monastery.[59] Mainz was home to the Benedictine priory of St. Alban's, which had the largest church in the area until the local cathedral (the Mainzer Dom) replaced it during the lifetime of Rabbi Judah.[60] The Mainz hinterland was home to several other priories and monasteries, and business dealings between the city's Jews and the church establishments in its vicinity were very common.[61] Later, after paying the cleric for the items he offered in local currency, Reuven overheard Shimon and other members of the *kahal* (affluent adult male members of the community) plotting to rob the cleric by threatening to report his criminal activity unless he paid them. Only then, Reuven claimed, did he realize that the objects he had purchased were stolen. Events unfolded very quickly.

It seems members of the Jewish community like Shimon had informers in town; not long after the cleric had sold the golden artifacts and received the payment from Reuven, the Jews learned he had been in the company of a prostitute.[62] The plotters apparently knew not only the exact amount of cash he was carrying on his person, but even the specific denominations of the coins.[63] Shimon, the plotters' ringleader, had devised a plan. Realizing that the cleric was probably fleeing the monastery from which he had stolen the gold, Shimon surmised that, even if the cleric were attacked and robbed, he would not report the theft to the authorities. Seeking to capitalize on the renegade cleric's vulnerability, Shimon suggested to his fellow plotters that he propose a business arrangement to a powerful local lord who was in debt to Shimon: the lord would apprehend the cleric, threaten to expose him, and take the cash on his person as hush money, which Shimon and the lord would then split between them. The lord would use his share of the coins to clear an old debt of three denarii to Shimon and pocket the rest. Shimon assumed that the cleric would not press charges against them, as he himself had committed a much worse crime—stealing from a house of God, selling the stolen goods,

TIME OF GREAT RISK, OPPORTUNITY, AND CHANGE   61

and consorting with a prostitute in breach of his sacred vows. Were he to file a complaint with the authorities, he would only be in worse trouble.

Reuven claimed that, once he learned of the conspiracy to extort money from the cleric, he spoke to Shimon in an attempt to thwart it. He was probably speaking the truth, as Reuven was in jeopardy of being implicated in abetting the cleric's crimes. Reuven thus warned Shimon that he would hold him accountable for any future loss he might suffer if his role was exposed. Shimon assured him that while the plan was foolproof, if something did go wrong, the lord involved in the scheme was on Shimon's side and would straighten things out for all involved.

Reuven, we learn from the responsum, was not overreacting—his worst fears came to pass. The text does not indicate just how it happened, but it states that, after the lord extorted the money from the renegade cleric and paid his debt to Shimon, the cleric's "deeds became known" and an investigation began.[64] The cleric was apprehended by a *sardiot* for questioning.[65] The official is said to have pressured (*dehako*) the cleric, which probably refers to torture or the threat of torture, after which he divulged information about his crime and its abettors, Reuven among them. Reuven was named as the man who had bought the stolen gold objects from the cleric and, as a result, suffered significant financial loss. He filed suit against Shimon before Rabbi Judah's court, charging that Shimon was responsible for the loss.

It should come as no surprise that Rabbi Judah ruled in favor of the respondent, Shimon. The court accepted Shimon's claim that Reuven's loss was an indirect outcome (*grama de grama*) of the former's scheme. Although Rabbi Judah asserted that a court could intervene in certain cases in which a person suffers indirect damage because of the actions of another, in this case, he found, the connection was too remote to support the premise that Shimon's actions had caused Reuven's loss. There were too many intermediary factors for there to be the clear cause-and-effect relationship that Reuven claimed. In his testimony, Shimon offered a legal argument that placed the case into the realm of "findings" (*metzi'ah*), rather than theft. As seen in the previous cases we discussed, this seems to have been the framework for viewing goods that had previously belonged to others (either Jews or Gentiles), but which due to human or natural circumstances were no longer in the possession of the original owner.

Shimon based his defense on the claim that he had not directly harmed Reuven, nor had he had any intention of doing so; the gold, he argued, had been *hefker* (ownerless) to begin with. Yes, the gold had belonged to a church, but once stolen and in the hands of the renegade cleric, the possessory ties between the church and the valuables were severed, rendering the gold ownerless. As such, it was there for the taking, and Shimon made a legitimate claim on the gold's value, using his alliance with the lord to extract the money from the cleric. As Shimon saw it, nothing he had done had anything to do, legally, with the fact that the cleric was eventually apprehended, interrogated, and his dealings with Reuven exposed.

Shimon may have had another basis for referring to the gold as a "find." According to rabbinic rulings based on a passage in the Talmud, while a Jew is forbidden to steal from a gentile, he is under no obligation to return a gentile's lost property (BT Baba Kama 113b).[66] By stating that he was merely claiming a "find," Shimon asserted that his actions should not be regarded by the court as violating the prohibition of stealing from a non-Jew. Shimon was apparently well-versed in Jewish law and could make a sophisticated argument.

The case offers much information on Jewish involvement in crime in the eleventh century, involving, as it does, two Jews who engage in shady ways of making money. Reuven buys and sells precious metals from a dubious source, although it is unclear whether he is aware that the seller is suspect. Shimon, for his part, openly behaves in a criminal manner, encouraging a third party to use violence and intimidation against a man in a precarious legal situation, so as to lay hands on his money. As in some of the previous cases examined, the Jew does not engage in violence himself; rather, he retains others to do so on his behalf.

Contrary to current standards, Reuven's contemporaries marked him, but not Shimon, as a criminal. Reuven's claim that he had no idea where the gold objects he purchased came from, or that they had been stolen, did not convince the gentile investigators. Reuven admitted in his statement to Rabbi Judah's tribunal that he did not ask many questions when the cleric showed up at his doorstep. Furthermore, when he spoke to Shimon about the latter's scheme, he was more concerned that he might lose money than about his reputation as an honest merchant.

Shimon's actions seem to be completely unexceptional to his contemporaries. Shimon and his associates did not plot in secret—they did so openly, at the entrance to Shimon's house, which is why Reuven, who happened to be passing by, was able to overhear them. Although the events that followed were violent and questionable from a moral perspective, none of the witnesses address that issue. While the reason may be the nature of the court records or the redaction of the text, the absence of any consideration of the moral issues is evident. Also interesting is the court's silence regarding the supposed moral implications of the deeds. The impression from the statements by the litigants and witnesses included in the responsum is that they are all confident about their legal status and social standing; there is no sense that they feel inhibited or endangered. While we cannot know for sure if this is typical of the times, it seems that cases like this were not uncommon in the better-documented Rhineland communities in the mid-eleventh century. This case vividly demonstrates that what may seem to a modern reader to be something out of a television series about a crime syndicate, may have in fact been a not uncommon occurrence in the business world of eleventh-century Germany.

Partners in Crime

The previous case featured two ad hoc business dealings between Jews and non-Jews: the cleric with Reuven and the lord with Shimon. Another of Rabbi Judah ha-Kohen's responsa addresses the case of merchants who traveled south from Cologne, up the Rhine, ferrying lamb's wool.[67] The wool was commandeered by a group of gentiles (*goyim*) whose rank and exact social standing is not disclosed in the text. The gentiles subsequently sold the commandeered wool to two Jews, referred to in the responsum text, once again, as Reuven and Shimon. The buyers were fully aware of the provenance of the merchandise. After purchasing the wool, they transported it from their town to

Mainz covertly (*ba-ḥashai*), and once they got it there they sought to sell the contraband as quickly as possible. The reason for their haste is not mentioned, but it stands to reason that it was because the goods were stolen. This urgency may also account for the fact that only one of the partners, Reuven, accompanied the goods to Mainz, while the other partner, Shimon, stayed behind in the town where they had purchased the wool.[68] In Mainz, the wool was bought by a third Jew, who promised to pay for it in two installments, the first upon striking the bargain, when the goods actually changed hands, and a second one at a future date. In the meantime, the Cologne wool traders who were the original owners of the goods had not lost hope of recovering their stolen property. They apparently tracked their merchandise to Mainz, where they took legal action to regain possession of the wool, which had already changed hands three times. The Jewish buyer, alias Levi, who now had the wool in his possession, feared that if the Cologne merchants' legal efforts in Mainz succeeded, he might lose his newly-acquired goods. Levi therefore used his connections and bribed both local officials (*sarei ha-'ir*) and local magistrates (*arka'ot*) in order to prevent the Cologne merchants from regaining control of the wool at his expense. That Levi paid out such bribes suggest that, had he not done so, the law would have restored the wool to its original owners. It is the bribes that brought the case before Rabbi Judah and made for his ruling to be included in a responsa collection. Levi, the buyer, demanded that the money he had paid as bribes be deducted from the second installment he owed to Reuven and Shimon. Levi claimed that the bribes saved the deal from being legally nullified, and he was thus entitled to have this sum deducted from the second installment. Rabbi Judah ruled in his favor. The last fact that the text reveals is that Reuven, who had taken the wool to Mainz, demanded that Shimon, who stayed behind, reimburse him for the discount he was forced to give to Levi, as he was the only representative of the partnership on the scene in Mainz.

This short responsum addresses two transactional relationships. Reuven and Shimon bought goods that had been commandeered by the gentiles. It is not clear whether the gentiles seized the wool at Reuven and Shimon's behest or whether the two Jews simply took

TIME OF GREAT RISK, OPPORTUNITY, AND CHANGE 65

advantage of an opportunity to purchase the stolen goods, as in some of the previous cases recounted above. Two other and no less important transactions are concluded between the two Jews, Shimon and Reuven, and a third Jew, Levi, who was willing to buy merchandise from a dubious source; and between Levi and the officials and magistrates he bribed. There is no evidence as to whether bribing city officials in eleventh-century Rhineland was considered a crime on a par with forcefully seizing goods on the road or waterway; similar sources indicate that such actions were hardly unusual.

As in the previous cases discussed, the Jews in this one were ready to profit from, if not to instigate, a criminal act, while preserving a distance between themselves and the actual illegal or violent seizure of the goods in question. Notably, in all the cases discussed so far, the Jews were not marginal individuals but rather respectable figures from the higher echelons of northern European urban society, equipped with political savvy, ties to local lords, and connections with magistrates and figures of authority.

Twisting the Truth

The last example differs slightly from the previous ones. It comes from the same collection of early eleventh-century Rhineland responsa attributed to Rabbi Judah ha-Kohen. In this case, the blatant criminal acts were committed directly by Jews.

The dispute involved a Jew, alias Reuven, misleading a non-Jewish customer about the true value of a silver object. A gentile, a regular customer of a Jewish dealer, inquired about purchasing a particular kind of silver vessel. Reuven, who did not have such an item in his own inventory, referred the client to a fellow Jew, alias Shimon, who had one. The gentile apparently preferred to deal with a merchant he knew and asked his Jewish acquaintance to act as an intermediary. Reuven left the buyer waiting in his home and went over to Shimon to procure the vessel. Shimon was prepared to sell it, but probably due to previous incidents, or because of Shimon's reputation, Reuven issued a caveat. He explained to Shimon that, as he was on friendly terms with the non-Jewish client, he did not wish to let him down in any way. He therefore explicitly asked Shimon to vouch for the authenticity and true value of the vessel, and to guarantee that it was made of pure silver.[69] Shimon disclosed to Reuven that the vessel was indeed made of silver, but not purely so. Rather, it was made of an alloy that contained some copper. The vessel weighed three pounds and Shimon sold it to Reuven for forty-seven denarii. Reuven returned to his home and sold the vessel to the non-Jewish customer for fifty denarii, collecting a three denarii commission for the brokerage. According to the responsum, the gentile took the artifact from Reuven's premises to his own home that very night before sunrise, suggesting he lived a fair distance away, possibly in the hinterland of the unnamed town in which the two Jews resided.

At a later date, Reuven visited the place where the gentile client lived. He was then confronted by the client, who accused him of telling him that the vessel was from pure silver, when it was actually alloyed with copper. The gentile forced Reuven to refund him the fifty denarii he had paid, probably by threatening him or perhaps by arresting or detaining him. He returned the vessel to Reuven. Reuven returned it to Shimon, complaining that he had been cheated and demanding he take the vessel back and reimburse him for its cost. Shimon refused, using the talmudic maxim: "you have checked the merchandise and you have agreed to it" (*savarta ve-kibalta*). The text suggests that it was at this point that the case came before a halakhic authority.

Acting as arbiter, Rabbi Judah ruled in Reuven's favor, writing that Shimon had deliberately cheated Reuven and his gentile buyer. According to Rabbi Judah, the seller didn't disclose the entire truth when saying that there was a bit of copper in the silver vessel, when in fact it was mostly made of copper. In Rabbi Judah's eyes Shimon's claim that Reuven had checked the merchandise and agreed to the sale may stand only if there is a minor dispute about the vessel's value but not if the entire transaction was based on misleading information. Rabbi Judah ruled that the transaction was void because it had been based on misleading information (*mekaḥ ta'ut*). Therefore, Shimon was obligated to refund the money he had received from Reuven.

Unlike the previous cases, in which the crime itself was committed by non-Jews, while Jews were in the second circle that benefited from the criminal deed, in this instance a Jew deliberately took advantage

TIME OF GREAT RISK, OPPORTUNITY, AND CHANGE 67

of a set of circumstances at another Jew's expense. Furthermore, the phrasing of the responsum indicates that Reuven had probably anticipated that Shimon might defraud him and thus issued an explicit caveat at the time of the transaction. Unlike the case of the renegade cleric, Rabbi Judah thought here that the warning was binding, rendering the sale invalid. As with the previous case, this one too came to be adjudicated due to a dispute between two Jews, one of whom claimed that he had suffered financial loss and damage to his reputation as a trustworthy merchant.

Taken together, these cases from eleventh-century Rhenish Jewish courts are clearly informative about issues of power and self-identity. They also offer insights about authority, especially moral authority, and the role of jurisprudential authority during this period. Finally, they portray the existence of an underworld, or a world of criminal activity, and the manner in which it manifested itself in the Jewish community at the time.

These cases are not new or unknown, but this is the first time they have been examined together from this perspective. They provide us with information about how criminals lived and the codes observed by people, some quite highly regarded, operating on the margins of the law and earning at least some of their living by extorting money, buying and selling stolen goods, and intercepting, by violent means, pillaged property. As dissected by halakhic jurists, they offer a glimpse of these people's motives. However, the responsa do not offer an account of the parties' introspection. Most of the characters appearing in these documents do not appear as three-dimensional human beings. They left no evidence by way of written accounts of their actions, let alone their thoughts. Nevertheless, these jurisprudential accounts offer some hints about the mindset and mentality of some Ashkenazi Jews in the mid-eleventh century.

We do not know how many eleventh-century northern European Jews made their living this way. We do know that Ashkenazi Jewish merchants traveled as far as Kiev, Russia, and eastern Poland, at considerable risk, to bring goods to sell in the Danube, Rhine, and

Mosel basins. Rabbi Judah ha-Kohen's responsa also address cases involving Jews who had large-scale business dealings with the Hungarian monarchy. The responsa I have presented here, however, show that eleventh-century Ashkenazi Jews did not have to travel far to encounter danger in their business affairs. It was an unquiet time. The responsum on the case of the renegade cleric shows that a number of members of the Jewish community were privy to Shimon's plot, and an even larger circle helped facilitate the scheme by providing information. These Jews seem to have simply been doing their best to survive by navigating the conflicting power centers and the treacherous and indeterminate legal standards of their time and place.

That time and place saw outbreaks of anti-Jewish violence, in 1007 in northern France and in 1012 in Mainz. But these were local eruptions of Jew-hatred, nothing to match for the riots and persecutions of 1096.[70] Jonathan Elukin argues, in *Living Together, Living Apart*, that Jews in medieval Christendom lived by and large a "normal" life, much less marked by persecution than commonly believed. Like some historians, I am not convinced by all of Elukin's claims. Yet his portrayal does seem to fit the atmosphere in the Rhineland region before 1096. Prior to the searing and deadly massacres of Jews set off by the First Crusade, day-to-day relations between Jews and Christians were not nearly as bleak as they have often been painted. In all the above cases, Jews wield financial power over others, Jews and non-Jews alike. Similarly, Jews and non-Jews cooperate intimately on money-making stratagems. The legal atmosphere is not one of utter lawlessness, but one in which lacunas in the law and its enforcement offer extensive opportunities.

For example, one of our Jewish contestants, having earned the trust, if not the respect, of local lords, moved from trading in stolen goods to providing the lords with cash loans. These rural lords probably needed the money to advance their social standing in a society that was changing with the gradual pacification of the realm and the economic growth that would mark the second half of the eleventh century. The responsa adduced here offer no indication that their protagonists were fearful on account of their ethnoreligious background.

TIME OF GREAT RISK, OPPORTUNITY, AND CHANGE 69

It may well be that, because of their own feudal system and its values, the landed and fighting nobility looked down on and despised the merchant class. But by the mid-eleventh century, the local aristocracy could not do without them. The fact that the merchant who served as an intermediary in transactions for a noble was itinerant and carried considerable cash was both the source of his power and his vulnerability. The era was one in which the warfare and lawlessness that had just recently prevailed was coming to an end, thanks to new standards and patterns of behavior that would later be exemplified in concepts like the late tenth-century *Pax Dei* (Peace of God) and initiatives such as *Treuga Dei* (Truce of God), first formulated in northern France in the eleventh century. In the early eleventh century, central governments began to demand from noblemen sums of cash that were not readily available to those who lived on small, fortified estates.[71] The new milieu provided business opportunities—risky but potentially lucrative ones—for Jews such as the traveling plunder dealer. By providing the lords with loans against goods given as collateral, the intermediary became a formidable economic force in the noblemen's lives. His ability to legally impound the valuables given as collateral for a loan put him in a powerful yet precarious situation. There was a great demand for his services and the law was on his side, but when he traveled beyond his hometown, the intermediary left the relative security he enjoyed within the local establishment and put himself outside the protection of its laws. In the rural lands of the Holy Roman Empire in the early eleventh century, the real law remained the power of the sword.

A similar impression of relative high legal standing emerges from the account of the Jews who dealt with the renegade cleric. There is no sense that either of them is apprehensive about doing business with this miscreant, nor do they fear the legal repercussions. The man who bought the stolen valuables from the cleric did not think that, if his involvement in the scheme was exposed, he would be singled out for more severe treatment simply because he was a Jew. There is no indication in the text that his religion or ethnic background played any significant role in the events recounted. His opponent in the case gives the impression of being even more uninhibited. He wielded the power of the information he received from associates and town contacts to orchestrate a plan involving a gentile lord that owed him a debt, apparently overdue. The responsum refers to the lord as a *sar*, which may indicate that he was the town's lord, ruler, or a high-ranking municipal official.[72] This is some indication that Jews enjoyed perhaps easy association with eminent members of local society. In any event, in neither of the Jews' cases was their religious affiliation an issue.

Were the Jews in these cases unusual, or was their behavior the norm before 1096? The evidence is too scant to permit more than speculation. It does seem to indicate, however, that at least some Jews, possibly even entire social cohorts within the Jewish community, felt very confident within the privilege system that governed their lives in the eleventh-century Rhenish communities. Some individuals, at least, were willing to take that confidence to its limits. Did that make them criminals? I doubt it. The parties in these cases, as in others of the time, were by no means marginal. The Jew who conspired with the lord to extort and rob the renegade cleric seems to have been a respected member of the *kahal*, a prominent member of the community with friends in high places and a social status that brought people to his doorstep, providing information and business intelligence. Given the circumstances of the eleventh century, it may well be that these Jews, whose behavior would today likely be deemed criminal, were just typical business people attempting to make money in the turbulent waters of their day.

In 1090, Emperor Heinrich IV conferred upon merchants of his realm the "stolen goods privilege," market protection rights that seem to have already been accepted practice.[73] Henceforth, if Jews engaging in financial transactions and lending on collateral were found with stolen goods, they were required to testify under oath how much they had paid for the purchased items. Under the terms of the privilege, it was up to the rightful owner to decide if he wanted to seek to regain his property. The purpose of the privilege was to protect both the dealer, Jews as well as others, and the original owner against economic losses. In case the seller was no longer able to identify the person who delivered the goods, he was to swear an oath about the value of the goods and was entitled to be compensated accordingly.

By the late eleventh century, Roman law was increasingly becoming the basis for the empire's legal system; by the early twelfth century, in keeping with that legal tradition, there is clear evidence of jurists favoring the original owners of the goods.[74] Such preferential treatment left open room for abuse, which is probably why the privilege was promulgated. Nevertheless, it was sharply criticized, including by Jewish authorities, who voiced their concern about the salvation and spiritual well-being of their coreligionists, as well as about the fate of the Jewish communities. One such critic was the early twelfth-century Speyer-based Rabbi Shmuel ben Kalonymus "the Pious."

A GUILTY CONSCIENCE NEEDS NO ACCUSER?

Several paragraphs in one of the opening chapters of *Sefer Ḥasidim* (*Book of the Pious*), a late twelfth or early thirteenth-century compendium describing the customs of a group of German pietists called Hasidei Ashkenaz, address repentant thieves and their problems. This section of the book is attributed by scholars not to Rabbi Judah the Pious of Regensburg (d. 1217), the man most associated with *Sefer Ḥasidim*, but rather to his father, Rabbi Shmuel ben Kalonymus the Pious, whose mystical aura and devotion led him to sometimes be referred to as a holy man (*kadosh*) and prophet (*navi*). Unlike his son Rabbi Judah, who sought to train a close circle of dedicated pietists, Rabbi Shmuel was more of a social reformer and a critic of the ethical habits of his twelfth-century Jewish contemporaries.[75] The first section of the Parma manuscript edition of the *Sefer Ḥasidim*, referred to as *Sefer ha-Yir'ah* (*Book of Awe*), attributed to Rabbi Shmuel, is a brief manual for those who seek to be knowledgeable God-fearing individuals.[76] Nearly all of its final paragraphs relate to theft and problems that arise when a thief seeks to atone for this transgression.

The first passage describes hypothetical thieves who must be provided with a clear avenue of atonement, free of unnecessary obstacles:

> He who stole or robbed, if he repented as a result of the fear of excommunication. Or if he was not placed under a ban of excommunication, but there are witnesses who attest that he returned the stolen objects. It is not permitted to speak vilely

of him, and he and his deeds should not be publicly discussed, even if he has sworn an oath that he had no stolen goods in his possession and later returned what he actually did take, he should not be shamed. We should not bar the door to those who seek penance.[77]

Rabbi Shmuel ben Kalonymus was concerned about thieves seeking to mend their ways. They acknowledged wrongly taking the belongings of others, and sought to turn back the clock by returning the stolen items to their owners. Such penitents were the butt of ridicule and gossip; their sincerity was questioned.[78] Seeking to encourage contrition and restitution, Rabbi Shmuel feared that the public practices meant to deter Jews from committing crimes could backfire and stand in the way of true penance. Ridicule, public shaming, and gossip were all powerful mechanisms for discouraging crime, especially in small and tightly knit societies like medieval Jewish northern European communities. They were effective, however, only with people who cared about their reputations. For those who had no interest in being seen as decent and respectable members of their communities, the deterrent was useless. On the contrary, the social standing of those who lived in a criminal underworld might actually be enhanced by accusations, innuendos, and reports of behavior deemed shameful by others.

According to Rabbi Shmuel, however, a thief who took the big step of admitting his guilt, feeling remorse, and seeking to atone for his sin cannot repent on his own. His community must be prepared to accept him.

In the paragraphs that follow, Rabbi Shmuel recounts instances in which thieves who embezzled community funds, or who shirked paying their community taxes under false pretenses, were moved by remorse (or other social factors) to make amends. Yet it was not that simple. For example, what should be done when the heirs of a deceased man realize that a parcel of land they inherited was stolen? How can they return it if the thief or his heirs were living in it? In another instance, a man stole money but, to salve his conscience, he made large charitable donations. How should he be regarded? Yet another case is that of a man who miscalculated his share of the profits from a business deal and thus cheated his business partner. What happens if the partner has traveled to a distant place and there is no way to compensate him? May the guilty man keep the money?[79]

Rabbi Shmuel does his best to supply answers to even the most extreme cases by prescribing elaborate techniques of reparation, penance, and mortification designed to turn the internal contrition into a socially acceptable penance. It is telling that these remedies appear in a brief guidebook to being a true God-fearing Jew. Furthermore, the work places a broad spectrum of financial acts under the rubric of theft, denying pretty much anyone a clear conscience. This text originates from one of the most extremely pious and penitentially preoccupied circles of medieval Ashkenazi Jewish society. As such, it seems likely that those financial actions that Rabbi Shmuel and those like him counted as theft were common practices in that time and place. In a business-oriented community, where financial negotiations, trade, interest, revenue, and taxation were daily matters, transgressions in this sphere were to be expected.

In contrast with the cases discussed earlier in this chapter, most of the victims of theft described in this discussion are not gentiles but Jews. Nevertheless, Rabbi Shmuel also addresses the potential for moral negligence involved in stealing from gentiles:

> And there is the matter of stealing from a gentile. This may bring about many evils, far more than the same with an Israelite. For when a Jew will come to that place [stealing from a gentile] they [the gentiles] will steal back. And thus this one sinner will cause harm to the rest of the Jews, furthermore he will impair the good reputation Jews had in that town.[80]

According to Rabbi Shmuel, not only is stealing from gentiles morally unacceptable, it is in fact much worse than stealing from a Jew because of the collateral damage it may cause.

The problem highlighted by Rabbi Shmuel seems to be absent from other eleventh-century texts. This may have to do with the genre differences between ethical texts like Rabbi Shmuel's and halakhic ones like responsa, but it may also reflect a change both in the general atmosphere and in some Jews' perception of how they were viewed by non-Jews. Rabbi Shmuel is apprehensive about such a change in attitude toward Jews as a collective. Behind the prospect of a *schande* (disgrace, in German) lay another problem, similar to the other issues on Rabbi Shmuel's list. If one Jew steals from gentiles, other Jews may be affected by the wrongdoer's transgression, a consequence that the thief may not anticipate, but for which he is to blame.

The Jewish victims would be not only the future business partners of these non-Jewish town dwellers, but the town's entire Jewish population. The presumption behind Rabbi Shmuel's position is that, on some level, even transgressors have moral sentiments and are fundamentally inclined to do good. It thus makes sense to alert them to the damage that stealing from non-Jews is likely to cause.

The "Walking Dead" Property Robber: On the Limits of Repentance

Rabbi Shmuel's admonition in *Sefer Ḥasidim* was neither the first nor the final effort made by Jewish ethical writers to encourage thieves to repent and make amends. *Sefer Ḥasidim* offers several examples of ethical admonitions made by Rabbi Judah the Pious (Rabbi Shmuel's son) to spur his disciples to repent their crimes.

One of book's rhetorical strategies is the use of exempla designed to edify and educate the pietists to whom it was addressed, and possibly even a larger audience. A less quoted versions of *Sefer Ḥasidim* offers the following exemplum:

> A story about a man who was wandering in the forest on a moonlit night. He chanced upon a man and he noticed that this person was dead, so he wanted to flee. The person called out to him and said: "Don't run away from me, I will not harm you; you know me, I am so and so the son of so and so." The man replied: "Yes, but aren't you dead?" The spirit then answered: "Because of a field that belonged to a certain person, that I have taken, I am not left to rest, and I am tormented in the forests."[81]

This ghost story is self-explanatory; the deceased's spirit cannot rest properly in his grave nor in the afterlife because of the sins he

A GUILTY CONSCIENCE NEEDS NO ACCUSER?

committed while alive. What is interesting, however, is the story that follows immediately after this one. It is not clear whether the author of this tale is Rabbi Judah himself, a disciple who heard the story from him, or a later copier of the manuscript, but it is worthy of attention, for it puts the ghost story in a larger context, while also discussing its theological aspects.

> I heard a similar story: When a certain gentile died (*nifgar*, lit. became a carcass) his servant was walking and chanced upon him in the night. The dead man said: "Don't run away from me, I will not harm you." The servant answered: "But you are dead, are you not?" The man answered: "Indeed I am! But I am tormented, for I drove someone off his land and took it by force. Now please go to my wife [the text may also be read 'my heir'] and ask that the land be returned to its rightful owner." The servant replied: "But they won't believe me!" The dead master answered: "Tell them to go tomorrow to a certain place and they will see me there." The servant returned to town and told everyone about the encounter with his dead master's ghost, saying: "This is what the man who died a few days ago said to me." He was asked: "Did he give you a sign?" The servant replied: "Yes, he told me that if you go to a certain place you will see him and then you will believe me." So they went to that place and they saw the dead man and they went looking for him in his grave but he was not to be found. The servant then told them what the dead master had told him: "Return the land to the man who was driven off it—then my master will rest in peace."
>
> And we should wonder: What good is all this worth in that world [the afterlife], if the man who died did not repent and did not proclaim on his deathbed that the land should be returned? We should make a distinction [*ḥiluk*], if he [the dead man] was deserving and he was banished from the Garden of Eden for his sins, or if he is tormented or tortured by thorns or by evil angels who mock him, it may actually benefit him if someone prays on his behalf or gives money to charity or if he stole and the heirs return the stolen property. But if he did not merit at all, anything done after his death is in vain, for he may not be delivered unless he decreed in his lifetime and the heirs followed suit.

The story and the ethical discussion that follows are enlightening. First, the text recounts two different stories, one about a Jew and one about a Gentile, both of whom were tormented in the afterlife because of land they had stolen while they were alive. The purpose of the meeting between the living and the dead man in both stories is to tell the living man why the dead man's spirit suffers and, in the second story, to convey a message to the heirs of the master's estate. In the latter case, its intention is to deliver the dead master from his otherworldly torments.

In the final paragraph, the writer distinguishes between the two versions of the story, with the aim of impelling people to abstain from thieving or, at the very least, repent on their deathbeds for their transgressions. He begins by questioning the purpose of the dead revealing themselves to the living, if the living cannot intercede in any way on their behalf. The author suggests that a line should be drawn, distinguishing between the person who was deserving (*zakhah*) and the person who was not (*lo zakhah*). The one who was deserving is the one who was either banished from the Garden of Eden or is being tormented in the afterlife. It is this person's soul that might benefit from intervention by relatives or friends: "It may actually benefit him if someone prays on his behalf or gives money to charity or if he stole and the heirs return the stolen property." The nature of this merit is not stated explicitly in the text; at first glance, the two dead men seem to have committed exactly the same crime. It stands to reason, however, that the critical difference between them is that one is a Jew and the other a non-Jew. The gentile tormented in the afterlife seeks to alleviate his suffering; the Jew in the first story only discloses information about the torments, rather than seeking to remedy the situation or make suggestions about what might be done. Perhaps the dead Jew trusted that the suffering would indeed cleanse him from the sin, while the gentile did not. It is as if the Jew has accepted his fate, while the gentile refuses to submit to his punishment in the afterlife. The story seems to imply that posthumously interceding on behalf of the dead in a manner advocated by Christians is superfluous unless some form of penance or at least recognition of the crime occurred in the sinner's life.

The moral lesson reverses the roles. While neither story offers a denouement, the ethical commentary that follows the stories suggests that it is the Jew, being of a meritorious people, who will eventually be delivered from torment, while the gentile has no such hope. It seems plausible that Jews who encountered this passage knew the talmudic maxim from the story of Onkelos the proselyte. When pondering whether to become a Jew or not, Onkelos used sorcery to call up the souls of prominent figures from the past. The talmudic sages who told the story use these characters to make a clear point: although the Jews may seem downtrodden in this world, their status in the next world shows that they are indeed the chosen people. So testify prominent figures such as the biblical Balʿam and the "evil-doer in Israel," a euphemism for Jesus: "Who is prominent in that world [the world to come]?" Onkelos asks their spirits, and twice he receives the same answer: "Israel [the Jews]."[82] The stories and commentary in *Sefer Ḥasidim* make the point explicit: even if a Jew suffers in the afterlife, he is indubitably in a better position than a Christian. It may seem that Jewish thieves and unscrupulous Jewish merchants suffer the same fate as their Christian counterparts in the afterlife, if they have not repented and made amends in life. But Jews, unlike Christians, suffer only for a time, as they have merit and are deserving of being delivered from their torments.

But, beyond contrasting Jews and Christians, the stories seek to bind together dead Jews and their living kin for the purpose of restitution. The tales are meant to frighten, and to impel Jews to repent and desist from evil deeds, return stolen property, and offer compensation for losses they or their forebears have caused.

FOR WE CAN DO NO WRONG: JEWISH COMMUNAL REGULATIONS ON THEFT

From the eleventh century onward, Jewish communal authorities, as well as ethical writers, did all they could to keep Jews from transgressing against non-Jews. The very fact that such a great effort was made means that such acts were serious and real concerns.[83] Further evidence can be found in sources from the High Middle Ages, such as community regulations. One of the famous collections of these is *Takanot Shum*, a compendium of the rules and procedures of the three largest Jewish communities of the middle Rhine region, Speyer, Worms, and Mainz (*Shum* is an acronym of their names in Hebrew). The regulations were formulated over time, beginning in the early eleventh century (some are attributed to Rabbi Gershom ben Judah of Mainz) and reaffirmed through the twelfth and the thirteenth centuries both in the middle Rhine area and in northern France. Designed to create a uniform code on matters that the communal authorities thought needed proper clarification, the regulations cover a host of issues.[84] Many of the regulations proscribed behavior not explicitly forbidden by the *halakhah*. Among them is an edict prohibiting the purchase of stolen objects of Christian religious significance. Attributed to the twelfth-century *Tosafist* (French and German medieval rabbis who created critical and explanatory glosses on the Babylonian Talmud), Rabbi Jacob ben Meir (Rabeinu Tam), it was formulated as a ban (*ḥerem*), meaning that violators were punished by excommunication.

> An ordinance under threat of the severe ban [*ḥerem*] that one should not accept stolen goods [*gneivot*], such as pictures and statues of the Christian cult [*to'evot*], or a chalice [*gaviah*] and liturgical vestments, Christian prayer book [*sefer tiflut*] and other books used in worship and their liturgical equipment [*meshamshei*], because of the danger emanating from them when found among Jews.[85]

The text is written in coded Hebrew, referring to the Christian objects of cultic use and worship using pejorative and derogatory dysphemisms.[86] Crosses and crucifixes are referred to with the Hebrew word *to'evot*, literally abominations, and the book (probably a missal) is referred to as a "book of profanities," using the homophonic Hebrew similarity between the word for prayers (*tefilot*) and the talmudic euphemism for sexual profanities (*tiflut*).[87] The ban was designed to prevent Jews who trafficked in stolen goods from buying and selling artifacts sacred to Christians. It was extremely dangerous to do so, as gentiles were likely to believe that the objects were obtained not for commercial purposes but for acts of religious desecration, mockery or sorcery. Such dealings thus put not only the trafficker but the entire community in danger. The regulation takes as a given that Jews habitually dealt in stolen goods and traded in them regularly; implicitly, it permitted Jews to buy, sell, or accept as collateral goods without reference to their provenance, as long as they were not objects of religious significance. We do not know to what extent this regulation was obeyed and enforced, though given the volatility of the issue it stands to reason that it was taken seriously.

Another such code comes from the Jewish community of Candia (modern-day Heraklion) on the island of Crete in the Mediterranean. In 1204, after the Fourth Crusade, initiated by Pope Innocent III, was diverted to Constantinople, many of the islands of the Mediterranean formerly under Byzantine rule were divided as spoils of war among the Italian city-states that had participated in the crusade. The island of Crete fell under Venetian rule and began receiving a constant trickle of Jewish immigrants from the European mainland. Thus we find in Candia an amalgam of Jewish traditions from the Greek Romaniote Jews of the Byzantine Empire, North African Jews, Venetian and other Italian city-state Jews, as well as Ashkenazi Jews who immigrated south to Italy and eventually on to Crete.

The text from Candia is a compilation of all of the community's regulations, assembled by the historian Rabbi Elia Capsali (c. 1485/90–c.1550/55), a member of the community.[88] According to Umberto Moshe David Cassuto and Elias Artom, the editors of the 1940 critical edition of this text, Rabbi Elia Capsali continued to work on the compilation as late as 1519. It incorporated regulations of the Candian Jewish community regulations, beginning with the first ten regulations, issued in 1228.

The critical edition is based on the Sasson manuscript. The initial pages of the manuscript were seriously damaged, but the third regulation, of importance for this work, is clear and legible:

> Regulation 3: Do not steal from [and] do not lie to gentiles.
> No one, neither a priest [*kohen*] nor a layman, may steal or lie to gentiles, nor cheat them [*lignov da'atam*, literally "to steal

their mind," meaning to trick and deceive]. For those who lie and steal from gentiles cause the Name [of the Almighty] to be defiled [*hillul ha-Shem*] and it is a criminal deed and it is registered. For they [the gentiles] will say there is no God in Israel "oh Ariel Ariel" (Isaiah 29:1). For it is written: "The remnant of Israel shall do no wrong" [Zephaniah 3:13],[89] and how is it that there are large or small stolen goods among the Hebrews "unless their Rock [the Almighty] had sold them, the Lord had given them up" [Deut. 32:30].

Therefore, in order to keep us away from this disgrace, and remove these foul voices and curses, we took this appropriate regulation [*takanah re'uyah*] upon ourselves and upon our offspring to the end of all time, and based on its merit we will hopefully receive greatness and proper standing.[90]

According to the introduction in the Sasson manuscript, the regulations were formulated by a committee of five and signed by fifteen of the community's dignitaries. The language suggests that Candian Jews were indeed stealing from, defrauding, and lying to gentiles, creating animosity toward the community. Its leaders were thus concerned not only with the ethical well-being, but also with the community's image and the potential for such behavior to instigate anti-Jewish polemics and other negative outcomes like legal sanctions or outright violence. Nevertheless, Jews who committed such acts were also guilty of desecrating the divine name. If the Jews were the bearers of God's tradition and they were caught violating His laws, they were not only transgressing specific Torah prohibitions but also giving the impression that the Jewish religion sanctioned such behavior.

Stealing from and swindling non-Jews were by no means the only transgressions that concerned the elders of Candia. But they were the crimes most likely to arouse the ire of forces outside the community. Notably, like many other Candian *takanot*, this one continued to appear in later iterations of the communal regulations. It might be a manifestation of the community's very traditional attitude, but it might also mean that it needed to be kept on the books because Jews continued to engage in such behavior. Perhaps this was due to the fact that the elders who issued the regulation did not stipulate any punishment or sanction against violators. Why they refrained from doing so is unclear. Possibly, they felt that Jews who swore a solemn oath in the synagogue as in other cases would not dare to renege on it. Another possibility is that this regulation was not truly meant to be enforced, but was rather enacted for the gentiles to see. The Jewish authorities, in Candia and elsewhere, seem to have been well aware that their authority to regulate the behavior of members of their community was largely limited to internal matters, and that there was little they could do to ensure compliance with their edicts when Jews had dealings with gentiles.

STEALING FROM JEWS

In most of the cases discussed thus far, the actual acts of theft and fraud were carried out by gentiles. Jews may have masterminded the crime, but were many times indirectly involved in the act itself, from which they profited, directly or indirectly. It was an important distinction in the context of medieval law, as can be learned from the origin of the English expression "caught red-handed," which draws a line between the "hands-on" perpetrator and any third party that may have been involved. The concept of being "caught red-handed" comes from fifteenth-century Scottish law, where it referred to killers or poachers who were caught with incriminating evidence on their persons. Similarly, under Germanic law, a murderer faced a much harsher sentence if his bloodstained clothes or the weapon he used were found, or if the unburied body of a murderer's victim was discovered. A similar logic operated with respect to theft. Unlike a felon caught "red-handed," that is, with the goods he stole in his possession, accomplices and conspirators were held to be less culpable, and were therefore judged with much less severity.

A typical case comes from Rabbi Haim Eliezer Or Zarua' (the son of the famous Rabbi Isaac ben Moses Or Zarua' of Vienna), centering on a Jew who claimed that another Jew had come to him and asked to borrow a horse. The Jew was holding the horse as collateral for a loan he had given to some non-Jews. When he lent the horse, he claimed, he had informed the borrower that he had reason to believe that the horse was a stolen one and, as such, there was good reason to believe that the owner would seek out the horse and confiscate it from the borrower—which is exactly what happened. The horse's owner also demanded reparations from the Jew in whose possession he had found the horse.[91] The Jews who lent and borrowed the horse were parties to the theft, but they clearly had no compunctions about benefiting from the deeds of non-Jewish thieves.

Jews in Ashkenaz, like their non-Jewish neighbors, owned gentile slaves or employed gentile household servants, and a common complaint was that these gentiles were filching items from the house.[92] Most of the slaves in northwestern Europe at this period were either Muslim captives from military campaigns in Iberia and the Mediterranean or men and women from the predominantly pagan Slavic frontier in central Europe.[93] Despite the ethnic and religious distinction between the masters and subordinates in these cases, which certainly meant that there was an element of bias on these grounds, the background to these accusations was principally the class differences between socially inferior service providers and the urban middle class, both Jewish and non-Jewish. Such accusations were leveled by both Jews and Christians against underlings no matter their religion and ethnicity.[94]

Some of these issues appear in exempla found in *Sefer Ḥasidim* and other writings produced by Ashkenazi Hasidim. They may be biased, as Rabbi Judah the Pious and his followers sought, as much as possible, to limit the contact between Jews and gentiles.[95] But as the exempla in question are not concerned with Jewish-gentile relations, the information they inadvertently offer about the subject can be taken to be reliable.[96] Given his position as a religious leader and scholar, Rabbi Judah would presumably not fabricate such material.

One of these passages tells of a Jewish man who didn't make serious efforts to suppress quarrels among his household employees in order to prevent them from conspiring to steal from him:

> A certain Jewish man had two gentile wet-nurses in his home, and there was a quarrel between them. They[97] said to him: "Why

do you tolerate a quarrel in your home?" To this he answered: "If they love one another they might steal from me but now they are each fearful of the other."[98]

Rabbi Judah condemns such behavior. In his view, theft is the lesser of the evils; the envy between the wet nurses should concern the master much more. Catalyzed by the rivalry the master had either engineered or neglected to suppress, seeking to win their employer's approbation, and hoping that that would be expressed monetarily, the wet nurses were liable to harm the Jewish infant or infants in their care.

A similar attitude can be seen in an exemplum that stresses how hard it is to control a gambling addiction. The story is presented as a dialogue between a Jewish slave owner and his guest. The guest offers to buy one of his host's domestic slaves.

> A man was about to sell one of his slaves to a guest. The guest told him that he would purchase the slave for the full price only if the owner would be truthful and list all the slave's shortcomings. So the slave owner said that the slave is a thief. To this the guest replied: "I'm taking him to a place where he will not understand the language and thus he won't be able to sell things that he steals, so he will not steal." The slave owner said: "He is a notorious glutton and he is tired and lazy." To this, the guest responded: "He has only one belly, which I will stuff with food, and I will beat him and hasten him so he doesn't sleep and loll around." Finally the slave owner said: "He has one other fault—he plays with dice.... To this the guest replied: get him out of my sight! I cannot sustain the whole world! A man who is addicted to gaming and gambling will stop at nothing, and he will steal and gamble and there is no stopping him. I do not want to purchase him."[99]

While the story's main purpose is to inform readers that gaming is the worst of all possible vices prevalent among household help (paid or owned), it also illustrates the lengths to which people would go to keep these domestics from stealing. The issue of theft is marginal to both the above stories, but they both show that it was an issue that preoccupied

Jews at the time. Another such example can be found in the Bologna edition of *Sefer Ḥasidim*. Here, a slave owner is encouraged to expel a slave from his household even "if he doesn't steal," implying that theft was often the reason why slaves and servants were dismissed.[100]

Yet another exemplum that offers insights tells of a rich man's son who realized that his father's wealth was diminishing due to household theft. The son contemplated an interesting countermeasure of questionable morality:

> A certain Jew was rich and had a large household. Many members of the household would steal his fortune. Now, the rich man had one son, and that son knew about the thefts. He said to his father: "But father, they are stealing everything from you! Why don't you keep an eye on them?" The father did not believe the son and would reprimand him. When the son came to realize that his father was not exercising caution in this matter he said: "I will steal all that is my father's, for if I don't the members of the household will take it all and my father will eventually end up stripped of his own clothes, and he will become a mockery to all. I had therefore better steal from my father and impoverish him, and in doing so I will sustain him, so saving my father's wealth for him instead of having it all stolen by others."[101]

It is not clear from the story whether the members of the household were servants or slaves, but clearly the father was either a man of poor judgment or, and this seems more likely from the text, his good sense had been clouded with age.[102] The son was not so much concerned with his father's honor as he was with his inheritance. To protect it, he devised a plan to keep his father's wealth out of the hands of these rivals. He would himself steal his father's assets, saving them from the clutches of those he identified as threats, after which he would use a part of the funds to provide for the old man's needs. The son recognized, however, that his plan was morally questionable, and he thus consulted a pietistic master (*ḥakham*), who sanctioned the extreme measure, on condition that the son maintain his father at the standard of living to which he was accustomed.[103]

Once a theft was committed in a household, a host of means were employed both to identify the culprits and their accomplices and to trace and retrieve the stolen goods. First and foremost, all possible suspects underwent a thorough and at times frightening interrogation, during which they were accused, threatened, and even subjected to physical violence. Magic might also be used, as recounted in the mystical writings of Rabbi Judah the Pious:

> Once one of the students had his clothes stolen, his rabbi [Judah] came and did something in the study hall [*beit ha-midrash*] and he was able to see the maidservant who had stolen from this place. He could see her walking through the marketplace and he also saw her putting the clothes away in a certain house and later moving the clothes to another location. After seeing this, the rabbi said: "If you look in that place you will find the clothes," and indeed they were found. I asked him [the rabbi]: "Did you manage to detect the theft through a revelation in a dream [*shema be-ḥalom ra'itah*]?" To that he responded: "Not so! I used an incantation to compel the angels to tell me [*hishba'ati malakhim*], once I did it suddenly I did not see the walls and the entire study hall in which I was sitting, all I saw was the thieving gentile woman. I could follow her tracks and I could see the places where she had put the clothes, all this I could vividly see."[104]

In addition to his ethical teachings, Rabbi Judah was an acclaimed mystic and was renowned for his abilities in the field of magic. He was considered by his contemporaries and later generations alike to be in possession of supernatural powers. His gravesite in the Regensburg Jewish cemetery was a medieval pilgrimage site until the expulsion of the city's Jews in 1519, when the cemetery was desecrated and destroyed. Most of the pilgrims sought his posthumous mystical intervention.[105] Both the writings of his contemporaries and subsequent hagiographic literature spoke of his supernatural vision. He was reputed to have had clairvoyant powers that enabled him to see the past and forecast the future. The tale of the student whose clothes were stolen, from the pietistic *Sefer ha-Kavod*, offers a glimpse at the exact mechanics of his supernatural abilities—Rabbi Judah employed the magical technique of binding angels with magical incantations and spells. Using these spells, he was able to pinpoint the culprit and locate the goods. The culprit in the story is identified as a non-Jewish maidservant. Apart from deterring potential offenders, who presumably would fear that their deeds were easily discernable to Jews with magical abilities, the story also shows magic could be employed to recover the stolen goods.

Rabbi Judah the Pious: Battling Crime and Exposing Thieves by Magical Means

Rabbi Judah the Pious's ability to identify criminals and locate stolen possessions also features in three of the hagiographic stories that circulated among Ashkenazi Jews after his death in 1217. A late-medieval Ashkenazi manuscript (MS Jerusalem 8°3182), published by Eli Yassif, includes a host of such folktales about Rabbi Judah.[106] Although the manuscript was penned in the sixteenth century, Yassif convincingly argues that some of the stories in this collection reflect events, experiences, and communal concerns from much earlier periods in medieval Ashkenaz, long before the tales were committed to writing. It is possible, though, that some of the stories were altered over time to fit other needs. The versions that we have today most probably took form in both Hebrew and the Yiddish vernacular during the fifteenth century.[107]

The three stories relevant to this discussion all tell of thefts and of Rabbi Judah's powers to detect the location of the stolen goods, bring the culprits to trial, and save a Jew implicated in the crime from grave peril. All three have other agendas, beyond the hagiographic aspect of demonstrating the power and magical abilities of a Jewish sage and mystic.

The first story concerns what seems to be an attempt to implicate a learned Jew in theft. A certain Rabbi Ephraim was entrusted with the treasures of the duke reigning in Regensburg.[108] "One night nine thieves arrived, all of them high-placed citizens of the city, and they took and stole all the money that the duke had deposited with the Jew."[109] Rabbi Ephraim raced to Rabbi Judah the Pious to obtain his aid in finding the thieves. At first Rabbi Judah was reluctant to intervene on Rabbi Ephraim's behalf, but after Rabbi Ephraim beseeched him and proclaimed him as his mentor ("as you have taught us, our teacher and master"), Rabbi Judah acquiesced. Rabbi Ephraim invoked a rabbinic maxim, from Mishna Sanhedrin 4:5, which Rabbi Judah is said to have taught him: "Anyone who saves the soul of an Israelite, it is as if he had saved the entire world." This quote cast his plight not as a mere monetary matter but rather as a life-threatening situation.

Unlike the earlier thirteenth-century accounts referred to previously, this hagiographic story does not indicate exactly what sort of magic Rabbi Judah employed. Instead, it cryptically recounts that Rabbi Judah warned Rabbi Ephraim to set his gaze on only one particular window in his study hall, and then he "did what he did and recited what he recited." Whatever they were, these magical words and actions were so potent that "it felt as if the study hall was levitating." Rabbi Judah repeated this procedure three times, each time performing a different action and uttering different words. Each time, the study hall ascended higher, until Rabbi Ephraim could see the culprits. From his magically elevated vantage point, Rabbi Ephraim saw that the thieves were uncertain how to dispose of the stolen treasure, and eventually buried it in a stable near a smithy not too far from a local privy. Once they knew the location of the buried treasure, Rabbi Judah instructed Rabbi Ephraim to make a mental note of the exact place. He then warned the victim of the theft that, to retrieve the treasure and save his family from disaster, he must follow Rabbi Judah's instructions precisely. He was to approach the duke, beg for his mercy, and recite certain words in his ear (probably also a magical incantation), which would impel him to bring the culprits to justice, rather than simply letting the duke reclaim the treasure. This is exactly what happened. In order not to awaken the culprits' suspicions, he had them summoned, along with their peers from among Regensburg's local patrician families, into the duke's court.[110] While they were there, Rabbi Ephraim accompanied the duke's men and quickly unearthed the stash, which they brought to the court and presented to all assembled. The thieves were tried, the Jew was acquitted, and the story concludes with the edifying sentence: "the Rabbi and his household were spared, to fulfill the saying in scripture: 'The righteous man is rescued from trouble, and the wicked man takes his place'" (Prov. 11:8).

The presence of both the duke and the burghers in supporting roles offers some possible information about when the story, in its current form, originated, even if its kernel crystalized either in Rabbi Judah's lifetime (d. 1217) or posthumously. The recorder of the story as we have it is in fact uncertain as to the name of the victim of the theft—he says it might have been either Rabbi Shmuel or Rabbi Ephraim—suggesting it was of little importance.[111] It is noteworthy that Rabbi Judah was initially reluctant to accept the magical challenge posed to him. Only after the petitioner appealed to his mystical powers, and after Rabbi Judah came to realize that the man's life and that of his family were in danger, did Rabbi Judah use his magical powers to find the stolen treasure and expose the thieves. Significantly, the storyteller states that, even after agreeing to help, Rabbi Judah made it clear that he would only make one attempt to aid Rabbi Ephraim. He also instructed Rabbi Ephraim exactly how to handle the situation and how to approach the duke, suggesting that he was familiar with diplomacy as well as magic.[112] Indeed, the diplomatic efforts are spelled out more explicitly than the magic. Though not the focus of the text, it is clear that, while the direct target of the theft was the rabbi in whose possession the treasure was entrusted, the target of the patricians who committed the robbery was, indirectly, the duke himself, probably as part of a power struggle.

The second of the theft stories in the Jerusalem manuscript describes Rabbi Judah's ability not only to locate stolen goods but also to stop burglaries in progress and bring the culprit to justice.[113] In contrast with the previous tale, in this case the thieves are simple burglars, not Regensburg patricians, whose crime had political undertones. In this story, two burglars break into Rabbi Judah the Pious's home under cover of the night. The Hebrew word used in the text is *ḥatru*, perhaps resonating a similar Hebrew word from Exodus 22:1 (*maḥ'teret*) or simply meaning that the burglars either tunneled under the floor or broke into the house through the walls.[114] The thieves were discovered by Rabbi Judah, who offered them even more of his belongings. Their arms laden with stolen goods, they left the house and Rabbi

Judah closed the door behind them. They suddenly found themselves frozen in place, standing petrified in the middle of the street with all the goods they took, as if spellbound.

The thieves, who understood that they were bound by magical means, beseeched Rabbi Judah to free them from the spell he had cast on them, but to no avail. By daybreak word got around the city and many of Regensburg's inhabitants, including several judges, arrived at the scene.[115] They suggested that the thieves cast away the stolen possessions and run for their lives. The thieves replied that they were frozen in place and unable to move, and thus could not dispose of the stolen goods. The burghers who were present at the scene approached Rabbi Judah and asked him to release the burglars and "send them to hell," as long as the stolen goods were returned. At this point, the storyteller relates that the burglars were not only equipped for a burglary but were also armed; furthermore, he explains that Rabbi Judah's home was targeted because it functioned as a bank of sorts.[116] Rabbi Judah told the burghers that the thieves had stolen not only his personal possessions but also deposits made with him by other Jews. He then acknowledged responsibility for the petrification, admitting that he had cast a spell on the burglars. He agreed to release the thieves on condition that the burghers promise that the culprits would be brought to justice. The burghers immediately arrested the thieves, tried them, and sentenced them to be hung, returning the stolen possessions to Rabbi Judah.

Aside from offering another instance of Rabbi Judah's use of magical powers, it portrays him as a firm opponent of vigilante justice. He refrains from sending the burglars to "hell" and asks that they be properly tried. The local system of justice seems to be held in high esteem by both Jews and the Christian burghers. This story, like others, exemplifies the tendency of medieval Ashkenazi Jews to rely on *recht* rather than *macht* (right of law rather than force).[117] In the story's imagined reality, the Jews are more powerful than their neighbors, as their reliance on the magical power wielded by the saintly Rabbi Judah freezes their opponents at the site of the crime. Yet the story stresses that Jews, embodied in the figure of Rabbi Judah, wanted to see justice served rather than simply to take revenge and recover their property. Perhaps the story was meant to convey this message to Jews who advocated direct action and had no patience for the slow, tedious, and, more often than not, biased legal proceedings of Regensburg's municipal courts. In the shifting political winds of the second half of the fifteenth century, when the stories took form, this most probably reflected the hope that Jews would receive the same treatment. The story also shows that, at the time, Jews had very little influence in German towns—it took no less a figure than a Jewish mystical master invested with magical powers to embody the Jewish aspirations to exercise some modicum of control over their lives.

The biblical dictum regarding a thief caught in the act, alluded to in this story, is very explicit: "If the thief is seized while tunneling, and he is beaten to death, there is no bloodguilt in his case" (Exod. 22:1). A Jew would probably not kill a non-Jewish thief who broke into his home, as no matter how angry and frustrated he might be when he happened on the burglar, the ramifications of finding the dead body of a Christian in the *Judengasse* (Jewish street) were probably greater. Nevertheless, Jews might not have had such compunctions about employing violence against an infiltrator from a lower social stratum.

USING MAGIC TO STEAL

The story of the petrified thieves tells how Rabbi Judah the Pious of Regensburg used his mystical powers to retrieve stolen goods. Medieval European Jewish folktales are but one textual platform that chronicles this phenomenon. Medieval magical manuals, mostly still unpublished, and an abundance of information that can be found in marginal notations of a magical nature in standard medieval Hebrew manuscripts, bear witness to countless attempts to prevent theft and retrieve stolen goods with the use of charms and magical formulae. Jewish society was hardly unique in this regard—the surrounding Christian society was no different. Magic of various types and origins was employed to this end both in Europe and in the Islamic realm, and was not restricted to individuals attempting to battle crime and retrieve stolen goods. Criminals, such as thieves and burglars, employed magical charms and incantations as well.

Exceptionally revealing are the instructions found among recipes for potions and medico-magical formulas listed in a Bibliothèque Nationale de France Hebrew manuscript from the early fifteenth century:

> The thieves that enter houses take with them the hand of a dead man [*yad ha-met*, mentioned earlier in the MS for medical uses].[118] They put it in the middle of the house and then all the household members tremble and fall asleep. And they take four lit candles and throw them to the four corners of the house and then they throw ground *diamant* dust on them [the spellbound household members], and it will seem to the household members that the house is rolling. While the thieves go about their business they take the dead hand and place it on the master of the house's heart and they ask him where the keys and the silver and gold are and he reveals all that he knows.[119]

The very existence of such manuals show that magical lore of this nature was circulated, copied, and used, just as the medical remedies were. The inclusion of spells and charms in a medical treatise is hardly surprising, given that the ingredients mentioned in the spell were commonly used medical ingredients at the time. The recipe appears in the form of a practical footnote or brief digression by the writer or copyist, no more than a passing comment mentioning the use of the hand of a dead man as one entry on a list of potent medico-magical ingredients.[120]

The ingredients mentioned in this recipe were known to possess evocative powers. From the fourteenth century onward, the use of diamonds, which, as a regal gem, had previously been restricted by royal decrees in many European countries, became more popular and their use slightly more widespread. This explains the diamond dust (a byproduct of the then emerging diamond cutting and polishing industry) in the recipe. Like many other gems, diamonds were thought to possess special powers, including the ability to relieve stress and insecurity and to clear the mind. It is not surprising, then, that the thieves mentioned in the charm used diamond dust as part of a magical potion designed to sedate the members of the household and get them to divulge information about the whereabouts of cash and valuables. The hand of the dead man may also have served like a truth serum, as well as a psychological deterrent, implying that a failure to comply with the thieves' demands would lead to death. Magic, then, was employed both by criminals, their victims, and the law, and was in no way alien to medieval European Jews.

PEOPLE OF THE BOOK: THE ROUGH WATERS AND THE SOLEMN BANKS OF THE STOLEN HEBREW BOOK MARKET

One of the first cases addressed in this chapter was a ruling by the late tenth-century Jewish luminary, Rabbi Gershom ben Judah of Mainz, about goods nearly lost when a river barge sank. This early European halakhic ruling served as the foundation for rulings in similar cases handed down by rabbinic courts in later times. Rabbi Gershom's responsum provides a clear portrayal of the social climate of eleventh-century Germany. Jewish communities were still grappling with the issue of authority within the community, and Jews who had good ties with the gentile establishment enjoyed a major advantage. With regard to the law, the Jews found themselves many times on similar footing with non-Jews. But the law's reach was limited at this time, so violence and crime were rampant.

Rabbi Gershom's ruling addressed a precious cargo of gold and gems that was nearly lost when a barge sank in a river. When considering the case, Rabbi Gershom pointedly refrained from adducing the Talmud's discussion of objects lost in a river, in tractate *Baba Metzia*. There, the context is an event in which the owner of the objects quickly loses hope of ever finding his property. A river, as a metaphor, also figures in other responsa.

The talmudic metaphor alluding to the actual river Biran in Mesopotamia that is invoked in some of these responsa provides the subtitle of this section. While Jews were hardly the only people to engage in the crimes of stealing and selling stolen goods in the medieval period, they stood out in a particular subset of thefts, that of Hebrew books. Books were high-value commodities in the Middle Ages, among the most precious objects in any book-owning household. Handwritten on paper, velum, or parchment, their production involved considerable time and expense. The most valuable books were illuminated codices, but books in general were valuable and rare objects. As in the surrounding society, Jews too owned handwritten copies of prayer books (*mahzorim* and *siddurim*), miscellanea (*mikhlolim*), the Pentateuch, and *haggadot*, the books used for the Pesach Seder; some of these were also illuminated. As such, they were particularly sought by thieves, as can be seen from a quick reading of a responsum by an early fourteenth-century Ashkenazi scholar who fled to Iberia, Rabbi Asher ben Yechiel (known also by the acronym of his name, Rosh).[121]

The case appears in the collection of Rabbi Asher's responsa, and is also cited in the great legal compendium composed by his son, Rabbi Jacob ben Asher. A poor woman married a man from a more affluent family. It was neither a love story nor a match made in heaven, but rather a financial transaction from which both sides benefited. The man, of unsound mind, was not a desirable match. Nevertheless, the woman's father agreed to the marriage, with her consent, most probably as a way of advancing her family's social and economic standing. When the husband's mental health deteriorated and he became violent, the woman decided to take action. Realizing that her husband's deteriorating mental state might soon render him incapable of giving her a divorce, she broke into the home of her husband's family and removed a number of books, which she held as guarantees for her economic well-being and as potential leverage in future negotiations over her children and her own financial security.[122] The scale of the theft is indicated by Rabbi Asher, who makes a point of reporting that the wife absconded with such a load of books that she required the help of a sympathetic member of the family.

Clearly, the case is not one of simple theft, the books taken as a means of ensuring that the husband's family would not cut off financial support for the wife and her children. It shows, however, just how valuable books were.[123]

Stealing a book from a Jewish household was as easy or difficult as stealing any other object from any other household, depending on how secured the valuable object was, but it was only worth the trouble in certain situations. In this case, the books were used as sureties, to be returned when the owners complied with the taker's demands. Hebrew books might also be worth the trouble and effort of stealing if the thief planned to use the book himself, or intended to sell it for its full value.[124]

Medieval European Jewish responsa portray a second-hand book market that at times put potential buyers in a moral bind. The market for second-hand books of a Jewish nature was much smaller than its Christian counterpart. If thieves wanted to receive the true market value of a Jewish book, they had to sell it to Jews, who could actually appreciate its true value.[125] In a much later period, during the Renaissance, Christian Hebraists became potential customers for such books, but during the High Middle Ages it was not easy to sell a book written in Hebrew and stolen from a Jewish household. Furthermore, many Hebrew books would be of use only to the learned rabbinic elite. While ritual books could be used by a larger number of people or communities, copies of the sacred legal Jewish texts (the Bible and its commentaries, copies of the Mishnah, Talmud, Tosefta, and other works of rabbinic culture) were more likely to interest the male scholarly elite. Scholars, eager to obtain rare and important works, were patrons of the secondary Hebrew book market. But they were also authors and editors, and as such were as concerned about the illegal market in copies, often corrupted, of their works as writers today are about the circulation of unlicensed electronic copies of books they have authored. They thus agonized over the moral and legal issues involved. Halakhists tried to work around the problem by establishing safety mechanisms that would assure buyers of the value of the books they bought while assuaging their moral compunctions.

A responsum addressing this issue was written by a fourteenth-century rabbi in Seville, Yom-Tov ben Avraham (also known by his acronym Ritva):[126]

> The Tosafot write that it is from these discussions that we learn that, with regard to books stolen by thieves from Jews and

sold to other Jews, one who purchases these books must return them to their lawful owners, if they [the original owners] offer to refund the money spent on the books. The original owners do not despair in finding the book. They know that these books are bound to make their way to Jewish hands. One does not despair of finding anything that may eventually surface in Jewish hands. But it is up to the original owner to compensate the purchaser of the books for his expense, since this is a regulation that is intended as a market stipulation [*takanat ha-shuk*], so that Jews will not refrain altogether from buying the books from the thieves and they [the books] will be left in their [the thieves'] hands.[127]

Ritva's rhetoric is telling. Although he explicitly mentions theft, he minimizes the ethical magnitude of the problem by placing it in the context of the *halakhah* of lost and found property. In this he follows in the wake of earlier halakhic authorities, both in Europe and the eastern Mediterranean. While this responsum addresses a case of theft, Ritva invokes the talmudic discussion about objects that have a distinct signature of ownership on them, but have fallen into a river or the sea.

According to that discussion, the owner of an object of value lost in a river or the sea generally despairs of ever finding it. Even though he can unambiguously identify the object as his, there is virtually no chance that an item lost in a large domain (like the stolen goods market) will ever be found and returned, in spite of the fact that some of the books bear identifying markers that testify to their ownership. Despair or forfeiture by the owner of an object (*ye'ush be'alim*) is a substantive concept in the Jewish laws of lost and found (*avedah u-metziah*), for it is the mental act of despair and forfeiture, or the lack thereof, that determines whether the lost object and its owner remain linked. Once the object is no longer in the owner's physical possession, this mental state remains the only such link. As long as an owner, under reasonable circumstances, has not despaired of regaining possession of a lost object, the finder of the object cannot gain legal possession of it. The finder is required to advertise the find so that the owner may hear of it.

If, however, the circumstances of the find indicate that it is reasonably certain that the owner has lost any expectation that the object may be returned, there is no such obligation. For example, if it was found in or alongside a large body of water, the legal presumption is that the owner has forfeited his ownership, as he has no hope of finding and regaining possession of it. The original owner's mental state obviates his claim to the object, rendering it *hefker* (ownerless). Thus, anyone who finds an object under such circumstances may take possession of it.

This principle is discussed in BT *Baba Metzia* 24b. The rabbis debate whether the original owner of an object that has fallen into a river despairs of finding it, thus losing his legal claim to the object. The editors of the talmudic passage distinguish between the sea, rivers, and one specific river in Babylonia, called the Biran. The implication is that, unlike the sea or other rivers, the Biran is "Jewish," as Jews owned the property along the banks and were thus the ones most likely to be both the losers and finders of an object lost there.[128] In other words, if a Jew lost something in the Biran, it would almost certainly be found by other Jews. As such, the owner of an object that fell into the Biran did not lose hope of regaining it, and thus any finder on the banks of the Biran was obligated to seek the owner and attempt to return the object.

The dilemma is clear in Ritva's responsum. The books sold by the thieves were obviously stolen from Jewish households. Yet once stolen, it was prima facie as if they had fallen into a river, and the original owner had no reason to believe that he would ever regain possession of them. In fact, however, it was not all that hard to determine and find the original owner of a stolen book. Most books had a colophon naming the owners.[129] Furthermore, unlike today's printed books, medieval codices usually had unique characteristics, such as the order of the texts copied in the codex, their size, the scribe's handwriting, marginal notations, the type of the binding, and other specific markers that distinguished one book from another, even if they contained the same text.

Books were often passed down from one generation to another as family heirlooms; the chances of such a book being sold by the family and appearing in the second-hand market were slim (but not entirely unrealistic).¹³⁰ The Jewish buyer of a second-hand Hebrew book ought thus suspect from the start that the book might be stolen. Ritva ruled that if the rightful owner surfaced and demanded it back, the buyer must comply, regardless of where or when he had purchased the book. The reclaimer was, however, required to compensate the buyer for whatever sum he paid for the book. Such a rule was necessary, Ritva argued, because if the buyers of such books were not protected against financial loss, they would cease to buy second-hand Hebrew books at all, fearing that they might be stolen and reclaimed by their rightful owners. If there were no buyers, thieves would be unable to sell stolen books, with the result that they would be lost or destroyed. Sticking to his metaphor, Ritva writes that the books might literally sink into the possession of the thieves (*yishtak'u be-yadam*) and be lost to the Jewish people forever.¹³¹ This relates not only to the loss of the book itself but also to the loss of its content, as Hebrew codices often contained an accumulation of knowledge that made them unique.

Ritva bases his ruling on the opinion of the Tosafot, a collection of exegetical glosses on the Talmud written by medieval rabbis, mostly of northern France, during the High Middle Ages. In the version of the Tosafot commentary that appears in the margins of the standard Vilna edition of the Talmud (1881), the passage adduced by Ritva is absent. This does not call its authenticity into question, however, as there were many glosses on the different tractates of the Talmud and not all were included in the compendium of Tosafot commentaries that appears in what came to be the standard traditional printed edition. Thus when Ritva refers to the Tosafot, he may be citing any of a set of commentaries on the Talmud written in this genre that were in circulation in his day but have since been lost.¹³²

He may have had in mind a passage written by Rabbi Isaac ben Moshe Or Zarua' of Vienna (c. 1180–c. 1250), who attributed similar ideas to Rabbi Isaac ben Shmuel ("the Elder") of Dampierre-Sur-Aube (d. 1189), an exegete and compiler of many prominent Tosafot glosses.¹³³ Another discussion of the issue can be found in a collection of responsa edited and published by Irving Agus in the 1950s.¹³⁴ A responsum attributed to Rabbi Ephraim of Regensburg takes up the same issue but, notably, reaches a different conclusion.¹³⁵

And a case had come before us[136] of one who bought books in Duringin [probably Thürigen or Thuringia] from the itinerant reprobate[137] peddlers who roam our kingdom [*malkhutenu*] and sell for six refined pieces of silver [*zekukim*—silver marks weighing about eight ounces each, or 240 grams]. It so happened that the original owner of the books had come and reclaimed the books. We have ruled in the original owner's favor and forced the buyer to return the books without receiving compensation, for this is a case of a "notorious thief," where the market stipulation does not apply.[138]

While the responsum offers only sketchy information, apparently it refers to a Jew who served as a middleman between reprobate peddlers who sold goods of dubious provenance, and learned Jews who were eager to purchase books. The books were apparently stolen in the Thuringia area, home to several Jewish communities, including affluent ones like Erfurt. Most likely, the books were stolen up north in Thuringia and sold to intermediaries, who transported them either to the west, to the relatively large Jewish centers in the Rhineland (where Rabbi Ephraim spent several years in Speyer), or south, to the area in and around the duchy of Bavaria, home to the Jewish communities of Nuremberg, Augsburg, and Regensburg (the city Rabbi Ephraim moved to, and where he lived until his death in 1175).

Rabbi Ephraim wrote that the buyers paid six *zekukim* for the books, a relatively large sum.[139] He then described how the previous owners, after learning that their books had been sold, traced the books and the buyers and petitioned a local court, probably in Regensburg, demanding the books be returned. The owners also demanded to be exempt from having to compensate the buyers. Rabbi Ephraim sided with the original owners, refusing to apply the market stipulation in this case. The market stipulation was intended to prevent the disincentive for commerce that would come into play if buyers feared losing the money they paid for goods that turned out to be stolen. However, Rabbi Ephraim thought that implementing the market stipulation rule in this case would be unjust, basing himself on the distinction the Talmud makes between regular cases, involving merchandise of dubious origin, where the market stipulation applies, and those involving a "notorious thief" (*ganav ha-mefursam*), in which case the provenance of the items is not simply dubious but rather presumptively stolen and the rule is not applied.

Why do the two rulings differ? While they come from disparate times and places, another distinction might hold the key—in the fourteenth-century case there are no Jewish intermediaries. Rabbi Ephraim refers explicitly to traders in stolen books who are known to be reprobates (*rekim*). He no doubt intended to curtail such commerce, which took place on and beyond the margins of regulated and legitimate trade. Rabbi Ephraim does not share Ritva's concern that stolen books, if not purchased, might be lost or destroyed by the thieves. In his view, apparently, once the Jewish books were back in Jewish hands, even those of Jewish dealers in stolen property, there was no real fear that they would disappear. While the dealers were probably not ideal guardians of important Jewish books, at least they or their kin would be aware of the books' importance and ensure that they not go missing. Unfortunately, Rabbi Ephraim's ruling actually exacerbated this very problem. If the Jewish intermediaries were to go out of business, the books these reprobates held might well indeed "sink" to the hands of non-Jews and be lost forever.

Ritva may have had other concerns about the books in the case he adjudicated; certainly his fear that the books would vanish once they fell into non-Jewish hands was well founded. Jewish books were primarily crucial vessels of Jewish lore, consulted daily by the medieval rabbinic elite. But they could be a source of danger if they fell into the wrong hands, especially from the thirteenth century onward, and certainly during Ritva's lifetime.

Jews learned through experience (such as the Paris trial against the Talmud in the 1240s and the Barcelona Disputation in 1263) that Christian access to Hebrew books could have deadly consequences. Jewish converts to Christianity and other Christian polemicists, especially from among the mendicant orders, used both instruction manuals written by converts that exposed inner Jewish discourse on Christianity and translations of Hebrew books in order to construct formidable intellectual cases against medieval Jewry. Hebrew books themselves were considered to contain heretical teachings, and were thus condemned to be burned. Jews who owned such books were, in Christian eyes, dangerous and heretical. Ritva, like other Jewish scholars, understood that, in the wrong hands, stolen Jewish books might not just represent a financial loss to individuals and a loss of their intellectual capital to Jewry, but could menace entire Jewish communities. In other words, even if stolen, they were best kept in Jewish hands.

A similar insight on the subject of second-hand Jewish books can be found in a responsum dating to half a century after Rabbi Ephraim's ruling but before Ritva's. Quoting his master and mentor, Rabbi Meir of Rothenburg, Rabbi Mordechai ben Hillel (known also simply as "the Mordechai") wrote of Jews who bought books pillaged from Jewish homes during riots:[140]

> And Rabbi Meir of Rothenburg presided over the case of a certain man who had identified his books that had been pillaged by gentiles from his home during the time of an evil decree [*yom ha-gezerah*]. And it is known to all that they [the gentiles] stole and robbed and sold the books to Jews. He [Rabbi Meir] ruled that the buyer should return the books without compensation, since those people who fall victim to gentile pillaging do not despair and forfeit their lost possessions.[141]

Rabbi Meir explained that buying from gentiles' books that had been stolen from Jewish homes should be seen as a selfless act of recovery and one should not seek to profit from it. The evil decree is not specified in the responsum, but it stands to reason that it may refer to the Mainz Pogrom of 1283 or the "good Werner" riots of 1287/1288. The earlier date, prior to Rabbi Meir's own incarceration, seems to be more likely.[142] In the wake of such riots, Jews tried to salvage as much Jewish property as possible. It was common knowledge that in the days after the riots there were many Jewish household goods on the market, some for bargain prices and with no owners to claim them.

Rabbi Haim Or Zarua' is quoted in later sources as having written that,[143] while the purchaser of such books may have to forfeit them if the rightful owner will appear and demand them, he will nevertheless have gained the merit of having fulfilled a commandment.[144] The commandment referred to is apparently the injunction to ransom captives, both human and sacred texts, which the Talmud states is a very important religious duty.¹⁴⁵

This situation was in no way unique, nor limited to the Christian European realm. The issue is addressed also in a number of responsa collected and translated from the Arabic that were copied (among other materials) into Rabbi Bezalel ben Avraham Ashkenazi compendium *Shita Mekubetzet* in the sixteenth century.¹⁴⁶ One of them, dating from the late twelfth century, deals with an even more sensitive subject, namely books stolen from a synagogue library. As such, the books fell under the halakhic category of *hekdesh*—sacred property. The author of the responsum, according to the compiler and translator Rabbi Bezalel, was no other than Maimonides (1138–1204):

> And you have asked: "How should we address the case of a person who bought holy books [*sifrei kodesh*] from a looting party that pillaged some synagogues in several cities and towns? Should we endorse the purchase or should we coerce him [to return the books] because he [is to be treated as if he himself] took the books from them? And if we decide to confiscate the books from him, is he entitled to compensation amounting to the sale price? And when we return the books, should they be returned to the same synagogue [from which each one came], or to another?"
>
> Answer: If the looting was sanctioned by royal authority, the purchase is deemed legal and the status of *hekdesh* [sacred property] is void. For even the Temple vessels that were pillaged lost their state of consecration, as they [the sages] adduced the verse: (Ezek. 7:22) "And robbers [*paritzim*] shall enter into it, and profane it."¹⁴⁷ However, if the synagogue was looted without a royal sanction, or they [the books] have plainly been stolen, the buyer should swear a solemn oath regarding the sum he paid to purchase [them], for which he may be compensated, and the books will be returned, just as in any other case in which it is found that a person's books or belongings have been stolen and identified.¹⁴⁸

Maimonides' ruling is unambiguous. Judging by the language, this towering halakhic adjudicator was appealed to by a local tribunal that was struggling with the case.¹⁴⁹ He distinguishes between two situations, one in which the looting of the synagogue and its belongings were sanctioned by the sovereign, in which case the books lose their consecrated status, and others in which there was no such sanction, but rather the synagogue was sacked by a mob or band of thieves. In the latter case, according to Maimonides, the rule that applies is not the standard one regarding stolen valuables. In the first case, the sanctity of the sanctuary has been violated, Maimonides maintains, and therefore the objects taken from it are no longer treated as sacred property (*hekdesh*), and the standard rule applies. In the latter case, however, the books retain this status. In the first case, Jews could purchase the stolen books without fear of violating any religious precepts and are entitled to compensation if the books were to be taken. What is at stake, in practical terms, is whether the buyer is compensated for the price of the stolen books he purchased. In the second case, that of looting or burglary, the books remain sacred property and are thus confiscated from the buyers, who receive no compensation. In the first case, where the books have lost their status as sacred property, the buyer must return the books to their original owner—in this case, the synagogue from which they were stolen—but the original owner must refund him the money he paid to purchase the books.

The cases considered up to this point address books obtained from a questionable source. None of the responsa so far discussed indicate who the buyers of the stolen books were, although presumably religious-rabbinic works were purchased by parties who needed them for study and reference. But members of the learned elite seldom acknowledged that they were the beneficiaries of larceny.

A responsum by the North African and Iberian sage Rabbi Isaac Alfasi (1013–1103) offers an ethical analysis of a case involving a student who stole books of exegesis (*perushim*) from a fellow-student.¹⁵⁰ The vague language of the responsum leaves open the question of whether the book in question contained exegetical notes on scripture or the Oral Torah (Mishnah, Tosefta, or Talmud), nor does it indicate whether the notes were a compilation or copy of the work of others, or perhaps the victim's own notes and innovations (*ḥidushim*). It was by no means an ordinary act of theft. In traditional Jewish culture, the study of Torah is not only an intellectual enterprise but also a religious obligation. When the owner of the book confronted the thief, the latter immediately swore a solemn oath not to return the book until he had copied it. While this might seem audacious to the modern reader, the mindset of both the thief and some of his peers and mentors was that the thief was in fact entitled to withhold the stolen codex until he had made a fair copy, as this was a fulfillment of a religious obligation. In his pleading, the thief acknowledged that he had obtained the book unlawfully, but justified doing so on the grounds that it was for the greater good of the study and dissemination of the Torah, which was why it was reasonable to withhold the book from its lawful owner until it was copied. Property rights and possession, categories that are usually seen as making sharp distinctions, took on a more fluid and ambiguous character in this case.

Sensing that this was a pivotal case, Alfasi offered a powerful rebuttal to the line of reasoning offered by the thief and the halakhists who supported him:

> The thief and the decisor are both in error and have acted in contradiction to the law. He who instructed that this is permitted is wrong, for it is said "the Holy One, Blessed Be He, despises the fulfillment of a commandment that involves a transgression" ... therefore, in his instruction to the thief, he both sinned and caused another to sin ... and he will not be credited with the merit of that commandment he wished to fulfill.

Although Alfasi's ruling had a major impact and was cited by later adjudicators, the fact that it had to be cited itself indicates that the ruling did not put an end to thefts like this one.

BATTLING THEFT BY PREACHING

Legislation in the form of communal edicts and legal adjudication addressed theft that had already occurred. But there were also preventative measures. In particular, some medieval Jewish leaders preached against theft, most often during communal gatherings, such as prayer services in synagogues on the Sabbath and holy days.

Unfortunately, while sermons and homilies were recorded in abundance in medieval Christian Europe, both in Latin and the vernacular, as well as in medieval Jewish Iberia, only fragments of these genres have survived from the Ashkenazi world.[151]

While we know that rabbis often delivered sermons, only a handful were recorded and transmitted, and even fewer were anthologized.[152] One of the few medieval Ashkenazi sources of this kind is a collection of notes for homilies and sermons delivered by Rabbi Haim Or Zarua'.[153] In his public remarks, he addressed halakhic matters, sought to instruct the public, to correct errors of observance and uproot entrenched but mistaken practices.

One of his sermons, delivered on a Shabbat when the weekly portion of Va'yetze, from the book of Genesis (28:10–32:4), was liturgically recited in the synagogue, consists of a long homily devoted almost entirely to theft, illegal acquisition of goods, financial and commercial fraud, and the criminal mishandling of funds. There is no direct indication as to why this homily was paired with this particular weekly reading, nor is there any information as to the geographical, political, and social context in which it was delivered or the precise events it was referring to.[154]

Nevertheless, it may well be that because theft and fraud are prominent in Va'yetze (which recounts how Laban the Aramean cheated Jacob, and the countermeasures employed by Jacob and his wives), preaching on this topic on this specific Shabbat seemed to be fitting. Furthermore, an anonymous thirteenth-century Ashkenazi polemical work, *Sefer Nitzaḥon Yashan* (*The Old Book of Polemics*, also known as *Nitzaḥon Vetus*) contains a brief reference to this weekly portion: "On most of the gentile holidays they read this chapter and preach [the Hebrew word refers to the barking of a dog, a dysphemism for preaching] about it."[155] This may have prompted Rabbi Haim Or Zarua''s sermon. Another possibility is that the sermon was a Jewish response to Christian accusations of Jewish dishonesty, prompted by the pejorative Christian reading of the story, from the portion read in synagogues the previous week, telling how Jacob gained the blessing of his father

Isaac at the expense of his brother Esau (Genesis 25:19–28:9). In the Christian reading, Jacob was the father of the Jewish people, and his deceit was taken, in Christian polemics, as emblematic of the Jewish duplicity. The sermon may have been aimed at countering this notion.

Rabbi Haim Or Zarua' began by invoking a talmudic homily adduced in Rashi's commentary on the Pentateuch. It comments on the verses relating how, while walking in the fields during the wheat harvest, Reuben, Jacob's eldest son, found mandrakes and brought them to his mother, Leah. While the specific mention of the time of year in the biblical verse (the wheat harvest season) seems superfluous, talmudic homilists saw it as a sign to future readers that, although Reuben was in the fields during the harvest, he did not pick crops belonging to others, but rather a wild plant that belonged to no one.[156] Rabbi Haim holds up Reuben's respect for the property of others as an example, stressing that theft is a grave sin, treated more severely by God than any other crime a person may have committed.

In the remainder of the sermon, Rabbi Haim considered everyday acts ranging from intentional fraud to occasional mistakes—misplacing valuable objects causing financial damage—and even various ways of avoiding internal and external taxation. In almost every area of social interaction, he told his listeners, a person was liable to encounter pitfalls that could implicate him in the crime of theft. People from every walk of life are prone to such transgressions, he stressed, even a king.

Although in general halakhic adjudicators subscribed to the idea that the will of the king is the law (*dina de-malkhuta dina*), this applies only if the king imposes taxes equally on all his subjects, and with their consent. If a king imposed excessive taxes, this was tantamount to theft and members of the Jewish community must not profit from it, even indirectly. For example, if a king or one of his lieutenants confiscated a house from a Jew, no other Jew should buy the house from the king, even if it was offered at a bargain price on the open market.[157]

Note that the reasoning Rabbi Haim offers for his ruling is not the usual one about the need for Jewish solidarity. Instead, he states that it is immoral to buy stolen property, even if it was confiscated by royal authorities. In general, the *halakhah* recognized that rulers had the power to seize private property or assets, and as such permitted

Jews to benefit from such confiscations, for example by buying such property from the ruler or his agent. Furthermore, Rabbi Haim extends the definition of theft to include actions never before placed under that rubric. One example is his unprecedented position on taxes. If a person dies before paying his Jewish communal taxes—even a small sum—Rabbi Haim maintained that his heirs may not divide the inheritance until the tax is paid. Neither may the eldest son factor in this sum when determining his double share of the inheritance allocated to him by the rule of the Torah.[158] The tax bill must be settled first. His argument for terming such actions theft makes it possible to deduce what some previous medieval European Jewish adjudicators did and did not include in that category.

In his sermon, Rabbi Haim also warned his listeners not to steal from a gentile, expanding this prohibition beyond the bounds set by previous authorities. In business dealings with non-Jews, he admonished, Jews should take care not to profit from the gentile's erroneous calculation. Previous halakhic authorities had distinguished between errors made by Jews and those made by gentiles. A Jew was forbidden to benefit from an error made by a fellow Jew, but not obliged to point such an error out to a gentile with whom he did business. However, these previous authorities had recognized that, while the Jew was not under obligation, there was reason for him to do so anyway. In doing so, and thus passing up an opportunity to profit from the mistake, the Jew would be enhancing the reputation of the Jews as an honest people, which would benefit the Jewish community as a whole. In halakhic terms, such an action was said to "sanctify the name [of God]." Rabbi Haim Or Zarua' suggested that such sanctification be made mandatory rather than optional.

Rabbi Haim ended this part of his sermon by reminding Jewish communal officials that, on matters of taxation, they should not exercise prejudice based on friendships and familial ties. He then asserted that the merits of Jews who acted righteously would safeguard Jewish assets. This apparently was meant to signal to his audience that they could protect their assets without resorting to illegal tactics. Rabbi Haim quoted the patriarch Jacob, hero of the weekly portion: "Had not the God of my father, the God of Abraham, and the Fear of Isaac, been with me, you would have sent me away empty handed" (Gen. 31:42). In an almost apotropaic fashion, Rabbi Haim used Jacob's staunch belief in the Almighty to suggest that the spirits of the righteous forefathers, watching over the Jews in their exile, safeguarded Jewish assets. Illegal tactics, fraudulent means, theft, and cheating were thus superfluous. His invocation of the Jewish people's righteous forefathers as guardians was much like the Christian invocation of guardian saints.

This homily, directed at Rabbi Haim's community—either in Regensburg, Wiener Neustadt, or Mainz—condemned a range of behaviors. Rabbi Haim forbade Jews to make a profit at the expense of another Jew, to take advantage of another Jew's mistakes, or to exploit a fellow Jew's downfall. Even profiting indirectly by purchasing confiscated or commandeered Jewish property from the king or his envoys, he maintained, is ethically unacceptable. But Rabbi Haim extended these prohibitions, already well ensconced in the halakhah, to include all forms of stealing or illegally profiting from a non-Jew. Presumably he was not addressing a hypothetical issue but rather the actual conduct of Jews in his community that he, as a communal leader and halakhic adjudicator, sought to limit and curb. One of the means of doing so most readily available to Rabbi Haim and other Jewish leaders was the well-established one of publically denouncing transgressors and their actions, with the aim of changing mores and community standards. The resulting social pressure would deter Jews from cheating gentiles and make those who did so contrite. To achieve this, the message had to be lucid, conveyed in a sermon on the holiest day of the week, in the sacred communal space of the synagogue. We can only guess about how effective these sermons were in admonishing the Jewish population and in generating the change from the patterns that Rabbi Haim Or Zarua' had highlighted in his sermons. The constant warnings against cheating and stealing from non-Jews suggest that, as in the case of his Christian contemporaries, these sermons were only partially successful in changing ingrained behavioral patterns.

THEFT WITHIN AND FROM THE COMMUNITY

This chapter has focused mainly on theft and financial transgressions between individuals, showing how social and communal mechanisms were employed to suppress such crimes. Another class of crime involved stealing from the Jewish community itself. Such violations ranged from outright theft of communal property to gross disrespect for community standards on financial matters, which many officials and congregants saw as a grave offense.

The Synagogue Break-in in Daroca

One of the best-documented examples of the theft of communal property comes from outside Ashkenaz, across the Pyrenees in Aragon in the early fourteenth century. The evidence comes from the responsa of Ritva, from which the case of the book thieves discussed above was also taken.[159] Exceptionally, this responsum is supplemented by a dossier of documents that Ritva used in judging the case, including dates and the names of those involved. Such an extensive record makes it possible to offer an account with a solid factual foundation, rather than relying on educated guesswork and speculation of the type that fleshing out other cases has required. While the crime was committed in Iberia, the case is germane to this book because Ritva was not the only halakhic adjudicator that was approached concerning this matter. A reference in the responsum indicates that Rabbi Asher ben Yechiel (Rosh), who relocated from Cologne in Ashkenaz to Toledo in Iberia in 1303, was also consulted by the community.[160] The opening lines of Ritva's dossier read:

> To Daroca: The [members of the] local *kahal* [communal lay leadership], may our Lord preserve sustain and aid them, have agreed to issue a decree [*takanah*] regarding Yitzhak, son of Avraham Medro, and regarding Avraham, son of Yosef, son of Palas. These men were apprehended in the synagogue in Daroca at night, while all the people of the community were sound asleep in their beds. At the time of their arrest they

> were in the midst of breaking the doors of the ark [*heikhal*] that holds the Torah scrolls, in an attempt to steal the silver. Both were incarcerated, yet they managed to escape from custody. A decree was issued regarding their case. Furthermore, a decree was also issued regarding Oro and Sabach as well as Nissim and Joseph and their mother Djamila [mother and siblings of the said Yitzhak son of Avraham Medro]. It stipulates that they are prohibited from residing here in Daroca for a specific time. And they went and apostatized.

The town of Daroca, located not too far from Zaragoza, Spain, has retained its medieval appearance, although the local synagogue, where the events that are discussed here took place, no longer stands.[161] In 1314, the year of the affair, Daroca was part of the crown of Aragon. Yitzhak, who was the older of the two, and Avraham were caught red-handed while breaking into the synagogue. They intended to steal the silver ornaments used to decorate the Torah scrolls.

In another document from the dossier, the community leaders express their disgust with the act, not only because it blatantly violated the sanctity of the sanctuary, but also because it displayed contempt for both communal property and the belief that God is all-seeing ("they acted as if God cannot see them").

This opening paragraph is followed by the petition Avraham's mother, Sati, made to the *kahal*. She protested the ban the *kahal* had placed on the two thieves after they had escaped from communal custody. The severity of the ban reflected the communal sense that the theft, and the malefactors' escape from custody, had breached sacrosanct community standards. She asked for the ban on her son and his accomplices be lifted, so that her son could repent his sins and be reintegrated into the community. Sati explained that unlike the Medros, a family of notorious criminals in Daroca, her son Avraham was a good boy who had fallen under a bad influence. Her husband's family was a good one, and she served as a midwife for all the Jewish women in Daroca and was "entrusted with all the matters of female dignity in Daroca." Her husband, Avraham's father, also did good deeds, volunteering to wash the dead prior to burial, as an act of charity. Sati beseeched the community to lift the ban of excommunication imposed on her son, which had been part of the decree issued against the absconded burglars. If he were allowed to return, she maintained, Avraham would be willing to do any form of penance imposed on him, for he was greatly ashamed of his part in the matter. She warned the community that, if the ban were not lifted, Avraham might join the Medro family in leaving the Jewish fold and converting to Christianity, possibly causing his younger sibling(s) to join him.[162] She asked the community to honor the Almighty and themselves and perform a *berakhah* (literally a blessing, but here used apparently to mean an act of mercy, above and beyond the strict letter of the law) and lift the ban so that Avraham could return to Daroca and put the thoughts of conversion out of his mind.

Sati's appeal is exceptional in two ways. First, she appeals to the "honor of the members of the *kahal*," reminding them that she is not only a practicing midwife but also "entrusted with the honor of all the Jewish women." Second, in contrast to most petitions in which Jewish women beseech medieval rabbinic courts or lay tribunals, there is no mention whatsoever of tears, weeping, or any other form of behavior usually attributed to women.[163] She may well have been issuing a veiled threat in citing her role as the community midwife, entrusted with the *dignity* of the Jewish women of Daroca, elegantly reminding the male elite that she was privy to many of their private secrets about their daughters and their wives' sex lives and extramarital affairs, along with miscarriages and abortions.[164] Perhaps this is why, rather than dismissing this plea, the *kahal* of Daroca sent the query forward to Ritva, requesting his legal intervention.

Apparently, to ensure that no member of the community violate the ban by having contact with the excommunicated outcasts, all the communal elders had taken an oath to uphold it. Furthermore, copies of the oath and decree had been sent to Ritva in Zaragosa and to Rosh, by then already residing in Toledo, for them to witnesses with their signatures, turning the oath into an unbreakable vow.[165] The problem was that it placed them in a legal bind when they were petitioned, and possibly threatened, by Avraham Palas's mother. By vowing to uphold the decree and obtaining the signatures of prominent rabbis on the

THEFT WITHIN AND FROM THE COMMUNITY 111

vow, the *kahal* in effect had renounced its independent authority to annul the punishment it had imposed. Its vow could only be voided under special circumstances and with rabbinic approval.

In the wake of Sati's plea, the leaders realized that, whatever they thought of the Medros family—whose exit from the community may in fact have been welcome—they had not foreseen that Avraham Palas might choose to convert. The *kahal* may have wanted to retract its harsh punishment, especially given Sati's subtle warning. But the only way they could do so was to obtain the sanction of the same halakhic authorities who had endorsed it. They therefore approached Ritva, in the hope that he would find a legal loophole that would make it possible for them to retract the decisions that had been made during the angry and anxious days following the synagogue break-in and the thieves' escape from detention.[166] His responsum shows how, after grasping the gravity of the situation, Ritva provided the Daroca community with a legal mechanism for retreating from their oath, thus paving the way for Avraham Palas's possible return to Daroca, enabling him to do penance and rejoin the community. Ritva suggested that since the community could not have anticipated that the events would lead to such serious consequences as someone leaving the fold and converting to Christianity, the vow was based on inadequate information. In light of this he ruled that the vow, although it was a public vow witnessed by many, was not binding as initially believed. He therefore ruled that the community may in fact reach out to Avraham Palas and enable him to do penance and eventually return to the community.

The Daroca case is informative in many ways. For example, there were probably many valuables in the synagogue, but the thieves targeted the Torah ornaments. This seems to indicate that, much like the Judaica market today, there was a lively market for such goods in medieval Iberia, and perhaps beyond the Pyrenees as well. The market value of the ornaments was much greater than the value of the precious metal they were made of. The case also highlights the extreme anticrime measures taken by the local community, exemplified by the draconian ban they placed on the culprits. The fine print of the oath included a list of sanctions that would be imposed on any member of the community who violated the terms of the excommunication, for example by maintaining contact or doing business with the Medros family or Avraham Palas. Among them:

> Any member of the Daroca community who had any contact with the banned individuals would himself be excommunicated for a full year.
>
> If the thieves, Isaac and Avraham, were apprehended in Daroca within the five years of their expulsion and excommunication, they would be arrested and then shaved in full public view in that section of the street, leading to the fort, that was in the possession of the Jews. Subsequently, they would be flogged, at the discretion of the local tribunal, in the amount of at least four lashes each, stark naked in the street, to honor the holy Torah they so gravely offended.

These regulations, including the threat of a humiliating public punishment executed in full view of both Jews and non-Jews alike, speaks to the community's vital need to ensure that the theft of community property be placed clearly out of bounds. In another provision, the community ruled that part of the fine any collaborator with the criminals would be required to disburse would be paid in the best available royally minted currency (not just any currency), so that the crown of Aragon would also benefit from the fine, thus creating a royal incentive to uphold the *kahal*'s decree. The heavy-handed measures included in the decree, designed to both punish the culprits and deter others, show that the community leaders viewed this crime as displaying more than the usual criminal contempt for the law.

The crime was a desecration of the inner sanctum—the Holy Ark where the Torah scrolls were kept—in a synagogue, a house of God. Not only was sacred property violated, but so were communal objects of religious significance, on which prayers and blessings for their donors were inscribed. Many of the ornamental decorations adorning the Torah scrolls, as well as the case, the ark, and the synagogue furniture were donated by community members in memory of deceased relatives. This made the violation of the space all the more egregious. The decree against the criminals expressed the rage of the city's Jews. They must have been even more incensed when the two culprits, who had been caught red-handed, managed to escape communal custody, highlighting the community's inability to control its own criminals.

The Winchester Incident

A very similar case comes from English Fine Rolls from the reign of King Henry III, in the first half of the thirteenth century. The king asked his sheriff in Hampshire to handle a dispute between the Jewish community of Winchester and a man named Cresse (probably a man whose Hebrew name was Gedaliyah) of Stamford:

> Concerning taking an inquisition. Order to the sheriff of Hampshire to inquire by the oath of twelve of the more lawworthy Jews of Winchester, by their roll, whether Cressus of Stamford, Jew, violently seized and took away the Apple of Eve from the synagogue of the Jews in the same city, to the shame and opprobrium of the Jewish community. If by that inquisition he shall be found guilty of that deed, then they are to distrain [impound] the rents, houses and chattels of Ceressus immediately to give one mark of gold to the king for that trespass. Witnessed as above. By the king.[167]

It seems that the "Apple of Eve" referred to was not an ornament for the Torah scrolls, but rather the communal *etrog*, the citron used in the ritual of the celebration of the Sukkot holiday.[168] It may be that Cresse stole the *etrog* because of the healing properties it was reputed to have—in particular, to cure his wife's infertility or ease her labor pains, or possibly to enhance his own virility.[169]

Like the case from Daroca, the Winchester affair also involves a Jew whose behavior not only offended the community but also violated the sacred space of the synagogue, by stealing a communal ritual object placed in that sacred space for safekeeping. Of course, a precious metal ornament specially dedicated to embellish the Torah scroll, and thus regularly situated in the sanctuary, differs from a piece of fruit used for liturgical purposes during one week of the year. Nevertheless, in both cases the communal authorities resorted to strong measures against the culprits. In both cases they outsourced the enforcement of the law within the community to an external agent. The English case seems even harsher, as Winchester's Jews appealed to the king himself against Cresse of Stamford. An appeal to the royal court was not an easy matter.

The king's instruction, dated January 19, 1252, was issued in royal presence in Geddington, the royal hunting lodge in Northamptonshire where King Henry III was staying en route from the wedding of the daughter of King Alexander of Scotland. In other words, the Winchester Jewish community's envoys had to travel to the itinerant royal court, some 120 miles to their north, ask for an audience with the king, and wait at court until such audience was granted. Meanwhile, the envoy or envoys had to bear the cost of their travel, not to mention fees or bribes in order to procure the writ in question. Alerting the non-Jewish authorities to a crime internal to the Jewish community was no simple matter under any circumstances, and this was no ordinary situation. Unfortunately, we do not know the outcome of the inquiry. David Carpenter says so explicitly in his account of the matter: "there appears to be no evidence as to the results of the inquiry mounted by the twelve law-worthy Jews of Winchester. Indeed, working through the indexes of the obvious printed sources, I have found no more about either the incident or Cressus of Stamford."[170] We may assume that, regardless of whether or not the *etrog* was returned to the Winchester synagogue, Cresse was fined for his acts of violence and larceny. However, the very existence of this case in the records of the non-Jewish authorities seems to be the exception that proves the rule. It would seem more likely that, for the most part, communal authorities chose to settle such matters within the bounds of the community.

2

"BE GONE THOU MAN OF BLOOD"

Murder and Murderers in Medieval European Jewish Society

If Priscus, a Jew who lived in Paris in the late sixth century, had not been murdered by Phatir, a fellow Jew who had recently converted to Christianity, we would never have known where the synagogue was in that city at the dawn of Jewish settlement in western Europe. According to the entry for the city's fifth and sixth arrondissements from the handy paperback edition of *The Complete Jewish Guide to France*:

> The Fifth Arrondissement, generally referred to as the Latin Quarter, is one of Paris's oldest areas of habitation. Many of the winding streets you see in this neighborhood, particularly those closest to the Seine, are hundreds of years old. So it is no surprise that the earliest Jewish inhabitants of Paris made their homes here along with other residents. Perhaps the earliest known synagogue was in the sixth century C.E. It stood in the vicinity of the present Church of St. Julian le Pauvre, one of the earliest churches in Paris, just across the river from the Notre-Dame. Nothing is really known about that community except that it existed. Nothing remains of it.[1]

The obscure origins of the Jewish community in Lutetia (modern day Paris) are clouded in sixth-century mists, as are the origins of most of the small number of Jewish communities north of the Alps during the late antique and early medieval period. There are neither archeological remains nor fragments of liturgical manuscripts to help pinpoint the location of this early Parisian synagogue. It was a Christian chronicler, Gregory of Tours, who recorded the assault and murder of a Jew who was on his way to the house of prayer on a Sabbath morning; in doing so, he offered historians and the authors of guidebooks a clue about the location of the building.[2] The author of the guidebook, probably aware of the story since she made a clear reference to the Church of Julian le Pauvre, chooses not to share it with her readers, telling them that virtually nothing is known of this community.

This chapter considers Jews who were involved in violent crimes, murder in particular, in medieval Europe. It shows how Jews reacted to the use of violence both within their communities and in the context of the larger non-Jewish society in which they lived, with particular attention to how Jewish communal authorities responded to the use of violence.

Violence and strife within societies were once seen as pathological. Legal anthropological research has more recently offered a new view, according to which conflict, and even violence, are inevitable, if not unavoidable, in every vibrant society. Violence is a part of the repertoire of normal social behavior, rather than an aberration.

Cain's murder of Abel, the first story told of human interaction after the expulsion from Eden, illustrates how ingrained violence is in human society. Theologically, violence and murder are manifestations of the fall of humans from the ideal of paradise. Medieval Christian and Jewish scholars saw murder as a byproduct of the fall of man and the drastic changes in the human condition brought about after the expulsion from paradise, the hard labor to which humankind was doomed outside Eden. The shortage of resources, the need to eke sustenance from the land, and the competition between farmers and herdsmen led to inequality, jealousy, and poverty, the engines of violence. In this view, while violence was unavoidable, it was to be treated as a sin and a deviation from acceptable normative behavior.

Violence, especially lethal violence, in Jewish communities in medieval northern Europe occurred against the background of the specific circumstances of Jewish life in that time and place. These were communities that enjoyed broad self-governing authority, but had only limited means of enforcement. They thus depended in large measure on voluntary adherence by members of the community to the authority of the communal leadership.

The taking of a human life is the ultimate crime. In premodern societies, where religion and theological concepts played a more significant role than they do today, premeditated murder was seen not only as a crime against a fellow human being but also an act of sacrilege, of contempt for God. According to the Bible, humans were created in the image of God, and this was taken to mean that an attack on a person's body was tantamount to an attack on God.[3] The same rationale lies behind the biblical prohibition against leaving the corpse of an executed criminal unburied (Deut. 21:22–23): "If a man is guilty of a capital offense and is put to death, and you impale him on a stake, you must not let his corpse remain on the stake overnight, but must bury him the same day. For an impaled body is an affront to God: you shall not defile the land that the Lord your God is giving you to possess." Taking a life also undermined the authority of those to whom God had delegated authority over life and death—kings, priests, and the judges.

In premodern times, however, not all lives were seen as equal, and therefore the import of, and punishment for, taking a human life depended on the status of the victim—a member of the community or a foreigner, man or woman, freeman or slave, aristocrat or commoner, rich or poor, as reflected in the Bible, the legal codices of the ancient Near East, as well as in Roman and Germanic Law.

Medieval society was probably more brutal than our own. Karen Hulttunen has noted that, before the sixteenth century, casual violence seems to have been a way of life for many people of all social ranks in western Europe.[4] As in other societies that subscribed to an ethos based on the "honor-shame" binary value system, even minor insults could prompt physical retaliation, family rivalries descended into vendettas and feuds, and personal scores were frequently settled through extralegal violence. During this period, in both non-Jewish and Jewish society, aggression and the willful infliction of pain on others were more tolerated than today; rather than intervening to stop a fight, bystanders were more likely to gather round to cheer it on. Most homicides were committed against people within the murderer's circle of acquaintance, namely neighbors and friends, or among strangers who met accidentally and ended up in a brawl. Less common was violence against blood relatives or kin. This suggests that many fatal assaults were sparked by sudden passions, often induced by drinking, gambling, and slights to honor, rather than by longstanding tensions.

When bureaucratized nation-states emerged in the modern era, they gradually assumed a monopoly over violence and social and behavioral control systems; in accordance with the Weberian model, political rulers aspired to supremacy and absolutist rule. Violence once more rampant among individuals was checked, government enhanced their policing efforts, and casual physical assault was more strictly suppressed and grew considerably less common in daily interactions. English homicide rates, for example, declined by some fifty percent between the thirteenth and the seventeenth centuries, and then dropped dramatically again between 1660 and 1800. Dying a violent death became less common.

Under this new social order, people sought to negotiate differences rather than take up arms to settle them. This was facilitated by a number of factors, including the gradual extension of what has been called the "civilizing process," with its demands for rational civic harmony, temperance, and emotional self-control.[5] Feudal culture, founded on concepts of personal honor, was gradually replaced by a modern bourgeois culture more attuned to property values. A new humanitarian sensitivity to cruelty and violence emerged, especially in the seventeenth and eighteenth centuries.

Although living as a *corpus separatum* and enjoying relative religious and judicial autonomy, medieval Jews were not completely divorced from larger societal trends. Jews followed and adopted social and religious mores and fashions from the non-Jewish society in which they were embedded, most specifically those characterizing urban medieval society. Therefore, it is hardly surprising that, in matters of crime and illegal activity, Jews did not deviate greatly from their non-Jewish neighbors.

The Hebrew word for murder, *retzah*, and murderer, *rotze'ah*, appear in medieval Jewish texts, but sometimes other less harsh terms are used, such *harigah* (manslaughter) or the more euphemistic *netilat nefesh* (literally, the taking of a soul). The subject of murder is also taken up indirectly, for example in discussions of mourning. Another aspect of murder is discussed in Hebrew sources when a Jew was accused of being an informer (*moser* or *malshin*) who disclosed information about grievances within the Jewish community to non-Jews in general and authorities in particular. Such a person faced retaliation by forces within the community or vigilantes. The first item in the collection of homilies and rulings by the fourteenth-century Austrian Jewish sage Rabbi Shalom of Wiener Neustadt, quoted by his disciple Rabbi Jacob ben Moses Molin (known as Maharil), is telling in this respect:

> Our teacher Rabbi Shalom made this comment in [the Passover] sermon [delivered on the Sabbath before the festival]: "Who is the man who is eager for life who desires years and good fortune? Guard your tongue against evil your lips from deceitful speech. Shun evil and do good, seek amity and pursue it" [Ps. 34:13–15]. All the more so he who denounces his fellow Jew and turns him in, to the hands of Gentiles. This person does not have a share in the world to come.[6]

Rabbi Shalom used the famous verse from Psalms and connected its two sections by linking them to the informer. It seems that in Rabbi Shalom's time and place, Jews denouncing fellow Jews and informing on coreligionists was becoming a serious social problem. That he used the platform of this high point in the calendar, the eve of the Jewish festival of Passover, during what would have been a well-attended sermon, indicates that this is a very high-profile matter. Note that Rabbi Shalom suggests that an informer will lose his share in the world to come, possibly because other internal communal measures have failed to suppress this sort of behavior.

AN ISRAELITE AND A LEVI ON THE EDGE OF TZARFAT: A CASE FROM LIMOGES, LATE TENTH CENTURY

The "horrifying incident from Limoges" refers to events that took place in that town in 992.[7] The account comes from an obscure Ashkenazi manuscript penned in the thirteenth or fourteenth century, first published in print by Avraham Berliner in 1878.[8] It recounts a murder case that is part of a Jewish "deliverance story," a genre typical of Jewish communities that had undergone serious perils and experienced what they understood to be a miraculous deliverance from disaster. Such stories are reminiscent of the biblical book of Esther and the tale of the deliverance of the Jews of Alexandria in 3 Maccabees.[9] While the Limoges incident ended well and the Jewish community was saved, the denouement remains a mystery, as the text, of which only one manuscript survives, ends abruptly. The scribe who presumably copied the text from an earlier source decided for some unknown reason to stop his work.

The story of the incidents of 992 is recounted in the form of a letter written to other communities by the Jews of Limoges (לימוניש); the surviving manuscript contains what appears to be a partial copy of the letter.[10] As there is no external confirmation of the events the letter relates, the story might be fictional. Nevertheless, it rings true for several reasons. The events are recounted in great detail, and while the single manuscript that contains the account dates to the late thirteenth or early fourteenth century, the original text, from which the story was copied, seems to have been written in close temporal proximity to the events it relates, when their memory was still vivid. Apart from the great detail, many of the specifics reflect the mental, political, and legal status of Jews living in Tzarfat (the northern and central areas of modern day France) in the late tenth century.[11] Peter S. Lehnardt, who has studied this text, recently argued that two other factors support the reliability of the text's self-professed date of 992. First, the form of the date is "nine hundred and twenty four years after the second destruction of the Temple." This method of dating also appears in the contemporaneous *Chronicle of Ahimaʻatz* from southern

Italy, and is typical of antemillennial Jewish texts in Europe.[12] In addition, the Hebrew of the text is almost entirely biblical, with almost no trace of postbiblical rabbinic influences. According to Lehnardt, this was typical of European Jewish Hebrew prose and poetry before the eleventh century. All this points to the text originating in the late tenth century.

The protagonist is Sehok ben Astar,[13] identified as an Israelite[14] and a native of the northern French city of Blois. Having abandoned the Jewish faith, he preferred "worshiping the foreign gods of Esau," Esau being the common medieval Jewish eponym for Christianity.[15] Tellingly, however, the text mentions no baptism or any other ceremonial or official conversion to Christianity. The implication is that Sehok displayed a form of hybrid religious affiliation, perhaps one that reflected his genealogy.[16] According to the account, following his break with the Jewish community and adoption of Christian practice (with or without formal conversion), Sehok also drifted away from his native Blois, abandoning not only his original faith and his family, but also the medieval ideal of *stabilitas*—commitment to community and stability in life.

Despite his Christian practices, Sehok, as he traveled among the "surrounding towns," identified as a Jew and took advantage of the Jewish network of social aid. He presented himself using words taken from the book of Jonah: "*'Ivri anokhi*," "I am a Hebrew ... and I worship the Lord, the God of heaven, who has made both the sea and the land" (1:9).[17] This allusion seems to be a deliberate literary way of portraying him as a Jewish renegade of sorts, while further deepening the tension between Sehok's religious behavior and his entreaty to the Jews. By identifying as a Hebrew, Sehok is said to have gained the assistance of "the house of Jacob," perhaps intimating that he worked his charms on Jewish women, who in turn sustained and provided him with food and livelihood "as is their custom, in every city to which he came."[18] The anonymous author relates a host of crimes that Sehok committed during his wanderings, exploiting the Jewish community's trust in him to steal their property and swindle and cheat them. When his crimes were discovered, he was banished and shunned by several Jewish communities in northern France.

As a result, he left the area of his native Blois and its surrounding towns and Jewish communities of the Loire valley, crossing into the area of Limoges.[19] His decision to head south was probably prompted by family ties. The author tells us that Sehok's maternal aunts lived in Limoges, described as a peripheral Jewish community on the edge of Tzarfat. Limoges is referred to as a walled city (*ha-birah*), suggesting its environs might have been perilous, as compared to the Loire Valley communities, of which Blois was one. Another explanation for referring to Limoges in this way might be that, in the tenth century, the city of Limoges grew around two foci, one being the abbey and the other the fortified residence of the viscount on the site of the future Castle of St. Martial, which would naturally be labeled *ha-birah* in Hebrew.[20] Sehok settled in Limoges where, we are told, one of his mother's sisters was married to a "stranger," probably meaning a Christian.

By this point, contemporary readers of the story would have thought the worst of Sehok, given his hybrid genealogy and the dubious social circles he traveled in. Yet in Limoges, where his history was unknown, Sehok seemed to have changed his ways, having risen to financial and public prominence and eventually taken over one of his aunt's households.[21]

The text relates that in Limoges, as in Blois, Sehok once achieving a prominent position, reverted to thieving, killing, fornicating, and swearing falsely—in short, he engaged in immoral and criminal behavior. Indeed, the list of his transgressions suggests that he violated almost every commandment in the Decalogue. But that may be an exaggeration; not every word of the text need be taken at face value.

After setting the scene, the text relates that Sehok and a neighbor, a member of the Limoges community of the Levite family (referred to in the text as *ha-Levi*, meaning "the Levite," which is how I will refer to him as well) were involved in a dispute over property. The language is somewhat ambiguous; Sehok either trespassed on his neighbor's land, or the dispute was a commercial matter. Whatever the case, Sehok pursued his claim ruthlessly, impugning the Levite's integrity, leveling other accusations against him, with the intention of defaming him and causing him to capitulate. But the Levite, no novice at Sehok's game, did not balk when Sehok apparently engaged in

AN ISRAELITE AND A LEVI ON THE EDGE OF TZARFAT

physical intimidation. Sehok then decided to get rid of his adversary, contracting two men from Blois to murder him. The hired killers lay in ambush with drawn swords for several nights, waiting for a chance to take the Levite by surprise.

But their wait was futile. The Levite was either warned in advance, or simply exercised caution, knowing that Sehok was liable to employ violence. He was most likely aware of the possible purpose of the presence of the people that Sehok had brought in from another city to help him, as the presence of strangers would not have passed unnoticed in a late tenth-century French town. The text relates that the Levite, fearing an assault, stayed home after dark and stopped attending the daily morning services in the local synagogue, probably in fear of an assault. But eventually the Levite let his guard down and resumed his daily early morning walk to synagogue.[22] Sehok's contract killers prepared to strike before dawn.[23] They lay in wait, and struck just as the Levite left his home. For whatever reason, it is only at this point in the text that the author discloses that the assailants from Blois were non-Jews.[24] The Levite cried out for help and "all the people congregated [in response] to the call." But it was too late; the Levite had been mortally wounded. With his last breath, however, he named the assassins, whom he identified as associates of Sehok's, "men he had no initial quarrel with."

The assassins, having been positively identified, fled town in great haste, without even collecting their pay. Apparently they did not return to Blois, where the agents of the feudal lord of the Limoges area would not have been able to apprehend them. The author relates that the outlaws sent envoys to Sehok in Limoges to demand their reward for killing his adversary. Sehok seems to have had no interest in paying up, so the assassins threatened to begin robbing travelers to the city. In the late tenth century, Limoges was not only a rising commercial center, but also a regional and superregional pilgrimage site. The demand, sent to Sehok in writing, deserves special scrutiny. The Hebrew is enigmatic; what follows is my attempt to render both the letter and the spirit:

> This is what so and so the murderer has said: "Send me my designated fee that I agreed to with you for killing a soul on

your behalf: a certain amount of money and a set of clothes.²⁵ Is there not one in your midst traveling with goods or a book? Do you not fear that I will confiscate these goods and clear your debt at another's expense? Why have I fled town on your behalf?"²⁶

That part of the wages agreed on for committing the murder was a new set of clothes lends verisimilitude to the story. There are two possible explanations for why new clothes were part of the deal. One was that the murderers would need to get rid of the bloodstained clothing they wore while performing the murder.²⁷ Many people in premillennial Europe, especially in the years before garment production became slightly more industrialized, owned only one set of clothing at any given time, wearing it until it wore out. Bloodstains would render the clothes unwearable both for aesthetic reasons and because they could incriminate the murderers. In Germanic law, as today, bloodstains on clothing or on a weapon could implicate a person in a murder. In legal systems with Germanic foundations, such evidence could also trigger the use of torture in interrogating a suspect.²⁸ A tenth-century killer thus needed a new set of clothes to put on immediately after the crime, in addition to his cash fee.

Sehok was not impressed by the murderers' threats to waylay travelers on the Limoges road. When they carried out their threat, however, he became a serious liability to the Limoges community. The local Jewish elders (*ziknei ha-aretz*, the elders of the land) attempted to negotiate with Sehok, but to no avail.²⁹ According to the text, Sehok reacted by harassing his fellow congregants and disrupting their estates. By this time, he had completely alienated himself from the community, to the point that he decided to destroy it by means of false accusations. To this end, Sehok attempted to plant incriminating evidence that would cause the Jewish community to be accused of employing magical means against the local feudal lord. To achieve this, he planted false evidence in the form of a crucified wax doll resembling the count in the local synagogue, in the ark where the scrolls of the Torah were kept.³⁰ He then sought to force the Jews into a trial by ordeal, in the form of a duel to the death, thus determining the fate of the entire community.³¹ But Sehok's plot failed and the community was saved. While the story abruptly ends at this point and does not say what ultimately happened to Sehok, he was presumably exposed as an imposter and executed by the Christian authorities for his misdeeds.

What does this early story, from the periphery of Jewish life in northern Europe, tell us about medieval Jewish responses to murder? It is important to keep in mind that the account is one-sided. We do not have accounts of these events from Sehok or his supporters, nor is there documentation of the case from either ecclesiastical or lay authorities in Limoges. Nevertheless, the story shares some features with the other violent incidents that will be considered in this section.

The first issue to be considered is the portrayal of Sehok's personality. The scholarly consensus is that the main intention of the account's author or authors was to commemorate the deliverance of the Limoges community from the accusations made by Sehok. They thus depicted Sehok in the worst possible way. Since the community was accused of sorcery and black magic, as well as, possibly, blasphemy and mockery of both the Christian ritual and the town's political leadership (the wax figure was said to resemble the crucified figure of the local count), it is no surprise that the author depicts Sehok himself not only as a blasphemer and an idol worshiper but also a criminal and instigator of a murder. The accusations against him, in particular those relating to his early years in Blois, thus need to be treated with caution. On the other hand, the fact that Sehok was able to hire thugs from Blois to abet him in his quarrels within Limoges's Jewish community indicates something about the circles he traveled in before his arrival in the city.

But this particular deliverance story has a subtext as well—it highlights the danger of individuals with hybrid religious identities. The author of the text, and possibly those who commissioned its composition, clearly believed that the presence of such liminal figures in the French Jewish community posed not only a moral but also an existential threat. Hybrid identities, mixed marriages, and blurred lines of demarcation between Jews and non-Jews spelled trouble. Sehok is evil not only because he was a scoundrel, but also because he was a Jewish turncoat, both in his religious practices and the company he kept, that of non-Jewish thugs who would kill a man for clothes and some money.

Yet while the author clearly condemns Sehok, doing all he can to portray him as despicable both before his arrival in Limoges and while he lived there, he does not refer to him as his neighbor's killer. Sehok is painted as a lax Jew who preferred to outsource the killing of a fellow Jew to non-Jewish henchmen from Blois rather than doing the deed himself. This detail offers further support for the veracity of the account, as it fits patterns that can be seen in later accounts by Jews of murder among their coreligionists. In the heat of a moment, of course, a Jew would not necessarily refrain from killing a fellow Jew—there were certainly circumstances in which a dispute over honor or money could and did escalate into a heated physical altercation that could have a fatal ending. Yet a recurring pattern in medieval accounts of murders within the Jewish community is that Jews who sought to kill another Jew almost always hired a non-Jewish assassin to do the deed. As the texts do not state the reason, I can only speculate. One possibility is that they were responding to a legal distinction between a person who himself committed murder and another who was involved in planning or abetting the crime but did not physically do the deed. That the actual killers were considered more culpable was one reason killers did not want to be discovered with bloody clothing or a murder weapon. The same distinction applied with regard to theft, as I showed in the previous chapter: traders in stolen goods were held less culpable than the thieves themselves.

Another possible explanation is that there were simply not many Jews with the training and experience to carry out a violent assault. There were far more non-Jews than Jews with access to weapons and military or paramilitary training. A third reason was that Jews and non-Jews both embraced the roles assigned to them by the medieval imagination. While Jews could be violent, as the next cases will show, they perhaps at least sought to keep up the appearance that the Christian majority society held the monopoly on violence.[32]

Another recurring trope in the stories in this chapter is the connection between immigration and crime. Sehok is an alien living in the Jewish community of Limoges. He may actually have been a stranger there, or the author might have labeled him as such as a literary device that, after the fact, distanced the community from him. According to the account, Sehok lived in the city for a few years before taking over his aunt's household and, later on, getting into a dispute with his neighbor. Nevertheless, it seems likely that Sehok only arrived in Limoges in his later years. There is no suggestion that he arrived with assets or capital; apparently he rose to prominence and played an influential part in the community and city power politics only as a result of taking over his aunt's assets. Furthermore, while the Levite was intimidated by Sehok, he himself had enough leverage in the community and around town to contain the impact of Sehok's slander. But the storyteller's description of Sehok as a marginal figure who gained power to which he was not truly entitled needs to be taken with a grain of salt. Nevertheless, the account of Sehok's crime makes two things clear. First, when he sought to hire murderers, he turned to his former place of residence. This indicates that while he was a man of some standing in Limoges, he was nevertheless not fully integrated into the city's communal politics. Second, Sehok seems to have had few scruples about leveling serious accusations against the members of the local Jewish community, who had sided with the murdered Levi and who blamed Sehok for many communal and local troubles. As a foreigner, he had very few genuine ties to the Jews of Limoges, apart from his own kin.

Sehok hired people he knew from Blois, rather than killers from Limoges, presumably because he believed that they would be loyal to him, and perhaps also because they would not be identified by Limoges locals. When they had to get out of town quickly after the murder, because their identity was exposed by the victim and before being paid, the killers lost much of the leverage they had on Sehok to ensure that he upheld his end of the bargain. When he failed to do so, they made their threat to attack travelers on their way to and from Limoges, which, in addition to being, by this time, a pilgrimage site in and of itself (the shrine of St. Martial), was an important stop on the Via Lemovicensis, one of the four major routes to the shrine of St. James "the Great," Santiago de Compostela.[33] As Sehok would be blamed for the robberies, they thought that this would intimidate him into paying up. Unfortunately, as the account ends abruptly, it leaves many questions remain unanswered.[34]

THE STATUS OF A MURDERER: WHAT'S IN A GAZE?

As already noted, there are hardly any sources that provide information about violence and murder involving medieval European Jews coming from the trial records of non-Jewish courts. Most of the material, especially until the late thirteenth century, arrives from Jewish communal material addressing social, religious, and ritual issues relating to perpetrators, abettors, and victims. What is the ritual status of a person with another person's blood on his hands? And how is that ritual status determined by the social class or group to which the killer belongs? These questions were not new ones—they were first posed with regard to priests, both those who served in the Temple while it stood and those of the post-destruction period.[35] While the Torah states explicitly that a priest who has had contact with a dead person becomes impure and thus unfit to perform the rituals incumbent on the priesthood, the rabbis ruled that a priest was also defiled by the blood shed on his behalf by another person. The reason given was that a priest who was party to a murder, even one he did not personally commit, clearly could not recite the priestly benediction, which calls on God to bring peace.[36] In the posttalmudic medieval period, these questions continued to be addressed in the writings of the heads of the Babylonian talmudic academies late in the first millennium. A mid-thirteenth-century Ashkenazi manuscript quotes the Babylonian master Sherira Gaon (906–1006):

> He who kills a soul *in our times*, we are unable to do anything to him. We cannot execute him, nor exact any other form of bodily punishment, nor can we exile him. All we can do is avoid him and not mix and mingle with him, and we should not pray in his presence nor should we look at his form. For the sages have said: "One may not behold the image of an evil person," and he is disqualified from testifying on any matter in the world, this is what Rabbi Sherira wrote.[37]

Rabbi Sherira Gaon, a typical representative of the Jewish self-governing system of late tenth century Islamic Baghdad, reflects many of the frustrations faced by Jewish leaders in both Christendom and Islam. With few tools of enforcement permitted to them, they were unable to compel members of their communities to conform to Jewish law. The problem was all the more acute when they had to deal with Jews who were prepared to employ violence or murder, or to arrange for a murder. Such people were contemptuous of the fundamentals that every community requires: respect for the law, moral behavior, and human decency. It is therefore not surprising to find this passage from Sherira Gaon quoted and his ruling reiterated almost three centuries after he died and more than two thousand miles to the west. Despite the cultural differences between tenth-century Iraq and thirteenth-century Germany, the reverence Ashkenazi rabbis had for the sages of Babylonia and their similar communal concerns effectively bridged the gap.[38]

A fundamental assumption of Sherira Gaon's, which held for Jews in medieval Europe as well, was that a Jewish criminal who displayed apparent disregard for human life nevertheless participated, wished to participate, or was expected to participate in the sacral communal worship space—the synagogue. During the Age of Faith, as the medieval era is sometimes known, religious performance was one of the defining features of people's communal affiliations. It was understood that all persons belonged to a religious community, regardless of the level of their actual reverence for the laws of the group to which they belonged. In medieval Jewish communities, limitations to or prohibitions against a transgressor's participation in public worship in the sacral space of the synagogue was one of the only ways for the community and its leaders to register its rejection and interdiction of misconduct.

Clearly, some of the protagonists of the cases recounted in this book had little or no regard for the law. They also had few, if any, inhibitions against employing violence or disobeying the leaders of their Jewish communities, who often lacked the means to counter violence, especially lethal violence. While the capacity for imposing sanctions and punishment varied from one community to another, in general it seems that most medieval Jewish communities had neither the legal ability nor the manpower to enforce their laws or properly punish individuals who had committed grave transgressions.

The most extreme avenues open to Jewish leaders were extradition to the non-Jewish authorities (*mesirah*) and excommunication (*ḥerem*). But there were less radical means at their disposal as well—sanctions in the sphere of ritual performance and the internal public sphere amounting to ostracism. The sanctions that Rabbi Sherira set forth in his ruling were intended to handicap the murderer socially, manifest communal contempt toward him, and signal to other members of the community that the offender's actions were reprehensible. By telling members of the community not only to refuse to allow a murderer to lead prayers but also to refrain from praying in his presence, or even gazing at him, Jewish authorities sought to mark the murderer and segregate him from Jewish society, labeling him as an outcast. Jewish leaders could also simply ignore the offender; his petitions for legal remedies could be ignored and he could be kept from benefiting from communal law and receiving legal succor. In all these ways, Jewish authorities could sometimes muster enough force to condemn and punish wrongdoers without involving extracommunal agencies.

Forbidding an offender from testifying, a penalty sanctioned by Rabbi Sherira, meant expunging him as a legal person. The prohibition against looking at the murderer, on the grounds that "one may not behold the image of an evil person," can be taken in its literal sense, and as a symbolic act of utter disregard, but it also had legal implications. By averting their gazes from the offender, other Jews dehumanized him and rendered him unable to obtain any form of compassion through visual contact. It also branded the murderer as a *rasha'*, an evil person. Furthermore, the sanction served to demarcate the boundaries of their community, placing the murderer outside and drawing an imaginary, yet salient, line between themselves and him.[39] Finally, turning their faces away from the murderer because of his evil actions and sins was an act of imitating God. In the literature that discusses the eternal punishment meted out to sinners in *gehennah* (hell), both Jewish and Christian traditions agree that one of the torments is that the damned souls yearn to behold God and beseech his forgiveness but are unable to do so.⁴⁰ The image comes from the Bible, where God is said to turn his gaze away from sinners: "And I will set My face against that man and will cut him off from among his people" (Lev. 20:3), and "Then My anger shall be kindled against them in that day, and I will forsake them, and I will hide My face from them. And I will surely hide My face in that day for all the evil which they shall have wrought" (Deut. 31:17–18). When the members of the community averted their gaze from the murderer, they could also not testify to his whereabouts, thus further enhancing his legal incapacitation. This process of symbolically marginalizing a murderer is at the center of Sherira Gaon's ruling.

But that ruling does not exhaust the subject. Before considering some cases of Jews who were involved in manslaughter or murder in medieval Europe, another Gaonic tradition known in medieval Europe needs to be examined.

"HE WHO KILLS IN OUR TIMES": FROM THE GAONIC PERIOD TO FIFTEENTH-CENTURY EUROPE

The need for a protocol for dealing with murderers in the Jewish community was not left unanswered. In addition to the above statement by Rabbi Isaac ben Moshe of Vienna (Or Zarua'),⁴¹ at least three complete medieval Jewish European manuscripts lay out rules for the proper response to murderers "in our times." All the three bear the title "The Verdict (*din*) of He Who Kills the Soul (*horeg et ha-nefesh*) in Our Times." One of the texts explicitly attributes the protocol to the Geonim, and it is followed by other penal ordinances (banishment, flogging) attributed to Amram Gaon (c. 810–875) and Nachshon Gaon (c. 820–879). This suggests that the remainder of the text copied in some of the manuscripts is based on Gaonic material as well.⁴²

One of them offers the Gaonic protocol, with medieval European adjustments appended. The protocol begins with the same statement quoted above, to the effect that Jews in "our time" cannot sentence a murderer to death or physical punishment; at most they can banish and ostracize such a person. The protocol assumes that some killers will feel remorse and that ostracism will spur them to undergo a procedure of atonement that will reintegrate them into the community. The protocol promises that if the murderer survives the penitential ordeal imposed on him, the halakhic authorities who imposed it will exonerate him, sanction his reintegration into the community, and forbid other Jews from rebuking him. The ordeal prescribed is a severe one, involving fasting, shaving the offender's head so as to humiliate him publicly, self-inflicted or other-inflicted bodily torment such as flogging, and a public confession of the misdeed.

Flogging is designed more as a ritual ordeal than a punitive measure. It should take place in public at the site of the crime, so that the blood of the penitent falls on the same spot where the blood of the victim had been spilled. Such measure-for-measure punishment seeks to balance the penalty and the crime, in the spirit of Genesis 9:6: "But for your own life-blood I will require a reckoning: I will require it of every beast; of man, too, will I require a reckoning for human life, of every man for that of his fellow man!"

After this ordeal of expiatory pain and bodily mortification, the procedure requires the penitent to beseech the physical remains of the slain person for forgiveness. This must be performed before witnesses. The killer is required to embark on a long journey into exile; he must not only leave his family and his social position, but also wander for a term of five years. Given the dangers of medieval travel and the era's low life expectancy, this was pretty much tantamount to a death sentence. In imposing this penalty, the rabbis drew on the biblical precedent of Cain, who after murdering his brother Abel was doomed to wander through the world. The biblical passage that describes Cain's exile consists of five words, from which come the protocol's five-year term. During this mendicant period, other communities are forbidden to extend aid beyond his basic needs; the murderer may not settle in another community. He is required to live humbly, eating only the most basic food; meat, wine, and ale are forbidden to him, except to fulfill religious requirements. Only after returning from this journey, and once again visiting his victim's grave to ask forgiveness, is the penitent finally absolved and reincorporated into the company of his coreligionists.

"HE WHO KILLS IN OUR TIMES" 133

This arduous penitential procedure is attributed to "an ordinance of the fathers," in the "tradition of the Geonim." It is supplanted, however, with similar protocols with a mitigated severity. One is attributed to "the rabbis of Rome" and the other to Rabbi Ephraim of Regensburg.

As these two texts are shorter than the full Gaonic protocol, I quote them in full. The first is that of the rabbis of Rome:

> And this is what the rabbis of Rome have decreed: Regarding one who cannot bear to suffer all that is written in the regulation of the Geonim [regarding a killer in our times]. He should go into exile for two years, wandering from one place to another. He is not to stay in one community for more than eight days, unless constrained to do so. He may not take or receive from any community more than he needs for his sustenance. During these two years he must fast daily, and on every Monday and Thursday he should be flogged as long as he is within a community. He should refrain from eating meat except on the Sabbath and festivals and he should not drink wine or ale or any intoxicating beverage except for *kiddush* and *havdalah* [the blessings over wine recited at the beginning and end of the Sabbath]. On the first week following his return home [after his two-year exile] he should take two or three people and go and prostrate himself on the grave of the slain person and say: "I declare to you, the bones of so and so. I have sinned and strayed off the righteous path, I have done injury to an innocent man [lit. blood] and I have transgressed the word of my Lord God, and all this is not worth it." He should do this all week twice a day. After this he may wed his betrothed if he is not married. And no man can prevent him from wedding his wife and no son of Israel may chastise him after he has accepted this judgment. And the sages are not at ease with one who does so and reprimands a killer. Furthermore, another eight years are to be imposed on him, during which he should fast every Monday and Thursday, and on the fast days in the evening he is to be flogged. He should also go on exile eight times during these eight years, each time for thirty consecutive days, adding up to a year. During this exile he should not stay in any given community more than three days, and when he goes into exile, and

upon his return, he should prostrate himself on the grave of the slain man and perform the acts mentioned above. He is not to eat meat or drink wine, and if he dies while in exile, he is to be buried in the graves of Israel [a Jewish cemetery, meaning that he has been accepted back into the community]. Once he concludes the eight-year period, he is as eligible as any other Jew to do anything.

The second text is attributed to Rabbi Ephraim of Regensburg.

> And this is what Rabbi Ephraim of Regensburg[43] has decreed. He should wander from place to place for three years throughout [the lands of the Jewish] Exile. He should refrain from meat and any beverage other than water alone, except on Shabbat and festivals. When he arrives in a community, he should fast and mortify his soul and flog his body in the morning and at night, and he should not eat meat at night and drink only water. He should sleep on the ground on a worn mattress. While on the road he need not fast, only on Mondays and Thursdays, and he should refrain from meat, wine, and ale, and also refrain from listening to music. He is to bathe his body [only] twice a year, [before] Passover and Yom Kippur, and then also wash his clothes. He may not shave his head nor his beard until three years have passed. He should have an iron fitting on his abdomen and the hand that committed the crime is to be tied to his groin with an iron chain, so that he cannot use it freely. All this is for three years. And if he can go to a place where the iron fitting can be removed on the eve of the Sabbath and returned upon the conclusion of the Sabbath, that is permitted, but if they cannot do this speedily enough, he should not remove them for the Sabbath. And the Rock of Israel will enable all the transgressors in Israel to repent and will forgive them and all the transgressions of Israel, amen.

These modified protocols indicate that the original atonement procedure was in fact implemented; presumably the revisions were the result of resistance to its draconian provisions. The more lenient procedure attributed to the rabbis of Rome begins with the statement: "Regarding one who cannot bear to suffer all that is written in the regulation of the Geonim." That the original protocol was appended twice, in two different places, Rome and Regensburg, suggests that it was consulted time and again, and revised to fit the needs of changing times. One of the concerns, as will become apparent below, was that there was considerable opposition to the imposition of exile as a punishment. Yet the fact that the procedure was modified rather than discarded indicates that rabbinic authorities viewed a penance of this sort to be essential. Above and beyond a felt need for a demanding punitive ritual that would express the community's revulsion for the crime of murder and for the murderer himself, the procedure was clearly based on the view that, regardless of the gravity of the sin, the transgressor remained a member of the community. It demonstrates that communal and rabbinic authorities felt responsible for the welfare of all Jews, both the blameless and sinners. The eventual outcome of the ritual was the reintegration of the killer into the community, either as an active member with full rights and privileges, or at least, following death and burial in the community cemetery, as a member in good standing. During the penitential period, the murderer is treated as less than a full Jew, but once he has endured his punishment, in either the full or modified form, he regains full standing. This sense of communal responsibility for all Jews can be seen in many aspects of Jewish life in medieval Europe, and is no doubt a corollary of minority status.

Despite the important role apparently played by the Gaonic protocol, in many of the cases that I address below there is no mention of it being implemented. The reason might be that the procedure was seen as too harsh, or that the crime was not seen as severe enough to justify invoking the protocol. Another possibility is that the protocol was seen less as a single procedure and more as a store of individual elements that could be imposed by communal authorities as circumstances required.

LETHAL INCLINATIONS, GENTILES, AND EXILE: THE HOMILIES OF RABBI JUDAH THE PIOUS

Another important Jewish figure in Regensburg was Rabbi Judah ben Shmuel "the Pious" (c. 1160–1217), a younger contemporary of Rabbi Ephraim who was mentioned above. Rabbi Judah the Pious is practically synonymous with the important and ascetic ethical manual attributed to him, *Sefer Ḥasidim*.[44]

The Familiar Murderer

The Parma manuscript of *Sefer Ḥasidim* includes a series of consecutive paragraphs relating to murder and how it is to be punished. Some of them are formulated as legal-moral rulings, while others are homilies on matters related to homicide and murder.[45] The homilies (*midrashim*) draw on Jewish traditions of late antiquity and, at first glance, seem to simply reiterate them. But a closer reading reveals the independent homiletics that are the staple of this work.

The subject of murder is first addressed in two brief homilies, one on Esau and the other on King David. The homilist, probably Rabbi Judah the Pious, took as his starting point the Bible's use of the adjective *admoni*, from the Hebrew word meaning "red," to describe both figures—presumably a reference to their having red hair.[46] Red hair, echoing the color of blood, was thought in both Jewish and Christian sources and lore to be an external manifestation of lethal inclinations and blood lust.[47] According to the homily, King David, mindful and apprehensive of this innate trait and its potential consequences, pleaded to the Almighty that this attribute be channeled only toward "the nations" (*ha-umot*), meaning non-Jews. The homily leaves it at that, but anyone familiar with the biblical narrative knows very well that, while King David indeed killed many foreigners, such as Goliath, he also used violence against members of his own nation.[48]

The homily encapsulates Rabbi Judah's values and his attitude toward the taking of a life. While killing is reprehensible in general, it is much more reprehensible to kill members of one's own nation or ethnic group. It is followed by a section addressing the penance imposed on a murderer (*rotze'aḥ*), one of the many original homiletic passages for which the book is best known. The presumption of this medieval midrash is that a murderer should be condemned to a five-year exile, based upon the five times that the Hebrew root *NVD* (נוד, to wander) appears in the Pentateuch. The homily alludes to the primordial murder of Abel by Cain, and the punishment imposed on the latter—to wander the earth in exile (Gen. 4:1–16).[49] The ensuing discussion invokes what seems to have been another tradition relating to the exile of a murderer, but in this case for three or even two years of exile—the exile imposed on Absalom after he kills his half-brother Amnon (2 Sam. 13–14, esp. 13:38 and 14:28).

Following his discussion of the duration of a murderer's exile, Rabbi Judah declares: "And if a man has a wife and small children, even though they are minors, he should go into exile in this manner in our times." In other words, there are two terms of exile as punishment for killing another human being: either a five-year exile or a reduced sentence of three years of exile, depending upon the murderer's family situation. It is important to stress that our discussions refer only to male murderers.

This last remark turns what at first seems to be a homily into a concrete legal ruling. The use of the phrase "our times" (*ba-zman ha-zeh*), namely the era in which Rabbi Judah lived, that is Ashkenaz of the late twelfth and early thirteenth century, suggests that Rabbi Judah and his audience were grappling with cases of this sort. Furthermore, the use of the story of Absalom portrays the murderer not as a ruthless and faceless stranger but as a member of the family, a member in good standing of the community rather than a lawless rogue on the margins of society.

The fuller version of *Sefer Ḥasidim* found in the large fourteenth-century Parma manuscript comprises more than 2,500 articles, including over 400 exempla.[50] One of the latter is conceptually linked to punishing a murderer with exile. Although it is a literary construct and not an eyewitness or legal account of an actual occurrence, the story includes credible life details that indicate a basis in actual events, or at the very least expresses Rabbi Judah's view of manslaughter in the Ashkenazi Jewish communities of his time. The exemplum has no title, but a good one would be "The Pious Murderer":

And there was a case of a man who killed a soul [*harag et ha-nefesh*], and he chose to provide livelihood to the heirs [of the victim] but did not go into exile. He said: "I know that if I am exiled among the Gentiles I will not be able to keep the Sabbath." He made himself an iron fitting and he wore it on his body like a belt and it tormented him, causing agony and grief. They said: this self-inflicted agony of torment is double the weight of that of the agony of exile. And he did all this so as not to eat gentile bread and violate the Sabbath.[51]

It seems that this exemplum was deliberately placed after the passage about the reduced term of exile. Its point of departure is the presumption that a murderer is to be exiled to perform penance, as stipulated in the Gaonic protocol (although the protocol is not explicitly referred to in the text). Just as concern for the well-being of the murderer's family was reason to reduce the sentence for manslaughter from five to three years of exile, here too circumstances mandate a mitigation of the sentence. These include the need for financial support for the victim's family, who were apparently poor, the religious well-being of the murderer, and the fear of a diminished sense of Jewish identity.[52] The standard punishment of exile was commuted to bodily mortification and providing for the dead person's family and children. The exemplum makes it clear that murders occurred, murderers were exiled, and that compromises were reached based on a host of social and religious considerations.

In the absence of an internal Jewish penal system with the power to mete out justice in accordance with the biblical and early rabbinic code, medieval European Jews had to grapple with the question of how to respond to the murder of a Jew by a fellow Jew. But even if Jewish communities in Ashkenaz had had the authority to impose a death sentence on murderers, they probably would not have done so. In fact, the talmudic sages had already obviated the imposition of capital punishment on such offenders.[53]

This state of affairs is salient in the above ruling by Sherira Gaon. The inability to implement proper judgment in capital offenses is ascribed by talmudic sages to the destruction of the Temple and its subsequent absence as a symbol of the link between God and man, a link that had enabled Jewish jurists to deprive a human being of the divinely bestowed right to live. In addition, it signified a diminished Jewish existence in the exilic period (BT *Megillah* 12b).[54]

In other words, the biblical and rabbinic treatment of capital offenses, murder in particular, was virtually obsolete by this time. The apologetic and polemic tenor of the imposition of exile on murderers is obvious. Originally, when the Jewish legal system chose to stop imposing capital punishment, it sought to signal to the imperial powers under whose rule they lived, the Roman and Parthian/Sassanian empires, that Jews had relinquished this power to the state. Once the Roman Empire adopted Christianity as the state religion, Jews needed to counter the Christian claim that Jewish communal authorities had condemned Jesus to death and handed him over to the Roman authorities for execution.[55] By suggesting that they did not have the ability to sentence anyone to death, the Rabbis showed that it was impossible to blame the Jews for the fate of the Christian Messiah.

As the Rabbis saw it, in the Diaspora, the only serious sanction that Jewish leaders retained was that of ostracism. The starting point for the author of *Sefer Ḥasidim* was thus that a murderer was to be exiled, not executed, and that the penalty could be administered in a number of ways. Expiation and penance could be performed by means of bodily mortification and financial penalties levied on the murderer. The communal fear of losing both victim and murderer seems to have loomed large over a sensitive individual like Rabbi Judah the Pious. Another concern Rabbi Judah had was with the penitent's loss of Jewish identity while in exile.

The murderer was to commit himself to the financial upkeep of the victim's family and heirs, and either go into exile or willingly mortify his body. While not stated explicitly, clearly the victim had been a male provider, meaning that his death left his family bereft not just emotionally but also financially, so that if they were not provided for, they would need to be supported by the community. Clearly influenced by the penitential practices in Christian society, especially in monastic circles, *Sefer Ḥasidim* subscribed to the idea of a calibrated penance.[56] Fearing that exile might cause him to lose his Jewish identity,

Rabbi Judah relates, the murderer devised an instrument for bodily mortification. Such double degradation, of both body and purse, is said to be twice as harsh as the agony of exile.[57] This does not mean that punishment by exile was abandoned altogether, nor was Rabbi Judah the innovator of the use of bodily mortification as a penalty. Rather, both were imposed in the internal Jewish penal system as part of the way in which the crime of slaying a fellow Jew was addressed.[58]

The concept of exile and financial compensation to the victim's family in cases of killing or murder resonates with both biblical and Germanic law. Exile is mentioned in the Bible as the punishment for an unintentional killer (Num. 35:6). A killer was to either flee to a specific town that was a place of exile or after being caught he was delivered there for a long sentence. It is not clear if this arrangement ever existed or was only a literary construct. In the medieval context, in absence of such a system (even if only as a literary construct) the punishment for unintentional killers seems to have been more like banishment from the community and the protections it could provide in accordance with the privileges that the Jews had been granted. No alternative Jewish community or penal colony was suggested. As such, exile here closely resembles the "outlaw" punishment for murder found in many Germanic codes.[59] Similarly, many of the ancient Germanic codes mandated the payment of compensation—*weregeld*—to the victim's family.[60]

Sefer Rokeah, the early thirteenth century halakhic compendium attributed to Rabbi Judah's disciple, Rabbi Elazar of Worms, includes a ruling that a murderer should be exiled wearing or carrying on his person at all times an iron fitting, designed to signify the sin of murder while simultaneously mortifying and tormenting the body.[61] Mortification of the body in this fashion is quite well known from Christian monastic circles. It is not clear to what extent the directives prescribed by Rabbi Eliezer were actually observed, but there is good reason to believe that at least some adherents of the Jewish Pietists' teachings implemented these penalties in meting out punishment for murders.

The need to impose severe penalties on Jewish murderers from within the community, and to demonstrate the offender's status as a member, and thus beneficiary, of the community, so common in

LETHAL INCLINATIONS, GENTILES, AND EXILE 141

minority groups, is also evidenced in other ways. In another passage in *Sefer Ḥasidim*, Rabbi Judah uses a verse from the book of Proverbs to make a strong claim against granting asylum to a Jewish fugitive with blood on his hands:

> If a murderer flees to you, do not accept him, be he a Jew or a Gentile.... If evil people and sinners flee to you and seek asylum under your wings, you should not provide them with protection or shelter, for if you do accept them, they will turn on you and their presence will cause either you or your offspring harm.... And you should not have pity on those who have no pity, for he who pities the merciless or accepts them, the Holy One, Blessed be He, will eventually turn you over into their hands. For it is said: "your life shall be forfeit for his life and your people for his people" (1 Kings 20:42), and it is written: "Show him no pity nor compassion" (Deut. 13:9) and this is why Saul was punished for the issue of Agag.[62]

The language is unequivocal, warning those who might grant a murderer sanctuary in their community of the consequences of allowing a condemned criminal to dwell and seek asylum in their midst. Typically, in terms of *Sefer Ḥasidim*'s language, Rabbi Judah warns that the evil consequences may come immediately, but might also only transpire during the life of the descendants (*zar'am/zar'o*) of those to whom he addresses his warning, a textual safeguard intended to make sure the prediction cannot be gainsaid.

Rabbi Judah makes no distinction in this regard between Jewish and non-Jewish murderers who might seek sanctuary in the town. Given that the rationale for the prohibition is the danger of having a murderer in the community, the murderer's religious affiliation is apparently not significant.[63] What matters is his personality. One might suppose that the greatest danger in harboring a criminal would be fear of legal retribution, but this does not seem to be the reason for the concern voiced here. *Sefer Ḥasidim* acknowledges the tendency for compassion, especially with regard to a coreligionist on the move if not on the run, yet explicitly demands that the beseecher's history be carefully checked in order to prevent granting sanctuary to an evildoer. A seemingly needy person might be a source of moral trouble, either in the immediate future or in the long run.[64]

Rabbi Judah expected Jews to deny suspected murderers asylum in their towns and communities. Presumably he did not issue his injunction in a void, but was rather reacting to a phenomenon or perhaps a specific incident, one that is not identified. While Rabbi Judah's language is unambiguous, the actual implementation of his decree may have been markedly different, or at least not as clear-cut as it is made out to be in his ethical writing.

Enacting Penance for Murder: The Story of Hai Gaon and the Murderer on the Mount of Olives

Lacking almost entirely authority to impose punishment on criminals, the Jewish communal legal system often had only one recourse—imposing severe penance.[65] One of the more intriguing exempla from *Sefer Ḥasidim* is the tale of the Babylonian sage Hai Gaon (d. 1038) and his pilgrimage to Jerusalem.[66] It reveals the ideas that circulated among Ashkenazi pietistic thinkers and halakhists, such as Rabbi Judah the Pious and possibly Rabbi Ephraim of Regensburg, who mitigated the "protocol of penance for a killer in our time" prescribed for grave sins of killing and murder. In general, they felt that such penance should involve not only symbolic acts but, as noted above, cause the offender actual pain and physical suffering.

The story, like many of the exempla in *Sefer Ḥasidim*, is framed by a larger discussion about the nature of the penance to be performed for grave sins and the manner in which the penitent himself may be part of determining the penance. However, Rabbi Judah felt that consulting with a pietistic wise man (*ḥakham*) was in order, as the judgment of the penitent might be clouded and the larger picture missed. The discussions and exempla thus underscore the pivotal role of a pietistic and rabbinic authority in this matter; the author shares the story of a penitent murderer in order to show the need for sincerity in penance, while emphasizing that there is always more than meets the eye.

> And all the above should not be taught to all and dispensed to every seeker but only to those penitents who really wish to purge themselves before the Holy One Blessed Be He. And so it happened in the days of Rabbi Hai[67] and Rabbi Evyatar Kohen Tzedek[68] in Jerusalem. A murderer appeared before them [seeking penance]. They ordered him flogged publicly on the Mt. of Olives [during the month of Elul] until he bled. While he was being flogged, the penitent murderer cried out "Beat me! Have no mercy on me! For I do not want to be summoned to trial before the Holy One Blessed be He."[69] So they flogged him mercilessly until his cheeks were swollen. Only then did he command to let him be.[70] And they let him recover for three weeks and then they buried him in the sand, leaving only a small pinhole size nozzle for air to barely flow. They tortured him and struck him until he was between life and death. All this was done three times until they knew and realized [דעו והבינו *da'u ve-hevinu*] that he was absolved [in the heavens], for he accepted and embraced all these abuses with love. Finally the murderer said: "But I have not been absolved yet," to which they replied: "We have heard from the Holy One Blessed Be He that you have been absolved."[71]

In the remainder of the text, Hai Gaon is portrayed in dialogue with the penitent murderer. As the storyteller, Rabbi Judah, sees it, the acts of severe penance transformed the penitent. The transgressor was absolved of his sins and his slate was wiped clean; but more than that, his painful ordeal created a form of intimacy between himself and his confessor, the overseer of his public penance, Hai Gaon.[72] It is for this reason that the storyteller uses the absolved murderer to drive the story forward, presenting him as Hai Gaon's intimate interlocutor as they both circle the Mount of Olives. The topic they discussed is a revelation the rabbi had while attending the liturgical procession during the ceremony on the Mount of Olives in Jerusalem on the Hoshaʿna Raba holiday (the last day of Sukkot, on the eve of Shemini Atzeret). The substance of this revelation is of extreme significance—it is eschatological and deals with the final redemption.

The storyteller, Judah the Pious, believed that a genuine rigorous contrition process, followed by painful bodily mortification coupled with a deeply penitent heart, would bring even the gravest sinner—a person who took another's life—back into the fold. In this Rabbi Judah was following the talmudic teaching attributed to Rabbi Abbahu of Caesarea: "In the place where penitents stand, even the wholly righteous cannot stand" (BT *Berakhot* 34b), as well as the logic behind the penitential protocol. His powerful message is that the murderer not only returns to the fold but actually reaches a higher spiritual plane, where he is worthy of delving into the mysteries of the final redemption and having the intimate experience of divine revelation. This was not always the case, as the stories that follow will show; it happened that, even after performing serious mortifications, penitents were hounded by their coreligionists.

The text, of course, does not depict historical events. The two "historical" figures portrayed in it may have never met. It does, however, have a historical setting. Most likely, the thirteenth-century German Jew Judah the Pious was, like medieval painters of biblical scenes, portraying a legend in a familiar landscape. As a result, the text says much more about Ashkenazi pietistic ideas of penance than it does about the lives of Middle Eastern Jews in eleventh-century Palestine. Rabbi Judah emphasizes the diligence of the penitent, driven by his preference to endure pain and suffering here and now rather than enduring divine retribution in the afterlife. In this, Rabbi Judah thought much like the Christian theologians of penance and contrition who were his contemporaries. They, too, advocated purging grave sins in this world so as to head off eternal damnation and hellfire, or at the very least long suffering in Purgatory.[73] The ritual suggested by the story is meant to simulate the pain suffered by the victim of the killing. It is followed by what seems to be a mock execution and subsequent burial, intended to bring the penitent as close as possible to the existential experience of death without crossing the mortal threshold. The result seems to be a feeling of expiation and rebirth, enabling the penitent's reentry not only into decent society but even to the intimate circle of the religious leadership, not as a member but as an observer. The text also exposes one of the most important factors in the penitential doctrine of the Ashkenazi Pietists, the need to receive the penance from a pietistic-religious authority.[74] More precisely, the purpose of the exemplum is to make this very point, namely that a sinner needs the guidance of a penitential supervisor to avoid further punishment in the afterlife.[75]

Inadvertent Murderers and Penitential Practices: Evidence from Medieval Responsa and Other Sources

The primarily moralistic and homiletic sources considered thus far have shown that some circles stressed that atonement required confession and bodily mortification, as well as penances such as exile, fines, and financial compensation. But they also recognized the need to mitigate the severity of such punishments, and in some cases questioned whether exile was indeed essential and advisable. The responsa literature offers further information relating to concrete cases.

Rabbi Isaac ben Moshe of Vienna (Or Zarua'), for example, adjudicated a case involving the unintentional death of a newborn infant as a result of his circumcision (see appendix 5). Sometime during the mid-thirteenth century, he received a letter from Rabbi Jacob ben Isaac ha-Lavan of Prague; the two had been close friends since the young Isaac Or Zarua' studied under Jacob's father, Rabbi Isaac ben Jacob ha-Lavan.

The original letter has not survived, but the case can be easily reconstructed from the responsum that Rabbi Isaac included in his eponymous halakhic work, *Or Zarua'*. It appears there along with a number of rulings by the author and other contemporary rabbinic authorities, between the subsection of the book devoted to rulings about prayer in general (*Hilkhot Tefilah*) and that addressing the rules applying to cantors and leaders of public prayer services (*Hilkhot Sheli'ah Tzibur*), which are parts of the first major section of this vast halakhic compendium. As in the case of the frontier communities in Poland, our knowledge about homicide, manslaughter, and other unnatural deaths in the Jewish community comes from cases that survived because of their impact on the sacred space of the communal liturgical meeting place, the synagogue.

The case concerns a *mohel*—ritual circumciser—named Matityah, most probably from Prague, who performed a circumcision ceremony that resulted in complications, eventually costing the infant his life. As an act of penance, Matityah was exiled from Bohemia, probably to neighboring Austria, where he lived as an itinerant. The responsum text states clearly that Matityah was impelled to do penance and go into exile by the community and its religious authorities.[76] In accepting this punishment, Matityah publically acknowledged his responsibility for the fatality and performed the penance that he and his community believed to be necessary. The responsum makes no mention of financial compensation, nor of bodily mortification. Apparently, money was either not at issue in this case, or the loss of life at this very early age was not seen to require such a payment.

Nevertheless, the infant's family did not consider an unspecified term of exile and penance sufficient. It is also unclear from the text if Matityah took upon himself or was instructed to perform any other form of penance apart from exile. When Matityah returned to Bohemia, the infant's family made his life miserable. The child's father claimed that Matityah had performed only halfhearted penance and that he had earned a living (*nistaker*) while in exile, implying that Matityah actually prospered rather than suffered during his time away. All Matityah did was relocate to another city, the father charged; he had not in fact wandered the roads "like a true penitent."[77] Accordingly, the father demanded that the community desist from praying in Matityah's presence and forbid him from leading the community in prayer. In other words, he was to live as an excommunicate in his own community, after having completed his term in exile.

The father's claims were indicative of the times. In contemporary non-Jewish society, exile and penance were closely associated. While especially salient in certain monastic circles in Ireland, Scotland, and in Irish and Scottish monastic communities on the continent, it was also conspicuous in southeast Germany in general and Regensburg (Rabbi Judah's city) in particular. The idea of exile as a punishment for manslaughter, a form of liturgical exile for the sake of penance, was well known, as was its later evolution into a pilgrimage. Early medieval Irish theologians called it a "blue martyrdom," and it was a rather widespread penitential practice intended especially for the sin of taking a life.[78] Matityah's case makes clear the role of the community and the way in which it dealt with such cases. In this case the community was split between supporters of the family and those of Matityah. Rabbi Jacob, perplexed by the case, shared his deliberations with his colleague, Rabbi Isaac. The father justified his demand on both ritualistic and communal grounds, as the synagogue served as both a Jewish sacral and public space. The demand to ban Matityah from attending services at the synagogue was meant to place Matityah outside both. Rabbi Isaac's response was unequivocal:

> It seems to me that the infant's father has no power to prevent you from praying with this Matityah. Rather, this is a matter for the public [*ha-tzibur*] to decide upon. Had he [Matityah] been a deliberate murderer [*horeg nefesh be-mezid*], even if the deceased's immediate kin did not prevent praying in his presence, the community itself would be expected to abstain from him. As Rabbi Sherira Gaon wrote: "Nowadays [*ba-zman ha-zeh*], he who kills a soul although we may not harm him at all, neither execute nor flog nor exile him, all we are left with is the ability to abstain from him and to prevent mixing and mingling with him. And we may not pray with him and we should even refrain from gazing upon him. For the Sages have said that one may not look at the face of a culprit, and he may not give any form of testimony."

Rabbi Isaac goes on to maintain that this ruling applies if the murderer has no intention of repenting. But in the case at hand, Matityah had had no intent to kill and accepted exile for the sake of penance. As such, his penance should be accepted and he should be considered as upright as any other member of the community.

But Rabbi Isaac adds a proviso. The murderer needed to perform an action to manifest the expiatory process that the penance he had undergone had brought about, immersion in a ritual bath (*tvilah*), to cleanse himself from the defilement of his sin.[79] This ritual, closely associated with purification from sin in both the Bible and rabbinic texts, is completely absent from both the full and the abridged and amended versions of the penance protocol. Indeed, in the abridged versions, the penitent actually is required to abstain from bathing while in the process of penance, perhaps as a manifestation of how his sin has defiled him both in soul and in body. *Or Zarua'* requires that the immersion come after his return to the community, similar to most of the purification processes described in the Torah. Regardless of the intentionality, in the minds of rabbinic authorities in Ashkenaz the act of killing another human being caused ritual defilement, and the murderer needed to be cleansed in the purifying water of a ritual bath.[80]

Rabbi Isaac then considers whether such a penitent could serve as a cantor, leading prayers in the synagogue. He rules that once the truly remorseful murderer has undergone ritual immersion (thus enacting the final phase of his penance), there are no legal grounds for the community to shun him or not to accept him as a prayer leader. Although Rabbi Isaac discusses both inadvertent murderers and the social reaction to an intentional murderer in his responsum, he makes no mention of capital punishment, simply because of the fact that, in the Jewish communities of northern Europe, executing murderers was not an option.

The case of Matityah, who had had accidentally caused a death while performing a mandatory religious ritual, also records non-rabbinic voices. While they come down to us secondhand, filtered through rabbinic writing, they nevertheless offer insights about the victim's family, their ideas about proper penance, and the nature of expiatory exile. These ideas, which may have had wider resonance in Jewish circles of that time, were not far removed from those of their non-Jewish neighbors, as well as the way the penitent killer understood the process.

The victim's family sought to enforce sanctions of a severity that the rabbis, and apparently some members of the community, believed to be overly harsh. The rabbis took it upon themselves to curb the vehemence and vengefulness of the victim's family. In so doing, they stressed the role of the community (*ha-tzibur*).

Rabbi Isaac Or Zarua' believed that both the murderer and the victim's family should defer to the leadership of the Jewish community to which they belonged. Apparently, it was Matityah who petitioned Rabbi

Jacob ben Isaac of Prague. As he saw it, he had paid his debt to society and performed his duty to God by going into exile. The responsum, most probably echoing material from Matityah's lost question, indicates that he charged that the victim's family was seeking to punish him unreasonably, by claiming that he had actually prospered in exile.

In this case, all the parties involved accepted rabbinic authority and the help extended by the rabbinic judicial system to resolve their grievances. This was not always the case. Rabbinic documents also offer accounts of cases in which one or more parties refused to submit to rabbinic decisions.

While inadvertent killers were not considered murderers, they were nevertheless seen as sinners, culpable in some sense for the loss of a life. A case such as this, termed an "accident that bordered on the deliberate" (*shogeg ha-karov le-mezid*), demanded that the perpetrator take action to restore the spiritual and communal equilibrium that his deed had disrupted. As in deliberate criminal acts, there were victims and their families involved; in some cases, the victim and the killer came from the same family, further complicating the matter. Rabbinic adjudicators often faced the need to regulate a community's attitude toward one of its members who had the blood of another member on his or her hands.

A MURDERER IN OUR MIDST: ADDRESSING EXTREME VIOLENCE IN THE COMMUNITY

How did communities and rabbinic authorities treat individuals who were intentionally violent, and how did they react to those who pushed violence to the ultimate extreme of deliberately taking a life, with total disregard for the moral and rabbinic penal code? What recourse, if any, did they have when faced with rogue murderers who had no scruples against committing violent, even deadly, crimes against fellow Jews— or against non-Jews, in which case they placed their entire community in danger? The penitential protocol instituted by the medieval Babylonian Geonim begins by offering a procedure—ostracism—for dealing with such criminals, but clearly there were many cases in which the protocol was not applicable and other methods were needed. While the documentation of how medieval European Jewish authorities handled such cases is sparse, the available records nevertheless offer enough information to be able to suggest some conclusions.

Contrary to the popular image that medieval Jews were peaceful within their communities and in their relations with non-Jews, violence was, in fact, ubiquitous in northern European Jewish communities. One of the first scholars to document this was Avraham Grossman, in his groundbreaking research on the early sages of Ashkenaz of the tenth and eleventh centuries. In an article published in 1981, highlighting findings from his dissertation, Grossman discussed violent individuals in early Rhineland Jewish communities and their impact on both their communities and Jewish legal procedures. He focused on the concepts of the *alam*, a violent individual, and the *gazam*, a person who threatens to use violence.[81]

The material unearthed by Grossman, from legal texts and his close readings of liturgical poetry (*piyyut*), depicts a social milieu of highly influential and affluent Jewish merchants who did not hesitate to threaten and commit violence against fellow members of their communities. Grossman shows that rabbinic authorities sought to check and curb this behavior, with varying success. The responsa do not offer statistical data, so there is no way of determining the frequency of such behavior.[82] Nevertheless, the fact that rabbinic and related texts from this time repeatedly address the use of violence and recorded statements made by communal officials and authorities indicating their helplessness in handling violent individuals, shows that the phenomenon was widespread.

My own reading of the sources indicates that violent behavior often erupted when a cycle of verbal invective spiraled out of control, until one of the parties responded with physical assault. In other cases, however, a violent attack was committed without provocation, verbal or otherwise. Most of the recorded cases were reported to communal or rabbinic authorities by victims seeking financial compensation and some sort of satisfaction. In other cases, communal and rabbinic authorities felt compelled to intervene of their own volition, when extreme violence threatened to redound on the community and its members. Communal authorities used the means available to them, most notably excommunication, in their attempts to curb such violent behavior.

A recently published brief responsum, written by Rabbi Isaac ben Avraham (Rizba), who lived in northern France in the late twelfth century, illustrates the limits of ostracism (*nidui*) as a penalty when it was imposed by an unnamed community against a man who used excessive violence against a fellow Jew.[83] Rabbi Isaac stresses that the banishment is meant not only to be punitive but also to compel the perpetrator to seek forgiveness from his victim. Only if he did so would he be able to receive absolution from the community and have the ban of excommunication lifted. In his responsum, Rabbi Isaac urges the victim to act benevolently and not withhold absolution: "And the victim who is now in the position to grant absolution [*moḥel*] should not behave cruelly towards the person seeking his forgiveness," he writes. Rabbi Isaac advised the rabbinic authorities from the community, who had sent the question to him: "And to you, my teachers, please try not to rebuff [the absolvent] and your manner should be a gentle and an easy one, so that he [the victim] may listen. Thus we may live up to the biblical maxim: 'therefore love truth and peace'" [Zech. 8:19].

Rabbi Isaac might seem to be displaying a troubling level of leniency toward the assailant. Perhaps this was a consequence of the voluntary nature of the Jewish communal judicial system. As I have already noted, and will highlight in another case below, Jews at this time always had the option of disregarding a rabbinic ruling or, even worse from the rabbinic and communal perspective, of submitting their grievance to the non-Jewish authorities. Jewish authorities did all they could to prevent this from happening, and condemned it in the strongest possible terms.[84] In his classic study *Tradition and Crisis*, Jacob Katz wrote:

> The belief that Jewish law was divinely inspired, in contrast to the merely human and conventional laws of the other nations, inevitably elevated the value of the former and lowered the latter. This view was strengthened by frequent warnings by communal authorities against Jews bringing their internal squabbles before non-Jewish courts [*'arka'ot shel goyim*]. Even cases in which the

Gentile courts found for the Jew and against the Christian did not affect this view in any fundamental sense since it was based on principles of faith rather than on any empirical observation.[85]

When someone did seek justice outside the internal Jewish system, there was very little the Jewish authorities could do. This concern appears repeatedly in the texts and subtexts of halakhic deliberations, as in the above responsum by Rabbi Isaac.

When it came to employing a very effective punitive instrument such as the act of excommunication (*nidui*), the question of proportionality was a major one. Indeed, the "protocol regarding a killer in our time," in both its full Gaonic and abridged European versions, stresses the efficacy of *nidui*. Rabbi Isaac's appeal to the local rabbinic authorities to exercise caution in imposing excommunication, followed by his advice to the victim not to exercise cruelty toward his assailant's attempt to seek absolution, may indicate that such sanctions were quite effective.[86] It may well be that Rabbi Isaac's conciliatory language was prompted by cases in which communities refused to accept penitents back into the fold, leading violent offenders to give up all hope of receiving penance within the communal system. This would have had grave consequences—they would seek justice elsewhere or, in extreme cases, convert to Christianity.[87]

In cases of murder, when violence between two Jews reached its most extreme, rabbinic writing exposes even deeper frustration. There is a strong sense of powerlessness when it comes to proper retribution. In a responsum from MS Parma 86, attributed to Rabbi Haim Eliezer Or Zaruaʻ, the author relates how he joined forces with others to proclaim that a certain person should be labeled "utterly evil" (*rashaʻ gamur*), excommunicated, and labeled an anathema (*shamta*), unfit for testimony in all Jewish judicial procedures. In his first sentence, Rabbi Haim writes: "Although I am not worthy, I cannot stand aside and cannot refuse to write of a certain person that he is utterly evil." This preamble indicates that Rabbi Haim's firmness in addressing the case was not matched by all the other rabbinic authorities before whom the case came, possibly due to fear and intimidation. Anathematization and branding an offender as "utterly evil" was also practiced by ecclesiastical courts in medieval Europe. Sanctions could be levied either on an individual, or even, in special cases, on entire communities or parishes. These sanctions could be imposed in a wide variety of cases, not just bearing on spiritual matters, that were entrusted to ecclesiastical courts. These sanctions, like bans, could be imposed at various scales: admonition, excommunication, aggravation, and reaggravation, to the point that the entire parish was put under interdict (*cession divinorum*), meaning that the Christians living there could not receive the sacraments.[88] A ban of excommunication could serve as a judicial measure (eradicating the convict's legal persona) but also as a powerful curse; labeling an offender "evil" or "utterly evil" (*rasha'* or *rasha' gamur*) may be both.[89]

Like Rabbi Haim, other thirteenth-century Jewish legal authorities reacted firmly to murder within the community. A responsum written by Rabbi Shabtai ben Shmuel of Zeitz (near Leipzig), a member of Rabbi Meir of Rothenberg's circle, discusses a Jewish man accused of manslaughter. There had been no eyewitnesses to this killing of a Jew, and it seems to have been unclear whether the accused man did the deed or if it was done at his behest by his gentile manservant. Rabbi Shabtai ruled that it was entirely irrelevant who had performed the actual murder. Given the halakhic maxim that the laws of agency (*shliḥut*) do not apply to gentiles, this ruling was a novelty. The Jew was to be labeled a murderer and ostracized as one. The language of the responsum is telling:

> On the evil deed that occurred involving this certain evil man, he who lacks the spirit of God in him [*ru'aḥ ha-Shem ein be-kirbo*],[90] he should be reprimanded with a piercing thorn.[91] And I heard while I was in Magdeburg that this man threatened the victim and this is why I resolved to convict him.... In the matter before us, there was no one in the field [at the scene of the crime] except the murderer and his gentile servant, and thus we cannot ascertain who actually killed the victim: the Jewish master or the gentile servant. If the Jew killed [the victim], he is to be regarded as an "utter murderer" [*rotze'aḥ gamur*] and if the servant killed, it was undoubtedly under specific orders from the

Jewish master. It therefore makes no difference, for the servant's deed is as if the master had done it. Regardless of whose actual hands committed the crime, we should have pity on his soul, for he has deviated from the righteous path and he needs penance. Indeed the God-fearing people should be zealous about this and abstain from any contact with this murderer and punish him and suppress him by any means of oppression, until his heart surrenders and he repents his evil deeds ... and I say if on matters of an alleged monetary debt we ban a person, it is all the more so in this matter that we should be harsh with him and ban him. And I agree with all of you about this matter, and this is a case where I call upon the murderer and say: Be gone, you man of blood, one so full of defilement. But if he submits to this admonishment he will be redeemed and will receive penance. [signed] Shabtai ben Shmuel.[92]

Anathema, expulsion from social interactions, and ritual excommunication were powerful instruments, but not effective on Jews who had little regard for the communal authorities, either because they lived on the margins of the community or had enough social and financial capital to grant them social standing independent of the community. As with other cases I have considered, even in these cases Jewish authorities left the door open to those who sought penance. After condemning the murder in no uncertain terms, Rabbi Shabtai nevertheless declares that if a murderer repents, accepting admonishment and punishment (and presumably compensating the victim's family financially), the communal authorities would absolve him. These sanctions apparently usually worked with inadvertent killers, who respected the law and wished to prove their contrition. Those who killed in self-defense also wanted official absolution for their act from rabbinic authorities, as in the case of the question posed to Rabbi Shalom of Neustadt by Jews living in Poland, discussed below.

Nevertheless, at times the communal authorities were completely powerless. That seems to have been the situation in the case of a Jewish man who habitually threatened to set fire to other people's property. The case came before an otherwise unknown rabbi, identified as "the martyr Isaac Klut," who apparently lived in Austria in the late thirteenth century. His ruling is adduced briefly in a responsum by Rabbi Isaac ben Mordechai, of the late thirteenth century. According to the quote, "the notorious Moses (*Moshe muhzak*) threatened to set the property of a fellow Jew on fire; he [Rabbi Isaac Klut] was asked what should be done with him and he answered: 'Whoever kills him first is worthy!'"[93]

In other words, Rabbi Isaac Klut encouraged members of his community to take the law into their own hands and commit an act of vigilante justice. It seems the arsonist was a Jew who had little regard for the law and over whom the communal authorities had no control. On top of that, the case was an urgent one—a fire could have spread and burned the homes of every member of the community and non-Jewish neighbors as well.

Labeling a Murderer: The Messy Business of Debt Collection

A Jew might be accused of murdering a fellow-Jew without actually doing the deed himself, as in the case above in which Rabbi Shabtai ben Shmuel of Zeitz suggested that an alleged killer might have ordered his gentile manservant to assault and kill a fellow Jew. Likewise, some Jews wielded violence indirectly when seeking to collect debts and enforce financial settlements. When creditors were faced with debtors who did not pay up, rabbinic authorities prescribed pressing legal charges within the internal Jewish system. But this could be effective only when both parties consented to the arbitration and agreed in advance to abide by the ruling. When debtors did not accept the authority of the Jewish court, creditors were known to hire non-Jewish ruffians to rough up a defaulter. Such a case appears in a responsum penned by Rabbi Meir of Rothenburg, which, like Rabbi Shabtai's responsum on the murder case, addresses the issue of indirect action.[94]

The case, brought before Rabbi Meir either by a fellow rabbi, a tribunal, or by an unspecified community's leadership, involved a man by the name of Alexander who had sent non-Jewish thugs to ensure that a Jewish business partner abided by a settlement they had reached.[95] While the exact nature of the settlement is not specified, it is clear that the gist of it was that, if they were to find themselves in conflict regarding their financial or business dealings, they would submit the quarrel to a non-Jewish arbitrator.⁹⁶ From the wording in the responsum, it is not altogether clear if they agreed to this orally or in a document drafted and signed by both. In any event, when Alexander's unnamed business partner did not abide by the agreement, Alexander sent non-Jewish enforcers to make sure his partner would make good on his promise. Things became messy and the fellow Jew was neither willing to have the matter decided in court nor to settle financially. The gentile thugs Alexander sent wanted to take money or possessions from the partner as collateral until the matter was resolved, but the partner stood his ground. A violent quarrel broke out, during which the gentiles killed the partner. Alexander's community applied to Rabbi Meir for guidance, as they were unsure how to categorize Alexander. Was he guilty of premeditated murder, or was he an unintentional murderer whose case was similar to those discussed above?

From a narrow Jewish legal standpoint, Alexander was not an accomplice to a murder. The Talmud rules that "agency cannot be vested in a non-Jew" (*ein shliḥut le-goy/le-nokhri*).⁹⁷ Jurisprudentially, a non-Jew could not act in the name of a Jew. If the gentile enforcers used violence and caused the partner's death, they were legally responsible for their own actions, regardless of the fact that they had acted at Alexander's behest. The legal category of agency (*shliḥut*) thus did not apply to the case. Each person involved was personally responsible for his own actions and not for those of any of the others. In other words, Alexander, who hired the non-Jewish enforcers and gave them instructions, could not be held responsible for their actions, even if he had explicitly told them to kill his partner (which he did not). He could be accused of inciting violence, but not of murder. The responsum says that Alexander invoked this claim in his defense.⁹⁸

Rabbi Meir rejected Alexander's claims and issued a harsh ruling against him. He was particularly outraged by the compact about settling grievances in a non-Jewish court. Although Alexander portrayed himself merely as having sought to harass his adversary, not kill him, Rabbi Meir maintained that the lethal outcome was no accident. It should have been anticipated and could not be seen as unintentional. In hiring non-Jews to rough up his partner, Alexander should have known that they were almost certain to kill the man. In Rabbi Meir's mind this was simply the nature of gentiles, especially in their dealings with Jews, and all the more so when Jewish financial assets were involved.[99]

Rabbi Meir thus ruled that Alexander had intentionally murdered his partner, even though he had not committed the act himself.[100] The literary metaphors describing the legal categories invoked by Rabbi Meir to describe the inevitability of a lethal outcome are also significant.[101] They cast the act as irresponsible, if not downright intentional. Accordingly, Rabbi Meir ruled that Alexander was complicit in the killing and should be treated as if he had committed the murder intentionally, with his own hands (*ba-yadayim*), a capital offense punishable by death according to Jewish law.

Rabbi Meir knew very well that, in Germany in his time, he and his coreligionists had no power to sentence Alexander to death. "It is up to the Almighty alone to punish the accused," he writes in the responsum. All that he and fellow rabbis or communal leaders could do was impose a severe penitential regime on the convicted man. He was doomed to the complete gamut of social ostracism, banishment, and a series of harsh penitential procedures designed to signal to the penitent, his community, and to his fellow Jews in general that he had committed a grave sin. But it was not just the community that needed to see Alexander put through this grueling regime; he, as a sinner, needed to endure it for his own good. In the poetically structured and rhymed envoi to the responsum, Rabbi Meir declares that Alexander, as a murderer, is to be punished as harshly as possible.

There is no way of knowing whether Alexander was indeed punished in accordance with Rabbi Meir's responsum. Enforcement of penitential practices varied; apparently they depended, as noted above, largely on the cooperation of the guilty person, and his determination to demonstrate his remorse. Factors such as the penitent's social status, religious observance, and personality played a crucial role in what was ultimately a predominantly voluntary system of communal justice. The unnamed person or body who brought the case before Rabbi Meir was most likely seeking the aid of this prominent halakhic authority to enforce Alexander's banishment. The purpose of the question was to force Alexander to acknowledge the gravity of his transgression and to facilitate the appropriate atmosphere for him to make amends and carry out proper penance. Rabbi Meir may well have seen this as an opportunity to set an example for other Jews on this and other related matters. By taking the case to a supercommunal authority like Rabbi Meir, the petitioner may also have sought to ostracize Alexander from wider social circles, not just within his own community. Interestingly, what is markedly absent from Rabbi Meir's responsum is the issue of financial compensation to the injured party, a central element when Rabbi Judah the Pious and Rabbi Isaac Or Zaruaʿ take up criminal cases.[102]

What was Rabbi Meir's motivation in labeling Alexander a murderer? Why was he so unequivocal and unforgiving? Alexander was not only guilty of violence and murder, as far as Rabbi Meir was concerned; in making his initial agreement with his business partner, he had also displayed contempt for the Jewish communal judicial system. It is entirely possible that Rabbi Meir wanted to make an example out of the case. Alexander's lack of faith in, or at the very least indifference to, the Jewish judicial procedure is not surprising given the growing atmosphere of crisis in Jewish circles in the last quarter of the thirteenth century and the early fourteenth century. There seems to have been a growing feeling, especially among affluent Jews, that the Jewish judicial system, based on the halakhic rulings of rabbis, could no longer provide the recourse it had in the past.[103] Part of Rabbi Meir's self-proclaimed mission was to bolster the Jewish legal system; to do so he had to come down strongly against any slight to it, especially vigilante actions and appeals to extracommunal non-Jewish systems of justice.[104]

Milo on the Run: A False Accusation from Thirteenth-Century York

Despite Rabbi Meir's attempt to bolster the standing of the Jewish legal system, criminal cases involving Jews came before non-Jewish courts when some of the parties involved were gentiles. These include cases of domestic violence. Although I devote the next chapter to domestic violence and crimes committed by and against women, Milo's case belongs in this chapter. I showed at the beginning of this chapter that evidence about violence within the Jewish community may sometimes be found in external sources. Domestic violence was no exception. In the absence of urban police forces, municipal prosecution, and a system of justice similar to our own, the information preserved is not of cases pursued by local authorities on their own initiative, but rather cases brought to their attention when one of the Jewish parties involved sued another Jewish party in a non-Jewish court. The *Curia Regis* rolls from thirteenth-century England provide an example of such a case.[105]

On the Sunday following Pentecost 1208, an itinerant English royal tribunal situated in York heard a case submitted by a local Jew named Milo. While rabbinic sources, the primary source of information for this chapter, do not normally offer a record of the judicial proceedings that produced rulings, this case from the English *Curia Regis* rolls provides a window into actual procedure.[106] The royal clerk who recorded the proceedings wrote that Milo petitioned the court, accusing three men of murdering his wife (whose name is not mentioned in the document). The three were William Makeblithe, Thomas Goldsmith, and a certain Robert, identified in the text as "Edmund's nephew." All three were most probably non-Jewish York locals. Given that Jewish courts had no jurisdiction over the accused men, taking the case to a non-Jewish court was Milo's only way of seeking justice for his murdered wife. As English Jews enjoyed royal protection, they had the right to bring non-Jews who offended them before a royal court.[107] The three alleged perpetrators were arrested and were held in custody by the local sheriff, acting on behalf of the crown, while awaiting trial.

When the trial commenced, however, there was a dramatic turn of events. The clerk recorded that "they are not suspected, neither by Jews nor by Christians" (*et ipsi non malecreduntur nec a Judeis nec a Christianis*). Instead, Milo himself had become a suspect. With his late wife's brother Benedict (Baruch) about to accuse his brother-in-law Milo of the murder in the royal court, Milo chose to flee rather than stand trial and defend himself against the accusations, leaving a trail of uncertainty and heavy suspicion behind. Regarding people who abjured the English realm in flight from judicial proceedings, William C. Jordan remarks: "Up through the year 1215 the fundamental mode of testing an indicted person's innocence of a felony in the absence of any *full* proof, such as a confession in open court, or the testimony of two eye-witnesses, or flight, which was regarded as a sure token of culpability, was the ordeal."[108] Once Milo fled, preferring to leave a cloud of suspicion hanging over him rather than endure trial, the royal authorities saw no further reason to adjudicate the case. Milo's flight had proven he was guilty. Subsequently, the three non-Jews accused by Milo and held in custody were released "under pledges to stand to right in case any shall accuse them." This was probably only a procedural precaution taken by the authorities, for it was by now clear that in the eyes of all those involved, accusers and officials alike, the three arrested men were not guilty of the crime.

The father of Benedict and the slain woman, Ursul, a physician, and another person named Isaac Negro (presumably another Jew) are recorded in the ledger as each paying half a mark to have Milo's original charge expunged. Acting on behalf of the Jewish community of York (*communae Judeorum Eboraci*),[109] this enabled Ursul's son, Benedict, to press charges against Milo for killing his sister. Now it was Milo who was accused by his coreligionist and former family members for the murder of his wife, their kin. It seems that Benedict had made some inquiries of his own into the matter and realized that "Milo killed [his] sister and that she was slain on account of Kelina[110] the Jewess, for Milo is alleged to have had an intrigue with her (*eo quod ipse Milo dicitur habuisse rem cum ea*)."

The Latin here is vague and makes it hard to tell exactly what sort of intrigue or business (*rem*) led Milo and Kelina to conspire against Milo's wife. Was it romance or money, or a combination of both? Why did Milo's wife have to be murdered? Why didn't Milo simply divorce her instead? The source answers none of these questions, so it is only possible to speculate. The ledger also relates that Kelina was arrested after Benedict accused her of being an accessory to the murder. She was probably interrogated, but was not prosecuted and was eventually set free. The circumstances of her release are not stated in the document, but since the most important issue for the court was the amount of money in the king's purse, the clerk did note that she was bailed or ransomed by another Jew, a man named Vivent, probably a relative of hers. Benedict was fined for making false and unsubstantiated accusations against Kelina, and obstructing justice. Both in charging Kelina and in revoking Milo's plea, the Jewish community of York was asked to be "in pledge," namely to be financially accountable in case the individuals involved did not make good on their financial commitment to the crown.

The document omits many details because its main purpose was not to provide an account of the case but rather to register the sums received by the king's envoys. Nevertheless, it provides important information about how Jews addressed crime, specifically murder in the domestic sphere.

The case of Milo of York is an outlier, in which a largely internal Jewish criminal affair came to be adjudicated not in a Jewish court but before a non-Jewish bench. Milo may have tried to pin the crime on non-Jews precisely so as to avoid causing a split within the Jewish community. Had the gentiles been convicted and the wife's family accepted that they were guilty, relations within the community would have remained solid. But in this case, the internal solidarity of the Jewish community was not upheld, as an internal conflict developed, pitting one family against another. Because the murder was not dealt with internally, it came to be recorded in a non-Jewish document.

While such cases were rare, they were not wholly anomalous. As in other kingdoms in Europe, the English king reserved his right and the right of the courts appointed and operated by the crown to try serious crimes, such as rape and murder even within the Jewish community, which usually enjoyed *immunitas*. As I have noted, most medieval legislative systems lacked a principle of equal standing before the law. Many individuals who took other people's lives were never tried, and if they were, punishment varied and was based on class privileges and economic status.[111] Milo accused non-Jews of murdering his wife. In the absence of first-person accounts of the marriage from Milo and his wife, there is no way of knowing what, if any, tensions there were in the relationship. While York's Jewish community backed Benedict and Ursul, that does not necessarily mean that Milo was guilty. He may have fled because he was not a native member of the community, and thus lacked the backing of one of the community's extended families;

he may have been convinced that forces stronger than he could fight were seeking to implicate him in a crime he did not commit. In any event, one thing this case has in common with others I have presented is the involvement of non-Jews in the violent and eventually lethal aspects of a conflict within the Jewish community. If Milo was indeed trying to cover up a crime he himself committed, the fact that he sought to pin it not on some other Jew but on non-Jews may indicate that he thought that members of the Jewish community would grant more credence to an accusation of murder against non-Jews than Jews.

Down the Pit, Head First: A Domestic Quarrel Gone Sour

Violence within the family seems to have been rare in medieval European Jewish communities, but Jewish sources record some cases in which domestic conflict turned fatal. One such case was addressed by Rabbi Meir of Rothenburg in a responsum about two Jewish men who married two sisters in the German town of Koblenz.[112]

One of the men believed that his friend and brother-in-law had become overly familiar with his wife. Enraged, he threatened to kill his rival. Sometime thereafter, the brother-in-law left town. All the indications were that he had embarked on a brief business trip, but he did not return as expected. A few days later, search parties were sent out to seek him, but returned empty-handed. A while later, three non-Jewish thieves arrived in another town, hoping to sell stolen goods to a Jew there. The thieves mentioned in passing that they had come across the body of a Jew buried in a peculiar way (fully clothed and thrown down a pit, head first). They also disclosed that the rumor among the criminals in the area was that the dead Jew had been murdered at the behest of his Jewish brother-in-law. The Jewish trader who heard this asked for more information about the dead man and where his body could be found. The thieves demanded to be paid one pound of sterling silver (*zakuk*) in exchange for the information. As this was a large sum of money, the merchant did not pay it right away. He may have needed time to raise the money, or perhaps he wanted time to obtain a financial guaranty that the family of the missing man would pay some or all of the money in exchange for the information.

His hesitation proved to be tragic, as the information was lost. It so happened that on that same day, the three thieves were caught either in the possession of stolen goods or in the act of robbery and were swiftly convicted; they were executed before sunset. They died without disclosing the whereabouts of the body. Sometime later, a lapsed Jewish convert to Christianity approached the family of the missing person and testified that he had seen the missing man alive and well in France (*Tzarfat*). The case came before a Jewish court because his wife had been left an *'agunah*, a "bound woman" who, in the absence of reliable evidence that her husband was dead, could not remarry. The court applied to Rabbi Meir in order to ascertain which of the testimonies should be favored, as both fell short of standard evidence admissible in a Jewish court. Which was the more reliable source, the testimony of three gentile thieves transmitted through a Jew with a dubious background, or the testimony of a Jew who had converted and then reverted to Judaism?

Previous scholarly interest in the case focused on the role of the lapsed Jewish convert and what the responsum says about the credibility of his testimony.[113] Here the point of interest is the murder itself. The responsum gives no indication that anyone was prosecuted for murder. As sketchy as the information provided by the responsum is, it offers, between the lines, a basis for offering hypotheses about aspects of the case and a reconstruction of the entire incident. For example, the responsum says nothing explicit about what circles the two brothers-in-law were involved in prior to the events recorded. The testimony of the gentile thieves indicates, however, that at least one of the two men had shady dealings or, at the very least, that the jealous husband knew where to turn when he needed to have someone murdered.[114] The events apparently proceeded rapidly, indicating that the jealous husband had no problem finding hired killers to carry out his vengeance and dump the body in a well, apparently not too far from the city. If this was the case, it conforms to a pattern: Jews who wished to do violence to fellow Jews, whether in the public or the domestic sphere, hired non-Jewish thugs for the purpose. There are hardly any cases of Jews roughing up or killing other Jews with their own hands. Premeditated murder was almost always outsourced to non-Jewish assassins.

The Limits of *Mesirah*: Informers and Informing during a "Time of Rage"

Informing on fellow Jews to the non-Jewish authorities was a grave offense in medieval Jewish communities.[115] It was a Jew's duty to other members of his community not to air dirty linen outside and not to place fellow Jews at the mercy of gentiles. During the Second Temple period, and in particular following the occupation of Judea by Rome in the mid-second century BCE, Jews detested informers. The category included those suspected of serving as paid informants to the Roman authorities. They were called *mosrim* (the Hebrew word for informers, literally meaning "those who hand over"). Almost as bad were Jews who provided the authorities with intelligence about fellow Jews in other matters like taxation.[116] Jews condemned *mosrim* in each of the three daily prayers instituted in the postdestruction period, at the end of the first and into the second century CE. One of the daily benedictions prescribed by the Sages, which rabbinic sources attribute to Shmuel ha-Katan, is called *birkat ha-minim*.[117] It was meant to serve as a deterrent and an anathema against a host of internal enemies, including heretics, collaborators, and informers.[118] The Talmud discusses two kinds of informers, those who inform about a person, and in doing so cause financial or physical damage to a fellow Jew, and those who inform about property and cause financial damage. Among the second group, the Talmud differentiates between those who inform under duress and those who inform voluntarily for personal or material gain.[119]

Medieval Jewish sages were well aware that social ostracism or a harsh penance were not always the most appropriate or effective measures against an informer. Sometimes physical retaliation by fellow Jews or an appeal to the non-Jewish authorities were the only way to deal with such people. *Mosrim* were usually treated very harshly. If the Jewish authorities had enough internal legal leeway and autonomy, they punished *mosrim* severely, excommunicating, banning, and ostracizing them. In extreme cases, they were exiled or even clandestinely eliminated.[120]

Nevertheless, Jews did not hesitate to take their legal grievances to non-Jewish courts and arbitrators, either as part of a business arrangement (as in the case of Alexander and his partner, the subject of one of Rabbi Meir's responsa) or, in a later period, simply because the non-Jewish authorities were more accessible, swifter to pass judgment, or easier to manipulate (by pitching one against the other, or offering bribes). In general, however, Jewish rabbinic authorities categorically banned the practice of seeking recourse outside the Jewish system. Moreover, in privileges granted to the Jews from as early as the eleventh century, Jewish authorities, with rabbinic sanction, did all they could to empower Jewish judicial bodies to adjudicate within the community.[121] There were exceptions, however, where Jewish courts were either willing to permit or forced to sanction Jews to petition non-Jewish courts, while not branding such a person a *moser*. Just such a case appears in the responsa collection of the late thirteenth-century rabbi Haim Eliezer ben Isaac Or Zaruaʿ.[122] It addresses what medieval Ashkenazi halakhists called a "time of rage" (or heat) (*sheʿat ha-zaʿam/ḥimum*).[123]

A "time (hour) of rage" is the legal term for the feeling of rage that overcame a Jew upon being released from captivity by non-Jewish individuals or authorities. Infuriated by the incarceration, humiliated, and possibly having suffered financial, physical, and mental abuse while confined, such a person was treated leniently by thirteenth-century halakhists, especially when he retaliated against the Jewish person or persons responsible for his incarceration and persecution. Even informing on such a person to the gentile authorities (*mesirah*) was treated with restraint under such circumstances, especially if it took place in close temporal proximity to the wronged party's own incarceration. In essence, it was an internal Jewish legal framework designed to enable vigilante retributive justice against those who would engage non-Jews in violence against another Jew.

From an analysis of several of the halakhic cases that discuss such situations, most of which date from the second half of the thirteenth century in Germany, in particular in the circle around Rabbi Meir of Rothenberg, it is clear that leniency was thought to be acceptable only in very close temporal proximity to the act of violence or forced incarceration that triggered the victim's rage or fury. Although there is no explicit exposition of the practice, and the term makes its appearance in the responsa literature almost without precedent, the implication is that the enraged victim was seen to be less than fully capable of exercising clear judgment, rendering him less than fully culpable for his actions, which thus fell short of actual *mesirah*.[124]

In a variety of halakhic contexts, the Hebrew words *za'am*, rage, and *ḥimum*, heat, are used interchangeably in order to denote uncontrollable rage and anger that causes a temporary state of diminished mental capacity and therefore responsibility for one's actions. Often powerless in any case to punish violence in their communities, the rabbis had an incentive to categorize certain violent acts as acceptable or understandable.[125]

One example is a responsum by Rabbi Meir of Rothenberg himself, addressed to a certain Rabbi Isaac. Rabbi Isaac had asked Rabbi Meir to render his opinion about exercising leniency in such cases. Rabbi Meir, stretching the category a bit further, ruled that a Jew who turned to gentile authorities while still in the heat of the humiliation and duress he suffered as a result of physical abuse inflicted by a fellow Jew was not to be punished by flogging and excommunication. He would still, however, be held responsible for any financial damage he caused to his adversary when he turned him over to the non-Jewish authorities. In a different case, a Jew, furious at being physically attacked by a fellow Jew in Würzburg turned in the assailant to the gentile authorities. In this case, the assailant was notoriously violent (*mu'ad le-hakot*). Under the circumstances, Rabbi Meir set aside his principled opposition to taking cases to gentile courts. In an ideal Jewish legal system, he wrote, such assailants would be sentenced to corporal punishment. As such a sentence could not be imposed by rabbis in his time, the assailants should not have the right to sue their victims who had turned them over to the gentiles and caused them financial damage. A Jew who routinely used violence against fellow Jews could not demand that Jewish courts award him compensation for the losses he suffered outside the Jewish judicial system.

Rabbi Meir concluded with the words: "And the high arm is broken… and the violent individuals will cease from doing so." Simha Emanuel suggested that, in the mid-thirteenth century, Jewish rabbinic courts were not always able to provide protection to the victims of violence within the community. To best address the problem, under the circumstances,

Jewish victims who turned their assailants over to the gentile authorities in the "heat of the moment," were not to be judged as *mosrim*. In this case, the "time of rage" exception was extended not only to those who, as a result of being informed on, had suffered at the hands of gentiles but also to those attacked by fellow Jews. According to Emanuel,

> These words of the respondent, as the many questions that arose in Germany in the second half of the thirteenth century, testify to the innate weakness of the inner Jewish system of justice. Jewish courts fell short in aiding those who were victims of such actions with a proper response, and reluctantly sanctioned turning the Jewish tormentors in to the hands of the non-Jewish authorities. Note that all the discussions focus on the possibility of suspending the sentences of Jews who were tormented and in their anger and rage informed on their assailants. There are hardly cases in which individuals executed their own private vigilante justice. The purpose of this legal leniency was to uphold a properly ordered society and maintain a system that would prevent slipping into chaos. Rabbis feared that, without this arrangement, inner communal violence would increase.[126]

In the late thirteenth century and early fourteenth century the category broadened beyond physical violence to include murder. In a difficult case brought before Rabbi Haim Eliezer ben Isaac Or-Zarua', a fight broke out during a feast, probably a wedding feast.[127] A man named Rabbi Shalom drew a knife, possibly after a verbal exchange. His brother and brother-in-law also drew swords and a fight broke out between Shalom, his family members, and another person. The other person was severely beaten and they, along with other "dignified people," possibly learned men or local communal leaders who were attending the festive gathering, were violently expelled from the feast. They were gravely insulted and retaliated by getting non-Jewish men to threaten the intimidators, thus drawing these non-Jews into the quarrel. From this point on, the chain of events is unclear, as the responsum provides little detail and what it offers is difficult to understand. Some facts, however, are clear. A Jew[128] who was close to one Rabbi Moshe and his father-in-law was asked by them to contact gentiles and ask them to attack Shalom's group. The unnamed Jew led the gentiles to Rabbi Shalom's doorstep, where a violent altercation ensued, ending with Shalom's death at the hands of the gentiles.[129] In an act of retaliation, Rabbi Shalom's relatives informed on the Jew who brought in the gentile assailants, as well as on Rabbi Moshe and his father-in-law, accusing them of murder. The non-Jewish authorities arrested the three men but, for reasons unknown, they managed to get released. The events were brought before Rabbi Haim, who encouraged the parties to resolve their very deep grievances with the aid of a local Jewish tribunal, headed by Rabbi Shabtai ben Shmuel of Zeitz (near Leipzig).[130] Rabbi Haim also offered his own insights.

Rabbi Haim maintained that Moshe and his kin were indeed entitled to inform on their assailants, especially immediately following the violent attack during the feast, while they were in a time of rage: "[In the case of a] person who turns to the authorities in a 'time of rage,' as the might of his rage is upon him and he cannot restrain his feelings of grief and shame, it is preferable that he turn to external justice and avenge his pride in this fashion, for if not, matters will end in bloodshed."[131]

Usually, Rabbi Haim wrote, informing on another Jew was justified only as preventative, namely if there was a clear indication that the injured party might instigate an act of revenge that might result in bloodshed. However, if the assailant were not a habitually violent person, and thus would not normally cause an escalation, the dispute should remain within the Jewish community. In the final sentence of the responsum, Rabbi Haim writes: "However, for murder, it is always a time of rage as, with regard to murder, scripture explicitly states that the murdered person's kin are relentlessly enraged and furious." In other words, in murder cases, the time of rage is not limited in time, but continues for as long as an act of revenge (*nekamah*) has not taken place. Thus, even if the victim's kin were to inform on the murderer years after the killing, the legal category of "time of rage" would still apply, and the informer should be treated with forbearance.

In his responsum, Rabbi Haim follows without reservation the precedent set by his mentor, Rabbi Meir, in the case of Alexander, the Jew who brought bloodthirsty gentiles into a quarrel between two Jews. Examining all the responsa that deal with the concept of "time of rage," Rabbi Haim makes a clear distinction between two different kinds of non-Jewish involvement in intra-Jewish altercations: non-Jewish judicial authorities (*ha-shofet*) and non-Jewish enforcers (*goyim*). The former seems to refer to a formal judicial system. In Jewish legal parlance, the establishment of and compliance with a system of laws and courts (*dinim*) is one of the requirements qualifying a gentile as a Noachide (*ben–Noah*, literally a son of Noah, a term designating non-Jews who observe the precepts incumbent on gentiles).[132] *Goyim* are described by both Rabbi Meir and Rabbi Haim as impulsive; anyone who involves them in a conflict between Jews is an evildoer; doing so indicates disregard for human life. The hotheaded nature of *goyim* and their proclivity for murder are taken as given. The intentions of such gentile enforcers are clear: "They came either to kill or to make the impression that such was their intention." As a result, the Jew who brought them into the conflict should be treated harshly: "He who brought the gentiles and drew them into the private doorways leading to the person who eventually lost his life [Rabbi Shalom] he is a murderer. His name should be announced in all the communities where he is known. His stench and shame should ascend so that he may be caught in the net that he himself cast."[133]

The culprit is to be singled out, marginalized, and ostracized by the Jewish communal and supercommunal system in the eastern German sphere, the area in which he lived. But there is nothing about penance and bodily mortification of the type that we find in the manual of penance for a murderer or like that Rabbi Meir imposed on Alexander. Perhaps the omission is connected to Rabbi Meir of Rothenberg's standing and influence. As one of the most prominent and respected halakhic masters in medieval Europe, Rabbi Meir could, at the height of his career, speak his mind freely and take unconventional positions without fear of repercussions. This was unusual, and many of his disciples (among them Rabbi Haim) who scattered far and wide over the western and eastern Ashkenazi world were unable to emulate him in this regard. Conceivably, Rabbi Haim took into account the circumstances that drove the evildoer to behave as he did. Perhaps he took into account the previous acts of hostility against Moshe and his allies as a factor in his ruling, a condition that did not apply in Alexander's case. Another possibility is that in this case, the evildoer, unlike Alexander, did not act alone; he had two accomplices, Rabbi Moshe and Moshe's father-in-law.

According to Rabbi Haim, Moshe and his father-in-law were not murderers.[134] Regardless of what the evildoer was told (or not) to do by the others, Rabbi Haim rules, he should have realized that the request was illegal, "for he should have feared the awful and terrible Lord God and not done so." Rabbi Haim maintained that the attitude of "merely following orders" is not an excuse. This position is firmly anchored in the halakhic tradition, according to which adults of sound mind and body have free will, and are thus able and expected to refuse to carry out immoral orders or requests from others, including an order to commit murder. Jewish legal thought even goes beyond this, making *shefikhut damim* (literally bloodshed, but understood as murder) one of three situations in which a Jew should accept martyrdom. If told that he can save his life only by killing another person, a Jew is required to refuse to do so and to accept death.[135] Rabbi Haim's use of the term *shefikhut damim* in his responsum is clearly meant to invoke this legal imperative.

Mourning a Killer: The Case of Shimon's Brother, from the Responsa of Rabbi Jacob Weil

The cases above address violence that ensued after one Jew informed on another (*mesirah*) to the gentile authorities. But *mesirah* sometimes happened in other contexts as well. Cases from the fifteenth century involve informers tipping the non-Jewish authorities off about a Jewish murderer or, alternatively, a Jewish murderer might be persuaded to turn himself in to the authorities after killing a fellow-Jew, as in the case at hand. Here, too, the story has come down to us incidentally, in the writings of Rabbi Jacob Weil, an important rabbinic figure from fifteenth-century Germany, where he served in the communities of Augsburg and Erfurt (c. 1385–c. 1455).[136] Rabbi Jacob was consulted by a learned Jewish man, Shimon, whose brother had committed murder, apparently of a fellow Jew, and, after turning himself in, was subsequently executed by the non-Jewish authorities. Shimon's question was not about the murder itself. The responsum indicates that there was disagreement within the family about how the brother should be mourned, if at all. Shimon maintained that it was incumbent on him to observe all the rules and rituals that apply to the immediate family of any deceased Jew. He sought sanction for his conduct and received it: "May the Lord be your help, my beloved Rabbi Shimon," Rabbi Jacob wrote to him. "You did well in mourning your brother, because he was not executed by order of the Sanhedrin and is no worse than those executed by order of the king, even though he was legally deserving of death."[137]

The background to Shimon's question was a talmudic injunction forbidding the relatives of a person executed by Jewish authorities and in accordance with Jewish legal procedure to mourn him. Rabbi Jacob stressed that this was not to case with Shimon's brother, who had been put to death by a non-Jewish court—in fact tortured to death in a cruel, painful, and gruesome manner, possibly because he was Jewish. For Rabbi Jacob, this clearly indicated that his family should mourn him. But there was one complication. The brother had either been persuaded or tricked into turning himself in to the non-Jewish authorities, even though it should have been obvious to him that this meant almost certain death. Should he then be considered a suicide, which would also mandate that his family not mourn him?[138] This information comes from a sentence toward the end of the responsum: "Someone told him 'leave freedom (ḥerut) and give yourself up so that you can achieve expiation (kaparah)', and so he did." The nature of the freedom referred to is not at all clear. In his analysis of this case, as part of a discussion about mourning murderers in medieval Jewish law, Pinchas Roth suggested:

> To "leave freedom" [ḥerut] is almost certainly a reference to sanctuary, such as a church, where medieval murderers fled as a matter of course.[139] According to Roman, canon, and German law, Jews were ineligible for legal asylum.[140] This case, then, may point to the gap between law and practice and provide evidence that Jews did, on occasion, take advantage of the law of

sanctuary and that this was respected by their pursuers, despite being unsupported by codified law.[141]

While I agree with Roth's general conclusion, I maintain that, in this particular case, *ḥerut* does not refer to sanctuary in a church property. The word may also designate the life of an outlaw. Shimon's brother had become an outlaw, living outside the Jewish community and its obligations, but also not enjoying its protection. *Ḥerut* means that he was out of the reach of the law. Yet, even in this state, Shimon's brother remained in contact with some members of the community, who eventually persuaded him to abjure the supposed freedom of the outlaw, turn himself in, and plead his case in a court. Perhaps they hoped that he would be able to prove his innocence, or would be treated leniently. Perhaps those who persuaded Shimon's brother to turn himself in thought they could pull strings or bribe officials to grant him clemency or maybe they thought that the authorities would let the Jewish community try him. (The use of the word *kaparah*, expiation, suggests that the person Shimon's brother was accused of killing was also a Jew.) If any of this was planned it fell through. Rabbi Jacob speculated that the murderer may have thought he would not be executed, or perhaps he was mentally unbalanced ("perhaps an evil spirit shook him up"). His death could therefore not be considered a suicide.

Rabbi Jacobs clearly believed that the murderer was treated with extreme cruelty because he was a Jew. Late medieval German laws prescribed specific forms of execution for Jews, intended to be particularly painful, humiliating, and derogatory.[142] Breaking their body on the wheel was not uncommon. Some were hung upside down, and then two dogs were hung by their legs at the victims' side, to maul him while he was suspended on the gallows. This form of execution, in which the Jew was hung like a carcass in a slaughterhouse, signaled that the Jew was no more than a beast. When Jews were condemned to such a death by a non-Jewish court, ecclesiastical authorities (especially mendicant friars) often sought to convert them just before the sentence was to be carried out, promising a reduction of the sentence to either a less humiliating, gruesome, or painful one, or a combination of the three. We do not know if Shimon's brother received such an offer. We do know that he was tortured, suggesting that, even if such an offer was made, he had turned it down; or, if he accepted it, his executioners refused to abide by the deal. There might be a connection to the brother's mental instability, hinted at by the text. If indeed the brother was, as the text suggests, mentally ill, his conversion, even on the gallows, would not have been very attractive to Christian propagandists. Rabbi Jacob suggests that his painful death, and the suffering he endured during the execution, granted him expiation, regardless of the crime he committed, since "just as the salt sweetens and cleanses the flesh, so does the pain of torture sweeten the judicial outcome."

On the Polish Frontier: Murder Cases from the Later Middle Ages
The Responsa of Rabbi Shalom of Neustadt and Rabbi Israel Bruna

The following two cases involve the killing of Jews by fellow Jews on the geographic margins of the Ashkenazi Jewish community in late fourteenth and first half of the fifteenth century in Poland.[143] As in many of the incidents discussed here, these come not from court records or judicial decisions relating directly to the crime. They appear, like the story of Shimon's brother, incidentally in documents devoted to subjects such as the rites of mourning or prayer. The first comes from a letter sent from an unnamed frontier Jewish community in Poland in the mid-fourteenth century to Rabbi Shalom of Neustadt in the Duchy of Austria, within the purview of the Holy Roman Empire.[144] The letter, published in a collection of Rabbi Shalom's rulings, customs and sermons known as *Minhagei Maharash*, came from a community seeking his guidance on prayer.

The issue was whether a particular man should be allowed to lead public prayers in the role of cantor (*ḥazan*). Two members of the community had been involved in a prolonged quarrel that escalated until threats of using violence were made; this led to one of them committing assault with a deadly weapon and killing the other.[145]

The community turned to Rabbi Shalom because most of the Jews who settled in Poland in this early period were of central European and German origin. There seems to have been a dearth of rabbinic authorities in this relatively new area of settlement, so it was quite common for the new settlers to send queries to rabbinic authorities in their respective countries of origin, in this case Austria.

The text does not give the names of the parties involved; for convenience I will call one Abraham and the other Isaac. The letter is vague about the nature of their quarrel, but the manner in which the events unfold implies that it was a dispute over money. Eventually, Abraham terrified Isaac by threatening to cut off his fingers, toes, and nose. The reference to fear might have been inserted by the killer, in his telling of the story, in an attempt to justify his deed, or it may be an observation of the communal authorities who investigated the incident and then forwarded their findings and assessment to Rabbi Shalom.[146] It was very common in medieval times for petitioners to display their emotions in court, and for adjudicators to take these emotions into account. Judicial records refer to both "authentic" emotions as well as "expected" emotional responses (shame, guilt, crying, trembling, anger, fear, etc.) Emotions like fear and anger could serve as motivators and justifications for certain behaviors.[147] That the reported feeling of intimidation was considered justified indicates that either Abraham was notorious for exercising violence or that there was a marked social discrepancy between the two parties, Abraham belonging to a more powerful social group than Isaac.

In medieval rabbinic literature, a person who behaved this way was generally, and derogatorily, labeled a *gazam* (intimidator) or *alam* (violent person); Abraham was no exception.[148] From this point onward he is referred to in the responsum as a *gazam*, and as such that his actions would eventually lead to his death. Following his threats, Abraham confronted Isaac and demanded that he provide guaranties and collateral to ensure that he would appear before a Jewish court (*beit din*) to settle their differences. Abraham promised that, if Isaac complied with this demand, he would cease to threaten violence. Isaac complied, but according to the telling of the events in the responsum Abraham nevertheless continued to threaten him, forcing Isaac to move to another town. The text does not indicate whether this was a temporary or permanent move, but in this time and place, leaving one's hometown or permanent dwelling was a serious matter, as the punitive use of forced exile indicates. If Isaac intended that the move rid him of Abraham's intimidations, he was disappointed. Ambushing him one morning when he was about to go to the synagogue, Abraham beat and injured Isaac severely. Isaac begged the assailant to leave him alone and spare him, but Abraham did not stop. At this point, Isaac drew a small knife he carried on his person, which, according to his testimony, he usually used for eating, and stabbed Abraham in his abdomen. The assailant dropped dead. Two women witnessed the fight.

As women are not considered valid witnesses under Jewish law, the text presents the incident from the point of view of the survivor, Isaac. Abraham, having been killed, could not provide his version of the altercation. The inevitable bias that results from this state of affairs requires caution. It may be that from Abraham's point of view, all he was doing was making sure Isaac would not slip away and avoid justice. In any case, the two women who witnessed the attack had not observed the events leading up to it.[149] Even assuming that the Jews in this Polish town had some jurisdiction over their community's affairs, given the lack of acceptable witnesses, a trial about the killing could not properly proceed in a Jewish court of law. Then again it may well be that the entire matter of the killing and the judicial deliberation over the validity of the testimonies was already settled in Poland before the case was forwarded to Rabbi Shalom, who was not asked about the this subject but rather about its liturgical ramifications: whether or not the killer could lead the community in prayer.

As in other cases from this period, the individuals involved were city-dwellers, probably merchants. The weapon used, a simple small knife usually used while eating, was an implement commonly carried by city folk, burghers, and wealthy peasants of their time, as depicted in the paintings of late medieval Flemish masters such as Hieronymus Bosch and Peter Bruegel the Elder.[150] The specific type of knife is mentioned, presumably, to support the claim that the killing was not premeditated, and that Isaac had not been carrying a sword or an assault weapon. Abraham and Isaac were involved in a violent altercation and although Abraham is said to have attacked Isaac and bruised him, there is no mention of any weapon used by him. Isaac claimed that he had acted in self-defense, using an implement that he kept on his person for nonviolent use, a claim Rabbi Shalom accepted. Abraham and Isaac seem to have been simple Jews fending for themselves in a semiurban frontier environment in Poland, who found themselves embroiled in a dispute that escalated beyond their intentions.

Once again, the only reason this case was included in Rabbi Shalom's collected rulings and responsa was that the Jews of this particular town, presumably the community authorities, referred a question to him. Rabbi Shalom was asked to render his judgment on whether the killer was indeed innocent of murder and therefore had not sinned. More specifically, they asked Rabbi Shalom to certify that Isaac could continue to lead the community in prayer on the High Holidays, as he had done previously.[151] Rabbi Shalom also addresses the possibility that Isaac might be stigmatized because of his deed: "And all those who humiliate the murderer on this account are to be punished."[152]

Rabbi Shalom ruled that Isaac should not only be reintegrated into communal prayer gatherings but also be reassigned to lead them on the High Holidays as he had done in the past. It seems that not everyone in the community accepted Isaac's side of the story and he probably suffered socially from the events. Rabbi Shalom accepted the petitioner's assertion that the killing was done in self-defense, and that, as such, the intimidator was to blame for his own death. While the text does not say so explicitly, Rabbi Shalom seems to have had in mind that penance and expiation are at the heart of the two High Holidays, Rosh Hashanah and Yom Kippur. He may have meant not only to permit but to positively mandate that the inadvertent killer lead the community prayer services on these holy days—not despite his involvement in a killing, but rather precisely because he sought absolution.

In stipulating that anyone who shamed Isaac would be punished, Rabbi Shalom ruled in the spirit of the Gaonic penitential protocol, or more specifically its abridged later versions, which said of those who call the penitent a sinner that "the spirit of the Sages is not at ease with him." Rabbi Shalom went one step further to stress that Isaac had, in fact, never sinned. By stating that anyone who claims that

Isaac is unworthy to lead prayers should be punished, Rabbi Shalom supports the claim that the killing was an act of self-defense and not murder. Yet the case may not have been as clear-cut as Rabbi Shalom thought. Clearly, some members of Isaac's community thought that although the killing was an act of self-defense, Isaac's precise legal status was not the issue. They may well have felt that acquittal of the grave sin of taking a life, or accepting punishment for committing such an act, was one thing, but leading a community in prayer during the High Holidays quite another. The petitioners, and Isaac himself, sought endorsement of Isaac's version of the story from a prominent rabbinic authority. The purpose was to dispel the dark social and religious clouds hanging over the man's head. The appeal was meant to provide the killer with a document stating that he had acted in self-defense and had rightfully been reaccepted by his community not only legally but socially as well, enabling him to serve as cantor during the High Holidays. This community's Jews seem to have taken the injunction to shun a killer quite seriously, or so Isaac feared, in the spirit of Psalms 51:5: "For I know my transgressions; and my sin is ever before me."[153] Otherwise, why would he or the community have troubled a far-off rabbinic authority like Rabbi Shalom of Neustadt? In fact, the appeal, if it came from Isaac himself, would indicate that he truly saw himself as an unintentional killer who had taken a life in self-defense, and was thus innocent of murder; a murderer with little regard for the law, human life, and morals would probably not go to the trouble of seeking a document of absolution from a rabbinic authority.

The letter by Rabbi Shalom shows that people involved in a killing were marginalized socially. It was an essential part of the protocol of penance, which banned the sinner from society in order to reaccept him, after his performance of duties and rituals, which included beseeching his dead victim for forgiveness. As is clear from the case of Isaac, being labeled a killer was all the more fraught in a small, tightly-knit community on a frontier of Jewish settlement, as Poland was in the fourteenth century. In the latter part of that century, there were cases of Jewish murderers who submitted to corporal punishment, including physical mutilation, as a way of "bartering" the social stigma for a physical one that would show that they had paid their debt for the crime. One example is a case documented by the fourteenth-century rabbi Menachem of Merseburg, who was active in eastern Germany:

> Reuven was willing to accept a punishment of his own volition, and his eye was gouged out. However, there are people [in the community] who persist in calling him a murderer and his sons the offspring of a murderer.[154] These people should be reprimanded and castigated, and if their behavior persists willfully despite the reprimand, they should be excommunicated.[155]

This brief passage relates that a man who had killed another Jew was willing to submit to severe and irreversible physical mutilation, apparently on the understanding that doing so would end his proscription by his community.[156] Ironically, physical mutilation of criminals could be a means of social marginalization, especially when the mutilation was performed on a visible part of the body, such as the forehead or face. In this case, the mutilation was meant to have the opposite effect, to move the criminal from the margins to the center. In submitting to having his eye gouged out, Reuven sought to shed the label of murderer that had been attached to him and which, he presumably feared, would also attach to his entire line.

According to the Gaonic protocol, a person who had killed and then submitted to the punishments and rituals it prescribed was to be protected from harassment by the slain person's relatives and other members of the community. While the text does not say so, perhaps the killer initially did not fulfill all the conditions of the protocol (either according to its severe original form or one of its subsequent modifications). Another possibility is that he did, but felt himself that he had not suffered sufficiently and thus accepted mutilation to settle his score with his victim and the victim's kin. Reuven saw mutilation as a proxy for the punishment he actually should have suffered for such a crime. He apparently believed that, in accepting this severe and disfiguring physical punishment, he would not only atone for his sin but also regain his social status. Yet this did not occur—the passage relates that the repentant offender and his family were persecuted by other members of the community, who called him a murderer and his children sons of a murderer.[157]

Rabbi Menachem's ruling shows just how important this issue was to communal and rabbinic authorities. If the rabbinic and communal system could not impel the public to accept the sentences, punishments, and penances they imposed on offenders, and if the offenders were not reaccepted into society after accepting their punishment and penances, there would be no incentive for future offenders to come forward and to accept such judgments and punishments. This tension between the official absolution and public opinion is evident throughout the period, unsurprisingly given that the Jewish judicial system was entirely dependent on voluntary compliance.

A Bad Brawl: A Polish Case from the Responsa of Israel Bruna

The second example from Poland comes from the responsa of Rabbi Israel Bruna, who was active in the second half of the fifteenth century in southern Germany.[158] Like the story of the killer from Rabbi Shalom's responsum, this case also originated in Poland.[159] The documents relating to it comprise a dossier of letters containing statements and testimonies, received by Israel Bruna in Regensburg from the communities of Lemberg (Lvov in modern-day Ukraine), Breslau (Wrozlav), and Poznan in Poland.[160] Rabbi Israel addressed his responsum to "the holy society (*Kadisha Havura*)[161] of Lemberg, concerning the murder that occurred in your town." The responsum addressed the murder of Nissan, a Jew, at the hands of two other Jews: Nahman and Simha. Rabbi Israel's assessment of the case was based on the documentation that arrived from the Polish communities mentioned above. The tribunals of these communities amassed information about the crime, interrogated witnesses, and relayed their findings, probably to the Lemberg community. It may well be that the involvement of Poznan and Wrozlav communities was needed because the suspects fled to or had come from those cities. The Lemberg community then forwarded the dossier to the south German rabbinic master Israel Bruna and asked him to render his opinion. As is often the case in the responsa literature, the published collection of Rabbi Israel's rulings provides only his response, not the questions posed to him. Based on his reply, it seems that the Polish Jews wanted to know which of the two implicated in the crime was guilty of the murder, and consequently who should pay compensation to the victim's family. The Lemberg community was also apparently uncertain about how to deal with one of the murderers, who expressed sincere remorse and wished to repent for his crime, as indicated by the fact that Rabbi Israel appended to his responsum a penitential program for the man.

The dossier indicates that Nissan, the victim, was confronted by two men, Nahman and Simha. Nahman struck Nissan first with a knife blow to the head, mortally wounding but not immediately killing him. Nissan staggered, barely able to stand on his feet. According to the letter of testimony from Breslau, "at that point Nahman grabbed Nissan by the head and shook it left and then right," apparently causing further damage. Nahman then shouted: "Beat him to death, Simha!"[162] Using a club—the word used in the text is *keule* (קוי״ל), a German word meaning a wooden club or bat—Simha knocked Nissan down, striking him repeatedly.

In his responsum, Rabbi Israel expresses his discomfort with the fact that, in their letter, the Lemberg communal authorities referred to Nahman simply by his name, while Simha was labeled "the murderer." Rabbi Israel argued that, although Nissan did not die immediately from the wound caused by Nahman's knife, both Simha and Nahman should be seen as murderers, sharing the burden of sin, guilt, and punishment.

The dossier does not offer the back story to the violence. The only reference to the events that preceded the attack is a phrase stating that Nissan had been the first to resort to violence: "and he took two wooden objects to throw at Simha." There is no elaboration. Did Nissan strike Simha and inflame him? Did he merely throw pieces of wood at Simha? How big were the wooden objects? Could they really have injured Simha or put his life at risk? Or did the action merely serve to humiliate or enrage him? All these details are missing, but the text may provide a clue.

In the responsum, Rabbi Israel turns the tables on Nahman. While the Lemberg community's petition seems to pin all the blame on

Simha, Rabbi Israel's agenda is to demonstrate that both men are liable and guilty. Rabbi Israel draws a clear distinction between Nahman, whom he sees as an irredeemable evildoer, and Simha, who, while an accomplice to the murder, eventually expressed remorse. He wished to repent, was prepared to pay compensation to Nissan's family, and was willing to undergo a penitential regimen. When Rabbi Israel addresses this penitential process, he mentions in passing that Simha was ordered apparently by the Lemberg community to stay away from saloons and taverns, as well as games of chance and gambling, "because this is what initiated the events that led to the killing." In other words, Nissim apparently died in a brawl over some sort of betting game.

Furthermore, the responsum examines to what extent those involved were drunk "as Lot" or "not as Lot." In other words, they were all inebriated to one extent or another.[163]

Rabbi Israel addresses many aspects of the crime, not all of which I will consider here. The conclusion he reaches is that both Nahman and Simha should be held accountable for the murder of Nissan and that both should pay compensation and repent. According to Rabbi Israel, both are liable for "a death sentence by the heavens" (*mitah bi-yedei shamayim*). Note that no one in fifteenth-century Jewish Germany thought that the Jewish judicial system could impose any form of corporal or capital punishment, even in murder cases. Given that, all that communal and rabbinic authorities could do was to label the murderers as murderers, and to demand financial compensation and public penance as a requirement for reintegration into communal life and Jewish civil society. The responsum makes no mention of charges having been brought against Simha or Nahman by the non-Jewish authorities, neither for murder nor brawling and disturbing the peace. Apparently, the gentile authorities in Lemberg abided by the privilege granted to the Jews of Poland by King Casimir III and reaffirmed by King Casimir the IV in 1453. The tenth clause of this extensive document states quarrels and brawls within the Jewish community would be judged only by Jewish elders.[164] In this case, both local Jewish authorities and authorities from outside Poland were involved.

According to Rabbi Israel,

> and to both of them I apply the biblical verse [Isa. 1:15]: "Your hands are full of blood," and on Nahman I apply the verse: "Out of the wicked cometh forth wickedness," for he has sinned and has caused Simha to sin as well, as we learn from the testimony that he shouted at Simha "beat him [Nissan] to death." He [Nahman] is therefore seen as a pursuer [*rodef*].[165]

Rabbi Israel invokes a battery of previous halakhic authorities, from the twelfth century northern French Tosafist Rabbi Jacob ben Meir Tam (d. 1171), through Rabbi Isaac ben Moses of Vienna (d. c.1230), to Rabbi Israel of Krems (d. c. 1420), and others. On the basis of these precedents, he rules that, although the murderer is supposedly condemned to death (even if it is "death by the heavens"), he is not exempt from paying financial compensation to the victim's family. "He should grant them livelihood, for he has severed their line of livelihood," he writes. The financial aspect seems to be the prominent driving force behind the query and the subsequent responsum.

Before concluding his judgment, Rabbi Israel addresses one last issue. A man named Moshe ben Asher, probably a member of the Breslau community (as his name is mentioned after that community's letter is cited) testified that the victim, Nissan, was not religiously observant. Nissan, on this account, was illiterate in Hebrew, lax in the observance of mandatory religious rituals, such as the daily donning of phylacteries (*tefillin*), and overall had "no vitality of Torah in him."[166] Such testimony seems at first glance to be irrelevant to the murder case. In modern-day legal procedure, the defense may bring character witnesses to support a plea that the sentence take into account a convicted person's character, merits, and contribution to society. But in this case the testimony is about the character of the victim, which seemingly has no bearing on the events of the murder itself. Moshe ben Asher was not testifying that Nissan had behaved belligerently, nor was he offering any new facts about the incident. What, then, was the purpose of testimony that discredited Nissan from a religious-ritualistic point of view?

Most likely, the testimony was meant to absolve the perpetrators of a murder charge and bearing the heavy financial consequences resulting from such a charge. Moshe ben Asher apparently wanted to label Nissan as what the Talmud terms an *'am ha-aretz*.[167] The talmudic Sages fiercely condemned the unlearned and laxly observant masses, whom they called *'amei ha-aratzot* (the plural of *'am ha-aretz*).[168] By invoking these allusions and language, Moshe ben Asher possibly believed that he could portray Simha's and Nahman's quarrel with Nissan as part of the age-old tension between the learned elite and the simple masses, thus reframing the events and possibly saving them from a murder conviction.

Rabbi Israel fiercely rejected the relevance of this claim. That Nissan was an *'am ha-aretz* did not mean that he could be harmed with impunity. In discussing the three men involved in the incident, Rabbi Israel offers his view of their natures—Nahman and Simha, as he depicts them, were notorious tavern trawlers, gamblers, and drunkards.[169]

The two cases from the Polish frontier have some things in common, but are nevertheless also markedly different. The case brought before Rabbi Shalom centered on a normative person who had enough knowledge of Jewish ritual practice to lead communal prayer as cantor. From the account in Rabbi Shalom's responsum, the killer seems to have made every attempt to avoid violence and to seek justice via the authorities in his community. When he was violently attacked, he defended himself, turning from a victim of terror and violence into an assailant. In the case that Rabbi Israel addressed in his responsum, all the parties involved seem to have been either upstanding Jews gone astray or lowlifes blatantly indifferent to rules and authority. Both responsa, however, come in answer to questions regarding the ritual status of a Jew who has killed a fellow Jew, underscoring the fact that Jewish religious and civil authorities could not impose corporal or capital punishment.

Who Owns the Soul? Ransoming a Penitent in the Fifteenth Century

Some murderers sought penance on their own. Alexander, labeled a murderer by Rabbi Meir of Rothenburg, was ordered to do penance.

The penance imposed on him differed from the Gaonic penitential protocol discussed at the beginning of this chapter, but bore some resemblance to the abbreviated and milder version of that protocol crafted by Rabbi Ephraim of Regensburg. The use of an iron fitting to mortify the body was a key element. This practice was meant both to humiliate the murderer and mortify his body with a metal fitting. Along with the requirement to fast, it would disfigure the murderer's body. We do not know for certain whether Alexander in fact underwent this program of penance, but even if he did not, he may have done even greater penance later, before he died. Rabbi Meir, who had passed judgment on Alexander in the mid-1270s, would be incarcerated by the German imperial authorities in 1286 while attempting to flee the Reich; he died in custody in 1293 without receiving a proper Jewish burial in a Jewish cemetery. Another document relates that a man named Alexander ransomed Rabbi Meir's body, fourteen years after the aged sage died in captivity in 1293. I have suggested elsewhere that it may be the same man, who sought to redeem himself in the eyes of the Jewish community, and possibly before the Almighty, by being buried alongside the halakhic master.[170] If this was indeed the case, it may have been a noble gesture that was seen as an act of penance.

In medieval European culture, and especially in medieval Germany, the practice of paying a ransom for a slain relative was very common and was seen as part of the penitential process. From as early as the medieval collections of legal material of the Frankish era (*lex salica*), a person's social status was defined and represented by the amount of *wergild* his kin would receive on his behalf if he were to be killed, whether accidentally or maliciously. Paying this money was an accepted means of preventing a blood feud, but also of compensating the family and the remaining kin of a slain individual. While the Hebrew Bible took a different attitude (see Numbers 35),[171] it is clear, on the basis of a host of Jewish sources, including many of the cases discussed here, that compensating the victim's kin was an integral part of the punishment and the penance levied on a murderer. Similar ideas circulated among the Ashkenazi Pietists.[172]

A responsum by Rabbi Jacob Weil[173] tells of just such a case, in which a penitent murderer offered monetary compensation to his victim's family:

> Regarding he who takes a soul [a murderer], the person who is first of kin[174] to the deceased should not take money from the murderer and absolve him. For this is what we find in the writings of Maimonides in the first chapter of the laws about murderers:[175] "The court is enjoined not to accept ransom from the murderer to save him from execution." Even if he gave all the money in the world, and even if the blood redeemer[176] was willing to forgive him, he should be executed. The rationale is that the soul of the victim is not the property of the blood redeemer, but the property of the Holy One, Blessed be He. And He commanded: "Do not accept ransom for the soul of a murderer" (Num. 35:31). This is what he [Maimonides] writes. And for this reason, I [Jacob Weil] believe that, even if a murderer repented and performed penance, we should not accept a ransom from him.[177]

Rabbi Weil emphasized his dissatisfaction with the practice and attempted to suppress it. He seems to have been reacting to a situation in which people who had been convicted of murder in the internal Jewish system, and who were performing penance, were either approached by the families of their victims, who demanded financial compensation, or themselves contacted the families and offered such compensation. Most likely, the compensation was offered in an attempt to mitigate the rigor of the physical and social penitential penalties, or to clear the killer's conscience. Rabbi Weil presumably sought to uphold an ethical system in which the souls of the deceased are owned neither by their kin nor by their killers, but rather entrusted to God. In the context of the salvation economy that gained currency in the fifteenth century, Rabbi Weil hoped to undermine the notion that the souls of murder victims were commodities in a reparations market, such that financial compensation to the injured party's kin would reduce the sentence or penance imposed on the perpetrator.

Perhaps this mindset was influenced by the Church's sale of papal indulgences, which promised a reduction of punishment in the afterlife in exchange for money. Like their Christian neighbors, Jews may have sought to ease their way into heaven by appeasing the families of those whom they had mortally wronged.[178] Such arrangements seem also to have troubled Rabbi Weil from a structural point of view—they had the potential to encourage the perpetrators and victims of crimes to circumvent the Jewish judicial system, transforming a killing from a public criminal offense, under the purview of Jewish courts, into a matter to be resolved between families.[179]

In Rabbi Weil's time, family feuds had become a common feature of German society, especially among nobles and the growing population of urban patricians. As Hillay Zmora has shown, in late medieval and early modern Germany, nobles feuded mostly not with strangers but with neighbors, relatives, and their feudal overlords. On the same model, the murder of a Jew by another Jew could easily become a feud between two families within the Jewish community. As Jews could not employ violence in the same way as their neighboring German landed and urban patricians did, there were not full-blown blood feuds between Jewish families, but such conflicts were indeed seen as family matters, leaving the rabbinic authorities out of the picture. Rabbi Weil sought to reverse that trend and reassert rabbinic authority. As urban society expanded in late medieval Europe, family vendettas were dangerous, as they could erupt in a cycle of violence. Christian religious and secular leaders thus sought to put an end to the practice. Their attempts at pacification, like Rabbi Weil's attempt to bring murder back into court, were only partially successful.[180]

In his concluding remarks to *A History of Murder*, Pieter Spierenburg connects the dots between the many components of his vast study, which spans seven centuries from the Middle Ages to the present. He seeks to explain the decline in murder rates during that time. "All the evidence combined," he writes, "provides powerful support for the theory of civilization." Diminishing murder rates become especially evident beginning in the late eighteenth century, and most of it can be attributed to a decline in honor killings, domestic violence, and infanticide. Spierenburg highlights a number of possible contributing factors: the rise of the European state system with its growing instruments of social control, the process of urbanization, and the growth of a differentiated economy.[181] He also points to social phenomena, such as the decline of feuding and its evolution into the stylized duel, which support his thesis that the change took place gradually.

While Spierenburg examined medieval Europe in general, I have focused in this chapter on murder among medieval European Jews, basing myself mostly on documentation produced by that community. The data on which this chapter is based is much more limited than that available to Spierenburg.[182] But like him, on the basis of my research I can reach some broad historical conclusions about society, in this case Jewish society. Here, too, the evidence points to gradual historical change over time with regard to murder. It is manifested in two separate aspects. The first is that of Jews who committed nonlethal and lethal violence within Jewish society; the second is the response to such violence.

A common thread that runs through all my work is my contention that Jews in medieval Europe were more like than unlike the Christians among whom they lived; in particular, I argue, they shared social codes of behavior. Rabbi Judah the Pious says as much in *Sefer Ḥasidim*: "For in every city and town the manner of behavior of the Jews resembles that of their non-Jewish neighbors in most places." From as early as the case of Phatir and Priscus in sixth-century Paris, through the cases from the German Jewish heartland in the Rhine, Mosel, Main, and Danube basins, to the eastern parts of Germany (Magdeburg, Zeitz) and further east into Poland, violent behavior among Jews differed little in its patterns from that of their non-Jewish neighbors.

There are, however, two marked differences. The first is that violence and lethal violence seems to have been less common among Jews. As noted by Spierenburg, one of the most prevalent reasons for killings in medieval European society was honor. At times, honor-related violence and the fatalities that came in its wake metastasized into fully blown feuds and vendettas between families and clans. The Jewish sources indicate that honor violence was much less frequent among Jews. This is not to say that Jews were not jealous of their honor—they were, very much so. The increasing number of responsa, especially from the fourteenth and fifteenth centuries, addressing shaming, name-calling, the spread of heinous rumors about lineage, and other honor-related matters indicates that this was a growing concern. Furthermore, there were certainly instances in which matters of honor developed from a verbal exchange into a physical altercation.

Nevertheless, among Jews, crossing the lethal threshold seems to have been another matter altogether. Perhaps this was due in part to the fact that fewer Jews bore real weapons, due to the growing control exerted by city councils and the over-policing of Jews. It may also be that Jews knew better than to draw attention to their internal squabbles. Furthermore, the option of *mesirah*, that is, of turning a Jewish adversary over to the gentile authorities, may have curbed violence. While Jewish law and authorities forbade doing this, a Jew acting in a "time of rage" could nevertheless do so without needing to fear repercussions. Most likely, all of these were contributing factors. Moving forward in time, violent deaths and fatalities appear more often in the sources, as the authority of Jewish community institutions seems to decline. Presumably, some such cases were better resolved in earlier periods, when the Jewish communal system of arbitration and justice had stronger leverage and control over members of the community.

Nevertheless, even in earlier times some had no compunctions about using violence and committing murder against other Jews who offended their honor, against business rivals, and to intimidate communal arbitrators and others.[183] They were the counterparts of members of the European nobility and urban patrician ruling class who used violence with impunity against individuals of inferior social status. But Jews who behaved in this manner seem to have been a minority within the Jewish minority in medieval Western Europe.

As communal power waned, there was a corresponding rise in the use of violence and the threat to use it within the Jewish community. Jewish sources testify to the growing inability of rabbinic courts and communal authorities to quash such violence. By the fifteenth century, as is evident in the case from Poland brought before Rabbi Israel of Bruna, lethal violence had become associated more with the margins of Jewish society. Rabbi Israel's consideration of the victim's religious observance and Jewish identity markers are significant in that they imply that the murdered man was only nominally a Jew, barely recognized as such. Over the course of the Middle Ages, murder shifted from being largely a tool of the higher echelons of Jewish society to a more common phenomenon in the lowest strata of Jewish society. The metamorphosis moves from Priscus and Phatir, who were members of the Neustrian royal entourage in sixth-century Paris to Nahman and Simha, the Jewish hoodlums of fifteenth-century Lemberg.

The Jewish self-image also changed over time. The documents considered in this chapter repeatedly voice the notion that Jews were less inclined to violence and murder than were the gentiles around them. These documents generally portray gentiles of all ranks and social standing, both noble and rural alike, as bloodthirsty ruffians, eager to engage in violence. That should not be surprising, given that throughout the European Middle Ages Jews suffered greatly from the violence of non-Jews, and were the victims of riots, pogroms, and random killings. This may explain why, in many of the cases, Jews availed themselves of non-Jews to commit acts of violence on their behalf.

That pattern runs through many of the cases in this chapter. Jews were involved in brawls that spiraled out of control, heated arguments that got out of hand, honor killings in the heat of the moment, and incidents of killing in self-defense. But when it came to a premeditated murder, both within the family and in the public sphere, the act was many a time outsourced to non-Jews. The rabbis who wrote the responsa discussed here sought to eradicate such behavior and to take a stand against it. Branding Jews who ordered the killing of fellow Jews as murderers was meant to make it clear that a Jew who ordered or hired a non-Jew to commit a murder was no less culpable than if he had done the act himself. The fact that rabbis had to invoke this rule again and again shows that, at least among the common people, it was not self-evident. Having said this, it is important to stress that, as Karen Halttunen remarks in her introduction to *Murder Most Foul:*

Medieval and Early Modern Homicide, "medieval societies were no less horrified by homicide than modern ones." This chapter shows that in this, too, Jewish society was like gentile society. Murder and homicide, Halttunen asserts, is an act that "rends the community in which it takes place, calling all relationships into question—mother and infant, husband and wife, lovers, friends, strangers, and mere acquaintances—and posing troubling questions about the moral nature of humankind."[184]

Finally, as has been demonstrated by Elishevah Baumgarten, Pieter Spierenburg, and recently by Dianne Berg, when it comes to murder, gender makes a difference. In the cases discussed in this section, the perpetrators are male, and so are nearly all the victims. There may be some exceptions (it is possible that Kelina was Milo of York's accomplice in the killing of his wife), but overall, murder was a man's business. This in itself is not surprising, since in medieval times the defense of both personal, familial, and clan honor was entrusted to men. Once a violation of honor had taken place, retribution, especially if the victim was a woman, was thought to be a male responsibility. Since, in the medieval honor-shame culture, honor issues accounted for many of the recorded killings, women's involvement was minor. When women killed, it was mostly in the domestic sphere, either involving romantic affairs or the deaths of infants, whether intentional or unintentional.[185]

The late thirteenth century east German rabbi Shabtai ben Shmuel of Zeitz (near Leipzig) said, speaking of an accused murderer: "Be gone thou man of blood, one so full of defilement, but if he surrenders to this admonishment he will be redeemed and will receive penance." Here, in a nutshell, lies the tension felt in Jewish communities in the Middle Ages between the need to rid a community of a murderer and the potent desire to keep even the most heinous criminals within the fold.

3

WOMEN AND CRIME

The case of the Jewish woman who stole valuable books from the home of her husband's family, briefly recounted in chapter 2, was addressed there among cases in which medieval Jews were involved in book theft. But the fact that the instigator of this particular crime was a woman deserves special attention.

Rabbi Asher became involved in the case after being approached by a Jewish tribunal before whom a suit against the woman was filed. In other words, it was a civil rather than a criminal case. The house she broke into, with the aid of a male relative, belonged to her husband's family, and the plaintiffs demanded that the books she stole be returned. The responsum offers only the scantest details, but they are enough to paint a tragic picture. The woman came from a poor family, whose father arranged her marriage to an apparently mentally unstable man from a wealthy family. The woman admitted to the tribunal that she had consented to the marriage in full cognizance of the fact that her husband was not of sound mind. Over time, however, her husband's condition deteriorated. The woman told the court that he "became more and more foolish by the day." When irritated or angered, he was prone to violent outbursts against property, livestock, and people around him. The responsum indicates that the woman was not only legally savvy but also assertive and ingenious. The husband's family had relinquished involvement in the couple's finances and she was clearly well aware that, were her husband's mental state to deteriorate further, she would have no legal way to dissolve the marriage. Under Jewish law, a divorce must be granted by a man to his wife, and a man who is not of sound mind cannot grant his wife a divorce because, from the legal point of view, he is not capable of understanding the act and all its implications and is thus unable to consent to it rationally. Were he to cease to provide for her, or if she were to move out of their common home because living with him was unbearable, she would be left financially bereft, as she could neither receive the divorce settlement mandated in their marriage contract nor remarry and thus gain the financial support of another man. In light of this, she asked a relative to help her break into the home of her husband's family home and take some valuable books she knew were there. The books were intended to serve either as leverage for negotiating a financial settlement with the family were the husband to squander all his assets, or as commodities that would sustain her and her children if her husband were unable to support her.

Another troubling story emerges from a different, somewhat earlier case:

> A certain man on whom pustules, strange boils like a *nega'*,[1] swelled up on his face, forced his wife to remain with him, even though she refused to be with him. She [then] became pregnant from him. But since he is considered violent [*muḥzak*], she fears for her life and is compelled to stay with him.... If he threatens her and forces her to be with him, she should be helped so that she does not fall into evil ways [*tarbut ra'ah*], and if he beats her or forces her to be with him, judgment must be rendered against him [on the charge of] beating another person.[2]

The case appears in a collection of rabbinic responsa found in an early fourteenth-century manuscript. This particular responsum, like many in this genre, has no introduction and, as in many cases discussed here and elsewhere, the question was omitted by the copyist. Typically, the name of the plaintiff, the abused wife, does not appear in the text, nor does her husband's. Either the husband was violent by nature, or his disease caused him to become so. The case came before an unnamed rabbinic tribunal, which forwarded it to a higher but also unnamed halakhic authority, because of the complexities the case presented.[3] According to the Jewish matrimonial code, had the woman petitioned the court and declared that she was repulsed by her husband's looks, smell, and overall appearance, the court could have ordered her husband to grant her a divorce, and if he refused, it could have imposed sanctions on him to compel him to do so. But this required that the wife invoke a specific halakhic formula reserved for such cases: she needed to declare that her husband *me'is alay* (lit. "he is repugnant to me"), or similar language. The wife did not do so, even though her behavior clearly expressed her repulsion nonverbally, most probably further infuriating her husband. Unfortunately, by not making the necessary legal claim, either because she was unaware of her rights or because she was afraid to do so, the woman tied the court's hands and left it with no legal basis for ending the marriage.

Seeking a way to help the wife, the court cited the husband's physical violence. The woman had been the victim of what would today be termed marital or spousal rape, and had become pregnant as a result. The members of the court also expressed their fear that the wife might take matters into her own hands, "fall into evil ways" (*tetzeh le-tarbut ra'ah*), meaning either that she was liable to run away with another man without properly divorcing her violent husband or, lacking financial and emotional spousal support, would prostitute herself so as to provide for herself and the future child. Regrettably, the text does not relate how the case was resolved, if it was.

In both these cases, a married woman was the victim of domestic violence.[4] In the first case, the wife chose to steal in order to guarantee her livelihood in the face of her husband's violence and mental deterioration. In the second, the court's concern seems to have been that the wife might prostitute herself in order to provide for herself and her unborn child. Both cases also give voice to the anxieties of the legal authorities regarding the implications of the domestic dispute for the community as a whole. Taken together, the cases demonstrate the complexities that the involvement of women in crime presented to Jewish communities and legal authorities.

METHODOLOGICAL PROBLEMS

In his work on medieval crime, Trevor Dean divided women's involvement into three parts: crimes committed by women, crimes committed against women, and the treatment of women as victims and offenders by courts and tribunals.[5] I will follow Dean's tripartite approach, though in fact there is a certain amount of overlap between the three categories. First, however, I need to expand on the methodological concerns I raised in chapter 1, which are even more problematic when it comes to women's roles.

According to Carol Lansing, "Female crime and victimization had distinct patterns different from those of men" because of the intrinsic bias of the documentation. Since the records were kept by men, the depictions of the crimes involving females were described differently. Such bias can be seen not only in legal codes and the court records, from the entire range of medieval European political and judicial systems, but also in literary sources, such as chronicles and historiographical treatises. All these were written by men and for men. Moreover, they were written from a male point of view. When reading about women in these records and accounts, the contemporary scholar must make an effort to see through the masculine bias, assumptions, and stereotypes, all the more when addressing the fraught topic of the nexus between women and crime.

All this is true of medieval Jewry as well. An overwhelming majority of the texts produced then were written by men for a male audience and thus represent a masculine perspective and reflect predominantly masculine concerns. In the general medieval European context there are but a handful of exceptions to this rule. The situation is even more acute with regard to Jewish material, which was composed primarily by the members of the male learned elite, in other words by either rabbis or men with rabbinic training. Among traditional Jews, this remains today an exclusively male preserve. The very essence of how crime was understood and perceived was a by-product of male engendering, especially in premodern times. What constituted a criminal violation was a male construct. The structuring and formulation of what was understood as a breach of law and legal norms were designed in masculine language with male self-perception in mind.

The extent to which these constructs are important is demonstrated by wife beating, an element of the cases with which this chapter began. In general, if the violence was not excessive and did not cause death or serious injury, it was not considered criminal behavior. This was particularly true of the high Middle Ages, when the increasing importance and influence of canon law and interest in Roman law reinforced the role of the man as *paterfamilias* (head of the household). As such, men were obligated to educate and discipline all members of their households, in which everyone else was subordinate to them—children, servants, slaves, and, no less, wives. While his wife was not on the same legal or social level as a maidservant or a female slave, she was equally subordinate to the domestic male hegemony. In this milieu, wife-beating was often considered not only permissible but mandatory.

But masculine constructs are not the sole obstacle to understanding medieval Jewish women's involvement in crime. Hebrew and talmudic Aramaic were incomprehensible to most medieval Jews, particularly to women, as inaccessible to them as Latin was to their Christian counterparts. Women had no opportunity to be initiated into Jewish sacred learning and legal dialogue. Thus when a woman's voice appears in medieval Jewish manuscripts, it is often a paraphrase of what she said in a vernacular language, not in the Hebrew that served as the language of legal documents and rulings.[6] Some sources might offer a direct quote translated from the vernacular, usually Yiddish, into Hebrew. Yiddish was even explicitly referred to as "women's speech," *weiber taitsch*, and was used in writing intended to explain things for women. An example of the importance of these gendered terms can be found in a responsum of the fifteenth-century Austrian master Rabbi Israel Iserlyn ben Petachia (1390–1460), author of the influential halakhic work *Terumat ha-Deshen*. It involved an accusation of adultery against a married woman who served as a live-in governess in the household of an affluent Jew. She was rumored to have had a sexual liaison with an unmarried Jewish manservant in that household. According to the responsum, when she was confronted by her employer and questioned about the allegations, the woman admitted that the servant had indeed visited her room at night. In admitting this, however, she exclaimed: "*aber er hat ni(ch)t recht bi mir gelegen*" ("but he did not really lie with me!"). Because the meaning of this Yiddish phrase was open to question, both the person posing the question and Rabbi Isserlyn considered it carefully, and as such it was quoted in the original Yiddish in the otherwise Hebrew-Aramaic text. It is one of the earliest verbatim quotes from women in the literature, a direct record of a woman's speech rather than a translation and paraphrase of what a woman said into legal Hebrew, as was the custom, then and in earlier sources.[7]

This distancing of women has been noted by a number of medieval Jewish historians over the past few decades.[8] As awareness has grown of their underrepresentation both in the sources that historians usually work with and in the scholarship historians produce, more have sought to balance the picture by focusing on female issues, asking questions from a female-gendered perspective, and critically evaluating male constructs. Scholars are now more attentive to submerged female voices in the source material, and by bringing them to the surface have been able to portray what issues concerned women in the past and how they expressed those concerns. But there is no getting around that the source material is extremely biased toward the male perspective; female voices can often only be heard between the lines.

When it comes to women's involvement in crime, the historian must bear in mind that the women under study were doubly, if not triply, marginalized. They were part of the Jewish minority, within that minority they were female, and among Jewish women, they were also part of a small group that were either victims or perpetrators of crime. As I stated at the start of this book, in the scholarly world Jewish involvement in crime has long been under-researched, and often deliberately avoided or simply overlooked, for a host of reasons. The role played by Jewish women has been even more marginalized. Even recent works that have addressed the role of women in medieval Jewish society have barely touched on the fundamental issues of what constituted crime with regard to women and the extent and profile of female involvement in crime.[9]

Gender and gender roles are key to understanding criminal acts performed by women. The question of whether or not a woman acted in accordance with normative roles determined how authorities viewed her behavior and how they reacted to it. The two stories above highlight rabbinical anxieties expressed as "lest she go astray" or "lest she fall into evil ways," which will appear frequently below as well. Women and female bodies were considered to be representations of the collective; violence against them, or their sexual violation, was seen as an attack on the entire collective. This raised a set of concerns that differed significantly from those engendered when a man committed or was a victim of a crime.

The two cases described briefly above also offer in their telling a fleeting glimpse of feelings like terror and fear expressed by the two women who had been the victims of their husband's physical and sexual violence. However, these emotions were conveyed by men, in the context of the courts, usually in an extremely truncated form. Although it is important to keep in mind that the expression of these emotions in the texts might well be a convention rather than a report of what the women actually said or felt, it is probably the closest we can get to the actual voices of medieval Jewish women.

PROSTITUTION

Jewish prostitutes do not make an appearance in medieval texts until late in that era, but Jewish men who patronized prostitutes are relatively well documented from the start. One early case is that of a cantor (*ḥazan*, also referred to as *shaliaḥ tzibur*, emissary of the public) appearing in an unsigned responsum that should probably be ascribed to the late tenth century Iberian rabbi Joseph Iben-Avitur.

Much like a Christian priest, the Jewish cantor was seen as a representative of the community that chose him to lead the services. In many communities it was a paid job that required skilled practitioners. Unlike a Christian priest, a Jewish cantor was not seen as the community's sole representative, as in Jewish tradition there is no need for mediation or intervention with the divine. Nevertheless, his role reciting the prayers in the sacred space of the synagogue was considered an important religious task. He was thus expected to uphold certain moral standards, especially if he was of the Jewish priestly descent (*cohen*), a status that enjoyed a certain aura even in the postdestruction era.

In the case that came before Rabbi Joseph, a cantor of priestly descent from an undesignated Jewish community, probably in Iberia, stood accused of immoral behavior. The man was a newcomer to the town who, not long after his arrival, was appointed to the well-paid position of communal cantor (*ḥazan*). Rumors about his immoral behavior and promiscuity began to spread soon thereafter. There is no mention of a wife or family, probably indicating that the man was single. The Jewish communal authorities first dismissed the rumors, which they attributed to the ill will of local candidates for the position angry at being supplanted by a stranger. But the rumors persisted, and evidence that they were true began to accumulate. The leaders decided to make inquiries, which determined that the community's representative before God lived a life of debauchery.

The cantor had made his home in a dubious part of town, where he had easy access to prostitutes. It was said that he had been caught in the act of having sex with a non-Jewish prostitute, in breach of the local law that prohibited such a liaison. In fact, the incident came to light because the gentile town authorities arraigned him for this offense, but he managed to have the charges dropped by paying a large bribe. He was also accused by fellow Jews of seducing and violating young boys. The most explicit and elaborate accusation against him came from a witness who claimed to have seen the cantor on the road (*ba-derekh*). According to the witness, the cantor was stalking a woman, attempting to procure her sexual services, probably presuming she was a prostitute. The witness reported that the woman did all she could to spurn the cantor's advances, but to no avail. In the face of his persistence, when she saw that she could not elude him, the woman faced him and unveiled herself. The woman declared she was Jewish, from a family the cantor knew, and demanded he leave her alone. It was only at this point that the cantor desisted. Other Jews testified that his public immoral behavior had attracted the attention of the town's non-Jewish inhabitants, who admonished the local

Jews for having chosen such a person to convey their prayers to the Almighty.[10] The question came before Rabbi Joseph because, following its inquiry, the community had dismissed the cantor. Some time thereafter, however, some members of the community sought to reinstate him, on condition that he repent and repair his ways.

Although this anecdote does not focus on women and is probably from Muslim Iberia in the tenth century rather than medieval Christian Europe, it offers some pieces of information touching on Jewish patronage of prostitutes in medieval times. First, the cantor resided in a part of town notorious for its sexual promiscuity, an area where prostitutes operated. In many parts of Europe, north and south alike, prostitution was restricted to specific areas.

Second, women were at times pursued by men who thought they were prostitutes or who tried to coerce them into providing sexual services. In her book *Common Women*, on prostitution in medieval England, Ruth Mazo Karras devotes an entire chapter to how women became prostitutes, where she documents the tactics used to recruit women into such work.[11] In some cases, women were harassed economically and deliberately driven to poverty in order to cause them to enter the "sex trade"; girls without families or with problematic or strained familial ties were particularly vulnerable, and the medieval Jewish community was no exception. In the case of the cantor, the woman he had stalked deterred him by stating her religious and family identity. Rabbi Joseph quotes her directly: "Reuven! Do you not know that I am Jewish? I am so-and-so, daughter of so-and-so, and you are bullying me excessively (*ve-atah madḥikeni kol kakh*)!" These words are probably a direct Hebrew translation of the oral testament of the eyewitness who reported the verbal exchange between the woman and the cantor, taken from the record of the communal committee of inquiry.

Both rabbinic and later non-Jewish archival sources indicate that Jewish men preferred to procure the services of prostitutes from outside their community, and even from outside the Jewish fold altogether. Notably, the same was true of Jewish women who sold their sexual services; in fact, one of the accusations leveled against Jewish prostitutes was that they consorted with non-Jews.

Bedding "the other" as a sexual outlet was not uncommon. Explicit evidence can be found in a passage from the *Sefer Agudah*, a halakhic compendium by the Erfurt-born rabbi Alexander ben Süslin Hacohen,[12] addressing a woman who wished to divorce her husband because he was fraternizing with prostitutes (*roʿeh zonot*, lit. shepharding prostitutes). Rabbi Alexander was willing to grant a divorce only if the allegation was substantiated by direct evidence of the act of coitus: "only if the witnesses saw him with the *non-Jewish prostitute* in coitus (*ke-derekh ha-menaʾafim*) or if the prostitute had given birth to a child from their sexual liaison." Rabbi Alexander not only notes that the prostitute was not Jewish, but cautions his rabbinic readers not to be hasty in passing judgment in such cases, due to the religious identity of the women on the one hand and the possible ramifications of such a liaison becoming public knowledge to non-Jewish authorities on the other. From the high middle ages there was a growing attempt by the municipal authorities in western Europe to curb Jewish patronage of non-Jewish prostitutes. In Rabbi Alexander's words: "for we have seen many perish over these allegations without a proper trial."[13]

Rabbi Alexander is referring to accusations against Jewish men who had sexual relations with non-Jewish women, ending with the man's prosecution and, in some cases, a death sentence. This situation is similar, although not identical, to that depicted in Rabbi Joseph Iben Avitur's responsum, where the cantor escaped prosecution for consorting with a non-Jewish prostitute only after bribing the Muslim authorities. In fourteenth-century Germany the situation was quite different.[14] Both Jewish sources and the archival evidence presented by Jorg Müller on sexual liaisons between Jews and non-Jews suggest that, while it was dangerous and at times even deadly for a Jew to procure the services of a non-Jewish prostitute, it was hardly rare.[15]

It is reasonable to assume that most paid sexual liaisons involving Jews took place between Jewish men and non-Jewish prostitutes, rather between non-Jewish men and Jewish prostitutes. Jews were a small minority, numerically inferior in the urban setting of medieval Europe, and premodern societies, especially smaller, tightly knit communities, closely supervised their women. Nevertheless, Jewish women are documented as providing sexual services to both Jewish and non-Jewish men.

Is *Znut* Prostitution?

The Hebrew word for prostitution is *znut*, and a prostitute is a *zonah*. In halakhic terms, *znut* is a much broader term. Often translated as "wantonness," it refers not only to prostitution, as the modern Hebrew connotation of the word suggests, but also to all sexual contacts between individuals who are not married to one another. Rashi (Rabbi Shlomo ben Isaac), the late eleventh century biblical and talmudic commentator, offered a definition of "wantonness": "A man who gives away his unmarried daughter for intercourse, not for the sake of matrimony."[16]

Nachmanides (Rabbi Moses ben Nachman, known in Jewish circles as Ramban), who lived in Barcelona in the thirteenth century, disputed Rashi's definition on the basis of a talmudic ruling (BT *Yebamot* 61:2) to the effect that if an unmarried man has sexual relations with an unmarried woman, and they do not intend to marry and did not have sex as a means of wedding one another,[17] it does not constitute *znut* and the woman is not a *zonah*. The disagreement between Rashi and Nachmanides demonstrates that biblical dictums, talmudic terms and concepts, and medieval commentators attempting to reconcile them with the societies they lived in and the people they knew leave much latitude and fluidity. More generally, the term refers to premarital or extramarital sexual relations between two individuals who do not wish their sexual activities to be considered as a consummation of marriage. It also refers to extramarital relations between a married woman and a married or unmarried man who is not her husband, as well as to sexual relations procured for some sort of payment.

The halakhic Hebrew source material needs to be handled with special caution in this regard. The modern criminological distinction between prostitution and extramarital sex was not necessarily recognized by medieval Jewish legal authorities. In the halakhic discourse, sexual expression outside marriage was, at the very least, unacceptable. Sexual activity that violated the marriage bond was, especially for women, intolerable and blatantly criminal. As such, many of the sources that address *znut* discuss men and women involved in sexual activities that have very little to do with prostitution. This use of the term in this manner persisted well into modern times.[18]

This is obviously a social construct; it is clear to many of the medieval commentators that the Bible, unlike their contemporaries, uses the word *zonah* to denote a woman who exchanges sexual favors for money or other methods of payment.[19] According to Deuteronomy 23:19, the income of a prostitute (אתנן זונה *etnan zonah*) may not serve as a gift to the Lord's Temple.[20] The Bible does not outlaw prostitution altogether, though there seems to be a strong bias against it, but it does forbid cultic prostitution (Deut. 23:18): "None of the daughters of Israel shall be a *cult prostitute [kedeshah]* nor shall any of the sons of Israel be a *cult prostitute [kadesh]*."[21]

The medieval Church accepted St. Jerome's definition of a prostitute: "A whore is one who is available to the lusts of many men." But other views were also current in Latin Europe, such as that of the Roman jurist Ulpian (Gnaeus Domitius Annius Ulpianus 170–223), for whom a prostitute was a person who engaged in sexual activity with a large number of customers for money or other material remuneration. As Jeffery Richards points out, promiscuity is the central element for Ulpian, not the exchange of goods or money for sexual favors. In this respect, the medieval rabbinic definition of *znut* and prostitution as defined by the Church are strikingly similar.

As we begin to see in the opening case of this section, prostitution was an integral part of medieval European urban life. It appears, for example, in a case from the mid-eleventh century that we discussed in chapter 1, involving valuables stolen from a church and sold to a Jewish merchant by a renegade cleric, who used the proceeds of the sale to pay for the sexual favors of a local prostitute.[22] Later works, like the *Chronicon de Rebus Gestis Ricardi Primi*, by the late twelfth-century English monastic chronicler Richard of Devizes of St. Swithin's house at Winchester, caution readers, especially monastic readers, about sexual promiscuity and the temptations that lurk in large urban centers such as London.[23] Jacques de Vitry, who would become the Bishop of Acre in the Latin Kingdom of Jerusalem in 1214, writes in his thirteenth-century chronicle about the very visible presence of prostitutes in Paris in his time:

> Prostitutes were everywhere in the streets and neighborhoods of the city, seeking to drag passing clerics by force into their brothels. If the clerics refused to enter they immediately shouted after them Sodomite! In one and the same building there might be a school upstairs and a brothel downstairs. While in the upper part the masters taught their pupils, in the lower part the prostitutes plied their nefarious trade. In one part the prostitutes quarreled with each other and their pimps, in the other part the scholars argued on scholarly matters.[24]

Prostitutes, like Jews, were tolerated in medieval Europe as practitioners of a trade that provided a vital social service. Like Jews, however, they were stigmatized as unclean. In many towns in medieval Europe, market regulations required Jews and prostitutes to purchase any food or goods they examined and touched, for fear they had polluted these objects and rendered them dangerous for others to consume or use. In other words, some medieval Christians viewed Jews and prostitutes as similar in some ways: they were deemed unclean and their touch was felt to be contaminating, transmitting moral uncleanliness. In the later Middle Ages, following the resolutions of the Fourth Lateran Council (1215), prostitutes, like Jews, were required by sumptuary laws to wear distinctive garments.[25]

Today, prostitutes are defined as people professionally involved in the sex industry. Some legal systems consider them criminals. Trafficking in women for sexual purposes and soliciting customers for a prostitute or a brothel are also criminal acts in many modern states, even where prostitution itself is not illegal. Medieval European attitudes were quite different. First, many women who provided sexual favors did so in exchange for food, shelter, protection, or work, and were not full-time prostitutes—that is, providing sexual services was not their primary livelihood. Many women traded sexual services for other goods incidentally, rather than on a regular basis. Not all prostitutes were seen as criminals.[26] The terms prostitute, whore, or harlot were often used to denote any woman with many sexual partners, not all of whom paid for the sexual favors they were granted. The same was true of the Hebrew terms *zonah* and *prutzah* (lit., penetrated). In some cases the Hebrew sources use the superlative *prutzah be-yoter*, indicating that the woman in question is not only sexually promiscuous but that she solicits customers or that her overall behavior is brazen. From biblical times and into late antiquity, the era during which talmudic literature took form, the term referred more to sexually promiscuous behavior than to selling sexual services.

Among medieval Jews, women who were promiscuous and those who provided sex for money were both seen as immoral and forbidden, socially, religiously, and legally. A woman who offered her body freely was not only religiously proscribed; she undermined male authority. But a woman could also be accused of wantonness, that is of being a *zonah* or *prutzah*, if she wore inappropriate clothing, certain hairstyles, or even used certain forms of speech or evinced irreverence. If she were unmarried, such behavior would make it harder to find a husband in decent and virtuous society. If she were married, wanton behavior could be grounds for a divorce with serious financial repercussions—her husband could send her away without being required to award her the financial compensation stated in her marriage contract. A married Jewish man who behaved shamelessly and fraternized with whores ran a similar risk. Jewish legal authorities viewed such behavior as grounds for a wife to be granted a divorce and payment of the obligation due her under the marriage contract, causing the husband serious economic damage, as in the case adjudicated by Alexander Süslin Hacohen.

Medieval Jews and Christians had different moral standards regarding sex and the role of women. According to Jöelle Koster,

> It is traditionally accepted that medieval society held a double standard regarding sexual behavior that allowed men sexual permissiveness and demanded sexual austerity from women. The irony remains that medieval men loaded woman with negative characteristics, they were considered fickle, libidinous, and inconsistent, prone to temptation and weak in terms of sexuality . . . yet men conceded that male concupiscence was problematic and a danger to civil order. By this circular rationale they acknowledged prostitution as a minor evil.[27]

Thus, even if was not legally proscribed, prostitution was a moral crime, a breach of the mores of decent and chaste society. With the rise of canon law beginning in the mid-twelfth century, and the growing power of Church enforcement mechanisms beginning in the thirteenth century, prostitution was increasingly seen as a crime. In James Brundage's words:

> Beyond their civil jurisdiction over marriage formation, canonical courts also exercised criminal jurisdiction over all types of extramarital sexual conduct. Thus fornication, adultery, bigamy, rape, incest, prostitution, and sodomy were all subject to ecclesiastical penalties and church courts . . . also tried to enforce regulations about sexual morals. Such cases brought numerous persons unwillingly into contact with the disciplinary mechanisms of canon law.[28]

Similar trends can be seen in medieval Jewish legal thinking, although Jewish men had been expected to exercise sexual temperance even before this time. Jews engaged in extramarital relations, of course, but Jewish legal thinkers, jurists, and ethical writers condemned them, and sexual promiscuity among men was also considerably disciplined, although not as strictly as among women.[29]

"Go Forth and Learn from the Righteous Gentile Lord": The Ethical Approach of *Sefer Ḥasidim*

One of the ethical writers who took up the subject of prostitution in his writing was the thirteenth-century author-compiler of *Sefer Ḥasidim* (*Book of the Pious*), Rabbi Judah ben Shmuel the Pious. Rabbi Judah was preoccupied with the repercussions of sexual promiscuity and determined to quell it. In one of his innovative exegetical passages he goes so far as to reprimand not only those who engage in *znut* but also those who indirectly instigate it by, for example, marrying a young woman to an old man, creating a situation by which the unbalanced sexual desires of both sides may create an incentive for the woman to seek sexual satisfaction outside the marriage, or introducing a man and a woman who might eventually have an illicit relationship with one another.[30] Elaborating on the biblical admonition "Do not degrade your daughter and make her a harlot [להזנותה *le'haznotah*], lest the land fall into harlotry [wantonness, תזנה הארץ *tizneh ha'aretz*] and the land be filled with depravity [זימה *zimah*]" (Lev.19:29), he suggests that the end verse be read not, as usual, in the passive voice, but in the active, in the sense "and you shall not cause the land to fill with harlotry," forbidding even unintentional facilitation of harlotry. In an exemplum (SHW § 58) building on this same innovative reading, Rabbi Judah praises a local Christian lord for not only regulating prostitution but for restricting the presence of prostitutes in the public sphere, especially during market days when many people frequent the town.

> Go forth and learn [*tze u-lemad*] from a gentile lord [*sar shel goyim*]. A certain bishop [*hegmon*] had a large marketplace in his locality. Many people would assemble there on the market days, as did many prostitutes. These prostitutes had a madam [*geveret*] supervising them. The bishop told his servant: "Take a considerable sum from my purse and hire the services of all the prostitutes, for tomorrow is the market day and they all come to the market. After you have hired them and paid the sum they require," said the bishop, "have them assembled in one house and make a fine bed for each and every one of them, provide them with food and drink and with fiber for spinning [to keep them busy] and keep them in that house until the market is over, only then you may let them return to their place." The servant did as he was told, he approached the madam and said: "Anything you desire I will give your women, even more than you would earn during the day of the market," and he gave her all that she wanted in payment. He then had them all put up in one house [outside of the town] and he kept them there until the market was over. Only then he let them return to the town. And he would do this whenever there was a market and the prostitutes would come. All the more so should Jews be mindful and segregate and safeguard themselves from any violation and deed facilitating transgression.

The exemplum demonstrates not only knowledge of the regulation of prostitution and the connection between markets and prostitution, but also knowledge of how brothels were run, by a woman who oversaw the prostitutes. Furthermore, it holds up as praiseworthy a Christian religious authority who is as concerned as pious Jews are with public morals and no less devoted to preventing vice. Jews, says the author of *Sefer Ḥasidim*, should emulate the bishop. In one manuscript, the text differs slightly, instructing the reader to learn this important lesson not from "a lord with authority among the gentiles" (*sar shel goyim*) but rather from the "righteous among the gentiles" (*kesherim shel goyim*).

Later in the thirteenth century, in 1276, the German King Rudolf von Habsburg attempted to curb prostitution in Vienna in a similar fashion. He placed the city's *hübschlerinnen* (a medieval German term for prostitutes) under the authority of its executioner, tantamount to outlawing their trade. Each Saturday these women paid the treasury a weekly tax, with a base rate of two pfennigs. After paying the tax, they were required to leave the city, as they were forbidden to remain in the city on Sundays, for religious reasons. King Rudolf's decree also forbade prostitutes from entering Vienna during the forty days of the Lent fast, under penalty of physical mutilation.[31]

In suggesting how to limit prostitution, Rabbi Judah's exemplum simultaneously displays his understanding of its causes and driving forces. When the steward assembles the prostitutes after making his offer, he provides them with food, drink, shelter, decent living quarters, payment, and yarn for spinning. Rabbi Judah viewed these as the essentials that would enable the prostitutes to refrain from soliciting clients and plying their trade at the fair. In other words, women became prostitutes because of financial exigency, hunger, thirst, and homelessness.[32] Some prostitutes, especially those who worked on the streets and not in brothels, had intercourse with their clients in any public space that could become "private" for a few moments—a dark alley, doorway, market stand, or vacant lot would do. Providing the prostitutes with shelter and a bed may have been a way to draw them into an enclosed space and prevent sexual acts from taking place in public.

The provision of fiber responds to medieval men's anxiety about the idleness of women. Both Jews and premodern non-Jews believed that idleness was a cause of wanton sexuality in women. Spinning fiber into yarn was considered an ideal occupation for a woman who was not engaged in any other household task. In Roman times, even noblewomen with many servants and slaves would spin as a sign of respectability and female decency. This notion still prevailed when the wool trade and the textile industry grew to large proportions, from the thirteenth century onward. The Franciscan preacher Berthold of Regensburg (1220–1272), proclaimed in his famous vernacular sermons in German that "men should fight and women spin," expressing ideas that circulated in the urban centers of Bavaria. Provision of yarn thus not only kept the prostitutes busy, but also served as a badge of dignity that marked them, in male eyes, as normative women, at least for a short time.

Judah the Pious holds up the bishop and his steward as role models for the Jewish community—they expend money, time, and effort to reduce the level of sexual promiscuity at a time when men might most easily be led astray. By spending his own money to compensate the madam and her prostitutes for their lost income, as well as to provide them with housing, food, drink, and a decent way to pass their time, the bishop managed to keep them off the streets and away from the fairground. While the pietistic agenda promulgated by Rabbi Judah and his disciples generally sought to keep Jewish-gentile relations to a necessary minimum, the exemplum indicates that there were apparently contacts that facilitated the exchange of ideas and other non-tangible commodities, such as moral principles and practices.

Rabbi Judah the Pious also made another comment indicating his familiarity with the treatment of prostitutes by Christian society. Rabbi Jacob ben Asher (Cologne 1269–Toledo 1343) quotes Rabbi Judah's interpretation of the verse from Genesis about the trial of Tamar, who was accused of harlotry (38:24): "About three months later, Judah was told, 'Your daughter-in-law Tamar has played the harlot; in fact, she is with child by harlotry.' 'Bring her out,' said Judah, 'and let her be burned.'"

Rabbi Judah, as quoted by Rabbi Jacob, wrote: "Judah did not condemn her to be burnt at the stake [as is the simple understanding of the text], but rather that her face should be branded as a sign that she is a whore." The interpretation is in keeping with the Jewish exegetical imperative to reconcile inconsistencies in the biblical text. Here the problems are that Judah is portrayed as judging a case in which he was a party, which is forbidden elsewhere in the Torah, and that the death penalty the Torah elsewhere mandates for a cultic prostitute is not burning but stoning; burning is reserved to a priest's daughter who had become a *zonah*. Judah was not a priest and Tamar was not his daughter. Rabbi Judah (like Nachmanides, who lived a generation later) resolved these contradictions by reference to the customs and practices he saw around him among non-Jews, one of which was the branding of prostitutes with a red hot iron. Furthermore, it seemed plausible to other Jewish exegetes, such as Rabbi Jacob ben Asher, who lived two generations later.

The Case of Sara and Isaac: Sexual Promiscuity, Infanticide, and a "License to Kill"?

On Monday, the 25th of Adar 5031 (March 16, 1271), a Jew named Isaac set out on a business trip from his home in a small town, probably on the outskirts of Erfurt, leaving his wife Sara behind. To the best of his knowledge, Sara was not pregnant at the time. He possibly made some provisions for her religious needs by arranging for another member of the community to come to their home to recite the *kiddush*, the blessing made over wine on the eve of the Sabbath and holidays, which a woman was not permitted to recite for herself. A year later, still on the road, Isaac heard rumors that his wife had given birth to a baby. He immediately went home, only to discover that his wife had gone to live with her parents in a different town, and that his community was awash with rumors about Sara's whereabouts during the previous year.[33] Talk of Sara's sexual promiscuity with non-Jews and her pregnancy was circulating not only in their hometown, but all over the small and tightly knit Jewish community in the region. No baby, however, was to be found.

Enraged and humiliated at having been cuckolded, Isaac was determined to settle the matter. He set out to find Sara at her parents' home, planning to petition the local Jewish court to compel Sara to accept a writ of divorce and to rule that her infidelity had voided his obligations under their marriage contract, meaning that he would not have to pay the sum stipulated for payment if the two of them separated. The local tribunal was initially reluctant to intervene, perhaps because both Isaac and Sara were visitors in town, not longtime residents. Faced with the court's inaction, Isaac availed himself of a traditional method of forcing the community to act—he disrupted prayers in the local synagogue and demanded justice.[34]

These extreme measures eventually impelled the local court to act. It commenced an inquiry and gathered evidence about the case. While it found confirmation of the rumors, Sara continued to refuse to accept a divorce. Desperate, probably because he wished to remarry, Isaac cast the writ of divorce (*get*) before the tribunal and pleaded with the court to sanction his actions. They should accept that, in casting the document before the judges, he had effectuated the divorce over Sara's objections; the court should thus pronounce the marriage null and void. The local rabbis, unwilling to proceed on their own with such an explosive and unusual case, decided to send it on to more senior and authoritative adjudicators. They forwarded Isaac's petition and the evidence they had gathered to four such figures:

> Our Rabbis, those close to us in Erfurt, and those more remote in Würzburg, and the great luminary Rabbi Meir of Rothenburg, may the Lord guide him, and the other rabbis in the Rhineland,[35] [please] discharge [*pitru*] Isaac from Sara, a stray cow [*para Sara*, a pejorative Hebrew pun], by sanctioning the action of casting down a writ of divorce in our presence [even without her consent].

The referral was signed by the members of the tribunal: Rabbi Moshe Azriel ben Rabbi Eliezer the Homilist (ha-Darshan) who presided over the tribunal, Eliezer son of Rabbi Yechiel OBM, and Ephraim son of Joel MBE.[36]

One of the four responses to the referral survives, that of Rabbi Meir of Rothenburg, who wrote a long and erudite answer.[37]

The Texts and Voices

The responsum consists of several texts, composing a dossier that shows what evidence Rabbi Meir had before him.[38] The first of these is the cover letter sent by the tribunal from the unnamed town near Erfurt, where Sara's parents resided. The material the tribunal sent to Rabbi Meir included affidavits and documents pertaining to the judicial inquiry that the court requested in the community in which Isaac and Sara had resided before Isaac left on his business trip. This responsum refers to that community as "the place of her dwelling" (*mekom yishuvah*), suggesting it was a rural location with a very small Jewish community, not a city or town. Another indication of the original community's small size is the fact that the testimony the local tribunal sought to obtain came from members of one single family (a certain Rabbi Shaltiel and his two sons). By Jewish legal standards this is problematic, since the testimonies of witnesses related to one another is thought to be of a lesser quality. The fact that the tribunal nevertheless sought such testimony anyway indicates that the community was so small that the judges had no way to collect testimony from two unrelated Jewish adult males.[39]

In the opening lines of his responsum, Rabbi Meir makes an unequivocal statement about Sara's moral character. The version of the dossier that is included in *Teshuvot Maimoniyot* begins with Rabbi Meir's response. Like many rabbinic responsa of the twelfth and thirteenth centuries, especially those not deliberately truncated by later copyists, this letter opens with a rhymed verse prologue that offers clues to what the respondent felt about the matter at hand:

> *How shall I open this case before you, O great ones of old*
> *Our rabbis who are laden with gold*
> *Your thighs are like fine jewelry*[40]
> *And I have not been able to make heads or tails of this story*
> *Of the wretched woman Gomer of Divlaim.*
> *Anything your mouth will utter*

> Will be like a command to all the Children of Israel on this matter
> And I, the youngster, discuss before you this matter
> As a student discussing before his master.[41]

Apart from the usual formulaic gestures and professions of humility, the passage offers a clear indication of Rabbi Meir's opinion of Sara's conduct. For him, as for many other rabbis, Sara was a prostitute, not simply an adulterous wife but an infamous whore. This is clear from his reference to her as Gomer of Divlaim, the harlot wife (*eshet znunim*) of the biblical prophet Hosea.[42] Rabbi Meir calls her *aluvah* as well, an adjective that can be translated as wretched, shameful, and vile, but which can also mean poor, humble, and pitiable. Despite some legal issues surrounding the authenticity of some of the testimonies against her, Rabbi Meir seems to have presumed from the outset that it was extremely unlikely that Sara had not committed the sexual transgressions of which she was accused. Nevertheless, by calling her *aluvah*, Rabbi Meir shows compassion for her and understanding of the circumstances that drove her to behave as she did.

The responsum tells a sad tale through a host of voices. One of them is that of Isaac, angry and humiliated, but also sorry, at least somewhat, for his neglect of Sara, which ended by bringing shame upon himself because of his wife's wantonness and the birth of a bastard daughter. Notably, Isaac disregards the charge of infanticide made against Sara, addressing only the accusations of prostitution and fornication.

Another voice is that of Sara's father, a man driven to the brink of a murderous outrage by the consequences of his daughter's behavior, which has sullied his family's reputation. He apparently considered murdering his daughter because of this stain on his honor. "I have one daughter," he told two of the members who served on the local rabbinic court, "and she has become pregnant from harlotry and she has given birth to a bastard from a gentile, for it has been over a year since her husband went away, and I cannot deny that she is an absolute and notorious whore (*zonah gmurah u-mefursemet*). She has given birth to a baby girl, and has killed the bastard [*mamzer*]."[43] In other words, it was public knowledge that Sara's child had been fathered not only by a man who was not her husband, but by a non-Jew. In terming his daughter "an absolute and notorious whore," he (or the men who wrote the text sent to Rabbi Meir) seems to be invoking Latin legal terms used in cases of sexual offences, "*fama publica*" (a prostitute of ill repute) and "*infamia*" (infamy).[44] At his own volition, before Isaac arrived, the father asked the local tribunal whether he was permitted to kill his own daughter because of the brazen misdeeds and the fear she would "fall into bad ways" (literally, "embrace evil culture,") a euphemism denoting that Sara would continue to be promiscuous and possibly earn her living as a prostitute. The father's voice offers a window into how common people felt about prostitution, which was not often committed to paper as rabbinical attitudes were. Of course, this does not mean that all or even most Jews thought it was acceptable or incumbent on them to kill a daughter who had dishonored her family, but clearly in this case the father was furious and unsure of how he ought to respond. It seems that it was Sara's mother who prevented her husband from acting impulsively and prevailed on him to consult the local rabbinic tribunal. She appears in the responsum as the voice of reason in this troubled household. Two members of the tribunal asked the father if there were not ways he could reprimand his daughter other than drowning her in a river. The father replied "Whenever I reprimand her, she threatens me that she will go and be among the gentiles, 'for I'm not the first woman who has been bad,' and she has fled the house many times, but *her mother* talks her into returning, and she returns. I fear she will take on evil ways and I beseech you in every way to let me kill her." In other words, Sara's mother not only attempted to mollify her husband but also to keep Sara in the Jewish fold.[45] We can't say for sure what the father was attempting by approaching the tribunal. Was he really seeking their approval for an act of angry zealotry or was the legal appeal an attempt to externally curb his own rage and aid him in restraining his feelings? In any event, the tribunal rejected his request to be allowed to kill his daughter. The dossier sent to Rabbi Meir also portrays the discomfort of two local tribunals: Rabbi Shaltiel's court (comprising himself and his two sons) and the regional rabbinic tribunal, presided over by Rabbi Moshe Azriel, the son of Eliezer the Homilist, which initially deliberated the case.

Other important voices accusing Sara of crimes belonged to the Jewish women of Sara's parents' town. In her *Crimes of Women in Early Modern Germany*, Ulinka Rublack discusses the concept of "gossip, silence and accusation" where she explores the dynamics of gossip and the way rumors traveled in female circles, among them discussions of unwanted pregnancies and accusations about infanticide. Here too we see how the talk of the town functions as a catalyst in drawing legal attention to Sara's case. When the case was referred by the second tribunal to the higher authorities (among them Rabbi Meir) it ends with the statement about how Sara's misdeeds have become "the talk of the town": "And indeed this case has become the talk of the local women, for she has fornicated and has blood on her hands."[46] That Sara had become the subject of gossip among women made the allegations of promiscuity and infanticide more worthy of special scrutiny and investigation. The Hebrew term used in quoting the women's gossip, unlike that used in the report of her father's testimony, may imply that Sara killed the infant child right after the birth or aborted her fetus close to the time of the expected delivery. The women say that Sara fornicated and has blood on her hands.

Sara's own voice in the matter appears in only two sentences. The first is her denial of the accusations that she had been pregnant out of wedlock. When the tribunal asks Sara about the pregnancy, she replies: "My husband [Isaac] left me full [with child]," denying his accusation that she had become pregnant as a result of extramarital relations during his absence. The next time Sara's voice is heard is in the judges' recounting of the conversation they had with Sara's father, who was threatening to kill her. In refusing to sanction such an act, they ask him whether he cannot admonish his daughter in any other way. The father objects, saying that "when he confronted his daughter about the pregnancy she 'threatened to go among the gentiles.'" This sounds like a euphemism for conversion. In one version of the story (the one in *Hagahot Maimoniyot*), Sara's response to her father includes the claim that: "I am not the first woman who has been bad." This statement shows that Sara saw her actions as part of a social phenomenon. It is not clear, however, whether she is referring to her sexual misconduct or to her threat to convert.

There are a few voices that are not heard in this story. Sara's "customers" are not mentioned among the evidence the court collected. If any of the clients were Jewish it seems that their wrongdoing either didn't matter to the court or that it did matter but the court could not seek them out. If they were not Jewish (like the alleged father of Sara's child) it would have been quite hard to arrange for a subpoena, given the jurisdictional obstacles. Another one of the voices not heard is that of the infant who lost her life. She had too much going against her, as the child of a presumed harlot, born out of wedlock from an illegitimate relationship between a married woman and a man other than her husband. Furthermore, her father, according to the tribunal and Sara's father, was a gentile. These circumstances, along with Sara's father's threats and the growing public animosity toward Sara once she could no longer conceal her pregnancy, sealed the baby's fate. Sara probably killed or abandoned her soon after birth.[47]

The other versions of the responsum almost all omit the narrative and cut straight to the halakhic chase, as is often the case in the responsa genre. However, even such truncated documents sometimes offer valuable information about the circumstances and the legal twists of a case and the individuals involved. One of the abbreviated versions of Rabbi Meir's responsum[48] reports that the woman, whose name is not given, was referred to as "the damned and the cursed."[49] This may simply be derogatory language expressing the scribe's or Rabbi Meir's view of her, but it may also suggest that Sara was subjected to some sort of public, ritualized humiliation and shaming in synagogue or elsewhere. If so, it was probably not as harsh as the way adulterous women were often treated in medieval Christian society. This was not because Jews were gentler, but rather because of their status as a minority society in medieval Europe. Jews could, of course, copy Christian behavior so as to show that they were no less diligent in enforcing morality than the gentiles were, but even acknowledging moral problems in the public sphere seems to have been a problem for Jews, and they preferred dealing with such cases internally without exposing the moral shortcomings of community members in public. Jews knew that they were being observed by their Christian neighbors and that the entire community might fall into disrepute because of individual members' misbehavior.

LEGAL ANALYSIS

While the case was one of carnal drama and scandal, Rabbi Moshe Azriel asked the Erfurt and Würzburg legal authorities and Rabbi Meir of Rothenburg to rule on two technical halakhic questions. The first was whether Isaac could legally divorce Sara despite her refusal to accept the writ of divorce. The second was whether Sara was entitled to financial compensation from Isaac, given the circumstances of her divorce. According to rabbinic law, in most divorce cases the wife is entitled to receive the sum of money stipulated in her marriage contract (*ketubah*) for such an eventuality. An adulterous or sexually wanton wife forfeited such compensation. The question posed by Rabbi Moshe Azriel and his colleagues was whether the witnesses who testified about Sara's immoral behavior were acceptable enough to make her suffer the economic ramifications of her sexual and moral misconduct.[50]

Normally a writ of divorce requires both the man and the woman's consent; he must proffer the *get* and she must accept it from him. As it is a legal procedure, the parties must be of sound mind and fully cognizant of the legal ramifications of the new status that the divorce created. In this case, however, Sara refused to take the *get* from Isaac, who then cast it down (*be-zrikah*) in the presence of the judges (*befaneynu*). Sara herself may not have even been present when he did so. Rabbi Moshe Azriel had accepted Isaac's act as effectuating the divorce, but sought as much rabbinic support as he could muster for this decision. The court probably felt compelled to consult supercommunal and superregional authorities due to the exceptional situation, specifically the need to validate the testimonies that led to the eventual divorce. Another reason was to ensure that the decision would not be overturned. There was no formal hierarchy among Jewish courts in medieval Europe. The Jews had no governmental system that paralleled that of their Christian contemporaries, who lived in communities and states with hierarchical religious and lay legal institutions. Jewish courts thus needed to ensure a broad legal consensus about their decisions.[51] It is also possible that Rabbi Moshe Azriel's court may have wanted to consult with additional adjudicators because of internal communal factors. One of the parties to the case or members of the community might have asked the tribunal to obtain the endorsement of a higher authority. The material and monetary implications of the case suggest there might have been people arguing that Sara should not be deprived of her right to refuse a divorce or to receive the compensation specified in her marriage contract simply on the basis of circumstantial evidence, no matter how convincing.

Moshe Azriel's regional tribunal accepted the writ of divorce in Sara's stead, deciding to do so after verifying to its own satisfaction that the facts in the case were indeed what they seemed to be. Rabbi Shaltiel's court, in the town where Isaac and Sara had resided before Isaac's departure, was asked to provide written testimony (*ktav 'edut*). Rabbi Meir's responsum makes it clear that the evidence was indeed circumstantial, meaning that it fell short of the Jewish legal requirements. For example, the allegation that Sara had been seen fondling two non-Jews in her home on the eve of Shavuot 1271 was confirmed by one eyewitness, rather than two, as Jewish evidentiary law requires. Another flaw in the procedure, in terms of Jewish law, was that Rabbi Shaltiel's local tribunal served as witnesses in the case and comprised only him and two of his sons. As they were all family members, their testimonies could not be taken as independent corroborating evidence; they together constituted a single source.

There could well have been, then, disagreement over whether Sara's alleged promiscuity was solely responsible for the divorce, a requirement for denying her the divorce settlement. Jewish law distinguishes between testimonies on matters of forbidden sexual conduct (*issur ve-heter*) and the monetary ramifications of such conduct (*mamonot*). Rabbi Meir made a clear distinction between the two, and thus, while he certainly did not sanction her behavior, was not eager to deprive Sara of what was legally hers according to her marital contract. In the end, though, following long legal deliberation, Rabbi Meir affirmed the regional tribunal decision to enable the divorce despite the unusual circumstances. He allowed Isaac to remarry, assuring him that he would not be in violation the ban of Rabbi Gershom, which had effectively dictated monogamy in northern European Jewish communities as of the early eleventh century, and endorsed the decision to deprive Sara of the divorce settlement stated in her marriage contract. Rabbi Meir also called on the readers of his responsum to use it to chastise women and ensure they did not transgress as Sara had. He invoked a biblical verse, Ezekiel 23:48: "Thus will I cause lewdness to cease out of the land, that all women may be taught not to do after your lewdness." Yet Rabbi Meir remained somewhat tentative, concluding with the following petition for further legal inquiry:

> And you should ask her [Sara] why is it that, when she was asked about her pregnancy in Elul of 5031 [August 1271], she denied it, and why she badmouthed those who made these allegations. Furthermore, you should delve into this matter and further, probe and purge it [be-drishah u-ve-ḥakirah] and leave no stone unturned. And if she cannot come up with a straight and logical explanation for her behavior, without any legal obfuscations, then you should deprive her of her marriage contract money and leave her only with the hard assets [nikhsei milug ve-nikhsei tzon barzel] she had brought with her into the marriage.

Notably, this apparently contradictory language does not appear in the Oxford manuscript as it does in the text before us in the printed editions:

> and there is no need to discuss this matter at great length, for it is obvious [pshita] that it is allowed and it is a commandment [mitzvah] to throw the get at her, and she is not entitled to the marriage contract settlement, neither one hundred two hundred nor the additional sums. She is only entitled to the sums she has earned him during the marriage which had not been spent yet, she may take that sum but all the rest she should lose without any warning. And this is also what Maimonides of blessed memory had decreed and farewell to you all, your loyal servant Meir ben Baruch, long may he live.

This discrepancy may be due to the fact that the published Oxford document is a later rendering of the text and events. The writer may not have had access to contemporary documents.

Social Analysis

Beyond its legal ramifications, the responsum addresses a number of social issues. The first question is why and how Sara ended up in such a situation. We know that her husband Isaac left her at home and set off on a long business trip. Sara was presumably a young woman, probably a newlywed, as there is no mention of children. Isaac was away for almost a year, and he and Sara lived in a very small Jewish community, far from Sara's family. She was presumably lonely, idle, and lacked support, both of her husband and her family. Apparently her need for love and affection grew acute. One of the people who testified about her sexual misconduct was a man who claimed under oath that he came by her house on the eve of the festival of Shavuot 1271 to perform some small religious duties; he told the court that Sara had no close family living nearby. Her social isolation and Isaac's prolonged absence either led the woman to fall prey to lustful and deceitful gentiles, or prompted her to make overtures to them. It is also possible that Isaac did not leave Sara with sufficient money and provisions to provide for her during his prolonged absence, forcing Sara to fend for herself once her funds ran out. On the other hand, Sara could presumably have left town and gone to stay with her family, as she indeed did when she discovered she was pregnant. Was Sara a victim of circumstances or a promiscuous hussy? Rabbi Meir's text leaves either possibility open.

Sara was alleged to have murdered her baby, and her father sought sanction to kill her. The evidence about the killing of the baby is sketchy; it is not clear whether a deliberate, self-induced miscarriage or postnatal infanticide by the distressed young mother is alleged. The accusation is barely addressed by the halakhic adjudicators. The father's request for halakhic permission to kill his daughter is also mentioned in the text and receives slightly more attention, as the regional tribunal of Rabbi Moshe Azriel points out its successful attempt to suppress the father's murderous outrage at what he understood to be his daughter's notorious behavior. The halakhic adjudicators use this request to highlight how attentive they were to the case. Murder seems to have become part of the father's equation because the sexual barriers between gentile men and Jewish women had been crossed.

Not all suspicious pregnancies were dealt with this way. As in the surrounding Christian society, a woman's social status and communal standing had a profound impact on how suspicions regarding her sexual conduct were addressed by her family and community. A source from the fourteenth century, found in the writings of Rabbi Shalom of Neustadt (Wiener Neustadt), refers to a case involving the wife of Rabbi Shlomil of Enns, in upper Austria. The unnamed wife gave birth to a child eleven months after her husband, the rabbi, had left town in order to learn "far away" (le-merḥakim).[52] Rabbi Shalom adduced a similar case, involving one of his disciples in Wiener Neustadt, who had also gone away. His wife gave birth twelve months after his departure. The texts about these women, found in the manuals of customs authored by Rabbi Shalom of Neustadt and Maharil respectively (Maharil quotes a case of Rabbi Shalom), appear in a section devoted to the rules of festivals; they are adduced as proof that a pregnancy may last much longer than anticipated. The compiler and editor of *Sefer Maharil*, Rabbi Salman of St. Goar, remarks: "Indeed eleven months after his [Rabbi Shlomil's] departure to go and seek knowledge in a distance his wife bore a child. And all testify that she is so pious and chaste that it is clear she had not fornicated and was not unfaithful to him."

The biological evidence quite clearly indicates that Rabbi Shlomil's wife was guilty of adultery. For her contemporaries (or at least some of them) her reputation as a chaste and pious woman is the fundamental fact that disproves from the start the *mala fama* accusation against her. Her social position as the wife of a member of the scholarly elite placed her beyond suspicion to the point that the community's decision-makers presumed that not she but rather their understanding of human conception and gestation was at fault. While modern observers might find this scientifically ludicrous, it was certainly socially sensible in medieval Germany, where an adulterous wife's life and livelihood were on the line. And from the medieval rabbinic perspective, there was a precedent for exceptional conception and birth in Jewish tradition. According to rabbinic lore, Ben Sira, the eponymous author of an apocryphal book of wisdom often quoted in the Talmud, was born under similarly unusual circumstances; indeed, Maharil cites the legend in his book, using language much like that he used in the case of Rabbi Shlomil's wife:[53]

> He [Maharil] said that Ben Sira was conceived from the semen of the prophet Jeremiah. The daughter of Jeremiah bathed after her father in a warm bath and conceived from her father's semen. She was impregnated and eventually gave birth. And all testify that she was extremely chaste, and therefore it is inconceivable that she had fornicated. And all agreed that she conceived and received the semen in the bathtub. And since the baby that was born was conceived without intercourse, he was called the "son of semen" [*ben zera'*]. However when he grew up and became acquainted and knowledgeable about this he was embarrassed by his name and changed it to Ben Sira, which has the same numerical value as Jeremiah [the numerical values of the letters in the names Sira and Jeremiah both equal 271].[54]

Maharil's and Rabbi Shalom's presumption of innocence in the cases of wives of prominent rabbis, taken alongside Sara's case, shows that a suspicious pregnancy could be read in different ways, depending on the social standing of the woman involved.

"She Was a Harlot"

Although Sara made the remark that "I am not the first woman who has been bad" the case of Isaac and Sara was probably atypical, extreme both in the family's reaction and in the relatively heavy involvement of communal authorities in the case. A contrasting case appears in a responsum of Rabbi Meir of Rothenberg's disciple, Rabbi Haim Eliezer Or Zarua'. The case apparently involves people living on the margins of what was considered decent society. The halakhic issues under discussion are the application of the laws of *yibbum* and *ḥalitzah*.[55] It begins with a brief question:

> A certain Jew had a son. The man [the father] reverted to doing evil for he took an unmarried Jewish woman [*yisraelit pnuyah*] and cohabited with her without properly wedding her [*be-lo ḥupah ve-kidushin*]. The man and his woman had left town and were away for several years, and during this time the woman bore him a son. And now the son the man had from his virtuous wife, to whom he was properly married, [himself married] but died childless, leaving his wife in need of the unmarried Jewish woman [for *yibbum*]. There are those who wished to redeem the widow from being in need of *yibbum* on the grounds that, when the unmarried Jewess went with the man and while she was involved with him [*kerukhah aḥarav*], she was suspected of having consorted with a few other of the sexually promiscuous men of our time, and she herself was very promiscuous.[56]

The woman in question was apparently the father's paramour and he didn't bother to formalize their relationship by marrying her, for unknown reasons. It may well be that his legal wife was alive and he thus could not marry his paramour because of the ban on polygamy of Rabbi Gershom. The question was whether the son born out of wedlock was legally the brother of the son the man had with his wife. If so, the widow would have been required to marry (or, more likely, to perform the *ḥalitzah* ritual with) a man of dubious lineage, the son of a harlot.

The request that Rabbi Haim was confronted with was to refrain from forcing the recently widowed and very decent woman from entering a forced and legally sanctioned levirate marriage with her deceased husband's half-brother, who may have been born of harlotry (*ben znunim*), thus tarnishing her reputation. The widow, or her family and supporters, apparently argued that she was under no obligation of *yibbum* because there was good reason to believe that the son of the paramour was not in fact her deceased husband's brother, but had rather been fathered by another of the paramour's lovers. Three factors corroborated the doubt about the status of the putative brother: the initial nature of the relationship between the father and his paramour, which was not a proper marriage; the paramour's bad reputation and alleged sexual promiscuity (she is referred to as a *prutzah*);

and the reputations of the men who allegedly had relations with her while she was in a relationship with the father. The language of the responsum also suggests that, at some point, the father and his paramour separated, adding more weight to the claim that the woman and her children should be declared unfit for marriage with members of decent society. Given the history of the couple's relationship it wasn't at all clear that the woman's son was indeed from the father and not another man.[57] The unnamed voices from the community (possibly the woman's kin) argued that the father's paramour was a harlot (*u-prutzah haytah*), and thus it should be presumed that any half-brother born of this out-of-wedlock union was of doubtful parentage, the implication being that the paramour was having sexual relations with other men while cohabiting with the father. While by non-Jewish standards the children born of this relationship would be considered the father's illegitimate children, the question in the Jewish context was whether they were to be considered the half-brothers of his sons from a previous marriage, and therefore eligible candidates for a levirate marriage or *ḥalitzah*.

The responsum, as it appears in the collection of Rabbi Haim's rulings, is truncated, but clearly comes down on the side of those who sought to absolve the widow of an obligation to marry the son of the illicit union.[58] It shows what normative Jewish society thought of the offspring of sexually promiscuous Jewish women who bore children outside of wedlock. In his ruling, Rabbi Haim discloses that the putative half-brother was already married; forcing him to enter into a levirate marriage would be in violation of Rabbi Gershom ben Judah of Mainz's ban on polygamy. Rabbi Haim concludes that overall in "our lands [Ashkenaz] we do not allow a *yibbum* at all." In light of this information, given the fact that *ḥalitzah* was the default practice, Rabbi Haim was trying as best he could work around the question of whether the wife could not marry again until she went through *ḥalitzah*. He sought to reconcile the formal demands of halakhah with the realities of life, rather than shape life in accordance with halakhah.

This responsum shows the extent to which the northern European Jewish conception of a decent and properly governed society (in which, for example, Rabbi Gershom's ban was binding) overrode what that society saw as divinely ordained biblical law. It was a society that condemned sexual promiscuity, while at the same time understanding that a woman who violated such taboos might be driven to do so by circumstances beyond her control. In such cases, rabbis often thought it more important to bring the transgressor back into normative society than to punish her according to the letter of the law.

Sexual Promiscuity: The Road to Conversion

In the process of adjudicating cases arising from the law mandating *yibbum* (levirate marriage), medieval rabbis wrote about aspects of family life that would probably otherwise never have been put to paper. In some of these cases, application of the law determined the social, economic, and religious fate of women. Women whose husbands had died without issue found themselves in legal limbo, in particular if their late husband's brother refused or was mentally unfit to participate in the *ḥalitzah* ritual, or if he was unable to do so because he could not be located or lived far away. Such women were unable to remarry at their own discretion and establish a family, and were left without the livelihood that, in their time and place, only a husband could provide. Rabbis feared that women in this position would be driven to seek sexual gratification and financial stability by cohabiting with a man outside a formal marriage, or by engaging in prostitution. Halakhic adjudicators thus sought out legal remedies that would release women from this bound state and the need to perform *ḥalitzah* to end it. Rabbis also understood that time was of the essence—women forced to wait an inordinate amount of time to be declared free to marry soon lost patience and took matters into their own hands.

One such case, with what appears to have been dire consequences, occurred in the years following the anti-Jewish riots of the Black Death. It appears in several responsa collections;[59] the fullest account is found in a responsum by Rabbi Jacob ben Moshe Halevi Mulin (Maharil), in which he recounts that his father, Rabbi Moshe ben Yekutiel Halevi Mulin, was involved in the case.[60]

A man who was murdered in the Black Death pogroms that swept through Europe in the summer of 1349 died childless. He was survived by a brother, and as such the man's widow and brother were subject to the law of *yibbum*. But the brother had converted to Christianity sometime between the marriage and the tragic death of the husband. The wife asked him several times to perform the ḥalitzah ceremony, so as to unbind her and enable her to marry freely. Her brother-in-law refused, declaring unequivocally (*be-feh maleh*) that he would not perform the ceremony, as he no longer adhered to the Jewish faith in any shape or form, for he was an apostate (the word used in the responsum is a German one, *ketzer*). The woman, who was from an affluent family, even offered to pay him, but to no avail.

After repeated refusals, the widow despaired, and began to fraternize with gentile men. Eventually, she became pregnant and gave birth to an illegitimate child. Sometime thereafter, she met a Jewish man and they began cohabiting; they were unable to marry officially, as she was still legally bound to her Christian brother-in-law. The case came to be adjudicated because, nearly twenty years after she had been widowed, the woman sought, for reasons not mentioned in the text, to make her relationship lawful. Presumably the trigger was that a child born of the relationship with the Jew sought to have his legal status resolved, for reasons of inheritance or in order to better his chances of marrying a woman of his own social position.

Not for the first time, the responsa literature tells us of a single woman who, unable to marry legally, and in need of love or sexual gratification, or both, took her fate into her own hands. Unlike Sara in the previous case, however, financial exigency was apparently not a factor, as the responsum tells us that the woman was affluent enough to offer her brother-in-law money. Another account of the case, found in the writings Rabbi Samuel of Schlettstadt (Sélestat, in modern-day lower Alsace, France), the compiler and abridger of *Sefer Mordechai*, relates that the woman also tried to procure a favorable ruling from a Jewish court, to no avail. According to Israel Yuval, who discussed this case in his book *Scholars in Their Time*, seeing that the Jewish legal system was unable or unwilling to help her, the woman decided to turn her back on Judaism altogether and to convert to Christianity.[61]

It is not clear whether the woman was involved in prostitution. But she certainly fell under the rabbinic definition of a sexually promiscuous woman, as she had, according to the responsa accounts, fraternized with non-Jewish men, given birth to a child from a relationship with a non-Jew, and later lived with a Jewish man without the benefit of marriage. There is reason, however, to question the assertion that she had fraternized with non-Jews and was impregnated by one of them. This may be information added in hindsight in order to paint a bleak picture of her for the learned Jewish readership, in light of subsequent events and the woman's eventual conversion to Christianity. Part of the reason this woman converted was that rabbinic courts failed to find a way to free her from being bound to her Christian brother-in-law. Perhaps the rabbis felt a need to defend their decision by tarnishing her good name further by including allegations of prostitution and misconduct with gentiles. The responsum speaks explicitly of a serious disagreement among the Jewish legal authorities that had discussed the case. Some who were unwilling to sanction her marriage to the Jew before it happened were willing to retroactively grant it legal credibility, while some others with a more stringent approach refused to sanction it even after the fact. It seems the more stringent opinion prevailed, causing the woman eventually to leave the fold altogether.

VERBAL ACCUSATIONS OF SEXUAL PROMISCUITY AND PROSTITUTION

Accusations of sexual promiscuity and prostitution were taken very seriously by both men and women in the medieval Jewish honor-shame culture. In this, Jewish society was no different than its surroundings. A person who applied such terms publically to another Jew was liable to be sued for defamation by the target of the allegation. A culture in which social information was conveyed by means of defamation, hearsay, and rumor defended its members from slander by taking such accusations seriously. The other side of the coin was that such allegations, if not refuted, were liable to attain the status of publicly known facts. Labels today used as general slurs or condemnations without reference to their literal meaning, such as "son of a bitch," "bastard," the German *Hurensohn* or French *fils de pute* ("whore's son"), were in medieval times attributions of specific and inferior lineage and legal status.[62] A case known from the responsa of Rabbi Meir of Rothenberg, quoted by his disciple Rabbi Mordechai ben Hillel of

Nürenberg, is a libel suit filed by a woman against a man who told her husband that she was cheating on him and called her a whore:

> And you have asked about Leah, who charged: "Reuven said to my husband: 'why are you intimate with a whore [*nafkat bra*]⁶³ like your wife?' And in that he defamed me [*ḥiraftani*]." To this Reuven answered that nothing of this sort ever happened—in fact, Leah speaks with grave disrespect for the deceased [*mevazah shokhnei 'afar*, lit., shames those who dwell in the earth].⁶⁴

The claim made by Leah, corroborated by witnesses, was that Reuven had accused her of being a prostitute, not only offending her in the extreme but also defaming her in the eyes of her husband. Rejecting her claim, Reuven in turn accused her of irreverence regarding a deceased family member. Given the context described in the responsum, I suspect that Leah may have made a similar allegation of sexual impropriety against Reuven's late mother.⁶⁵ As early as the mid-thirteenth century, the responsa literature offers verbatim quotations of such language in the vernacular using French and German terms used by those spreading the rumors. According to a ruling by Rabbi Yehiel of Paris, quoted by his disciple Rabbi Meir of Rothenburg,

> We do not call for a ban denouncing someone as a transgressor [*ḥerem avaryanut*] simply because of using terms such as bastard [*mamzer*], son of a menstruating woman [*ben ha-nidah*], but rather only if one pronounces the words in the language of idolaters [*la'az*, an acronym for *leshon 'avodah zarah*] like *fils de pute*.

Rabbi Yehiel seems to have made this distinction because of the much graver social implications of slander voiced in a phrase and a language understood by all strata of society, both Jews and non-Jews alike. But a different approach can be found in a truncated responsum by Rabbi Menachem of Merseburg, who lived in eastern Germany in the fourteenth century. The case involved a Jew who called a fellow Jew a *Hurensohn*.⁶⁶ Rabbi Menachem ruled more leniently about the use of a colloquial term; he apparently understood such terms less literally and thus took them less seriously.

"If We Keep Upholding the Law on This Matter We Are Debauchers": Rabbi Judah Mintz Saves Rachel from Prostitution in Padua

Most of the accusations in the previous cases were of sexually promiscuous behavior. It is only in the fifteenth century that attempts to prostitute Jewish women appear in Jewish sources. While the crime itself most probably had a much earlier pedigree, there is little, if any, evidence of it. But changes in the status of Jews in late medieval Europe, in particular their growing segregation, led to changes in Jewish involvement in prostitution. A case from northern Italy offers a glimpse of that social metamorphosis.

Sometime during the late fifteenth century, Rabbi Judah Mintz (Judah ben Eliezer Halevi of Mainz, known as Mahari Mintz)[67] of Padua decided to share publically the reasons he had issued a ruling in the case of the marriage of a woman named Rachel to one Rabbi Mordechai Popstilen. In his ruling, he set aside talmudic and posttalmudic legal tradition to allow Rachel to marry. Rachel had given birth only five months earlier, and was thus forbidden to marry under Jewish law, as she was nursing a child from a previous relationship. The prohibition, which had roots in the Talmud and was reaffirmed by the Geonim and again by the twelfth-century Jewish sage Rabbi Jacob ben Meir Tam, grew out of the fear that a woman who remarries while still caring for an infant from a previous partner might have an incentive, conscious or unconscious, to neglect or even kill the child.[68] A man was prohibited from marrying a widowed or divorced woman, or one who had had a child out of wedlock, who was nursing a child, or who had a child under the age of twenty-four months. In halakhic parlance, it was referred to as the prohibition against marrying "the wet-nurse of another" (*meyaneket ḥavero*). The rule was widely accepted *halakhah*, and by the fifteenth century it was observed in both Sephardi and Ashkenazi communities, after being included in Rabbi Jacob ben Asher's halakhic compendium *Arba'ah Turim (Tur Even ha-Ezer* §81–82) in the fourteenth century. Rabbi Judah summed up his deliberations:

> And for all these reasons and tribulations I thought it clear that I must rule that this woman should not be halakhically regarded as "the wet-nurse of another," and I allowed her to marry a man, although it was still within the period that she was considered nursing and defined as prohibited to remarry. For I say these are difficult times, and in these cases we may differ. Furthermore, I am not alone in my ruling, my colleagues, may God protect them, they too thought it fit to exercise leniency on this matter and I have gone to great length in exploring this matter for I think my conclusion is a novel one, and what I saw fit to do I have written down and I sign, the wary Judah Mintz.

Judah Mintz had good reasons to be wary. The picture the details of this case paint are unsettling from a traditionalist's point of view.[69]

Mordechai Popstilen and Rachel were people of dubious repute with regard to their sexual behavior. In taking Rachel, a single mother, into his home, Mordechai may simply have been performing an act of charity, but Judah Mintz seems to have been the wiser. Hints in the text suggest Mordechai and Rachel had some previous acquaintance either from their country of origin or from the road to and in northern Italy; the latter seems more plausible. It is clear, however, that regardless of this previous acquaintance Mordechai was not the father of the nursing infant.

According to the responsum, Rachel was a young unmarried woman from Germany. At the time, the number of Jewish communities in Germany had declined dramatically, in the wake of a wave of expulsions that swept through Germany in the fifteenth century. There were not many communities left that she could have come from.[70] The sort of life Rachel led before her arrival in Italy is also unclear, although there are hints in the text that she was not chaste. In a later period, in early modern Germany, the word *zonah* was not used only to mean a woman engaged in the prostitution trade, but more generally to designate women of shady sexual reputations. It could designate a woman who engaged in sexual relations that were characterized as *be'ilat znut* (lit., intercourse out of wedlock). Such a woman was usually not a professional prostitute, but simply a woman who had had intercourse with a man who was not her husband. Most such women were of lower social standing, working as housemaids or domestic caregivers, where they often were seduced or forced into sexual relationships with male servants, or with the master or other male members of the household. If they became pregnant, they were at times dismissed from their job. The only way for such a woman to reenter "decent" Jewish society was to marry and serve as a wet-nurse, or marry a well-off householder (ba'al bayit) who would legally marry her but in fact employ her in his domestic service. As Rabbi Judah terms Mordechai a man of some means, this may be the background to his interest in or willingness to marry Rachel. Mordechai could have been a widower or a divorcee who was willing to settle for a stable relationship with a young woman of questionable repute while providing her with the status of a married woman.[71]

While Rabbi Judah did not think highly of Rachel's morals, he does not reproach her explicitly. His opinion of her is buried in the lengthy and convoluted legal analysis that forms the body of the responsum, not in its opening exposition or the verdict it reaches. As most readers probably skipped or skimmed the technical legal discussion and focused only on the facts of the case and the final judgment, they may well not have noted what the author thought of Rachel. But in the midst of his legal analysis, Rabbi Judah offers his opinion about her sexual looseness: "for we should be apprehensive that she will revert to her old bad habits, for she had already besmirched [her reputation] in the land of Ashkenaz, and it had already then come to public knowledge."

Rabbi Judah does not term Rachel a prostitute, but rather a woman of dubious morals. As travel was hazardous, especially for a pregnant woman or one with a newborn baby, she must have had urgent reasons to leave Germany to join the growing Ashkenazi community in northern Italy. Presumably the reasons were that she had been compelled to leave her home in Germany after getting pregnant while working as a servant there. She arrived in Padua, which had been under Venetian rule since 1405, when the child was but a couple of months old.

Explaining his unprecedented ruling, Rabbi Judah wrote:

> We are overwhelmed by corrupted individuals to the point that, if we rule in this matter in accordance with Jewish law [*din Yisrael*], the procuring/pandering of prostitutes will be unavoidable [*i efshar mi-lir'ot zonot*]. And this is the least of our troubles. For they [the procurers] rent properties among us in our streets and homes and there is a "breach, there is an outcry from all our sides and in our quarters."[72]

Rabbi Judah was convinced that desperate times call for desperate measures. The impression is that he had despaired of correcting the morals of Padua's Jews by the usual means of chastising the community in sermons and exhortations. Stronger measures were required. From the discussion in his halakhic manifesto, however, it seems that even more radical attempts had reached a dead end. Rabbi Judah describes how some chaste Jews in Padua had turned to the local Christian authorities (*arka'ot shel goyim*) in order to curb other elements in the community who were trying to establish Jewish brothels and prostitute Jewish girls. But this did not help, as the gentile authorities turned a blind eye to prostitution, or even actively facilitated it: "For the non-circumcised [gentiles] think that regulating prostitution and settling prostitutes in the markets and in houses is a heavenly decree [*mitzvah*], for it is seen in their eyes as deliverance from the greater evil of fornicating with a married woman [*isur eshet ish*]."

Rabbi Judah speaks of these as clandestine endeavors to reach an understanding with the local municipal authorities to suppress such establishments. But local authorities were unwilling to cooperate for, as he states, they thought of prostitution as a lesser evil. They preferred men to satisfy their sexual desires with prostitutes in brothels rather than to do so by committing the mortal sin of adultery with married women.

In the face of this and in order to uphold the standards of the written letter of the halakhah, Rabbi Judah preferred to deviate from the established law that forbade an unmarried nursing mother to marry within twenty-four months of the child's birth. Rabbi Judah felt that he had no choice but to allow Rachel and Mordechai to marry, even though such marriage was forbidden by the Talmud. Not to allow them to marry would be to abet the town's Jewish whoremongers, the violent *paritzim* (sexually licentious men, probably affluent), who imposed a reign of terror that intimidated the community's upstanding members.

Rabbi Judah contextualizes his ruling by condemning Padua as a very immoral city, with prostitutes plying their trade on every street corner. In fact, however, Padua was not unique. European cities at this time institutionalized and taxed prostitution, so that it helped fill the city coffers. As Peter Clark writes in his broad overview, *European Cities and Towns*:

> Traditionally, drinking-houses were linked to prostitutes, and during the fourteenth and fifteenth centuries prostitution developed as a more organized service trade in town. Between 1350 and 1500, cities such as Venice, Florence, Siena, Seville, Augsburg, Dijon, and London opened official brothels, both to discourage sexual crime and to promote urban income.[73]

After offering his view of the moral standards of Padua and its residents, Rabbi Judah recounts the chain of events that led him to make his untraditional ruling. No sooner had Rachel set foot in Padua, and while still residing in temporary quarters,[74] she was approached by local Jews, who either knew about her and her reputation before her arrival or learned who she was once she came. They tried to coerce her to prostitute herself. At the time, Padua apparently had an intricate network of informants who identified new arrivals who might be recruited into the sex industry and passed the information on to the appropriate people. Rachel was relatively easy prey, as she was new in town, young, and the unmarried mother of a newborn child. She was all alone and apparently had no local family—in other words, no one to protect her and support her financially, and no visible means of earning a living. In referring to what the *paritzim* wanted Rachel to do, Rabbi Judah does not use the word *zonah*, prostitute. Instead, he writes that the *paritzim* wanted Rachel to be a woman *mufkeret la-kol*.

Playing on the legal term *hefker*, literally meaning "forfeited," the label *mufkeret la-kol* encapsulated one of the deepest anxieties of both Jewish women and halakhic authorities. Not only was prostitution morally unacceptable, it also harbored problems of a more philosophical nature. A sexually promiscuous woman who was *mufkeret la-kol*, forfeited to all, undermined the fundamental principle that men owned women. Jewish marital laws are governed by the notions of ownership and belonging. When a couple is betrothed to one another, they become part of an ownership system. In Jewish tradition it is customary for the man to ask the woman's consent to his "ownership" over her, before the actual act of betrothal, which is symbolized by his granting her money or a ring. The husband is therefore called a *ba'al*, a Hebrew term meaning both husband and owner. The sexual act of coitus, consummating the marriage, is called both *bi'ah*, meaning entry, and also *be'ila*, becoming the owner. A woman in a status of *mufkeret la-kol* undermined this system, for she was literally ownerless, with no prospect even of future ownership. Rabbi Judah was convinced that this situation could only be remedied by wedlock, as he believed that once married, the *paritzim* would leave Rachel alone.[75]

The situation described by Rabbi Judah was, to the best of my knowledge, unheard of before his time. Indeed, he says as much in his concluding lines. Medieval Jewish women with more than one partner, or who had sexual relations with non-Jews, appear in documents from that time, as do Jewish men who had sexual relations with non-Jewish women. But the Padua case is the earliest evidence of something that resembles a Jewish sex industry of the kind known from much later, in the nineteenth century. According to Rabbi Judah's account, the procurers, the *paritzim*, intimidated the local Jews who sought to suppress prostitution. The support the paritzim enjoyed from local non-Jewish authorities was to the detriment of inner Jewish attempts to curb the problem. In justifying his ruling, Rabbi Judah claimed that Rachel was barely able to turn down the offers of the *paritzim*, either because of her dire economic situation before marrying Mordechai, or due to the intense pressure they exerted, or a combination of both. Rabbi Judah reported that her prospective groom, Mordechai, helped her relocate twice within a short time, seeking to help her escape from the procurers hounding her.[76] These men threatened Rachel that they would ensure she would never be hired for respectable domestic service and would not be able to afford to support herself and her baby.[77]

Considerable information about the medieval sex industry in Padua can be gleaned from between the lines of Rabbi Judah's manifesto, including bullying and intimidation techniques much like those used today. Other matters remain unclear. For example, why was Rachel pursued so relentlessly by the *paritzim*? Was a woman in her situation all that unique? And why is it the first incident of prostitution known among the Jews of medieval Europe? Could it really be that that prostitution as a profession did not exist among Jews previously?

In order to try an answer these questions we need to look beyond Padua at the greater European picture. Beginning in the fourteenth century, municipal councils in both southern and northern Europe increased their efforts to regulate the lives of their denizens, with a special emphasis on the public arena. European city councils were as concerned about the moral well-being of their citizenry as they were with public sanitation and health. Brothels, which had formerly operated rather freely in the urban sphere, were gradually placed under restrictions in northern and southern Europe, and were often overseen, if not actually operated, by the city council and city elders. The income from prostitution and brothels was taxed and rules and regulations about prostitution were enacted by local legislatures. During this period, city councils adopted ecclesiastical language and tone, seeking to prevent sexual relations between Christians and Jews. This included banning Jews from using the sexual services provided in taverns, bathhouses, brothels, and other establishments where men were accustomed to seek sexual satisfaction. While violations of the ban were at times met with corporal punishment or banishment from the city, this penalty could be commuted into a fine, albeit a heavy one.

In some cases, Jews were sentenced to corporal punishment, such as branding or facial disfigurement. For example, in Nördligen, Germany, in 1470, a nonresident Jew named Moses of Andernach was convicted of having paid for sexual relations with a Christian woman. Some of his encounters with her took place in the house of another woman, who acted as the go-between. This woman, Hermanin, confessed that she too had had sexual relations with Moses, in return for an unspecified payment. Moses was branded, as were the two women, who were also expelled from the city. This was an extreme penalty, and most probably it was imposed and not converted into a fine only because Moses was a traveler and not a resident of the city. The judges and town elders seem to have been more scandalized by the fact that Moses had paid for sex than by the act itself.[78] Apparently the growing physical and financial consequences of being caught *in flagrante delicto* with a Christian woman, even if she was a prostitute, prompted Jews to create their own sex industry in which Jewish women sold their bodies.

This is the possible background to Rabbi Judah's manifesto. It explains why the Padua *paritzim* worked so hard to force Rachel into prostitution. It also lies behind the refusal of the non-Jewish authorities to help the members of the Jewish community who sought to suppress the *paritzim*. The city administration's goal was to ensure that regulated sexual services were available to its Christian male citizens in prescribed locations, and probably secondarily to encourage the city's Jews to provide such services for their own men.

The Padua case, in the fifteenth century, might represent the dawn of a Jewish sex industry in Europe—one of bordellos and pimps and full-time hustlers. There is scant documentary referencing to Jewish brothels, professional prostitutes, madams, and other institutions of the sex trade before this time. The opposite is true of urban Christian communities. Again, when Jewish sources prior to the fifteenth century refer to *znut*, the reference is to women having sexual relations out of wedlock, not professional prostitutes.

In his declarative ruling, Rabbi Judah Mintz not only warns against a morally reprehensible phenomenon, but also fashions a creative counterweight to the *paritzim* and their allies. In ruling that a nursing woman could marry, even though she was prima facie prohibited from doing so within twenty-four months after childbirth, he demonstrated how a halakhic adjudicator could stand up to powerful entrepreneurs involved in establishing an infrastructure of Jewish prostitution. As it stood, the halakhic system was creating a supply of workers for the

Jewish sex trade in the form of young women who, for one reason or another, were unable to provide for their sexual, emotional, and material needs by entering into a legal Jewish marriage. Allowing such women to marry would sharply reduce the pool of potential recruits for the procurers. Rabbi Judah's groundbreaking ruling aimed to do precisely this.

Punishments for Sexual Transgressions

There are almost no accounts of punishment meted out to Jewish women accused of *znut* in the sense of sexual license. However, Jewish jurists did write about cases in which such women sought to repent and change their ways. Motivating such attempts were a guilty conscience, desire to be accepted by normative society, or desire to marry, as seen above.

One such document is a letter addressed to Maharil (Rabbi Ya'acov ben Moshe Halevi Mulin), active in Mainz and Worms in the late fourteenth and early fifteenth century. The writer identifies himself as Rabbi Yohanan, apparently the spiritual leader of a smaller community.[79]

Rabbi Yohanan tells Maharil that he received a packet of unsigned letters from a distant location. The letters were written in Yiddish "in female form," presumably meaning that their author referred to herself in the feminine gender. Rabbi Yohanan confessed that he had found it difficult to decipher the obscure and enigmatic text of the letters. He was thus forwarding the originals to Maharil, whom he addressed as *raish galota*, the exilarch.[80] His hope was that the great scholar would be able to rule on the woman's petition after making sense out of the letters. Aware, however, that reading the letters was no easy task, and that a sage of Maharil's standing would have limited time to devote to the matter, Rabbi Yohanan assisted Maharil—and today's scholars—by offering a brief digest of what he had been able to divine from the letters. As the letters themselves have not survived, the digest is the only account we have.

The author of the letters wrote that she had been married to her husband for ten years. Her husband was away for the first two years of their marriage, either pursuing religious studies or, more probably, on business. During this time she had fornicated with two other men. The woman asked Rabbi Yohanan to prescribe her *teshuvah*, that is, a penitential regime. According to Rabbi Yohanan, he did not know the name of the woman, her husband, or the individuals with whom she had relations during these two years. The courier who brought the letters to Rabbi Yohanan was willing to disclose only the city from which the packet had been sent. Rabbi Yohanan demanded that the woman supply the missing information. In response, the woman confessed to having sinned several times, and also disclosed that she was "still under her husband" (that is, still married to and dependent on him) and wished to remain anonymous, fearing how her husband would react if he learned of her behavior and what it would mean for the four children that she had borne him. Rabbi Yohanan, realizing that the case raised serious halakhic issues (for example, were her children *mamzerim*? Could they inherit their father's property?), wrote back that he would need to consult "higher authorities" on the matter.

Presumably, the anonymous woman was sincerely contrite and genuinely accepting religious culpability for her clandestine sexual misdeeds. While determined to undergo a penitential process, she conditioned it on protecting her children and avoiding her own public humiliation as well as her husband's.[81] Cognizant of the explosive nature of her confession, she was determined to ensure that the father of her children not learn of her adultery. She thus provided only the information she felt was relevant. She also insisted on knowing what the implications were for her marriage. According to *halakhah*, an unfaithful wife was forbidden from having sexual relations both with her husband and with the person or persons she had had sexual encounters with. But the black-and-white legalistic approach manifested by Rabbi Yohanan's referral was different from what the woman had wished and envisioned. It was also different from the spirit of penance that was typical of the Pietists of Ashkenaz, which carried over into later Ashkenazi society.[82] The woman's idea of confession does bear a striking resemblance, however, to the more commercial philosophy of penance adopted by the Church, which instituted a literal market economy of salvation and contrition, in the form of indulgences, which became very popular in the fourteenth century and spurred the criticism that eventually brought about the Reformation.[83]

We do not know from the digest how the woman sought to atone for their sins. Was she offering a payment to Rabbi Yohanan in return for *teshuvah*? Was her social standing coercive of his cooperation? It does seem, however, that given her position in the negotiations with Rabbi Yohanan, the anonymous plaintiff in this case was not a woman of low standing, living on the margins of Jewish society. Unlike Rachel from Padua, the woman who turned to Rabbi Yohanan for penance was a married woman most probably of high social standing seeking to gain religious salvation without losing social face. Her name and the name of her family as well as their reputation was important to her. She negotiated her penance from a position of power. Nevertheless, the possibility of public humiliation if exposed as an adulteress served as a powerful deterrent to penance in matters that remained largely within the domestic sphere and were exposed only when one of those harboring the secret approached authorities and sought penance.

Jewish leaders also used the effect of parents' immoral behavior on their children, both legitimate and illegitimate. The idea that a child might suffer as punishment for his parents' transgressions is ancient and can be traced to the biblical maxim (Jer. 31:28; Ezek. 18:2) "The fathers have eaten sour grapes, and the children's teeth are set on edge." While some of the biblical prophets cited this belief only in order to counter it and to teach rather that each person is responsible and punished only for his own sins, others did stress that the Almighty does at times visit punishment on the righteous for the sins of previous generations. In seeking to enforce sexual norms in the private sphere of the home, religious authorities admonished their flocks that even transgressions performed in secret would eventually manifest themselves in full public view. For example, they declared that a child conceived sinfully while his mother was menstruating would be inflicted with leprosy.[84] Similarly, in a sermon delivered in the Jewish community of the Austrian town of Wiener Neustadt in the second half of the thirteenth century, the local preacher, Rabbi Haim Eliezer Or Zaruaʿ, warned his listeners that if a man had sexual relations with a non-Jewish woman, even the children born legitimately from his Jewish wife would never become Torah scholars.[85]

One of the ways rabbinic authorities shamed women who sexually transgressed and conceived out of wedlock was a significant theatrical modification to the rite of circumcision, meant to make it clear that the child was a *mamzer* (bastard), born of an illicit sexual union between a married woman and a man other than her husband. Maharil's book of rulings and customs includes an account of such a ceremony:

> I witnessed a deed, and years later our Lord and Master Mahari Segel [Maharil] himself recalled this when we discussed his teaching us *halakhah*. Once he had to deal with a circumcision of a *mamzer* who was born to the wife of a man [*eshet ish*]. The ceremony took place on a Sabbath, and Maharil allowed hot water to be brought from the local gentile bakery on the eve of the Sabbath to wash the boy prior to the ceremony. And Rabbi Gumprecht, Maharil's brother, performed the circumcision [*haya mohel*], and he [the infant] was circumcised in the synagogue courtyard by the synagogue entrance, unlike the other legitimate children, who are circumcised by the doorway inside the synagogue. And the rabbi [Maharil] ordered his brother to recite the blessing, but only halfway, up to the words *koret ha-brit*, and no further. For from that phrase onward it is all a request and plea to the Almighty to sustain the child after the circumcision blood has been let so that he may live. This should not be pleaded for in the case of a *mamzer* as it is not fitting for the holy Israelites to sustain the *mamzerim* among them. He [Maharil] further decreed that those assembled for the ceremony refrain from reciting the remainder of the prayers commonly recited by the crowd on this occasion: "As he has entered the covenant, so may he then enter Torah, the marriage canopy, *mitzvot* [observance of religious precepts], and good deeds" as they are accustomed to say about legitimate children. He then decreed that the child would be named Kidor, invoking the verse in Deuteronomy 32:20 "For they are a perverse generation [*ki dor tahapukhot hemah*], sons in whom is there is no faithfulness,"[86] and indeed so we have learned in the second chapter of the tractate Yoma [BT *Yoma* 83b]. Then the rabbi [Maharil] ordered the town's sexton to

> announce after the ceremony in a loud voice that "All should be informed that the child who has been circumcised is a *mamzer*, so his offspring shall not mix with ours." And Maharil told us [his circle of disciples when he was reminiscing on the matter] that when this boy was ten years of age he died, and Maharil wrote it down and thought of it as a good sign that he was gathered from our midst [*ne'esaf mi-tokhenu*].[87]

The idea that the death of an innocent child should be welcomed because his parents were sinners is hard to accept today, but the historian must seek to understand why it made sense to Maharil. The author of the quoted passage was Maharil's disciple and personal secretary, Rabbi Salman of St. Goar. Rabbi Salman offers an eyewitness report of a deviation from the way circumcisions were commonly conducted in a case in which the infant boy was a *mamzer*. In Europe of the late fourteenth and early fifteenth centuries, circumcisions were customarily performed in the public space of the synagogue, rather than, as had once been the case, in the private sphere of the home.[88] Most circumcision rituals were carried out at the entrance to the synagogue, most likely for the practical reason that this delicate surgery required good lighting. Rabbi Salman's testimony appears in the context of an account of the laws of circumcision as presented in a digest of customs for rabbinic use. As such, it offers virtually no information about the surrounding circumstances, or of the mother's subsequent fate. In surrounding German Christian communities, conceiving a child adulterously was considered a grave sin. As such, some women in these circumstances committed infanticide (which was punishable by beheading); if the child survived, the mother would be sentenced to harsh punishment, the nature of which depended on the severity of the case, the particular circumstances, and the social position of those involved.[89] In extreme cases it would be a death sentence; more commonly, it was banishment or public shaming.

Rabbi Salman offers no background details. He does not relate if and how the mother of this child was punished, for example. Neither does he say who paid for the ceremony, or whether the child was abandoned by his parents. We also do not know why Maharil's brother,

Rabbi Gumprecht, performed the circumcision. It may well be that he was the community *mohel* but, if so, why was he explicitly named in the text? Was it because the community's regular *mohel* was unwilling to perform it? Or could it be that Maharil wished to put a special emphasis on the circumcision ceremony by attending the ceremony himself and having his own brother perform the ritual, so that he could public condemn extramarital sexual relations?

The account also leaves other questions unanswered. The child was defined halakhically as a *mamzer*, yet he was nonetheless circumcised at the synagogue on a Sabbath. Though the act of circumcision involves a number of actions that are normally prohibited on the Sabbath, the command to circumcise a boy on the eighth day after his birth is considered so important that it overrides the laws of the Sabbath. But in cases where there is doubt about whether the infant requires circumcision, the ceremony is delayed until after the Shabbat. Such a doubt exists with regard to the circumcision of a *mamzer*, so it is surprising that Maharil demanded that the laws of the Sabbath be violated for this child regardless of his halakhic status, given his enforcement of other ceremonial modifications. He altered the regular circumcision ceremony protocol by performing the circumcision outside the synagogue door, in order to advertise to the community both the mother's deed as well and the child's problematic legal status.[90] In doing so, Maharil deliberately blocked the child's future integration into the community through marriage, as a *mamzer* is not allowed to marry a normative Jewish woman. He also branded the child for life by naming him Kidor. When Rabbi Salman wrote of this incident, more than a decade after it took place, he related that "[the ceremony was] unlike [that of] other legitimate children, who are circumcised by the doorway inside the synagogue."

The incident shows the way a message of grave halakhic consequences could be disseminated and seared into communal collective memory, although there is no certainty about the latter. After all, the record of the act came from the learned male elite; there is no guarantee that other members of the community followed his lead in their ideas and feelings. The ceremony was altered both in place and in substance, the *mamzer*'s legal status was publicly announced by the sexton, and the child was given an odd name that branded him with his outcast status. Nevertheless, intended to ensure that the boy would not marry into the normative Jewish community when he came of age, it was an act that shamed his mother, and perhaps his father and other members of his family.[91]

Significantly, the case that immediately precedes the story in the book, also recounted by Rabbi Salman of St. Goar as Maharil's secretary, centers on public humiliation and the preservation of dignity. This account too was prefaced by Rabbi Salman as a personal memory of an occasion he witnessed:

> A certain unmarried woman bore a child, and she gave it to a certain person, stating that he was the father; the man proclaimed, however, that this was not his son. And they [probably members of the community] wanted to give the boy a name and call him so-and-so, son of so-and-so. Maharil warned them they should not humiliate him [the alleged father] in such a manner [naming the son after the father] for he does not admit to this [being the father]. During the child's circumcision ceremony the *ba'al brit* [the man who brought the child to be circumcised, who was not the child's father but probably a relative from the mother's side—the text does not tell us] recited the benediction "to bring him [the child] into the covenant of Avraham our father." However when the *mohel* who performed the ceremony came to the proclamation "Thank the Lord, for it is good and his grace is eternal" [*hodu la-Adonay ki tov, ki le-'olam ḥasdo*] he altered the verse and omitted the words "it is good," since he believed the child should not be called good, for he was the child of a relationship involving fornication [*znut*]. This *mohel* was reprimanded by Maharil, and Maharil demanded that the *mohel* repeat the verse, for the child's status is like a child born within wedlock.[92]

The account portrays the communal milieu that was the backdrop to Maharil's ruling in the subsequent passage, discussed above. Apparently, some members of the community, as well as some of the religious practitioners, thought it best to alter the circumcision ceremony so as to reflect their judgment of the child and the child's putative father. This modification of the ceremony was not an improvisation of the moment. Up until Maharil's time, in the early fifteenth century, and even for a while thereafter, Jewish culture in Ashkenaz was predominantly oral. Although literacy was relatively widespread, it was largely restricted to sacral literacy; while most male Jews learned to read Hebrew, they did not necessarily write it. Like many other medieval European communities, they were heavily reliant on custom and performance. The practice of customs was of such importance that the slightest change or modification of a recurring performative practice was profoundly meaningful and imparted a message to the community.[93] Both accounts of the "altered circumcision" do not state that Maharil recorded the *mamzer*'s birth or the circumcision in writing in communal records (although there may have been such). For all those involved, it was the change in the ceremony's location and the altered ritual and liturgy that would shape communal memory. Like many of his contemporaries, Maharil was well aware that such departures from standard procedure would make a profound impression on those who participated in and witnessed the ceremony. He did ask the sexton to spread word of the *mamzer*'s birth all over town, and when the sexton did so of his own volition, it was merely to confirm what had already been seen at the ceremony.

Two hundred years after Maharil's death in 1427, in a society made more literate by the advent of print, gossip, hearsay, and memory still remained important means of perpetuating and signifying breaches of mores. In *The Crimes of Women in Early Modern Germany*, Ulinka Rublack stresses the importance of orally transmitted knowledge, especially in matters of moral behavior that could disgrace families and bring about a serious deterioration of social and legal status, with material repercussions. In some extreme cases, rumors that were corroborated to one extent or another could lead to corporal and even capital punishment. Body gestures, facial expressions, and minute deviations and changes in dress and daily behavior were meticulously noted, committed to memory, and spoken of. If this was true of Germany in the seventeenth century, it was no doubt the case two hundred years earlier as well. The two accounts of the circumcisions of children born out of wedlock underline how public practice and memory could determine an infant's future reputation and course of life.[94]

VIOLENCE IN THE DOMESTIC SPHERE

This chapter began with two cases of domestic violence in which Jewish men targeted and victimized Jewish women. They show that domestic violence was a fact of life for Jews in medieval Europe. If the surviving documentary evidence of the crimes and acts of violence that are the subject of this book is sparse and difficult to parse, that is all the more the case with transgressions that took place within the private confines of the home.[95] Furthermore, women were also not the only victims of domestic violence—children were also beaten, sometimes in the guise of attempts to educate them.[96] While Jewish law does not sanction domestic violence, neither does it categorically forbid it. Avraham Grossman has already shown that marriage at a very early age and medieval educational approaches were factors, and that Mediterranean and northern European cultures and traditions differed in their attitudes.[97] The extant material shows that Jewish European legal authorities sought to curb such violence, but with little success. One example is a ruling by Rabbi Simcha of Speyer, of the late twelfth century, in a letter quoted by his disciple, Rabbi Isaac of Vienna in his halakhic compendium *Or Zarua'*: "And there was a case of a man who was accustomed to beating his wife, and our master Rabbi Simcha of blessed memory was asked about this and he answered that the husband should be compelled to divorce her."[98] In fact, many women who filed for divorce in rabbinic court claimed to be victims of domestic violence.

The woman in this case was the daughter of a certain Rabbi Jeremiah, who petitioned Rabbi Simcha on her behalf.[99] Neither her name nor that of her abusive husband is given. The petition relates that, in addition to beating his wife, he also publicly abused and shamed her; the petition also hints at sexual violence and mistreatment. Rabbi Simcha sided with the plaintiff and said she was entitled to a divorce. However, he suggested to the husband that a divorce might be averted by means of arbitration between him and his wife, but that entering into such a process would require the husband to commit to refrain from further violence and mistreatment. Otherwise, Rabbi Simcha ruled, the rabbinic court would compel the husband to grant his wife a divorce. He even sanctioned the use of non-Jewish enforcers to compel the husband to capitulate. Although to a modern observer this would seem far from sufficient, by medieval Jewish rabbinic standards this was a great effort since dissolving the marriage by the court without the consent of the husband was not an option. The fact that the petition was filed by the abused woman's father, who was a member of the rabbinic elite, was no doubt a factor in the categorical nature of the decision. There is good reason to believe that a woman whose family did not have cachet with the rabbinic authorities, or who had no family to help her, would have been much less likely to gain a favorable ruling from a senior halakhic figure.

Domestic violence among Jews in the Middle Ages had a number of causes. It could have been the result of a marriage between a man and woman of very different social status, economic background, age, or health. In some cases, it was a corollary of financial hardship that developed over time; in others the husband was simply brutal and crude. Violence and abuse could also be a symptom of mental decline, as in the first case adduced in this chapter, from the writings of Rabbi Asher ben Yechiel of the late thirteenth century.[100] In that case the wife sought protection because her husband had squandered the family's resources, but also because she had been the victim of severe violence: When the woman's family described her situation they mentioned that "when someone angers him [the husband], he hits and kills, throws and kicks and bites." The reference to killing, incidentally, seems to relate to domestic animals, not human beings. This case presented a unique legal problem, as the halakhic requirement is that both parties be *compos mentis* when the deed of divorce, the *get*, is written and handed by the husband to his wife. When one of the sides is not in his or her right mind, there are serious doubts about the validity of the act. In this case, the husband was clearly mentally disturbed.

Other cases of wife-beating also go hand-in-hand with financial abuse. In one such case, a husband—a renowned rabbinic scholar by the name of Yechiel ha-Kohen—did not just beat his wife, Chana, but also sought to transfer all his assets so that, if he divorced her, she would not be able to receive the financial settlement to which her marriage contract entitled her. This case came before Rabbi Meir of Rothenburg, who in a responsum written after 1281 and probably before 1286, reprimanded his rabbinic colleague:[101]

> Here we have heard the cry of the noble[102] and dear mistress Chana whose clamor was brought to us constantly. Her kin, the magnates of the land [*eilei ha-aretz*, lit., the rams of the land], complain about you, Rabbi Yechiel ha-Kohen, that you are humiliating her by beating her, as well as by disgraceful acts [*bizyonot*] and that you have deliberately divested yourself of your assets in order not to pay her the sum allocated in the marriage contract. And this was never done among the Jews and it shall never be. We have also heard much more, until we could hear no more. I have therefore resolved to inform you, in an attempt to steer you off this path, for this is behavior does no honor to you and you should cease acting in this way. Since you, thank God, have a good reputation, and you are gloriously famous do not tarnish it. Furthermore, you will not prevail.

As in the case addressed by Rabbi Simcha Or Zaruaʻ, it was the wife's affluent family who intervened on her behalf with the halakhic adjudicator. He concludes his letter with an admonition:

> For this kind of behavior [deliberately divesting oneself of assets so as to avoid paying a divorce settlement] was already decreed against by the sages, and a regulation was issued even before the decree, [at it applies all the more so] to the widow of a martyr and virtuous wife [*eshet hayil*], a scion of the magnates of the land who is worthy of every measure of honor.

It seems that Yechiel was Chana's second husband, and that her first husband died a martyr.[103] Like Rabbi Simcha before him, Rabbi Meir employed a range of techniques to convince Rabbi Yechiel to end his violent and financially abusive behavior.

In the cases we saw above, men's brutality was many times unprovoked, or at least no evidence to provocation was left in the texts. While cases of intentional, premeditated, cold-blooded domestic murder are rare, at times domestic violence and wife-beating could be fatal and women died directly or indirectly of beating and abusive behavior. I have not found, however, recorded cases of a Jewish woman killing or wounding her husband, even though such cases are known from the surrounding Christian society. The reason may be that divorce, while rare, was an option in Jewish society, and was not for Christians. Jewish women had recourse to the courts to seek a way out of an abusive marriage (especially if the woman had support from her own kin) and, as we have seen, made use of it.

As in many instances of violence and murder, the gender roles were maintained, or at least presented in this manner in the legal narratives. Almost all the recorded cases of marital violence involve a husband acting violently toward his wife. It is men who threaten and commit violence, in extreme cases lethal violence, premeditated or not.[104] References to violent acts perpetrated by women usually pertain to child abuse, infanticide, and the unnatural death of children.[105]

Crib Death, Infanticide, and the Role of Women

Infant crib deaths and other cases of infant mortality were often attributed to women. Women were considered responsible for these deaths even if there was no evidence of foul play.

In the chapter on murder, I also considered the cases of unintentional killers. These were people who caused another person's death completely by accident or, more often, during a physical altercation, when the intent was to hurt the adversary but not kill him. A common subset of this category was unintentionally causing the death of an infant or child, for example in the case involving a failed circumcision that ended in the death of the infant boy. Although the *mohel* accepted exile as penance, the child's parents maintained that it was not sufficiently rigorous. Another, more common, cause of death among children was abandonment, documented by Elisheva Baumgarten in her groundbreaking book *Mothers and Children*. Abandonment sometimes occurred when a woman sought to remarry, and this motivated rabbinic law on when a widow or divorcee could remarry. As we saw earlier in the case of Rachel from Padua, this law was the background of Rabbi Judah Mintz's fifteenth-century ruling, and he had to explain why he decided to circumvent it.

The decree by Rabbi Jacob ben Meir restricted remarriage within twenty-four months of childbirth, considered the mandatory nursing period. The reason was the fear of child neglect. "In the case of remarriage," writes Baumgarten, "we can see that despite the belief in the 'natural love' of mothers to their children, under certain conditions, this love wasn't trusted as sufficient. If mothers were suspected of not cherishing their children when they were desperate to remarry, stepmothers were often portrayed as an outright danger to their stepchildren."[106] The initial concern voiced in the Talmud and reiterated in Rabbi Jacob's decree was that of child neglect, which may even lead to death. The discussions in the Talmud, in late antiquity, voice the ancient Rabbis' concern that a divorced or widowed woman who married within the nursing period was more likely to neglect her existing child. While in general pregnancy was encouraged, as it was thought to strengthen the bonds between the newlyweds, the concern was that it would come at the expense of the existing infant.

Another form of child mortality blamed on women occurred when children died in their sleep. Some of these infants died in their beds or cribs within the first year of their lives, of what we today call Sudden Infant Death Syndrome (SIDS).[107] It is a phenomenon that puzzles modern medicine, and was no less mysterious in medieval times. Under the conditions of urban life in medieval Europe, such deaths would have been more frequent than they are today.

Some infants and children died in communal beds shared by parents and children. Given the crowded living conditions in medieval cities, even among the affluent and especially during harsh northern European winters, some infants and younger children were either crushed by their parents or siblings in their sleep or suffocated for a host of other possible reasons.[108] A collection of thirteenth-century responsa published by Simcha Emanuel includes five entries that address such cases, attesting to how common and how alarming they were and the extent of judicial interest they raised.[109]

VIOLENCE IN THE DOMESTIC SPHERE 249

The accounts are clearly gendered in nature. Women are most often blamed for the deaths. And they, too, like the *mohel* Matthias who inadvertently killed an infant boy, seek a way to do penance. But, in the women's cases, the penitential regime does not include exile. The rabbis who addressed the cases believed that the proper place for women, especially married women, was in the home, and thus their penance took place there. The possibility that a woman might go on the road, to some unknown place, probably never crossed the rabbis' minds. On the basis of the evidence, however, the authorities viewed regular fasts, the mildest of the bodily mortification rituals used for penance, as acceptable for women, though halakhic opinions varied. Some rabbis demanded a stricter approach, while others were more lenient.

The longest document known on this subject, attributed to Rabbi Elchanan ben Shmuel (probably a resident of Magdeburg) of the mid-thirteenth century, takes the lenient approach. In the opening statement to this account he addresses the case of a woman who seeks to perform penance for the death of an infant. If the woman were to insist on a harsh penance, Rabbi Elchanan writes, he would not stand in her way but, as she asked his counsel, he would offer advice in accordance with the lenient opinions. He claims that, in fact, the Geonim themselves specified a form of penance for such cases:

> A woman who has found her child dead by her [*etzlah*] should fast for an entire year. These are fifty-two weeks, on Mondays and Thursdays, so as to fast two days of fasting every week, not including the days on which fasting is forbidden by Scripture and the Rabbis. On those days she should not fast, for the decree of the Lord and that of the Rabbis takes precedence over her sin. These days are Hanukkah and Purim, and all the days of the month of Nissan, and the intermediate days of the festivals [*ḥol ha-moed*] and the first days of the month [*rashei ḥodashim*]. And all those Mondays and Thursdays that she will not be fasting she should make up after the end of the year. She should have a wooden board where she will mark every day that she missed fasting until the year ends. After the year has ended she should count the number of missed days and she must make up for

them during the following year and mark those days on another wooden board until the account is balanced. And on those days of penance, she should refrain from meat and wine. And since our beverages are mostly thick ale she should refrain from them and prefer drinking diluted ale. She should bathe only twice a month. This is what I gathered from the writings of those who are less stringent on this matter.[110]

This protocol resembles the Gaonic "manual of penance" for a male murderer or killer, discussed in chapter 2, but there are also significant differences. The penitential requirements for a woman, as laid out here, are not as stringent as those for men, and they seem to take into account both the mother's guilt feelings and the age of the infant, who is referred to in the text as "the recently born" (*ha-valad*) rather than the usual "youngster" (*katan*) or nursling (*tinok*).

One element that appears here but which is glaringly absent from the male manual of penance is the calculation of the fast days missed due to holidays and other days on which fasting is prohibited. This protocol specifies how such lost days should be tracked, mandating that they be recorded on a wooden board. The reasons for this difference can only be guessed. Is it because women were thought to experience grief more intensely and thus would lose count of the lost fast days? In the normal course of things, women were required to keep count of the days of and after their menstrual period, so should have been recognized to be reliable counters. Was it because of the unusual circumstances that they were ordered to count with the aid of the wooden device? Was the practice and the device suggested to visually exhibit the status of a penitent? Also notable is Rabbi Elchanan's psychological observation that there are women who seek penance from a rabbinic authority and seek guidance and others who are harsher toward themselves and do not seek guidance. His response is to suggest a more lenient penance to those who seek counsel.

Although the protocol is not as harsh as that prescribed for men, it does suggest that these women were seen as sinners and thought to bear guilt for the death of their newborns of the same sort that men did when they killed other men. In both cases, the killers were sinners and needed penance of a similar nature. Indeed, one of the texts in Simcha Emanuel's collection of responsa from Rabbi Meir of Rothenburg and his circle states this explicitly: "And it is also said in the name of Rabbi Shmuel, in the name of Rabbi Judah Katz: [When] women find their newborns dead by their side on their beds, we think of this as a deliberate killing and not as an accident, and we should be stricter with them."

The person who forwarded the information, one Rabbi Shmuel ben Isaac, quotes a certain Rabbi Judah Katz.[111] The adjudicator maintained that a woman in whose bedchamber a child was found dead, even if she was not at fault, was required to perform penance. Neither her grief nor her feelings should be taken into account. But this harsh attitude is balanced by other voices. A copyist wrote in the margin of an unsigned responsum:

> A responsum that I found regarding a woman who found her child dead in her bed. If she is not nursing and not pregnant and if she is fit she should fast for a year.[112] But this is only if her husband allows it. And if she is young (*baḥurah*), and is not accustomed to fasting, they [she and her husband] should fast on Mondays and Thursdays until they complete [together tally a total of] 354 days of fasting.[113]

It is clear from this anonymous halakhic adjudicator that, while fasting for a year was considered a penitential practice suitable for women, it could be accomplished in a less arduous way than that required of men by being carried out over an extended period of time. It also had to be sanctioned by the woman's husband (following what seems to be a homily on the spirit of the biblical dicta in Numbers 30:1–16, according to which vows made by a married woman must be sanctioned by her husband). Furthermore, if the woman is young, she and her husband are to fast together. In his conclusion, the anonymous author offers advice to husbands: "It is better, if possible, that [women] should not lay the children by their side, especially if they feel that the infant has no need to lie there."

Rabbi Meir of Rothenburg also responds to a question about the proper penitential regime for women in the case of the death of an infant under similar circumstances and offers a complete list similar to the female manual of penance, highlighting the days on which the penance should be performed and on which days it should not, such as festivals and the Sabbath. He concludes, however, that this woman should not fast while pregnant or nursing, and that she should not lay her child by her side in her bed. One of Rabbi Meir's contemporaries, Rabbi Chaim Paltiel of Magdeburg, takes a slightly different, yet still extremely gendered, approach. Unlike the other respondents who may have received the appeals of individuals they were not familiar with or were relating to the phenomena in general, he seems to have known the father of the dead infant he was replying to:

> I am deeply saddened by the incident and you should know that the Geonim ruled that [when] a woman who finds her child dead next to her [in her bed], it is an accident that borders on a deliberate deed. Nevertheless, I cannot be stringent with the woman with regard to fasting. For some women miscarry as a result of excessive fasting. And her penance will be within a 365 day period, Mondays and Thursdays, or forty consecutive days or three consecutive days and nights. But it is impossible for a woman who is of the age of pregnancy [*bat herayon*].[114] And it is good that she calculate how many Monday and Thursday fasts are in 365 days excluding Hanukkah and the month of Nissan and the intermediate days of the festivals when one may not fast, and she should fast one day a week until she completes [her fasting period], and give as much charity as she can, and peace to all, Chaim Paltiel.

Rabbi Chaim takes the gender-infused directive one step further. In his system of values, female fertility supersedes the need to repent for the loss of an infant's life. By safeguarding the mother's fertility, the social body can be confident that, while one child was lost, the mother's ability to conceive other children will not be compromised. He wants the woman thought to have unintentionally caused the death of her child to conceive again quickly, and wants to avert an evil cycle of death and miscarriage.[115] The penance for the recently deceased infant and the concern to avert a future miscarriage brought on by excessive penitential fasting demonstrate just how gendered the ruling is. Notably, he does not require the woman's husband to participate in his wife's regime of fasting. Instead, he charges the woman with calculating the exact number of days she is required to fast, and to distribute them over the course of the year so that she can fulfill the requirement without detriment to her reproductive capacity. In this respect, his ruling leaves a certain amount of agency to the woman.

The effect of these legal determinations on the community appears to be relatively minimal. As opposed to the case of the failed circumciser, where communal strife erupted over the fact that Matthias was accepted as part of the community and was allowed to lead it in prayer, in the case of women whose infants died in their beds the community seems not to get involved. After all, although women frequented the synagogues to participate in public prayer, they did not lead it. Furthermore, there seems to be a consensus regarding the role of women, and the matter of guilt and blame are not addressed. No one contested the notion that when a child is found dead in the family bed, the blame rests on the mother. Did women also feel that in such cases it was the mother to blame? As the voices of women are barely audible in these proceedings, there is no basis for even an educated guess.

These unfortunate incidents offer another example of a motif that appears time and again in many of the cases and examples discussed in this chapter. Male writers and adjudicators judged female involvement in what they saw as criminal or at the very least sinful acts on the basis of the differential gender roles and attitudes of their time and place. Furthermore, all these writers were male, and only men made rulings in such cases.

In bringing cases of putative crimes committed by women to the forefront, I have sought to read beyond the male perspective and to be attentive to all the voices the sources offer, including muffled female voices. I have also endeavored to understand the motivations for the actions that were perceived as crimes that required penance, motivations only hinted at in the texts. Most of the chapter focused on prostitution, on the face of it a crime committed by women. But the sources show that women were not independent agents in this activity. They were often subject to pressure from men—pimps, procurers, and clients. Furthermore, women who flouted the norms and laws of Jewish society to find sexual satisfaction, emotional attachment, and to gain the financial support of a man outside of marriage were also called prostitutes—that is, criminals—and were treated as such, even when those very norms and laws made it impossible for them to marry.

A specifically Jewish sex trade seems to have come into being only on the threshold of the early modern era. At this time, Jews were gradually pushed out of the public sphere and barred from municipal institutions like the local brothels, at the same time that city and church authorities began to regulate and curtail prostitution. Jews were forbidden to patronize gentile prostitutes and to enter those parts of the city where gentile prostitutes were allowed to ply their trade. This led to the inception of a Jewish prostitution industry. Through the medieval period, most accusations of female sexual promiscuity, which meant sexual relations with a number of men or men other than their spouses, were usually referred to as *pritzut*. Prostitution in the form of an actual profession—the exchange of sexual favors for material gain—are few. The case of Rachel, from the late medieval period, in which procurers sought to prostitute a young single mother with very few prospects for marriage or livelihood, is very similar to cases known from the modern period.

In the nineteenth century, in eastern Europe, Jewish girls were offered positions as caregivers and governesses in the homes of affluent Jews in North and South America. This lucrative offer included a free ticket to a life of what seemed to be opportunity outside the realm of eastern Europe and the Pale of Settlement in the Russian empire. Many such women fell prey to an organized network of procurers and pimps who violently abused them on the journey, usually raping and violating them while they were on their way to the New World. These women viewed themselves, because of the norms of their society, as "damaged goods." Bereft of the support of their families and communities they were easily drawn into the American sex trade.[116] In the fifteenth century, Rachel's status as an immigrant likewise made her a perfect mark for local Jewish procurers. The immigrant's marginality as an outsider, with limited knowledge of local language and mores, and lacking a social network, was exacerbated by Rachel's problematic social status as a single mother and her inability to earn her own keep because she had an infant to care for. There is not enough documentation to determine whether the situation in Padua was typical of other cities at the time, and whether other girls were targeted in the same way. But Rabbi Judah Mintz, who ruled in her case, certainly felt that the moral state of northern Italy's Jewish community had seriously deteriorated, to the point that he was prepared to set aside longstanding halakhic norms to allow Rachel to escape her plight by accepting an offer of marriage.

CONCLUSION

The story of life on earth as told in many popular accounts presents a continuous chain of evolutionary development leading inexorably from one-celled creatures to invertebrates to fish, then amphibians, then reptiles, then mammals, culminating in human beings. But the paleontologists who do the fieldwork that lies behind this story will tell you that what they see in the strata of an outcropping of rock is neither continuous nor inexorable. The fossils of one stratum are separated by millions of years from those immediately above and below. The paleontologists must piece together a tree of life from the surviving fossils, which are the remains of an infinitesimal percentage of the animals and plants that have lived on earth. The links between them can only be surmised, based on careful anatomical analysis, against the background of information provided from other beds of fossils and other fields, such as geology, biology, genetics, and meteorology. Likewise, the evidence collected and presented in this book seeks to piece together a picture of crime in medieval Jewish society on the basis of a small data set of documents that survived not because they were written for the use of historians but because they were important to their writers and readers for reasons entirely unrelated to history. They come from locations hundreds and even thousands of miles apart and span centuries.

Other historians have written studies based on the criminal records of a kingdom, a county, or a town, so as to produce an account of crime at a specific time or in a certain place. I have done something quite different in my use of the Jewish sources on which this book is based.

Although many come from the responsa literature, the sources are of diverse genres, composed by writers with different interests, philosophies, and concerns, or culled by medieval compilers because of their usefulness as records of legal proceedings and decisions. While some rabbis and halakhic authorities appear multiple times in the preceding chapters, the questions they grappled with do not necessarily represent a single community or even a single region.

Most of the sources I cite in this book do not focus on crime. The information about crime that I glean from them appears as marginal comments or background to other matters. This literature does not, therefore, provide the comprehensive and fine-grained image that a historian seeks to project. I, and my readers, can only fill in the empty spots between bits of data that represent distant points in space and time.

Yet, like a paleontologist, I am confident that, by using sophisticated methods and reading between the lines, I have been able to offer an account of how, where, when, and why medieval Jews were involved in crime, as perpetrators, accessories, or victims. I cannot provide statistics, or count the exact number of Jews who were engaged in theft or murder, nor can I say how common acts of murder or rape were in this community. But I have shown what sorts of criminal threats medieval Jews thought they were facing, and how some of them responded to these threats under the unique circumstances of their lives.

When I began this research, I believed that one of my main sources of information would be *Nimukim* (lit., reasons), a brief compendium of Jewish legal rulings by Rabbi Menachem of Merseburg. Rabbi Menachem lived in the eastern German town of Merseburg, located today in the south of the modern German state of Saxony-Anhalt on the river Saale, not too far from Halle. He was probably a member of the local Jewish court in the fourteenth century. Unlike many of the large responsa collections discussed at length in this book, Rabbi Menachem's *Nimukim* is no more than a small booklet, really little more than a list of cases and decisions.

In one of the only scholarly articles ever written about *Nimukim*, Eric Zimmer suggests that it is actually an abridgment of a much larger compilation called *Me'il Tzedek* (lit., coat of justice), a no longer extant

CONCLUSION 259

work attributed to Rabbi Menachem in other contemporary and later sources.[1] When I first read through *Nimukim*'s short headings, digests one or two lines long for each entry, the sense was that I was peeking into a world of irreverence for law, contempt for norms, and disregard for crime. Almost half of the entries, 44 out of the total 104, have to do with taxes levied by Jewish communities so as to meet the assessments imposed by gentile authorities on the communities as a whole. That is, they were about people who had evaded paying the levies imposed on them, or who claimed they were exempt from paying the taxes as stipulated in community regulations, or Jews who preferred to settle their fiscal issues with the Christian authorities privately, rather than through the Jewish community. The remaining headings comprise a long list of criminal violations: fraud, theft, petty violence, name-calling, and spreading rumors about loose moral behavior. Every entry begins with the Hebrew word *din*, which can mean justice, a verdict, a ruling, or the like. *Nimukim*'s list of offenses suggests that the late medieval Ashkenazi community ranked tax violations high on the scale of severity. They were crimes against the collective, worthy of a day or more in court. The work's ranking of offenses has not been noted by other writers and merits further research. *Nimukim* also lists cases involving theft, violence, and fatalities, including even a threat of arson, although not premeditated murder.

It may well be that some of the entries in this list are cases that were brought before Merseburg's rabbinic court and were therefore recorded by Rabbi Menachem. But close examination shows that quite a few of the entries are clearly quotes and abridgments of rulings made by other courts and rabbis. In fact, much of the material is taken from the responsa of Rabbi Meir of Rothenburg. Some entries are short expositions that address the list of communal and supercommunal regulations drafted and reiterated by representatives of the Shum communities of the Rhineland. In other words, even a concise digest like *Nimukim*, which may seem at first glance to offer the rulings of a single person in a single location, in fact offers a much wider view of Ashkenazi Jewish jurisprudence up to the fourteenth century.

To the best of my knowledge, there is no other list of the kinds of cases that were addressed by the Jewish legal system of medieval

Europe. There are responsa and court rulings in individual cases, but no enumeration of what kinds of actions were considered crime. Only much later, on the brink of the modern period, does the Jewish legal literature come to resemble the more systematic and detailed accounts produced by the jurisprudence of medieval Christian Europe. The first comprehensive record of the proceedings of a rabbinic court, including deliberations of the adjudicators prior to issuing their verdict, comes from Metz in the late eighteenth century; medieval documents of this sort were either never produced, or have yet to be discovered.[2] In the absence of such medieval records, I have faced the challenge of piecing together the stories of crimes, court cases, and punishments from the fragments of information found in responsa, correspondence, and other medieval documents.

One notable feature of *Nimukim* is the relatively high number of references to cases in which non-Jewish political, fiscal, and juridical authorities were involved in internal Jewish matters. Most of these cases discuss Jews who preferred to pursue their grievances against fellow Jews by petitioning gentile authorities rather than a Jewish tribunal. The number of such cases is high, given that appealing to authorities outside the community was strongly discouraged, in keeping with the talmudic interdict, reiterated time and again in subsequent halakhic texts, against Jews who brought their grievances before gentile courts (*arka'ot shel goyim*). Doing so was termed *mesirah*, informing on a Jew and handing him over to the gentiles. The prohibition was taken so seriously that rabbinic authorities in mid-thirteenth-century Ashkenaz were willing to tolerate violent acts against such a *moser*, or informer, by their victims, when those victims were released and sought revenge. Acts of vengeance by Jews who had been released after being incarcerated and tortured, and by the relatives of those who had been killed by gentile authorities, were tolerated in the period in which the victim or his kin was still caught up in what the rabbis called "the hour of rage," as I recounted in chapter 2. Similar attitudes appear in the communal regulations of the Rhineland communities. Yet at the same time, Jewish authorities, rabbis included, sometimes called on local non-Jewish authorities to assist them in suppressing what they saw as criminal behavior within the Jewish community. In the case of prostitution, writers on ethics such as Rabbi Judah the Pious in the thirteenth century, praised non-Jewish authorities for their efforts to curtail the practice, and called on Jewish authorities to emulate them. In the fifteenth century, Rabbi Judah Mintz had no compunctions about encouraging the gentiles to punish Jewish procurers and prostitutes in his native Padua, but to no avail. A Jewish appeal to non-Jewish authorities was often brought on because the Jewish authorities had little power, beyond communal pressure, to enforce their decisions. They could neither imprison nor administer corporal or capital punishment.

Communal pressure was not an insignificant means of enforcement, but it only worked if both sides to a dispute conformed to their social roles and the rules of the community. If a Jew chose not to accept these rules, the community could only counter his criminal behavior by invoking external forces. When Milo of York tried to pin the murder of his wife on non-Jews, his own Jewish community exposed his accusation as a lie, and they, if not the communal leadership itself, asked the gentile authorities to intervene. They did so regardless of the fact that all the people implicated in the killing were Jews. In the case of the burglary from the Daroca synagogue, the gentile authorities were not called in to investigate, but they were asked to help enforce the Jewish community's ban against the perpetrators.

The Jewish community's ability to control crime relied on a measure of reverence for Jewish law and the autonomous Jewish authorities, who had an interest in keeping certain matters within the community. Their ability to punish culprits rested on the latter's willingness to accept the blame for the crimes they committed and to suffer the consequences. In certain cases, violators caught in the act indeed preferred to so submit, as the judgment and punishment they were likely to receive outside the confines of the community could be much harsher.

Jewish criminals who caused serious injury to their fellow Jews were expected by rabbinic authorities and the Jewish community to express contrition and submit to punishment and penance. Only in the most extreme cases were perpetrators excommunicated, that is, banished from the community, as in the Daroca case, or as stipulated in the manual of penance for men accused of taking a life. Rabbinic authorities and communities had a range of other measures for disciplining offenders and administering justice. These included temporarily suspending the offender's legal persona by refusing to accept his testimonies, prohibiting the offender from participating in public prayer with his community, and disqualifying him from the honor of leading public prayer. Not all were effective.

In apportioning blame in murder cases, medieval Ashkenazi rabbis made no clear distinctions between the person who actually performed the murder and the person who ordered the killing by hiring or asking another person to carry it out. From a legal, penitential, and social point of view, the person who initiated the murder was no less guilty than the actual perpetrator, whether the latter was a Jew or a gentile acting at a Jew's behest. In the case of theft, however, the apportionment of blame was the reverse. The culprit was the person who actually committed the theft, whereas those who stood to benefit from it, and who may even have commissioned a robbery, were not generally culpable. The sources do not explain the reason for these two different ways of viewing guilt. Perhaps it was due to the gravity of murder, and the need to ensure that a person who ordered a killing would not walk away blameless. Another reason might have been that the rabbis saw that those who ordered murders tended to be rich and powerful, while those who actually did the killing at their behest were usually poor and defenseless.

The available sources also provide a socioeconomic profile of medieval Jewish criminals. When I began my research, I assumed that I would find that most criminals came from the lower strata of medieval Jewish society. In fact, the evidence I have presented shows that Jewish offenders came from all walks of life, from the most distinguished and affluent to the most disenfranchised. The cases from the eleventh-century courts of Rabbi Gershom ben Judah and Rabbi Judah ha-Kohen the Elder of Mainz, the case appealed to Rabbi Meir of Rothenburg in the thirteenth century concerning the death of a man during an attempt to collect a debt from him, and the case of Sara, wife of Isaac, who was accused of prostitution with gentiles and with killing the child she conceived adulterously, all demonstrate that crime and breaching the law were not confined to any one class. The Daroca case shows that people from very different social backgrounds might collaborate in a crime. Jews also colluded in crime with non-Jews, just as they collaborated in many other aspects of life in medieval Europe. The clearest case of prostitution discussed in this book, found in the writing of the late medieval rabbi Judah of Mainz, shows that, while not only poor women committed sexual transgressions, it was easier for procurers to entice indigent women without the support of family and community into the sex trade. Members of the Jewish elite found it much easier, however, to get away with such crimes. Medieval Jews lived in hierarchical societies, and the network of contacts and availability of money gave the elite a clear advantage, all the more so given that, in medieval times, equality before the law was not seen as fundamental to justice.

Most of the sources that I discussed in this book are rabbinic and halakhic. A few come from non-Jewish courts or legal systems. While there is no surviving evidence of nonrabbinic law enforcement and judicial authorities, there is reason to believe that such existed, but that they kept no records or, if they did, that these have since been lost.

An indication of this can be found in the account of the 1096 Crusader riots in Cologne written by Rabbi Shlomo bar Shimshon, who lived in the twelfth century. His account begins with a paean to the city's Jewish community: "Cologne, the pleasant city where the assembled flock was gathered—and Heaven brings merit through meritorious individuals—from there emanated life, sustenance and permanent law [*din kavua‘*] to our brothers so widely dispersed."[3] Rabbi Shlomo does not indicate who dispensed this "permanent law" or what kind of arbitration authority or tribunal administered justice in the city. But while the rabbinic figures of the middle Rhine area in the eleventh century are well known thanks to the groundbreaking work of Avraham Grossman, virtually nothing is known about eleventh-century rabbis from Cologne.

I surmise that there were very few rabbinic figures in Cologne, and that those there were did not have the standing of their middle Rhine contemporaries. *Din kavua‘* may well refer to a Jewish nonrabbinic arbitration system functioning in this city of commerce and trade, where the commercial mercantile elite administered justice among the Jewish merchants who gathered in town, especially during the city's famed fairs. But for this cryptic reference, we would not know of the existence of such a system, as it left us no written records. Such systems most probably existed in other places as well, and lasted into the late Middle Ages. The rabbinic courts, which produced most of the surviving medieval Ashkenazi legal documents, may not have been the sole judicial and enforcement system in Jewish communities, but they were probably the only ones that produced documentation.

The surviving records show clearly that, although Jews committed crimes, collaborating both with each other and with gentile criminals, there were, proportionally, fewer Jewish than gentile criminals. My findings show that, among Jews, outright criminal acts, such as theft, robbery, and extortion, were the exception, rather than the rule. Nevertheless, it was not at all uncommon for merchants, both Jews and gentiles, to act in the gray areas in attempts, for example, to evade taxes, wriggle out of contracts, or market goods that they knew were stolen.[4]

I have focused on clear and evident crimes, while also touching on the penumbra and gray areas around them. But there are others aspects of crime that await scholarly attention. Taxation was a major issue for Ashkenazi Jews, and many responsa address cases involving people who attempted to avoid internal Jewish and external gentile taxation. The language used in these cases at times resembles the language used with regard to criminals. This issue deserves an in-depth inquiry, as the subject did not fall within the purview of this book.

When I began this book during a sabbatical year in New York City, I was under the impression that the material available was extremely limited, barely enough to provide the kernel of a book project. In the end, I found enough documentation that I had no choice but to restrict my attention to three areas—theft, murder, and crimes committed by and against women. But these cover only a portion of the actions that medieval Jews defined as criminal.

APPENDIX 1

"Lest She Go Astray"

"Lest She Go Astray." A Responsum by Rabbi Gershom ben Judah of Mainz. In The Responsa of Rabbenu Gershom Meor Ha'golah, *ed. Shlomo Eidelberg (New York: Yeshiva University, 1955), 103–5 §37.*

I, Gershom ben Yehuda, signed below, was asked this following question: A man was accustomed to traveling to many places, mostly walled cities and castles, usually within a one or two day ride from his hometown. This man used to both buy goods and sell goods to the castle lords, which were all his business acquaintances [*ma'arifisch shelo*]. At times, when they were short of coins, they would give him collateral against the gold and silver that they owed him. He also used to exchange goods with them, bartering the goods for livestock that they plundered from their enemies. The livestock's market value would increase under his care, and he would then travel back to his home town and sell it for a better price, and he would make a fine profit on it. This man went about this business for six or seven years. Now, the local villagers, as well as some of their masters, the lords, bore a grudge against this man, for they said: "This Jew provokes our enemies against us for he is there, always ready to procure the plunder, which is why they [the castle lords who were the Jew's business partners] make a habit of sacking and pillaging us, for they are sure of their profit." Furthermore, some of the castle lords quarreled with him occasionally over the items he held as bonds and collateral for their debts. During these disputes over the interest [*neshekh*] and payment, the said lords more than once abducted him and intimidated him about the bonds he would sell. At times they had also held him for ransom, but he was rescued; in other instances, other Jews were held for ransom on his account, and he caused them to lose money for his sake. Once they [his business partners] even held his sons for ransom until he took their place and was taken away in their stead, but then he was rescued. And he did this, and he and others would go back and forth between his home and the castles until the time came when the king of France, accompanied by his troops and some troops from Burgundy who came to his [the king's] aid had set a siege on a certain walled city not too far from this man's hometown, about a half a day's walk away. His townsmen made it their habit during this campaign to go forth and sell provisions to the French army and buy loot and booty. And this said man had earlier sojourned in that district, as he was accustomed to do, but this time he stayed there for three months. Now, the troops would plunder all that was near them, and those who had their castles nearby would send the booty to their homes, and upon their return from the king's campaign they would carry abundant plunder with them. Some of these plundering lords were this man's enemies. And even before the campaign had ended, rumors spread that he had been caught by his enemies on the way, incarcerated, and later they had taken him to their place. A few witnesses came forth and told his kin that he had been imprisoned in a faraway place, for they had heard that he was taken by his more remote enemies. Others testified that he had been killed. Later, other people arrived and told his kin: "I know the place where he is detained," while others said "I know where he was seen dead, if you choose one of you to accompany me and pay my fee, I will come down and show him to you." Another one said: "The offer made to your envoy to show the Jew to you is a false one, and its entire purpose is to extort money from you, as you [the relatives] know that there will never be a trace of him in these parts." And many envoys were dispatched [by his family] over this matter, and they discovered no sign of him. Furthermore, two Jews from among his kinsmen set out to find him and have returned with nothing; meanwhile the cost of the envoys rose to a great deal and this whole affair had been dragging on for a whole year.

APPENDIX 2

The Plundered Goods Caravan

The Plundered Goods Caravan. A responsum attributed to Rabbi Gershom ben Judah of Mainz. In Teshuvot Geonim Kadmonim, *ed. David Cassel (Berlin: Friedlander Buchdruckerei, 1848), 32b §93.*

And yet again, a Jew said to his fellow Jew: "The people from a certain city have conquered my town and pillaged my belongings. The merchants of that city are on their way to your city to sell these plundered goods. Can you, with the aid of the lords of your town, raid their caravan, take my pillaged goods, and return them to me?" The Jew answered: "Were it possible, I would raid them myself for my own sake for I too have lost money there." When the merchants arrived in that [the second Jew's] city, the local Jew risked his life and, by using the might of some local gentiles, whom he paid to do this, he had their caravan ransacked. When the first Jew heard of this, that the merchants fell victim to a raid, he came and said to his fellow Jew: "Give me the money and goods that you have taken from these merchants, for I told you about them, and furthermore I pointed them out to you." To this, the second Jew answered: "I risked my life and I pillaged these gentiles, and now you want me to surrender my goods to you? Not only that, I am now endangered [*mesukan ba-davar*] by what I did." The plaintiff then tried to force him to go to court and imposed himself on him [the second Jew] until he succumbed and gave him one pound [*litra*] as a compromise, but then the man who gave the pound of silver later regretted it.

Answer: Thus I have been instructed from the heavens! The plaintiff's claim is futile and the defendant should not pay him at all. Although the plaintiff pointed out the merchants to the defendant, and although he told him to plunder them and give him the booty, we have a *mishnah* that states: "If a man riding on an animal sees a lost article and says to his friend: 'Give it to me,' and the latter picked it up and said: I acquired it [for myself]' [then] it is his." Even more so here, as the defendant initially said: "If I could raid them [the merchants], I would do so for my own sake, for I have also lost a considerable fortune out there [in the pillaged town]." And the raid he carried out was not on the plaintiff's behalf, for he [the defendant] had also suffered losses, both initially, when some of his goods were pillaged in that town, and again when he paid the gentiles to participate in the raid with him. Therefore, the plaintiff has no claim whatsoever with the defendant. Furthermore, [with regard to] the pound that was promised, there is no reason it should be paid, since it is clear even from the plaintiff's own words that the defendant does not owe him anything. The case here is not a case in which we invoke the rule of: "He paid so that he would not be taken to court," for in this matter there is no need either for a judge [to investigate the matter] nor for a court hearing. The only reason this pound [payment] came into being is that he [the plaintiff] annoyed and aggravated him [the defendant] with his nonsense, and he eventually succumbed [and consented] to give the aggravating person a pound to placate him, or because he cared for him and pitied him. Now it looks as if the plaintiff, after having acquired a bit, wants much more, and as such we rule against it and this is my judgment!

APPENDIX 3

The Renegade Cleric

The Renegade Cleric. A responsum by Rabbi Judah ha-Kohen the Elder of Mainz. In Meir b. Baruch of Rothenburg, The Responsa of Meir of Rothenburg, *ed. Jacob Farbstein (Jerusalem: Machon Yerushalayim, 2014), 1:426–27 §844.*

Reuven and Shimon came to the court. Reuven claimed: "A cleric came to my house and brought some gold which I then purchased from him. After he had left my home, I happened to pass by Shimon's house, where I saw some members of the community [*miktzat ha-kahal*] just leaving it and talking to one another, saying: 'I have seen that certain cleric today and I have seen in his pocket six denarii in new coins. He was found in the house of a whore and I know he will not be returning to his father's house, for he is a scoundrel [*reik*].' Shimon also said [regarding the theft that the cleric had committed, and the goods he had exchanged for the coins later seen in his purse]: 'If one were to steal the coins from the cleric, he would certainly not lose [probably meaning that the theft is a sure gain] for he [the renegade cleric] is on the run and afraid. This is because he has already become infamous as a thief, and therefore will surely flee [and not press charges for the theft]. I [Shimon] have already devised a plan in my mind. I will approach my acquaintance [*ma'arufiah sheli*] and tell him that he can steal from this renegade cleric. This way he will be able to finally pay me back [a debt of] three denarii that he [the acquaintance] owes me.'

"When I [Reuven] heard this from Shimon, I was terrified! I immediately told him: 'Be advised! I have purchased some of these stolen goods! If you implicate the cleric, I fear that word of my role [as an accessory] will get around as well. I therefore warn you that, if I suffer a loss due to your machinations, I will hold you accountable, and I will demand that you pay me back.' To this Shimon answered: 'I reject your warning. Besides, this lord [Shimon's acquaintance] has a liking for me, and if I confide in him and warn him not to cause me harm, especially after revealing to him the coins he will steal, he will not implicate me, and the whole matter will not become known.' Shimon then went ahead and ignored my warning. It came to pass that, in fact, after the lord released the renegade cleric, his deeds had become known, and an official apprehended the cleric and pressured him until he had revealed all the information about what he had stolen, and all that he had sold. [Revuen said:] 'In light of these developments I [Reuven] suffered financial losses. I therefore demand that you [Shimon] compensate me for all my losses, both of capital [*keren*] and from profit [*revah*].'"

To this Shimon had answered, "I have not committed any crime! For I have not informed on any of the assets that are in your possession, nor have I intentionally caused you any form of loss. All I wanted to do was to seize the opportunity to take a finding [an ownerless object or money] from a renegade cleric, for whoever is first at the scene gets the finding. Furthermore, the one I have spoken to [my acquaintance, the lord] had not caused you [Reuven] any financial damage. All that transpired is that rumors began to circulate, which caused the cleric to be arrested, and you have lost what you have lost."

APPENDIX 4

Letter of Deliverance

Letter of Deliverance of a Community in France from the Year 992. Translated by Peter S. Lehnardt, modified by Ephraim Shoham-Steiner. The Hebrew original can be found in the Palatina Library, Parma, Italy, Cod. Parm. 2342 (de Rossi 541) fol. 286r–287r. The text was transcribed and published by Avraham Berliner, "Ma'aseh Nora mi'ktav yad asher be'Parma," Otzar Tov 4 (1878), pp. 49–52. Avraham M. Habermann reprinted Berliner's copy of the text in his Sefer Gzerot Ashkenaz ve'Zarfat *(Jerusalem: Tarshish, 1946), 11–15.*

A letter [of] the community of Limo[g]es, a book about God's deliverance, who acted for those who observe His covenant and who keep His commands.

[Introduction]

[1] In the year 924 from the day the Temple was destroyed the second time, this book was written as a memorial for the children of Israel for all time, so that they may tell their children [unto] the last generation children will be born, for they shall learn and know their God's deliverance and His powerful hand, who did not withhold His kindness from his servants who serve Him truly. For He has pardoned them by His compassion to give them a remnant in their exile, in order to establish His covenant with Abraham, with Isaac and with Jacob. And this is the matter of this open letter, which is written down in the script of truth.

And there stood up a scion of wickedness, [from] the root of the snake, from the land of Tzarfat [Northern France], who [was] in the city of Bloyes [Blois], and his name [was] Sehok son of Aster the Israelite. And he did evil in the eyes of the Lord, the God of Israel, to anger Him by his misdeeds, and he abandoned His law and His rulings and His traditions that He commanded Moses His servant. And he went and worshipped the god of the gentiles and the idols of the sons of Esau [the Christians], that cannot see and cannot hear, and cannot eat and cannot smell. To these he adhered, to worship them and to prostrate before them. And he did not recognize the God of strongholds, and he behaved worse than anybody before him....

[3] And it was later on, and he said in his heart: "I shall go and set out to tour the towns, and accustom myself in the gatherings to the gentile people and their god and to each and every folk." And he set out from there [Blois] and came to the towns of the congregations of Israel that he found. And he misled them with the words of his deceit, saying to them: "I am a Hebrew!" And the House of Jacob [the women] had mercy on him and sustained him according to their custom. For in every city he arrived in [except for] two or three in which he did not [succeed to] commit a crime, because [there] they hated him on account of his countless misdeeds and the evil of his heart. He made stealing his profession and of any joint venture fraud; and with his tongue he increased blasphemies and he stuck to a twisted way [of life]. And he despised kindness [missing text] to distort it; and succeeded and [continued] to do [so] until the time of his final defeat. In each of the unfortified towns [probably a reference to the Latin word *oppida*, meaning an unwalled city] in the country, he attempted to settle but did not succeed, because everybody who knew him and heard about his deeds expelled him altogether to exile.

[4] After all [this] he set out and went and came to the town Lemo[g]eys, the fortified city [probably a reference to the Germanic word *burg*, meaning walled compound or city], [to the] tiny community of a few at the periphery of Tzarfat. And here the sisters of the one who gave birth to him settled there in the city, and one of them had [missing text], and her man was a foreigner [a non-Jew]. And the wicked person [Sehok] came to them, and lived with them for many days; and

he took the daughter of his mother's sister and became the governor and the judge in her house. And he raised his heart in its haughtiness, his evil lip never tired; and his evil misdeeds never ceased, until the rising of the wrath of God in reward to his acts of evil. Stealing, and murdering, and committing adultery and perjury and burning incense before the Ba'al [worshiping idols], all these he did; and mocking the law and withholding charity and stealing from the poor and suffering, and putting a burden on the righteous, and giving a hand to the sons of 'Esau. And he did much evil more than everybody before him and [even] the common people.

[5] And there was a quarrel between him and a Levi who settled in the neighborhood near to him, and the adversary [Sehok] wished to appropriate his [the Levi's] house. And realizing that the Levi had the upper hand and that he could not tarnish him by his deceit, he [Sehok] devised in his heart the worst of evil, up to the most extreme, and he plotted things against him [the Levi] against his very soul [*nafsho*]. And he took counsel with two foreigners from the town of his origin [lit., descent, that is Blois], and he hired them to doom [*le-abed*] an innocent and blameless [person]. And they [the mercenaries from Blois] went around and lay in ambush for him during the nights; each one with his sword, and they had not been his foes before. And one day the Levi arose before sunrise, at the crack of the dawn, intending to go the house of God, according to his established daily custom; and he did not know that someone lay in wait for him outside the house. And when he passed beyond the threshold of his home, they rose upon him and the two uncircumcised smote him with the[ir] sword[s]. And he cried out loudly, and the town was aroused by the sound of his scream; and all the people got up and came and found him smitten with the sword, and his body cast by the road. And they lifted him up and brought him home, and he was still breathing. And they asked him to say who had stabbed him, and he told to them the names of the man-slaughterers.

And the man-slaughterers were residents of the town of birth of the adversary, and were known to him [the adversary] from before, and his friends and his companions, [and] those with whom he took counsel. And while they were on the run for their lives, they sent, two or three times, emissaries to the adversary to say to him:

This is what so and so and so and so [the murderers] said: Send us the wage on his behalf that he agreed upon with you for killing the soul at your behest: this [amount of] money and this [kind of] cloak. Because if not, when a person comes around there, from here and beyond, carrying a book and his [merchandise], he will need to be worried that it will be taken, [because the murderer(s)] shall carry it off as booty for the sake of his wage. Because why should he [otherwise] have left the city on your account [go into exile for the murder that you have ordered]?

And he [the adversary] turned his heart away, and he was reluctant to hear their appeal, and did not turn his face to them [the emissaries], and covered his ears from listening, and shut his eyes from seeing, because God hardened his heart. And, when the murderer heard that he [the adversary] was not paying any attention, he captured on that account a person who had walked there from the walled town of the one killed. In spite of all this, he [the adversary] did not turn away from all his infuriating misdeeds, and continued even more to commit very evil deeds, and did not abandon the ways of mischief to turn his heart to the law of God.

[6] And he was a person of contention to all the people, and hounded many and trampled them. And when the elders of the country rebuked him, he came to hate them. And he robbed in his corruption, [every] person and his neighbor, a man and his hereditary land. To many delegations he did not listen, and to what was transmitted to him he did not lend an ear. And he was ridiculing God's law and on the wisdom of the holy ones. To all the gentiles of the country he gave counsel with malice lips to bereave the people of the holy ones [the Jews]; to bring the God-fearers to devastation, and to alter the statute of God's law. He said to burn that which is more desirable than gold and much fine gold [the Torah], to obliterate them, not to leave root or branch of them, of the keepers of the resource [for action, the Torah]. And it was in his eyes a disdain to cause harm only to the community he was living in; and he wanted to destroy, to kill and extinguish the rest of Israel that is to be found, from young man to old, infant and women, on one day and to despoil them utterly.

APPENDIX 5

The Case from Poland

The Case from Poland: Rabbi Shalom of Neustadt. In Shalom b. Isaac Zekel of Neustadt, Decisions and Customs, *ed. S. Spitzer (Jerusalem: Machon Yerushalayim, 1997), 40 §95.*

They sent a question from Poland to our Master Rabbi Shalom, regarding two Jews who lived there in a city and had a quarrel. Eventually one of them threatened the other that he would cut off his nose, his hands, and his feet. This caused the threatened man to fear the offender, at which point the offender confronted him and asked him to provide some guaranties and collateral to appear before a Jewish court. If he would do so he will stop making threats. Nevertheless, all this did not stop the threats, for he kept on threatening. The threatened party then left the town and moved to another town. This proved futile, for the offender followed him and waylaid him in the morning when he was about to go to the synagogue he hit him and bruised him severely. The person under attack asked the assailant to leave him be and not to kill him, and still the assailant kept on striking him. It was at this point that the person under attack drew a small knife he carried with him, which he usually used for eating, and shoved that knife into the assailant's abdomen, and the assailant dropped dead. Witnessing these events were two women. The Jews of this place sent a query to Rabbi Shalom to make a statement that the killer is not guilty of murder and has not sinned. They further asked that he not be considered unacceptable and that he could continue to lead the community in prayer on the high holidays, as he had done previously. Rabbi Shalom answered that the killer should be expiated, and that they should hold the assailant accountable for his own death, for he rightfully committed this deed in an attempt to save his own life. And anyone who humiliated the assault victim, who had killed, should be punished. And I have seen other rabbis that have expressed their agreement that the victim of the assault who had done the killing is the just party in the matter.

APPENDIX 6

The Manual of Penance

The Manual of Penance appears in manuscript in both the Palatina Library, Parma, Italy, Cod. Parm. 1237 (fol. 168 r) and in BL (Add. MS 27075 fol. 165 r), http://www.bl.uk/manuscripts/Viewer.aspx?ref=add_ms_27075_fs001r, from which this translation is taken. This version was published by Moshe Hershler in Sinai *(66) 1970: 173–77.*

He who kills a soul in our times. We have no authority in our hands to harm him. We cannot execute or incarcerate him nor can we exile him. But we may avoid him and not mix and mingle with him. It is forbidden even to look at him, as the sages have said: "One must not gaze at the figure of an evil doe" (BT *Megilah* 28a). He is disqualified for any testimony whatsoever. He is not counted among the public and they cannot pray with him nor dine nor drink with him. He is to be banished all his life and a letter of excommunication shall be sent wherever he goes. If he dies while he is banished, the court should have his coffin stoned and he may not be buried in the graves of Israel. He must not be eulogized and the relevant prayers for the deceased should not be recited on his behalf. He must not be mourned and his memory is not to be invoked in a fine way. All the above applies if he steadfastly refused to accept the rule of the communities and he does not express regret and accept the sentence. But, if he shows remorse for the blood of his brother that he spilled and he is willing to accept justice, he should be sentenced in accordance with his wishes, as is evident from the case of Cain and in accordance with the Decree of our Fathers and the tradition of the Geonim.

And this is his sentence: the full measure of justice is to be imposed on him: he is to be banished, so that he will go to the place where the slayed person was killed and he should be there for three months and fast each and every day. On the day of his arrival to that place he should shave his head and beard and he should be bound in the place where the blood was spilt. There he should be flogged and whipped with no limit with leather lashes made of calf skin and donkey skin with iron tips like shackles, with iron nails at their ends, so that anywhere the whip hits it will draw blood. If he dies during this flogging they should not be seen as liable and his death will be seen as expiating all his transgressions. But if he survives this beating, they should go on beating him every Monday and Thursday and Monday for three months with these whips three times a day. And on these days of flogging during the three months he should go three times a day and prostrate himself and weep over the bones of the said slain person and he should say: The bones of so-and-so, I have suffered on your behalf, please forgive me, I have sinned. and I have deviated from the righteous path. I have spilt innocent blood, I have transgressed the commandments of my Lord God, and all this was not worth it for me. He should bring with him three people to bear witness and he should repeat this formula three times a day morning and evening and receive forty lashes. He then should give his assets to the poor as much as he can for it is said (Dan. 4:24): "break off thy sins by almsgiving, and thine iniquities by showing mercy to the poor."

After three months he should leave his place of dwelling and go on exile to other places for five years. And why have they decreed five years? It is in accordance with the five references to words denoting exile mentioned with regard to Cain. And they are: *na ve-nad*; *na ve-nad*, and *nod*. During these five years he should fast daily and receive flogging every Monday and Thursday. He may not drink wine or ale or honey and anything that is intoxicating neither on the Sabbath nor on the festivals and he should not eat meat neither on Sabbath nor on festivals. He should not stay in one congregation for more than eight days, excepting the Sabbath and festivals, or if he is incapacitated or bedridden. He may not take or receive from any community anything beyond his sustenance, and he should proclaim wherever he goes that he is a murderer for it is said (Deut. 19:4): "This is the case of a manslayer." During the five years when he is in exile, he should fast daily and receive flogging every Monday and Thursday once a day. If he dies during his exile he should be buried among the graves of Israel honorably but if he does not die during his exile, after his return from it, having been away for five years, the slain person's blood avengers may not touch neither him nor his descendants, nor those who act at his behest. From this moment on he is eligible for everything, like all the rest of the people of Israel. And where is this promise from? From the story of Cain, for God has told Cain (Gen. 4:15): "Whosoever slayeth Cain, vengeance shall be taken on him sevenfold," and it is subsequently written, "And the Lord set a sign for Cain, lest any finding him should smite him." Rav Nachman said: he who accepts justice and penance upon himself after having transgressed and performed penance he will be reintegrated into the life of this world and his moral debt will be obliterated and this is the ruling of *halakhah*....

And this is what the Rabbis of Rome have decreed:

For him who cannot bear to suffer all that is written in the regulation of the Geonim [regarding a killer in our times].

He should go into exile for two years, wandering from one place to another. He should not stay in one community for more than eight days, unless he is compelled to. He may not take or receive from any community more than he needs for a living. During these two years he must fast daily, and on every Monday and Thursday he should be flogged as long as he is within a given community. He should refrain from eating meat except on the Sabbath and festivals, and he should not drink wine or ale or any intoxicating beverage except for *kiddush* and *havdalah*. On the first week of his arrival back to his home [after his two years of wandering in exile] he should take two or three people and he should go and prostrate himself on the grave of the slain person and say: "I answer to thee, the bones of so-and-so. I have sinned and deviated from the righteous path I have hurt innocent blood and I have transgressed the word of my Lord God and all this is not worth it." He should do this all week twice a day. After this he may wed his fiancé if he is not yet married. And no man can prevent him from wedding his wife, and no son of Israel may chastise him after he had accepted his sentence. And he who does this and reprimands a killer, the sages are not at ease with him. Furthermore, he should be fined with another eight years during which he should fast every Monday and Thursday and on the fast days in the evening he should be flogged. He should also go into exile during these eight years eight times, each time for thirty consecutive days so that it would add up to a year. During this exile he should not stay in any given community more than three days, and when he goes into exile and upon his return he should prostrate himself on the grave of the slain man and perform the acts mentioned above. He shall not eat meat nor drink wine, and if he dies while in exile he shall be buried in the graves of Israel. Once he concludes the eight-year period he is as eligible as any other Jew to do anything.

And this is what Rabbi Ephraim of Regensburg has decreed. He should wander from place to place for three years all over the exile. He should refrain from meat and any beverage but water alone, except on Shabbat and festivals. When he arrives in a community he should fast and mortify his soul and flog his body in the morning and in at night and he should not eat meat at night and drink only water. He should sleep on the ground on a worn pallet. When he is on the road he does not need to fast, only on Mondays and Thursdays, and he should refrain from meat, wine, and ale, and also refrain from listening to music. Twice a year he should bathe his body and then also wash his clothes, for Passover and on the Day of Atonement. He may not shave his head nor his beard until three years have passed. He should have an iron fitting on his abdomen and his transgressive hand should be tied to his groin with an iron chain so that he cannot use it freely. All this is for three years. And if he can go to a place where the iron fitting can be removed on the eve of the Sabbath and returned upon the conclusion of the Sabbath, then that is acceptable, but if they cannot do this speedily enough, he should not remove them for the Sabbath. And the Rock of Israel will supply us with the ability for all the transgressors in Israel to repent and he will forgive them and to all the transgressions of Israel, amen.

APPENDIX 7

A Ḥazan Who Has Killed a Soul

A Ḥazan Who Has Killed a Soul: Rabbi Isaac b. Moshe of Vienna (Or Zaruaʻ). In The Book of Or Zaruaʻ, *3 vols., ed. Jacob Farbstein et al. (Jerusalem: Machon Yerushalayim, 2010), 1:105–7 §112.*

A man who has killed a soul unintentionally if he may lead prayer?

A double dose of heavenly salutations upon you as is right for royalty. My lord Rabbi Jacob b. Isaac the learned of distinguished lineage. I have made it my business to reply to your letter. It seems to me that the baby's father has no power to force you to quit praying in the presence of the said Matthias. Rather it is up to the public. Of course if the killer was an intentional killer, even if the victim's relatives would not have demanded it, the public should have refrained from praying with the killer as Rav Sherira the Gaon has stipulated: "He who kills a soul in our times we can't harm him, neither execute him nor flog or exile him, all we can do is refrain from him and prevent him fraternizing with us. And it is forbidden to pray with him and one should not gaze upon him for the sages said that one should not gaze at the image of an evil man. And he is also not fit to testify any sort of testimony." This is what he [Rav Sherirah] wrote.

Indeed, there is no difference between an intentional and an unintentional killer in that we should refrain from him as long as he hasn't repented. However, if he had done penance and repented he is considered a completely righteous individual instantly even if he hadn't yet accepted any of the penalties. Nevertheless, he needs to immerse in water and to rinse himself and cleanse himself from the sin that defiled him for the transgression is ritually defiling as it is said in the Midrash *Shoher Tov* on Psalms 51: "Wash me thoroughly from mine iniquity, and cleanse me from my sin"; from this we may conclude that all that have sinned is defined by the uncleanliness of the dead and he can be cleaned only by sprinkling him with special cleansing waters with Hyssop. And David too has stipulated: "Purge me with hyssop, and I shall be clean" (Ps. 51: 9). Is it possible to think that David himself was defiled? It is only possible if we understand that it was sin that had defiled him. And indeed this is what I learned from our master my teacher Rabbi Simcha of blessed memory [Rabbi Simcha of Speyer, d. c. 1225] that all penitents need ritual immersion as it is said in the third chapter of *Avot* D'Rabbi Nathan about a certain girl that was captured, etc., and when she was redeemed from captivity she was immersed. For all the days she was amongst the gentiles she ate their food and now she was immersed so that she may be purified. Although the defiled foods of the gentiles do not contaminate the body nevertheless she was immersed in order to purify her from the transgression of eating these foods. And although I have stipulated that all those who do penance need immersion nevertheless the immersion is not deemed as a prerequisite for the penance itself and it does not withhold the acceptance of the penance. But rather, all those who transgressed, regardless of their transgression once they have considered repenting they are deemed righteous again. Nevertheless he should agonize and mortify his body to expiate the deed he has done.

APPENDIX 8

A Responsum by Meir of Rothenburg

A responsum by Meir of Rothenburg. Quoted in the collection of his disciple Rabbi Haim Eliezer b. Isaac Or Zarua'. In Teshuvot Maharakh Or Zarua' *[Responsa]* Derashot ve'Piskei Halakhot *[Sermons and Adjudications], ed. Menachem Avitan (Jerusalem, 2002), §141.*

The word of my teacher Rabbi Meir of blessed memory.

I greet you, but I am very bitter, and my scent has weakened and withered.

Oh what can I say about this Israelite who has turned his back to the righteous path and has exchanged good for evil? Our "sons have fainted, they lie at the heads of all the streets as a wild bull in a net" (Isa. 51:20), "just as when a wild bull falls into a trap, no one has mercy upon it, so with the property of an Israelite, as soon as it falls into the hands of heathen oppressors, no mercy is exercised towards it" [BT *Baba Kama* 117a], and all the more so in this case, when we have the hand of another Jew in the middle, that the heathen enforcers feel that it is entirely lawful "to destroy, to slay, and to cause to perish" (Esther 3:13). What can I answer you my rabbis about this bad deed and terrible occurrence; his judgment is not in our hands, but rather in the hands of the Almighty. And who would know how this Alexander may seek absolution from this crime. I feel that we should be more stringent with him than with a regular case of a Jew who tells his fellow Jew to go and kill someone. And although we know that: "Where the words of the Master [God] are contradicted by words of a disciple [humans], whose words should be followed?" [BT *Baba Kama* 56a and BT *Kiddushin* 43a], clearly the word of God should be followed, and therefore, surely the person who committed the crime cannot say he was "only operating at the behest of another." He who committed the crime is liable for his own deeds, in matters of the heavens to one, and in the matters of earth to another. In that case, as it is likely that he would not act accordingly, because "Where the words of the Master [God] are contradicted by words of a disciple [humans], whose words should be followed?" But if, as in our case, he sent gentiles, they are considered as instruments of damage, and it is similar to a case where one entrusts a minor or a fool or imbecile with setting a field ablaze and handing him all the instruments of damage [firewood, fuel, and a flame]. This person is liable also to the laws of men and not only to the laws of heaven, for the noncircumcised are only too happy, and already start splitting the spoils when they have an opportunity to fall upon a Jew. And I wonder who let this man [Alexander] capture his legal foe using the aid of gentiles? And even if we accept his claim that all he intended was to bring his legal foe to justice, this is not acceptable.

[I omit part of the Talmudic discussion.]

It therefore seems to me that he [Alexander] is in need of penance like a murderer who has killed with his bare hands. And his situation is similar to that of a person who forced his fellow man into water or into a fire and to "one who bound his fellow man and then caused a column of water to inundate him" [BT *Sanhedrin* 78b], and it is as if he had killed him with direct force, for the situation here is similar to one who kills with his own arrows. For we assume as a given that a man would not confront another [when outnumbered], not for his body or for his possessions [he would rather flee than be caught and killed, so there is no contributing blame on the part of the slain person]. Thus, when these gentiles pursued the slain person, they meant to kill him for if he had stood up to them, they would surely have slain him. And since they were like a lion sitting on his boundaries, he [Alexander] is a criminal and has done damage, and anything that the gentiles have done is as if they were his direct arrows. And indeed we need no supporting evidence in this matter save his own admission on the matter.

I therefore decree that he requires penance like a murderer, this was like a fire blown off its track by a regular wind. Its damage was predictable. He should bind himself with an iron fitting and should be flogged as well. He should be humiliated publicly and privately and go into exile and wander and shift about until his face discloses his falsehood and his profile shows his lies, and then maybe he will be absolved. He should hide from the wrath of God on His day, for on that day he will have to repent and cleanse his sin with lye, but his face will still be blackened by constant fasting for a year or two, and anything you my esteemed rabbis will demand of him. For I agree with you and demand even more. I wish you much peace and ease. Your humble disciple, Meir son of Baruch, may he live.

APPENDIX 9

The Death of the Wife of Milo

The Death of the Wife of Milo. In F. W. Maitland, ed., Select Pleas of the Crown *(Latin transcripts and English translations from Curia Regis rolls), vol. 1, AD 1200–1225 (London: Selden Society, 1888), Trinity AD 1208, plea 103, p. 57.*

William Makeblithe and Thomas Goldsmith and Robert, Edmund's nephew, were arrested for the death of the wife of Milo the Jew of York upon the appeal of the said Milo.

And they are not suspected neither by Jews nor by Christians [*et ipsi non malecreduntur nec a Judeis nec a Christianis*]. But Milo himself is suspected of the said death.

And when Benedict brother of the slain woman was about to appeal Milo, he [Milo] fled [*ipse Milo fugit*]. And Milo does not charge those who were arrested.

And so let the said William, Thomas, and Robert be under pledges to stand to right in case any shall accuse them. Let the sheriff take the names of their pledges, and they give twenty shillings to the king, to wit, each of them a half mark on the pledge of Walter Goldsmith, Adam Goldsmith, and Clarenbald.

And let Milo's pledges to prosecute be in mercy, to wit, Ursell the physician [*medicus*] and Isaac Black [*Niger*] each for a half-mark on the pledge of the commonalty of the Jews of York [*communae Judeorum Eboraci*].

And Benedict, Ursell's son, appealed the said Milo for that he learned by an inquiry he made that Milo killed [Benedict's] sister [Milo's wife] and that she was slain on account of Kelina the Jewess, for Milo is said to have had an intrigue with her [*eo quod ipse Milo dicitur habuisse rem cum ea*].

And Kelina was arrested, but is not suspected.

So let her be under pledge and she gives a half-mark for which Vivent the Jew is pledge.

And let Benedict upon whose appeal, which is null, she was taken and imprisoned be in mercy for his false appeal in a half-mark for which the commonalty of the Jews is pledged.

APPENDIX 10

A Responsum by Rabbi Haim Eliezer Or Zarua'

A Responsum by Rabbi Haim Eliezer ben Isaac Or Zarua'. In Teshuvot Maharakh Or Zarua' *[Responsa]* Derashot ve'Piskei Halakhot *[Sermons and Adjudications]*, ed. Menachem Avitan (Jerusalem, 2002), §25. (This translation is provided by Dr. Rachel Furst of Ludwig Maximilian University, Munich.)

Will you quarrel forever and multiply altercations, relatives of R. Shalom, the murdered one, and their opponents?

And are there not in your midst, praise the Lord, blessed is God, learned and wise men—my teacher Rabbi Shabtai son of the honorable Rabbi Shmuel and his court? And you should have acted in accordance with their instructions and [thus] suppressed the dispute. And what benefit is there to the relatives of the murdered one? Even if they could manage to defame R. Moshe and his father-in-law, will they bring R. Shalom back to life thereby? Even though he [Shalom] began to draw his knife and his brothers and brothers-in-law drew swords, until they drove respectable people from the feast in dispute and altercation, like the story of Kamtza and Bar Kamtza, and the altercation intensified until blood was shed. If at that point they [Moshe and his father-in-law] would have complained to the non-Jews [the authorities], I would not have held them accountable for whatever loss R. Shalom and his brothers and brothers-in-law would have incurred thereby. For [it is like] a person who is about to strike his fellow; the victim will not restrain himself with regard to his body [i.e., his life], certainly not with regard to his money, as wrote my teacher R. Meir, may the righteous and holy one merit eternal life.

It is worth considering whether it is permissible for any [uninvolved] person to save the victim of violence, even at the expense of the perpetrator's life, if there is no other means of saving him. For behold, Rav Kahana broke the neck of the one who said, "I will indeed show [my fellow Jew's property to the authorities]." And *Sefer ha-Mitzvot* explained that it is because he is like a thief who enters stealthily [*ha-ba be-maḥteret*]. And this is despite the fact that logically, in that case, it does not fit to say that a person does not restrain himself with regard to his money—for a person does not fight a royal authority that takes his money. Certainly here, where a person is about to attack his fellow—and a person does not restrain himself with regard to his body [i.e., his life]—and lest he thereby come to spill blood, it is permissible for any person to break his neck. For so too in [the case of] a thief who comes stealthily. Is it entirely clear whether the homeowner will rise against him to kill him? Maybe he will injure him or cut off his hand or his foot, and take his money and leave. Rather, lest it come to the shedding of blood, the Torah said, "he has no bloodguilt," and all the more so here. And once his life is forfeited, surely so is his money, according to the opinion that it is permissible to physically destroy the money of an informer. And even the opinion that prohibits this, here, in order to save the victim, the one who destroys is exempt like a pursuer [*rodef*] who was pursuing an attacker and broke someone else's utensils, who is exempt [from paying damages]. And [this is] not strictly legal, but if it were not so, no one would [attempt to] save his fellow from an attacker. And here, too, since he is about to strike and will surely strike—it is permissible for any person to tell the [non-Jewish] judge and demand that he be detained, even if he will lose all his money as a result.

And, similarly, I assert that this is the reason our rabbis excused one who complains [to the authorities] during [his] "hour of rage" [*shaʿat ha-zaʿam*]: because his rage overpowers him and he cannot restrain himself due to his pain and shame, such that if he does not complain and take revenge via the [non-Jewish] judge, he will avenge his shame even at the expense of his life. And lest he thereby come to shed blood, it is permissible to complain to the [non-Jewish] judge; and it is permissible even for others [to do so], as I explained previously. But, surely, if an upstanding person [*adam kasher*] struck, and it happened coincidentally that he struck, and it is known that he will not continue but will rather regret [his actions]—it is prohibited to [make him] lose his money. And in any case, in this terrible episode, if after he [Shalom] shamed them and drove them from the feast, and they [Moshe and his father-in-law] departed the said group, they would have complained to the non-Jewish [authorities] and thereby resolved not to take further revenge——it would seem right to absolve them of responsibility for any damages they would have caused their shamers thereby. In fact, according to all the testimonies, the non-Jews came to kill or to menace; but regardless, the one who is known to have brought the non-Jews and to have drawn half the length [of his sword] and ushered them into the home of the murdered one—he is an outright murderer. And indeed, he should be denounced in all the communities that know him, and let his stench and his shame rise, and may he be trapped in his [own] net. However, R. Moshe and his father-in-law—why should they be trapped? And even if it were so, that they told that villain to bring non-Jews—does one listen to the words of the master or the words of the student? And even King Saul, when he told Avner and Amasa to attack Nov, the city of priests, they declined to do so; certainly this evil murderer—even if it were so that they told him to do this terrible thing, he should have feared God, the venerable and the awesome, and he should not have done it. Even though it is questionable whether one who tells an apostate to kill is responsible [for the deed], as an apostate who does not fear God will surely perform [the act] rather than heed the words of the Master; nonetheless, this evil murderer may not have been presumed to act this way [to flout God] from the outset—and, therefore, there is no need to elaborate on this.

And all this I wrote even if it were so that they [Moshe and his father-in-law] told him [the villain] to do it. But I have not seen any clear testimony on this at all. And it is appropriate to castigate all those who call R. Moshe and his father-in-law "murderers" with regard to this terrible episode, and so too, to clear their names, that they did not tell that villain to do it. I have not seen any clear testimony about this either, for who knows what they whispered together when they came to the [Jewish] court after they were chased out—and heaven forbid, we must not suspect R. Moshe of this terrible thing. Nonetheless, to ban and excommunicate those who open their mouths against them on this matter, without constraint—it is not possible due to [the prohibition], "Do not place a stumbling-block before the blind," for it is clear they will transgress. And just as it is a positive commandment to say that which will be heeded, so is it a positive commandment not to say that which will not be heeded.

Indeed, this is my final word: that there is absolutely no murder verdict for Moshe and his father-in-law in this terrible episode, and so should it be proclaimed in my name in any place they wish. And with regard to the complaints that the relatives of the murdered one submitted [to the non-Jewish authorities] and, according to their [Moshe and his father-in-law's] claims, caused them to lose their money thereby—it seems that they [Shalom's relatives] should not be charged, for the laws of informing are *kenas* [financial penalties], as per the Jerusalem Talmud. And [with regard to the claim that] it is written in *Sefer ha-Mitzvot* in the name of R. Isaac b. Abraham that wherever the matter will become commonplace if they do not impose penalties, they should charge [the informer] as though it were a direct injury, and here too it might become commonplace—[in fact], praise the Lord blessed be God, for a number of years we have not heard a complaint about murder until now. And there are other reasons, but it is not appropriate to write them all. And what they wrote, that they [Shalom's relatives] did not complain during "the hour of rage"—they were incorrect. For with regard to murder, it is forever "the hour of rage," as it is written, "When his heart is fired up." And if the blood avenger killed the murderer several years later, when he encountered him, we still consider it "When [his heart] is fired up." And One who confesses and gives them up will find mercy.

Peace, the forlorn Haim Eliezer b. Rabenu Isaac, may his soul rest in Eden.

APPENDIX 11

The Case of Isaac and Sara

The Case of Isaac and Sara. In Meir b. Baruch of Rothenburg, The Responsa of Meir of Rothenburg, *ed. Jacob Farbstein (Jerusalem: Machon Yerushalayim, 2014), 384–88 §341 (310).*

"We shall pass over before" [Num. 32:32] our rabbi's concern [about] the bad deed that has been reported to us. For Rabbi Isaac has come to us and has shouted and screamed. He screamed about his wife Sara that he had left in the month of Adar in the year 5031 [March 1271], when he traveled to a distance in an attempt to make a profit so that he could sustain his home. He had left her empty [not with child] and he did not return to her until he heard in the place where he was that his wife had transgressed [*zantah*] and had conceived in harlotry and had given birth. Now he has returned to his kingdom [this may suggest that Isaac went on business to a place outside the German realm] and he came before us in the month of Av 5032 [July 1272] and found his wife here. He pleaded before us and even wished to keep us from prayer [*rotzeh le-vatel tmideynu*] until we decided to probe, investigate, and look into the matter.

And we asked her [the wife, Sara] about the matter, and she said: "My husband left me full [with child]." To this he said: "This was never true, as is known to all, as I left town in Adar [March 1271] and she delivered the next Adar [March 1272]. We [the tribunal that discussed the case] have sent for the people of her place of residence [*bnei yishuvah*], to Rabbi Shaltiel and his two sons, and asked them to testify under penalty of *ḥerem* [excommunication], and they did so, testifying under oath that indeed she had borne a *mamzer* [bastard]," as you will see in the letter of Rabbi Shaltiel (the signatures on the document are validated for we have done so using reliable witnesses who know these signatures). We also heard one witness who appeared before us, who testified under oath before us that, last year on the eve of the festival of Shavuot in 5031 [May 23, 1271], he went over to her house to make *kiddush* [the traditional Sabbath and festival benediction over wine at the beginning of the main meals, usually performed by men for all the members of the household] for her, and he had found her in the company of disreputable gentiles [*goyim rekim u-poḥazim*]; they were playful and intimate with her [*saḥaku imah*] and they were embracing and he fondled her. He left them in the house. We have assumed that it was in and around that time that she had conceived. And there are some individuals who testified that they have seen her now [recently], on Purim of 5032 [February 23, 1272], with a very bulging belly here [in the town of the tribunal]. Furthermore, before the bad rumor spread around this town, Sara's father appeared before the undersigned and asked to consult us so that we should instruct him whether he may kill his daughter by drowning her in the river and ridding the world of her presence. We asked him why he wished to do so, to which he replied: "I have one daughter and she has become pregnant from harlotry and she has given birth to a *mamzer* from a gentile, for it has been over a year since her husband went off, and I cannot deny that she is an absolute and notorious whore [*zonah gmurah u-mefursemet*]. She has given birth to a baby girl, and has killed the *mamzer* [bastard], and I fear she will leave altogether and associate with bad company." We asked him: "Can you not put this matter right in any other fashion?" To which he replied: "Whenever I reprimand her she threatens me that she will go and be among the gentiles, 'for I am not the first woman who has been bad,' and she has fled the house many times, but then her mother talks her into returning, and she returns. I fear she will associate with bad company, so I beseech you in every way to let me kill her." We have not permitted him to do so, for as it is written in tractate *Sanhedrin* "but he who pursues idol worship, we do not save him [from himself by killing him, even though by this deed, according to Jewish tradition, the person loses his share in the world to come, allocated to every Jew regardless of the justness of his deeds]." And even he who fornicates with an Aramean, whom we know may be killed by zealots, if those zealots consult a legal authority, and do not act out of pure zeal, those they consult with may not rule and sanction the zealous act. And even more so in our case.

And we have sent all the rest of the evidence to Rothenburg to the great luminary, our teacher Rabbi Meir, may he live. And indeed this case has become the subject of local female gossip [in Hebrew, נושאות ונותנות בה מוזרות בלבנה, an expression taken from tractate *Sota* 6:1, meaning that women speak of her as they spin at night] about how she has fornicated and has blood on her hands. And have recorded it all down as it came to pass. For they [the husband, and maybe the father] have come before us, and we have accepted the testimonies, validated them, and delved into the matter and investigated. It is therefore our opinion that in this case we should not say "let us help them patch it up," but rather we should assist in severing this marital bond. Now, our rabbis, those close to us in Erfurt, and those more remote in Würzburg, and the great luminary Rabbi Meir of Rothenburg, may the Lord guide him and the other rabbis of the Rhineland, discharge Isaac from Sara, a stray cow [*parah Sara*, a pun on the name Sara[1]] by accepting Isaac's *get* [writ of divorce] that was performed in our presence. We have written and signed this: Moshe Azriel ben Rabbi Eliezer Hadarshn; Eliezer son of Yechiel of blessed memory; Ephraim ben Yoel may he rest in Eden.

NOTES

INTRODUCTION

1. Derek Wilson, *The Tower of London: A Thousand Years* (London: Allison & Busby, 1982), 34–38.
2. See Willis Johnson, "Textual Sources for the Study of Jewish Currency Crimes in Thirteenth Century England," *British Numismatic Journal* 66 (1996): 21–32.
3. Cecil Roth, *A History of the Jews in England* (Oxford: Clarendon Press, 1964), 75–76; Robin R. Mundill, "Edward I and Final Phase of Anglo-Jewry," in *The Jews in Medieval Britain: Historical Literary and Archaeological Perspectives*, ed. Patricia Skinner (Woodbridge, UK: Boydell Press, 2003), 55–70, esp. 61–62; Mundill, *The King's Jews: Money, Massacre and Exodus in Medieval England* (New York: Continuum, 2010), 154–55.
4. Meir b. Baruch of Rothenburg, *The Responsa of Meir of Rothenburg*, ed. Jacob Farbstein (Jerusalem: Machon Yerushalayim, 2014), §274 (formerly 246). Also Zefira Entin-Rokeah, "Money and the Hangman in Late-13th-century England: Jews, Christians and Coinage Offences Alleged and Real," *Jewish Historical Studies* 31 (1990): 83–109.
5. Jörg R. Müller, "Eine Jüdische Diebesbande im Südwesten des Reiches in der ersten Hälfte des 14. Jahrhunderts," in *Beziehungsnetze aschkenasischer Juden während des Mittelalters und der frühen Neuzeit*, ed., Jörg R. Müller Forschungen zur Geschichte der Juden, A20 (Hannover: Hahnsche Buchhandlung, 2008), 71–116.
6. Maria R. Boes, "Jews in the Criminal-Justice System of Early Modern Germany," *Journal of Interdisciplinary History* 30 (1999): 407–35; Boes, "Zweifach im Visier: Jüdische Opfer von Straftaten und Rechtsprechung

im Römisch-Deutschen Reich der Frühen Neuzeit," *Zeitschrift für Historische Forschung* 39 (2007): 221–41. See also O. Ulbricht, "Criminality and Punishment of the Jews in the Early Modern Period," in *In and Out of the Ghetto: Jewish Gentile Relations in Late Medieval and Early Modern Germany*, ed. R. Po-chia Hsia & H. Lehmann (Cambridge, Cambridge University Press, 1995), 49–70.

7. See for example *Medieval Handbooks of Penance: A Translation of the Principal "Libri Poenitentiales" and Selections from Related Documents*, ed. John T. McNeill and Helena M. Gamer (Cambridge: Cambridge University Press, 1990); Rob Meens, *Penance in Medieval Europe, 600–1200* (Cambridge: Cambridge University Press, 2014).
8. BT tractate *Rosh Hashana* 17a. The Talmud discusses the definition of "*posh'ei yisra'el*." The answer is: those who do not don phylacteries (*tefilin*).
9. Gavin I. Langmuir, "Thomas of Monmouth: Detector of Ritual Murder," *Speculum* 59 (1984): 820–46.
10. Mitchell B. Merback, *The Thief, the Cross and the Wheel: Pain and the Spectacle of Punishment in Medieval and Renaissance Europe* (Chicago: University of Chicago Press, 1998), 101–57.
11. Paul J. Hunter, *Before Novels: Cultural Contexts of Eighteenth-Century English Fiction* (New York: Norton, 1992), 180–83; Lennard Davis, *Factual Fictions: The Origins of the English Novel* (Philadelphia: University of Pennsylvania Press, 1997), 123–37. I wish to thank my friend Yael Shapira for calling this topic to my attention.
12. On this concept of a "holy community" and the Jewish self-image see Israel Jacob Yuval, "Heilige Städte, heilige Gemeinden: Mainz als das Jerusalem Deutschlands," in *Jüdische Gemeinden und Organisationsformen von der Antike bis zur Gegenwart*, ed. Robert Jütte und Abraham P. Kustermann, Aschkenas Beiheft 3 (Vienna: Böhlau, 1996), 91–101; Ivan G. Marcus, "A Pious Community in Doubt: Jewish Martyrdom among Northern European Jewry and the Story of Rabbi Amnon of Mainz," in *Essays in Hebrew Literature In Honor of Avraham Holtz*, ed. Z. Ben-Yosef Ginor (New York: Jewish Theological Seminary Press, 2003), 21–46; Jeffrey R. Woolf, "'Qehillah Qedosha': Sacred Community in Medieval Ashkenazic Law and Culture," in *A Holy People: Jewish and Christian Perspectives on Religious Communal Identity*, ed. Marcel Poorthuis & Joshua Schwartz, Jewish and Christian Perspectives Series 12 (Leiden: Brill, 2006), 217–36; Haym Soloveitchik, "A Note on Deviance

in Eleventh Century Ashkenaz," in *Collected Essays* (Oxford: Littman Library of Jewish Civilization, 2013), 1:278–82.

13. Shulamit Shahar, *Marginal Groups in the Middle Ages*, Broadcasted University Series (Tel Aviv: Ministry of Defense, 1995), 7–8 (Hebrew). See also Aron Gurevich, *Historical Anthropology of the Middle Ages*, ed. Jana Howlett (Chicago: University of Chicago Press, 1992), 30, 42–46.

14. S. D. Goitein, *A Mediterranean Society: The Jewish Communities of the Arab World as Portrayed in the Documents of the Cairo Geniza*, 6 vols. (Berkeley: University of California Press, 1967–93). Goitein surveys the whole range of Jewish Mediterranean culture as reflected in the documents found in the Cairo Geniza. Robert Bonfil, "Myth, Rhetoric, History? An Inquiry into Megillat Ahimaaz," in *Culture and Society in Medieval Jewry: Studies Dedicated to the Memory of Haim Hillel Ben-Sasson*, ed. Robert Bonfil, Menahem Ben-Sasson, and Joseph Haker (Jerusalem: Merkaz Zalman Shazar, 1989), 99–135; more recently: Robert Bonfil, *History and Folklore in a Medieval Jewish Chronicle: The Family Chronicle of Ahima'az ben Paltiel* (Leiden: Brill, 2009); Ivan G. Marcus, "The Historical Meaning of Hasidei Ashkenaz: Fact, Fiction, or Cultural Self-Image?" in *Gershom Scholem's 'Major Trends in Jewish Mysticism' Fifty Years After: Proceedings of the Sixth International Conference on the History of Jewish Mysticism*, ed. Joseph Dan and Peter Schäfer (Tübingen: Mohr-Siebeck, 1993), 103–13. Marcus, *Rituals of Childhood: Jewish Acculturation in Medieval Europe*. New Haven, CT: Yale University Press, 1996. More recently: Elisheva Baumgarten, *Mothers and Children: Jewish Family Life in Medieval Europe* (Princeton, NJ: Princeton University Press, 2004); ibid, *Practicing Piety in Medieval Ashkenaz: Men Women and Everyday Religious Observance* (Philadelphia: University of Pennsylvania Press, 2014); David I. Shyovitz, *A Remembrance of His Wonders: Nature and the Supernatural in Medieval Ashkenaz* (Philadelphia: University of Pennsylvania Press, 2017). Also my own previous contribution to this field: Ephraim Shoham-Steiner, *On the Margins of a Minority: Leprosy, Madness, and Disability among Jews of Medieval Europe*, trans. Haim Watzman (Detroit: Wayne State University Press, 2014).

15. One such groundbreaking study is Michel Mollat, *The Poor in the Middle Ages: An Essay in Social History*, trans. Arthur Goldhammer (New Haven: Yale University Press, 1986). Other studies worth mentioning are those of Robert Jütte, *Poverty and Deviance in Early Modern Europe* (Cambridge: Cambridge University Press, 1994).

16. Caroline Dunn, *Stolen Women in Medieval England: Rape, Abduction, and Adultery 1100–1500* (Cambridge: Cambridge University Press, 2013), 204–30.
17. Jay Berkovitz, *Protocols of Justice: The Pinkas of the Metz Rabbinic Court 1771–1789*, Studies in Jewish History and Culture 44, 2 vols. (Leiden: Brill, 2014).
18. Judah ben Shmuel Ha'hasid, *Sefer Hasidim (Das Buch der Frommen)*, ed. Judah Wistinetzki (Frankfurt: Wahrmann Verlag, 1924), SHW §1301. See Ivan G. Marcus, *Piety and Society: The Jewish Pietists of Medieval Germany* (Leiden: Brill, 1981), 131. See also Ephraim Shoham-Steiner, "'For in Every City and Town the Manner of Behavior of the Jews Resembles Their Non-Jewish Neighbours': The Intricate Network of Interfaith Connections—A Brief Introduction," in *Intricate Interfaith Networks in the Middle Ages: Quotidian Jewish Christian Contacts*, History of Daily Life, vol. 5, ed. Ephraim Shoham-Steiner (Turnhout: Brepols, 2016), 1–32.
19. Theodore J. Rivers, trans. and ed., *Laws of the Alamans and Bavarians* (Philadelphia: University of Pennsylvania Press, 1977).
20. Trevor Dean, *Crime in Medieval Europe, 1200–1550* (London: Pearson, 2014), 4.
21. Dean, *Crime in Medieval Europe*, 5–7.
22. Maureen Mulholland and Brian Pullan, eds., *Judicial Tribunals in Europe and England: The Trial in History, vol. 1*, Manchester University Press: Manchester 2003, 1–17.
23. Dean, *Crime in Medieval Europe*, 9.
24. John H. Langbein, *Prosecuting Crime in the Renaissance: England Germany France* (Cambridge, MA: Harvard University Press, 1974), 131–57.
25. Alfred Haverkamp, "Juden und Städte—Verbindungen und Bindungen," ed. Christoph Cluse, in *Europas Juden im Mittelalter: Beiträge des Internationalen Symposiums in Speyer vom 20–25 Oktober 2002*, ed. Christoph Cluse (Trier, Ger.: Kliomedia, 2004), 13–29; A. Haverkamp, "The Jews of Europe in the Middle Ages: By Way of Introduction," in *The Jews of Europe in the Middle Ages (Tenth to Fifteenth Centuries): Proceedings of the International Symposium held in Speyer 20–25 October 2002*, ed. Christoph Cluse, Cultural Encounters in Late Antiquity and the Middle Ages, CELAMA 4 (Turnhout: Brepols, 2004), 1–16; A. Haverkamp, *Jews in the Medieval German Kingdom*, trans. Christoph Cluse (Trier, Ger.: Universitätsbibliothek, 2015) <urn:nbn:de:hbz:385-9169>; A. Haverkamp, "The

Beginning of Jewish Life North of the Alps with Comparative Glances at Italy (ca.900–1100)," in *Diversi Angoli di Visuale Fra Storia Medievale e storia Degeli Ebrei: In Ricordo di Michele Luzzati*, ed. Anna Maria Pult-Quagila & Alessandra Veronese (Pisa: Pacini Editore, 2016), 85–102. See also Eva Haverkamp, "The Jews in Christian Europe: Ashkenaz in the Middle Ages," in *The Wiley-Blackwell History of Jews and Judaism*, ed. Alan T. Levenson (Malden, MA: Wiley, 2012), 169–206.

26. Shlomo Eidelberg, "Trial by Ordeal in Medieval Jewish History: Laws, Customs and Attitudes," *Proceeding of the American Academy of Jewish Research* 46/47: Jubilee Vol. Part 1 (1979–80): 105–20; Elisheva Baumgarten, "Seeking Signs? Jews, Christians and Proof by Fire in Medieval Germany and Northern France," in *New Perspectives on Jewish-Christian Relations in Honor of David Berger*, ed. Elisheva Carlebach and Jacob J. Schacter (Leiden and Boston: Brill, 2012), 205–25.

27. See Michael Toch, "*Die Juden im Mittelalterlichen Reich*," in *Enzyklopädie deutscher Geschichte* (Munich: R. Oldenbourg, 1998), 44:109–11.

28. Hanna Vollrath, "The Western Empire Under the Salians," in *The New Cambridge Medieval History*, ed. David Luscombe and Jonathan Riley-Smith (Cambridge: Cambridge University Press, 2004), vol. 4, pt. 2, 38–68.

29. Aaron Kirshenbaum, *Jewish Penology: The Theory and Development of Criminal Punishment among the Jews throughout the Ages* [in Hebrew] (Jerusalem: Magness Press, 2013), 332–37. An English summary of the book may be found on pp. vii–xlviii.

30. On this matter and the limits that kept communal Jewish authorities from employing punitive measures, see Guido Kisch, "The Jewry-Law of the Medieval German Law-Books: Part 1," *Proceedings of the American Academy for Jewish Research* 7 (1935–1936): 61–145, and "Part 2, The Legal Status of the Jews," *Proceedings of the American Academy for Jewish Research* 10 (1940): 99–184, vii–xlviii. This is an abridgment of the considerably more detailed Hebrew version.

31. Kirschenbaum, *Jewish Penology*, 336.

32. On this title: Esriel Hildesheimer, "Bishoph ha'Yehudim" [in Hebrew], *Sinai* 105 (1990): 142–65. Kenneth R. Stow, *Alienated Minority: The Jews of Medieval Latin Europe* (Cambridge, MA: Harvard University Press, 1992), 160. Avraham Grossman suggests that this title was granted to Rabbi Shlomo ben Shimshon of Worms as part of the privilege granted to this city's Jews by Emperor Heinrich IV in 1190. See Avraham

Grossman, *The Early Sages of Ashkenaz: Their Lives Leadership and Works (900–1096)* [in Hebrew] (Jerusalem: Magnes Press, 1989), 340.

33. Avraham Grossman, "The Attitude of the Early Scholars of Ashkenaz towards the Authority of the 'Kahal'" [in Hebrew], *Shenaton Ha'Mishpat Ha'Ivri* [Annual of the Institute for Research in Jewish Law] 2 (1975): 175–99.
34. Stow, *Alienated Minority*, 160–64.
35. Louis Finkelstein's *Jewish Self-Government in the Middle Ages* (New York: Philipp Feldheim, 1964) examines the legal documents of the rabbinical synods that produced these *takanot*. This invaluable collection is to date one of the most important sources of knowledge of the local and regional institutions of the Jewish self-governing mechanisms in medieval Europe. More recently, a full edition of the famous communal regulations of the Rhineland communities of Speyer, Worms, and Mainz has appeared: Rainer J. Barzen, *Taqqanot Qehillot Šum. Die Rechtssatzungen der Jüdischen Gemeinden von Mainz, Worms und Speyer im hohen und späten Mittelalter*, Monumenta Germaniae Historica: Hebräische Texte aus dem mittelalterlichen Deutschland 2 (Wiesbaden: Harrassowitz Verlag, 2019).
36. See, for instance, the regulations attributed to Rabbi Gershom ben Judah of Mainz (Meor ha'Gola d. 1028): Israel Schepansky, *The Takanot of Israel, vol. 4 Communal Ordinances* [in Hebrew] (New York and Jerusalem: Mosad Harav Kook and Yeshiva University Press, 1991), 78–104.
37. Rudolf Glanz, "The 'Jewish Execution' in Medieval Germany," *Jewish Social Studies* 5 (1943): 3–26.
38. Guido Kisch, *The Jews in Medieval Germany: A Study of Their Legal and Social Status* (New York: Ktav Publishing, 1970), 171–73; Finkelstein, *Jewish Self-Government*, 6–95.
39. Merav Schnitzer-Maimon, *Rape between Halakha and Reality: Attitudes towards Sexual Coercion of Women in Medieval Jewish Communities of Northern France and Germany* [in Hebrew] (Tel Aviv: Tel Aviv University Press, 2017), 21–76.
40. Eric Zimmer, *Harmony and Discord: An Analysis of the Decline of Jewish Self-Government in Fifteenth Century Central Europe* (New York: Yeshiva University Press, 1970), 90–103, 211–16, esp. 90–92. Jews attempted, for as long as they could, to associate themselves with the patrician segment of medieval urban society. As merchants, and later as bankers and financiers, the affluent families that in many cases formed the

social and economic backbone of the Jewish communities tirelessly attempted to gain high social standing within the urban system, even when the tables were already turning against them in the late fourteenth century.

41. Salo W. Baron, *A Social and Religious History of the Jews: Under Church and Empire* (New York: Columbia University, 1965), 9:135–54; Guido Kisch, *Jews in Medieval Germany*, 107–28. More recently see David Abulafia, "The King and the Jews: The Jews in the Ruler's Service," in *The Jews of Europe in the Middle Ages (Tenth to Fifteenth Centuries)*, ed. Christoph Cluse (Turnhout: Brepols, 2004), 283–93.

42. Fernand Braudel, *On History*, trans. Sara Matthews (Chicago: University of Chicago Press, 1982), 64–82. A fine example of such a study in the historical inquiry of crime is Pieter Spierenburg's *A History of Murder: Personal Violence in Europe from the Middle Ages to the Present* (Cambridge: Polity Press, 2008).

43. See Michael Toch, *The Economic History of European Jews: Late Antiquity and Early Middle Ages* (Leiden: Brill, 2013), 65–102.

44. Johanes Heil, "Getting Them In or Keeping Them Out? Theology, Law, and the Beginnings of Jewish Life in the Rhine Valley in the 10th and 11th Centuries," in *Jews in Early Christian Law: Byzantium and the Latin West, 6th-11th Centuries*, ed. John Tolan et al. (Turnhout: Brepols, 2014), 211–28, esp. 216.

45. Debra Kaplan, *Beyond Expulsion: Jews Christians and Reformation Strasburg* (Stanford, CA: Stanford University Press, 2011). Lucia Raspe, "Sacred Space, Local History and Diasporic Identity: The Graves of the Righteous in Medieval and Early Modern Ashkenaz," in *Jewish Studies at the Crossroads of Anthropology and History: Authority, Diaspora, Tradition*, ed. Ra'anan Bustan, Oren Kosansky, and Marina Rostow (Philadelphia: University of Pennsylvania Press, 2011), 147–63.

46. David Napolitano, review of: *Public Justice and the Criminal Trial in Late Medieval Italy: Reggio Emilia in the Visconti Age*, by Joanna Carraway-Vitiello, *The Medieval Review* (January 29, 2017).

47. Andrew McCall, *The Medieval Underworld* (New York: Barnes & Noble Books, 1979); Dean, *Crime in Medieval Europe*. And more recently Larissa Tracy, ed., *Medieval and Early Modern Murder: Legal, Literary, and Historical Contexts* (Cambridge: D. S. Brewer, 2018).

48. See Kenneth R. Stow, *Alienated Minority: The Jews of Medieval Latin Europe* (Cambridge, MA: Harvard University Press, 1992). Also Stow,

"Conversion, Apostasy, and Apprehensiveness: Emicho of Flonheim and the Fear of Jews in the Twelfth Century," *Speculum* 76 (2001): 911–33.

49. On the myth of deicide see Jeremy Cohen, *Christ Killers: The Jews and the Passion from the Bible to the Big Screen* (Oxford: Oxford University Press, 2007), 73–102, for the theological implications and the history of this myth. For a discussion on Christian religious art see 185–209, and for the role of Jews as Christ-killers in the passion plays, see 211–29. For a slightly different view see Sara Lipton, *Dark Mirror: The Medieval Origins of Anti-Jewish Iconography* (New York: Metropolitan Books, 2014), 1–11. On the impact of the myth of ritual murder, see Israel J. Yuval, *Two Nations in Your Womb: Perceptions of Jews and Christians in Late Antiquity and the Middle Ages*, trans. Barbara Harshav and Jonathan Chipman (Berkeley: University of California Press, 2006), 159–204; Robert Chazan, *From Anti-Judaism to Anti-Semitism: Ancient and Medieval Christian Constructions of Jewish History* (Cambridge: Cambridge University Press, 2016), 109–35.

50. Edward Peters, *The First Crusade: The Chronicle of Fulcher of Chartres and Other Source Materials* (Philadelphia: University of Pennsylvania Press, 1971), 129.

51. Within the Christian theological framework, the Jewish arch-villain Judas Iscariot was accused of the third crime in the unholy trinity of deicide, homicide, and suicide. On Judas's suicide see Alexander Murray, *Suicide in the Middle Ages, vol. 2, The Curse on Self-Murder* (Oxford University Press: Oxford 2000), 323–64.

52. Jeremy R. Cohen, *Christ Killers*, 103–9. See Yuval, *Two Nations in Your Womb*, 205–56.

53. On the blood libel see Gavin Langmuir, *History, Religion, and Antisemitism* (Berkeley: University of California Press, 1990). See also Yuval, *Two Nations in Your Womb*, 135–256. On later accusations of Jewish sacrilege tied to these allegations, see Magda Teter, *Sinners on Trial: Jews and Sacrilege after the Reformation* (Cambridge, MA: Harvard University Press, 2011).

54. On Jewish moneylending in medieval Europe see Robert Bonfil, *The Book of Moneylender and Borrower* [in Hebrew] (Jerusalem: Shazar Publishing, 2015), 44–94. On the ingrained hatred toward moneylenders in western Europe, see Rowan William Dorin, "Banishing Usury: The Expulsion of Foreign Moneylenders in Medieval Europe, 1200–1450," (PhD diss., Harvard University, 2015).

55. Jeremy R. Cohen, *The Fraiers and the Jews: The Evolution of Medieval Anti-Judaism* (Ithaca, NY: Cornell University Press, 1984), 226–41.
56. Examples of *maskilim* mocking Hasidim can be found in Jonatan Meir, *Imagined Hasidism: The Anti-Hasidic Writings of Joseph Perl* [in Hebrew] (Jerusalem: Mossad Bialik, 2013).
57. On this manuscript, Montefiore 98, see Ephraim Shoham-Steiner, "Making a Living in Early Medieval Ashkenaz" in *Jüdische Kultur in dem SchUM Städten: Literatur—Musik—Theater*, ed. Karl E. Grözinger, Judische Kultur: Studien zur Geistesgeschichte, Religion und Literatur, vol. 26 (Wiesbaden: Harrassowitz Verlag, 2014), 64–82, esp. n9.
58. Avraham Grossman, who noticed its absence from the nineteenth-century collection, salvaged it from oblivion and found it to be a fine illustration of the main argument of an article he published in 1975, discussing the rabbinic sanctioning of early Ashkenazi communal regulations like the laws of *ma'arufia*. See Grossman, "Attitude of the Early Scholars," 175–199. However, even Grossman chose to print the responsum in an appendix, without discussing it in the body of his article.
59. On this see Chaim Rabin, "Jewish Secret Languages," in *Encyclopedia of Modern Jewish Culture*, ed. Glenda Abramson (New York: Routledge, 2005), 1:496; Gilman Sander, *Jewish Self-Hatred: Anti-Semitism and the Hidden Language of the Jews* (Baltimore: Johns Hopkins University Press, 1986), 22–67.
60. This Zionist worldview and the historical narrative that it implied have been discussed recently by David Myers and Amnon Raz-Krakotzkin. See David N. Myers, "History as Ideology: The Case of Ben Zion Dinur, Zionist Historian 'Par Excellence,'" *Modern Judaism* 7 (1988): 167–94; Myers, "Is There Still a 'Jerusalem School?' Reflections on the State of Jewish Historical Scholarship in Israel," *Jewish History* 23 (2009): 389–406. A. Raz-Krakotzkin, "Geschichte, Nationalismus, Eingedenken," in *Jüdische Geschichtsschreibung heute: Themen, Positionen, Kontroversen: ein Schloss Elmau-Symposium*, ed. M. Brenner and D. Myers (Munich: C. H. Beck, 2002), 181–204.
61. On Jewish Orthodox historiography see Israel Bartal, "True Knowledge and Wisdom: On Orthodox Historiography," *Studies in Contemporary Jewry* 10 (1994): 178–92, and more recently Yoel Finkelman, "Nostalgia, Inspiration, Ambivalence: Eastern Europe, Immigration, and the Construction of Collective Memory in Contemporary American Haredi Historiography," *Jewish History* 23 (2009): 57–82; Nahum Karlinsky, "The

Dawn of Hasidic–Haredi Historiography," *Modern Judaism* 27 (2007): 20–46; Kimmy Kaplan, "Innovating the Past: The Emerging Sphere of the 'Torah-true Historian' in America," *Studies in Contemporary Jewry* 21 (2005): 270–87; K. Kaplan, "'Absolutely Intellectually Honest': A Case-Study of American Jewish Modern Orthodox Historiography," in *Creation and Re-Creation in Jewish Thought: Festschrift in Honor of Joseph Dan on the Occasion of His Seventieth Birthday*, ed. Rachel Elior and Peter Schäfer (Tübingen: Mohr-Siebeck, 2005), 339–61.

62. Irving Howe, *World of Our Fathers: The Journey of the East European Jews to America and the Life They Found and Made* (New York: New York University Press, 2005); Dan Miron, *Image of the Shtetl and Other Studies of Modern Jewish Literary Imagination* (Syracuse, NY: Syracuse University Press, 2000).

63. John G. Bellamy, *Crime and Public Order in Later Medieval England* (London: Routledge & Kegan Paul, 1973).

64. James Buchanan Given, *Society and Homicide in Thirteenth-Century England* (Stanford, CA: Stanford University Press, 1977).

65. As Thomas Green wrote in his review of the book in *Speculum*: "James Given has produced the first systematic book-length treatment of the sociology of medieval English crime." Thomas A. Green, review of *Society and Homicide in Thirteenth-Century England*, by J. B. Given, *Speculum* 54 (1979): 137–40.

66. Barbara A. Hanawalt, *Crime and Conflict in Medieval Europe 1300–1348* (Cambridge, MA: Harvard University Press, 1979). See Bellamy, *Crime and Public Order*.

67. Andrew McCall, *Medieval Underworld*. On Gurr's theory see Ted R. Gurr, "Historical Trends in Violent Crime: A Critical Review of the Evidence," *Crime and Justice: An Annual Review of Research* 3 (1981): 295–360.

68. Norbert Elias, *The Civilizing Process*, 2 vols. trans. Edmund Jephcott (Oxford: Oxford University Press, 1978).

69. Manuel Eisner, "Modernization Self-Control and Lethal Violence: The Long-term Dynamics of European Homicide Rates in Theoretical Perspective," *British Journal of Criminology* 41 (2001): 618–38, and later, Eisner, "Long-Term Historical Trends in Violent Crime," *Crime and Justice* 30 (2003): 83–142. For a discussion of the early medieval period see also Guy Halsall, ed., *Violence and Society in the Early Medieval West* (Woodbridge, UK: Boydell Press, 1998).

70. Spierenburg, *History of Murder*.

71. Xavier Rousseaux, "Crime, Justice and Society in Medieval and Early Modern Times: Thirty Years of Crime and Criminal Justice History," *Crime History and Societies* 1 (1997): 87–118.
72. Dean, *Crime in Medieval Europe*.
73. Avraham Grossman, "Offenders and Violent Men in Jewish Society in Early Ashkenaz and their Influence upon Legal Procedure" [in Hebrew], *Shenaton Ha'Mishpat Ha'Ivri* (Annual of the Institute for Research in Jewish Law) 8 (1981): 135–52.
74. Ilana Luria, "Informers and Mafiosi: Violent Factionalism and Fear in the Jewish Communities of Fourteenth-Century Valencia" [in Hebrew], *Zmanim: A Historical Quarterly* 29 (1988): 48–55.
75. Yom Tov Assis, "Crime and Violence among the Jews of Spain (13th–14th Centuries)" [in Hebrew], *Zion* 50 (1985): 221–40; Assis, *The Golden Age of Argonese Jewry: Community and Society in the Crown of Aragon 1213–1327* (London: Littman Library of Jewish Civilization, 1997), 288–96.
76. Esther Cohen, "Jewish Criminals in Late Fourteenth-Century France" [in Hebrew], *Zion* 46 (1981): 146–54.
77. Shlomo Simonson, "Jewish Vagabonds in Medieval European Communities" [in Hebrew], *Ha'uma* 2 (1963): 103–7.
78. Israel J. Yuval, "Hospices and their Guests in Jewish Medieval Germany," *Proceedings of the World Congress of Jewish Studies*, division B, vol. 1 (1989), 125–29; Yaakov Guggenheim, "Social Stratification of Central European Jewry at the End of the Middle Ages: The Poor," *Proceedings of the World Congress of Jewish Studies*, division B, vol. 1 (1989), 130–36; Guggenheim "Von den Schalantjuden zu den Betteljuden: Jüdische Armut in Mitteleuropa in der Frühen Neuzeit," in *Juden und Armut in Mittel- und Osteuropa*, ed. Stefi Jersch-Wenzel (Cologne: Böhlau, 2000), 55–69.
79. Zefira Entin-Rokeah, "Crime and Jews in Late 13th-Century England: Some Cases and Comments," *Hebrew Union College Annual* 55 (1984): 95–137.
80. Entin-Rokeah, "The Jewish Church Robbers and Host Desecrators of Norwich (ca.1285)," *Revue des Etudes Juives* 141 (1982): 331–62.
81. See note 6 in the introduction.
82. Müller, "Eine Jüdische Diebesbande," 71–116.
83. Guy Geltner, *The Medieval Prison: A Social History* (Princeton: Princeton University Press, 2014).

84. The members of the Daroca community were probably also aware of the shortcomings of their communal detention. On the idea of the banishment and marginalization of unwanted individuals, see Bronislav Geremek, "The Marginal Man," in, *The Medieval World*, ed. Jacques Le-Goff, trans. Lydia G. Cochrane (London: Collins & Brown, 1990), 347–72. On the case from Daroca see Yom Tov ben Avraham Ishbili (Ritva), *Responsa* [in Hebrew], ed. Joseph Kapah (Jerusalem: Mosad Harav Kook, 1978), §158. On this case, see Assis, "Crime and Violence among the Jews of Spain." This incident received only a very short citation in Assis's book, *Golden Age of Aragonese Jewry*, 200, 218, 289.

1. "THE THIEVES THAT GO FROM HOUSE TO HOUSE"

1. MS Bibliothèque Nationale de France, Hebr. 1122 fol. 4 verso.
2. The website of the National Archives (formerly the PRO) in London offers statistics on crimes committed in eight English counties over almost fifty years (approximately the average life span) between 1300 and 1348: theft, 73.5 percent of all offenses; murder, 18.2 percent; receiving stolen goods, 6.2 percent; arson, counterfeiting coins, rape, treason, and all others, 2.1 percent. See "Were the Middle Ages Lawless and Violent?" The National Archives [UK], accessed Jan. 4, 2011, http://www.nationalarchives.gov.uk/education/candp/crime/g01/default.htm, accessed Jan. 4, 2011.
3. See the discussion of Sehok ben Astar in chapter 2.
4. William Chester Jordan, *From England to France: Felony and Exile in the High Middle Ages* (Princeton: Princeton University Press, 2015), 16n47.
5. James Brodman, *Charity and Welfare: Hospitals for the Poor in Medieval Catalonia* (Philadelphia: University of Pennsylvania Press, 1998), 85. On poverty in medieval Europe see Michel Mollat's classic, *The Poor in the Middle Ages*. See also Jütte, *Poverty and Deviance*, 21–44; Gerhard Jaritz, ed., *The Sign Language of Poverty*, Forschungen des Instituts für Realienkunde des Mittelalters und der frühen Neuzeit: Diskussionen und Materialien 8 (Vienna: Verlag der Österreichischen Akademie der Wissenschaften, 2007).
6. On the marketplace as a scene of crime and of punishment see J. Masschaele, "The Public Space of the Marketplace in Medieval England," *Speculum* 77 (2002): 383–421.

7. Peter Johanek, "Merchants, Markets and Towns," in *The New Cambridge Medieval History*, ed. T. Reuter (Cambridge: Cambridge University Press, 1999), 3:70, Cambridge Histories Online, accessed Apr. 5, 2011 DOI:10.1017/CHOL9780521364478.004. The maxim "*mercatores, id est Judei et ceteri mercatores*" can be found in Julius Aronius, ed., *Regesten zur Geschichte der Juden im im Fränkischen und Deutschen Reiche bis zum Jahre 1273*, in Auftrage der Historischen Commission für Geschichte der Juden in Deutschland (Berlin: Verlag von Leonhard Simion, 1902), 52–53 §122. These Jews highly valued the ability to procure a legal arrangement enabling them to avoid tolls and customs, as can be seen from the *Memorbuch* of Worms. The book's third entry, commemorating the people who performed good works for the community, refers to a Jewish couple, Isaac and Bella, who "managed to abrogate the customs at Koblentz." See Avraham Berliner, "ha' Memorbuch shel Quehilta Wormisa" [in Hebrew], *Kovtz al Yad* 3 (1886): 5.
8. M. Doberl, ed., *Monumenta Germaniae selecta ab anno 768 usque ad annum 1250*, in *Selected Historical Documents of the Middle Ages*, trans. and ed. E. F. Henderson (London: George Bell and Sons, 1896).
9. M. Parisse, "Lotharingia," in *The New Cambridge Medieval History*, vol. 3 c.900-c.1024 (Cambridge: Cambridge University Press, 1999), Cambridge Histories Online, accessed Apr. 5, 2011, DOI:10.1017/CHOL 9780521364478.013.
10. A clear distinction needs to be made between northwestern Europe and the Iberian Peninsula, due to the different nature of the dominant religion, forms of political tradition and government, and the language and culture that are the backdrop to the primary source material. During this period, and until the first real advances of the Spanish Reconquista, Iberia was under Muslim rule, with a very different legal and cultural tradition from northwestern Europe. It is in the Rhineland that many of the ground rules governing Ashkenazi life were laid down and communal arrangements formulated, making it a highly significant era in Jewish history. I have made similar distinctions in my analysis of related but somewhat different matters in my *On the Margins of a Minority*, 6–10.
11. For a recent discussion of the traditional view of the beginnings of Jewish life north of the Alps see A. Haverkamp, "Beginning of the Jewish Life North of the Alps"; Heil, "'Getting Them In or Keeping Them Out'?"

12. See Ivan G. Marcus, "A Jewish Christian Symbiosis: The Culture of Early Ashkenaz," in *Cultures of the Jews: A New History*, ed. David R. Biale (New York: Schocken Books, 2002), 449–518.
13. This claim, critiqued by Robert S. Lopez and others, generally overlooked, if not actually disregarding for apologetic reasons, early Jewish involvement in what may be labeled as criminal activity. Robert S. Lopez, review of *Urban Civilization in Pre-Crusade Europe: A Study of Organized Town Life in North–Western Europe during the Tenth and Eleventh Centuries, Based on Responsa Literature*, by Irvin A. Agus, *Speculum* 42 (1967): 340–43.
14. Michael Toch, *Economic History of European Jews*, 87–97.
15. Michael Toch mentions this case in passing in his *Economic History of European Jews*, 97. He uses it to highlight the fact that Jews used the ma'arufiah system of clients not only with the rich and able but also with the poor.
16. The Hebrew text was published as part of the appendix to an article by Avraham Grossman over five decades ago. Avraham Grossman, "The Attitude of the Early Scholars of Ashkenaz towards the Authority of the 'Kahal'" [in Hebrew], *Shenaton Ha'Mishpat Ha'Ivri* [Annual of the Institute for Research in Jewish Law] 2 (1975): 175–99. The article dealt with the reactions of the early Ashkenazi sages (among them Rabbi Gershom) to the rule of the *kahal* (the Jewish communal organization composed of the affluent and economically able lay male elite). Grossman noted that this specific responsum is part of a large collection found in MS Montifiore 98 that served as the basis for the collection of responsa by the sages of France and Lorraine (*Teshuvot Chachmei Zarfat ve' Lotair, Wien 1881*) published by Joel Müller, a member of the Wissenschaft des Judentums school. The manuscript itself was for many years kept in London Jews' College Montefiore Library collection, until it was put on auction and sold to a private collector, a Mr. Feinberg, in 2004. In his book, *The Early Sages of Ashkenaz*, Grossman discusses the merits of this specific manuscript. The fourteenth-century Ashkenazi scribe seems to have been very meticulous. Unlike many of his contemporaries, he did not omit the questions in the manuscript and codices he was copying from, but rather preserved them, even if they digressed at length. Some of the collections of responsa he was copying from were edited during the lives of their eleventh-century authors themselves, making this manuscript collection highly trustworthy and accurate.

17. On the laws of *ma'arufiah* see Shlomo Eidelberg, "'Maarufia' in Rabbenu Gershom's Responsa," *Historia Judaica* 15 (1953): 59–66. Avraham Grossman dealt with the text because the *ma'arufiah* regulations were a halakhic innovation of the Ashkenazi community and thus served as a test case for how rabbinic authority related to these regulations.
18. For the most recent discussion of the term *ma'arufiah*, its origin, development, and meaning, see Richard Steiner, "Linguistic Traces of Jewish Traders from Islamic Lands in the Frankish Kingdom" [in Hebrew], *Leshonenu* 73 (2011): 347–70.
19. For more information on this see Irving A. Agus, *Urban Civilization in Pre-Crusade Europe: A Study of Organized Town-Life in Northwestern Europe during the Tenth and Eleventh Centuries, Based on the Responsa Literature* (New York: Yeshiva University Press, 1965), 2:205.
20. There is no certainty as to whether the lower court was a rabbinic court that had adjudicated the suit according to talmudic law. It could well have been a court of the plaintiff's peers. All that is known for certain is that the suit then came before Rabbi Gershom, a halakhic scholar, so that he could rule on the question of who "owned" the partnership. The suit may have been referred by the original court itself. It could be that one of the parties involved was not happy with the first ruling and that the court, seeking to satisfy all parties, hoped that Rabbi Gershom's ruling would be seen as definitive.
21. In this specific case, the Jews and the Gentile thieves are not said to have eaten together but, according to the responsum, offering food and drink was customary upon the successful conclusion of a business deal—a convention it mentions several times. Apparently, it was important enough that it could not have been skipped even if one of the business partners was absent.
22. The exact nature of the business is not disclosed in the text, but presumably, if he was not an owner of vines himself (quite possible in this period in the Rhineland region), Reuven may have been in the business of supplying credit to viticulture, discussed at length in Haym Soloveitchik, *Wine in Ashkenaz in the Middle Ages: Yeyn Nesekh, A Study in the History of Halakhah* [in Hebrew] (Jerusalem: Shazar Press, 2008). Other possibilities may be that he supplied food and drink to the harvesters or that he was responsible for examining the crop so as to ascertain the quality of the harvest and thus estimate the revenue from the wine it

would yield. We also know that, during the grape harvest, town Jews relocated to wine-growing areas near the towns to oversee and participate in the process of producing the wine, to ensure that wine intended for Jewish consumption was produced in accordance with *halakhah*. See Adiel Schremer, "History, Halakhah, and Religious Identity in the Halakhic Discourse of Rabbinic Sages in Medieval Ashkenaz" [in Hebrew], *Zion* 81 (2016): 31–66.

23. The thieves apparently reported, on the basis of their reconnaissance, that the goods they were after were locked in a cupboard, or more likely a chest, that could be breached only with special tools.
24. As late as the mid-twelfth century, the Assize of Clarendon (1166) in England stipulated that thieves and robbers who were apprehended were put to the trial of water. See David C. Douglas, ed., *English Historical Documents* (London: Oxford University Press, 1981), 2:441–44. On Jews and trial by ordeal see Elisheva Baumgarten, "Seeking Signs?," 205–25, esp. n. 2 and 3, with references to the seminal studies by Peter Brown, Robert Bartlett, and Paul Hyams.
25. Shlomo Eidelberg, *The Responsa of Rabbenu Gershom Me-Or ha'Golah* [in Hebrew] (New York: Yeshiva University Press, 1955), 154–58 §67. See also Eidelberg, "Trial by Ordeal in Medieval Jewish History."
26. Esther Benbassa, *The Jews of France: A History from Antiquity to the Present*, trans. M. B. DeBevoise (Princeton: Princeton University Press, 1999), 3–12.
27. See Eidelberg, "Trial by Ordeal," 112n109, and also Kisch, *Jews in Medieval Germany*, 138–39.
28. The Jewish sources also express constant distrust, on the ground that local authorities did not consistently comply with agreements made with the Jews.
29. See Toch, *Die Juden*, 109–11.
30. The ruling is not Rabbi Gershom's innovation. It is attributed to his predecessor, Rabbi Meshulam b. Kalonymus (c. 950–c. 1010) in *Teshuvot Geonim Kadmonim* §136 and is later quoted and expanded in Rashi's commentary on the Talmud in BT *Kidushin* 59a.
31. On rabbis employing scribes to write their responsa see Aryeh Grabois, "The Use of Letters as Communication Medium among Medieval European Jewish Communities," in *Communication in the Jewish Diaspora: The Pre-Modern World*, ed. Sophia Menache (Leiden: Brill, 1996), 93–105, esp. 102–5.

32. On this see Avraham Grossman, "Social Structure and Intellectual Creativity in Medieval Jewish Communities (Eighth to Twelfth Centuries)," in *Studies in Medieval Jewish History and Literature*, ed. Isadore Twersky and Jay M. Harris (Cambridge, MA: Harvard University Press, 2000), 3:1–20.

33. "Until the time came when the king of France, accompanied by his troops and some troops from Burgundy who came to his aid, had laid siege to a certain walled city [or castle] not too far from this man's hometown, about a half day's walk away." This vague bit of information in the responsum is actually an important clue for dating the case. It most likely refers to a thirteen-year-long war that broke out after the death of Henry I, Duke of Burgundy, in 1002, between two claimants to his title: his nephew, Robert the Pious, king of France; and his stepson, Otto-William, Count of Burgundy, a vassal of the emperor, whom Henry had adopted and named his heir some time before. If so, the events discussed in the case brought before Rabbi Gershom probably occurred during that war and before Rabbi Gershom's death in 1028. See "Burgundy Duchy, Dukes of Burgundy," Foundation for Medieval Genealogy, updated Nov. 2016, accessed Jan. 26, 2017, chap. 3, Dukes of Burgundy (capet) [956]-1361, 3a. Dukes of Burgundy 956–1031, http://fmg.ac/Projects/MedLands/BURGUNDY.htm#_Toc359691839 version 3.

34. The full text of the responsum in translation can be found in appendix 1.

35. Rabbi Gershom was approached either by the local rabbinic or more likely by lay communal authorities; it is unclear whether the question came from Mainz or elsewhere. It may have been brought by relatives of Reuven's who stood to lose a share of his estate if his wife married Shimon. The original tribunal had received evidence that did not meet the usual standards (there was only one witness, testimony from non-Jews, hearsay, and other forms of circumstantial evidence). They asked Rabbi Gershom to determine whether this evidence could be accepted.

36. Had there been children, they would have been mentioned. According to *halakhah*, the Jewish court assumes guardianship of orphaned children and is supposed to provide for them. The absence of any reference to children is significant.

37. *Huḥzeku*, from the Hebrew *ḥazakah*, the legal Hebrew term for a presumption.

38. This disregards the usual requirement for two eyewitnesses, as mandated by biblical law (Deut. 19:15).
39. With fewer assets to pay taxes from, and with fewer agricultural yields and livestock, villagers (peasants, serfs, freeholders, and sharecroppers) paid their lords less and thus caused the lords indirect loss. The damage to the village infrastructure due to homes, hamlets, fields, and livestock sheds being ransacked or burned down during these raids only added to the cost.
40. On the image of the Jew as moneylender and usurer see Sara Lipton, *Images of Intolerance: The Representation of Jews and Judaism in the Bible Moralisée* (Berkeley: University of California Press, 1999), 31–63. And Lipton, *Dark Mirror*, 132–33, 156–57. On Jewish money lending and its meaning in the eyes of Christians in medieval times, see the recent annotated version by Robert Bonfil of the medieval Jewish work on money lending, interest rates, and credit economy, *Book of Moneylender and Borrower*.
41. On hostage-taking as a means of guaranteeing debt, see Jean-Claude Schmitt, *The Conversion of Herman the Jew: Autobiography, History, and Fiction in the Twelfth Century*, trans. Alex J. Novikoff (Philadephia: University of Pennsylvania Press, 2010), 204–6. In this instance the Jew (Judah/Herman) who provided the loan and didn't ask for an object as pledge was forced by his kin to accompany the debtor as a "debt reminder." The reverse, a twelfth-century Jew taking a bishop and an imperial counselor hostage for a debt, would have been inconceivable. See also Adam Kosto, *Hostages in the Middle Ages* (Oxford: Oxford University Press, 2012), 2–78.
42. On this period and the role of castles in it see Patrick J. Geary and Heinerich Fichtenau, *Living in the Tenth Century: Mentalities and Social Orders* (Chicago: University of Chicago Press, 1993), 350–60. In many ways a text like the responsum analyzed here complements the historical narrative of Geary and Fichtenau.
43. The responsum is from an edition called *Teshuvot Geonim Kadmonim*, ed. David Kassel (Berlin, 1848), §93. The nineteenth century *Wissenschaft des Judentums* editor of this collection, David Kassel, and Shlomo Rappaport (Shi"r), who studied the manuscript before him, thought that the medieval compiler was Rabbi Joseph Bonfils (Rabbi Joseph Tuv 'Elem), whom they identified as a rabbinic scholar of the twelfth century in northern France. They assumed that the material compiled

by Rabbi Joseph Tuv 'Elem was Gaonic, namely first-millennium Babylonian material that he had access to. They were correct about the access—Rabbi Joseph Bonfils indeed had access to a considerable amount of Babylonian material. Nevertheless, the text discussed here is neither his own halakhic ruling, nor is it Babylonian. Basing himself on the work of Avraham Epstein, Avraham Grossman showed that the world depicted in this responsum, and certain locutions, such as "So I have been instructed from the heavens," indicate that it is an Ashkenazi text from the late tenth and early eleventh century. While it is not signed, it is most likely from the pen of Rabbi Gershom ben Judah. See Grossman, *Early Sages of France*, 74. Grossman prefers Epstein's Ashkenazi reading of these texts. On the ties between Rabbi Joseph Bonfils and Babylonia see Avraham Grossman, "Communication among Jewish Centers during the Tenth to the Twelfth Centuries," in *Communications in the Jewish Diaspora: The Pre-Modern World*, ed. Sophia Menache (Leiden: Brill, 1996), 107–39, esp. 122–24.

44. The full text of the responsum in translation can be found in appendix 2.
45. Recourse to Jewish networks in times of stress and need can be seen in many of the cases discussed in this book, for example the incident of Sehok in chapter 2.
46. On this phrase as a staple of Rabbi Gershom's responsa and its meaning in these early times in Ashkenaz see Grossman, *Early Sages of Ashkenaz*, 153–54. See also Israel M. Ta-Shma, "Ashkenazi Jewry in the Eleventh Century," in *Creativity and Tradition: Studies in Medieval Rabbinic Scholarship, Literature and Thought*, ed. Israel M. Ta-Shma (Cambridge, MA: Harvard University Press), 1–36; Talya Fishman, *Becoming the People of the Talmud: Oral Torah as Written Tradition in Medieval Jewish Cultures* (Philadelphia: University of Pennsylvania Press, 2011), 120–40.
47. S. Eidelberg, ed., *Responsa of Rabbi Gershom Ben Judah Meor Hagola*, 154 §67. For a full list of quotes of this responsum see Mordechai b. Hillel Hacohen, *Sefer Mordechai Ha'Shaloem: Tractate Baba Kama*, ed. A. Halperin (Jerusalem: Machon Yerushalayim, 1992), 201–2 §163. A translation of this responsum can be found in Agus, *Urban Civilization*, 1:70–73. Eidelberg maintains that the barge sank near Mainz, on the basis of a reference in the text to a supercommunal assembly that sanctioned the ban discussed in the responsum. In later centuries, such supercommunal gatherings were indeed held at times in Mainz, but there is no evidence of such a gathering at this time. There is,

however, documentation of such meetings in the eleventh century in Cologne, usually during the large commercial fairs. On the supercommunal gatherings in Cologne in conjunction with its trade fairs see Eva Haverkamp, *Hebräische Berichte über die Judenverfolgungen während des Ersten Kreuzzugs*, Monumenta Germaniae Historica, Hebräische Texte aus dem mittelalterlichen Deutschland (Hannover: Hahnsche Buchhandlung, 2005), 1:573. For a translation of this text into English see Shlomo Eiedelberg, trans. and ed., *The Jews and the Crusaders: The Hebrew Chronicles of the First and Second Crusades* (Madison: University of Wisconsin Press, 1977), 49–59. On the travel options in these early times see Kenneth Stow, "By Land or by Sea: The Passage of the Kalonymides into the Rhineland in the Tenth Century," in *Communication in the Diaspora: The Pre-Modern World*, ed. Sophia Menache (Leiden: Brill, 1996), 59–73. Ephraim Shoham-Steiner, "Lions and Serpents, Rabbis and Parnasim: A Clash over Synagogue Decorations in Medieval Cologne," *Jewish History* 31 (2017): 129–64. In light of the above, I suggest that the events took place in the lower Rhine area near Cologne, probably no further south than Koblenz.
48. On the word *yohar* for precious stones in these early texts see Haggai Ben-Shammai, "Yohar: The Transformations of a Middle-Persian Word in Judaeo-Arabic and in Medieval Hebrew" [in Hebrew], *Tarbitz* 81 (2012): 397–408.
49. Gershom ben Judah of Mainz, *Responsa of Rabbenu Gershom Meor Hagolah*, 154–58 §67.
50. BT *Baba Metziah* 24a.
51. On cases where the eleventh-century Jews of northern France undermined a communal ban because they thought the communal authorities had conflicts of interest and biases, see the famous responsum by Rabbi Eliezer ben Isaac (Hagadol) of Mainz and Rabbi Judah ben Meir Hacohen of Mainz to the Troyes community: *Sefer Kolbo* [in Hebrew], ed. Avraham David (Jerusalem: Feldheim 1990–2009), 8:71–88 §142. See also the discussion by Avraham Grossman, *Early Sages of Ashkenaz*, 189–95.
52. I am grateful to my friend Simcha Emanuel for calling this source and its variants to my attention.
53. The Hebrew words *dinim* (rulings or judgments) and *dayanim* (jurists or judges) may be spelled the same, דינים, but are pronounced differently. *Sefer ha-Dinim* itself no longer exists, like many other books lost in

transition and in transmission during the Middle Ages. Later, with the invention of the printing press, many manuscripts that had previously been copied and thus preserved were not printed, and thus fell into obscurity and, finally, into oblivion. See Simcha Emanuel, *Fragments of the Tablets: Lost Books of the Tosaphists* [in Hebrew] (Jerusalem: Magnes Press, 2006). Extracts from *Sefer ha-Dinim* from the manuscripts that became the source for the Prague edition of Rabbi Meir of Rothenburg's responsa collection were published in a facsimile edition: Yehudah Hacohen, *Sefer Hadinim: Teshuvotav melokatot mimkorot shonim*, ed. Avraham. Grossman (Jerusalem: Dinur Center, 1977). See also Simcha Emanuel, "Sridim hadashim, misefer ha'dinim shel Rabbi Yehudah Hacohen," *Qovetz Al Yad* 20 (5771/2011): 81–103. Rabbi Judah was a largely overlooked medieval European Jewish figure until Avraham Grossman revived interest in him in his groundbreaking book *The Early Sages of Ashkenaz* of 1981. Grossman showed that Rabbi Judah was seen at the time not merely as a local Mainz adjudicator and legal consultant, but as a supercommunal authority. The responsa signed by him or attributed to him show that he was approached time and again by Jews of his own native Mainz, of neighboring Rhineland cities, and even from as far away as Hungary and elsewhere on the outer margins of the medieval central European range of travel and commerce. Indeed, Jews from as far away as the frontier town later known as Przemyśl, at the foot of the Carpathian Mountains in Poland, as well as the Jews of Kiev in the Ukraine, sent questions and matters to be resolved by Rabbi Judah in Mainz, testimony to his fame as an adjudicator. Grossman suggests that Rabbi Judah may have slipped into obscurity because his role as a judge, possibly presiding over the Mainz tribunal, overshadowed his other intellectual activities. See Grossman, *Early Sages of Ashkenaz*, 175–210. On Rabbi Judah's interregional connections see Ta-Shma, "Ashkenazi Jewry in the Eleventh Century," 1–36.
54. Grossman, *Early Sages of Ashkenaz*, 199 n. 107.
55. The text is from the Prague edition of Rabbi Meir of Rothenberg's responsa, §844: Meir b. Baruch of Rothenburg, *Responsa*, ed. Jacob Farbstein (Jerusalem: Machon Yerushalayim, 2014), 1:426–27. The text originates from the Prague collection of Rabbi Meir's responsa based on MS Prague Jewish Museum 20 §205. An abridged version of this discussion appeared in Shoham-Steiner, "Making a Living in Early Medieval Ashkenaz."

56. An English translation of the responsum appears in appendix 3.
57. Both parties most likely spoke in a local language used by Rhineland Jews (a Romance language or Middle High German) but their testimonies and affidavits were set down in Hebrew, the language in which all medieval Jewish legal proceedings were recorded. During the fourteenth century rabbis began to use both Hebrew and Yiddish vernacular in their accounts of the exchanges in rabbinical courts. See, for example, the responsa of the fifteenth-century rabbi Jacob ben Judah Weil (1390–1453), where the Hebrew account of court cases include some sentences in the original Yiddish used by the parties in the court: Jacob b. Judah Weil, *Responsa of Rabbi Jacob Weil* [in Hebrew], ed. Yonatan Shraga Domb (Jerusalem: Machon Yerushalayim, 2001), §147. On the use of vernacular languages among Jews in northern Europe see the recent discussion by Kirsten A. Fudeman, *Vernacular Voices: Language and Identity in Medieval French Jewish Communities* (Philadelphia: University of Pennsylvania Press, 2010).
58. Bloch published his edition of Rabbi Meir's responsa in Budapest in 1895. The manuscript that Bloch used also included earlier material dating to the eleventh-century sage Rabbi Judah ha-Kohen. In preparing the manuscript for publication, Bloch replaced the Hebrew word *galaḥ*, meaning a tonsured Christian cleric (either a monk or a priest) with the Hebrew word *ganav*, thief. The recent reproducers of the original Prague edition followed Bloch's lead, and in their 2014 edition the text reads "*ganav*," obscuring the fact that the manuscript reads "*galaḥ*," priest. The culprit was indeed a thief, but it is significant that he was a Christian cleric.
59. Even at this early period, monasteries and other Christian institutions had close dealings with Jews. Precious metal artifacts, books, and ceremonial clothes were sold to Jewish merchants, or extended as collateral for loans taken from Jews for cash. This matter surfaces in both Jewish and Christian sources. For instance: *Teshuvot Geonei Mizrach U'Ma'arav* §152.
60. The Mainz Cathedral was built under the resourceful Archbishop Willigis of Mainz (940–1011, archbishop from 975). The cathedral suffered extensive damage from a fire on the day of its inauguration in 1009 and was rebuilt under Willigis's successor, Archbishop Bardo. All this construction took place during the lifetime of Rabbi Judah.

61. In a lecture at the "Beyond the Elite" conference at the IIAS in Jerusalem (Feb. 2015), Eva Haverkamp offered a convincing presentation about the strong ties between the Mainz Jewish community and the Disibodenberg monastery. The monastery, a day's walk (52 km., approx. 10 hours) southwest of Mainz, was rebuilt in the late tenth century by Archbishop Willigis.
62. The responsum is difficult to date, but a small detail offers a clue. During the second half of the eleventh century, Archbishop Siegfried I of Mainz (1059–1084) completed building the cathedral that his predecessor had started. He also imposed Pope Gregory VII's rule of celibacy on the archbishopric's clergy, siding with the pope against the emperor. The renegade priest in the case at hand used the money he received from selling the gold to visit a brothel immediately after the transaction, perhaps in reaction to this decree of celibacy. There is a slight inconsistency, as Rabbi Judah seems to have died in or around 1050, while Siegfried ascended his see only in 1059, according to the coinage issued to commemorate his reign. In fact, however, we have no solid death date for Rabbi Judah ha-Kohen. An overlap between the two thus remains possible; the fact that Rabbi Judah is referred to in many contemporary sources as "the elder" (*ha-Zaken*) seems to indicate that he lived to a ripe old age. If indeed born in 975 (a presumption without a solid factual basis), he would have been eighty-five years old in 1060. During Rabbi Judah's lifetime, the Mainz and Erfurt mints issued new coinage signifying almost every new archbishop's reign, five times in total. On Mainz coinage and minting, see the illuminating report found in Künker Auktion 130, *The De Wit Collection of Medieval Coins, 1000 Years of European Coinage*, pt.2: Germany, Switzerland, Austria, Bohemia, Moravia, Hungary, Silesia, Poland, Baltic States, Russia and the golden Horde (Osnabrück: Numismatischer Verlag Künker, 2007), 200–204.
63. This detail further corroborates the hypothesis that the entire story took place in Mainz. Not every city could mint its own coins. In 1084, Bishop Rüdiger Huzmann of Speyer demanded that, in exchange for the generous privilege he granted the Jews, the latter pay the Speyer priory a lump sum every year in *local coin*.
64. Perhaps the lord did not act discreetly and confronted the cleric in a public place with witnesses. Alternatively, word of the robbery

might have spread through the town, prompting officers of the law to investigate.

65. The talmudic word *sardiot*, the title the responsum uses for this investigative official, is a Hebrew/Aramaic corruption of the Greek word στράτιωης, meaning a captain or an official entrusted with law enforcement authority. In the eleventh-century Hebrew of medieval German rabbinic Jews, the word meant what we would today call a police officer or an investigator. On this see Rashi's commentary on BT *Yoma* 11a, where he explains the word *kasdor* in the text (a corruption of the Latin word *quaestor*) as "a name of an official like a *sardiot* and it is an officer [*shoter*]." Rashi was not an immediate contemporary of Rabbi Judah ha-Kohen. He was born in the northern French town of Troyes, but he spent many years studying in the Rhineland talmudic academies of Mainz and Worms in the third quarter of the eleventh century, a short while after Rabbi Judah ha-Kohen's death.

66. A lengthy and interesting discussion on the matter may be found in Rabbi Shlomo Luria's Talmud exegesis *Yam Shel Shlomo* on BT *Baba Kama* 113B.

67. Meir b. Baruch, *Responsa*, 1 §186. Cologne was an important commercial hub, for wool and lambskin in particular, from the eleventh century through the High Middle Ages. On this and on the very intricate ties between Cologne and the English wool market see Joseph P. Huffman, *Family, Commerce, and Religion in London and Cologne: Anglo-German Emigrants (c.1000–c.1300)* (Cambridge: Cambridge University Press, 1998), 9–13.

68. While there is no way to know in which of the towns on the Rhine between Cologne and Mainz the exchange took place, two seem slightly better candidates than others: Bonn, on the banks of the Rhine, which had a Jewish community that was martyred in 1096, and Koblenz, at the confluence of the Mossel and Rhine rivers, about halfway between the two larger cities.

69. The finest silver objects are made from silver of 92.5 percent purity, known today as sterling silver. Silver is usually alloyed with copper to give it strength while preserving the ductility and appearance of the precious metal. The issue in this case was just how much copper had been added. As early as the eleventh century, coins minted by the Norman conquerors in England (after 1066) were made of an amalgam of silver and other metals. The fine 92.5 percent silver known as sterling

appears as early as the twelfth century in northern Germany. The responsum under discussion, dating to the end of the 1050s at the latest (Rabbi Judah died no later than 1060), may be a very early record of local German nobles' or affluent individuals' awareness of the particulars of the silver alloy used to make precious objects.

70. See Robert Chazan, "1007–1012: Initial Crisis for Northern European Jewry," *Proceedings of the American Academy for Jewish Research* 38/39 (1970–71): 101–17.

71. On the origins, purview, and impact of these modes of pacification, Pax Dei (Peace of God) and Treuga Dei (The Truce of God), see R. I. Moore, "The Peace of God and the Social Revolution," in *The Peace of God: Social Violence and Religious Response in France around the Year 1000*, ed. Thomas Head and Richard Landes (Ithaca, NY: Cornell University Press, 1992), 308–26. On the government of the Ottonian Empire in the early eleventh century, see David A. Warner, ed., *Ottonian Germany: The Chronicon of Thietmar of Merseburg*, Manchester Medieval Sources (Manchester, UK: Manchester University Press, 2001).

72. The fact that the renegade cleric was then turned over to other authorities, who interrogated him, is not surprising, as they were probably lay officials working for local ecclesiastical authorities. This suggests that the incident did not take place in Mainz, where the local ruler was the archbishop, an ecclesiastical prince, whose officers had apprehended and interrogated the priest. Another possibility is that the event did take place in Mainz, but that the authorities interrogating the cleric were from the place of his origin.

73. Alexander Patschovsy, "The Relationship between the Jews of Germany and the King (11th–14th Centuries): A European Comparison," in *England and Germany in the High Middle Ages*, ed. Alfred Haverkamp and Hanna Vollrath (Oxford: Oxford University Press, 1996), 193–218, esp. 197–99.

74. The revived study of Roman law in the West is tied traditionally to the recovery of the Digest (c. 1070 CE), after which glossators expounded on the texts and annotated (glossed) them. From the early twelfth century, the study of Roman law was becoming more common and influential. See Kenneth Pennington, "Roman and Secular Law," in *Medieval Latin: An Introduction and Bibliographical Guide*, ed. Frank A. C. Mantello and A. G. Rigg (Washington DC: Catholic University of America Press, 1996), 254–66.

75. On this see Ephraim Shoham-Steiner, "Exile, Immigration and Piety: The Jewish Pietists of Medieval Germany, from the Rhineland to the Danube," *Jewish Studies Quarterly* 24 (2017): 234–60.
76. Marcus, *Piety and Society*, 136–43; Marcus, *Sefer Hasidim and the Ashkenazic Book in Medieval Europe* (Philadelphia: University of Pennsylvania Press, 2018), 37–39.
77. SHW §20.
78. Similar concerns were voiced at this time about Jews who had accepted baptism during the Crusade and had returned to the Jewish faith. See Mordechai b. Hillel Hacohen, *Sefer Ha'Mordechai*, referring to 91B §210–11.
79. SHW §21–22.
80. SHW §23.
81. Princeton University Sefer Hasidim Database (PUSHD), Jewish Theological Seminary manuscript 2499 folio 12 recto.
82. BT *Gittin* 57a.
83. Legal material from medieval Germany found in German medieval law books also corroborates this notion: Guido Kisch, *Jewry Law in Medieval Germany: Laws and Court Decisions Concerning Jews*, Texts and Studies, vol. 3 (New York: American Academy for Jewish Research, 1949), 78.
84. On the history of communal regulations and specifically on the *Shum* regulations, see Menachem Elon, *Jewish Law: History, Sources, Principles* (Jerusalem: Magnes Press, 1988), 1:632–40. Avraham Grossman, "Ashkenazim to 1300," in *An Introduction to the History and the Sources of Jewish Law*, ed. Neil. S. Hecht et al. (Oxford: Oxford University Press, 1996), 299–321.
85. See Barzen, *Taqqanot Qehillot Šum*, N.6.\4 p. 607.
86. On Jewish use of polemical dysphemisms in the Jewish chronicles depicting the events of the First Crusade (1096), see Anna Sapir-Abulafia, *Christian-Jewish Relations 1000–1300: Jews in the Service of Medieval Christendom* (London: Routledge, 2014), 135–66, esp. 143–46.
87. The use of dysphemisms in reference to Christians, their cultic objects, and their clergy was common in medieval Hebrew. The use of dysphemism is of course not unique to Jews. On this phenomenon in early Christianity see Jeremy F. Hultin, *The Ethics of Obscene Speech in Early Christianity and Its Environment* (Leiden: Brill, 2008).
88. For a brief biography of Rabbi Elia, see Aleida Paudice, "Elia Capsali," Historians of the Ottoman Empire (University of Chicago), accessed

July 5, 2017, https://ottomanhistorians.uchicago.edu/en/historian/elia-capsali.

89. The entire verse referred to here is pertinent: "The remnant of Israel shall do no wrong, and speak no falsehood, a deceitful tongue shall not be in their mouths; only such as these shall graze and lie down, with none to trouble them." On the meaning of taking oaths in medieval society, see Robert Fossier, *The Axe and the Oath: Ordinary Life in the Middle Ages*, trans. Lydia G. Cochrane (Princeton, NJ: Princeton University Press, 2010). See also Ephraim Shoham-Steiner, "'And in Most of Their Business Transactions They Rely on This': Some Reflections on Jews and Oaths in the Commercial Arena of Medieval Europe," in *On the Word of a Jew: Religion, Reliability, and the Dynamics of Trust*, ed. Michael B. Hart and Nina Caputo (Bloomington: Indiana University Press, 2018), 36–61, and the bibliography there.

90. Elias S. Artum and Humbertus M. D. Cassuto, eds., *Statuta Iudaeorum Candiae Eorumque Memorabilia* [in Hebrew] (Jerusalem: Mekize Nirdamin, 1940), 4.

91. Haim Eliezer b. Isaac Or Zaruaʿ, *Teshuvot Maharakh Or Zaruaʿ (Responsa) ve'Piskei Halakhot* (Sermons and Adjudications) [in Hebrew], ed. Menachem Avitan (Jerusalem: 2002), 250 §260.

92. On non-Jewish household servants see Carmel Muskin, "Gentile Slaves and Servants in Medieval Ashkenaz" [in Hebrew], *Tura: Studies in Jewish Thought* 1 (1989): 235–45.

93. On slavery in medieval Europe and its Mediterranean outposts see William D. Phillips, *Slavery from Roman Times to the Early Transatlantic Trade* (Minneapolis: University of Minnesota Press, 1985); Reuven Amitai and Christoph Cluse, eds., *Slavery and the Slave Trade in the Eastern Mediterranean (c. 1000–1500 CE)* (Turnhout: Brepols, 2017). Michael Toch has recently offered a forceful refutation of the hoary claim that the medieval slave trade was dominated by Jews. According to Toch, "One commodity habitually mentioned by scholars—slaves—should be struck from the list. German and French Jews and indeed other European ones did not practice the slave trade to a significant degree and they certainly did not dominate it." See his *Economic History of European Jews*, 94, 178–90.

94. See Yacov Guggenheim, "Meeting on the Road: Encounters between German Jews and Christians on the Margins of Society," in *In and Out of the Ghetto: Jewish-Gentile Relations in Late Medieval and Early Modern*

Germany, ed. Ronnie Po-chia Hsia and Hartmut Lehmann (Cambridge Cambridge University Press, 1995), 125–36; Frank Rexroth, *Deviance and Power in Late Medieval London*, trans. Pamela E. Selwyn (Cambridge: Cambridge University Press, 2007), 1–24.

95. On Judah the Pious's perspective on this subject, see Peter Schäfer, "Jews and Christians in the High Middle Ages: The *Book of the Pious*," in *The Jews in Europe in the Middle Ages (Tenth to Fifteenth Centuries): Proceedings of the International Symposium Held at Speyer 20–25 October 2002*, ed. Christoph Cluse (Turnhout: Brepols, 2004), 29–42. Minimizing contact with gentiles was also a staple of extreme piety among Jews of later periods as well. Rabbi Shalom of Neustadt, who lived in Austria in the mid-fourteenth century, tells of one Rabbi Moshel, a member of the Neustadt Pietists (*ha-ḥasidim min Neustadt*) who made a practice of wiping the doorknobs touched by his non-Jewish servants.

96. Eli Yassif, *The Hebrew Folktale: History, Genre, Meaning*, trans. Jacqueline S. Teitelbaum (Bloomington: Indiana University Press, 1999), 297–320.

97. Either other members of the household or of the Jewish community.

98. SHW 67 §159.

99. SHW §1428.

100. "It is better at times to distance one member of the group for the benefit of other members, as it is written [in scripture]: 'Expel the scoffer and contention departs, [quarrel and contumely cease]' (Prov. 22:10), and this is so with regard to male and female slaves as well. Even if they do not steal and they do not vex anyone else within the household, it is better that way. For they [those hurt by the problematic slave] will seek to take revenge on him who could have reprimanded but refrained from doing so or could have banished the slave but did not" (*Sefer Hasidim: Judah ben Shmuel he-ḥassid*, ed. Reuven Margalioth [Jerusalem: Mosad Harav Kook, 1957], §189).

101. SHW §1730.

102. On aging in the Middle Ages, see Shulamith Shahar, *Growing Old in the Middle Ages: "Winter Clothes Us in Shadow and Pain"* (New York: Routledge, 2004), 36–98.

103. Within the literary system of Ashkenazi Pietistism, the *ḥakham* (sage) is not the same as a rabbi. On the difference between the two and the pietistic nature of the counsel provided by the *ḥakham*, see Irving A. Agus, "The Use of the Term Hakham by the Author of the Sefer Hassidim

and Its Historical Implications," *JQR* 61 (1970): 54–62; Marcus, *Piety and Society*, 72–74.

104. This account was published from MS Oxford Bodli. 1567 fol. 49v. The manuscript is a mystical tractate by the medieval German pietists. The full Hebrew text can be found in Joseph Dan, "Demonological Stories in the Writings of Rabbi Judah Hehasid," *Tarbitz* 30 (1961): 273–89, esp. 274.
105. On Jews visiting and praying at the graves of meritorious dead, see Elliott Horowitz, "Speaking to the Dead: Cemetery Prayer in Medieval and Early Modern Jewry," *Journal of Jewish Thought and Philosophy* 8 (1999): 303–17. Ephraim Shoham-Steiner, "'For a Prayer in That Place Would Be Most Welcome': Jews, Holy Shrines and Miracles—A New Approach," *Viator* 37 (2006): 369–95.
106. Eli Yassif, *Ninety-Nine Tales: The Jerusalem Manuscript Cycle of Legends in Medieval Jewish Folklore* [in Hebrew] (Tel Aviv: Tel Aviv University Press, 2013), 253–55. Other stories about Rabbi Judah's mystical powers appear on 176 and 193–97.
107. Josef Bamberger, "The Praise of the Ashkenazi Pietists: Outline of the Jewish Hagiography in Ashkenaz in the Middle Ages," (PhD diss., Bar-Ilan University, 2005), 207–12.
108. During the time the story took its current form, the local duke in the Regensburg area of Bavaria was the Duke of Bavaria Landshut. I suggest that the story reflects a political rivalry between the city council's patrician families and the duke during the decade of the duke's reign in Regensburg (1486–96). If so, the duke in question is Duke George the Rich (Georg der Reich) von Wittelsbach of Bavaria Landshut.
109. Yassif, *Ninety-Nine Tales*, 253–55 §85.
110. The duke's court was not in town. According to the story, the rabbi had to ride there. If the story indeed originated in the late fifteenth century, the court of the duke would have been Trausnitz, the Wittelsbach family castle, overlooking the town of Landshut.
111. Both these men were contemporaries of Rabbi Judah the Pious, of the late twelfth century. The reference to them is probably an internal literary device interpolated into the story to enhance its credibility as a true account from the time of Rabbi Judah. See Shoham-Steiner, "Exile, Immigration and Piety."
112. Rabbi Judah hailed from the Kalonymide family, renowned among German Jewry not only as Torah scholars and wonder-workers, but also as

highly skilled diplomats and petitioners on behalf of the Jewish community. Some of the stories in MS Jerusalem center on forebears of Rabbi Judah Hasid who represented Jewish interests to the imperial court. Rabbi Judah himself is mentioned in a story as interceding on behalf of the Jews of Regensburg when they were accused of a blood libel. The story (included in Yassif, *Ninety-Nine Tales*, 255–56 §87) portrays Rabbi Judah as an advocate (*melitz*) on behalf of a Jewish defendant in a blood libel accusation when he appeals to the city council and magistrates. There were at least two blood libels in Regensburg in 1474–75 implicating, among others, the city's rabbi, Rabbi Israel Bruna. See Ronnie Po-chia Hsia, *The Myth of Ritual Murder: Jews and Magic in Reformation Germany* (New Haven, CT: Yale University Press, 1988), 67–85.

113. Yassif, *Ninety Nine Tales*, 254–55.
114. Many of the homes in the German towns during the late Middle Ages were of the *fachwerkhaus* type. Built of an amalgam of straw and clay over wooden frames, they were very well insulated against cold weather, but not being built of stone they were not very sturdy, and easily broken into. None of the homes of Regensburg's medieval Jewish quarter have survived; most were razed and demolished in the aftermath of the expulsion of the Jews from the city in 1519. See Raphael Straus, *Regensburg and Augsburg*, trans. Felix E. Gerson, Jewish Communities Series (Philadelphia: Jewish Publication Society of America, 1939), 162.
115. This detail suggests that the writer knew about the town's routine legal procedures at the time he put down the story. Judges were supposed to inquire into rumors of foul play even if none of the parties involved pressed charges.
116. The accusation that the infiltrators were armed explains the severe sentence in the final scene. In some medieval codes of law, if a thief was caught red-handed, but returned the goods and paid a fine, he received a reduced sentence and sometimes his life was spared, in exchange either for a reduced corporal punishment or banishment instead of capital punishment. But an armed robber was almost always given a harsher sentence.
117. A similar agenda can be detected in another story from this cycle, in which the storyteller has Rabbi Judah present an explicit dichotomy: "What do you wish? Proper judgment or violence?" Yassif, *Ninty Nine Tales*, 255.

118. This may allude to the medieval French term *mort main*, upon which the modern legal term *mortmain* is based, meaning ownership of real estate by a corporation or legal institution that can be transferred or sold in perpetuity. The term is usually used in the context of its prohibition. Gideon Bohak of Tel Aviv University called my attention to the use of human and animal body parts in an attempt to extract confessions or secrets from people. For instance, in a case of a woman suspected of adulterous conduct, one recipe suggests placing a toad's tongue on the woman while she is asleep, thus casting a spell which would prompt her to talk (probably in her sleep) about her clandestine whereabouts.

119. I used the microfilmed copy from the Institute of Microfilmed Hebrew Manuscripts in the National Library of Israel (film no. 15066).

120. Other magical recipes appear in Moshe Idel's discussion of the thirteenth-century Jewish mystic Rabbi Nehemia ben Shlomo, the "Prophet of Erfurt." See Moshe Idel, "Rabbi Nehemia ben Shlomo the Prophet on the Star of David and the Name *Taftafia*: From Jewish Magis to Practical and Theoretical Kabbalah," in *Ta-Shma: Studies in Judaica in Memory of Israel M. Ta-Shma*, vol. 1, ed. Avraham (Rami) Reiner et al. (Alon Shevut: Tenuvot Press, 2011), 1–76, esp. 27.

121. The case appears in one of Rabbi Asher's Ashkenazi responsa, written either while he still resided in Cologne or in response to questions sent to him by individuals or tribunals in Germany after his move to Iberia in the early fourteenth century. See Asher b. Yehiel, *Responsa* [in Hebrew], ed. Shlomo Jodlov (Jerusalem: Machon Yerushalayim Press, 1994), 179–80 §43:3. On the responsa of Rabbi Asher see Ephraim Elimelech Urbach, "The Responsa of R. Asher b. Yehiel in Manuscripts and Printed Editions" [in Hebrew], *Shenaton Ha'Mishpat Ha'Ivri (Jewish Law Annual)* 2 (1975): 1–153. For additional information on questions sent to Rabbi Asher from Germany after he had immigrated to Iberia see Shlomo Toledano, "Kovtzi Teshuvot Harosh Bekitvei Yad U'bidfusim" (MA thesis, Hebrew University of Jerusalem, 1995), 103–15. This case will also be discussed in the section on crime and women.

122. Jewish matrimonial law stipulates that both parties to a divorce, husband and wife, must be sane and of sound mind. If one of the parties is mentally ill or otherwise incapable of understanding the legal and sexual implications of the divorce, the procedure is invalid.

123. In another earlier rabbinic responsum, from Bonn in the thirteenth century, Rabbi Eliezer ben Joel Halevi took up the will and testament of a Strasburg Jew forwarded to him by the Jewish tribunal in that city. The man listed among his belongings an "improper book" (*sefer pasul*), meaning a book in Latin, containing Christian religious material (probably a missal or a biblical codex). Most likely, he held it as collateral for a loan. Eliezer b. Joel ha-Levi, *The Book of Ra'avia* [in Hebrew], vol. 3, ed. David Deblitzki (Bnei-Brak, 2005), 364–65 §1005.

124. A book written on velum or parchment could also be sold to scribes or copyists. Due to the relatively high price of such writing materials, processed parchment was highly valued, so scribes scraped the ink off unwanted manuscripts so that the parchment could be reused. On this see Georges Declercq, "Codices Rescripti in the Early Medieval West," in *Early Medieval Palimpsests*, Bibliologia: Elementa Ad Librorum Studia Pertinentia 26, ed. Georges Declercq (Turnhout: Brepols, 2007), 3–22.

125. Thousands of pages of medieval Hebrew books were sold for their material, especially during the later Middle Ages, when large quantities of books were confiscated by Christian religious and lay authorities. These books were either shredded or erased and turned into single palimpsest pages or used as palimpsest codices for writing. Folios were used as binding material for archival documents and dossier files, filling for book covers, and other staples of the parchment and book industry. Collections of these materials, discovered in recent years, are referred to as the "European Genizah." See Simcha Emanuel, "The European Genizah and Its Contribution to Jewish Studies," *Henoch* 19 (1997): 313–40. Note in particular the work of Prof. Mauro Perani of the University of Bologna and Prof. Andreas Lehnardt at the Johannes Gutenberg Universität in Mainz. Both dedicate their research to uncovering these books. A sample of the vast work on the topic can be seen in M. Perani, "The 'Italian Genizah': An Updated Report on Fifteen Years of Research," in *European Association for Jewish Studies Newsletter* 2 (Oct. 1996–Feb. 1997): 15–22. For a digital database of this material see http://www.hebrewmanuscript.com/hebrew-fragments-databases.htm.

126. Yom-Tov ben Avraham Asevilli was born in Seville in 1250 and lived there until his death in 1330. He studied with Rabbi Aharon Halevi of Gerona and with Rabbi Shlomo ben Aderet of Barcelona.

127. Bezalel b. Avraham Ashkenazi, *Shitah Mekubetzet on BT Baba Metziah* (Tel Aviv, 1967), vol. 10 *Baba Metziah*, fol. 24b.
128. The Biran was probably one of a network of irrigation canals to be found in Mesopotamia under Sassanid Persian rule. The channels required constant maintenance. Jews presumably frequented the canals in the areas where they lived.
129. On the importance of colophons in medieval Hebrew codicology see Malachi Beit-Arié, "Hebrew Codicology: Historical and Comparative Typology of Medieval Hebrew Codices based on the Documentation of the Extant Dated Manuscripts until 1540 Using a Quantitative Approach," ed. Zofia Lasman, preprint internet version 0.6 (2017), 91–132, National Library of Israel, accessed August 13, 2017, http://web.nli.org.il/sites/NLI/English/collections/manuscripts/hebrewcodicology/Pages/default.aspx.
130. The responsa of Rabbi Isaac Iben Migash, who lived in Eliossana/Lucena in Andalusia in the early to mid-twelfth century, and those of Moses Maimonides, whose father Rabbi Maimon the Adjudicator (Rabbi Maimon ha-Dayan) was a disciple of Migash's, suggest in their discussions of the sale of such items that used Jewish books may have found their way to the second-hand market after being confiscated by the crown for various reasons. See Bezalel b. Avraham Ashkenazi, *Shitah Mekubetzet on BT Baba Metziah*, fol. 24b. In his discussion on BT *Baba Kama* 114b, the thirteenth-century rabbi Isaac ben Moshe Or Zarua' of Vienna mentions that, in his commentary, Rashi understood the rabbinic ruling "he who sees his books or utensils in the hands of another" to mean that the identification occurs before forfeiture (*ye'ush*). See Isaac b. Moshe, *The Book of Or Zarua'* [in Hebrew], ed. Jacob Farbstein et al. (Jerusalem: Machon Yerushalayim, 2010), 3:149–51 §453–55.
131. The word *yishtak'u*, and other derivations of the Hebrew root *sh-k-'* (to sink), almost always bears a negative connotation in rabbinic literature, appearing usually in the context of the fear of losing someone or something to evil.
132. On this phenomenon see Simcha Emanuel's groundbreaking research: Emanuel, *Fragments of the Tablets*.
133. Isaac b. Moshe, Book of *Or Zarua'*, 3:149–51§453–55.
134. Agus gave the collection the title *Responsa of the Tosaphists*; it is based primarily on the Goldschmit manuscript kept at the Jewish Theological Seminary library in New York. The manuscript is a typical Ashkenazi

composite, and is based on one of the most popular halakhic compendia of the thirteenth century, the *Great Book of Rabbi Mordechai ben Hillel of Nirenberg* [d.1298], with additional responsa material compiled by one of Rabbi Mordechai's students in the early fourteenth century. Rabbi Mordechai's book is an encyclopedia of halakhic material from the eleventh to the thirteenth century.

135. Irving A. Agus, ed., *Responsa of the Tosaphists: Unpublished Responsa Culled from Various Manuscripts* (New York: Talpioth Press Yeshiva University, 1954), 96–97 §33.

136. The reference to "us" in the plural probably refers to the local tribunal in Regensburg, discussed at length by Ephraim E. Urbach in *The Tosafists: Their History, Writings, and Methods* [in Hebrew], 2 vols. (Jerusalem: Mosad Bialik Publishers, 1986), 170–77, and notes there. On this tribunal see Ephraim Kanarfogel, "R. Judah he-Hasid and the Rabbinic Scholars of Regensburg: Interactions, Influences, and Implications," *JQR* 96 (2006): 17–37.

137. The Hebrew term here is *rekim*, meaning "empty." It may refer to either beggars (who are empty of assets) or reprobates who are empty of good deeds and virtues but full of misdeeds and sin. The biblical word *rekim* is frequently paired with *benei bliyal* (evildoers) (2 Chron. 13:7) or *poḥazim* (criminals) (Judg. 9:4). In my opinion, the second sense is most likely in this context. The word clearly had negative connotations in the Middle Ages, as in Rashi's commentary on 2 Chron. 13:7, where he explains *rekim* as *resha'im* (evil men).

138. The quote is attributed simply to Rabbi Ephraim. While the name may refer to a few possible candidates, it seems most likely the turbulent and fiery Rabbi Ephraim ben Isaac of Regensburg (1110–75), an Ashkenazi sage who studied under Rabbi Jacob ben Meir Tam in northern France. Rabbi Ephraim returned to the Rhineland and settled in Speyer, but later, due to a heated debate over religious matters, removed himself to the south German town of Regensburg on the Danube, where he lived until his death. The compiler of the manuscript, probably a student of Rabbi Mordechai ben Hillel (d. 1298), states that he copied the responsum from Rabbi Ephraim's book. Rabbi Ephraim wrote a number of legal works, and the book that most fits the following entry and may have served as its source is the lost work known as *The Four Aspects* (*Arba' Panim*), dealing chiefly with torts (*dinei nezikin*). In his detailed study of the Tosafists, the late Ephraim. E. Urbach acknowledges that

this brief responsum is indeed an extract from this book. See Urbach, *The Tosafists*, 170–77, and notes there. On immigrants to Regensburg see Shoham-Steiner, "Exile, Immigration and Piety."

139. The word *zekukim* comes from the Hebrew root z-k-k, which means to purify or to distill. This medieval Hebrew root refers to the purity of the metal alloy in the coins. In the late twelfth century, the word *zakuk* was used to refer to marks, the local currency. See Irving A. Agus, "The Amount of a Ketuba" [in Hebrew], *Horev* 5 (1939): 143–68.

140. Such events became ever more frequent during Rabbi Mordechai's own lifetime and thereafter. Indeed, this may have been the fate of Rabbi Mordechai's own book collection when he and his family were murdered in the Rindfleisch riots in Nuremberg in 1298.

141. Mordechai, *Sefer Ha'Mordechai*, §163.

142. On the anti-Jewish riots in the late thirteenth-century Germany see Jörg Müller, "Erez Gezerah—'Land of Persecution': Pogroms against the Jews in Regun Teutonicum 1280–1350," in *The Jews in Europe in the Middle Ages (Tenth to Fifteenth Centuries): Proceedings of the International Symposium Held at Speyer 20–25 October 2002*, ed. Christoph Cluse (Turnhout: Brepols, 2004), 245–59, esp. 248–50.

143. Rabbi Haim Eliezer ben Isaac Or Zarua' was a mid- to late thirteenth-century disciple and contemporary of Meir of Rothenburg. The quote is from Rabbi Israel of Krems am Donau, the late thirteenth and early fourteenth-century editor of the influential *Hagahot Ashri*, discussing Rabbi Asher ben Yehiel (Rosh). Many of these matters were discussed by Isaac Zeev Kahana, "Keniyat u'mekhirat sefarim ba'halakha," *Mekhkarim be'Sifrut ha'Teshuvot*, ed. Isaac Zeev Kahana and Haim Zeev Hirshberg (Jerusalem and Ramat Gan: Mosad Harv Kook, 1973), 258–71.

144. See Maharshal, *Yam Shel Shlomo*, BT Baba Kama *Sefer Nezikin*. In his detailed account of the Tosafists, the late Ephraim. E. Urbach acknowledges the possibility that the following short responsum entry is indeed an extract from this book. See Urbach, *The Tosafists*, 170–77, and notes there.

145. This may also be the experience behind Rabbi Mordechai's ruling. A student of Meir of Rothenburg, his wife was the daughter of Rabbi Yehiel of Paris, Rabbi Meir's mentor and one of the Jewish defenders of the Talmud in the Paris Trial of the 1240s. The burning of the books in Paris was probably a formative experience for her. Rabbi Meir's

position is hardly surprising given that he had witnessed the consignment of many copies of the Talmud to the flames in Paris during the early 1240s. The burnings prompted Rabbi Meir to compose a *kinah* (liturgical lament), "Sha'ali Serufa ba-Esh" (Ask, you who have been burnt in the fire). It is recited to this day as part of the liturgy on the fast of the Ninth of Av.

146. Rabbi Bezalel Ashkenazi (c. 1520–84) was born in Palestine. He studied in Cairo under the famous Rabbi David ben Zimra, along with other prolific students, among them the famous Rabbi Yitzhak Luria Ashkenazi, who would later be known as the Ari (the Lion), the founder of Lurianic kabbalah. In Cairo he had access to the famously well-stocked library of Rabbi David ben Zimra. Using these resources, he put together a compendium called *Shitah Mekubetzet* (The compiled method), a commentary on the Talmud that anthologized many other medieval commentaries, especially, but not exclusively, from the Tosafists. He returned to Jerusalem and was appointed the chief rabbi.

147. According to Rabbi Bezalel, Maimonides was referring to BT *'Avodah Zarah* 52b.

148. Bezalel b. Avraham Ashkenazi, *Shitah Mekubetzet: Baba Metziah*, ed. B. Brochman (Jerusalem: Vagshal, 2006), fol. 24B.

149. Since this responsum was translated from Arabic, caution needs to be exercised in evaluating the language used.

150. Rabbi Isaac Alfasi, *She'elot u'Teshuvot Ha'rif*, ed. Ya'acov Asher Rozman (Jerusalem: Machon Yerushalayim, 2008), pt.1, 80–81 §133. This edition is based on the Livorno printing of Rabbi Alfasi's responsa (1781). A newer version of this responsum, based on the MS Moscow-Ginzburg 566, was published by Rabbi Avraham Shoshana: "Kovetz Teshuvot Ha'rif Ha'khadashot," *Yeshurun* 12 (2003): 15–31, esp. 22–24 §115. The responsum also appears in a collection of responsa attributed to Rabbi Shlomo ben Aderet by Rabbi Haim Falagi in Livorno in 1825. Rabbi Falagi's attribution is mistaken, however. I suspect that, when he produced the latter work, the printer still had the plates of Alfasi's material, and that he simply appended them to the later work, by another Iberian master. Rabbi Isaac was born in North Africa in the early eleventh century, moving to the Iberian Peninsula as a result of an intracommunal confrontation. For the last fifteen years of his long life he lived in Lucena, part of the Emirate of Cordova, where he died at the age of ninety.

151. The exception is Rabbi Elazar b. Judah of Worms's Passover sermon. See Rabbi Elazar Vormensis, *Oratio ad Pascam* [in Hebrew], ed. Simcha Emanuel (Jerusalem: Mekize Nirdamim, 2005). Notably, Rabbi Moses of Coucy of northern France embarked on a preaching tour of Iberia in the 1230s, seeking to persuade that region's Jews to reembrace practices that served as Jewish positive identity markers (such as wearing *tefilin* and *tzitizit*). On Rabbi Moses as a preacher see Judah D. Galinsky, "Rabbi Moses of Coucy as Pietist, Preacher, and Polemicist: His Intellectual Accomplishments and Communal Activity" (MA thesis, Yeshiva University, 1993).

152. On the significance of medieval Christian preaching see two colections of articles edited by Prof. Beverly M. Kienzle (et al.): *De Ore Domini: Preacher and Word in the Middle Ages* (Kalamazoo, MI: Medieval Institute Publications, 1989) and *Medieval Sermons and Society: Cloister, City, University*, Textes et études du Moyen Age 9 (Louvain-la-Neuve: Brepols, 1998). On the difference between Jewish adjudicators and academic teachers and preachers see Ephraim Kanarfogel, "From Germany to Northern France and Back Again: A Tale of Two Tosafist Centers," in *Regional Identities and Cultures of Medieval Jews*, ed. Javier Castano et al. (Liverpool: Littman Library, 2018), 149–72. For a brief summary of the role of preaching in both religious cultures see Jonathan Adams and Jussi Hanska's introduction to *The Jewish-Christian Encounter in Medieval Preaching*, ed. Jonathan Adams and Jussi Hanska (New York: Routledge, 2015), 2–8. On the attempt to enhance Jewish religiosity see Baumgarten, *Practicing Piety in Medieval Ashkenaz*, 1–19.

153. On Rabbi Haim Eliezer see Noah Goldstein, "Rabbi Hayyim Eliezer ben Issac Or Zarua: His Life, His Work, and a Digest of His Responsa," (PhD dissertation, Yeshiva University, 1959). On his life and work see Yehoshua Horowitz, "Rabbi Haim *Or Zarua* ve'Yahaso le'Hevrah shel ha'Goyim" [in Hebrew], in *Hevrah ve'Historia*, ed. Yehezkel Cohen (Jerusalem: Israeli Ministry of Education, Dept. for Torah Culture, 1980), 93–102. Rabbi Haim also left behind a digest of the sermons he delivered, which were copied and preserved in manuscripts that survived into the age of print: MS Parma Palatina Cod. Parm. 2413 (Catalogue De-Rossi 1264). This manuscript was copied in Weiner Neustadt, Austria, in 1450 by Moshe ben Eliezer Halevi Mintz (brother of Rabbi Judah Mintz). The second manuscript is MS Russian State Library

Moscow-Ginzburg 85. Both served as the basis for Rabbi Menachem Avitan's 2002 edition. See Haim Eliezer b. Isaac Or Zarua', *Teshuvot Maharakh*, 1–75.
154. Most probably Wiener Neustadt.
155. David Berger, ed., *The Jewish Christian Debate in the High Middle Ages: A Critical Edition on the Nizzahon Vetus* (Philadelphia: Jewish Publication Society, 1979), 56–57; 17; 246–47.
156. See Gen. 30:14 and BT *Sanhedrin* 99b.
157. On this see Shmuel Shilo, "Dina De-malkhuta Dina," *Encyclopedia Judaica*, 2nd ed., ed. Michael Berenbaum and Fred Skolnik (Detroit: Macmillan, 2007), 6:51–55; Salamon Farber, "On the principle of Dina de-Malkhuta Dina," *Judaism: A Journal of Jewish Life and Thought* 26 (1977): 117–22; Aaron Kirschenbaum, "The Sovereign Power of the State: A Proposed Theory of Accommodation in Jewish Law," *Cardozo Law Review* 12 (1991): 925–40.
158. According to biblical law, it is the eldest son's birthright to inherit a double share of his father's property (Deut. 21:17).
159. Rabbi Yom-Tov b. Avraham Ishbili of Zaragosa, in the early fourteenth century the Crown of Aragon. Yom-Tov b. Avraham Ishbili (Ritva), *Responsa* [in Hebrew], ed. Joseph Kapah (Jerusalem: Mosad Ha'rav Kook, 1957).
160. The responsum appears in the printed edition of Ritva's responsa, See Yom-Tov b. Avraham Ishbili, *Responsa*, ed. Joseph Kapah (Jerusalem: Mosad Ha'rav Kook, 1957), 187–90. Rabbi Joseph Kapah used the National Library of Israel (NLI), Jerusalem, MS Heb. 4°8676 (formerly MS Jerusalem-Joseph Kapah 84) as the basis for his edition. The responsum itself can be found on pages 80b–82a in the manuscript. A scan of the manuscript is available online on the NLI KTIV website: https://web.nli.org.il/sites/nlis/en/manuscript.
161. After a long decline over the fifteenth century, the local Jewish community of Daroca was expelled, along with many others in the United Kingdom of Spain, by royal decree in the spring of 1492. Thereafter, the local synagogue and hospital were sold and eventually razed. A parking lot now stands on the site of the synagogue, next to the Colegiata Santa María de los Sagrados Corporales in Daroca.
162. The Hebrew text reads אחרי. As the Hebrew alphabet includes only consonants, there is no way to determine whether the word is in the singular or the plural.

163. On the social, theological and legal role of tears and crying as a female attribute in medieval Europe see Jean Claude Schmitt, "The Rationale of Gestures in the West: A History from the Third to the Thirteenth Centuries," in *Advances in Non-Verbal Communication: Sociocultural, Clinical, Esthetic and Literary Perspectives*, ed. Fernando Poyatos (Amsterdam: John Benjamins, 1992), 77–97, and Elina Gerstman, ed., *Crying in the Middle Ages: Tears of History* (London: Routledge, 2012).
164. On such cases in medieval Iberia in the late thirteenth and early fourteenth century, see Rabbi Shlomo b. Adrat, *Responsa*, ed. Haim Zalman Dymitrovski (Jerusalem: Mosad Harav Kook, 1990–2015), 1:531–33 §1187. For a broader discussion on this see Baumgarten, *Mothers and Children*, 169–83.
165. In halakhic terms, the rabbis' signatures changed the status of the oath from one sworn in private to one sworn in public. According to talmudic law, a public oath is unbreakable (נדר שנידר על דעת רבים אינו ניתן להפרה).
166. The members of the Daroca *kahal* probably appealed to Ritva rather than to Rosh for two reasons. The first was that Zaragosa was closer to Daroca than Toledo and time was of the essence. The second was that it is clear from other sources that the Rosh held very stringent views on the possibility of reversing a public vow. He came from Ashkenaz, where spoken oaths were taken much more seriously. On oaths and their relevance in Ashkenaz see Ephraim Shoham-Steiner, "'And in Most of Their Business Transactions.'"
167. Chancery Fine Rolls 1251–2, no.173. For the image of the entry from the National Archives/Public Record Office, see Henry III Fine Roles Project, www.finerollshenry3.org.uk/content/fimages/C60_49/m20.html, 10 entries down. The entry is not in the *originalia* roll. The Latin reads: "Mandatum est vicecomiti Suhampton' quod inquirat per sacramentum xii. de legalioribus Judeis Winton' super rotulum suum utrum Cressus de Stanford Judeus rapuit et asportavit a scola Judeorum eiusdem civitatis violenter pomum eve indedecus et oprobrium communitatis Judeorum Winton' vel non. Et si per Inquisicionem illam culpabilis sit de facto illo, tunc statim distringant ipsum Cressum per redditus, domus et catalla sua ad dandum Regi unam marcam auri pro transgressione illa. Teste ut supra. per Regem."
168. In an eye-opening article published online, Evyatar Marienberg and David Carpenter discuss what it was that Cresse from Stamford stole

and why the king found it necessary to intervene in the matter: "The Stealing of the 'Apple of Eve' from the Thirteenth Century Synagogue of Winchester," Henri III Fine Rolls Project: Fine of the Month: December 2011, The National Archives and Kings College London, http://frh3.org.uk/content/month/fm-12-2011.html.

169. Evyatar Marienberg, *La Baraita de Niddah: Un texte juif pseudo-talmudique sur les lois religieuses relatives à la menstruation* [The Baraitade-Niddah: A pseudo-talmudic Jewish text about the religious laws concerning menstruation] (Turnhout: Brepols, 2012).

170. Since Marienberg and Carpenter's publication in Dec. 2011, the project has expanded, more documents have been entered into the system, it is fully digitized, and a search feature was introduced into the database. A search in the larger digital database of the Henri III Fine Rolls Project performed in August 2017 yielded similar results to those found by Carpenter in 2011.

2. "BE GONE THOU MAN OF BLOOD"

1. Toni L. Kamins, *The Complete Jewish Guide to France* (New York: St. Martin's Griffin, 2001), 65. A similar reticence is also apparent in "A Short History of the Jews in Paris," in the same book (44–45), which makes no mention of the murder case. "Long before Benjamin of Tudela [the twelfth-century Jewish traveler], in the sixth century CE the area near the church of St. Julian le Pauvre (just south of Notre Dame) in the Fifth arrondissement was the site of a synagogue."

2. The story of Priscus the Jew's murder by Phatir the Convert appears in Gregory of Tours, "The History of the Franks," in *Historia Francorum*, Monumenta Germaniae Historica, Scriptores rerum Merovingicarum i, 1., ed. Bruno Krusch and Wilhelm Levison (Hanover: Hahn Verlag, 1937–51), bk. 6:17. I have relied on the well-informed and meticulous translation of the Latin text that appears in Walter Goffart, "To See Ourselves as Others See Us," in *Christians, Jews, 'Others' in Late Antiquity*, ed. Jacob Neusner and Ernst R. Frerichs (Chico, CA: Scholars Press, 1985), 473–97. The text was also reprinted in Goffart's collection of essays as "The Conversion of Avitus of Clermont and Similar Passages in Gregory of Tours," in *The Fall of Rome and After* (London: Hambledon Press, 1989), 293–307. For the earlier scholarship on these events see 293n1. Goffart noticed that the portrayal of all the figures

involved in the story stemmed from Gregory's favorable bias toward King Guntram, his dislike of King Chilperic, and his ties with Bishop Avitus of Clermont, to which he attributed a much more successful attempt to convert the Jews of his city (*Historia Francorum*, bk. 5:11) than that of King Chilperic. On this event see also Michel Rouche, "Les baptêmes forcés des Juifs en Gaule mérovingienne et dans l'Empire d'Orient," in *De l'antijudaïsme antique à l'antisemitisme contemporian*, ed. V. Nikiprowitzky (Lille: Presses Universitaires de Lille, 1979), 105–27; and: Brian Brennan, "The Conversion of the Jews of Clermont 576," *Journal of Theological Studies* n.s. 36 (1985): 321–37. The Latin reads "*cum pueris suis,*" which could also mean "people at his service."
3. For an exhaustive discussion of these aspects, see Yair Lorberbaum, *In God's Image: Myth, Theology, and Law in Classical Judaism* (Cambridge: Cambridge University Press, 2015), 100–223. See also Maimonides, *Mishne Torah*, Sefer Shoftim, Hilkhot Sanhedrin 15:6.
4. See Karen Hulttunen, *Murder Most Foul: The Killer and the American Gothic Imagination* (Cambridge MA: Harvard University Press, 1998), 9.
5. Elias, *Civilizing Process*; Tatiana Savoia Landina and François Dépelteau, eds., *Norbert Elias and Violence* (New York: Palgrave Macmillan, 2017).
6. Rabbi Shalom b. Isaac Zekel of Neustadt, *Decisions and Customs of Rabbi Shalom of Neustadt* [in Hebrew], ed. Shlomoh J. Spitzer (Jerusalem: Machon Yerushalayim, 1997), 1 §1. See Rabbi Jacob b. Moses Molin, *The Book of Maharil: Customs* [in Hebrew], ed. Shlomoh J. Spitzer (Jerusalem: Machon Yerushalayim, 1989), 12–13 §6. The sermon given by the local rabbi on the Sabbath before Passover was an opportunity for him to display his erudition and to address pressing matters on the communal agenda. See Rabbi Elazar Vormensis, *Oratio ad Pascam*, 42–45.
7. I wish to thank my colleague and friend Peter S. Lehnardt from the Department Hebrew Literature at Ben-Gurion University for sharing with me his thoughts and invaluable ideas on this subject. I am also grateful to him for permitting me to use a yet unpublished draft version of a new edition of this text that he is preparing. Katelyn Mesler's forthcoming annotated edition of the text has also contributed greatly to my understanding. However, I am using Lehnardt's translation, which can be found in the appendix, rather than Katelyn Mesler's.

8. Avraham Berliner, "Ma'aseh Norah mi'Ktav Yad Asher be'Parma" [in Hebrew], *Otzar Tov* 4 (1878): 49–52. Berliner's account was republished in Avraham Moshe Habermann, *Gezerot Ashkenaz ve-Zarfat* (Jerusalem: Tarshish Publishing, 1946), 11–15. Berliner copied the text from the last pages of MS Parma 2342 (de Rossi 541). This manuscript, like many other Ashkenazi *Likutim* books, is a typical miscellany. Originally a larger manuscript that was split in half to be sold separately, probably for commercial purposes, it was eventually identified as being related to MS Parma 2295 (de Rossi 563). National Library of Israel, fol. 286r–287r (293–95 in the scanned version), accessed Apr. 19, 2017, https://web.nli.org.il/sites/nlis/en/manuscript.

9. On this genre see Yassif, *Hebrew Folktale*, 304–5. Yassif sees these stories as belonging to the category of a historical legend and explains their use in creating a collective memory.

10. More than half a century ago, Robert Chazan argued that the events took place not in Limoges but in Le Mans, based on the fact that the Hebrew name of the town is given as Limones. See Chazan, "The Persecution of 992," *Revue des Etudes Juives* 129 (1970): 217–21. The story is briefly discussed in Simon Schwartzfuchs, *A History of the Jews in Medieval France* [in Hebrew] (Tel Aviv: Hakibbutz Hameuchad, 2001), 67–68. It is my impression that this is improbable since in the late tenth century Le Mans was still referred to simply as Mans. Only after the Capetian expansion of the eleventh century and the inclusion of other cities with similar names, such as Amiens, did the city's name change to Le Mans, creating the possibility of a Hebrew misrepresentation when written לימוניי״ש. The Hebrew represents the Romance pronunciation of the name of the locality, obscuring the written letter G in Limoges. On the first century of Capetian rule in the area see Damien Kempf, "Capetian France (987–1328): Introduction," *French Historical Studies* 37 (2014): 169–72. Also Henri Gross, *Gallia Judaica: Dictionnaire géographique de la France d'après les Sources rabbiniques* (Paris: Peeters, 2011), 308–9.

11. Tzarfat is the medieval Hebrew term used in rabbinic literature to describe northern France. See Grossman, *Early Sages of Ashkenaz*, 13–45.

12. On the text of the *Chronicle of Ahima'atz* see Bonfil, *History and Folklore in a Medieval Jewish Chronicle*. By the late eleventh century, Jewish texts provide dual dating, both from the destruction of the Second Temple and from the creation of the world, as is the case with the

Hebrew Chronicles of the 1096 crusader riots. For these, see the recent edition in the Monumenta Germaniae Historica series: E. Haverkamp, *Hebraische Berichte*.

13. The Hebrew reads שחוק בן אסתר. The name Sehok is an unusual one, and may be, as Chazan suggests, a pejorative play on the Hebrew name Yitzhak (Isaac), or an allusion to Job 12:4 (I thank Peter Lehnardt for this reference). The Hebrew lettering also accommodates the possibility that the name should be read as *Shaḥuk* (worn away), which has a pejorative connotation deriving from the talmudic curse ישחקו עצמותיו (may his bones be worn away), frequently used against people considered to be enemies of the Jewish community, such as Emperor Hadrian.

14. The reference may allude to the fact that Sehok was neither a *kohen* (a member of the Jewish priesthood) nor a Levite (a member of the tribe of Levi). This is significant because one of the story's characters is a Levite and another is a Christian priest, referred to in the text as *Kohen la-baʿal* (literally and pejoratively, a priest of the pagan god Baʿal). Another possible intertextual reference may be to the biblical story of the blasphemer (Lev. 24:10). The blasphemer is said to be "the son of an Israelite woman, whose father was an Egyptian." It may be that, in terming Sehok an Israelite, the author is alluding to the biblical blasphemer. Sehok's parent is named Aster, or Esther. As it would be unusual, in the Ashkenazi milieu, for a man to be identified as the son of his mother, it seems more likely that the name of Sehok's father was Aster, Astre in Old French, meaning star. Sehok himself would then be "son of the star," the meaning of the name of the second-century Jewish revolutionary and false messiah Bar Kokhva. Although the language of the text would seem to suggest a connection with the substance of the story of the blasphemer, it seems more likely that the author may have wanted to intimate that Sehok was also the son of an intermarried couple, as was the blasphemer in Leviticus.

15. See Gerson D. Cohen, "Esau as Symbol in Early Medieval Thought," in *Jewish Medieval and Renaissance Studies*, ed. Alexander Altman (Cambridge, MA: Harvard University Press, 1967), 19–48.

16. In his monumental book on religious conversion, Arthur D. Knock makes a distinction between being powerfully drawn to the practices of another religion, a state he defines as "adhesion," and actual conversion, requiring the convert to turn his back completely on his

former religion and sever all ties to his former world. Although modern scholarship has rejected the dichotomy suggested by Knock, preferring a more spectrum-like model for religious conversion in traditional societies, I believe that the concept of adhesion may correctly describe the state of affairs in Sehok's case. See Knock, *Conversion: The Old and New Religion from Alexander the Great to Augustine of Hippo* (New York: Clarendon Press, 1933), 14–20. After all, despite the events he describes, the author of the text under consideration, writing in hindsight, refers to Sehok as an Israelite rather than as a convert to Christianity.

17. The choice of *'Ivri*, Hebrew, the term used by the prophet Jonah, rather than *Yehudi*, Jew, is consistent with the text's preference for biblical rather than Rabbinic Hebrew.

18. "וירחמו עליו בית יעקב ויכלכלוהו כמשפטם בכל קרית בואהו." The reference to "the house of Jacob" (*beit Ya'akov*) may be just a literary trope, but it could also have other connotations. God tells Moses before his ascent to Mt. Sinai (Exod. 19:3): "Thus shalt you say to the house of Jacob, and tell the children of Israel." The standard Rabbinic interpretation of this verse is that the words *beit Ya'akov* "refers to the women," while "the children of Israel" refers to the men (Yalkut Shimoni Shmot §276; Shemot Raba 28).

19. On the political divisions in France at this time see Chazan, "Persecution of 992."

20. In the Middle Ages, Limoges comprised two towns, the City and the Chateau. The City was first governed by the Abbots of St. Martial, who claimed to have received their authority from Emperor Louis the Pious (825). Later, the viscounts of Limoges claimed this authority. See Paul Louis Grenier, *La cité de Limoges: Son évêque, son chapitre, son consulat (XIIe-XVIIIe siècles)* (Paris: Picard, 1907), 12–13.

21. The exact meaning of the text is disputed. It says of Sehok that he ויקרח his aunt's household. Berliner and Haberman both maintain that the letter ר is a scribal interpolation and that the word should ויקח, which would suggest that Sehok married his aunt. I disagree. The word ויקרח may mean "he shaved them bald," suggesting that Sehok dispossessed his relatives of their property and took over their estate, leaving them "bald" of their assets.

22. Another indication that the text comes from a time close to the events (tenth century) is the use of the term *beit ha-Elohim* for "synagogue."

It is a direct translation of the Germanic word *Gotthus*. I thank Peter Lehnardt for this insight.

23. When it first refers to Sehok hiring men from Blois, it says there were twelve of them. But only two are mentioned as committing the murder.

24. The author uses the term *'arelim* (ערלים, uncircumcised) to describe the assassins.

25. The poetic Hebrew reads: כה אמר פלוני ופלוני המרצח: שלחה לנו משכורתו אשר כרת עמך בהורגו את הנפש בגללך כה כסף וכה שלמה. האם אין בלכת שם איש מזה והלאה נושא ספר ומרטלותו (?) יגורהו בחרמו וישלול לו שלל למען שכרו כי מדוע חדל בעבורך את העיר? MS Parma 2342 fol. 293. The reference here to מרטלותו may be to the Abby of St. Martial in Limoges. St. Martial was the patron saint of Limoges, around whose tomb the city of Limoges began to take shape in about the ninth century.

26. It is not clear exactly how the author of the story came to know of the letter's contents. Perhaps he made it up. But its enigmatic formulation leads me to suspect that it may well be authentic. Perhaps the author had access to the letter following Sehok's downfall. In such cases, the criminal was arrested and executed, and his assets confiscated (note that this is the denouement of the Book of Esther, the model deliverance story on which the Limoges story seems to be based). This case ended no differently. Most likely, the incriminating letter was found among Sehok's possessions in the aftermath of his downfall. Another possibility is that the author of the story learned of it from testimony offered by someone in Sehok's inner circle, perhaps in the process of trying to arrange a plea bargain or pardon.

27. High-quality garments were held in very high regard in medieval Europe, especially before the changes in weaving techniques and the evolution of the production of textiles that followed the Crusades, in the thirteenth century. Before this, most Europeans of nonnoble backgrounds wore homespun clothing. See Désirée Koslin, "Value-Added Stuffs and Shifts in Meaning: An Overview and Case-Study of Medieval Textile Paradigms," in *Encountering Medieval Textiles and Dress: Objects, Texts, Images*, ed. Désirée Koslin and Janet Snyder (New York: Palgrave-Macmillan, 2003), 237–40.

28. Barbara J. Shapiro, "'Fact' and the Proof of Fact in Anglo-American Law (ca.1500–1850)," in *How Law Knows*, ed. Austin Sarat et al. (Stanford, CA: Stanford University Press, 2007), 25–71.

29. The expression alludes to Prov. 31:23, "he sits among the elders of the land," that is, the community's judges, not necessarily a rabbinical court but possibly the lay leadership, of the type referred to as the kahal in early medieval Germany. See Grossman, "Attitude of the Early Scholars."

30. See Kati Ihnat and Katelyn Mesler, "From Christian Devotion to Jewish Sorcery: The Curious History of Wax Figurines in Medieval Europe," in *Entangled Histories: Knowledge, Authority, and Jewish Culture in the Thirteenth Century*, ed. Elisheva Baumgarten, Ruth Mazo Karras, and Katelyn Mesler (Philadelphia: University of Pennsylvania Press, 2017), 134–58, esp. 156–57, and notes on 303–9. Ihnat and Mesler suggest that Christian sources clearly demarcate between mock crucifixion and sorcery: "While the Jewish author was aware of both kinds of Christian accusations, he did not understand how Christians conceived of the boundaries that separated mock crucifixion and sorcery. In this Jewish account, unlike Christian ones, there is slippage between the two types of abuse" (157).

31. On the Jewish avoidance of trial by ordeal see Shlomo Eidelberg, "Trial by Ordeal in Medieval Jewish History: Laws, Customs and Attitudes," *Proceedings of the American Academy for Jewish Research (PAAJR)* 46–47 (1979–80): 105–20.

32. On this see Ephraim Shoham-Steiner, "Criminal Cooperation between Jews and Christians in Medieval Europe: A View from Some Inner Jewish Sources," in *Medieval Ashkenaz: Proceedings of the 17th World Congress of Jewish Studies in Honour of Alfred Haverkamp*, ed. Christoph Cluse and Jörg R. Müller (Forschungen zur Geschichte der Juden, A 30), Wiesbaden: Harrassowitz, 2021 (forthcoming).

33. See Walter Starkie, *The Road to Santiago: Pilgrims of St. James* (Berkeley: University of California Press, 1965), 25–28.

34. Perhaps the fact that Blois was also a stop on one of the pilgrim routes to Santiago de Compostela gave the murderers the idea that the pilgrimage route that ran through Limoges would be an effective target. Blois was an important stop on the Via Touronensis, named after the city of Tours, through which it also ran.

35. After the destruction of the Temple, the most important ritual duty incumbent on Jewish priests (*kohanim*) was (and remains to this day) the public recitation of the priestly benediction (Num. 6:23–27), which ends with the word *shalom* (peace). For this task they were expected

to maintain a level of ritual purity. When the Torah is read in public during prayer services, a *kohen* is called up first to do so. Another ceremony they participate in is *pidyon ha-ben*, the ritual in which a woman's first-born son is redeemed from the obligation of serving in the Temple (Exod. 13: 14–15).

36. This issue is part of a larger one on ritual purity, spiritual purity, and the ties between performer and performance in the liturgical sphere. Medieval Jewish sources often address the ritual purity of a murderer and that of a lapsed convert to idolatry (i.e., Christianity) simultaneously. See, for example, Gershom b. Judah of Mainz, *Responsa of Rabbenu Gershom Meor Ha'gola*, 57–61.

37. Similar language appears in a ruling by an earlier mid-ninth-century Gaonic sage, Rav Natronai Gaon (head of the Sura Talmudic academy in Iraq, 853–58): "We cannot flog him, but in order not to let him off, so that he doesn't think we sanction his behavior, we excommunicate him and we torment him and we make sure he is ostracized." See Kirschenbaum, *Jewish Penology*, 497 and n. 18. The quote from Sherira Gaon is found in a responsum by Rabbi Isaac ben Moshe of Vienna in his vast compendium *Sefer Or Zarua'*, 1:105 §112.

38. The Ashkenazi world was well aware of the rulings of the Babylonian sages known as the Geonim. Recently, Haym Soloveitchik has suggested that the relationship between the two centers of learning ran much deeper than previously realized. See "The 'Third Yeshiva of Bavel' and the Cultural Origins of Ashkenaz—A Proposal," in Soloveitchik, *Collected Essays* 2:150–215.

39. The belief that evil is physically manifested in a criminal's face has a long history, and lay at the basis of the pseudoscience of physiognomy. A strong manifestation of this belief in the nineteenth century may be found in Oscar Wilde's novel *The Portrait of Dorian Gray*: "Sin is a thing that writes itself across a man's face. It cannot be concealed. If a wretched man has a vice, it shows itself in the lines of his mouth, the drop of his eyelids, the molding of his hand even."

40. See Martha Himmelfarb, *Tours of Hell: An Apocalyptic Form in Jewish and Christian Literature* (Philadelphia: University of Pennsylvania Press, 1983), 104–5, 142–43.

41. Rabbi Isaac ben Moshe of Vienna (c. 1180–1250) is the father of the aforementioned Rabbi Haim Eliezer ben Isaac Or Zarua'. Rabbi Isaac was a resident of Vienna while his son resided in Wiener Neustadt

and later moved westward to central Germany in the late thirteenth century. It seems Rabbi Isaac died when his son was a young boy. Rabbi Haim was nicknamed Or Zaruaʿ after his father's famous compendium.

42. The text is from BL Add MS 27075 fol. 165r. The manuscript can be accessed on the British Library's website, http://www.bl.uk/manuscripts/Viewer.aspx?ref=add_ms_27075_fs001r, accessed Dec. 19, 2018. The other manuscript witnesses are from the Palatina Library in Parma, Cod. Parm. 3012 fol. 362r and Cod. Parm. 2092 fol. 168r. These texts were published by Moshe Hershler, "Tesuvot Geonim ve'Quadmonim be'Seder Tikin ve'Onashim be'Dinei Nefashot ba'Zman ha'zeh," *Sinai* 66 (1970): 173–77, reprinted in Yizhak Jodlov and Shlomo Zalman Havlin, eds., *Toratan shel Geonim* (Jerusalem: Vagshal Press, 1992), 6:388–93. An English translation of the text from the BL manuscript can be found in the appendix.

43. The manuscript reads רינושבורג, which seems to be a distorted version of Regensburg. Rabbi Ephraim arrived in Regensburg in the mid-twelfth century. He was a colleague of Rabbi Jacob ben Meir (Rabbeinu Tam), with whom he engaged in a number of halakhic disputes, some of them ferocious. Another colleague and correspondent of Rabbi Ephraim's was Rabbi Joel Halevi of Bonn and Cologne (father of Rabbi Eliezer ben Joel Halevi, Ra'avya). Rabbi Ephraim was a member of the Regensburg rabbinic court and a well-known scholar in the mid-twelfth century. On Rabbi Ephraim, see Urbach, *Tosafists*, 1:199–207, and Ephraim Kanarfogel, *The Intellectual History and Rabbinic Culture of Medieval Ashkenaz* (Detroit MI: Wayne State University Press, 2013), 39–44, 74–75.

44. The literature on *Sefer Ḥasidim* is vast and constantly growing. Three of the most important studies are Haym Soloveitchik, "Three Themes in Sefer Hasidim," *AJS Review* 1 (1976): 311–57; Marcus, *Piety and Society*; and Marcus, *Sefer Hasidim and the Ashkenazic Book in Medieval Europe* (Philadelphia: University of Pennsylvania Press, 2018).

45. SHW MS Parma H 3280, §175–76.

46. On the significance of body hair in biblical culture see Susan Niditch, *My Brother Esau is a Hairy Man: Hair and Identity in Ancient Israel* (New York: Oxford University Press, 2008).

47. See G. Cohen, "Esau as Symbol in Early Medieval Thought," 19–48, esp. 19–30. See also Ruth Mellinkoff, "Judah's Red Hair and the Jews," *Journal of Jewish Art* 9 (1982): 31–46, and Mellinkoff, *Outcasts: Signs*

of Otherness in Northern European Art of the Late Middle Ages, 2 vols. (Berkeley: University of California Press, 1994), 1:155–60.

48. The biblical David was both directly and indirectly responsible for a number of lethal acts of violence much closer to home. These include the deaths of Uriya the Hittite (2 Sam. 11:16) and his own son, Absalom ben Ma'acha (2 Sam. 18:14), who were seen as a threat to royal interests or potential opponents and were dealt with violently by David's henchmen. On his deathbed, the aged King David listed the names of his political rivals and asked his heir, Solomon, to make sure they were disposed of as soon as he ascended the throne (1 Kings 2:1–9).

49. This clearly alludes to the five-year term of exile mandated in the Gaonic protocol, but which is not mentioned explicitly in *Sefer Ḥasidim*.

50. On the reception history and the history of research on *Sefer Ḥasidim*, see the recent work of Ivan G. Marcus, *"Sefer Hasidim" and the Ashkenazic Book in Medieval Europe* (Philadelphia: University of Pennsylvania Press, 2018).

51. SHW §176. The concern about being able to observe the laws of the Sabbath "among the gentiles" is a frequent trope in the writings of Rabbi Judah the Pious, and appears multiple times in *Sefer Ḥasidim*. As Rabbi Judah saw it, the Sabbath was a defining marker of Jewish identity. See SHW §902 and Ephraim Shoham-Steiner, "The Humble Sage and the Wandering Madman: Madness and Madmen in an Exemplum from Sefer Hasidim," *Jewish Quarterly Review* 96 (2006): 38–49. Here Rabbi Judah couples his concern about observance of Shabbat with another observance he saw as a bedrock of Jewish identity—refraining from eating food—in this case, bread—prepared by non-Jews.

52. In medieval times, being exiled for five years from a community was tantamount to a death sentence. In a case of theft from a synagogue in medieval Aragon, the perpetrators were exiled from the community for five years. It is clear from the text that the intention was perpetual exile. See Yom Tov ben Avraham Asyballi, *The Responsa of Rabbi Yom Tov ben Avraham Asyballi* (Ritva) [in Hebrew], ed. Joseph Kapah (Jerusalem: Mosad Harav Kook, 1957), §159.

53. Kirshenbaum, *Jewish Penology*, 54–61.

54. In tractate *Sanhedrin* of the BT, the "clouded judgment" that befell Jewish jurists as a result of the destruction of the Temple in fact began forty years before the actual destruction, which took place in 70 CE: "Forty years before the destruction of the Temple in Jerusalem, the

Great Sanhedrin exiled itself from its chambers on the Temple Mount [*lishkat hagazit*, the Chamber of Hewn Stone] and sat in *hanut* ... this means that they no longer judged capital cases" (BT *Sanhedrin* 41a). This is part of a notion ubiquitous in the BT that there were premonitions and signs that foretold the destruction of the Temple (BT *Rosh Hashana* 31b, *Yoma* 39b). Some of these statements include intimations of both Jewish apologetics and anti-Christian polemic. The Sanhedrin's inability to try capital offenses forty years before 70 CE would mean that a Jewish tribunal could not have been involved in condemning Jesus to death circa 30 CE. This ruling also included some serious anti-Christian apologetic overtones. See BT tractate *Avoda Zara* 8b and Maimonides, *Mishne Torah*, Hilkhot Sanhedrin 13:13.

55. Paul Winter, *On the Trial of Jesus*, 2nd ed., ed. T. A. Burkill and Geza Vermes (Berlin: De Gruyter, 1974), 27–43, 110–30; Haim Cohen, *The Trial and Death of Jesus* [in Hebrew] (Tel Aviv: Dvir, 2012). J. H. H. Weiler, "The Trial of Jesus," *First Things* 6 (2010), accessed Feb. 4, 2016, http://www.firstthings.com/article/2010/06/the-trial-of-jesus.

56. My translation of the Jewish pietistic ideal of *teshuvat ha-mishkal*. See SHW 39–43 §37–43.

57. Although Rabbi Judah accepts that exile was the appropriate punishment for taking a life, he seems to have had serious reservations about it, consistent with his concerns about travel in general. See Ahuva Liberles-Noiman, "Space and Distance in Sefer Hasidim" (MA thesis, Hebrew University of Jerusalem, 2014).

58. A ruling by Rabbi Israel of Bruna reads, toward its end: "And it is well known that Rabbi Eliezer of Worms received a tradition (*kabbalah*) from 'the Pious' of blessed memory [Rabbi Judah the Pious] that the penance of a murderer is that he should go into exile with mortifying iron fittings for three years. He should engage in similar grave mortifications for these three years." See Israel b. Haim of Bruna, *Responsa*, §265.

59. Milton Haight Turk, ed., *The Legal Code of Ælfred the Great* (Clark NJ: Lawbook Exchange, 2004), par. 6.

60. *Weregeld*, also spelled *wergild* or *weregild* (Old English "man price"), was the amount of compensation paid by a person committing an offense to the injured party under ancient Germanic law. In the case of a death, depending on the local code (e.g., Lex Salica, Lex Ripuaria, Lex Alamannorum) the sum was paid to the family. The amount varied based on the injured party's gender, age, and social status. In Alamanic law,

from the eighth century, a distinction was made between an accidental killing and a premeditated act of lethal violence. In certain instances, part of the *weregeld* was paid to the king and lord—these having lost, respectively, a subject and a vassal. The *weregeld* was at first informal but was later regulated by law. See also Ulrich Stutz, *"Römerwergeld" und "Herrenfall": Zwei kritische Beiträge zur Rechts und Verfassungsgeschichte der fränkischen Zeit* (Berlin: De Gruyter, 1934). More recently, Lisi Olive, *The Body Legal in Barbarian Law* (Toronto: Toronto University Press, 2010), 203–46.

61. Elazar ben Judah of Worms, *Sefer Rokeah*, ed. Noah Kazachkov and Joseph Benjamin Rubin (Jerusalem: Zichron Aharon Press, 2014), 1:54, Hilchot Teshuvah §23.

62. The quote is from SHW §181; see also the Bologna edition, Judah ben Shmuel he-ḥassid, *Sefer Hasidim*, ed. Reuven Margalioth (Jerusalem: Mosad Harav Kook, 1957), §684 The King Agag mentioned in the passage was the captured King of the Amalekites slain by the prophet Samuel at Gilgal after King Saul's war of annihilation against that nation (1 Sam. 15:33).

63. In many cases of premeditated murder, Jews hired non-Jews to do the actual killing; in such cases the hired assassin might become a fugitive who would turn up on the doorstep of the Jew who hired him.

64. From the thirteenth century on, similar concerns about vagabonds and vagrants are evident both in the general European society and among Jews: Mollat, *The Poor in the Middle Ages*; Guggenheim, "Meeting on the Road"; Guggenheim, "Von den Schalantjuden zu den Betteljuden"; Elliot Horowitz, "'(Deserving) Poor Shall Be Members of Your Household': Charity, the Poor, and Social Control in the Jewish Communities of Europe between the Middle Ages and the Beginning of Modern Times," in *Religion and Economy: Connections and Interactions: Collected Essays*, ed. Menachem Ben-Sasson (Jerusalem: Shazar Publishing, 1995), 209–32; Ephraim Shoham-Steiner, "Poverty and Disability: The Medieval Jewish Perspective," in *The Sign Languages of Poverty*, Forschungen des Institut für Realienkunde des Mittelalters und der frühen Neuzeit: Materialien und Diskussionen, vol. 8, ed. G. Jaritz (Vienna: Verlag der Österreichischen Akademie der Wissenschaften, 2007), 75–94.

65. On the practice of penance and confession in contemporaneous medieval society, especially in the German lands, see Peter Biller,

"Confession in the Middle Ages: Introduction," in *Handling Sin: Confession in the Middle Ages*, ed. Peter Biller and A. J. Minnis (York UK: York Medieval Press, 1998), 3–33, esp. 3–7. Biller points out the importance of confession in the late twelfth- and early thirteenth-century Rhineland based on the exempla of Dialogus Miraculorum by Caesarius of Heisterbach (1180–1240). On the relationship between this collection of stories and *Sefer Ḥasidim*, see Joseph Dan, "Rabbi Judah the Pious and Caesarius of Heisterbach: Common Motifs in Their Stories," *Scripta Hierosolymitana* 22 (1971): 18–27. On Jews in this collection see Ivan Marcus, "Images of the Jews in the Exempla of Caesarius of Heisterbach," in *From Witness to Witchcraft: Jews and Judaism in Medieval Christian Thought*, ed. Jeremey R. Cohen (Wiesbaden: Harrassowitz Verlag, 1996), 247–56.

66. SHW §630.
67. The leader of Babylonian Jewry circa 1000.
68. Rabbi Evyatar ben Eliyahu Kohen-Tzedek (c. 1042–1112) was the last known Gaon (leader) of the Palestinian *yeshivah* (talmudic academy). The Latin conquest of the Levant and the establishment of the Frankish presence in the Near East occurred during his tenure. The Palestinian academy had migrated from Jerusalem to Tyre. The chance that the two figures actually met in Jerusalem is slim, as Hai Gaon died in 1038. The *Sitz im leben* of this story is the first half of the eleventh century. During this time Babylonian Jews made pilgrimages to Jerusalem and conducted the ceremony on the Mount of Olives that is described in the text. Furthermore, we know that European Jews attended such events and could have reported about them. See Mark Hirshman, "The Priest's Gate and Elijah ben Menahem's Pilgrimage" [in Hebrew], *Tarbiẓ* 55 (1985): 217–27. See also the remarks by Avraham Grossman and Elchanan Reiner in the same issue, 275–90. Also Mark Hirshman, "'R. Elijah Interpreted the Verse Concerning Pilgrims' (Shir Rabba 2, 14, 7): Another Medieval Interpolation and Again R. Elijah" [in Hebrew], *Tarbiẓ* 60 (1990): 275–76.
69. The statement by the murderer seems to allude to a text in one of the minor tractates appended to the Babylonian Talmud. Tractate *Semaḥot* chap. 8 article 11. The text there sympathetically highlights King David's penitential regimen, as exemplified in Ps. 51:4–5: "Wash me thoroughly from mine iniquity, and cleanse me from my sin. For I know my transgressions; and my sin is ever before me." The tractate *Semaḥot*

text reads: "David said to his Father [the Lord]: Lash me! For it says [in the Psalms]: 'Wash me thoroughly from mine iniquity, and cleanse me from my sin.'"
70. The text does not specify who ordered this.
71. SHW §630.
72. Similar psychological bonds between a sinner and his confessor could be seen in the surrounding Christian society. Later inquisitors and the heretics they interrogated developed similar relationships. See the recent work of John Arnold, *Inquisition and Power: Catharism and the Confessing Subject in Medieval Languedoc* (Philadelphia: University of Pennsylvania Press, 2013), 11–14 and 74–109. (I thank my friend Pinchas Roth for this important reference.)
73. One of the most influential sources for penitential practice that circulated in many manuscripts in Germany during the eleventh and twelfth centuries is Burchard of Worms's *Decretum*. The 1584 edition of the *Decretum*, printed in Cologne and based on Vatican manuscripts identified as dating back to Burchard's lifetime in the eleventh century, is considered by scholars to be the best text of this work. Although the work was probably kept in episcopal libraries and not accessible to parish priests, it had considerable influence on pastoral care. See G. Austin, "Jurisprudence in the Service of Pastoral Care: The Decretum of Burchard of Worms," *Speculum* 79 (2004): 929–52. On this manual and its influence even beyond monastic circles see Meens, *Penance in Medieval Europe*, 148–54. For the role of the confessor and the psychological relationship between him and the sinner see Erik Berggren, *The Psychology of Confession* (Leiden: Brill, 1975), 36–49. On the development of confessional theory in medieval times up to the twelfth century, see Meens, *Penance*, esp. 190–213. For other manuals of penance in medieval Europe see Sara M. Hamilton, *The Practice of Penance, 900–1050* (Martlesham Suffolk UK: Boydell and Brewer, 2001).
74. On the importance of authority in the Christian doctrine of confession and penance see Berggren, *Psychology of Confession*, 19–35.
75. Until recently, most scholars maintained that this mode of guided penance for serious offenses was an innovation of the Ashkenazi pietistic circle associated with the figures of Rabbi Shmuel the Pious, his son Rabbi Judah the Pious, and Rabbi Judah's close disciple, Rabbi Eliezer ben Judah of Worms. But Rami Reiner and Pinchas Roth have found evidence that this template may have originated earlier than

the late twelfth century, and was associated with figures not previously thought to have been involved in guided penance, such as the mid-twelfth-century Tosafist Rabbi Isaac of Dampierre. Rabbi Isaac is recorded having a discussion about guided penance with a lapsed Jewish convert to Christianity who sought his advice and was advised to perform guided penance. See Avraham (Rami) Reiner and Pinchas Roth, eds., *The Responsa of Rabbi Isaac the Elder of Dampierre: Annotated Edition with Forward and Notes* [in Hebrew], §98. See also Simcha Emanuel, ed., *Responsa of Rabbi Meir of Rothenburg and his Colleagues*, vol. 1 [in Hebrew] (Jerusalem: World Union of Jewish Studies, 2012), 489–90 §188.

76. Self-imposed exile is known from as early as the aftermath of the 1096 Crusader riots. See Daniel Soukup, "Apostatrix Gens: The First Crusade and Criticism of the Reversions of Jews in Cosmas's Chronica Boëmorum (Chronicle of the Bohemians)," *Colloquia Mediaevalia Pragensia* 7 (2015): 9–25, esp. 20. But Mathias was driven into exile: "and especially this Matthias that had already accepted the penance levied upon him by the rabbis." The text of the responsum can be found in Isaac b. Moshe of Vienna, *Or Zarua'*, pt. 1 §112.

77. Note that the father invoked the Christian image of the wandering penitent, as opposed to Rabbi Isaac's view of penance.

78. In the penitential handbook written by the sixth-century Irish monk Colombanus, a layman who killed his neighbor was sentenced to go into exile. See Meens, *Penance in Medieval Europe*, 56; Clare Stancliffe, "Red, White and Blue Martyrdom," in *Ireland in Early Mediaeval Europe: Studies in Memory of Kathleen Hughes*, ed. Dorothy Whitelock et al. (Cambridge: Cambridge University Press, 1982), 21–46; Yitzhak Hen, "Martyrim Kekhulim: Aliya La'regel Ve'kaparat Avonot B'yemei Ha'beynayim Ha'mukdamim," in *Ut Videant et Contingant: Essays on Pilgrimage and Sacred Space in Honor of Ora Limor*, ed. Yitzhak Hen and Iris Shagrir (Ra'anana: Open University Press, 2011), 125–34, and see the extensive bibliography on the subject quoted there.

79. Although Rabbi Isaac mandated ritual immersion as a symbol of penance, he nevertheless ruled that "although I have said that all the penitents require ritual immersion, I stipulate that [a failure to perform] the immersion does not forestall absolution."

80. On a similar practice in a different context in medieval Ashkenaz, see Ephraim Kanarfogel, "Returning to the Jewish Community in Medieval

Ashkenaz: History and Halakha," in *Turim: Studies in Jewish History and Literature Presented to Bernard Lander*, vol. 1, ed. Michael A. Schmidman (New York: Touro College Press, 2007), 67–97.

81. Grossman, "Offenders and Violent Men."
82. Not everyone in the Jewish community consulted rabbis, and even when they did, not all the rulings were preserved. Many rulings that were recorded for further use were nevertheless lost over time, and even those that did survive until the age of print were not always published with this new technology. See Emanuel, *Fragments of the Tablets*, 12–52, and his more recent *Hidden Treasures from Europe* [in Hebrew] (Jerusalem: Mekize Nirdamim, 2015), 1:13–63.
83. Emanuel, *Responsa of Rabbi Meir of Rothenburg and his Colleagues*, 2:730 §367. Rizba was a prominent northern French Tosafist, the nephew of Rabbi Shmuel ben Meir (Rashbam) and Rabbi Jacob ben Meir (Rabbenu Tam). His father was Rabbi Avraham of Sens, and he served as head of the talmudic academy in Dampierre-sur-Aube after the death of Rabbi Isaac the Elder (Ri ha-Zaken) in the last quarter of the twelfth century. He died c. 1200.
84. Esriel Hildesheimer, "The Provision against Gentile Courts in Late Medieval Ashkenaz: Halakhah and Practice," *Proceedings of the World Congress of Jewish Studies* [in Hebrew], div. C, vol. 1: Jewish Thought and Literature (1989): 217–24.
85. Jacob Katz, *Tradition and Crisis: Jewish Society at the End of the Middle Ages*, trans. Bernard Dov Cooperman (New York: New York University Press, 1993), 268. Katz mentions the observation made by Rabbi Judah the Pious in *Sefer Ḥasidim*, that sometimes the gentiles are just, while the Jews are much less so (SHW §1301).
86. A lesser punitive measure often used by rabbinic authorities against violent offenders was revoking the offender's right to testify in Jewish courts. This sanction was usually conjoined with branding him officially as an evildoer (*rasha'*) and sinner (*hote*), as in one of Rabbi Meir of Rothenburg's reponsa: "And you have asked about he who hit his fellow Jew and has not sought forgiveness and thus has not mended his twisted ways (*ivututo*). Be advised that of course he is unacceptable as a witness . . . and he is also called an evildoer, and this is also the ruling of Maimonides and the other Geonim." See Emanuel, *Responsa of Rabbi Meir of Rothenburg and His Colleagues*, 2:792.

87. A case where such a threat is made can be found in the responsa of the early fourteenth century Aragonese Rabbi Yom-Tov ben Avraham Ishbili (Ritva), q.v.: *Responsa*, 187–90 §159.
88. I thank my colleague Dr. Christoph Cluse from Trier University for discussing these matters with me and referring me to the relevant literature. On this see Brian A. Pavlac, "Excommunication and Territorial Politics in High Medieval Trier," *Church History* 60 (1991): 20–36. For a broader context see Elisabeth Vodola, *Excommunication in the Middle Ages* (Berkeley: University of California Press, 1986). Notably, Vodola focuses on the mid-thirteenth century Pope Innocent IV as the person who, as Kenn Pennington put it, "ameliorated the use of excommunication" in the Church. See Kenneth Pennington, review of *Excommunication in the Middle Ages*, by Elisabeth Vodola, *Speculum* 63 (1988): 242–44.
89. Richard. H. Helmholz, "Excommunication in Twelfth-Century England," *Journal of Law and Religion* 11 (1994): 235–53.
90. Although the expression is a metaphor, it encapsulates the view that, when a criminal capitulates to evil and seeks another person's death, his soul vacates his body. The word *ru'aḥ* appears in the Bible in the sense of the divine soul that God gives to human beings. Isaiah 11:3 speaks of the person who is imbued with divine spirit: "the spirit of wisdom and understanding, the spirit of counsel and might, the spirit of knowledge and of the fear of the Lord." The assertion that the spirit of God is not upon the murderer means that these blessings are withheld as well.
91. It is not at all clear whether this is a reference to an actual physical punishment or a metaphor invoked by Rabbi Shabtai.
92. Emanuel, *Responsa of Meir of Rothenburg and His Colleagues*, 1:566–67 §255.
93. וגם אמר לי שמעשה היה בימי הקדוש יצחק קלוט ז"ל ומשה מח' [ככל הנראה כינוי למוחזק א.ש.] גיזם לחבירו בדליקה ושאלו ממנו והשיב להם: משה מח' כל הקודם להורגו זכה.

See Emanuel, *Responsa of Meir of Rothenburg and His Colleagues*, 2:765–69 §393–94. These two responsa discuss the crime of potentially lethal arson at length. On arson as an extremely serious hazard and cause of anti-Jewish strife, see Simcha Emanuel, "Fires and Crimes in the Late Middle Ages: Testimonies from Halakhic Literature" [in Hebrew], in *Studies in Jewish History Presented to Joseph Hacker* ed. Yaron Ben-Naeh et al. (Jerusalem: Shazar, 2014), 157–69.

NOTES TO CHAPTER 2   355

94. A slightly different version of the argument presented here was published in Ephraim Shoham-Steiner, "Burial *ad sanctos* for a Jewish Murderer? Alexander Wimpfen and Rabbi Meir of Rothenburg," *JSQ* 23 (2016): 124–41. The responsum by Rabbi Meir appears in a few collections of his halakhic rulings and responsa compiled by his students (Rabbi Moshe ha-Kohen of Rothenburg's collection *Teshuvot Maimoniyot*), as well as in the responsa collection of Rabbi Haim Eliezer ben Isaac Or Zaruaʻ. For the sake of accuracy, I consulted the new printed edition of Rabbi Haim, *Teshuvot Maharakh*, 131–32 §141. In addition, I consulted one of the more complete and relatively early manuscripts of this responsa collection from the Hebrew Manuscript collection at the city and university library at Frankfurt am Main, Universitätsbibliothek Ms. Heb. qu. 4, 214–15, accessed: January 27, 2016, http://sammlungen.ub.uni-frankfurt.de/mshebr/content/titleinfo/1885701.

95. In translating and briefly analyzing this responsum, Irving Agus reconstructed the question posed to Rabbi Meir, which was not included in any of the versions preserved in the writings of Rabbi Meir's disciples. Agus also omitted the introduction Rabbi Meir wrote to his own responsum, which included not only a poetic exordium but also the name of the defendant, a detail that is not often included in responsa. Irving A. Agus, *Rabbi Meir of Rothenburg: His Life and His Works as Sources for the Religious, Legal, and Social History of Jews of Germany in the Thirteenth Century* (Philadelphia: Dropsie College for Hebrew and Cognate Learning, 1947), 2:678 §783.

96. The ruling was cited by later rabbinic authorities. Rabbi Menachem of Merseburg, in the fourteenth century: "It was ruled: Reuven ordered to have his opponent arrested by non-Jews. We should be more stringent with him than with a Jew who ordered a fellow Jew to kill another Jew, for in that case we hold that in all likelihood it will not come to pass [i.e., the Jew who was ordered to commit the murder would not carry out the order]. However, when gentiles are involved, they are considered to be hazardous, and therefore he who ordered them to go forth and kill requires absolution as a cold-blooded murderer." Rabbi Shlomo Luria (1510–1573) of Poland, the sixteenth century: "Maharam [Rabbi Meir] ruled in a responsum found in *Teshuvot Maimoniyot* (Nezikin §14) regarding a man who wanted to capture his fellow Jew and compel him to settle in court. Once the debtor refused, he let non-Jewish enforcers capture him. They beat him and killed him. And Maharam ruled that he

should be treated like a murderer with all that this status entails." For the Hebrew original, see Rabbi Shlomo Luria, *Yam Shel Shlomo on BT Baba Kama*, chap. 8, § 65 (printed in the standard editions of the BT). *Teshuvot Maimoniyot* is the collection of Ashkenazi responsa compiled by Rabbi Meir of Rothenburg's disciple, Rabbi Meir ben Yekutiel Ha-Kohen of Rothenburg (b. c. 1260) as an addendum to Maimonides' code of law, *Mishneh Torah*. Rabbi Meir perished in the Rindfleisch anti-Jewish riots (1298).

97. BT *Baba Metzia* 71b. This is also true of the case adjudicated by Rabbi Shabtai.
98. The responsum offers no real account of the positions taken by the parties involved. Nevertheless, Alexander's position can be understood from his claim that "even according to his version of the events, all he wished was for the enforcers to impel the other party to settle in court."
99. In Jewish rhetoric, non-Jews were commonly depicted as greedy and craving Jewish blood and money, mirroring gentile portrayals of Jews as greedy and bloodthirsty. This trope about Jews became more ubiquitous in the second half of the thirteenth century, with the intensification of the blood libel and ritual murder accusations. To quote Israel Yuval, there was no "mutual denial or rejection of one another's religious symbols; rather each side adopted and reinterpreted part of the other's repertoire." See Israel J. Yuval, "Jews and Christians in the Middle Ages: Shared Myths, Common Language," in *Demonizing the Other: Antisemitism, Racism and Xenophobia*, Studies in Antisemitism 4, ed. Robert S. Wistrich (Jerusalem: Harwood Academic Publishers, 1999), 88–107. On Jews in Christian literary imagery and art see Miri Rubin, *Gentile Tales: The Narrative Assault on Late Medieval Jews* (New Haven, CT: Yale University Press, 1999); John D. Martin, *Representations of Jews in Late Medieval and Early Modern German Literature*, Studies in German Jewish History 5 (Bern: Peter Lang, 2004), 155–82; Lipton, *Images of Intolerance*, 30–53; Debra Higgs Strickland, *Saracens, Demons, and Jews: Making Monsters in Medieval Art* (Princeton, NJ: Princeton University Press, 2003), 95–155; Lipton, *Dark Mirror*, 129–67.
100. The term "reasonable man" is not mentioned in the text. It is a modern legal term used in Israeli jurisprudence to refer to common sense and communal knowledge, with regard to the predictable outcomes of certain actions. See Alan D. Miller and Ronen Perry, "The Reasonable Person," *New York University Law Review* 87 (2012).

101. He refers, for example, to a talmudic discussion of a case in which a field is set ablaze (משלח את הבערה) by individuals considered by talmudic law to be of diminished mental capacity (a deaf-mute, imbecile, or minor). According to Rabbi Meir, setting a field ablaze is a dual infraction. First, it is irresponsible, since fire, a force of nature, cannot be controlled and contained. Sending a minor, a deaf person, or an imbecile (חרש שוטה וקטן) to do the task is even more irresponsible. Rabbi Meir refers to BT *Baba Kama* 22b, where the Talmud rules that a person is responsible for the actions of a minor, a deaf mute, or an imbecile if he gave them the means to start a fire and they did so. See also the responsa of Rabbi Haim Eliezer ben Isaac Or Zaruaʻ (in the Avitan edition 24–25 §25 and 132–33 §142.)
102. It may be that the compilers of Rabbi Meir's responsa intentionally omitted this bit of information; the financial settlement might not have been legally innovative and therefore of little relevance for later copyists and readers. Another possibility is that Alexander had already paid financial compensation to his partner's family for the loss of life (a fact that Alexander did not contest). The main point of contention was Alexander's intent in contracting the gentile enforcers. I incline towards the latter explanation. The length of the responsum indicates that it was not abridged by later copyists and compilers, apart from the omission of the query.
103. On this see Simcha Emanuel, "German Sages in the Thirteenth Century: Continuity or Crisis?," *Frankfurter Judaistische Beiträge* 39 (2014): 1–19. On the role of Halakhah as a system of arbitration and the settlement of financial and other disputes in the early period of settlement and establishment in the Rhineland, see Ephraim Shoham-Steiner, "Making a Living in Early Medieval Ashkenaz."
104. Rabbi Meir did all he could to stop Jews from performing justice on their own and from turning to non-Jewish courts. See Joseph Isaac Lifshitz, *R. Meir of Rothenberg and the Foundations of Jewish Political Thought* (New York: Cambridge University Press, 2016), 82–149.
105. The *Curia Regis* rolls record proceedings before the King's Bench (later known as the Court of Common Pleas) and *corum rege* (before the king himself). The Bench was the most powerful of the English law courts, dealing with treason and other serious crimes. Jews appear in these rolls because, in medieval England, they enjoyed royal protection and paid their taxes directly to the king and his court.

106. F. W. Maitland, ed., *Select Pleas of the Crown*, vol. 1 AD 1200–1225 (London: Selden Society, 1888), 57, Trinity AD 1208, plea 103. The record is from the Easter and Trinity Term of the Curia Regis of 1208 during the Reign of King John. All quotes in both Latin and English in this section are from this edition. See appendix for text.

107. See Barrie Dobson, "The Medieval York Jewry Reconsidered," in *Jews in Medieval Britain: Historical, Literary and Archaeological Perspectives*, ed. Patricia Skinner (Woodbridge UK: Boydell, 2003), 145–56.

108. Jordan, *From England to France*, 9–10 n16.

109. This entry is the first we hear of such an entity as suggested by Dobson, "The Medieval York Jewry," 152n34.

110. Some scholars suggested that the reading here should be *Belina*, which is a more reasonable reading echoing the Hebrew names Tova or Yaffa. The paleography of the B and K in these records is very similar. See Joseph Jacobs, *The Jews in Angevin England: Documents and Records from Latin and Hebrew Sources* (London: David Nutt, 1893), 233.

111. Assis, *The Golden Age of Aragonese Jewry*, 288–98.

112. On Jews in Koblenz see Zvi Avneri, ed., *Germania Judaica*, vol. 1: Von den ältesten Zeiten bis 1238 (Tubinegen: J. C. B. Mohr-Siebeck: 1963), 144–47 and vol.2/1: Von 1238 bis zur Mitte des 14 Jahrhunderts (1968), 407–14. The responsum appears in the writings of two of Rabbi Meir's disciples. One version appears in the commentary of Rabbi Mordechai ben Hillel ha-Kohen on the BT tractate *Ketubot* §301 (printed in the standard versions of the BT by the Widow and Brothers Rohm edition from Vilnius 1881) The other version of the responsum appears in Rabbi Meir ha-Kohen of Rothenburg's *Teshuvot Maimoniyot*, an Ashkenazi responsa collection printed as an addendum to Maimonides's *Mishneh Torah*. The text appears in *Hilkhot Ishut* (marital affairs) §10. For the text of the question see the appendix.

113. Jacob Katz, *Exclusiveness and Tolerance: Studies in Jewish-Gentile Relations in Medieval and Modern Times* (London: Oxford University Press, 1961), 54–55.

114. Rabbi Meir preferred and accepted the inadvertent testimony of the three gentile thieves, believing it to be more credible than that of the lapsed convert. He ruled that the wife should be freed from her marriage and allowed to remarry, even though the evidence had been provided by non-Jews and was mere hearsay, with no corroborating eye-witness testimony and without actual physical evidence produced

to facilitate the statement. Moreover, the witnesses themselves could no longer be interrogated.

115. I am indebted to my friend Moshe Dovid Chechik for bringing the Hour of Rage cases to my attention and for discussing them with me.

116. Tax collectors were also seen as collaborators and informers. Jesus's association with them and the fact that among his adherents were well-known tax collectors has produced a vast literature on Jewish attitudes toward this profession in his era, more than I can possibly cite. I suggest: John R. Donahue, "Tax Collectors and Sinners: An Attempt at Identification," *Catholic Biblical Quarterly* 33 (1971): 39–61; Hyam Maccoby, "How Unclean Were Tax-Collectors?," *Biblical Theology Bulletin* 31 (2001): 60–63; Timothy A. Friedrichsen, "The Temple, a Pharisee, a Tax Collector, and the Kingdom of God: Rereading a Jesus Parable," *Journal of Biblical Literature* 124 (2005): 89–119; and most recently, Yair Furstenberg, *Purity and Community in Antiquity: The Traditions of the Law between Second Temple Judaism and the Mishnah* (Jerusalem: Magnes Press, 2016), 334–38.

117. Rabbinic sources about this sage are limited, and do not all agree about when he lived. If he indeed was in charge of formulating the prayer against the heretics and informers, he would fit best in the first generation following the destruction of the Temple, c. 70–110 CE. See BT *Berakhot* 28b Megila 17b. For contradicting opinions see BT *Sota* 48b; *Sanhedrin* 11a; and Jerusalem Talmud *Sota*, chap. 9 Halakhah 13.

118. Ruth Langer has written extensively on *birkat ha-minim*, which is aimed at both Jewish heretics and informers. For the earliest textual evidence see Uri Ehrlich and Ruth Langer, "The Earliest Texts of 'Birkat Haminim,'" *HUCA* 76 (2005): 63–112, and for a full overview of the historical phenomenon, Ruth Langer, *Cursing the Christians? A History of the Birkat HaMinim* (Oxford: Oxford University Press, 2012). Christians were well aware of this practice, as can be seen in the testimony of the inquisitor Bernardus Gui in his *Practica Inquisitionis Heretice Pravitatis* (1320), where the benediction is mentioned explicitly. See J. H. Yerushalmi, "The Inquisition and the Jews in France in the Time of Bernard Gui," *Harvard Theological Review* 63 (1970): 317–76. For an English version of Gui's manual see Bernard Gui, *The Inquisitor's Guide: A Medieval Manual on Heretics*, trans. and ed. Janet Shirley (Welwyn Garden City, UK: Ravenhall Books, 2006). Chapter 6 discusses the Jews.

119. Scholarship has addressed the issues of the *moser* and *mesirah* from the legal point of view. See Paul H. Vishny, "The Informer as a Defendant in Jewish Criminal Procedure," in *Meyer Waxman Jubilee Volume: On the Occasion of His Seventy-Fifth Birthday*, ed. Judah Rosenthal et al. (Chicago and Jerusalem: College of Jewish Studies Press and Mordecai Newman Publishing House, 1966), 122–36. Eliyahu C. Ben-Zimra, "'Informers' in the Teachings of the Early European Scholars" [in Hebrew], in *Jubilee Volume in Honor of Moreinu Hagaon Rabbi Joseph B. Soloveitchik*, ed. Shaul Israeli Norman Lamm and Yitzchak Raphael (Jerusalem and New York: Mosad Harav Kook and Yeshiva University, 1984), 732–85 (Hebrew). More recently: Israel Moshe Ta-Shma, "Rabbi Isaac of Dampierre's Responsum Concerning Informers: On the Halakhic Value Attributed to Aggadic Material by Ashkenazic Tradition" [in Hebrew], *Zion* 68 (2003): 167–74.
120. See preceding note.
121. Aronius, *Regesten zur Geschichte der Juden*, §168. And see Guido Kisch, *Jewry-Law in Medieval Germany*, 37–67.
122. Haim Eliezer b. Isaac Or Zaruaʽ, *Responsa*, new responsa 276–77 §18. See also references there, esp. Avraham Joseph Havatzelet, "Teshuvot Rabbenu Azriel ben Rabbi Yehiel" [in Hebrew], *Tzfunot: Tora Quarterly* 1 (1989): 5–14, esp. 13.
123. I am deeply indebted to my friend Moshe Dovid Chechik for enlightening me on this matter, which has received little attention from scholars. The Hour of Rage touches on the fine line between the halakhic categories of the informer (*moser*) and that of the enraged individual.
124. See my discussion of the sense of the diminished criminal liability of the *furiosus*: *On the Margins of a Minority*, 123–26.
125. Emanuel, *Responsa of Rabbi Meir of Rothenburg and his Colleagues*, 1:620 §292, 645 §311.
126. Emanuel, *Responsa of Rabbi Meir of Rothenburg and his Colleagues*, 1:620 §292.
127. The case is discussed in Haim Eliezer ben Isaac Or Zaruaʽ, *Responsa*, 24–25 §25. Some of the text is quoted in another responsum: 132–33 §142.
128. The name of this person is not disclosed but he is labeled as an "evildoer" (*rashaʽ*) by Rabbi Haim and later on referred to as a murderer (*rotze'aḥ gamur*).

129. Rabbi Haim is referring to the talmudic story about Kamtza and Bar Kamtza (BT *Gitin* 55b), a rabbinic tale of the events that led to the great Jewish war of 66–70 CE and the subsequent destruction of the Temple. The subtext invokes the analogy that petty hatred (*sinat ḥinam*) was the reason for the downfall of Judea and brought about social strife, civil war, and destruction in the first century and will be the cause of Jewish downfall in medieval Ashkenaz as well.
130. See n. 94 above.
131. Haim Eliezer b. Isaac Or Zarua', *Responsa*, 24–25 §25.
132. In rabbinic law, a Noachide is a gentile who abides by the seven commandments to civilized cultures listed in the Mishnah in BT *Sanhedrin* 56a: 1) to have laws and courts for the society, 2) to refrain from blasphemy, 3) to refrain from idolatry, 4) to refrain from a set of six forbidden sexual relationships, 5) to not murder, 6) to not steal, 7) to not eat flesh removed from a living animal.
133. Haim Eliezer b. Isaac Or Zarua', *Responsa*, 24–25 §25.
134. Rabbi Haim made a serious effort both to cast doubt on the part played by the other two men in the conspiracy, and to show that, regardless of their role, the evildoer had acted at his own volition and should thus bear the full burden of responsibility. The question is why Rabbi Haim seems to have gone out of his way to clear the two. Were they of higher social standing than the evildoer? Was it because Moshe bore the title of rabbi? On the meaning of the appellation "rabbi," see Avraham (Rami) Reiner, "The Role and Significance of Titles Used to Describe the Deceased on the Tombstones in the Würzburg Cemetery," in *Die Grabsteine vom Judischen Friedhof in Würzburg aus der Zeit vor dem Schwarzen Tod*, ed. Karlheinz Müller, Simon Schwarzfuchs, and Avraham (Rami) Reiner (Würzburg: PH.C.W. Schmidt, 2011), 235–62.
135. This idea appears in the Talmud and in Gaonic literature: see BT *Sanhedrin* 74a; and Ahai Gaon, *Sheeltot de Rav Ahai Gaon: A Critical and Annotated Edition*, ed. Shlomo Kalman Mirsky (New York and Jerusalem: Sura Research and Publication Foundation Yeshiva University and Mosad Harav Kook, 1963), 3:40–48 §44.
136. Bernard Rosenzweig, *Ashkenazic Jewry in Transition* (Waterloo, Canada: Wilfrid Laurier University Press, 1975), 11–18.
137. The case appears both in Jacob Weil's collection of responsa as well as in the responsa of his contemporary, Rabbi Moses Mintz. See Jacob Weil, *Responsa* [in Hebrew], ed. Yonatan Shraga Domb (Jerusalem:

Makhon Yerushalayim, 2001), 142–43, no. 114. See also Moses Mintz, *Responsa* [in Hebrew], ed. Yonatan Shraga Domb (Jerusalem: Machon Yerushalayim, 1991), 518–19, no. 106. For this passage I have used the translation of this specific responsum by Pinchas Roth in: Pinchas Roth, "Mourning Murderers in Medieval Jewish Law," in *Murder Most Foul: Medieval and Early Modern Homicide*, ed. Larissa Tracy (Cambridge: D. S. Brewer, 2018), 77–95.

138. BT *Semachot* 2:1–4; Doc Zlotnick, trans., *The Tractate "Mourning" (Semahot)* (New Haven, CT: Yale University Press, 1966), 33–34; Benjamin Gesundheit, "Suicide: A Halakhic and Moral Analysis of Masekhet Semahot, chapter 2, laws 1–6," *Tradition: A Journal of Orthodox Jewish Thought* 35 (2001): 34–51. On this section of the responsum, see Yechezkel Lichtenshtein, "Suicide as an Act of Atonement," *Jewish Law Annual* 16 (2006): 51–91, esp. 79. See also my analysis of a Jewish adolescent suicide from England: Ephraim Shoham-Steiner, "'Vitam finivit infelicem': Madness, Conversion and Adolescent Suicide among Jews in Late Twelfth-Century England," in *The Constructed Jew: Jews and Judaism through Medieval Christian Eyes*, ed. Merrell L. Price and Kristine. T. Utterback (Turnhout: Brepols, 2013), 71–90.

139. Karl Shoemaker, *Sanctuary and Crime in the Middle Ages, 400–1500* (New York: Fordham University Press, 2011); Jordan, *From England to France*.

140. Kisch, *Jews in Medieval Germany*, 188. And specifically Glanz, "'Jewish Execution' in Medieval Germany."

141. Roth, "Mourning Murderers."

142. Glanz, "'Jewish Execution' in Medieval Germany"; Kisch, *Jews in Medieval Germany*, 186–87; Merback, *The Thief, the Cross, and the Wheel*, 187–88; Merback, *Beyond the Jewish Badge: Anti-Judaism and Antisemitism in Medieval and Early Modern Visual Culture* (Leiden: Brill, 2007), 263.

143. By the sixteenth century Poland would no longer be a marginal Jewish community. In the late fourteenth and the early fifteenth century, however, it was a frontier land for Jews. The first case discussed here comes from Shalom ben Isaac Zekel of Neustadt, *Decisions and Customs of Rabbi Shalom of Neustadt* [in Hebrew], ed. Shlomoh J. Spitzer (Jerusalem: Machon Yerushalayim, 1997), §95.

144. On the life and times of Austrian Jewry in this period and slightly later see Shlomo Eidelberg, *Jewish Life in Austria in the Fifteenth Century:*

As Reflected in the Legal Writings of Rabbi Israel Isserlein and His Contemporaries (Philadelphia: Dropsie College for Hebrew and Cognate Learning, 1962). For a more recent study see Martha Keil and Klaus Lohrmann, eds., *Studien zur Geschichte der Juden in Österreich* (Vienna: Böhlau Verlag, 1994). On the Jews in Vienna and its surroundings in the Middle Ages see Klaus Lohrmann, *Die Wiener Juden im Mittelalter* (Berlin: Philo Verlag, 2000). On the medieval Jews of Wiener Neustadt, see Werner Sulzgruber, "Die Geschichte der jüdische Gemeinde in Wiener Neustadt," in David Jüdische Kulturzeitschrift, accessed Aug. 29, 2016, http://david.juden.at/kulturzeitschrift/66-70/68-sulzgruber.htm.

145. For a bibliographical essay on the Jews of Poland in this early period, see Gershon D. Hundert and Gershon C. Bacon, *The Jews in Poland and Russia: Bibliographical Essays* (Bloomington: Indiana University Press, 1984), 38–42. Aleksander Gieysztor, "The Beginnings of Jewish Settlement in the Polish Lands," in *The Jews in Poland*, ed. Chimen Abramsky et al. (Oxford: Blackwell, 1986), 15–21. Anthony Polonsky et al., eds., *The Jews in Old Poland 1000–1795* (New York: I. B. Tauris, 1993), 13–22. Documents related to the early period of settlement can be found in Shmuel A. Arthur Cygielman, *Jewish Autonomy in Poland and Lithuania until 1648* (Jerusalem: Shlomo Natan, 1997), 13–44. None of the surveys relating to medieval Polish Jewry discusses the responsa and halakhic sources from Poland in this early period. Another source that reflects on the life of Jews in the late fourteenth and early to mid-fifteenth century is the work of Yosselyn ben Moshe Höchstadt, *"Lequet Yosher,"* who served as a self-appointed secretary of the Jewish master Rabbi Isserlyn ben Petachya of Wiener Neustadt in the first half of the fifteenth century. See, for example, Yosselyn b. Moshe, *Lequet Yosher: Orach Chaim* [in Hebrew] (Jerusalem: Machon Yerushalayim, 2010–13), Hilkhot Melachot Shabbat [62–63] §30 p. 134.

146. I tend to accept the second statement. Due to its jurisprudential importance, details that were relayed in the description of the events tend to be crucial. On the legal procedures of courts in medieval Ashkenaz and its periphery see Avraham (Rami) Reiner, "Rabbinical Courts in France in the Twelfth Century: Centralization and Dispersion," *Journal of Jewish Studies* 60 (2009): 298–318; Ephraim Kanarfogel, "Unanimity, Majority, and Communal Government in Ashkenaz during the High Middle Ages: A Reassessment," *Proceedings of the American Academy of Jewish Research* 58 (1992): 79–106; Kanarfogel, "Religious Leadership

during the Tosafist Period: Between the Academy and the Rabbinic Court," in *Jewish Religious Leadership*, ed. Jack Wertheimer (New York: Jewish Theological Seminary, 2004), 1:265–305. More recently, the yet unpublished doctoral dissertation by Rachel Fürst, "Striving for Justice: A History of Women and Litigation in the Jewish Courts of Medieval Ashkenaz," Ph.D. diss., Hebrew University of Jerusalem (2014).

147. On emotions in the medieval society see Barbara H. Rosenwein, *Anger's Past: The Social Uses of an Emotion in the Middle Ages* (Ithaca NY: Cornell Univerity Press, 1998). More recently, Rosenwein, *Emotional Communities in the Early Middle Ages* (Ithaca NY: Cornell Univerity Press, 2006).

148. On the first appearances of *gazamim* and *alamim* (intimidators and violent individuals) in medieval European legal writing, and their attempts to influence rabbinic courts, see A. Grossman, "Offenders and Violent Men."

149. On this matter see Fürst, "Striving for Justice."

150. In late medieval Germany, the Jewish right to bear arms was gradually restricted as part of the general deterioration in Jews' legal privileges, as they became *servi camerae regis*—chattels of the king. But this was not the case in the eastern marches of the Holy Roman Empire, and especially beyond its eastern borders. See Kisch, *Jews in Medieval Germany*, 111–28.

151. In medieval Ashkenaz, men who served as *ḥazanim* (cantors, leaders of prayer) on the High Holidays were thought to possess special spiritual and mystical powers. See Ephraim Kanarfogel, "The Appointment of Ḥazzanim in Medieval Ashkenaz: Communal Policy and Individual Religious Prerogatives," in *Spiritual Authority: Struggles over Cultural Power in Jewish Thought*, ed. Howard Kreisel et al. (Beersheva: Mosad Bialik, 2010), English section pp. 5–31. As Isaac lived in a frontier community, he may well have been one of a handful of men who were capable of leading prayer services. Although not stated explicitly, it stands to reason that frontier communities at this time generally lacked Jews who were minimally knowledgeable on religious matters, and who could read Hebrew, two requirements for leading prayers.

152. The Hebrew reads: וכל המבייש את המוכה ההורג מחמת זה ענוש יענש

153. Sociologists who have investigated the social consciousness of marginalized individuals have found that some tend to view the world through "sociological glasses," sensing themselves to be in conflict with the

world around them. This feeling is caused in part by shame and alienation. The embarrassment felt by marginalized people is also expressed in their daily contacts with others. See John J. Macionis, *Sociology*, 12th ed. (Upper Saddle River NJ: Pearson Prentice-Hall. 2008), 5.

154. Descendants of criminals were distressed by the bad reputation of their ancestors. It was a serious matter among Jews in medieval and early modern times. For example, a series of responsa from the mid-sixteenth century relates that the two sons, Avraham and Ephraim, of Shlomo Shneur (שלמה יטיל שניאור a.k.a Emericus Fortunatus or Imre Szerencses), a high-ranking Jewish convert to Christianity, asked for a rabbinic decision clearing them of their father's transgression and declaring that his misdeeds should not affect their standing in the community. From their petition it seems that their community had branded them as "the offspring of a convert," refusing them certain ritual roles; when they were called to the Torah, their father's name was not mentioned, as was customary. See Meir ben Isaac Katzenellenbogen of Padua (1473–1565), *Responsa and Rulings* (Venice 1553), §87; Moses Isserles (1520–72), *Responsa*, ed. Asher Ziv (Jerusalem: Mosad Ha'rav Kook, 1971), §41.

155. The treatise of Rabbi Menachem ben Pinchas of Merseburg (eastern Germany, fourteenth century), known as the *Nimukim* (Explanations), is apparently an abridged version of a larger but lost work, *Robe of Righteousness* (*Me'il Tzedek*, alluding to Isaiah 61:10), a compendium of his halakhic rulings, responsa, and legal teachings. The *Nimukim* were eventually printed alongside the first edition of responsa by Rabbi Menachem's better-known contemporary, Rabbi Jacob Weil. There is relatively little scholarship about Rabbi Menachem. See Eric Zimmer, "Rabbi Menachem mi-Merseburg ve-Nimmukav" [in Hebrew], *Sinai* 78 (1976): 75–88.

156. The person who was convicted of murder was not necessarily the person who actually performed the act. Rabbi Hezekiah ben Mano'aḥ (Hizkuni, c. 1250–1310) writes, in his commentary on the Pentateuch, regarding the commandment "thou shall not murder" (Exod. 20:13): "Thou shall not murder: either by hand or by speech or even by silence, such as in a case when a secret of a murderer is revealed to you and you choose not to disclose it" הן ביד הן בלשון הן בשתיקה, כגון שנתגלה לך סוד הרוצח ואין אתה מגלה הסוד. See Hizkiya ben Mano'ach, *Hizkuni Pirushei Ha'Torah le'Rabbenu Hizkiya ben Mano'ach*, ed. Haim Dov Chavel (Jerusalem: Mosad

Ha'Rav Kook, 1981), 258. On this biblical exegete, his life, and his times see Yosef Priel, "The Exegetical Method of Rabbi Hezekiah Ben Manoah (Hizquni) on the Torah," PhD diss., Bar Ilan University (2010), 324–34. Priel asserts that this exegete was a late thirteenth-century northern French commentator. I'm inclined to accept his sound and judicious suggestion.

157. Being called names and having a bad social reputation is a recurring theme in rabbinic writing and rulings in fourteenth- and fifteenth-century Ashkenaz. Another case discussed in *Nimukim* concerns a man who was called *hurensohn* (Judeo-German for "whoreson," meaning that his mother was a prostitute or bore him out of wedlock). This did not necessarily mean that he was considered a *mamzer* (bastard) under Jewish law; it might simply imply that his parents were not wed when he was conceived. Another similar pejorative was calling a man a *ben shifḥah* (son of a maidservant or female slave). The *Nimukim* and other late medieval responsa collections (especially those from the fifteenth century), such as those of Rabbi Jacob ben Moshe Mulin (Maharil) and his disciple Rabbi Jacob Weil, include many references to such issues. Jews were sensitive about such insults because lineage (*yuḥasin*) was taken very seriously in Jewish society. It was an indication of a person's character and determined marriage choices and social and economic connections. In a society that kept very few written records, being associated with the family of a criminal or offender could have grave consequences. If rumors of such an association were not suppressed, they would continue to circulate; the longer they did, the more difficult it would be to expunge them and undo the damage. See Elchanan Reiner, "*Yihus* and Libel: Maharal, the Bezalel Family, and the Nadler Affair," in *Maharal—Overtures: Biography Doctrine Influence*, ed. Elchanan Reiner (Jerusalem: Shazar Press, 2015), 101–26. On bodily mutilation as punishment for crime in medieval Europe see Dean, *Crime in Medieval Europe*, 114–43.

158. Rabbi Israel ben Haim of Bruna, *Responsa*, §265. Rabbi Israel himself had a life fraught with quarrels and conflict. On his life and times see Avraham Fuchs, "Historical Material in the Responsa of Rabbi Israel Bruna," PhD diss., Yeshiva University (1974), accessed Aug. 31, 2016, http://www.fuchs.org/AvrahamFuchs/DR_Thesis/mobile/index.html. I wish to thank my friend Avraham (Rami) Reiner, who called this responsum to my attention.

159. There is no indication in the text why the letters containing the testimonies arrived in Regensburg from so far and wide. It may be that the Lemberg community issued a *ḥerem* that called on other Jewish communal authorities to collect whatever information they had on the murder of Nissan in Lemberg. From the wording of the responsum it seems the two men accused of the deed were either Lemberg locals or were living there (possibly under arrest until the matter was resolved).

160. In the mid-fifteenth century, Regensburg was one of the largest and most influential Jewish communities that remained in Germany. From about 1470, and especially after the events of 1475 in Trent, the city burghers continually pushed local authorities to expel the Jews from the city. In 1519 they succeeded when the emperor rescinded his long-standing edict protecting the Jews. On the history of Jews of Regensburg see Straus, *Regensburg and Augsburg*; more recently, Siegfried Wittmer, *Judisches Leben in Regensburg: Vom frühen Mittelalter bis 1519* (Regensburg: Universitätsverlag, 2001). On the Trent blood libel and its long-reaching influence in southern Germany in general, and Regensburg in particular, see Ronnie Po-chia Hsia, *Trent 1475: Stories of A Ritual Murder Trial* (New Haven, CT: Yale University Press, 1992), 95–98; Paul Oskar Kristeller, "The Alleged Ritual Murder of Simon of Trent (1475) and Its Literary Repercussions: A Bibliographical Study," *Proceedings of the American Academy for Jewish Research* 59 (1993): 103–35.

161. The "holy society" of Lemberg most likely refers to the learned members of the town's Jewish community, who probably served as members of the local tribunal (who had sent the query to Rabbi Israel in the first place). This term should not be confused with the similar term *ḥevra kadisha*, which refers, to this day, to a Jewish community's burial and charity society. For a similar contemporaneous use of the same term see the letter of Rabbi Israel Iserlyn b. Petachia of Wiener Neustadt (1390–1460) to the *Havura Kadisha* of Regensburg, written while Rabbi Israel Bruna resided in Regensburg, concerning the controversy over the rabbinate in that city between Rabbi Israel and a certain Rabbi Anshyl. *Terumat ha-Deshen, Responsa and Rulings*, §126 (appears also in Jacob Weil's responsa). The sequence of the words *Kadishe Havureh* is very odd in Hebrew or Aramaic. It may represent the local Yiddishized pronunciation.

162. The Hebrew is enigmatic: "הכה תכה ניסן למיתור." The last word, *lemitortz*, is the most problematic. My colleague Orit Hirt-Ramon suggests that

it is an amalgam of the Hebrew word למיתה to which a Slavic suffix C or CZ, has been added. Alternatively, she proposes, the word might be a mispronunciation or a copyist's inaccurate transcription of the Slavic word mrtc (death). It may also be a scribal error; in this period most copyists were more familiar with German-Yiddish than with Slavic languages.

163. The reference is to the biblical Lot, son of Haran, the nephew of Abraham. Lot is described in Gen. 19:30–38 as having been intoxicated by his daughters in a cave at Tzo'ar, to the point that he was not aware that they had sexual relations with him.

164. Shmuel Arthur Cygielman, *The Jews of Poland and Lithuania until 1648: Prolegomena and Annotated Sources* (Jerusalem: Zalman Shazar Publishing, 1991), 54.

165. The talmudic term "pursuer" (*rodef*) refers to a person who is chasing someone with the intention of killing him. Once someone is defined as a pursuer he may be apprehended, so as to prevent (or "rescue") him from committing the sin of murder, even if to do so it is necessary to kill him. Marilyn Finkelman, "Self-Defence and Defence of Others in Jewish Law: The Rodef Defence," *Wayne Law Review* 33 (1987): 1257–87.

166. אין בו לחלוחית.

167. In late antiquity, the talmudic Sages employed the term '*am ha-aretz* in order to demarcate themselves from the masses. In talmudic literature the term '*am ha-aretz* is sometimes used to as a synonym for "the common people." On '*am ha-aretz* see the classic work of Aharon Oppenheimer, *The Am ha-Aretz: A Study in the Social History of the Jewish People in the Hellenistic-Roman Period* (Leiden: Brill, 1977). For a more recent treatment: Yair Furstenberg, "Am Ha-aretz in Tannaitic Literature and Its Social Contexts," *Zion* 78 (2013): 287–320. For a comprehensive study of this term and the history of scholarship on it see Jonathan Aaron Pomeranz, "Ordinary Jews in the Babylonian Talmud: Rabbinic Representations and Historical Interpretation," PhD diss., Yale University (2016), 49–122. The use of the term in posttalmudic rabbinic literature is a desideratum.

168. See BT *Pesachim* 49b.

169. On the history of gambling see David G. Schwartz, *Roll the Bones: The History of Gambling, Casino Edition* (Las Vegas NV: Winchester Books, 2013), 22–41.

170. Shoham-Steiner, "Burial *ad sanctus* for a Jewish Murderer?"

171. The biblical code in Num. 35:9–34 discusses the establishment of cities of asylum for unintentional murderers and a system of justice for trying murderers. The code specifically states that no ransom should be accepted: "Moreover you shall take no ransom for the life of a murderer, that is guilty of death; but he shall surely be put to death. And you shall take no ransom for him that is fled to his city of refuge, that he should come again to dwell in the land, until the death of the priest" (Num. 35:31–32).
172. Marcus, *Piety and Society*, 126–28.
173. On Jacob Weil (1390–1456) see Rosenzweig, *Ashkenazic Jewry in Transition*.
174. The Hebrew reads *go'el ha-dam*, literally the blood redeemer/avenger. The biblical blood avenger was the kin closest to the deceased, who was entrusted by the clan to find the murderer and avenge the killing, and in doing so balance blood with blood to restore equilibrium.
175. Maimonides, *Mishneh Torah*, Sefer Nezikin, Hilkhot Rotze'aḥ u-Shemirat Nefesh [The Book of Torts, Laws of Murderers, and the Protection of Life], chap. 1:4.
176. The kinsman who, according to biblical law, is charged with avenging the death.
177. Jacob Weil, *Responsa*, §61.
178. On indulgences in Germany in this period see Bernard Moeller, "Religious Life in Germany at the Eve of the Reformation," in *Contesting Christendom: Readings in Medieval Religion and Culture*, ed. James L. Halverson (Lanham MD: Rowman & Littlefield, 2008), 189–98.
179. On family feuds and their dynamics in late medieval and early modern Germany see Hillay Zmora, *State and Nobility in Early Modern Germany: The Knightly Feud in Franconia 1440–1567* (Cambridge: Cambridge University Press, 1998), and more recently, *The Feud in Early Modern Germany* (Cambridge: Cambridge University Press, 2011). On the grave challenges to the inner Jewish judicial system at the time, focusing on some of the challenges dealt with by Rabbi Jacob Weil of Ulm, see Zimmer, *Harmony and Discord*.
180. Spierenburg, *History of Murder*, 19–32.
181. Spierenburg does not mention medical advances, which were an important factor in domestic deaths, especially infant mortality.
182. Jordan, *From England to France*.
183. Grossman, "Offenders and Violent Men."

184. Karen Halttunen, *Murder Most Foul: The Murderer and the American Gothic Imagination* (Cambridge, MA: Harvard University Press, 1998), 1.
185. Dianne Berg, "Monstrous Un-Making: Maternal Infanticide as Female Agency," in *Murder Most Foul: Medieval and Early Modern Homicide*, ed. Larrisa Tracy (Suffolk UK: Boydell, 2017). This aspect will be discussed in the third section of this book on Jewish women's involvement in crime.

3. WOMEN AND CRIME

1. *Nega'* is the word used in the book of Leviticus to denote the biblical affliction also called *tzara'at*. On this source from a different angle see Shoham-Steiner, *On the Margins of a Minority*, 64–66.
2. The text is MS Oxford Bod. 692. Most of the material found in the manuscript was published by Kupfer in the 1970s. Our case is cited in Efraim Kupfer, *Responsa et Decisiones: Ad fedem codicis Bodleianensis 692 edidit prefatione et notis instruxit* [in Hebrew] (Jerusalem: Mekize Nirdamim, 1973), 243 §156.
3. Judging by the ruling and its similarity to other rulings, the respondent was most likely either Rabbi Meir of Rothenburg or one of his disciples.
4. Domestic violence by husbands toward their wives was not considered a crime in many cases and in most medieval European legal systems. See the concise discussion in Eva Salisbury, "Domestic Abuse" in *Woman and Gender in Medieval Europe: An Encyclopedia*, ed. Margaret Schaus (New York: Routledge, 2006), 219–21. On domestic violence in canon law see James A. Brundage, "Domestic Violence in Classical Canon Law," in *Violence in Medieval Society*, ed. Richard Kaeuper (Rochester NY: Boydell Press, 2002), 183–95, and, in the same volume, Barbara A. Hanawalt, "Violence in the Domestic Milieu of Late Medieval England," 197–214. And more recently on medieval England, Dunn, *Stolen Women in Medieval England*.
5. Dean, *Crime in Medieval Europe*, 72.
6. This use of the vernacular was not gendered. Jewish men who appeared in court probably also spoke it. But Jewish legal texts were written in Hebrew, intermixed with talmudic Aramaic, as this was the convention of the genre.
7. Even this verbatim quote is not from the woman's testimony in the court. Rather, it is a transcription of the words she said when she was

confronted by her employer. In the original text the quote is in German in Hebrew letters: אב״ר ע״ר הו״ר ני״ט רעב״ט ביי״א מי״ר גלעג״ן. See Israel Iserlyn ben Petachia, *Terumat ha-Deshen*, 2:422–24 §222.
8. Among them Judith Baskin, Elisheva Baumgarten, Rene Levin-Melamed, and Sharon Koren.
9. For example, in his groundbreaking book on the role of Jewish women in medieval European Jewish culture, *Pious and Rebellious: Jewish Women in Medieval Europe*, trans. Johnathan Chipman (Waltham, MA: Brandeis University Press, 2004), Avraham Grossman did not address the role of women in crime, even though he devoted an entire chapter to violence against women (chap. 10, n10). His chapter on the "rebellious wife" addresses married women who refrained from sexual relations with their husbands, despite the obligation to physically cohabit as a married couple. Grossman's "The Murderous Wife" subchapter ("*ha-Ishah ha-Katlanit*"), the title of which promises a consideration of women who killed their husbands, in fact refers to a twice-widowed woman, and would be better rendered as "The Lethal Wife." It was widely believed in late antiquity and the Middle Ages that a twice-widowed woman should not be allowed to marry again, lest her third husband die as well.
10. The text was printed by Rabbi Joel Müller in *Responsen der Lehrer des Ostens und Westens* [in Hebrew] (Berlin: Deutsch, 1888), 41b §171. Joel Müller mistakenly identifies the respondent as Rabbi Joseph Tuv-Elem (Bonfil) of northern France (980–c. 1050), but Avraham Grossman correctly ascribes it to Rabbi Joseph Iben-Avitur. See Grossman, *Early Sages of Ashkenaz*, 189n65.
11. Ruth Mazo Karras, *Common Women: Prostitution and Sexuality in Medieval England* (New York: Oxford Univerity Press, 1996), 48–64.
12. Rabbi Alexander lived in Erfurt, Frankfurt, and Worms during the first half of the fourteenth century. There is a scholarly debate whether he was martyred in 1349 or not. A lament about the fate of the Erfurt community in 1349 mentions him explicitly, but this may be because he hailed from the city and represented the city's claim to intellectual fame. Oddly, later masters do not mention him as a martyr. His book *Sefer ha-Agudah* (Book of the Bundle) is one of the encyclopedic works that preserved medieval Ashkenazi legal thinking and rulings. Unlike his contemporary, Rabbi Jacob ben Asher, who also compiled a halakhic compendium for practical use (*Sefer Arba'ah Turim*, Book of

Four Columns), the *Agudah* is structured according to the Babylonian Talmud's tractates, much like another Ashkenazi encyclopedic compilation of a generation earlier, *Sefer Mordechai*, by Mordechai ben Hillel. The text in question appears in the glosses (*hagahot*) on this work written by Rabbi Moshe Iserles (who lived in Kraków in the sixteenth century), which appear in the standard printing of BT *Yebamot*, chap. 6 §52, where *Sefer Agudah* is also quoted. My friend Pinchas Roth, who found this reference, also found an abbreviated entry on this matter in a National Library of Israel manuscript: MS Montefiore Ms. 108 §373 (currently MS Jerusalem Ms. Heb. 38°8860) fol. 39r. The MS was consulted with Ktiv, Dec. 12, 2017: http://web.nli.org.il/sites/NLI/English/digitallibrary/pages/viewer.aspx?&presentorid=MANUSCRIPTS&docid=PNX_MANUSCRIPTS000199292-1#|FL52367365.

13. This is a reference to cases in which Jews were prosecuted in late medieval non-Jewish courts for fathering children with Christian women. On this matter see Jörg Müller, "Sexual Relations between Christian and Jews in Medieval Germany according to Christian Sources," in *Iggud: Selected Essays in Jewish Studies*, vol. 2, History of the Jewish People and Contemporary Jewish Society, ed. Gershon Bacon et al. (Jerusalem: World Union of Jewish Studies, 2009), 19–32.

14. David Nirenberg suggests that the question of gender is crucial to the issue of how sexual relations were perceived by society. See David Nirenberg, *Communities of Violence: Persecution of Minorities in the Middle Ages* (Princeton, NJ: Princeton University Press, 1996), 163–68. This issue is emphasized in Ora Limor, review of *Communities of Violence: Persecution of Minorities in the Middle Ages*, by David Nirenberg [in Hebrew], *Zion* 63 (1998): 476–82.

15. See n13 above.

16. Rashi addresses the issue in his commentary on the levitical prohibition: "Do not degrade your daughter and make her a harlot [להזנותה], lest the land fall into harlotry [wantonness, תזנה הארץ] and the land be filled with depravity [זימה]" (Lev. 19:29).

17. The Babylonian Talmud stipulates, in the first passage of tractate *Ketubot*, which address matrimonial issues, that a woman is betrothed in three distinct manners: either by a monetary payment (*kesef*), by contractual agreement (*shtar*), or by consenting to sexual intercourse (*bi'ah*).

18. In the Jewish community in Altona in the eighteenth century, unmarried young Jewish maidservants who became pregnant out of wedlock were listed in the communal register with the label *zonah*. See Elisheva Carlebach, "Fallen women and Fatherless Children: Jewish Domestic Servants in Eighteenth Century Altona," *Jewish History* 24 (2010): 295–308.
19. The Hebrew word *zonah* is of feminine gender, and thus refers to women. As there is no parallel masculine term, in modern Hebrew a male prostitute is referred to as a *zonah me-min zakhar*, a *zonah* of the male sex. Biblical Hebrew has male and female forms for cultic prostitutes (*kadesh* קדש for a male and *kedeshah* קדשה for a female), but sometimes the latter simply means a harlot, as in the story of Judah and Tamar (Gen. 38:21). Both are forbidden, and sexual acts with them are labeled as illicit and contrary to the Israelite form of worship.
20. The Bible has a specific term for this tainted form of profit, *etnan*, found both in Deuteronomy and in the book of prophet Michah (1:7). Medieval commentators wrestled with the meaning of the word, agreeing that it came from the Hebrew root NTN, to give. The *etnan* is thus the gift to the prostitute in exchange for her sexual favors. Interestingly, the *etnan* to the prostitute is paired with the "price of a dog," מחיר כלב; both are objectionable gifts to the Lord's Temple because of their origin. Most commentators accepted the standard talmudic interpretation that if a person wishes to offer a lamb as a sacrifice in the Temple but acquires the lamb by trading a dog for it, the lamb may not be brought as a sacrifice. The fifteenth-century Iberian commentator Don Isaac Abarbanel understood "the price of a dog" differently, maintaining that it meant the fee of a male prostitute. "Dog," he maintained, is a euphemism for a male prostitute. In the ancient Near East, the term *kelev* or its derivatives did indeed denote a male cultic prostitute. The cuneiform sign UR.SAL for *assinnu* (a male devotee of Ishtar who took on feminine characteristics) means both "dog" and "man/woman," while in Greek the word *kinaidos* ("dog-like"; Latin *cinaedus*) was used for men who were flamboyantly effeminate and encouraged homosexual advances.
21. Here I follow the translation of the *Standard American Bible* (1995) which, in my opinion, better captures the original Hebrew than the King James Version and the JPS Bible, the latter of which reads: "There

shall be no whore of the daughters of Israel, nor a sodomite of the sons of Israel."

22. The text is from the Prague edition of Rabbi Meir b. Baruch of Rothenberg's responsa, 426–27§844. The text originates from the Prague collection of Rabbi Meir's responsa based on MS Prague Jewish Museum 20 §205.

23. John T. Appleby, trans. and ed., *The Chronicle of Richard of Devizes of the Time of King Richard the First* (London: Thomas Nelson & Sons, 1963), 65–66.

24. J. Richards, *Sex Dissidence and Damnation: Minority Groups in the Middle Ages* (London: Routledge, 1990), 116. Jacques de Virty's and Richard of Devizes' accounts should not be accepted uncritically, as both were clerics and may have been the victims of ridicule by prostitutes, as Jacques reports. However, in a slightly later period (the first official count of households took place in 1328) Paris had some 200,000 inhabitants, a full several thousand of whom were prostitutes. On life in medieval Paris see Simone Roux, *Paris in the Middle Ages*, trans. Jo Ann McNamara (Philadelphia: University of Pennsylvania Press, 2009), 38–41.

25. Jöelle Koster, "Prostitution," in *Woman and Gender in Medieval Europe: An Encyclopedia*, ed. Margaret Schaus (New York: Routledge, 2006), 674–78, esp. 677.

26. Karras, *Common Women*, 48–64.

27. Koster, "Prostitution," 674–78.

28. James A. Brundage, *Medieval Canon Law* (New York: Routledge, 1995), 75.

29. *Sefer Ḥasidim* takes an extreme position, but for the Ashkenazi Pietists, the most important goal was to safeguard the sanctity of marriage and avoid undermining it as an institution. On this see Judith R. Baskin, "From Separation to Displacement: The Problem of Women in 'Sefer Hasidim,'" *AJS Review* 19 (1994): 1–18, and more recently, Baskin, "Women and Sexual Ambivalence in 'Sefer Hasidim,'" *Jewish Quarterly Review* 96 (2006): 1–8.

30. SHW § 1526.

31. Harry Kühnel, "Laster und Lust" in *Alltag in Spätmittelalter*, ed. Harry Kühnel et al. (Graz, Austria: Editions Kaleidoskop, 1986), 38–46.

32. On the nexus between poverty and prostitution see Lidia L. Otis, *Prostitution in Medieval Society: The History of an Urban Institution in*

Languedoc (Chicago: University of Chicago Press, 1985), 64–65, and Karras, *Common Women*, 114–28.

33. On the Jews living in rural areas in medieval Germany see Rainer Josef Barzen, "Ländliche Jüdische Siedlungen und Niederlassungen in Aschkenas, Vom Hochmittelalter bis ins 16. Jahrhundert: Typologie, Struktur und Vernetzung," *Aschkenas* 21 (2013): 5–35.

34. Disrupting prayers was a venerable means of drawing communal attention to grievances that had not received a proper response from the legal authorities. Samuel Krauss, *Korot Batei ha'Tephilah be'Yisrael* [The History of the Prayer Houses in Israel] [in Hebrew] (New York: Ogen Press, 1956), 302–16; Finkelstein, *Jewish Self-Government in the Middle Ages*, 15–18, 119, 128–29. See Avraham Grossman, "The Origins and Essence of the Custom of 'Stopping-the-Service'" [in Hebrew], *Milet* 1 (1983): 199–220. On a similar custom in the Jewish communities in Islamic lands see Menahem Ben-Sasson, *"Ha-tzeaqa el ha-tzibur be-beit ha-keneset be-artzot ha-islam be-reshit yemei ha-beinayim"* [The Call to the Public in Synagogues in Islamic Lands in the Early Middle Ages] [in Hebrew], in *Keneset Ezra: Literature and Life in the Synagogue*, ed. Shulamit Elizur (Jerusalem: Yad Ben Zvi, 1994), 327–50. This recourse was taken in a variety of cases. See Shoham-Steiner, *On the Margins of a Minority*, 113 and nn. 27–28. See also Patrick J. Geary, "'L'humiliation des saints," *Annales Histoire Sciences Sociales* 34 (1979): 27–42.

35. The Hebrew reads ושאר רבותינו שבריינוס ("the rest of our rabbis who reside in the Rhine region"), most probably a reference to the super-communal organization of Rhenish Jewish communities.

36. Rabbi Moshe Azriel ben Rabbi Eliezer "the Homilist" was the great-grandson of Rabbi Judah the Pious of Regensburg. Rabbi Eliezer, the Homilist's father, was Rabbi Moses, the son-in-law of Rabbi Judah the Pious (Moshe married Rabbi Judah's daughter, Golda). See Avigdor Aptovitzer, *Introduction to the Book of Ra'avia* (Jerusalem: Stybel Publishing, 1938), 344, and Urbach, *The Tosafists*, 445 n24, and also Daniel Abrams, "Sefer Hayihud le' Rabbi Elazar ha-Darshan," *Kovetz al Yad* 22, n.s., 12 (1994): 149–60.

37. The case is recounted in Rabbi Meir ha-Kohen of Rothenburg's compilation of Ashkenazi legal rulings, halakhic verdicts, and responsa, *Teshuvot Maimoniyot*, in the form of a commentary on Maimonides' *Mishneh Torah*. When Maimonides's halakhic magnum opus became

popular in Ashkenaz during the second half of the thirteenth century, it became necessary to point out the discrepancies between his rulings and northern European halakhic traditions. Meir ha-Kohen took on this assignment and wrote a commentary called *Hagahot Maimuniyot (Maimonidian Glosses)*, in which he noted these differences. He also referred his readers to the relevant European responsa. The one discussed here appears in *Teshuvot Maimoniyot,* Nashim 25. Rabbi Meir ha-Kohen was a disciple of Rabbi Meir of Rothenburg, accompanying his aged master during the latter's incarceration and imprisonment in Alsace between 1286 and his death in 1293. Rabbi Meir ha-Kohen was martyred in Rothenburg during the 1298 Rindfleisch riots. The responsum is also quoted in the recent large collection of Rabbi Meir's responsa. See Meir b. Baruch, *Responsa*, 2:384–88 §341 (310). Another version of the responsum was published by Isaac Z. Kahana, "Responsa of Or Zarua' and Maharam ben Baruch from an Oxford Manuscript" [in Hebrew], *Sinai* 8 (1940)—*Sinai* 14 (1944), 30–31§ 227. (I used a bound copy found at the Judaica Reading Room in the National Library of Israel, signed ב 157.2). The case was recently discussed at length by Rachel Fürst, who used it to study female agency in rabbinic courts. See her "Striving for Justice," 20–25.

38. Due to its exceptional importance, its richness, and its multifaceted nature, I chose to bring forth the entire first exposition of the case as it appears in *Teshuvot Maymoniyot*, which apparently represents the "cover letter" received by Rabbi Meir when he was first referred to the case by the regional tribunal of Moshe Azriel in the fall of 1272 (5032). See appendix 1.

39. When the testimonies of Rabbi Shealtiel and his sons are taken into consideration, they are regarded as the testimony of a single witness (*'ed ehad*).

40. An allusion to the verse in Song of Songs 7:2: "The rounding of thy thighs is like the links of a chain."

41. The translation is my own. I have tried to convey in this translation both the spirit of the text as well as the sense of the rhymed prose without deviating from the meaning. The Hebrew text, written by Rabbi Meir of Rothenberg, who was rising to prominence at this time, reads as follows: איך אפתח תחילה בגדולים/ לרבותינו מפז מסולאים/ חמוקי ירכיה כמו חלאים/ ואני לא מצאתי ידיים ורגלים/ בעסק העלובה הזאת גומר בת דיבליים/ ואשר יצא מפיהם כל עד ישראל יעשו אותו / ואני צעירם פתחתי מן הצד כתלמיד הדן לפני רבו.

42. This euphemism for prostitution and harlotry appears also in other versions of the responsum, where copiers and later compilers chose to omit the rhymed prose and some of the details but maintained the biblical reference to Gomer. See also Isaac Z. Kahana, "Responsa of Or Zarua' and Maharam bar Baruch," 30–31 §227.

43. Sara's child was a girl, but the word *mamzer* appears here in the male form, as it does in the Hebrew Bible. In medieval Ashkenaz, the word may have been used interchangeably for either a male or a female bastard, although the Palestinian Talmud uses the Aramaic feminine cognate, *mamzerta* (*Kidushin* 3:12, p. 64:3).

44. On the use of these terms in medieval legal discourse see F. R. P. Akehurst, "Good Name, Reputation and Notoriety in French Customary Law," in *Fama: The Politics of Talk and Reputation in Medieval Europe*, ed. Thelma Fenster and Daniel Lord Smail (Ithaca NY: Cornell University Press, 2003), 75–94. Jesus Angel Solorzano Telechea, "Fama Publica, Infamy and Defamation: Judicial Violence and Social Control of Crimes against Sexual Morals in Medieval Castile," *Journal of Medieval History* 22 (2007): 398–413.

45. A much later case, known from the writings of the late fifteenth-century rabbi Joseph Colon of northern Italy, involves a Jewish mother who took her young child and fled to a convent following what seems to have been a domestic quarrel or dispute. It seems that the woman wanted to convert to Christianity, but eventually decided not to convert her child. Later she was persuaded to return to the Jewish community. The case came before Rabbi Joseph. The woman was married to a Jew of priestly lineage. She was suspected of having had sexual intercourse with non-Jewish men during her time outside the Jewish community. If so, she would be forbidden to her Jewish husband. See Rabbi Joseph Colon, *Responsa*, ed. Shmuel Baruch Hacohen Deutsch and Elyakim Slesinger (Jerusalem: Oraysoh Publishing, 1988), 316–24 §160. On this source see Gerald I. Blidstein, "The Personal Status of Apostate and Ransomed Women in Medieval Jewish Law," *Shenaton Ha-Mishpat Haivri* (Annual of the Institute for Research in Jewish Law) 3–4 (1976–77): 35–116. See also Rachel Fürst, "Captivity, Conversion, and Communal Identity: Sexual Angst and Religious Crisis in Frankfurt, 1241," *Jewish History* 22 (2008): 179–221.

46. The Hebrew translated here as "the talk of the local women" is נושאות ונותנות בו מוזרות בלבנה, a phrase taken from the Mishnah, tractate *Sotah*,

chap. 6:1. The passage records a controversy between Rabbi Eliezer and Rabbi Joshua regarding a woman suspected of adultery. Rabbi Eliezer holds the opinion that if a person is jealous of his wife it is enough that he had heard a rumor that she was unfaithful to set in motion the *sotah* ritual, performed when a man suspects his wife of committing adultery. Rabbi Joshua thinks that this is too harsh, and maintains that the ritual should be used only when a woman's sexual misconduct becomes the subject of gossip by women spinning and knitting at night. See Ya'akov N. Epstein, ed., *Mavo le'Nosach ha'Mishna* [in Hebrew] (Jerusalem: Magnes Press, 2000), 1:84–86, and Menachem Kahana, ed., *Sifri Zuta Devarim* [in Hebrew] (Jerusalem: Magnes Press, 2002), 351–59; Miriam Peskowitz, *Spinning Fantasies: Rabbis, Gender and History* (Berkeley: University of California Press, 1997), 136–39; Lisa Gruschcow, *Writing the Wayward Wife: Rabbinic Interpretations of Sotah* (Leiden: Brill, 2006), 105. I thank my friend Jason Rogof for helping me find some of these references.

47. On the methods of infanticide in early modern Germany see Ulinka Rublack, *The Crimes of Women in Early Modern Germany*, Oxford Studies in Social History (Oxford: Clarendon Press, 2001), 163–96, esp. 164–65, 171. See also George Duby, ed., *The History of Private Life*, vol. 2, Revelations of the Medieval World, trans. Arthur Goldhammer (Cambridge MA: Belknap Press, 1988), 220–24; 489–99; Roland C. Finucane, *The Rescue of the Innocents: Endangered Children in Medieval Miracles* (New York: St. Martin's Press, 1997). On infanticide in medieval Jewish communities, see the pioneering work of Zfira Entin-Rokeah, "Unnatural Child Death among Christians and Jews in Medieval England," *Journal of Psychohistory* 18 (1990): 181–226. More recently and with a broader scope Baumgarten, *Mothers and Children*, 174–78. More on infanticide see later in the chapter.

48. Isaac Z. Kahana, "Responsa of Or Zarua' and Maharam ben Baruch from an Oxford Manuscript," *Sinai* 8 (1940)–*Sinai* 14 (1944): 30–31 §227.

49. אבל זה הארורה והמקוללת שכפרה ואמרה (!).

50. While Sara's father had approached two members of the tribunal about killing his daughter, and had disclosed to them information about her behavior, he was not legally fit to testify. First, because the testimony of relatives is not admissible; second, most of the information he offered was hearsay, as he was not himself a witness to her behavior.

Furthermore, the tribunal was not in formal session when he discussed his grievances with two of its members.

51. In this respect, the Shum supercommunal organization was an exception. This supercommunal organization of the Rhineland was ratified by a regional set of rules and a series of meetings that solidified the organization. See Reiner Barzen, "'Kehillot Schum': Zur Eigenart der Verbindungen zwischen den jüdischen Gemeinden Mainz, Worms, und Speyer bis zu Mitte des 13. Jahrhunderts," in *Jüdische Gemeinden und ihr christlischer Kontext in kulturräumlich vergleichender Betrachtung von der Spätantike bis zum 18. Jahrhundert*, ed. Christoph Cluse, Alfred Haverkamp, and Israel J. Yuval (Hannover: Verlag Hahnsche Buchahandlung, 2003), 389–404. Barzen, "Jewish Regional Organization in the Rhineland: The 'Kehillot Shum' around 1300," in *The Jews in Europe in the Middle Ages (Tenth to Fifteenth Centuries): Proceedings of the International Symposium Held at Speyer 20–25 October 2002*, ed. Christoph Cluse (Turnhout: Brepols, 2004), 233–42. For a detailed account see Barzen, *Taqqanot Qehillot Šum*. For a comparison with other Jewish supercommunal regional structures see Joseph Schatzmiller, "Community and Super-Community in Provence in the Middle Ages," in *Jüdische Gemeinden und ihr christlischer Kontext in kulturraumlich vergleichender Betrachtung von der Spätantike bis zum 18. Jahrhundert*, ed. Christoph Cluse, Alfred Haverkamp, and Israel J. Yuval (Hannover: Verlag Hahnsche Buchahandlung, 2003), 441–48.

52. Jacob ben Moshe Halevi Mulin, *The Book of Maharil: Customs* [in Hebrew] (Jerusalem: Machon Yerushalayim, 1989), 178–79. See the parallel text in Rabbi Shalom ben Isaac Zekel of Neustadt, *Decisions and Customs*, 19–20 §35.

53. Jewish tradition sought to associate or attribute authorship of the major books of the Apocrypha quoted in the Talmud to scriptural figures. The legend was familiar to both Jews and Christians in medieval Europe through the *Ben Sira Alphabet*, a tenth-century compilation based on the original apocryphal book. It relates that the prophet Jeremiah was ambushed in a bathhouse by wicked men of the tribe of Ephraim. They wanted to molest him sexually and forced him to ejaculate his semen into a tub in the bathhouse. Later on, the prophet's daughter bathed in the same pool and conceived from the semen left in the water. Her son was Ben Sira, who, as a result of this incestuous conception, was both Jeremiah's son and grandson.

54. A parallel tradition can be found in *Toldot Yeshu*. See David Biale, "Counter-History and Jewish Polemics against Christianity: The Sefer Toldot Yeshu and the Sefer Zerubavel," *Jewish Social Studies* 6 (1999): 130–45, and Peter Schäfer et. al., eds., *Toledot Yeshu (The Life Story of Jesus) Revisited: A Princeton Conference* (Tübingen: Mohr Siebeck, 2011).
55. *Yibbum*—or levirate marriage—is mandated by biblical law (Deut. 25:5–10). The brother of a man who has died without heirs is obligated to marry the widow in order to maintain the deceased brother's lineage. However, if either of the parties refuses to go through with the marriage, they must perform a ceremony known as *ḥalitzah*, a symbolic act in which they relinquish their right to enter into this marriage. Over the centuries, the practice of *yibbum* declined and *ḥalitzah* became standard, as in this case. See Solomon Schechter and Joseph Jacobs, "Levirate Marriage (Hebr. 'yibbum')," *Jewish Encyclopedia* (1906), accessed Jan. 4, 2018, http://www.jewishencyclopedia.com/articles/9859-levirate-marriage. See also Grossman, *Pious and Rebellious*, 90–101.
56. Haim Eliezer b. Isaac Or Zarua', *Responsa*, 43 §50. On Rabbi Haim Eliezer see Noah Goldstein, "Rabbi Hayyim Eliezer ben Issac Or Zarua: His Life, His Work, and a Digest of His Responsa," PhD diss., Yeshiva University (1959). On his life and work see Y. Horowitz, "Rabbi Haim Or Zarua'."
57. The Hebrew reads: "בעודה הולכת עמו וכרוכה אחריו"—while she was still walking with him and involved with him."
58. Rabbi Haim draws a parallel between this case and another one in which the brother in question had converted to Christianity. A passage in the Babylonian Talmud, tractate *Yebamot* 70a, addresses the issue. Raba's opinion is that had the wife known that this would be her fate (to be compelled into a levirate marriage with a convert) she would not have consented to the initial marriage in the first place. Rabbi Haim offers the same argument in the present case—had the widow known that she would end up in a levirate marriage with the son of a harlot, she would not have married her deceased husband in the first place.
59. The fullest and probably the most accurate version can be found in Ya'acov b. Moshe Halevi Mulin, *Responsa of Rabbi Ya'acov Mulin–Maharil*, ed. Yitzchok Satz (Jerusalem: Machon Yerushalayim, 1979), 322–23 §205 (233) and n12.
60. On anti-Jewish violence in this period see Müller, "*Erez Gezerah*—'Land of Persecution.'" On the Black Death and the anti-Jewish violence see

Alfred Haverkamp, "Die Judenverfolgungen zur Zeit des Schwarzen Todes im Gesellschaftsgefüge deutscher Städte," in *Zur Geschichte der Juden im Deutschland des späten Mittelalters und der frühen Neuzeit*, ed. Alfred Haverkamp (Stuttgart: Hiersemann, 1981), 27–93; František Graus, *Pest, Geissler, Judenmorde: Das 14. Jahrhundert als Krisenzeit* (Göttingen: Vandenhoek & Ruprecht, 1987), 155–390; Rosemary Horrox, ed., *The Black Death* (Manchester UK: Manchester University Press, 1994), 207–26; Christoph M. Cluse, "Zur Chronologie der Verfolgungen zur Zeit des 'Schwarzen Todes,'" *Forschungen zur Geschichte der Juden* 14 (2002): 223–42.

61. The text uses the euphemism *yatzah le-tarbut ra'ah*, literally, "went out to bad culture," meaning conversion. See Israel J. Yuval, *Scholars in Their Time: The Religious Leadership of German Jewry in the Late Middle Ages* (Jerusalem: Magnes Press, 1988), 80–83.

62. This was, of course, true of the surrounding society as well. See, for example, Rublack, *Crimes of Women*, 16–20.

63. The term *nafkat bra* appears in Aramaic translations of Hebrew scripture in the sense of "prostitute." The literal meaning is "she who has gone out." In his scriptural commentary, Rashi glosses the term (Judg. 19:2): "every time the term *zonah* [whore] appears, it is the same as the [Aramaic] term *nafkat bra*, for the woman leaves her husband and goes out to fornicate with others." I have no idea why Rabbi Meir, or the person who wrote down or copied his responsum, chose to use this Aramaic word to describe the woman's behavior. We also do not know which exact word was used between the two parties to the case, or the word that appeared in the woman's petition, which has not survived. I believe that the term was used to translate a colloquial term for harlotry and sexual promiscuity, so as not to confine the discussion to the legal question of the precise definition of the words *znut* and *zonah*. On the Aramaic term, see, for instance, Floris Sepmeijer, ed., *A Bilingual Concordance to the Targum of the Prophets*, vol. 12, Jeremiah, chaps. 1–7 (Leiden: Brill, 1998), 203.

64. Rabbi Mordechai ben Hillel Hacohen, *Sefer Ha'Mordechai*, chap. Hakhovel, §80–82.

65. Rabbi Meir ruled that, if the accusation about Leah insulting a dead person was corroborated by witnesses, she should ask the dead person's forgiveness in the presence of ten adult men at his or her grave.

66. Menachem of Merseburg, "Nimukei Rabbi Menachem of Merseburg," [in Hebrew], in *The Responsa of Rabbi Jacob Weil*, ed. Bezalel Landoi (Jerusalem: Tiferet Torah, 1988), 171–82.
67. We know very little about Rabbi Judah Mintz. He seems to have been born in Mainz, Germany, in the early fifteenth century; in any case, he was a victim of the 1462 expulsion from that city. He then moved to northern Italy and settled in Padua, where he taught at the local yeshiva and lived until his death at a very ripe old age, in around 1509. Tradition has it that Rabbi Judah's book collection and his correspondence were destroyed in a fire that consumed his study. Only sixteen of his responsa survived, and those were printed along with the responsa of his younger disciple and his granddaughter's husband, Rabbi Meir Katzenellenbogen of Padua. On the migration of Ashkenazi Jews from Germany to northern Italy in the fifteenth century see Angela Möschter, *Juden im Venezianischen Treviso* (1389–1509), Forschungen zur Geschichte der Juden, vol. 19 (Hannover: Hahnsche Buchhandlung, 2008), 72–91. Although Möschter focuses on the northern Italian city of Traviso and on the migration of Jews from Nuremberg to this area, many of her findings are applicable to other Jews in nearby towns.
68. This talmudic prohibition grew out of the fear that without it the woman would have an incentive to neglect her child, leading to either intentional or unintentional infanticide. For a well-informed survey of the possible obstacles to remarriage see Tamar Salmon-Mack, *On Marriage and Its Crises in Early Modern Polish and Lithuanian Jewry* [in Hebrew] (Tel Aviv: Hakibbutz Hameuchad, 2012), 89–134.
69. Unusually, both the woman and the man in the case are named. Most often, respondents and the editors of responsa did not disclose the names of the individuals in rulings. It may well be that Rabbi Judah was prompted to disclose the names of the parties because of the nature and novelty of the case. I suspect that it may have been his way of indicating his displeasure with their individual behavior and the overall phenomenon it represented. Although Rabbi Judah agreed to facilitate the marriage, for the sake of the people named in the responsum (Mordechai and Rachel), he did so ex post facto, seeking to make it clear that he in no way condoned their actions.
70. Clearly, the responsum was composed after 1462, the year Jews were expelled from Mainz. Rabbi Judah was among those Jews that left Mainz in that year and settled in northern Italy. While undated, the

internal evidence indicates that he was already residing in Padua when he wrote it, in other words, some time during the four decades between his arrival there and his death in 1509.

71. Mordechai apparently could afford to rent temporary lodgings for Rachel in Padua until the legal issue was settled and she could marry him. He also had enough money to move her from one rented room to another, which might have required additional payment for terminating the rental contract. The move was necessary because the text indicates that the first lodgings were located in a neighborhood of bad repute and *paritzim* harassed her.

72. An ironic reference to Ps. 144:14: "with no breach, and no going forth, and no outcry in our broad places," changing the negative to positive.

73. Peter Clark, *European Cities and Towns 400–2000* (Oxford: Oxford University Press, 2009), 55–56.

74. Rachel's temporary place of dwelling is referred to in the text as an "encampment house" (*beit mahaneh*), literally meaning a hostel or a boardinghouse.

75. Leah Otis points out that the medieval belief that prostitution endangered women and offered them a bad moral example was one of the major motivations for regulating it and confining prostitutes to designated parts of cities and towns. This was done not only because allowing men a sexual outlet with prostitutes was seen as preferable to them having liaisons with the wives of other men, but also to ensure that the chaste wives and daughters of citizens with impeccable reputations were not exposed to a bad moral example. See Otis, *Prostitution in Medieval Society*, 100–113, esp. 103–5. German towns instituted ordinances clearly aimed at demarcating prostitutes from decent women. Late fifteenth-century Würzburg had a detailed dress code for whores, prohibiting them from wearing luxurious dresses, on pain of a fine of ten guilders and the confiscation of the garments. See Merry E. Wiesner, "Paternalism in Practice: The Control of Servants and Prostitutes in Early Modern German Cities," in *Gender, Church and State in Early Modern Germany: Essays* (New York: Routledge, 2013), 94–113, esp. 103.

76. Mordechai is described as moving Rachel from her temporary dwellings in the boardinghouse to other accommodations and then again to yet another, much less appealing residence on the outskirts of Padua right above the cemetery, in the undertaker's home. On the cemeteries

in Padua see David Malkiel, *Stones Speak: Hebrew Tombstones from Padua 1529–1862* (Leiden: Brill, 2014), 1–8.

77. The job Rachel most likely could have hoped to get was as a housemaid, although this is not explicit in the text, which only speaks of *sekhirut*, literally, wage labor.
78. See Jörg Müller's work on interreligious sexual encounters. See also his reference to Norbert Schnizler's 2002 article in his note 9.
79. The document survived in MS British Museum Or. Add. 27.111 and was published by the late Haim Hillel Ben-Sasson almost half a century ago. See Haim H. Ben-Sasson, "Mishnato ha'Khevratit shel Rabbi Yohanan Luria," *Zion* 27 (1962): 166–98, 193, n145.
80. The exilarch was the lay leader of the Jewish community in Mesopotamia in Talmudic and early medieval times; here it is used as an honorific for a master of Jewish legal scholarship. It is evidence of Maharil's standing among the halakhists of his age. See Yuval, *Scholars in Their Time*, 208–64.
81. This attempt to seek a penitential recipe would be in line with the rituals of the Devotio Moderna movement, which became very popular in Germany at this time. See Harry Kühnel, "Devotio Moderna: Die Neue Frommigkeit," in *Alltag im Spätmittelalter*, ed. Harry Kühnel et al. (Graz, Aus.: Verlag Styria, 1986), 111–14.
82. Jacob Elbaum, *Repentance and Self-Flagellation* [in Hebrew] (Jerusalem: Magnes Press, 1992).
83. Harry Kühnel, "Frömmigkeit ohne Grenzen," in *Alltag im Spätmittelalter* ed. Harry Kühnel et al. (Graz, Aus.: Verlag Styria, 1986), 92–110. On the abuse of the sale of indulgences in late medieval Europe see R. N. Swanson, *Indulgences in Late Medieval England: Passports to Paradise?* (Cambridge: Cambridge University Press, 2007), 113–78.
84. See Shoham-Steiner, *On the Margins of a Minority*, 35.
85. Haim Eliezer b. Isaac Or Zarua', *Teshuvot Maharakh*, §11, Sermon on the weekly portion Va'erah, 14–16.
86. The translation is that of the New American Standard Version of the Hebrew Bible, 1995. The translation most often used by Jewish scholars is, "for they are a very forward generation, children in whom there is no faithfulness." The name of the boy, Kidor, is deliberately intended to invoke the verse's first two words.
87. Ya'acov ben Moshe Halevi Mulin, *Book of Maharil*, 485–86, Hilkhot Milah §20.

88. See Baumgarten, *Mothers and Children*, 55–89.
89. See Rublack, *Crimes of Women*, 134–96. And see Gerhard Jaritz, "Leben um zu Leben," in *Alltag in Spätmittelalter*, ed. Harry Kühnel et al. (Graz, Austria: Verlag Styria, 1986), 157–64.
90. On the importance of the performance, and of paying attention to every deviance from a prescribed performance, see Richard Schechner, *Performance Studies: An Introduction* (London: Routledge, 2002), 124–29, 151–56.
91. The name given to a Jewish male at his circumcision ceremony was his *shem kodesh* (sacral name), used mostly for religious purposes (in the synagogue, Jewish rituals, and Hebrew documents). Most Jewish males and females had other names and aliases that they used in their daily interactions with both fellow Jews and Christians. See Lilach L. Assaf, "The Language of Names: Jewish Onomastics in Late Medieval Germany, Identity and Acculturation," in *Zugehörigkeit: Spätmittelalterliche Praktiken der Namengebung im europäischen Vergleich*, ed. Christof Rolker und Gabriela Signori (Konstanz, Germany: Konstanz University Press, 2011), 149–60.
92. Ya'acov b. Moshe Halevi Mulin, *Book of Maharil*, 485–86, Hilkhot Milah §19.
93. Custom was of such great import in medieval Ashkenazi society that it sometimes overrode *halakhah*. See Israel M. Ta-Shma, *Early Franco-German Ritual and Custom* [in Hebrew] (Jerusalem: Magnes Press, 1994), 13–108. On the later medieval Ashkenazi customs and their impact see Eric I. Zimmer, *Society and Its Customs: Studies in the History and Metamorphosis of Jewish Customs* [in Hebrew] (Jerusalem: Shazar, 1996).
94. The potency of this mechanism is also evident in a responsum by Rabbi Israel b. Haim of Bruna (c. 1400–1480), the rabbi of Regensburg in the second half of the fifteenth century. The case involved a child whose priestly descent was questioned on the grounds that his mother was alleged to be "extremely promiscuous" (*prutzah be-yoter*). See his *Responsa*, §68. One of the pieces of evidence adduced in support of the mother's chastity and the son's legitimacy was that, at the time of or soon after the child's birth, there had been *no ritual deviation* to indicate that his status was problematic, or that anyone had knowledge of such a problem. They claimed that the child's circumcision took place in the synagogue and not in the courtyard. Children who were suspected to be *mamzerim* were circumcised in the synagogue courtyard

by the building's doorway from its external side. In this case there was no such evidence and the mother and boy claimed that the absence of such memory attested to the fact that there was no legitimacy problem and that all the rumors about the mother's alleged promiscuity were indeed false.

95. Avraham Grossman was one of the first scholars in Jewish studies to address the topic of domestic violence in the Jewish Middle Ages. See his groundbreaking article adapted from a lecture delivered at the World Congress of Jewish Studies (1989): "Medieval Rabbinic Views on Wife-Beating 800–1300," *Jewish History* 5 (1991): 52–63.

96. Mordechai Frishtik, "Physical Violence by Parents against Their Children in Jewish History and Jewish Law," *Jewish Law Annual* 10 (1992): 79–97. See also Tali M. Berner, *In Their Own Way: Children and Childhood in Early Modern Ashkenaz* [in Hebrew] (Jerusalem: Shazar Publishing, 2018), 59–63.

97. Avraham Grossman, "Child Marriage in Jewish Society in the Middle Ages until the Thirteenth Century," *Pe'amim* 45 (1990): 108–25, and Grossman, "Medieval Rabbinic Views on Wife Beating 800–1300."

98. Isaac ben Moshe of Vienna, *Book of Or Zaruaʻ*, vol. 3, 46–47, Pirquei Baba Kama §160–61.

99. On the mechanics of divorce laws in medieval Ashkenaz, see Rachel Fürst, "Marriage before the Bench: Divorce Law and Litigation Strategies in Thirteenth-Century Ashkenaz," *Jewish History* 31 (2017): 7–30.

100. See Shoham-Steiner, *On the Margins of a Minority*, 120–22.

101. The case appears in Emanuel, *Responsa of Meir of Rothenburg and his Colleagues*, vol. 2, § 459, p. 893. This R. Yechiel ha-Kohen may be the same one who collected material included in a collection of R. Meir b. Barukh's responsa. See the same collection, vol. 1, § 116. He may possibly also be a person of the same name referenced in Haim Eliezer ben Isaac Or Zaruaʻ, *Teshuvot Maharakh*, § 191, 178–79. I thank Rachel Fürst for calling my attention to this man and to his possible whereabouts.

102. The word in Hebrew is מעטירה, which literally means "crown-wearing," from the Hebrew noun "עטרה," crown or diadem. I believe that Rabbi Meir was trying to convey a sense of dignity and Chana's high pedigree.

103. The first husband is referred to as a martyr (קדוש), and not simply as "the slain" (הנהרג), which denotes any violent death, including as the result of involvement in criminal activity. It may indicate that he was killed during the riots of the 1280s. See Müller, *Eretz Gezerah*, 245–59.

104. Grossman, *Pious and Rebellious*, 231–39.
105. See chap. 2 section, "Inadvertent Murderers and Penitential Practices." On this see also Entin-Rokeah, "Unnatural Child Death." See also Rublack, *Crimes of Women*, 163–96.
106. Baumgarten, *Mothers and Children*, 170–72.
107. "Sudden Infant Death Syndrome (SIDS): Overview," *National Institute of Child Health and Human Development*, updated June 27, 2013, https://www.nichd.nih.gov/health/topics/sids.
108. On the size of medieval urban homes, especially in Germany, see Helmut Hundsbichler, "Wohnen," in *Alltag im Spätmittelalter*, ed. Harry Kühnel (Gratz, Aus.: Styria Verlag, 1986), 254–70; Entin-Rokeah, "Unnatural Child Death"; Duby, *History of Private Life*, 220–24, 489–99; and Finucane, *Rescue of the Innocents*.
109. Emanuel, *Responsa of Rabbi Meir of Rothenburg and His Colleagues*, 1:54 §333; 2:740–44 §375–78. On this matter see Ephraim Elimelekh Urbach, "Al Grimat Mavet be'Shgaga u'Mavet ba'Arisah," *Asufot* 1 (1987): 319–32. See also Baumgarten, *Mothers and Children*, 176–78. Given that only a small fraction of the responsa written have survived, the fact that we have documentation of five cases from a short interval in the mid-thirteenth century is telling. See Haym Soloveitchik, "Can Halakhic Texts Talk History?," *AJS Review* 3 (1978): 153–96.
110. Emanuel, *Responsa of Rabbi Meir of Rothenburg and His Colleagues*, 2:740–41 §375. The Hebrew reads: "אשה שמצאה וולד מת יש מרבותינו שמחמירים עליה ויש שמקילים. ואיני רשאי להחמיר עליה דשמא הא מילתא להא דאמרינן הנסקלין והנשרפין ידונו בקלה. ושמא לא דמיא הא מילתא להא דאמרינן 'המחמיר תבוא עליו ברכה' דהני מילי לגבי אדם אם רוצה להחמיר על עצמו תבוא עליו ברכה אבל השואל להורות לו אינו רשאי להחמיר בדבר אלא כיון שיש מרבותינו שמקילים אחריהם אורה. וכך מצאתי כתוב: פסקו הגאונים אישה שמצאה וולד מת אצלה דינה להתענות שנה, והם נ"ב שבועות ב"ה ובכל שבוע ב' תעניות, לבד מימים הנאסרים בהספד ובתענית, בין מדברי תורה בין מדברי סופרים שבהם לא תתענה. דגזירת המקום וגזירת רבותינו קדמה לחטא זה. והם: חנוכה ופורים וכל ימי ניסן וחול המועד וראשי חודשים. וכל אותם ב' וה' שלא תתענה בהם צריכה להשלים אחר השנה. וטוב שיהיה לה עץ אחד וכל ב' וה' שלא תתענה בו תרשום על העץ פגימה עד סוף השנה. ואחר השנה תמנה כמה פגימות יש, ויהיה עץ אחר ותשלים כל הימים שלא התענית בהם. ותתענה בכל שבוע ב' וה' ובכל יום שתתענה בו תרשום על העץ פגימה עד שתשלים בחשבון כל הפגימות שהיו על העץ הראשון. וכל הימים שתתענה לא תאכל בשר ולא תשתה יין. ואחרי שמשקין שלנו שיכר עב אז לא תשתה שיכר עס אלא שיכר דק, ולא תרחוץ כי אם פעמים בחודש כך היבנתי מדברי המקילים בדבר זה. . . ."

111. In his introduction to the copious halakhic material he included in his two-volume edition of the *Responsa of Rabbi Meir of Rothenburg and His Colleagues*, Simcha Emanuel notes that, while we have very little information about the rabbis named here, many of the places they refer to are in the vicinity of Magdeburg in Germany. He thus presumes that they operated in Magdeburg and its environs, and surmises that there was probably a scholarly center in the area. See 1:104–11.
112. This did not mean fasting every day but rather fasting on Mondays and Thursdays for an entire year.
113. MS Oxford 641(O Add. Fol. 34, fol. 57); Emanuel, *Responsa of Rabbi Meir of Rothenburg and his Colleagues*, 2:744 §378.
114. The text here is from Baumgarten, *Mothers and Children*, 237 n115. Baumgarten's masterful translation of this responsum is based on her understanding of the term "*bat herayon*" as "pregnant woman," basing herself on BT *Sota* 25b and Rashi's commentary on the word *eilonit* in that passage. I disagree. I think that the text relates to a larger group of women, not only those who are pregnant, but rather all women of fertile age who may potentially become pregnant. Excessive fasting is known to have a tremendous impact on menstruation and fertility of women, as exhibited in acute anorexia. See Elizabeth R. Hoffman, Stephanie C. Zerwas, and Cynthia M. Bulik, "Reproductive Issues in Anorexia Nervosa," *Expert Review of Obstetrics and Gynecology* 6 (2011): 403–14, accessed Sept. 14, 2016, http://www.ncbi.nlm.nih.gov/pmc/articles/PMC3192363/.
115. Other rabbis were not as accommodating. See Baumgarten, *Mothers and Children*, 237n115.
116. On the criminal organization known as the Zvi Migdal syndicate see Isabel Vincent, *Bodies and Souls: The Tragic Plight of Three Jewish Women Forced into Prostitution in the Americas* (New York: Harper Collins, 2005).

CONCLUSION

1. Zimmer, "Rabbi Menachem mi'Merseburg ve'Nimukav."
2. Berkovitz, *Protocols of Justice*. Other complete or partial records of this sort can be found in as yet unpublished manuscripts scattered in various libraries, but they, too, come from a much later period. On collecting, evaluating, and digitizing some of these sources see "The Pinkassim

Project," National Library of Israel, accessed Feb. 10, 2018, http://web.nli.org.il/sites/NLI/English/collections/jewish-collection/pinkassim/Pages/default.aspx. For a preliminary bibliography list on these *pinkassim* see, on the same website, "Pinkassim Project Bibliography," http://web.nli.org.il/sites/NLI/English/collections/jewish-collection/pinkassim/Documents/PinkassimBibliography.pdf.

3. Based on R. Solomon's 1096 chronicle, in Eidelberg, *Jews and the Crusaders*, 49. I have made a few small stylistic modifications in Eidelberg's translation and added the word "permanent." The Hebrew expression דין קבוע stresses the permanence of the Jewish juridical system in Cologne.

4. Much remains to be learned about Jewish involvement in crime, not just in medieval times but in the early modern period. From that later period, much more extensive and orderly documentation survives, both from the Jewish milieu and gentile society. These make it possible to offer a more nuanced picture of everyday life in Jewish communities. The work of Maria Boes has shown that the archives of the late medieval and early modern period can also make a great contribution to the study of medieval Jewry.

The Jews of Regensburg are a case in point. The research of my colleague Eva Haverkamp and her students on archival material from the city of Regensburg, kept in the Bavarian State Archives in Munich, has shown that there are new avenues to be explored with regard to Jewish involvement in crime as well as to criminal collaboration between Jews and non-Jews. Another avenue of research is an in-depth examination of the situation in Iberia, only marginally touched upon in this book. The late Yom Tov Assis took up this issue in his seminal study on the Jews in the kingdom of Aragon up to the fourteenth century, but the records of other Iberian realms and their Jewish communities still remain to be studied. Much remains to be learned from the responsa collected by Rabbi Asher ben Yehiel's son, Rabbi Judah ben Asher, printed today under the title *Zikhron Yehudah*. Of similar importance is the world of Jews under Islamic rule, about which the Cairo Geniza documents offer a wealth of material. This includes both the earlier Geniza material studied by, among others, Shelomo Dov Goitein, Mordechai Akiva Friedman, and Miriam Frenkel, and the later periods of the fourteenth to seventeenth centuries written on by scholars such as Dotan Arad.

APPENDIX 11

1. It seems that Sara was last seen pregnant on the month of Adar and had given birth in close temporal proximity to the special Sabbath of *Parah*, when alongside the weekly portion, Jews read in the Torah about the Red Heifer (*parah aduma*, Num. 19), symbolizing the purification rituals to be enacted before the festival of Passover.

BIBLIOGRAPHY

All Hebrew names are rendered according to *Encyclopedia Judaica*, edited by Michael Berenbaum and Fred Skolnik, 2nd ed. (Detroit: Macmillan, 2007). Translation of biblical verses is based upon and adapted as necessary from *Tanakh: JPS Hebrew-English Tanakh: The Traditional Hebrew Text and the New JPS Translation*, 2nd ed. (Philadelphia: Jewish Publication Society, 2000). K represents the Hebrew letters *kaf* and *qof*. H represents both the letters *he* and *ḥet*. The digraph tz represents Hebrew *tzadi*. Mishnah, Tosefta, and Midrash refer to the bodies of literature; mishnah, tosefta, and midrash refer to specific passages within the respective bodies of literature.

ABBREVIATIONS

AJS Review	Association of Jewish Studies Review
BT	Babylonian Talmud (Vilnius 1881)
JQR	Jewish Quarterly Review
M	Mishna
PAAJR	Proceedings of the American Academy of Research
PT	Palestinian Talmud
SHW	*Sefer Hasidim* (Wistinezki, ed.)
T	Tosefta

PRIMARY SOURCES

Agus, Irving A., ed. *Responsa of the Tosaphists: Unpublished Responsa Culled from Various Manuscripts*. New York: Yeshiva University, 1954.

Ahai Gaon. *Sheeltot de Rav Ahai Gaon: A Critical and Annotated Edition*. Edited by Shlomo Kalman Mirsky. 5 vols. Jerusalem: Sura Research and Publication Foundation, Yeshiva University, and Mosad Harav Kook, 1960–77.

Aronius, Julius, ed. *Regesten zur Geschichte der Juden im Fränkischen und Deutschen Reiche bis zum Jahre 1273*. Historischen Commission für Geschichte der Juden in Deutschland. Berlin: Verlag von Leonhard Simion, 1902.

Artum, Elias S., and Humbertus M. D. Cassuto, eds. *Statuta Iudaeorum Candiae Eorumque Memorabilia*. [In Hebrew.] Jerusalem: Mekize Nirdamin, 1940.

Asher b. Yehiel. *Responsa*. [In Hebrew.] Edited by Shlomo Jodlov. Jerusalem: Machon Yerushalayim Press, 1994. Avneri, Zvi, ed. *Germania Judaica*. Vol. 2/1, Von 1238 bis zur Mitte des 14. Jahrhunderts. Tübingen: J. C. B. Mohr-P. Siebeck, 1968.

Berkovitz, Jay. R. *Protocols of Justice: The Pinkas of the Metz Rabbinic Court, 1771–1789*. 2 vols. Leiden: Brill, 2014.

Bezalel b. Avraham Ashkenazi. *Shitah Mekubetzet: Baba Metziah*. [In Hebrew.] Edited by B. Brochman. Jerusalem: Vagshal, 2006.

Cassel, David, ed. *Teshuvot Geonim Kadmonim*. [In Hebrew.] Berlin: Friedlander, 1848.

David, Avraham, ed. *Sefer Kolbo*. [In Hebrew.] 8 vols. Jerusalem, 1990–2009. Doberl, M., ed. *Monumenta Germaniae selecta ab anno 768 usque ad annum 1250*. In *Selected Historical Documents of the Middle Ages*, translated and edited by E. F. Henderson. London: George Bell and Sons, 1896.

Douglas, David C., ed. *English Historical Documents*. Vol. 2, 1042–1189. London: Oxford University Press, 1981.

Elazar b. Judah of Worms. *Elazar Vormensis Oratio ad Pascam*. [In Hebrew.] Edited by Simcha Emanuel. Jerusalem: Mekize Nirdamim, 2005.

———. *Sefer Rokeah*. Vol. 1. [In Hebrew.] Edited by Noah Kazachkov and Joseph Benjamin Rubin. Jerusalem: Zichron Aharon Press, 2014.

Elbogen, Ismar, ed. *Germania Judaica*. Vol. 1, Von den ältesten Zeiten bis 1238. Tübingen: J. C. B. Mohr-Siebeck, 1963.

Eliezer b. Joel ha-Levi. *The Book of Ra'avia*. [In Hebrew.] 4 vols. Edited by David Deblitzki. Bnei-Brak, 2005.

Emanuel, Simcha, ed. *Responsa of Rabbi Meir of Rothenburg and his Colleagues*. [In Hebrew.] 2 vols. Jerusalem: World Union of Jewish Studies, 2012.

Epstein, Ya'akov N. *Mavo le'Nosach ha'Mishna*. [In Hebrew.] 2 vols. Jerusalem: Magnes Press, 2000.

Gershom ben Judah of Mainz. *The Responsa of Rabbenu Gershom Meor Ha'gola*. [In Hebrew.] Edited by Shlomo Eidelberg. New York: Yeshiva University, 1956.

Gregory of Tours. "The History of the Franks." In *Historia Francorum: Monumenta Germaniae Historica, Scriptores rerum Merovingicarum I, 1*, book 6:17, edited by Bruno Krusch and Wilhelm Levison. Hannover: Hahn Verlag, 1937–51.

Gui, Bernard. *The Inquisitor's Guide: A Medieval Manual on Heretics*. Translated and edited by Janet Shirley. Welwyn Garden City, UK: Ravenhall Books, 2006.

Habermann, Avraham Moshe. *Gezerot Ashkenaz ve-Zarfat*. Jerusalem: Tarshish, 1946.

Hacohen, Yehudah. *Sefer Hadinim: Teshuvotav melokatot mimkorot shonim*. [In Hebrew.] Edited by Avraham Grossman. Jerusalem: Dinur Center, 1977.

Haim Eliezer b. Isaac Or Zarua'. *Teshuvot Maharakh Or Zarua'* [Responsa] *Derashot ve'Piskei Halakhot* [Sermons and Adjudications]. [In Hebrew.] Edited by Menachem Avitan. Jerusalem, 2002.

Henry III Fine Roles Project. "Images for C 60/49. m20." National Archives and Kings College London. http://www.finerollshenry3.org.uk/content/fimages/C60_49/m20.html.

Hizkiya ben Mano'ach. *Hizkuni Pirushei Ha'Torah le'Rabbenu*. [In Hebrew.] Edited by Haim Dov Chavel. Jerusalem: Mosad Ha'Rav Kook, 1981.

Isaac Alfasi. *She'elot u'Teshuvot Ha'rif*. [In Hebrew.] Edited by Ya'acov Asher Rozman. Jerusalem: Machon Yerushalayim, 2008.

Isaac the Elder of Dampierre. [in Hebrew] Edited by Avraham (Rami) Reiner and Pinchas Roth. Jerusalem: Mekitzei Nirdamim, 2020.

Israel b. Haim of Bruna. *Responsa*. [In Hebrew.] Edited by Moshe Herschler. Jerusalem: Tiferet Hatorah, 1960.

Isaac b. Moshe of Vienna. *The Book of Or Zarua'*. 3 vols. [In Hebrew.] Edited by Jacob Farbstein et al. Jerusalem: Machon Yerushalayim, 2010.

Israel Iserlyn b. Petachia. *Terumat ha-Deshen* [Responsa and Rulings]. [In Hebrew.] 2 vols. Edited by Shmuel Avitan. Jerusalem, 1991.

Jacob b. Judah Weil. *Responsa of Rabbi Jacob Weil*. [In Hebrew.] Edited by Yonatan Shraga Domb. Jerusalem: Machon Yerushalayim, 2001.

Jacob b. Moshe Halevi Mulin—Maharil. *The Book of Maharil: Customs*. [In Hebrew.] Edited by Shlomo Spitzer. Jerusalem: Machon Yerushalayim, 1989.

———. *Responsa*. Edited by Yitzchok Satz. Jerusalem: Machon Yerushalayim, 1979.

Jacobs, Joseph. *The Jews in Angevin England: Documents and Records from Latin and Hebrew Sources*. London: David Nutt, 1893.

Joseph b. Shlomo Colon. *Responsa*. [In Hebrew.] Edited by Eliyahu Dov Pines. Jerusalem: Machon Yerushalayim 1984.

———. *Responsa*. [In Hebrew.] Edited by Shmuel Baruch Hacohen Deutsch and Elyakim Slesinger. Jerusalem: Oraysoh, 1988.

Jodlov Yizhak and Shlomo Zalman Havlin, eds., *Toratan shel Geonim* [in Hebrew]. Jerusalem: Vagshal Press, 1992.

Judah b. Shmuel Ha'hasid. *Sefer Hasidim (Das Buch der Frommen)*. Edited by Judah Wistinetzki. Frankfurt: Wahrmann Verlag, 1924.

Kahana, Isaac Z. "Responsa of Or Zarua' and Maharam ben Baruch from an Oxford Manuscript." [In Hebrew.] *Sinai* 8 (1940)–*Sinai* 14 (1944).

Kahana, Menachem. *Sifri Zuta Devarim*. [In Hebrew.] Jerusalem: Magnes Press, 2002.

Kupfer, Efraim, ed. *Responsa et Decisiones: Ad fedem codicis Bodleianensis 692 edidit prefatione et notis instruxit*. [In Hebrew.] Jerusalem: Mekize Nirdamim, 1973.

Maimonides. *Mishne Torah*. 8 vols. [In Hebrew.] Edited by Shabtai Frenkel. Jerusalem: Shabtai Frenkel 2005.

Maitland, Frederic. W., ed. *Select Pleas of the Crown*. Vol. 1. AD 1200–1225. London: Selden Society, 1888.

Margliyot Reuven. *Sefer Hasidim*. Jerusalem: Mosad Harav Kook, 1957.

Meir b. Baruch of Rothenburg. *The Responsa of Meir of Rothenburg*. 3 vols. Edited by Jacob Farbstein. Jerusalem: Machon Yerushalayim, 2014.

Meir b. Isaac Katzenellenbogen of Padua. *Responsa and Rulings*. Venice, 1553.

Menachem of Merseburg. "Nimukei Rabbi Menachem of Merseburg." [In Hebrew.] In *The Responsa of Rabbi Jacob Weil*, edited by Bezalel Landoi, 171–82. Jerusalem: Tiferet Torah, 1988.

Mordechai b. Hillel. *Sefer Ha'Mordechai on Tractate Baba Kama*. Edited by Avraham Halperin. Jerusalem: Machon Yerushalayim, 1992.

Moses Isserles. *Responsa*. Edited by Asher Ziv. Jerusalem: Mosad Ha'rav Kook, 1971.

Moses Mintz. *Responsa*. [In Hebrew.] Edited by Yonatan Shraga Domb. Jerusalem: Machon Yerushalayim, 1991.

Müller, Joel, ed. *Responsen der Lehrer des Ostens und Westens*. Berlin: Deutsch, 1888.

———. *Responsa by the sages of France and Lorraine (Teshuvot Chachmei Zarfat ve' Lotair)*. Wien 1881.

Shalom b. Isaac Zekel of Neustadt. *Decisions and Customs*. [In Hebrew.] Edited by Shlomoh J. Spitzer. Jerusalem: Machon Yerushalayim, 1997.

Shlomo b. Adrat. *Responsa*. 3 vols. Edited by Haim Zalman Dymitrovski. Jerusalem: Mosad Harav Kook, 1990–2015.

Shoshana, Avraham. "Kovetz Teshuvot ha'Rif ha'Khadashot." *Yeshurun* 12 (2003): 15–31.

Wistinezki, Y., ed. *Sefer Hasidim*. (SHW). Berlin: Mekitzei Nirdamim, 1891.

Yom-Tov b. Avraham Ishbili (Ritva). *Responsa*. [In Hebrew.] Edited by Joseph Kapah. Jerusalem: Mosad Ha'rav Kook, 1957.

Yosselyn b. Moshe. *Lequet Yosher: Orach Chaim*. Jerusalem: Machon Yerushalayim, 2010–13.

Zlotnick, Doc, trans. *The Tractate "Mourning" (Semahot)*. New Haven, CT: Yale University Press, 1966.

SECONDARY SOURCES

Abrams, Daniel. "Sefer Hayihud le' Rabbi Elazar ha'Darshan." *Kovetz al Yad* 22 (n.s.12) (1994):149–60.

Abulafia, David. "The King and the Jews: The Jews in the Ruler's Service." In *The Jews of Europe in the Middle Ages (Tenth to Fifteenth Centuries)*, edited by Christoph Cluse, 283–93. Turnhout, Belg.: Brepols, 2004.

Adams, Jonathan, and Jussi Hanska. "Introduction." In *The Jewish-Christian Encounter in Medieval Preaching*, edited by Jonathan Adams and Jussi Hanska, 2–8. New York: Routledge, 2015.

Agus, Irving A. "The Amount of a Ketuba." [In Hebrew.] *Horev* 5 (1939): 143–68.

———. *Rabbi Meir of Rothenburg: His Life and His Works as Sources for the Religious, Legal, and Social History of Jews of Germany in the Thirteenth Century*. 2 vols. Philadelphia: Dropsie College for Hebrew and Cognate Learning, 1947.

———. *Urban Civilization in Pre-Crusade Europe: A Study of Organized Town-Life in Northwestern Europe during the Tenth and Eleventh Centuries Based on the Responsa Literature*. 2 volumes. New York: Yeshiva University Press, 1965.

———. "The Use of the Term *Hakham* by the author of the *Sefer Hassidim* and Its Historical Implications." *JQR* 61 (1970): 54–62.

Akehurst, F. R. P. "Good Name, Reputation and Notoriety in French Customary Law." In *Fama: The Politics of Talk and Reputation in Medieval Europe*, edited by Thelma Fenster and Daniel Lord Smail, 75–94. Ithaca NY: Cornell University Press, 2003.

Amitai, Reuven, and Christoph Cluse, eds. *Slavery and the Slave Trade in the Eastern Mediterranean (c. 1000–1500 CE)*. Turnhout: Brepols, 2017.

Appleby, John T., trans. and ed. *The Chronicle of Richard of Devizes of the Time of King Richard the First*. London: Thomas Nelson & Sons, 1963.

Aptovitzer, Avigdor. *Introduction to the Book of Ra'avia*. Jerusalem: Stybel Publishing, 1938.

Arnold, John. *Inquisition and Power: Catharism and the Confessing Subject in Medieval Languedoc*. Philadelphia: University of Pennsylvania Press, 2013.

Assaf, Lilach L. "The Language of Names: Jewish Onomastics in Late Medieval Germany, Identity and Acculturation." In *Zugehörigkeit: Spätmittelalterliche Praktiken der Namengebung im europäischen Vergleich*, edited by Christof Rolker and Gabriela Signori, 149–60. Konstanz: Konstanz University Press, 2011.

Assis, Yom Tov. "Crime and Violence among the Jews of Spain (13th-14th Centuries)." [In Hebrew.] *Zion* 50 (1985): 221–40.

———. *The Golden Age of Aragonese Jewry: Community and Society in the Crown of Aragon 1213–1327*. London: Littman Library of Jewish Civilization, 1997.

Austin, G. "Jurisprudence in the Service of Pastoral Care: The Decretum of Burchard of Worms." *Speculum* 79 (2004): 929–52.

Bamberger, Josef. "The Praise of the Ashkenazi Pietists: Outline of the Jewish Hagiography in Ashkenaz in the Middle Ages." PhD diss., Bar-Ilan University, 2005.

Baron, Salo W. *A Social and Religious History of the Jews*. Vol. 9, *Under Church and Empire*. New York: Columbia University Press, 1965.

Bartal, Israel. "True Knowledge and Wisdom: On Orthodox Historiography." *Studies in Contemporary Jewry* 10 (1994): 178–92.

Barzen, Rainer J. "Jewish Regional Organization in the Rhineland: The 'Kehillot Shum' around 1300." In *The Jews in Europe in the Middle Ages (Tenth to Fifteenth Centuries): Proceedings of the International Symposium held at Speyer 20–25 October 2002*, edited by Christoph Cluse, 233–42. Turnhout: Brepols, 2004.

———. "'Kehillot Schum': Zur Eigenart der Verbindungen zwischen den jüdischen Gemeinden Mainz, Worms, und Speyer bis zu Mitte des 13. Jahrhunderts." In *Jüdische Gemeinden und ihr christlischer Kontext in kulturräumlich vergleichender Betrachtung von der Spätantike bis zum 18. Jahrhundert*, edited by Christoph Cluse, Alfred Haverkamp, and Israel J. Yuval, 389–404. Hannover: Verlag Hahnsche Buchandlung, 2003.

———. "Ländliche Jüdische Siedlungen und Niederlassungen in Aschkenas. Vom Hochmittelalter bis ins 16. Jahrhundert: Typologie, Struktur und Vernetzung." *Aschkenas* 21 (2013): 5–35.

———. *Taqqanot Qehillot Šum: Die Rechtssatzungen der Jüdischen Gemeinden von Mainz, Worms und Speyer im hohen und späten Mittelalter*. Monumenta Germaniae Historica: Hebräische Texte aus dem mittelalterlichen Deutschland 2. Wiesbaden: Harrassowitz Verlag, 2019.

Baskin, Judith R. "From Separation to Displacement: The Problem of Women in 'Sefer Hasidim.'" *AJS Review* 19 (1994): 1–18.

———. "Women and Sexual Ambivalence in 'Sefer Hasidim.'" *Jewish Quarterly Review* 96 (2006): 1–8.

Baumgarten, Elisheva. *Mothers and Children: Jewish Family Life in Medieval Europe*. Princeton, NJ: Princeton University Press, 2004.

———. *Practicing Piety in Medieval Ashkenaz: Men, Women and Everyday Religious Observance*. Philadelphia: University of Pennsylvania Press, 2014.

———. "Seeking Signs? Jews, Christians and Proof by Fire in Medieval Germany and Northern France." In *New Perspectives on Jewish-Christian Relations: In Honor of David Berger*, edited by Elisheva Carlebach and Jacob J. Schacter, 205–25. Leiden: Brill, 2012.

Beit-Arié, Malachi. *Hebrew Codicology: Historical and Comparative Typology of Medieval Hebrew Codices Based on the Documentation of the Extant Dated Manuscripts until 1540 Using a Quantitative Approach*. Edited by Zofia Lasman. Preprint internet version 0.6 (2017). National Library of Israel. Accessed Aug. 13, 2017. http://web.nli.org.il/sites/NLI/English/collections/manuscripts/hebrewcodicology/Pages/default.aspx.

Bellamy, John G. *Crime and Public Order in Later Medieval England*. London: Routledge & Kegan Paul, 1973.

Benbassa, Esther. *The Jews of France: A History from Antiquity to the Present*. Translated by M. B. DeBevoise. Princeton, NJ: Princeton University Press, 1999.

Ben-Sasson, Haim H. "Mishnato ha'Khevratit shel Rabbi Yohanan Luria." *Zion* 27 (1962): 166–98.

Ben-Sasson, Menahem. "Ha-tzeaqa el ha-tzibur be-beit ha-keneset be-artzot ha-islam be-reshit yemei ha-beinayim" [The Call to the Public in Synagogues in Islamic Lands in the Early Middle Ages]. [In Hebrew.] In *Keneset Ezra: Literature and Life in the Synagogue*, edited by Shulamit Elizur, 327–50. Jerusalem: Yad Ben Zvi, 1994.

Ben-Shammai, Haggai. "Yohar: The Transformations of a Middle-Persian Word in Judaeo-Arabic and in Medieval Hebrew." [In Hebrew.] *Tarbiz* 81 (2012): 397–408.

Ben-Zimra, Eliyahu C. "'Informers' in the Teachings of the Early European Scholars." [In Hebrew.] In *Jubilee Volume in Honor of Moreinu Hagaon Rabbi*

Joseph B. Soloveitchik, edited by Shaul Israeli Norman Lamm and Yitzchak Raphael, 732–85. Jerusalem: Mosad Harav Kook and Yeshiva University, 1984, 732–85.

Berg, Dianne. "Monstrous Un-Making: Maternal Infanticide as Female Agency." In *Murder Most Foul: Medieval and Early Modern Homicide*, edited by Larrisa Tracy. Suffolk UK: Boydell, 2018.

Berger, David, ed. *The Jewish-Christian Debate in the High Middle Ages: A Critical Edition on the Nizzahon Vetus*. Philadelphia: Jewish Publication Society, 1979.

Berggren, Erik. *The Psychology of Confession*. Leiden: Brill, 1975.

Berkovitz, Jay. *Protocols of Justice: The Pinkas of the Metz Rabbinic Court 1771–1789*. Studies in Jewish History and Culture 44. 2 vols. Leiden: Brill, 2014.

Berliner, Avraham. "Ha' Memorbuch shel Quehilta Wormisa." [In Hebrew.] *Kovtz al Yad* 3 (1886): 1–66.

———. "Ma'aseh Norah mi'Ktav Yad Asher be'Parma." [In Hebrew.] *Otzar Tov* 4 (1878): 49–52.

Berner, Tali M. *In Their Own Way: Children and Childhood in Early Modern Ashkenaz*. [In Hebrew.] Jerusalem: Shazar Publishing, 2018.

Biale, David. "Counter-History and Jewish Polemics against Christianity: The Sefer Toldot Yeshu and the Sefer Zerubavel." *Jewish Social Studies* 6 (1999): 130–45.

Biller, Peter. "Confession in the Middle Ages: Introduction." In *Handling Sin: Confession in the Middle Ages*, edited by Peter Biller and A. J. Minnis, 3–33. York UK: York Medieval Press, 1998.

Blidstein, Gerald I. "The Personal Status of Apostate and Ransomed Women in Medieval Jewish Law." *Shenaton Ha-Mishpat Haivri (Annual of the Institute for Research in Jewish Law)* 3–4 (1976–77): 35–116.

Boes, Maria R. "Jews in the Criminal Justice System of Early Modern Germany." *Journal of Interdisciplinary History* 30 (1999): 407–35.

———. "Zweifach im Visier: Jüdische Opfer von Straftaten und Rechtsprechung im Römisch-Deutschen Reich der Frühen Neuzeit." *Zeitschrift für Historische Forschung* 39 (2007): 221–41.

Bonfil, Robert. *The Book of Moneylender and Borrower*. [In Hebrew.] Jerusalem: Shazar Publishing, 2015.

———. *History and Folklore in a Medieval Jewish Chronicle: The Family Chronicle of Ahima'az ben Paltiel*. Studies in Jewish History and Culture, vol. 22. Leiden: Brill, 2009.

———. "Myth, Rhetoric, History? An Inquiry into Megillat Ahimaaz." In *Culture and Society in Medieval Jewry: Studies Dedicated to the Memory of Haim Hillel Ben-Sasson*, edited by Robert Bonfil, Menahem Ben-Sasson, and Joseph Haker, 99–135. Jerusalem: Merkaz Zalman Shazar, 1989.

Braudel, Fernand. *On History*. Translated by Sara Matthews. Chicago: University of Chicago Press, 1982.

Brennan, Brian. "The Conversion of the Jews of Clermont 576." *Journal of Theological Studies* n.s. 36 (1985): 321–37.

Brodman, James. *Charity and Welfare: Hospitals for the Poor in Medieval Catalonia*. Philadelphia: University of Pennsylvania Press, 1998.

Brundage, James A. "Domestic Violence in Classical Canon Law." In *Violence in Medieval Society*, edited by Richard Kaeuper, 183–95. Rochester: Boydell Press, 2002.

———. *Medieval Canon Law*. New York: Routledge, 1995.

Carlebach, Elisheva. "Fallen Women and Fatherless Children: Jewish Domestic Servants in Eighteenth-Century Altona." *Jewish History* 24 (2010): 295–308.

Cawley, Charles. "Burgundy Duchy, Dukes of Burgundy." Version 3, update Nov. 2016. Chap. 3, "Dukes of Burgundy (Capet) [956]-1361, 3a. Dukes of Burgundy (956–1031)." Accessed Jan. 26, 2017. http://fmg.ac/Projects/MedLands/BURGUNDY.htm#_Toc359691839.

Chazan, Robert. *From Anti-Judaism to Anti-Semitism: Ancient and Medieval Christian Constructions of Jewish History*. Cambridge: Cambridge University Press, 2016.

———. "1007–1012: Initial Crisis for Northern European Jewry." *Proceedings of the American Academy for Jewish Research* 38/39 (1970–71): 101–17.

———. "The Persecution of 992." *Revue des Etudes Juives* 129 (1970): 217–21.

Clark, Peter. *European Cities and Towns 400–2000*. Oxford: Oxford University Press, 2009.

Cluse, Christoph M. "Zur Chronologie der Verfolgungen zur Zeit des 'Schwarzen Todes.'" *Forschungen zur Geschichte der Juden* 14 (2002): 223–42.

Cohen, Esther. "Jewish Criminals in Late Fourteenth-Century France." [In Hebrew.] *Zion* 46 (1981): 146–54.

Cohen, Gerson D. "Esau as Symbol in Early Medieval Thought." In *Jewish Medieval and Renaissance Studies*, edited by Alexander Altman, 19–48. Cambridge MA: Harvard University Press, 1967.

Cohen, Haim. *The Trial and Death of Jesus*. [In Hebrew.] Tel Aviv: Dvir, 2012.

Cohen, Jeremy R. *Christ Killers: The Jews and the Passion from the Bible to the Big Screen*. Oxford: Oxford University Press, 2007.

——. *The Fraiers and the Jews: The Evolution of Medieval Anti-Judaism*. Ithaca, NY: Cornell University Press, 1984.

Cygielman, Shmuel A. Arthur. *Jewish Autonomy in Poland and Lithuania until 1648*. Jerusalem: Shlomo Natan Publishing, 1997.

——. *The Jews of Poland and Lithuania until 1648: Prolegomena and Annotated Sources*. Jerusalem: Zalman Shazar Publishing, 1991.

Dan, Joseph. "Demonological Stories in the Writings of Rabbi Judah Hehasid." *Tarbitz* 30 (1961): 273–89.

——. "Rabbi Judah the Pious and Caesarius of Heisterbach: Common Motifs in Their Stories." *Scripta Hierosolymitana* 22 (1971): 18–27.

Davis, Lennard. *Factual Fictions: The Origins of the English Novel*. Philadelphia: University of Pennsylvania Press, 1997.

Dean, Trevor. *Crime in Medieval Europe, 1200–1550*. New York: Routledge, 2014.

Declercq, Georges. "Codices Rescripti in the Early Medieval West." In *Early Medieval Palimpsests*, Bibliologia: Elementa Ad Librorum Studia Pertinentia 26, edited by Georges Declercq, 3–22. Turnhout: Brepols, 2007.

Dobson, Barrie. "The Medieval York Jewry Reconsidered." In *Jews in Medieval Britain: Historical Literary and Archaeological Perspectives*, edited by Patricia Skinner, 145–56. Woodbridge UK: Boydell, 2003.

Donahue, John R. "Tax Collectors and Sinners: An Attempt at Identification." *Catholic Biblical Quarterly* 33 (1971): 39–61.

Dorin, Rowan William. "Banishing Usury: The Expulsion of Foreign Moneylenders in Medieval Europe, 1200–1450." PhD diss., Harvard University, 2015.

Duby, George, ed. *The History of Private Life*. Vol. 2, *Revelations of the Medieval World*. Translated by Arthur Goldhammer. Cambridge MA: Belknap Press, 1988.

Dunn, Caroline. *Stolen Women in Medieval England: Rape, Abduction and Adultery 1100–1500*. Cambridge: Cambridge University Press, 2013.

Ehrlich, Uri, and Ruth Langer. "The Earliest Texts of 'Birkat Haminim.'" *HUCA* 76 (2005): 63–112.

Eidelberg, Shlomo. *Jewish Life in Austria in the Fifteenth Century: As Reflected in the Legal Writings of Rabbi Israel Isserlein and His Contemporaries*. Philadelphia: Dropsie College for Hebrew and Cognate Learning, 1962.

———, trans. and ed. *The Jews and the Crusaders: The Hebrew Chronicles of the First and Second Crusades*. Madison: University of Wisconsin Press, 1977.

———. "'Maarufia' in Rabbenu Gershom's Responsa." *Historia Judaica* 15 (1953): 59–66.

———. "Trial by Ordeal in Medieval Jewish History: Laws, Customs and Attitudes." *Proceeding of the American Academy of Jewish Research* 46–47 (1979–80): 105–20.

Eisner, Manuel. "Long-Term Historical Trends in Violent Crime." *Crime and Justice* 30 (2003): 83–142.

———. "Modernization, Self-Control and Lethal Violence: The Long-term Dynamics of European Homicide Rates in Theoretical Perspective." *The British Journal of Criminology* 41 (2001): 618–38.

Elbaum, Jacob. *Repentance and Self-Flagellation*. [In Hebrew.] Jerusalem: Magnes Press, 1992.

Elias, Norbert. *The Civilizing Process*. 2 vols. Translated by Edmund Jephcott. Oxford: Oxford University Press, 1978.

Elon, Menachem. *Jewish Law: History, Sources, Principles*. 4 vols. Translated by Bernard Auerbach and Melvin J. Sykes. Jerusalem: Magnes Press 1994.

Emanuel, Simcha. "The European Genizah and Its Contribution to Jewish Studies." *Henoch* 19 (1997): 313–40.

———. "Fires and Crimes in the Late Middle Ages: Testimonies from Halakhic Literature." [In Hebrew.] In *Studies in Jewish History Presented to Joseph Hacker*, edited by Yaron Ben-Naeh et al., 157–69. Jerusalem: Shazar Publishing, 2014.

———. *Fragments of the Tablets: Lost Books of the Tosaphists*. [In Hebrew.] Jerusalem: Magnes Press, 2006.

———. "German Sages in the Thirteenth Century: Continuity or Crisis?" *Frankfurter Judaistische Beiträge* 39 (2014): 1–19.

———. *Hidden Treasures from Europe*. Vol. 1. [In Hebrew.] Jerusalem: Mekize Nirdamim, 2015.

———. "Sridim Hadashim, Misefer Ha'dinim shel Rabbi Yehuda Hacohen." *Qovetz Al Yad* 20 (5771/2011): 81–103.

Entin-Rokeah, Zefira. "Crime and Jews in Late 13th-Century England: Some Cases and Comments." *Hebrew Union College Annual* 55 (1984): 95–137.

———. "The Jewish Church Robbers and Host Desecrators of Norwich (ca.1285)." *Revue des Etudes Juives* 141 (1982): 331–62.

———. "Money and the Hangman in Late-13th-Century England: Jews, Christians and Coinage Offences Alleged and Real." *Jewish Historical Studies* 31 (1990): 83–109.

———. "Unnatural Child Death among Christians and Jews in Medieval England." *Journal of Psychohistory* 18 (1990): 181–226.

Farber, Salamon. "On the Principle of Dina de-Malkhuta Dina." *Judaism: A Journal of Jewish Life and Thought* 26 (1977): 117–22.

Finkelman, Marilyn. "Self-Defence and Defence of Others in Jewish Law: The Rodef Defence." *Wayne Law Review* 33 (1987): 1257–87.

Finkelman, Yoel. "Nostalgia, Inspiration, Ambivalence: Eastern Europe, Immigration, and the Construction of Collective Memory in Contemporary American Haredi Historiography." *Jewish History* 23 (2009): 57–82.

Finkelstein, Louis. *Jewish Self-Government in the Middle Ages*. New York: Philipp Feldheim, 1964.

Finucane, Roland C. *The Rescue of the Innocents: Endangered Children in Medieval Miracles*. New York: St. Martin's Press, 1997.

Fishman, Talya. *Becoming the People of the Talmud: Oral Torah as Written Tradition in Medieval Jewish Cultures*. Philadelphia: University of Pennsylvania Press, 2011.

Fossier, Robert. *The Axe and the Oath: Ordinary Life in the Middle Ages*. Translated by Lydia G. Cochrane. Princeton, NJ: Princeton University Press, 2010.

Friedrichsen, Timothy A. "The Temple, a Pharisee, a Tax Collector, and the Kingdom of God: Rereading a Jesus Parable." *Journal of Biblical Literature* 124 (2005): 89–119.

Frishtik, Mordechai. "Physical Violence by Parents against Their Children in Jewish History and Jewish Law." *Jewish Law Annual* 10 (1992): 79–97.

Fuchs, Avraham. "Historical Material in the Responsa of Rabbi Israel Bruna." PhD diss., Yeshiva University, 1974. Accessed Aug. 31, 2016. http://www.fuchs.org/AvrahamFuchs/DR_Thesis/mobile/index.html.

Fudeman, Kirsten A. *Vernacular Voices: Language and Identity in Medieval French Jewish Communities*. Philadelphia: University of Pennsylvania Press, 2010.

Fürst, Rachel. "Captivity, Conversion, and Communal Identity: Sexual Angst and Religious Crisis in Frankfurt, 1241." *Jewish History* 22 (2008): 179–221.

———. "Marriage before the Bench: Divorce Law and Litigation Strategies in Thirteenth-Century Ashkenaz." *Jewish History* 31 (2017): 7–30.

———. "Striving for Justice: A History of Women and Litigation in the Jewish Courts of Medieval Ashkenaz." PhD diss., Hebrew University of Jerusalem, 2014.

Furstenberg, Yair. "Am Ha-aretz in Tannaitic Literature and Its Social Contexts." *Zion* 78 (2013): 287–320.

———. *Purity and Community in Antiquity: The Traditions of the Law between Second Temple Judaism and the Mishnah.* [In Hebrew.] Jerusalem: Magnes Press, 2016.

Galinsky, Judah D. "Rabbi Moses of Coucy as Pietist, Preacher, and Polemicist: His Intellectual Accomplishments and Communal Activity." MA thesis, Yeshiva University New York, 1993.

Geary, Patrick J. "L'humiliation des saints." *Annales Histoire Sciences Sociales* 34 (1979): 27–42.

———, and Heinrich Fichtenau. *Living in the Tenth Century: Mentalities and Social Orders.* Chicago: University of Chicago Press, 1993.

Geltner, Guy. *The Medieval Prison: A Social History.* Princeton, NJ: Princeton University Press, 2014.

Geremek, Bronislav. "The Marginal Man." In *The Medieval World*, edited by J. Le Goff and translated by Lydia G. Cochrane, 347–72. London: Collins and Brown, 1990.

Gerstman, Elina, ed. *Crying in the Middle Ages: Tears of History.* London: Routledge, 2012.

Gesundheit, Benjamin. "Suicide: A Halakhic and Moral Analysis of Masekhet Semahot, Chapter 2, Laws 1–6." *Tradition: A Journal of Orthodox Jewish Thought* 35 (2001): 34–51.

Gieysztor, Aleksander. "The Beginnings of Jewish Settlement in the Polish Lands." In *The Jews in Poland*, edited by Chimen Abramsky et al., 15–21. Oxford: Blackwell, 1986.

Gilman, Sander. *Jewish Self-Hatred: Anti-Semitism and the Hidden Language of the Jews.* Baltimore: Johns Hopkins University Press, 1986.

Given, James Buchanan. *Society and Homicide in Thirteenth-Century England.* Stanford: Stanford University Press, 1977.

Glanz, Rudolf. "The 'Jewish Execution' in Medieval Germany." *Jewish Social Studies* 5 (1943): 3–26.

Goffart, Walter. *The Fall of Rome and After.* London: Hambledon Press, 1989.

———. "To See Ourselves as Others See Us." In *Christians, Jews, 'Others' in Late Antiquity*, edited by Jacob Neusner and Ernst R. Frerichs, 473–97. Chico, CA: Scholars Press, 1985.

Goitein, S. D. *A Mediterranean Society: The Jewish Communities of the Arab World as Portrayed in the Documents of the Cairo Geniza.* 6 vols. Berkeley: University of California Press, 1967–93.

Goldschmidt, Daniel. *Mahzor le'Yamim Noraim: Lefi Minhag Beni Ashkenaz le'chol Anfeyhem.* Vol. 1, Rosh Ha'Shana. [In Hebrew.] Jerusalem: Koren Publishing, 1970.

Goldstein, Noah. "Rabbi Hayyim Eliezer ben Issac Or Zarua: His Life, His Work and a Digest of his Responsa." PhD diss., Yeshiva University, 1959.

Grabois, Aryeh. "The Use of Letters as Communication Medium among Medieval European Jewish Communities." In *Communication in the Jewish Diaspora: The Pre-Modern World,* edited by Sophia Menache, 93–105. Leiden: Brill, 1996.

Graus, František. *Pest, Geissler, Judenmorde: Das 14. Jahrhundert als Krisenzeit.* Göttingen: Vandenhoek & Ruprecht, 1987.

Green, Thomas A. Review of *Society and Homicide in Thirteenth-Century England,* by J. B. Given. *Speculum* 54 (1979): 137–40.

Grenier, Paul Louis. *La cité de Limoges: Son évêque, son chapitre, son consulat (XIIe–XVIIIe siècles).* Paris: Picard, 1907.

Gross, Henri. *Gallia Judaica: Dictionnaire géographique de la France d'après les Sources rabbiniques.* Paris: Peeters, 2011.

Grossman, Avraham. "Ashkenazim to 1300." In *An Introduction to the History and the Sources of Jewish Law,* edited by Neil S. Hecht et al., 299–321. Oxford: Oxford University Press, 1996.

———. "The Attitude of the Early Scholars of Ashkenaz towards the Authority of the 'Kahal.'" [In Hebrew.] *Shenaton Ha'Mishpat Ha'Ivri* [Annual of the Institute for Research in Jewish Law] 2 (1975): 175–99.

———. "Child Marriage in Jewish Society in the Middle Ages until the Thirteenth Century." *Pe'amim* 45 (1990): 108–25.

———. "Communication among Jewish Centers during the Tenth to the Twelfth Centuries." In *Communications in the Jewish Diaspora: The Pre-Modern World,* edited by Sophia Menache, 107–39. Leiden: Brill, 1996.

———. *The Early Sages of Ashkenaz: Their Lives Leadership and Works 900–1096.* [In Hebrew.] Jerusalem: Magnes Press, 2001.

———. *The Early Sages of France: Their Lives, Leadership, and Works.* [In Hebrew]. Jerusalem: Magnes Press, 1995.

———. "Medieval Rabbinic Views on Wife-Beating 800–1300." *Jewish History* 5 (1991): 52–62.

———. "Offenders and Violent Men in Jewish Society in Early Ashkenaz and Their Influence upon Legal Procedure." [In Hebrew.] *Shenaton Hamishpat Ha'ivri* [Annual of the Institute for Research in Jewish Law] 8 (1981): 135–52.

———. "The Origins and Essence of the Custom of 'Stopping-the-Service.'" [In Hebrew.] *Milet* 1 (1983): 199–220.

———. *Pious and Rebellious: Jewish Women in Medieval Europe*. Translated by Johnathan Chipman. Waltham MA: Brandeis University Press, 2004.

———. "Social Structure and Intellectual Creativity in Medieval Jewish Communities (Eighth to Twelfth Centuries)." In *Studies in Medieval Jewish History and Literature*, vol. 3, edited by Isadore Twersky and Jay M. Harris, 1–20. Cambridge, MA: Harvard University Press, 2000.

Grözinger, Karl Erich. "Jüdische Wundermänner in Deutschland." In *Judentum im Deutschen Sprachraum*, edited by Karl Erich Grözinger and Elvira Grözinger, 190–221. Frankfurt am Main: Suhrkamp, 1991.

Gruschcow, Lisa. *Writing the Wayward Wife: Rabbinic Interpretations of Sotah*. Leiden: Brill, 2006.

Guggenheim, Yaakov. "Meeting on the Road: Encounters between German Jews and Christians on the Margins of Society." In *In and Out of the Ghetto: Jewish-Gentile Relations in Late Medieval and Early Modern Germany*, edited by Ronnie Po-chia Hsia and Hartmut Lehmann, and translated by Pamela E. Selwyn, 125–36. Cambridge: Cambridge University Press, 1995.

———. "Social Stratification of Central European Jewry at the End of the Middle Ages: The Poor." *Proceedings of the World Congress of Jewish Studies*, division B, vol. 1 (1989): 130–36.

———. "Von den Schalantjuden zu den Betteljuden: Jüdische Armut in Mitteleuropa in der Frühen Neuzeit." In *Juden und Armut in Mittel- und Osteuropa*, edited by Stefi Jersch-Wenzel, 55–69. Cologne: Böhlau, 2000.

Gurevich, Aaron. *Historical Anthropology of the Middle Ages*. Edited by Jana Howlett. Chicago: University of Chicago Press, 1992.

Gurr, Ted R. "Historical Trends in Violent Crime: A Critical Review of the Evidence." *Crime and Justice: An Annual Review of Research* 3 (1981): 295–360.

Halsall, Guy, ed. *Violence and Society in the Early Medieval West*. Woodbridge: Boydell Press, 1998.

Halttunen, Karen. *Murder Most Foul: The Murderer and the American Gothic Imagination*. Cambridge, MA: Harvard University Press, 1998.

Hamilton, Sara M. *The Practice of Penance, 900–1050*. Martlesham: Boydell and Brewer, 2001.

Hanawalt, Barbara A. *Crime and Conflict in Medieval Europe 1300–1348*. Cambridge, MA: Harvard University Press, 1979.

———. "Violence in the Domestic Milieu of Late Medieval England." In *Violence in Medieval Society*, edited by Richard Kaeuper, 197–214. Rochester, NY: Boydell Press, 2002.

Havatzelet, Avraham Joseph. "Teshuvot Rabbenu Azriel ben Rabbi Yehiel." [In Hebrew.] *Tzfunot: Tora Quarterly* 1 (1989): 5–14.

Haverkamp, Alfred. "The Beginning of Jewish Life North of the Alps with Comparative Glances at Italy (c. 900–1100)." In *Diversi Angoli di Visuale Fra Storia Medievale e storia Degeli Ebrei: In Ricordo di Michele Luzzati: Atti del Convegno Pisa 1–2 Febbraio 2016*, edited by Anna Maria Pult-Quagila and Alessandra Veronese, 85–102. Pisa: Pacini Editore, 2016.

———. *Jews in the Medieval German Kingdom*. Translated by Christoph Cluse. Trier, Ger.: Universitätsbibliothek, 2015.

———. "The Jews of Europe in the Middle Ages: By Way of Introduction." In *The Jews of Europe in the Middle Ages (Tenth to Fifteenth Centuries): Proceedings of the International Symposium held in Speyer 20–25 October 2002 (Cultural Encounters in Late Antiquity and the Middle Ages CELAMA 4)*, edited by Christoph Cluse, 1–16. Turnhout: Brepols, 2004.

———. "Juden und Städte—Verbindungen und Bindungen." In *Europas Juden im Mittelalter: Beiträge des Internationalen Symposiums in Speyer vom 20–25 Oktober 2002*, edited by Christoph Cluse, 13–29. Trier, Ger.: Kliomedia, 2004.

———. "Die Judenverfolgungen zur Zeit des Schwarzen Todes im Gesellschaftsgefüge deutscher Städte." In *Zur Geschichte der Juden im Deutschland des späten Mittelalters und der frühen Neuzeit*, edited by Alfred Haverkamp, 27–93. Stuttgart: Hiersemann, 1981.

Haverkamp, Eva. *Hebräische Berichte über die Judenverfolgungen während des Ersten Kreuzzugs*. Monumenta Germaniae Historica, Hebräische Texte aus dem mittelalterlichen Deutschland, vol. 1. Hannover: Hahnsche Buchhandlung, 2005.

———. "The Jews in Christian Europe: Ashkenaz in the Middle Ages," In *The Wiley-Blackwell History of Jews and Judaism*, edited by Alan T. Levenson, 169–206. Malden MA: Wiley, 2012.

Heil, Johannes. "Getting Them in or Keeping Them Out? Theology, Law, and the Beginnings of Jewish Life in the Rhine Valley in the 10th and 11th

Centuries." In *Jews in Early Christian Law: Byzantium and the Latin West, 6th–11th Centuries*, edited by John Tolan et al., 211–28. Turnhout: Brepols, 2014.

Helmholz, Richard. H. "Excommunication in Twelfth-Century England." *Journal of Law and Religion* 11 (1994): 235–53.

Hen, Yitzhak. "Martyrim Kekhulim: Aliya La'regel Ve'kaparat Avonot B'yemei Ha'beynayim Ha'mukdamim." In *Ut Videant et Contingant: Essays on Pilgrimage and Sacred Space in Honor of Ora Limor*, edited by Yitzhak Hen and Iris Shagrir, 125–34. Ra'anana: Open University Press 2011.

Hershler, Moshe. "Tesuvot Geonim ve'Quadmonim be'Seder Tikin ve'Onashim be'Dinei Nefashot ba'Zman ha'zeh," [in Hebrew] *Sinai* 66 (1970): 173–77. Reprinted in Yizhak Jodlov and Shlomo Zalman Havlin, eds., *Toratan shel Geonim* (Jerusalem: Vagshal Press, 1992), 6:388–93.

Hildesheimer, Esriel. "Bishoph ha'Yehudim." [In Hebrew.] *Sinai* 105 (1990): 142–65.

———. "The Provision against Gentile Courts in Late Medieval Ashkenaz: Halakhah and Practice." [In Hebrew.] *Proceedings of the World Congress of Jewish Studies*, division C, vol. 1, Jewish Thought and Literature (1989): 217–24.

Himmelfarb, Martha. *Tours of Hell: An Apocalyptic Form in Jewish and Christian Literature*. Philadelphia: University of Pennsylvania Press, 1983.

Hirshman, Mark. "The Priest's Gate and Elijah ben Menahem's Pilgrimage." [In Hebrew.] *Tarbiz* 55 (1985): 217–27.

———. "'R. Elijah Interpreted the Verse Concerning Pilgrims' (Shir Rabba 2, 14, 7): Another Medieval Interpolation and Again R. Elijah." [In Hebrew.] *Tarbiz* 60 (1990): 275–76.

Hoffman, Elizabeth R., Stephanie C. Zerwas, and Cynthia M. Bulik. "Reproductive Issues in Anorexia Nervosa." *Expert Review of Obstetrics and Gynecology* 6 (2011): 403–14. Accessed Sept. 14, 2016. http://www.ncbi.nlm.nih.gov/pmc/articles/PMC3192363/.

Horowitz, Elliot. "'(Deserving) Poor Shall Be Members of Your Household': Charity, the Poor, and Social Control in the Jewish Communities of Europe between the Middle Ages and the Beginning of Modern Times." [In Hebrew.] In *Religion and Economy: Connections and Interactions: Collected Essays*, edited by Menachem Ben-Sasson, 209–32. Jerusalem: Shazar Publishing, 1995.

———. "Speaking to the Dead: Cemetery Prayer in Medieval and Early Modern Jewry." *Journal of Jewish Thought and Philosophy* 8 (1999): 303–17.

Horowitz, Yehoshua. "Rabbi Haim Or Zarua' ve'Yahaso le'Hevrah shel ha'Goyim." In *Hevrah ve'Historia*, edited by Yehezkel Cohen, 93–102. Jerusalem: Israeli Ministry of Education, Dept. for Torah Culture, 1980.

Horrox, Rosemary, ed. *The Black Death*. Manchester: Manchester University Press, 1994.

Howe, Irving. *World of Our Fathers: The Journey of the East European Jews to America and the Life They Found and Made*. New York: New York University Press, 2005.

Huffman, Joseph P. *Family, Commerce, and Religion in London and Cologne: Anglo-German Emigrants (c.1000–c.1300)*. Cambridge: Cambridge University Press, 1998.

Hultin, Jeremy F. *The Ethics of Obscene Speech in Early Christianity and Its Environment*. Leiden: Brill, 2008.

Hulttunen, Karen. *Murder Most Foul: The Killer and the American Gothic Imagination*. Cambridge MA: Harvard University Press, 1998.

Hundert, Gershon D., and Gershon C. Bacon. *The Jews in Poland and Russia: Bibliographical Essays*. Bloomington: Indiana University Press, 1984.

Hundsbichler, Helmut. "Wohnen." In *Alltag im Spätmittelalter*, edited by Harry Kühnel, 254–70. Graz, Aus.: Styria Verlag, 1986.

Hunter, Paul J. *Before Novels: Cultural Contexts of Eighteenth-Century English Fiction*. New York: Norton, 1992.

Idel, Moshe. "Rabbi Nehemia ben Shlomo the Prophet on the Star of David and the Name *Taftafia*: From Jewish Magis to Practical and Theoretical Kabbalah." In *Ta-Shma: Studies in Judaica in Memory of Israel M. Ta-Shma*, vol. 1, edited by Avraham (Rami) Reiner et al., 1–76. Alon Shevut: Tenuvot Press, 2011.

Ihnat, Kati, and Katelyn Mesler. "From Christian Devotion to Jewish Sorcery: The Curious History of Wax Figurines in Medieval Europe." In *Entangled Histories: Knowledge, Authority, and Jewish Culture in the Thirteenth Century*, edited by Elisheva Baumgarten, Ruth Mazo Karras, and Katelyn Mesler, 134–58. Philadelphia: University of Pennsylvania Press, 2017.

Jaritz, Gerhard. "Leben um zu Leben." In *Alltag in Spätmittelalter*, edited by Harry Kühnel et al., 157–64. Graz, Aus.: Styria Verlag, 1986.

———, ed. *The Sign Language of Poverty*. Forschungen des Instituts für Realienkunde des Mittelalters und der frühen Neuzeit: Diskussionen und Materialien. Vienna: Verlag der Österreichischen Akademie der Wissenschaften, 2007.

Johanek, Peter. "Merchants, Markets and Towns." In *The New Cambridge Medieval History*, vol. 3, c. 900–c. 1024, edited by T. Reuter, 64–94. Cambridge: Cambridge University Press, 1999.

Johnson, Willis. "Textual Sources for the Study of Jewish Currency Crimes in Thirteenth Century England." *British Numismatic Journal* 66 (1996): 21–32.

Jordan, William Chester. *From England to France: Felony and Exile in the High Middle Ages*. Princeton, NJ: Princeton University Press, 2015.

Jütte, Robert. *Poverty and Deviance in Early Modern Europe*. Cambridge: Cambridge University Press, 1994.

Kahana, Isaac Zeev. "Keniyat u'mekhirat sefarim ba'halakha." In *Mekhkarim be'Sifrut ha'Teshuvot*, edited by Isaac Zeev Kahana and Haim Zeev Hirshberg, 258–71. Jerusalem and Ramat Gan: Mosad Harv Kook, 1973.

Kamins, Toni L. *The Complete Jewish Guide to France*. New York: St. Martin's Griffin, 2001.

Kanarfogel, Ephraim. "The Appointment of *Hazzanim* in Medieval Ashkenaz: Communal Policy and Individual Religious Prerogatives." In *Spiritual Authority: Struggles over Cultural Power in Jewish Thought*, edited by Howard Kreisel et al., 5–31. Beersheva: Mosad Bialik, 2010.

———. "From Germany to Northern France and Back Again: A Tale of Two Tosafist Centers." In *Regional Identities and Cultures of Medieval Jews*, edited by Javier Castano et al., 149–72. Liverpool: Littman Library, 2018.

———. *The Intellectual History and Rabbinic Culture of Medieval Ashkenaz*. Detroit MI: Wayne State University Press, 2013.

———. "Religious Leadership during the Tosafist Period: Between the Academy and the Rabbinic Court." In *Jewish Religious Leadership*, vol. 1, edited by Jack Wertheimer, 265–305. New York: Jewish Theological Seminary, 2004.

———. "Returning to the Jewish Community in Medieval Ashkenaz: History and Halakha." In *Turim: Studies in Jewish History and Literature Presented to Bernard Lander*, vol. 1, edited by Michael A. Schmidman, 67–97. New York: Touro College Press, 2007.

———. "R. Judah he-Hasid and the Rabbinic Scholars of Regensburg: Interactions, Influences, and Implications." *JQR* 96 (2006): 17–37.

———. "Unanimity, Majority, and Communal Government in Ashkenaz during the High Middle Ages: A Reassessment." *Proceedings of the American Academy of Jewish Research* 58 (1992): 79–106.

Kaplan, Debra. *Beyond Expulsion: Jews, Christians and Reformation Strasburg*. Stanford CA: Stanford University Press, 2011.

Kaplan, Kimmy. "'Absolutely Intellectually Honest': A Case-Study of American Jewish Modern Orthodox Historiography." In *Creation and Re-Creation in Jewish Thought: Festschrift in Honor of Joseph Dan on the Occasion of His Seventieth Birthday*, edited by Rachel Elior and Peter Schäfer, 339–61. Tübingen: Mohr-Siebeck, 2005.

———. "Innovating the Past: The Emerging Sphere of the 'Torah-true Historian' in America," *Studies in Contemporary Jewry* 21 (2005): 270–87.

Karlinsky, Nahum. "The Dawn of Hasidic–Haredi Historiography." *Modern Judaism* 27 (2007): 20–46.

Karras, Ruth Mazo. *Common Women: Prostitution and Sexuality in Medieval England*. New York: Oxford University Press, 1996.

Katz, Jacob. *Exclusiveness and Tolerance: Studies in Jewish-Gentile Relations in Medieval and Modern Times*. London: Oxford University Press, 1961.

———. *Tradition and Crisis: Jewish Society at the End of the Middle Ages*. Translated by Bernard Dov Cooperman. New York: New York University Press, 1993.

Keil, Martha, and Klaus Lohrmann, eds. *Studien zur Geschichte der Juden in Österreich*. Vienna: Böhlau, 1994.

Kempf, Damien. "Capetian France (987–1328): Introduction." *French Historical Studies* 37 (2014): 169–72.

Kienzle, Beverly Mayne, et al., eds. *De Ore Domini: Preacher and Word in the Middle Ages*. Kalamazoo, MI: Medieval Institute Publications, 1989.

———et al., eds. *Medieval Sermons and Society: Cloister, City, University* (Textes et études du Moyen Age, 9). Louvain-la-Neuve: Brepols, 1998.

Kirshenbaum, Aaron. *Jewish Penology: The Theory and Development of Criminal Punishment among the Jews throughout the Ages*. [In Hebrew.] Jerusalem: Magnes Press, 2013.

———. "The Sovereign Power of the State: A Proposed Theory of Accommodation in Jewish Law." *Cardozo Law Review* 12 (1991): 925–40.

Kisch, Guido. "The 'Jewish Execution' in Medieval Germany." *Historia Judaica* 2 (1943): 103–32.

———. *Jewry-Law in Medieval Germany: Laws and Court Decisions Concerning Jews*. Texts and Studies, vol. 3. New York: American Academy for Jewish Research, 1949.

———. "The Jewry-Law of the Medieval German Law-Books: Part 1." *Proceedings of the American Academy for Jewish Research* 7 (1935–36): 61–145.

———. "The Jewry-Law of the Medieval German Law-Books: Part 2, The Legal Status of the Jews." *Proceedings of the American Academy for Jewish*

Research 10 (1940): 99–184. Pp. vii–xlviii is an abridgment of the considerably more detailed Hebrew version.

———. *The Jews in Medieval Germany: A Study of Their Legal and Social Status*. New York: Ktav Publishing, 1970. First published 1949 by University of Chicago Press.

Knock, Arthur D. *Conversion: The Old and New Religion from Alexander the Great to Augustine of Hippo*. New York: Clarendon Press, 1933.

Koslin, Désirée. "Value-Added Stuffs and Shifts in Meaning: An Overview and Case-Study of Medieval Textile Paradigms." In *Encountering Medieval Textiles and Dress: Objects, Texts, Images*, edited by Désirée Koslin and Janet Snyder, 237–40. New York: Palgrave-Macmillan, 2003.

Koster, Jöelle. "Prostitution." In *Women and Gender in Medieval Europe: An Encyclopedia*, edited by Margaret Schaus, 675–78. New York: Routledge, 2006.

Kosto, Adam. *Hostages in the Middle Ages*. Oxford: Oxford University Press, 2012.

Krauss, Samuel. *Korot Batei ha'Tephilah be'Yisrael* [The History of the Prayer Houses in Israel]. [In Hebrew.] New York: Ogen Press, 1956.

Kristeller, Paul Oskar. "The Alleged Ritual Murder of Simon of Trent (1475) and Its Literary Repercussions: A Bibliographical Study." *Proceedings of the American Academy for Jewish Research* 59 (1993): 103–35.

Kühnel, Harry. "Devotio Moderna: Die Neue Frömmigkeit." In *Alltag im Spätmittelalter*, edited by Harry Kühnel et al., 111–14. Graz, Aus.: Verlag Styria, 1986.

———. "Frömmigkeit ohne Grenzen." In *Alltag im Spätmittelalter*, edited by Harry Kühnel et al., 92–110. Graz, Aus.: Verlag Styria, 1986.

———. "Laster und Lust." In *Alltag im Spätmittelalter*, edited by Harry Kühnel et al., 38–46. Graz, Aus.: Verlag Styria, 1986.

Künker Auktion 130. *The De Wit Collection of Medieval Coins, 1000 Years of European Coinage*. Part 2: Germany, Switzerland, Austria, Bohemia, Moravia, Hungary, Silesia, Poland, Baltic States, Russia, and the Golden Horde. Osnabrück, Ger.: Numismatischer Verlag Künker, 2007.

Landina, Tatiana Savoia, and François Dépelteau, eds. *Norbert Elias and Violence*. New York: Palgrave Macmillan, 2017.

Langbein, John H. *Prosecuting Crime in the Renaissance: England, Germany, France*. Cambridge, MA: Harvard University Press, 1974.

Langer, Ruth. *Cursing the Christians? A History of the Birkat HaMinim*. Oxford: Oxford University Press, 2012.

Langmuir, Gavin I. *History, Religion, and Antisemitism*. Berkeley: University of California Press, 1990.

———. "Thomas of Monmouth: Detector of Ritual Murder." *Speculum* 59 (1984): 820–46.

Liberles-Noiman, Ahuva. "Space and Distance in Sefer Hasidim." MA thesis, Hebrew University of Jerusalem, 2014.

Lichtenshtein, Yechezkel. "Suicide as an Act of Atonement." *Jewish Law Annual* 16 (2006): 51–91.

Lifshitz, Joseph Isaac. *R. Meir of Rothenberg and the Foundations of Jewish Political Thought*. New York: Cambridge University Press, 2016.

Limor, Ora. Review of *Communities of Violence: Persecution of Minorities in the Middle Ages*, by David Nirenberg. [In Hebrew.] *Zion* 63 (1998): 476–82.

Lipton, Sara. *Dark Mirror: The Medieval Origins of Anti-Jewish Iconography*. New York: Metropolitan Books, 2014.

———. *Images of Intolerance: Representations of Jews and Judaism in the Bible Moralisée*. Berkeley, 1999.

Lohrmann, Klaus. *Die Wiener Juden im Mittelalter*. Berlin: Philo Verlag, 2000.

Lopez, Robert S. Review of *Urban Civilization in Pre-Crusade Europe: A Study of Organized Town Life in North–Western Europe during the Tenth and Eleventh Centuries Based on Responsa Literature*, by Irvin A. Agus. *Speculum* 42 (1967): 340–43.

Lorberbaum, Yair. *In God's Image: Myth, Theology, and Law in Classical Judaism*. Cambridge: Cambridge University Press, 2015.

Luria, Ilana. "Informers and Mafiosi: Violent Factionalism and Fear in the Jewish Communities of Fourteenth-Century Valencia." [In Hebrew.] *Zmanim: A Historical Quarterly* 29 (1988): 48–55.

Maccoby, Hyam. "How Unclean Were Tax-Collectors?" *Biblical Theology Bulletin* 31 (2001): 60–63.

Macionis, John J. *Sociology*. 12th ed. Upper Saddle River NJ: Pearson Prentice Hall, 2008.

Malkiel, David. *Stones Speak: Hebrew Tombstones from Padua 1529–1862*. Leiden: Brill, 2014.

Marcus, Ivan G. "The Historical Meaning of Hasidei Ashkenaz: Fact, Fiction, or Cultural Self-Image?" In *Gershom Scholem's 'Major Trends in Jewish Mysticism' Fifty Years After: Proceedings of the Sixth International Conference on the History of Jewish Mysticism*, edited by Joseph Dan and Peter Schäfer, 103–13. Tübingen: Mohr-Siebeck, 1993.

———. "Images of the Jews in the Exempla of Caesarius of Heisterbach." In *From Witness to Witchcraft: Jews and Judaism in Medieval Christian Thought*, edited by Jeremey Cohen, 247–56. Wiesbaden, Ger.: Harrassowitz Verlag, 1996.

———. "A Jewish Christian Symbiosis: The Culture of Early Ashkenaz." In *Cultures of the Jews: A New History*, edited by David R. Biale, 449–518. New York: Schocken Books, 2002.

———. *Piety and Society: The Jewish Pietists of Medieval Germany*. Leiden: Brill, 1981.

———. "A Pious Community in Doubt: Jewish Martyrdom among Northern European Jewry and the Story of Rabbi Amnon of Mainz." In *Essays in Hebrew Literature in Honor of Avraham Holtz*, edited by Z. Ben-Yosef Ginor, 21–46. New York: Jewish Theological Seminary Press, 2003.

———. *Rituals of Childhood: Jewish Acculturation in Medieval Europe*. New Haven, CT: Yale University Press, 1996.

———. *"Sefer Hasidim" and the Ashkenazic Book in Medieval Europe*. Philadelphia: University of Pennsylvania Press, 2018.

Marienberg, Evyatar. *La Baraita de-Niddah: Un texte juif pseudo-talmudique sur les lois religieuses relatives à la menstruation* [The Baraitade-Niddah: A Pseudo-Talmudic Jewish Text about the Religious Laws Concerning Menstruation]. Turnhout: Brepols, 2012.

———, and David Carpenter. "The Stealing of the 'Apple of Eve' from the Thirteenth-Century Synagogue of Winchester." Fine of the Month: December 2011. Henri III Fine Rolls Project. National Archives and Kings College London. http://frh3.org.uk/content/month/fm-12-2011.html.

Martin, John D. *Representations of Jews in Late Medieval and Early Modern German Literature*. Studies in German Jewish History 5. Bern: Peter Lang, 2004.

Masschaele, J. "The Public Space of the Marketplace in Medieval England." *Speculum* 77 (2002): 383–421.

McCall, Andrew. *The Medieval Underworld*. New York: Barnes & Noble Books, 1979.

McNeill, John T., and Helena M. Gamer, eds. *Medieval Handbooks of Penance: A Translation of the Principal "Libri Poenitentiales" and Selections from Related Documents*. Cambridge: Cambridge University Press, 1990.

Meens, Rob. *Penance in Medieval Europe 600–1200*. Cambridge: Cambridge University Press, 2014.

Meir, Jonatan. *Imagined Hasidism: The Anti-Hasidic Writings of Joseph Perl.* [In Hebrew.] Jerusalem: Mossad Bialik, 2013.

Mellinkoff, Ruth. "Judah's Red Hair and the Jews." *Journal of Jewish Art* 9 (1982): 31–46.

———. *Outcasts: Signs of Otherness in Northern European Art of the Late Middle Ages.* 2 vols. Berkeley: University of California Press 1994.

Merback, Mitchell B. *Beyond the Jewish Badge: Anti-Judaism and Antisemitism in Medieval and Early Modern Visual Culture.* Leiden: Brill, 2007.

———. *The Thief, the Cross and the Wheel: Pain and the Spectacle of Punishment in Medieval and Renaissance Europe.* Chicago: University of Chicago Press, 1998.

Miller, Alan D., and Ronen Perry. "The Reasonable Person." *New York University Law Review* 87 (2012): 323–92.

Miron, Dan. *Image of the Shtetl and Other Studies of Modern Jewish Literary Imagination.* Syracuse, NY: Syracuse University Press, 2000.

Moeller, Bernard. "Religious Life in Germany at the Eve of the Reformation." In *Contesting Christendom: Readings in Medieval Religion and Culture*, edited by James L. Halverson, 189–98. Lanham, MD: Rowman & Littlefield, 2008.

Mollat, Michel. *The Poor in the Middle Ages: An Essay in Social History.* Translated by Arthur Goldhammer. New Haven, CT: Yale University Press, 1986.

Moore, R. I. "The Peace of God and the Social Revolution," In *The Peace of God: Social Violence and Religious Response in France around the Year 1000*, edited by Thomas Head and Richard Landes, 308–26. Ithaca, NY: Cornell University Press, 1992.

Möschter, Angela. *Juden im Venezianischen Treviso (1389–1509).* Forschungen zur Geschichte der Juden, vol. 19. Hannover: Hahnsche Buchhandlung, 2008.

Mulholland, Maureen, and Brian Pullan, eds. *Judicial Tribunals in Europe and England: The Trial in History.* Vol. 1. Manchester: Manchester University Press, 2003.

Müller, Jörg. "Erez Gezerah—'Land of Persecution': Pogroms against the Jews in Regun Teutonicum 1280–1350." In *The Jews in Europe in the Middle Ages (Tenth to Fifteenth Centuries): Proceedings of the International Symposium Held at Speyer 20–25 October 2002*, edited by Christoph Cluse, 245–59. Turnhout: Brepols, 2004.

———. "Eine Jüdische Diebesbande im Südwesten des Reiches in der ersten Hälfte des 14. Jahrhunderts." In *Beziehungsnetze aschkenasischer Juden während des Mittelalters und der frühen Neuzeit*, edited by Jörg R. Müller,

Forschungen zur Geschichte der Juden, A 20, 71–116. Hannover: Hahnsche Buchhandlung, 2008.

———. "Sexual Relations between Christian and Jews in Medieval Germany According to Christian Sources." In *Iggud: Selected Essays in Jewish Studies*, vol. 2, History of the Jewish People and Contemporary Jewish Society, edited by Gershon Bacon et al., 19–32. Jerusalem: World Union of Jewish Studies, 2009.

Mundill, Robin R. "Edward I and Final Phase of Anglo-Jewry." In *The Jews in Medieval Britain: Historical, Literary and Archaeological Perspectives*, edited by Patricia Skinner, 55–70. Woodbridge, UK: The Boydell Press, 2003.

———. *The King's Jews: Money, Massacre and Exodus in Medieval England*. New York: Continuum, 2010.

Murray, Alexander. *Suicide in the Middle Ages*, vol. 2: *The Curse on Self-Murder*. Oxford: Oxford University Press, 2000.

Muskin, Carmel. "Gentile Slaves and Servants in Medieval Ashkenaz." [In Hebrew.] *Tura: Studies in Jewish Thought* 1 (1989): 235–45.

Myers, David N. "History as Ideology: The Case of Ben Zion Dinur, Zionist Historian 'Par Excellence.'" *Modern Judaism* 7 (1988): 167–94.

———. "Is There Still a 'Jerusalem School?' Reflections on the State of Jewish Historical Scholarship in Israel." *Jewish History* 23 (2009): 389–406.

Napolitano, David. Review of *Public Justice and the Criminal Trial in Late Medieval Italy: Reggio Emilia in the Visconti Age*, by Joanna Carraway-Vitiello. *The Medieval Review*, Jan. 2017.

Niditch, Susan. *My Brother Esau Is a Hairy Man: Hair and Identity in Ancient Israel*. New York: Oxford University Press, 2008.

Nirenberg, David. *Communities of Violence: Persecution of Minorities in the Middle Ages*. Princeton, NJ: Princeton University Press, 1996.

Olive, Lisi. *The Body Legal in Barbarian Law*. Toronto: Toronto University Press, 2010.

Oppenheimer, Aharon. *The Am ha-Aretz: A Study in the Social History of the Jewish People in the Hellenistic-Roman Period*. Leiden: Brill, 1977.

Otis, Lidia L. *Prostitution in Medieval Society: The History of an Urban Institution in Languedoc*. Chicago: University of Chicago Press, 1985.

Parisse, M. "Lotharingia." In *The New Cambridge Medieval History*, vol. 3, c. 900–c. 1024, edited by T. Reuter. Cambridge: Cambridge University Press, 1999. Cambridge Histories Online. Cambridge University Press. Accessed Apr. 5, 2011. DOI:10.1017/CHOL9780521364478.013.

Patschovsy, Alexander. "The Relationship between the Jews of Germany and the King (11th–14th Centuries): A European Comparison." In *England and Germany in the High Middle Ages*, edited by Alfred Haverkamp and Hanna Vollrath, 193–218. Oxford: Oxford University Press, 1996.

Paudice, Aleida. "Elia Capsali." Historians of the Ottoman Empire. University of Chicago, 2006. Accessed July 5, 2017. https://ottomanhistorians.uchicago.edu/en/historian/elia-capsali.

Pavlac, Brian A. "Excommunication and Territorial Politics in High Medieval Trier." *Church History* 60 (1991): 20–36.

Pennington, Kenneth. Review of *Excommunication in the Middle Ages*, by Elisabeth Vodola. *Speculum* 63 (1988): 242–24.

———. "Roman and Secular Law." In *Medieval Latin: An Introduction and Bibliographical Guide*, edited by Frank A. C. Mantello and A. G. Rigg, 254–66. Washington DC: Catholic University of America Press, 1996.

Perani, Mauro. "The 'Italian Genizah': An Updated Report on Fifteen Years of Research." *European Association for Jewish Studies Newsletter* 2 (Oct. 1996–Feb. 1997): 15–22.

Peskowitz, Miriam. *Spinning Fantasies: Rabbis, Gender and History*. Berkeley: University of California Press, 1997.

Peters, Edward. *The First Crusade: The Chronicle of Fulcher of Chartres and Other Source Materials*. Philadelphia: University of Pennsylvania Press, 1971.

Phillips, William D. *Slavery from Roman Times to the Early Transatlantic Trade*. Minneapolis: University of Minnesota Press, 1985.

"The Pinkassim Project." National Library of Israel. Accessed Feb. 10, 2018. http://web.nli.org.il/sites/NLI/English/collections/jewish-collection/pinkassim/Pages/default.aspx.

"The Pinkassim Project Bibliography." National Library of Israel. Update June 26, 2014. http://web.nli.org.il/sites/NLI/English/collections/jewish-collection/pinkassim/Documents/PinkassimBibliography.pdf.

Po-chia Hsia, Ronnie. *The Myth of Ritual Murder: Jews and Magic in Reformation Germany*. New Haven, CT: Yale University Press, 1988.

———. *Trent 1475: Stories of a Ritual Murder Trial*. New Haven, CT: Yale University Press, 1992.

Polonsky, Anthony, et al., eds. *The Jews in Old Poland 1000–1795*. New York: I. B. Tauris, 1993.

Pomeranz, Jonathan Aaron. "Ordinary Jews in the Babylonian Talmud: Rabbinic Representations and Historical Interpretation." PhD diss., Yale University, 2016.

Priel, Yosef. "The Exegetical Method of Rabbi Hezekiah Ben Manoah (Hizquni) on the Torah." PhD. diss., Bar Ilan University, 2010.

Rabin, Chaim. "Jewish Secret Languages." In *Encyclopedia of Modern Jewish Culture*, vol. 1, edited by Glenda Abramson, 496. New York: Routledge, 2005.

Raspe, Lucia. "Sacred Space, Local History and Diasporic Identity: The Graves of the Righteous in Medieval and Early Modern Ashkenaz." In *Jewish Studies at the Crossroads of Anthropology and History: Authority, Diaspora, Tradition*, edited by Ra'anan Bustan, Oren Kosansky, and Marina Rostow, 147–63. Philadelphia: University of Pennsylvania Press, 2011.

Raz-Krakotzkin, A. "Geschichte, Nationalismus, Eingedenken." In *Jüdische Geschichtsschreibung heute: Themen, Positionen, Kontroversen: Ein Schloss Elmau-Symposium*, edited by M. Brenner and D. Myers, 181–204. Munich: C. H. Beck, 2002.

Reiner, Avraham (Rami). "Rabbinical Courts in France in the Twelfth Century: Centralization and Dispersion." *Journal of Jewish Studies* 60 (2009): 298–318.

———. "The Role and Significance of Titles Used to Describe the Deceased on the Tombstones in the Würzburg Cemetery." In *Die Grabsteine vom Jüdischen Friedhof in Würzburg aus der Zeit vor dem Schwarzen Tod*, edited by Karlheinz Müller, Simon Schwarzfuchs, and Avraham (Rami) Reiner, 235–62. Würzburg: Verlag PH.C.W. Schmidt, 2011.

Reiner, Elchanan. "*Yihus* and Libel: Maharal, the Bezalel Family, and the Nadler Affair." In *Maharal—Overtures: Biography, Doctrine, Influence*, edited by Elchanan Reiner, 101–26. Jerusalem: Shazar Press, 2015.

Reuter, Timothy, ed. *The New Cambridge Medieval History*. Cambridge: Cambridge University Press, 1999. Cambridge Histories Online. Accessed Apr. 5, 2011. DOI:10.1017/CHOL9780521364478.004.

Rexroth, Frank. *Deviance and Power in Late Medieval London*. Translated by Pamela E. Selwyn. Cambridge: Cambridge University Press, 2007.

Richards, J. *Sex Dissidence and Damnation: Minority Groups in the Middle Ages*. London: Routledge, 1990.

Rivers, Theodore J., trans. and ed. *Laws of the Alamans and Bavarians*. Philadelphia: University of Pennsylvania Press, 1977.

Rosenwein, Barbara H. *Anger's Past: The Social Uses of an Emotion in the Middle Ages*. Ithaca, NY: Cornell University Press, 1998.

———. *Emotional Communities in the Early Middle Ages*. Ithaca, NY: Cornell University Press, 2006.

Rosenzweig, Bernard. *Ashkenazic Jewry in Transition.* Waterloo, Can.: Wilfrid Laurier University Press, 1975.

Roth, Cecil. *A History of the Jews in England.* Oxford: Clarendon Press, 1964.

Roth, Pinchas, "Mourning Murderers in Medieval Jewish Law." In *Murder Most Foul: Medieval and Early Modern Homicide,* edited by Larissa Tracy, 77–95. Cambridge: D. S. Brewer, 2018.

Rouche, Michel. "Les baptêmes forcés des Juifs en Gaule mérovingienne et dans l'Empire d'Orient." In *De l'antijudaïsme antique à l'antisemitisme contemporian,* edited by V. Nikiprowitzky, 105–27. Lille: Presses Universitaires de Lille, 1979.

Rousseaux, Xavier. "Crime, Justice and Society in Medieval and Early Modern Times: Thirty Years of Crime and Criminal Justice History." *Crime, History and Societies* 1 (1997): 87–118.

Roux, Simone. *Paris in the Middle Ages.* Translated by Jo Ann McNamara. Philadelphia: University of Pennsylvania Press, 2009.

Rubin, Miri. *Gentile Tales: The Narrative Assault on Late Medieval Jews.* New Haven, CT: Yale University Press, 1999.

Rublack, Ulinka. *The Crimes of Women in Early Modern Germany.* Oxford Studies in Social History. Oxford: Clarendon Press, 2001.

Salisbury, Eva. "Domestic Abuse." In *Women and Gender in Medieval Europe: An Encyclopedia,* edited by Margaret Schaus, 219–21. New York: Routledge, 2006.

Salmon-Mack, Tamar. *On Marriage and Its Crises in Early Modern Polish and Lithuanian Jewry.* [In Hebrew.] Tel Aviv: Hakibbutz Hameuchad Publishing, 2012.

Sapir-Abulafia, Anna. *Christian-Jewish Relations 1000–1300: Jews in the Service of Medieval Christendom.* London: Routledge, 2014.

Schäfer, Peter. "Jews and Christians in the High Middle Ages: The *Book of the Pious.*" In *The Jews in Europe in the Middle Ages (Tenth to Fifteenth Centuries): Proceedings of the International Symposium Held at Speyer 20–25 October 2002,* edited by Christoph Cluse, 29–42. Turnhout: Brepols, 2004.

———, et al., eds. *Toledot Yeshu (The Life Story of Jesus) Revisited: A Princeton Conference.* Tübingen: Mohr Siebeck, 2011.

Schatzmiller, Joseph. "Community and Super-Community in Provence in the Middle Ages." In *Jüdische Gemeinden und ihr christlischer Kontext in kulturräumlich vergleichender Betrachtung von der Spätantike bis zum 18.*

Jahrhundert, edited by Christoph Cluse, Alfred Haverkamp, and Israel J. Yuval, 441–48. Hannover: Verlag Hahnsche Buchhandlung, 2003.

Schechner, Richard. *Performance Studies: An Introduction*. London: Routledge, 2002.

Schechter, Solomon, and Joseph Jacobs. "Levirate Marriage (Hebr. 'yibbum')." In *Jewish Encyclopedia* (1906). Jewishenclyclopedia.com. Accessed Jan. 4, 2018. http://www.jewishencyclopedia.com/articles/9859-levirate-marriage.

Schepansky, Israel. *The Takanot of Israel*. [In Hebrew.] Vol. 4, *Communal Ordinances*. New York: Yeshiva University Press and Mosad Harav Kook, 1991.

Schmitt, Jean-Claude. *The Conversion of Herman the Jew: Autobiography, History, and Fiction in the Twelfth Century*. Translated by Alex J. Novikoff. Philadelphia: University of Pennsylvania Press, 2010.

———. "The Rationale of Gestures in the West: A History from the Third to the Thirteenth Centuries." In *Advances in Non-Verbal Communication: Sociocultural, Clinical, Esthetic and Literary Perspectives*, edited by Fernando Poyatos, 77–97. Amsterdam: John Benjamins Publishing, 1992.

Schnitzer-Maimon, Merav. *Rape between Halakhah and Reality: Attitudes towards Sexual Coercion of Women in Medieval Jewish Communities of Northern France and Germany*. [In Hebrew.] Tel Aviv: Tel Aviv University Press, 2017.

Schremer, Adiel. "History, Halakhah, and Religious Identity in the Halakhic Discourse of Rabbinic Sages in Medieval Ashkenaz." [In Hebrew.] *Zion* 81 (2016): 31–66.

Schwartz, David G. *Roll the Bones: The History of Gambling, Casino Edition*. Las Vegas, NV: Winchester Books, 2013.

Schwartzfuchs, Simon. *A History of the Jews in Medieval France*. [In Hebrew.] Tel Aviv: Hakibbutz Hameuchad, 2001.

Sepmeijer, Floris, ed. *A Bilingual Concordance to the Targum of the Prophets*. Vol. 12, *Jeremiah, Chapters 1–7*. Leiden: Brill, 1998.

Shahar, Shulamith. *Growing Old in the Middle Ages: 'Winter Clothes Us in Shadow and Pain.'* New York: Routledge, 2004.

———. *Marginal Groups in the Middle Ages*. The Broadcasted University Series. Tel Aviv: Ministry of Defense, 1995.

Shapiro, Barbara J. "'Fact' and the Proof of Fact in Anglo-American Law (ca.1500–1850)." In *How Law Knows*, edited by Austin Sarat et al., 25–71. Stanford, CA: Stanford University Press, 2007.

Shilo, Shmuel. "Dina de-Malkhuta Dina." In *Encyclopedia Judaica*, vol. 6, edited by Michael Berenbaum and Fred Skolnik, 2nd ed., 51–55. Detroit: Macmillan, 2007.

Shoemaker, Karl. *Sanctuary and Crime in the Middle Ages, 400–1500*. New York: Fordham University Press, 2011.

Shoham-Steiner, Ephraim. "'And in Most of Their Business Transactions They Rely on This': Some Reflections on Jews and Oaths in the Commercial Arena of Medieval Europe." In *On the Word of a Jew: Religion, Reliability, and the Dynamics of Trust*, edited by Mitchel B. Hart and Nina Caputo, 36–61. Bloomington: Indiana University Press, 2018.

———. "Burial *ad sanctos* for a Jewish Murderer? Alexander Wimpfen and Rabbi Meir of Rothenburg." *Jewish Studies Quarterly* 23 (2016): 124–41.

———. "Criminal Cooperation between Jews and Christians in Medieval Europe: A View from Some Inner Jewish Sources." In *Medieval Ashkenaz: Proceedings of the 17th World Congress of Jewish Studies in Honour of Alfred Haverkamp*, edited by Christoph Cluse and Jörg R. Müller. Forschungen zur Geschichte der Juden, A 30. Wiesbaden: Harrassowitz, 2020.

———. "Exile, Immigration and Piety: The Jewish Pietists of Medieval Germany, from the Rhineland to the Danube." *Jewish Studies Quarterly* 24 (2017): 234–60.

———. "'For a Prayer in That Place Would Be Most Welcome': Jews, Holy Shrines and Miracles—A New Approach." *Viator* 37 (2006): 369–395.

———. "'For in Every City and Town the Manner of Behavior of the Jews Resembles Their Non-Jewish Neighbours': The Intricate Network of Interfaith Connections—A Brief Introduction." In *Intricate Interfaith Networks in the Middle Ages: Quotidian Jewish-Christian Contacts*, History of Daily Life, vol. 5, edited by Ephraim Shoham-Steiner, 1–32. Turnhout: Brepols, 2016.

———. "The Humble Sage and the Wandering Madman: Madness and Madmen in an Exemplum from Sefer Hasidim." *Jewish Quarterly Review* 96 (2006): 38–49.

———. "Lions and Serpents, Rabbis and Parnasim: A Clash over Synagogue Decorations in Medieval Cologne." *Jewish History* 31 (2017): 129–64.

———. "Making a Living in Early Medieval Ashkenaz." In *Jüdische Kultur in dem SchUM Städten: Literatur—Musik—Theater*, Jüdische Kultur: Studien zur Geistesgeschichte, Religion und Literatur, vol. 26, edited by Karl E. Grözinger, 64–82. Wiesbaden: Harrassowitz Verlag, 2014.

———. *On the Margins of a Minority: Leprosy, Madness, and Disability among the Jews of Medieval Europe*. Translated by Haim Watzman. Detroit: Wayne State University Press, 2014.

———. "Poverty and Disability: The Medieval Jewish Perspective." In *The Sign Languages of Poverty*, Forschungen des Institut für Realienkunde des Mittelalters und der frühen Neuzeit, Materialien und Diskussionen, vol. 8, edited by G. Jaritz, 75–94. Vienna: Verlag der Österreichischen Akademie der Wissenschaften, 2007.

———. "'Vitam finivit infelicem': Madness, Conversion and Adolescent Suicide among Jews in Late 12th-Century England." In *The Constructed Jew: Jews and Judaism through Medieval Christian Eyes*, edited by Merrell L. Price and Kristine. T. Utterback, 71–90. Turnhout: Brepols, 2013.

Shyovitz, David I. *A Remembrance of His Wonders: Nature and the Supernatural in Medieval Ashkenaz*. Philadelphia: University of Pennsylvania Press, 2017.

Simonson, Shlomo. "Jewish Vagabonds in Medieval European Communities." [In Hebrew.] *Ha'uma* 2 (1963): 103–7.

Solorzano Telechea, Jesus Angel. "Fama Publica, Infamy and Defamation: Judicial Violence and Social Control of Crimes against Sexual Morals in Medieval Castile." *Journal of Medieval History* 22 (2007): 398–413.

Soloveitchik, Haym. "Can Halakhic Texts Talk History?" *AJS Review* 3 (1978): 153–96.

———. *Collected Essays*. 2 vols. Oxford: Littman Library of Jewish Civilization, 2013–14.

———. "Three Themes in Sefer Hasidim." *AJS Review* 1 (1976): 311–57.

———. *Wine in Ashkenaz in the Middle Ages: Yeyn Nesekh, A Study in the History of Halakhah*. [In Hebrew.] Jerusalem: Shazar Press, 2008.

Soukup, Daniel. "Apostatrix Gens: The First Crusade and Criticism of the Reversions of Jews in Cosmas's Chronica Boëmorum (Chronicle of the Bohemians)." *Colloquia Mediaevalia Pragensia* 7 (2015): 9–25.

Spierenburg, Pieter. *A History of Murder: Personal Violence in Europe from the Middle Ages to the Present*. Cambridge, UK: Polity Press, 2008.

Stancliffe, Clare. "Red, White and Blue martyrdom." In *Ireland in Early Mediaeval Europe. Studies in Memory of Kathleen Hughes*, edited by Dorothy Whitelock et al., 21–46. Cambridge: Cambridge University Press, 1982.

Starkie, Walter. *The Road to Santiago: Pilgrims of St. James*. Berkeley: University of California Press, 1965.

Steiner, Richard. "Linguistic Traces of Jewish Traders from Islamic Lands in the Frankish Kingdom." [In Hebrew.] *Leshonenu* 73 (2011): 347–70.

Stow, Kenneth R. *Alienated Minority: The Jews of Medieval Latin Europe*. Cambridge, MA: Harvard University Press, 1992.

———. "By Land or by Sea: The Passage of the Kalonymides into the Rhineland in the Tenth Century." In *Communication in the Diaspora: The Pre-Modern World*, edited by Sophia Menache, 59–73. Leiden: Brill, 1996.

———. "Conversion, Apostasy, and Apprehensiveness: Emicho of Flonheim and the Fear of Jews in the Twelfth Century." *Speculum* 76 (2001): 911–33.

Straus, Raphael. *Regensburg and Augsburg* (Jewish Communities Series). Translated by Felix N. Gerson. Philadelphia: Jewish Publication Society of America, 1939.

Strickland, Debra Higgs. *Saracens Demons and Jews: Making Monsters in Medieval Art*. Princeton, NJ: Princeton University Press, 2003.

Stutz, Ulrich. *"Römerwergeld" und "Herrenfall": Zwei kritische Beiträge zur Rechts und Verfassungsgeschichte der fränkischen Zeit*. Berlin: De Gruyter, 1934.

"Sudden Infant Death Syndrome (SIDS): Overview." *A to Z List*. National Institute of Child Health and Human Development. Accessed Jan. 19, 2017. https://www.nichd.nih.gov/health/topics/sids/Pages/default.aspx.

Sulzgruber, Werner. "Die Geschichte der jüdischen Gemeinde in Wiener Neustadt." David Jüdische Kulturzeitschrift. Judisches Leben Online. Hagalil .com. Accessed Aug. 29, 2016. http://david.juden.at/kulturzeitschrift/66-70/68-sulzgruber.htm.

Swanson, N. *Indulgences in Late Medieval England: Passports to Paradise?* Cambridge: Cambridge University Press, 2007.

Ta-Shma, Israel M. "Ashkenazi Jewry in the Eleventh Century." In *Creativity and Tradition: Studies in Medieval Rabbinic Scholarship, Literature and Thought*, edited by Israel M. Ta-Shma, 1–36. Cambridge, MA: Harvard University Press, 2006.

———. *Early Franco-German Ritual and Custom*. [In Hebrew.] Jerusalem: Magnes Press, 1994.

———. "Rabbi Isaac of Dampierre's Responsum Concerning Informers: On the Halakhic Value Attributed to Aggadic Material by Ashkenazic Tradition." [In Hebrew.] *Zion* 68 (2003): 167–74.

Teter, Magda. *Sinners on Trial: Jews and Sacrilege after the Reformation*. Cambridge, MA: Harvard University Press, 2011.

Toch, Michael. "Die Juden im Mittelalterlichen Reich." In *Enzyklopädie deutscher Geschichte*, vol. 44. Munich: R. Oldenbourg, 1998.

———. *The Economic History of European Jews: Late Antiquity and the Early Middle Ages*. Leiden: Brill, 2013.

Toledano, Shlomo. "Kovtzi Teshuvot Harosh Bekitvei Yad U'bidfusim." MA thesis, Hebrew University of Jerusalem, 1995.

Tracy, Larissa, ed. *Medieval and Early Modern Murder: Legal, Literary and Historical Contexts*. Cambridge: D. S. Brewer, 2018.

Turk, Milton Haight, ed. *The Legal Code of Ælfred the Great*. Clark, NJ: Lawbook Exchange, 2004.

Ulbricht, O. "Criminality and Punishment of the Jews in the Early Modern Period." In *In and Out of the Ghetto: Jewish-Gentile Relations in Late Medieval and Early Modern Germany*, edited by R. Po-chia Hsia and H. Lehmann, 49–70. Cambridge: Cambridge University Press, 1995.

Urbach, Ephraim Elimelekh. "Al Grimat Mavet be'Shgaga u'Mavet ba'Arisah." *Asufot* 1 (1987): 319–32.

———. "The Responsa of R. Asher b. Yehiel in Manuscripts and Printed Editions." [In Hebrew.] *Shenaton Ha'Mishpat Ha'Ivri (Jewish Law Annual)* 2 (1975): 1–153.

———. *The Tosafists: Their History, Writings, and Methods*. [In Hebrew.] 2 vols. Jerusalem: Mosad Bialik Publishers, 1986.

Vincent, Isabel. *Bodies and Souls: The Tragic Plight of Three Jewish Women Forced into Prostitution in the Americas*. New York: Harper Collins, 2005.

Vishny, Paul H. "The Informer as a Defendant in Jewish Criminal Procedure." In *Meyer Waxman Jubilee Volume: On the Occasion of His Seventy-Fifth Birthday*, edited by Judah Rosenthal et al., 122–36. Chicago and Jerusalem: College of Jewish Studies Press and Mordecai Newman Publishing, 1966.

Vodola, Elisabeth. *Excommunication in the Middle Ages*. Berkeley: University of California Press, 1986.

Vollrath, Hanna. "The Western Empire under the Salians." In *The New Cambridge Medieval History*, vol. 4, 1024–1198, part 2, edited by David Luscombe and Jonathan Riley-Smith, 38–68. Cambridge: Cambridge University Press, 2004.

Warner, David A., ed. *Ottonian Germany: The Chronicon of Thietmar of Merseburg*. Manchester Medieval Sources. Manchester: Manchester University Press, 2001.

Weiler, J. H. H. "The Trial of Jesus." *First Things* 6 (2010). Accessed Feb. 4, 2016. http://www.firstthings.com/article/2010/06/the-trial-of-jesus.

"Were the Middle Ages Lawless and Violent?" Crime before 1450. National Archives [UK]. Accessed Jan. 4, 2011. http://www.nationalarchives.gov.uk/education/candp/crime/g01/default.htm.

Wiesner, Merry E. *Gender, Church and State in Early Modern Germany: Essays by Merry E. Wiesner*. Abingdon, UK: Routledge, 2013.

Wilson, Derek. *The Tower of London: A Thousand Years*. London: Allison and Busby, 1982.

Winter, Paul. *On the Trial of Jesus*. Edited by T. A. Burkill and Geza Vermes. Berlin: De Gruyter, 1974.

Wittmer, Siegfried. *Jüdisches Leben in Regensburg: Vom frühen Mittelalter bis 1519*. Regensburg: Universitätsverlag, 2001.

Woolf, Jeffrey R. *The Fabric of Religious Life in Medieval Ashkenaz (1000–1300): Creating Sacred Communities*. Leiden: Brill 2015.

———. "'Qehillah Qedosha': Sacred Community in Medieval Ashkenazic Law and Culture." In *A Holy People: Jewish and Christian Perspectives on Religious Communal Identity*, Jewish and Christian Perspectives Series 12, edited by Marcel Poorthuis and Joshua Schwartz, 217–36. Leiden: Brill, 2006.

Yassif, Eli. *The Hebrew Folktale: History, Genre, Meaning*. Translated by Jaqueline S. Teitelbaum. Bloomington: Indiana University Press, 1999.

———. *Ninety-Nine Tales: The Jerusalem Manuscript Cycle of Legends in Medieval Jewish Folklore*. [In Hebrew.] Tel Aviv: Tel Aviv University Press, 2013.

Yerushalmi, J. H. "The Inquisition and the Jews in France in the Time of Bernard Gui." *Harvard Theological Review* 63 (1970): 317–76.

Yuval, Israel Jacob. "Heilige Städte, heilige Gemeinden: Mainz als das Jerusalem Deutschlands." In *Jüdische Gemeinden und Organisationsformen von der Antike bis zur Gegenwart*, Aschkenas Beiheft 3, edited by Robert Jütte and Abraham P. Kustermann, 91–101. Vienna: Böhlau, 1996.

Yuval, Israel J. "Hospices and Their Guests in Jewish Medieval Germany." *Proceedings of the World Congress of Jewish Studies*, division B, vol. 1 (1989): 125–29.

———. "Jews and Christians in the Middle Ages: Shared Myths, Common Language." In *Demonizing the Other: Antisemitism, Racism and Xenophobia*. Studies in Antisemitism 4, edited by Robert S. Wistrich, 88–107. Amsterdam: Harwood Academic Publishers, 1999.

———. *Scholars in Their Time: The Religious Leadership of German Jewry in the Late Middle Ages*. Jerusalem: Magnes Press, 1988.

———. *Two Nations in Your Womb: Perceptions of Jews and Christians in Late Antiquity and the Middle Ages*. Translated by Barbara Harshav and Jonathan Chipman. Berkeley: University of California Press, 2006.

Zimmer, Eric. *Harmony and Discord: An Analysis of the Decline of Jewish Self-Government in Fifteenth-Century Central Europe*. New York: Yeshiva University Press, 1970.

———. "Rabbi Menachem mi'Merseburg ve'Nimmukav." [In Hebrew.] *Sinai* 78 (1976): 75–88.

———. *Society and Its Customs: Studies in the History and Metamorphosis of Jewish Customs*. [In Hebrew.] Jerusalem: Shazar, 1996.

Zmora, Hillay. *The Feud in Early Modern Germany*. Cambridge: Cambridge University Press, 2011.

———. *State and Nobility in Early Modern Germany: The Knightly Feud in Franconia, 1440–1567*. Cambridge: Cambridge University Press, 1998.

CITATIONS INDEX

BIBLE

Genesis
- 4:1–6   137
- 4:15   279
- 9:6   132
- 19:30–38   368n163
- 25:19–28:9   105
- 28:10–32:4   104
- 31:42   107
- 38:16   45
- 38:24   208

Exodus
- 13:14–15   345n35
- 19:3   342n18
- 20:13   365n156
- 22:1   88, 90

Leviticus
- 10:1–7   57
- 19:29   206, 372n16
- 20:3   131
- 24:10   341n14

Numbers
- 6:23–27   344n35
- 11:15–30   57
- 11:24–30   57
- 19   390n1
- 30:1–16   251
- 32:32   295
- 35   184
- 35:6   140
- 35:9–34   369n171
- 35:31–32   369n171
- 35:31   185

Deuteronomy
- 13:9   141
- 19:4   279
- 19:15   315n38
- 21:17–18   131
- 21:17   336n158
- 21:22–23   117
- 23:18   202, 373–74n21
- 23:19   202
- 25:5–10   380n55
- 32:20   239, 384n86
- 32:30   80

Judges
- 9:4   332n137
- 19:2   380n63
- 1 Samuel 12:1   57

CITATIONS INDEX

2 Samuel
11:16	347n48
13–14	137
13:38	137
14:28	137

1 Kings
2:1–9	347n48
20:42	141

Isaiah
1:15	182
11:3	354n90
29:1	80
51:20	285
61:10	365n155

Jeremiah 31:28 — 238

Ezekiel
7:22	101
18:2	238
23:48	218

Micah 1:7 — 373n20

Zephaniah 3:13 — 80, 325n89

Psalms
34:13–15	119
51	284
51:4–5	350–51n69
51:5	177
51:9	284
144:14	383n72

Proverbs
11:8	88
22:10	326n100
31:23	141, 344n29

Job 12:4 — 341n13

Song of Songs 7:2 — 476n40

Esther 3:13 — 285

Daniel 4:24 — 278

Ezra 10:8 — 57

2 Chronicles 13:7 — 332n138

NEW TESTAMENT

Matthew
26:15	22
27:25	20–21

JEWISH WRITINGS

Babylonian Talmud (BT)

'Avodah Zarah 52b — 334n147

Baba Kama
22b	357n101
56a	286
113b	62
114b	331n130
117a	285

Baba Metzia
24b	92, 96
71b	356n97

Berakhot 28b — 359n117

Gitin 55b — 361n129

Ketubot
1	372n17
301	358n112

Kiddushin
43a	286
59a	44, 314n30

Megillah
12b	139
28a	277

Rosh Hashanah
17a	300n8
28a	57
31b	348n54

Sanhedrin
11a	359n117
41a	347–48n54
56a	361n132
74a	361n135

78b	286	70a	380n58
Semaḥot		*Yoma*	
2:1–4	362n138	11a	322n65
8:11	350–51n69	39b	348n54
Sota		83b	239
6:1	297	Jerusalem Talmud/Palestinian	
25b	388n113	Talmud	
48b	359n117	*Kidushin* 3:12	377n43
Sukkah 26a	36	*Sota* 9:13	359n117
Yebamot		Mishna	
6:52	372n12	*Sanhedrin* 4:5	359n117
61:2	201	*Sotah* 6:1	377–78n46

MANUSCRIPTS

London	
British Library Add. Ms. 27075	277–82, 346n42
British Library Or. Add. 27.111	384n79
National Archives/Public Record Office, Chancery	
Fine Rolls 1251-2, no. 173	337n167
National Library of Israel	
fol. 286r–287r	340n8
Jerusalem 8°3182	86, 88, 328n112
Jerusalem Heb. 4°8676	336n130
Montefiore 98	23, 312n16
Montefiore 108/Jerusalem Heb. 38°8860	372n12
New York Jewish Theological Seminary, Goldschmit MS	97, 331–32n134
Oxford, Bodleian Library	
692	370n2
1567	327n104
Paris, Bibliothèque Nationale de France, Hebr. 1122	35, 91
Parma, Palatina Library	
Cod. Parm. 86 *(Or Zarua')*	152
Cod. Parm. 1237	277–82
Cod. Parm. 2092	346n42
Cod. Parm. 2295 (de Rossi 563)	340n8
Cod. Parm. 2342 (de Rossi 541)	120, 271–74, 340n8
Cod. Parm. 2413 (de Rossi 1264)	335n153

Parma, Palatina Library *(continued)*
    Cod. Parm. 3012   346n42
    Cod. Parm. H 3280 *(Sefer Hasidim)*   71, 136, 137, 346n45
Princeton Theological Seminary 2499 *(Sefer Hasidim)*   324n81
Russian State Library
    Moscow-Ginzburg 85   335–36n153
    Moscow-Ginzburg 566   334n150
Sasson manuscript   79–81

GENERAL INDEX

abandonment/neglect of children, 247–48
Abarbanel, Don Isaac, 373n20
Abel, murdered by Cain, 116, 132, 137, 278–79
Absalom, slaying of Amnon by, 137
'agunah (bound woman), 47–48, 163
Agus, Irving, 97, 331n134, 355n95
Ahai Gaon, 361n135
Aharon Halevi of Gerona, 330n126
alam and *gazam*, 150, 174, 364n148
Alexander (Jew involved in debt collection leading to murder), 155–58, 164, 168–69, 183–84, 285–87, 356n98, 357n102
Alexander (king of Scotland), 114
Alexander ben Süslin Hacohen, 200, 204, 371–72n12
'am ha-aretz/*'amei ha-aratzot*, 183, 368n167
Amnon, slain by Absalom, 137
Amram Gaon, 131
Annales school, 19
anti-Jewish bias/violence: arson and, 354n93; Black Death, anti-Jewish riots of, 224; blood libel (ritual murder and host desecration), 3, 6, 21, 27, 328n112, 356n99, 367n160; in capital punishment of Jews, 171, 172–73; in context of medieval crime and criminal reporting, 1, 3–5, 16, 20–22, 28; Crusades and, 21, 68, 263; deicide, accusations of, 20–21, 139, 306n49, 348n51; dysphemisms, Christian use of, 324n87; Hebrew books, Christian use of, 99–100; Jewish belief in thuggishness of gentiles and, 189, 356n99; money/moneylending, association of Jews with, 22, 50, 306n54, 316n40, 356n99; riots and pogroms, 68, 100, 189, 224, 263, 333n140, 333n142, 340–41n12, 352n76, 356n96, 376n37, 386n103 (*see also specific events*); thieves/thieving and, 68, 104–5

apostasy. *See* conversion
"apple of Eve" *(etrog)* stolen from synagogue in Winchester, England, 113–14
Arad, Dotan, 389n4
Aragon. *See* Iberian peninsula
Arba'ah Turim (Jacob ben Asher), 228
archons, 15
Ari (Yitzhak Luria Ashkenazi), 334n146
aristocracy: merchant class, relationship with, 68–69; plunder economy and, 46–47, 49–50
arson, 154–55, 354n93, 357n101
Artom, Elias, 79
Asher ben Yechiel. *See* Rosh
Assis, Yom-Tov, 27, 28, 310n84, 389n4
Assize of Clarendon (1166) on trial by ordeal for thieves and robbers, 314n24
asylum/sanctuary, denied to murderers, 141–42, 278–79
Attribute of Judgment *(Midat ha-Din)*, 1, 2
Avitus of Clermont, 338–39n2
Avraham ben Yosef ben Palas, 108–13
Avraham of Sens, 353n83

banishment. *See* exile; ostracism
Barcelona Disputation (1263), 99
Bardo of Mainz, 320n60
Baron, Salo, 25
bathing, ritual, 147–48, 284, 352n79

Baumgarten, Elishevah, 190, 247–48, 388n114
beit din (rabbinic court), 11, 15, 57, 174
Bellamy, James, 25
Benedict (Baruch; brother-in-law of Milo of York), 159, 160–61, 289, 290
Benjamin of Tudela, 338n1
Ben Sira and *Ben Sira Alphabet*, 221, 379n53
Berg, Dianne, 190
Berliner, Avraham, 120, 342n21
Bernardus Gui, 359n118
Berthold of Regensburg, 208
Bezalel ben Avraham Ashkenazi, 101–2, 331n130, 334n146
Bialik, Chaim Nachman, 24
Biller, Peter, 349–50n65
Binyamin b. Shmuel, 1–2
Biran (river), 92, 96, 331n128
birkat ha-minim, 164, 359n118
Black Death, anti-Jewish riots of, 224
Bloch, Moshe Arieh, 320n58
Blois: Limoges incident (992) and, 121–23, 125–27, 272–73, 343n23; Santiago de Compostela, on pilgrimage route to, 344n34
blood libel (ritual murder and host desecration), 3, 6, 21, 27, 328n112, 356n99, 367n160
Boes, Maria, 27–28, 389n4
books: buying back pillaged Hebrew books, 100; Christian use of Hebrew books, 99–100, 330n125; colophons, 96, 331n129; Jewish will and

testament listing "improper book" (containing Christian religious material), 330n123; theft of Hebrew books, 92–103, 191–92; woman in troubled marriage, book theft by, 93, 191–92, 193; writing materials, reused for, 330nn124–25
Bosch, Hieronymus, 175
branding, as punishment for prostitution, 209, 234–35
bribes and bribery, 17, 55–56, 64–65, 114, 165, 172, 198
Brueghel, Peter, the Elder, 175
Brundage, James, 205
Burchard of Worms, 351n73

Caesarius of Heisterbach, 350n65
Cain and Abel, 116, 132, 137, 278–79
Cairo Geniza, 389n4
Candia (Heraklion, Crete), community regulations from, 79–81
cantors: community position of, 173, 197–98, 364n151; penitent murderers as, 148, 173, 177, 183; prostitutes, consorting with, 197–200
capital punishment: communal Jewish authorities' inability to impose, 11, 14, 16, 129–30, 131–32, 138–39, 157, 181; death of penitent murderers while being flogged, 278; by gentile authorities, 261; in medieval context, 11, 14, 16, 17, 29; mourning of executed murderers, 170–73; murder and, 138–39, 148, 157, 171, 181, 183; theft and, 36, 44, 163, 328n116; torture and cruelty towards Jews suffering, 171, 172–73; women's crimes and, 209, 240, 243
Capsali, Elia, 79
Carolingians, 14, 43
Carpenter, David, 114, 337–38n168, 338n170
Casimir III (king of Poland), 181
Casimir IV (king of Poland), 181
Cassuto, Umberto Moshe David, 79
Catholicism. *See* Christianity/Church authorities
Chaim Paltiel of Magdeburg, 252
Chana, wife of Yechiel ha-Kohen, 246
Charlemagne, 14, 43
Chazan, Robert, 340n9
children: abandonment/neglect of, 247–48; circumcision, unintentional death of newborn from, 145–49, 247, 249, 253, 283–84; circumcision rite for illegitimate children, modification of, 239–44; descendants/offspring of criminals, 178–79, 365n154, 366n157; domestic abuse of, 244; infanticide, 212, 214, 215, 219, 228, 240, 382n68; lineage insults involving mother/conception, 178, 225–28, 365n154, 366n157; *mamzer* (illegitimate child), 212, 227, 239–41, 296, 366n157, 377n43

children *(continued)* nursing mother allowed to marry to prevent her involvement in prostitution, 228–36, 248, 254–55; SIDS cases, 248–53; stepmothers and, 248; suffering from parental immorality, 237, 238–44; women's presumed role in infant deaths, 247–53
Chilperic (Frankish ruler), 339n2
Christianity/Church authorities: confession in, 349–50n65, 351nn72–73; dysphemisms, use of, 324n87; excommunication, 152–53; extortion plot against Christian cleric selling stolen gold items to Jew, 58–63, 68, 69–70, 202, 269–70; family feuds and, 186; Hebrew books, use of, 99–100; indulgences, 186, 237–38; Jewish will and testament listing "improper book" (containing Christian religious material), 330n123; Lateran IV (1215), 203; on prostitution and sexual transgression, 202–5, 206–9; Protestant Reformation/ Catholic Counter-Reformation, 19; selling and pawning of Christian objects to Jewish merchants, 320n59. *See also* anti-Jewish bias/violence; conversion
Christ Killers (Cohen), 21
Christ killing. *See* deicide
Chronicle of Ahima'atz, 120–21, 340–41n12
Chronicon de Rebus Gestis Ricardi Primi (Richard of Devizes), 202
circumcision: modification of rite for illegitimate children, 239–44, 385–86n94; name given at, 241–42, 385n91; unintentional death of newborn from, 145–49, 247, 249, 253, 283–84
"civilizing process" framework, 26
Clarenbald (in Milo of York case), 289
Clark, Peter, 232
clothing in medieval society, 124, 203, 204, 343n27, 383n75
coats, partnership between Jewish and gentile thieves to steal, 23, 307n58
Cohen, Esther, 27
Cohen, Jeremy, 21
coin clipping, English Jews accused of, 3–4
Cologne: as commercial hub for wool and lambskin, 322n67; Jewish presence in, 39, 263–64; lamb's wool taken by gentiles and sold to Jews for resale, 63–65; supercommunal assemblies at, 318n47
Colon, Joseph, 377n45
colophons, 96, 331n129
Columbanus, penitential handbook of, 352n78
Common Women (Karras), 199
communal ban. *See* excommunication; exile; ostracism

GENERAL INDEX 435

communal Jewish authorities, 10–11, 14–17, 261–62; acceptance of punishment and expiation, enforcing, 178–79; discouragement of pursuing grievances outside of, 11, 15, 16, 17, 151–52, 155, 158; inability to impose severe punishment, 11, 14, 16, 129–30, 131–32, 138–39, 157, 181, 345n37; languages used in Jewish legal proceedings, 320n57; murderers, communal status and treatment of, 118–19, 128–35, 277–82; power of, 261–62; reliability of testimony of converted Jew versus gentile thieves, 163; in Sara and Isaac case, 210–11, 213; sunken barge case used to support, 54–58; supercommunal organizations, 16, 30, 55, 58, 158, 169, 216, 259, 317–18n47, 319n53, 375n35, 379n51; testimony in Jewish courts, revocation of murderers' right of, 353n86; theft, Jewish communal regulations on, 77–81; women not allowed as witnesses, 175

Complete Jewish Guide to France, The (Toni L. Kamins), 115, 338n1

confession in middle ages, 132, 145, 160, 237, 329n118, 349–50n65, 351nn72–73

Continental/Roman legal system, 12–13, 70–71, 323n74

conversion: anti-Jewish polemic and, 1, 99; descendants/offspring of converts, 365n164; hybrid religious affiliation/identity, 121, 125, 272, 341–42n16; Jews accepting baptism during Crusades and then returning to Judaism, 324n78; of Jews sentenced to torture and execution, 172–73; murder and, 115–16, 121, 152, 163, 172–73, 187, 189, 338–39nn1–2; reliability of testimony of converted Jew versus gentile thieves, 163; by thieves under community ban, 109–11; women and, 214, 224–26, 235, 377n45; *yibbum* and *ḥalitzah* when brother-in-law of widow has converted, 224–26, 380n58

corporal punishment, 16, 17, 29, 36, 44, 132, 166, 177, 181, 183, 234, 243, 261, 328n116

courts. *See* Christianity/Church authorities; communal Jewish authorities; gentile authorities; laws and legal systems

credit. *See* debt/credit

Cresse (Gedaliyah) of Stamford, 113–14, 337–38nn167–168

Crime and Conflict in Medieval Europe (Hanawalt), 26

crime and Jews. *See* Jews and crime in medieval Europe

Crimes of Women in Early Modern Germany (Rublack), 214, 243

Crusades, 21, 68, 79, 263, 324n78, 324n86, 341n12, 343n27, 352n76

Daroca (Aragon): expulsion of Jewish community of (1492), 336n161; punishment of attempted theft from synagogue of, 28–29, 108–13, 261, 263, 310n84, 347n52
David (biblical king), and murder, 136, 347n48
David ben Zimra, 334n146
Dean, Trevor, 26, 33, 194
death penalty. *See* capital punishment
debt/credit: hostage taking as means of guaranteeing, 316n41; money/moneylending, association of Jews with, 22, 50, 306n54, 316n40, 356n99; murder, debt collection leading to, 155–58, 285–87; viticulture, supplying credit to, 313–14n22
Decretum (Burchard of Worms), 351n73
deicide, accusations of, 20–21, 139, 306n49, 348n51
deliverance story, Limoges incident (992) as, 120–27, 271–74
descendants/offspring of criminals, 178–79, 365n154, 366n157
Devotio Moderna, 384n81
diamond dust, as magical potion, 35, 91–92
diminished mental capacity, 93, 191–92, 245, 357n101

divorce. *See* marriage and marital law
domestic violence. *See* women and crime
duel, trial by, 43, 124–25. *See also* trial by ordeal
Dunn, Caroline, 9
dysphemisms, 78, 104, 210, 328nn86–87

economic issues. *See* financial/economic issues
Edward I (king of England), 4
Eidelberg, S., 317–18n47
Eisner, Manuel, 26
Elazar/Eliezer b. Judah of Worms, 140, 335n151, 348n58, 351n75
Elchanan ben Shmuel, 249–50
Elias, Norbert, 26
Eliezer ben Isaac of Mainz (Hagadol), 318n51
Eliezer ben Joel Halevi (Ra'avya), 33n123, 346n43, 375n36
Eliezer ben Yechiel, 210, 297
Elukin, Jonathan, 68
Emanuel, Simcha, 166–67, 248, 251, 388n111
emotional displays in court, treatment of, 174
emotional responses of women, 110, 197
England: Assize of Clarendon (1166) on trial by ordeal for thieves and robbers, 314n24; coin clipping, English Jews accused of, 3–4; crime statistics (1300–1348), 310n2;

GENERAL INDEX   437

Curia Regis rolls, 159, 289, 357n105; expulsion of 1290, 4, 27; legal system in, 12–13; Milo of York, murder of wife of, 158–62, 190, 289–90; prostitution in, 199; taxes paid directly to king by Jews in, 357n105; Winchester, theft of *etrog* from synagogue in, 113–14
Entin-Roke'ah, Zefira, 27
Ephraim ben Isaac of Regensburg: biographical information, 332–33n138, 346n43; books, on theft of, 97–99, 100; magic used to recover theft from, 86–88; murderers, on penitential protocols for, 133, 134, 184, 280–81, 282
Ephraim ben Joel, 210, 297
episcopus Iudaeorum, 15
Epstein, Avraham, 317n43
equal standing before the law, lack of, 116, 161, 182–83
etnan, 202, 373n20
etrog ("apple of Eve") stolen from synagogue in Winchester, England, 113–14
Europe, medieval, Jews and crime in. *See* Jews and crime in medieval Europe
European Cities and Towns (Clark), 232
European Genizah, 330n125
Evyatar ben Eliyahu Kohen-Tzedek, 143, 350n68
excommunication: as Christian practice, 152–53, 354n88; *nidui*, 32, 151, 152–53
exile: of murderers, 132–35, 137–40, 146–47, 278–82, 347n52, 352n76; as penance in gentile communities, 146–47, 352n78; theft from synagogue, community ban imposed as punishment for, 109–11, 347n52. *See also* ostracism
expulsions of Jews: from England (1290), 4, 27; from Mainz (1462), 382n70; from Regensburg (1519), 85, 367n160; from Spain (1492), 336n161

fachwerkhaus construction, 328n114
Falagi, Haim, 334n150
family feuds, 184, 186, 187–88, 369n174
fertility of women, pentitential regimes protecting, 252–53, 388n114
Fichtenau, Heinrich, 316n42
financial/economic issues: divorced woman's access to financial settlement, 210, 216–19, 245–46; money/moneylending, association of Jews with, 22, 50, 306n54, 316n40, 356n99; murderer, financial compensation paid by, 138, 139, 146, 158, 180–83, 184–86, 257n102, 348–49n60; pawnbroking, association of Jews with, 50; plunder economy, 46–47, 49–50

financial/economic issues *(continued)* plundered goods, financial dispute over successful attempt to reclaim, 52–54, 267–68; viticulture, supplying credit to, 313–14n22. *See also* debt/credit

Finkelstein, Louis, 304n35

fire, setting, 154–55, 354n93, 357n101

First Crusade (1096), 21, 68, 263, 324n86, 341n12, 352n76

flogging of murderers, as penance, 132, 143, 278, 280, 281

food and drink: Jewish and gentile business partners sharing, 41, 313n21; prohibition on eating food prepared by gentiles, 41, 347n51

Fourth Crusade (1204), 79

Fourth Lateran Council (1215), 203

France: anti-Jewish violence in, 68; Limoges incident (992), 120–27, 271–74, 340n10; prostitution in, 202–3, 374n24. *See also specific towns*

Fürst, Rachel, 376n37

Gamaliel, Rabbi, 57

Gaonic protocols for dealing with murderers, 128–35, 277–82, 345n38

gazam and *alam*, 150, 174, 364n148

gaze, aversion of, from murderers, 128–31

Geary, Patrick J., 316n42

Gedaliyah (Cresse) of Stamford, 113–14, 337–38nn167–168

gender: domestic violence and gender roles, 247; female criminality and gender roles, 197; masculine construction of records and lack of female voice, 194–96, 197; murder, males as main perpetrators and victims of, 190; occupational division of labor, 208; ownership of women, prostitution and sexual transgression challenging, 233; sexual double standard and, 204. *See also* women and crime

gentile authorities: *Curia Regis* in England, 159, 289, 357n105; informers and informing, 15, 119, 164–70, 255–56n96, 291–94; Jewish discouragement of pursuing grievances with, 11, 15, 16, 17, 151–52, 165, 260; Jewish interaction with, 260–61; limitation of Jewish contact with gentiles, as principle, 82, 326n95; *messiah* (appealing to non-Jewish authorities), 130, 164–70, 188, 260; Milo of York, murder of wife of, 158–62, 289–90; mourning of murderers executed by, 170–73; prostitution, treatment of, 202–5, 206–9, 231, 232, 234–35, 261, 383n75; synagogue theft referred to, 113–14. *See also* Christianity/Church authorities

gentile servants/slaves. *See* servants/slaves, gentile

George der Reich von Wittelsbach of Bavaria Land shut, 327nn108–9
Germanic codes on murder, 140, 348–49n60
German lands: family feuds in, 186; Iberian peninsula compared, 311n10; Jewish expulsions from, in 15th century, 229, 382–83n70; Jewish right to bear arms in, 364n150; late tenth to mid-eleventh century, changes of, 38–39; laws and legal systems in, 13, 14. *See also specific towns*
Gershom ben Judah of Mainz: 'agunah (bound woman), compassion for, 47–48; coats, on partnership beween Jewish and gentile thieves to steal, 23, 44–45, 307n58; communal regulations attributed to, 78; disappearance/death of Jewish merchant of stolen goods, on remarriage of wife, 46–52, 265–66; forbidding Jews to use non-Jewish courts, 16; lay leaders, reaction to rule of, 312n16; *ma'arufia* rights, case involving, 39–46; plundered goods, financial dispute over successful attempt to reclaim, 52–54, 267–68; polygamy banned by, 218, 223; regulations attributed to, 304n36; socioeconomic profile of criminals and, 262; sunken barge, unlawful taking of recovered goods from, 54–58, 92
Geschichte von Unten school, 19
Given, James Buchanan, 25, 308n65
Goffart, Walter, 338–39n2
Goitein, S. D., 301n14
Goldschmidt, Daniel, 1
Goldsmith, Thomas, 159, 289
Goldsmith, Walter and Adam, 289
"good Werner" riots (1287/1288), 100
Grätz, Heinrich Zvi, 25
Great Book of Rabbi Mordechai ben Hillel of Nirenberg, 332n134
Green, Thomas, 308n65
Gregory of Tours, 116, 338–39n2
Gregory VII (pope), 321n62
Grossman, Avraham: on domestic violence, 244, 371nn9–10, 386n95; on murder, 150; on rabbinic figures of middle Rhine area, 263; on theft, 15, 27, 44, 303–4n32, 307n58, 312–13nn16–17, 317n43, 319n53
Guggenheim, Yaakov, 27
guided penance, 351–52n75
Gumprecht (brother of Maharil), 239, 240–41
Guntram (Frankish ruler), 339n2
Gurr, Ted, 26

Haberman, Avraham M., 342n21
ha-Darshan (Moshe Azriel ben Rabbi Eliezer the Homilist), 210, 213, 216, 217, 219–20, 297, 375n36
Hadrian (Roman emperor), 341n13

Hagadol (Eliezer ben Isaac of Mainz), 318n51

Hagahot Ashri, 333n143

Hai Gaon and murderer on the Mount of Olives, 142–45, 350n68

Haim Eliezer ben Isaac Or Zarua': actual thief versus parties benefiting from theft, on differentiation of, 81–82; on anathematization, 152; biographical information, 81, 333n143, 345–46n41; on book theft, 100–101; on children of Jewish/gentile parents, 238–39; debt collection leading to murder, citation of Meir of Rothenburg on, 285–87; digest of sermons, 335–36n153; on diminished mental capacity, 357n101; *Or Zarua'*, 152, 291–94; preaching against theft, 104–7; "time/hour of rage," on murders committed in, 165–70, 260, 291–94, 361n134; on *yibbum* and *ḥalitzah*, 221–24, 380n58

halakhah: as arbitration and dispute settlement mechanism, 357n103; communal regulations proscribing behavior not strictly forbidden by, 78; concept of, 10; on confiscations by rulers, 105–6; custom overriding, 385n93; on expiation of murder, 279; on free will and ability to realize a request is illegal, 170; gentiles, laws of agency not applicable to, 153, 156; lost/found property and book theft, 95–97; *ma'arufia* rights sanctioned by, 44; on marriage of women nursing a child, 228, 248, 382n68; *me'is alay* (he is repugnant to me) claims, women suing for divorce on grounds of, 193; on orphaned children, 315n36; on pursuing grievances against other Jews in non-Jewish courts, 11; sunken barge case, cited by halakhic authorities, 54, 55; on "time of rage," 165–66; on wine intended for Jewish consumption, 314n22

ḥalitzah. See *yibbum* and *ḥalitzah*

Halttunen, Karen, 117, 189–90

Hanawalt, Barbara, 26

hand of a dead man, thieves using, 35–36, 91, 92, 329n118

Hasidim Hasidei, 71, 82

Haskalah (Jewish Enlightenment), 22

Haverkamp, Eva, 321n61, 389n4

Hebrew books. See books

Hehlerrecht, 14, 46

Heinrich IV (emperor), 14, 38, 70, 303n32

hellfire and damnation, 89, 130, 144

Henry I (duke of Burgundy), 315n33

Henry III (king of England), 113–14

ḥerem, 16, 32, 40, 55, 78, 130, 227, 296, 367n159

Hermanin (prostitute/brothel madame), 235

ḥerut, 171–72
Hezekiah ben Mano'aḥ (Hizkuni), 365–66n156
highway crimes, 17, 36, 124, 274
Hillel, Rabbi, 57
hiring others to commit a crime: murder, 123–24, 126, 127, 153–54, 155–58, 163, 167–69, 189, 262, 273–74, 286, 349n63; thievery, 37, 44, 46, 81–82, 262
Hirt-Ramon, Orit, 367–68n162
"Historical Trends in Violent Crime" (Gurr), 26
History of Murder, A (Spierenburg), 186–87
Hizkuni (Hezekiah ben Mano'aḥ), 365–66n156
Höchstadt, Yosselyn ben Moshe, 363n145
"holy societies" *(Kadisha Havura)*, 179, 367n161
homilies and sermons: Haim Eliezer ben Isaac Or Zaruaʻ, digest of, 335–36n153; Judah the Pious on murder, 136–45; Sabbath before Passover, importance of sermon on, 119, 339n6; theft, preaching against, 103–7
honor and honor cultures, 117–18, 187–88, 190
hostages. *See* ransom
host desecration. *See* blood libel
"hour/time of rage," murders committed in, 165–70, 260, 291–94, 361n134
Howe, Irving, 24
Huzmann, Rüdiger, of Speye, 321n63

Iberian peninsula: compared to northwestern Europe, 311n10; Daroca (Aragon), punishment of attempted theft from synagogue of, 28–29, 108–13, 261, 263, 310n84, 347n52; expulsions of Jews from (1492), 336n161; Muslim rule and Reconquista, 311n10
Ihnat, Kati, 344n30
illegitimate children: circumcision rite for, modification of, 239–44, 385–86n94; infanticide and, 212, 214, 215, 219, 228, 240; *mamzer* as term for, 212, 227, 239–41, 296, 366n157, 377n43; Sara and Isaac case, rumors/evidence of pregnancy and sexual promiscuity in, 209, 210, 212–13, 214, 217, 218, 220–21, 295–97
immigration and crime, connections drawn between, 126–27, 349n64
indulgences, 186, 237–38
infanticide, 212, 214, 215, 219, 228, 240, 382n68
informers and informing, 15, 119, 164–70, 255–56n96, 291–94
Innocent III (pope), 79
Innocent IV (pope), 354n88
Isaac Alfasi, on book theft, 102–3, 334n150
Isaac ben Abraham, 294
Isaac ben Avraham (Rizba), 151, 152, 353n83
Isaac ben Jacob ha-Lavan of Prague, 145

Isaac ben Moshe Or Zarua' of Vienna: biographical information, 345–46n41; on domestic abuse, 244; on murder, 131, 145–49, 182, 283–84; *Or Zarua'*, 145, 148, 283–84; on theft, 81, 97, 333n130
Isaac ben Shmuel the Elder of Dampierre-Sur-Aube (Ri ha-Zaken), 97, 352n75, 353n83
Isaac Black/Negro/Niger, 160, 289
Isaac Iben Migash, 331n130
Isaac Klut, 154–55
Iserles, Moshe, 372n12
Iserlyn, Israel ben Petachia, of Wiener Neustadt, 195–96, 367n161
Israel ben Haim of Bruna, 179–83, 189, 328n112, 348n58, 366n158, 367n161, 385–86n94
Israel of Krems am Donau, 182, 333n143
Italy: Jews expelled from German lands migrating to, 229, 382–83n70; Padua, organized prostitution and brothels in, 228–36, 254–55

Jacob ben Asher, 208–9, 228, 371n12
Jacob ben Isaac ha-Lavan of Prague, 145, 147, 149
Jacob ben Meir Tam, 78, 182, 228, 248, 332n138, 346n43
Jacob ben Moses Molin (Maharil), 119, 220, 221, 236, 239–43, 366n157

Jacques de Vitry, 202–3, 374n24
Jewish communal authorities. *See* communal Jewish authorities
Jewish identity, loss of: hybrid religious affiliation/identity, 121, 125, 272; immigration and crime, connections drawn between, 126–27; by murderers in exile/ostracized, 139–40; by thieves under community ban, 109–11, 347n52
Jewish priesthood, 128, 198, 341n14, 344–45n35
Jews and crime in medieval Europe, 1–33, 257–64; anti-Jewish bias and, 1, 3–5, 16, 20–22, 28 (*see also* anti-Jewish bias/ violence); communal Jewish authorities and, 10–11, 14–17, 261–62 (*see also* communal Jewish authorities); defining crime, 5–6; gentile authorities, interaction with, 260–61 (*see also* Christianity/ Church authorities; gentile authorities); in historical context, 7–8, 11–12; historiography of, 19, 22–28; Jewish/rabbinic sources on, 1–2, 257–60, 263–64; low percentage of Jewish criminals compared to gentiles, 264; medieval European concepts of crime and punishment, 12–18; methodology and sources, 3, 8–11, 28–33, 194–97, 257–60, 263–64, 389n4; nature of

Jewish criminal engagements, theories about, 31–32; reasons for studying, 6–8; scarcity of historical information, 3, 9, 22, 29, 263–64; socioeconomic profile of, 262–63; temporal and geographic scope, 9–10, 19–22; voluntary and involuntary marginals, 2–3. *See also* laws and legal systems; murder and murderers; thieves and thieving; women and crime

Joel Halevi of Bonn and Cologne, 346n43

Jordan, William C., 36, 187

Joseph Bonfil/Tuv 'Elem, 316n43, 371n10

Joseph Iben-Avitur, 197–200, 371n10

Judah and Tamar, story of, 45, 208–9, 373n19

Judah ben Asher, 389n4

Judah ben Meir ha-Kohen of Mainz (Judah ha-Zaken/Judah Ba'al Sefer ha-Dinim): on communal bans, 318n51; dating of, 320n60, 321n62, 322n65; on extortion plot against Christian cleric selling stolen gold items to Jew, 58–63, 68, 69–70, 202, 269–70; historical interest in/ significance of, 319n53; on lamb's wool taken by gentiles and sold to Jews for resale, 63–65; on misleading buyer about value of silver object, 65–67; socioeconomic profile of criminals and, 262, 263

Judah ben Shmuel the Pious of Regensburg: blood libel case handled by, 328n112; dating of, 327n111; on gentile slaves/servants stealing from Jewish masters, 82, 83, 85–86; graveside as medieval pilgrimage site, 85, 325n106; guided penance and, 351n75; Kalonymide family origins, 327–28n112; on limiting contact between Jews and gentiles, 82, 326n95; magic used to identify thieves and locate stolen possessions by, 85–90; moral concerns of thieving, engagement with, 71, 74–75; on murder, 136–45, 187, 348nn57–58; on prostitution and sexual transgression, 205–9; Sabbath observation, concern about, 347n51; Sara and Isaac case, relationship to rabbis involved in, 375n36. See also *Sefer Ḥasidim*

Judah Sar ha-Birah, 4

Judas Iscariot, 22, 306n51

Kadisha Havura ("holy societies"), 179, 367n161

Kahana, Rav, 292

Kamtza and Bar Kamtza, 361n129

kaparah, 171, 172

Karras, Ruth Mazo, 199

Kassel, David, 316–17n43

Katz, Jacob, 151–52, 353n85

Katz, Judah, 251
Kelina (paramour of Milo of York), 160–61, 190, 290, 358n110
kidnapping, ransom, and violent death, 47, 49–52
Kisch, Guido, 18, 303n30
Knock, Arthur D., 341–42n16
Koster, Jöelle, 204

lachrymose school of Jewish history, 25
Langmuir, Gavin, 6
languages used in Jewish legal proceedings, 320n57
Lansing, Carol, 194
Lateran IV (1215), 203
laws and legal systems: anti-Jewish bias and, 16; Continental/Roman system, 12–13, 70–71, 323n74; court records, as source material, 29; criminal trials, 13; *Curia Regis* in England, 159, 289, 357n105; *dina de-malkhuta dina* (the will of the king is the law), 105; emotional displays in court, treatment of, 174; English system, 12–13; equal standing before the law, lack of, 116, 161, 182–83; extreme violence, crimes and punishments involving, 17; immunities and privileges granted to Jews, 13–14, 43, 161, 181; languages used in Jewish legal proceedings, 320n57; late medieval change in legal attitudes toward crime, 20; multiplicity of jurisdictions, 10, 12; rule of law, Jewish reliance on, 89–90; supercommunal mechanisms, 16; *takanot*, 10, 16, 54, 80, 304n35. *See also* Christianity/Church authorities; communal Jewish authorities; gentile authorities; *halakhah*; trial by ordeal
lay leaders in Jewish communities, 15, 54, 55, 312
Lehnardt, Andreas, 330n125
Lehnardt, Peter S., 120–21
Lemburg, distribution of responsibility of two murderers in, 179–83, 189, 367n159
lex salica, 184, 348n60
Limoges: Santiago de Compostela, on pilgrimage route to, 127, 344n34; St. Martial and, 122, 127, 342n20, 343n25; two towns of, 342n20
Limoges incident (992), 120–27, 271–74, 340n10
lineage insults, 178, 225–28, 365n154, 366n157
Living Together, Living Apart (Elukin), 68
loans. *See* debt/credit
Lopez, Robert S., 312n13
lost/found property, *halakhah* on, 95–97
Louis the Pious (Holy Roman emperor), 342n20
Luria, Ilana, 27

Luria, Shlomo, 355–56n96
Lurianic kabbalah, 334n146

ma'arufia, 39–46, 59–60, 307n58, 312n15, 313nn17–18
magic: crucified wax doll, malefactor's use of, 124, 344n30; identifying thieves and recovering stolen goods with, 85–86; used to commit theft, 35–36, 90–92
Maharam (Meir ben Yekutiel Ha-Kohen of Rothenburg), 355–56n96
Maharil (Jacob ben Moses Molin), 119, 220, 221, 236, 239–43, 366n157
Mahzor le'Yamim Noraim (Goldschmidt), 1
Maimonides (Moses ben Maimon): addenda to work of, 356n96, 358n112; on book theft, 101–2, 331n130, 334n147; on divorce settlements, 218; on financial compensation for murder, 185; Meir of Rothenburg's commentaries on, 375–76n37; testimony in Jewish courts, revocation of murderers' right of, 353n86
Maimon the Adjudicator (Maimon ha-Dayan), 331n130
Mainz: anti-Jewish violence in, 68; cathedral of, 60, 320n60, 321n62; coinage of, 321nn62–63; expulsion of Jews from (1462), 382n70; extortion plot against Christian cleric selling stolen gold items to Jew, 58–63, 68, 69–70, 202, 269–70; Jewish presence in, 39; lamb's wool taken by gentiles and sold to Jews for resale, 63–65; rabbinic judicial and arbitrational authority in, 15; supercommunal assemblies at, 317–18n47; thieving, Jewish communal regulations on, 78
Mainz Pogrom (1283), 100
Makeblithe, William, 159, 289
malshin, 15
mamzer (illegitimate child), 212, 227, 239–41, 296, 366n157, 377n43
marginalized individuals, voluntary and involuntary, 2–3, 20, 26, 127, 131, 169, 177, 178, 196, 255, 364–65n153
Marienberg, Evyatar, 337–38nn168–170
Market Stipulation *(takanat ha-shuk)*, 14, 46, 57, 95, 98
marriage and marital law: *'agunah* (bound woman), 47–48, 163; book theft by woman married to man with diminished mental capacity, 93, 191–92, 193, 245; disappearance/death of Jewish merchant of stolen goods and remarriage of wife, 46–52, 265–66; domestic abuse, husband compelled to divorce wife due to, 244–45; financial settlement, divorced woman's access to, 210, 216–19, 245–46

446　GENERAL INDEX

marriage and marital law *(continued)* fornicating woman, implications of actions for marriage of, 237–38; *me'is alay* (he is repugnant to me) claims, women suing for divorce on grounds of, 193; mental health of parties to divorce, 329n122; nursing mother allowed to marry to prevent her involvement in prostitution, 228–36, 248, 254–55; pit, missing Jew found by thieves buried head first in, 162–63, 358–59n114; polygamy, ban on, 218, 223; prostitutes, woman desiring to divorce her husband for consorting with, 200, 204; in Sara and Isaac case, 210, 216–19. See also *yibbum* and *ḥalitzah*

martyrdom, Jewish acceptance of, 170

maskilim, 22

Matityah (Matthias), unintentional death of newborn due to circumcision by, 145–49, 247, 249, 253, 283–84

McCall, Andrew, 26

medieval Europe, Jews and crime in. *See* Jews and crime in medieval Europe

Me'il Tzedek (Menachem of Merseburg), 258–59

Meir ben Baruch of Rothenburg: on accusations of sexual transgression, 226–27; on deaths of infants, 252; on diminished mental capacity, 357n101; discouraging vigilantism and appeals to non-Jewish courts, 357n104; on domestic abuse, 246; on murder, 153, 155–58, 162–63, 165–70, 183–84, 285–87, 292, 353n86; ransoming of body of, 183–84; responsa, as source material, 259; Sara and Isaac case referred to, 210–11, 295, 297 *(see also* Sara and Isaac case*)*; socioeconomic profile of criminals and, 262; on theft, 4, 319n53, 319n55, 333n143, 333n145

Meir ben Yekutiel Ha-Kohen of Rothenburg (Maharam), 355–56n96

Meir ha-Kohen of Rothenburg, 358n112, 375–76n37

Meir of Regensburg, 100

Menachem ben Pinchas of Merseburg, 178–79, 227–28, 258–59, 355n96, 365n155

merchants and merchant class: aristocracy, relationship with, 68–69; Jewish affiliation with, 37, 39, 311n7

Meshulam b. Kalonymus, 314n30

mesirah, 130, 164–70, 188, 260

Mesler, Katelyn, 344n30

Metz *beit din*, 11

metzi'ah, 53, 63

Midat ha-Din (Attribute of Judgment), 1, 2

Milo of York, murder of wife of, 158–62, 190, 289–90

Minhager Maharash (Shalom of Wiener Neustadt), 173
Mintz, Judah, 228–36, 255, 335n153, 382–83n70, 382n67
Mintz, Moses, 361n137
Mintz, Moshe ben Eliezer Halevi, 335n153
money/moneylending, association of Jews with, 22, 50, 306n54, 316n40, 356n99
Mordechai ben Hillel Hacohen of Nürenberg (the Mordechai): on accusations of sexual transgression, 226–27; on fasting penance for women with child found dead in her bed, 358n112; *Great Book of Rabbi Mordechai ben Hillel of Nirenberg*, 332n134; on Jews accepting baptism during Crusades and then returning to Judaism, 324n78; on recovery of pillaged Hebrew books, 100, 332n134, 333–34n145, 333n140; Rindfleisch riots, death in, 333n140; *Sefer Mordechai*, 225, 317n47, 372n12; student of, 332n138
mort main, 329n118
moser/mosrim (informers), 15, 119, 164–70
Moses ben Maimon. *See* Maimonides
Moses ben Nachman (Nachmanides; Ramban), 201, 209
Moses of Andernach, 234–35
Moses of Coucy, 335n151
Moshe Azriel ben Rabbi Eliezer the Homilist (ha-Darshan), 210, 213, 216, 217, 219–20, 297, 375n36
Moshe ben Asher, 182
Moshel of Neustadt, 326n95
Mothers and Children (Baumgarten), 247–48, 388n111
Mount of Olives, Hai Gaon and murderer on the, 142–45, 350n68
mourning for executed murderers, 170–73
Müller, Joel Hacohen, 23, 312n16, 371n10
Müller, Jörg, 28, 200
murder and murderers, 115–90; behavior of victims/community toward expiated perpetrator, 145–49, 151, 176–79, 283–84; Cain and Abel, 116, 132, 137, 278–79; character of victim, relevance of, 182–83; descendants/offspring of, 178–79, 365n154, 366n157; domestic violence resulting in murder, 247; family feuds, 184, 186, 187–88, 369n174; free will and responsibility issues, 170; gentile assassins/thugs, Jewish use of, 123–24, 126, 127, 153–54, 155–58, 163, 167–69, 189, 262, 273–74, 286, 349n63; Germanic codes on, 140, 348–49n60; Hebrew terms for, 119; historical insights about, 186–90; honor/honor cultures and, 117–18, 187–88, 190; infanticide, 212, 214, 215, 219, 228, 240, 382n68

murder and murderers *(continued)*
  informers and informing, 15, 119, 164–70, 255–56n96, 291–94; intentional, severe, and habitually violent offenders, 149–55; Jewish community, murders within, 136–42; Judah the Pious on, 136–45; low percentage of Jews as perpetrators and victims, 17–18, 187–89; males as main perpetrators and victims, 190; in medieval society, 117–19, 150–51, 190; ransoming souls/bodies, 183–86, 369n171; self-defense, 175–76, 183, 275–76, 368n165; sexual promiscuity, father's desire to kill daughter for, 212–13, 214, 219–20, 296–97, 378–79n50; soul, murderers losing, 153, 354n90; in urban versus suburban/rural environments, 17; violence viewed as normal social behavior, 116–17

murder and murderers, cases of: circumcision, unintentional death of newborn from, 145–49, 247, 249, 253, 283–84; debt collection leading to murder, 155–58, 285–87; Hai Gaon and murderer on the Mount of Olives, 142–45, 350n68; Limoges incident (992), 120–27, 271–74, 340n10; Milo of York, murder of wife of, 158–62, 190, 289–90; mourning executed murderers, 170–73; pit, missing Jew accused of philandering found buried head first in, 162–63, 358–59n114; prayers, quarrel over leading, 173–79, 183, 275–76, 364n151; Priscus, murdered by Phatir, 115–16, 187, 189, 338–39nn1–2; "time/hour of rage," murder committed in, 165–70, 260, 291–94, 361n134; two murderers, distribution of responsibility of, 179–83, 189

murder and murderers, punishment of: asylum/sanctuary, denied to murderers, 141–42, 278–79; atonement and penitential rituals, 132, 142–45, 146, 277–82; communal status and treatment of murderers, protocols for, 118–19, 128–35, 277–82; enforcement of penance for, 151–52, 157–58; exile imposed on murderers, 132–35, 137–40, 146–47, 278–82, 347n52; financial compensation paid by murderer, 138, 139, 146, 158, 180–83, 184–86, 257n102, 348–49n60; flogging of murderers, as penance, 132, 143, 278, 280, 281; inability of Jewish community to severely punish, 129–30, 131–32, 138–39, 157, 181, 345n37; Jewish identity, exiled/ostracized murderer's loss of, 139–40; mock execution and burial of murderers, 143,

144; ostracism of murderers, 128–32, 139, 146–47, 148, 153–54, 277, 283–84; physical mutilation, 178; ritual bathing following penance by murderer, 147–48, 284, 352n79; self-mortification, 132, 139–40, 184; testimony in Jewish courts, revocation of right of, 353n86

Murder Most Foul: Medieval and Early Modern Homicide (Halttunen), 189–90

Nachman, Rav, 279
Nachmanides (Moses ben Nachman; Ramban), 201, 209
Nachshon Gaon, 131
Napolitano, David, 20
Nathan, Rabbi, 284
Natronai Gaon, 345n37
neglect/abandonment of children, 247–48
Nehemia ben Shlomo, 329n120
Neustadt pietists, 326n95
nidui, 32, 151, 152–53
Nimukim (Menachem of Merseburg), 258–60
Nirenberg, David, 372n14
Noachides, 169, 361n132
non-Jewish authorities. *See* gentile authorities
Nuremberg, Rindfleisch riots (1298) in, 333n140, 356n96, 376n37

oaths and oath-taking, 325n89, 337n166

offspring/descendants of criminals, 178–79, 365n154, 366n157
Onkelos the proselyte, 77
ordeal. *See* trial by ordeal
Orthodox Jewish historiography, 22, 24
Or Zarua' (Haim Eliezer Or Zarua'), 152, 291–94
Or Zarua' (Isaac ben Moshe of Vienna), 145, 148, 283–84
ostracism: anathematization/excommunication, Christian, 152–53; ḥerem, 16, 32, 40, 55, 78, 130, 227, 296, 367n159; limitations as punishment, 149–51, 154; of murderers by Jewish community, 128–32, 139, 146–47, 148, 153–54, 277, 283–84; theft from synagogue, community ban imposed as punishment for, 109–11, 347n52. *See also* excommunication; exile
Otis, Leah, 383n75
Ottonian empire. *See* German lands
Otto-William, Count of Burgundy, 315n33
"outlaw" punishment for murder in Germanic codes, 140

Padua, organized prostitution and brothels in, 228–36, 254–55
papal indulgences, 186
Paris: Priscus, murdered by Phatir in, 115–16, 187, 189, 338–39nn1–2; prostitution in, 202–3, 374n24

Paris *(continued)*
  trial against Talmud (1240s), 99, 333–34n145
pawnbroking, association of Jews with, 50
Peace (Truce) of God, 37–38, 69
penance, penitence, and penitential regimes. *See* punishment and penitential regimes
Pennington, Kenn, 354n88
Perani, Mauro, 330n125
Phatir, murdering Priscus, 115–16, 187, 189, 338–39nn1–2
physical punishment, 16, 17, 29, 36, 44, 132, 166, 177, 181, 183, 234, 243, 261, 328n116
physiognomy, 345n49
pietists and pietism: guided penance and, 351–52n75; on murder, 140, 142, 144–45, 184; prostitution/sexual transgression and, 237, 374n29; on theft, 71–77, 84, 85, 326–27n103, 326n95
pit, missing Jew accused of philandering found buried head first in, 162–63, 358–59n114
piyyutim, as sources, 1–2, 31, 150
plunder economy, 46–47, 49–50
plundered goods, financial dispute over successful attempt to reclaim, 52–54, 267–68
Poland: Jewish settlement in, 362n143, 363n145; murder cases in, 173–83; prayers, quarrel over leading, 173–79, 183, 275–76, 364n151; two murderers, distribution of responsibility of, 179–83, 189
polygamy, ban on, 218, 223
Popstilen, Mordechai, 228–36, 382n69, 383n71, 383n76
prayers: disruption of, as method of forcing community action, 210, 375n34; led by man causing unintentional death of newborn from circumcision, 145–49, 253, 283–84; murder resulting from quarrel over leading, 173–79, 183, 275–76, 364n151
preaching. *See* homilies and sermons
Priel, Yosef, 366n156
Priscus, murdered by Phatir, 115–16, 187, 189, 338–39nn1–2
prostitution and sexual transgression, 197–244; abused women resorting to, 192, 193; accusations and rumors of, 226–28, 377–78n46; cantor consorting with prostitutes, 197–200; children's suffering from parental immorality as persuasion against, 237, 238–44; Christian cleric selling stolen goods to visit prostitute, 60, 61, 202; defining and delineating, 201–5; divorce of husband for consorting with prostitutes, 200, 204; efforts to control prostitution, 206–8; gender-based double standard regarding, 204; gentiles, Jewish prostitutes and Jewish clients seeking sexual relations with,

199–200; governess associating with Jewish manservant, 195–96; government regulation of prostitution, 207, 232, 234–35, 383n75; infanticide and, 212, 214, 215, 219, 228, 240; Jewish men resorting to, 197–201; lineage insults involving mother/conception, 178, 225–28, 365n154, 366n157; nursing mother allowed to marry to prevent her involvement in prostitution, 228–36, 248, 254–55; organized sex industry, 231–36, 254–55; ownership of women, challenging, 233; punishments and penitential regimes, 209, 234–35, 237–38; repentance and change, motivations for, 236–44; *Sefer Ḥasidim* (Judah the Pious) on, 205–9; socioeconomic profile of, 262–63; suspicious pregnancy of Rabbi Shomil's wife belied by her reputation, 220–21; by women unable to marry legally, 221–26; *yibbum* and *ḥalitzah*, problems with, 221–26. *See also* Sara and Isaac case

Protestant Reformation, 19

punishment and penitential regimes: branding, as punishment for prostitution, 209, 234–35; Columbanus, penitential handbook of, 352n78; communal Jewish authorities, enforcement of punishment and expiation by, 178–79; communal Jewish authorities' inability to impose severe punishment, 11, 14, 16, 129–30, 131–32, 138–39, 157, 181, 345n37; corporal punishment, 16, 17, 29, 36, 44, 132, 166, 177, 181, 183, 234, 243, 261, 328n116; for death of infant, 249–53; fertility of women, penitential regimes protecting, 252–53, 388n114; guided penance, 351–52n75; for prostitution and sexual transgression, 209, 234–35, 237–38; *teshuvah*, 32, 237, 238. *See also* capital punishment; murder and murderers, punishment of

Purgatory, 144

purity, ritual, 128, 147–48, 284, 345n36, 352n79

Ra'avya (Eliezer ben Joel Halevi), 33n123, 346n43, 375n36

Raba, 36, 380n58

rabbis, scholars, and sages: *beit din* (rabbinic court), 11, 15, 57, 174; judicial and arbitrational authority of, 15–16; mediation of sources by, 30; pietistic differentiation of rabbis and *ḥakham* (sages), 326–27n103; preaching against theft, 103–7; responsa, as source material, 29–30. *See also specific individuals by name*

Rachel (nursing mother), 228–36, 248, 254–55, 382n69
Ramban (Nachmanides; Moses ben Nachman), 201, 209
Rami (Avraham Reiner), 351–52n75
ransom: of body of Meir b. Baruch of Rothenburg, 183–84; debt, hostage taking as means of guaranteeing, 316n41; kidnapping and violent death, 47, 49–52; of souls/bodies of murderers, 183–86
Rappaport, Shlomo (Shi"r), 316–17n43
Rashbam (Shmuel ben Meir), 353n83
Rashi (Shlomo Yitzhak/Shlomo ben Isaac), 45, 105, 201, 314n30, 322n65, 331n130, 372n16, 388n114
"reasonable man" standard, 356n100
red hair and lethal inclinations, 136
"red-handed," felons caught, 81, 328n116
Red Heifer, 390n1
Regensburg: books stolen and resold in, 98; expulsion of Jews from (1519), 85, 367n160; *fachwerkhaus* construction in, 328n114; grave of Judah the Pious as medieval pilgrimage site, 85; importance of Jewish community of, 367nn159–60; magic used to identify thieves and locate stolen possessions in, 86–90
Reiner, Avraham (Rami), 351–52n75
rekim, 332n137
religious objects: dysphemisms, use of, 78, 328n87; Jewish will and testament listing "improper book" (containing Christian religious material), 330n123; prohibition of purchase of stolen objects with Christian religious significance, 78–79; punishment by banishment of attempted theft from synagogue, 28–29, 108–13, 310n84; selling and pawning of Christian objects to Jewish merchants, 320n59; Winchester, England, theft of *etrog* from synagogue in, 113–14
repentance. *See* punishment and penitential regimes
responsa, as source material, 29–30, 38–39, 259
"Reuven," as standard alias for first party in responsa, 41
Richard of Devizes, 202, 374n24
Richards, Jeffery, 202
Ri ha-Zaken (Isaac ben Shmuel the Elder of Dampierre-Sur-Aube), 97, 352n75, 353n83
Rindfleisch riots (Nuremberg, 1298), 333n140, 356n96, 376n37
ritual murder accusations. *See* blood libel
ritual purity, 128, 147–48, 284, 345n36, 352n79
Ritva (Yom-Tov ben Avraham Asevilli/Ishbili): biographical information, 330n126; on book theft and *halakhah* on lost/found property, 94–97,

99, 100; on murder, 354n87; on synagogue theft, 108–13, 337n166
Rizba (Isaac ben Avraham), 151, 152, 353n83
Roman Catholicism. *See* Christianity/Church authorities
Rome, rabbis of, on treatment of murderers, 133–35, 279–80, 281–82
Rosh (Asher ben Yechiel): on book theft, 93, 191–92; on domestic abuse, 191–92, 245; *Hagahot Ashri* discussing, 333n143; synagogue theft, consulted on, 108, 110, 337n166
Roth, Pinchas, 171–72, 351–52n75, 372n12
Rousseaux, Xavier, 26
Rublack, Ulinka, 214, 243
Rudolf von Habsburg, 207
rural and suburban areas. *See* urban versus suburban/rural environments

St. Martial and Limoges, 122, 127, 342n20, 343n25
Salman of St. Goar, 220, 240–43
Samuel of Schlettstadt, 225
sanctuary/asylum, denied to murderers, 141–42, 278–79
Santiago de Compostela, pilgrimage routes to, 127, 344n34
Sara and Isaac case, 209–21, 295–97; father of Sara's desire to kill her, 212–13, 214, 219–20, 296–97, 378–79n50; infanticide charges, 212, 214, 215, 219; Isaac's view of, 209–10, 212, 295; Jewish women in community, view of, 214, 297, 377–78n46; legal analysis of, 216–19; marital law and divorce issues in, 210, 216–19; Meir of Rothenburg, referral to, 210–11, 295, 297; moral character of Sara, judgments of, 211–12, 214, 215–16; mother of Sara, view of, 213, 296; non-Jewish alleged father of Sara's child, 212–13, 215; referral to experts by community and regional authorities, 210–11, 213; Sara's view of, 210, 214, 221, 295–96; sexual promiscuity and pregnancy of Sara, rumors/evidence of, 209, 210, 212–13, 214, 217, 218, 220–21, 295–97; social analysis of, 219–21; socioeconomic profile of criminals and, 262; texts and voices in, 211–16
sardiot, 61, 322n65
Sati (mother of Avraham ben Yosef ben Palas), 109–11
Scholars in Their Time (Yuval), 225
Sefer Agudah (Alexander ben Süslin Hacohen), 200, 371–72n12
Sefer ha-Dinim (Judah ben Meir ha-Kohen), 58, 318–19n53
Sefer ha-Kavod, 85–86
Sefer ha-Mitzvot, 292, 294

Sefer Hasidim (Judah the Pious): on influence of non-Jewish society, 12; on murder, 12, 136, 137, 139, 141, 142, 187, 347n51, 353n85; on prostitution and sexual transgression, 205–9, 374n29; on theft, 71–77, 82–85

Sefer Maharil (Salman of St. Goar), 220

Sefer Mordechai (Mordechai ben Hillel), 225, 317n47, 372n12

Sefer Nitzahon Yashan/Nitzahon Vetus (The Old Book of Victory), 104

Sefer Rokeah (Elazar of Worms), 140

Sehok ben Astar and Limoges incident, 120–27, 271–74, 340n10, 341–42n16, 341nn13–14, 342n21

self-defense, 175–76, 183, 275–76, 368n165

self-mortification by murderers, 132, 139–40, 184

sermons. *See* homilies and sermons

servants, Jewish: governess associating with Jewish manservant, 195–96; male *paterfamilias* as in control of, 195; sexual abuse of maidservants, 230, 373n18; "son of a maidservant" as lineage insult, 366n157

servants/slaves, gentile: expelling/dismissing, 84, 326n100; limitation of Jewish contact with gentiles and, 82, 326n95; murders, ordered to perform, 153–54; "son of a maidservant or female slave" as lineage insult, 366n157; stealing from Jewish masters, 82–86

sexual transgression. *See* prostitution and sexual transgression

Shabtai ben Shmuel of Zeitz, 153–54, 155, 190, 291, 354n91

Shalom of Wiener Neustadt, 119, 154, 173–79, 183, 220, 275–76, 326n95

Shaltiel, Rabbi, and sons (in Sara and Isaac case), 211, 213, 217, 296, 376n39

Shamai, Rabbi, 57

shefikhut damim, 170

Sherira Gaon, 128–30, 138, 147, 283

"Shimon," as standard alias for respondent, 41

Shi"r (Shlomo Rappaport), 316–17n43

Shita Mekubetzet (Bezalel ben Avraham Ashkenazi), 101–2, 331n130, 334n146

Shlomo bar Shimshon, 263

Shlomo ben Aderet of Barcelona, 330n126, 334n150

Shlomo Shneur (Emericus Fortunatus/Imre Szerencses), 365n154

Shlomo Yitzhak/Shlomo ben Isaac (Rashi), 45, 105, 201, 314n30, 322n65, 331n130, 372n16, 388n114

Shmuel ben Isaac, 251

Shmuel ben Kalonymus the Pious, 71–74, 351n75

Shmuel ben Meir (Rashbam), 353n83

Shmuel ha-Katan, 164, 359n117

GENERAL INDEX   455

Shum communities, 78, 259, 324n84, 379n51. *See also* Mainz; Speyer; Worms
SIDS cases, 248–53
Siegfried I of Mainz (archbishop), 321n62
silver: misleading buyer about value of silver object, 65–67; qualities and grades, 66, 322–23n69
Simcha of Speyer, 244–45, 284
Simcha Or Zarua', 246
Simonson, Shlomo, 27
slaves and slavery: Jewish lack of involvement in slave trade, 325n93; male *paterfamilias* as in control of, 195. *See also* gentile servants/slaves
Solomon bar Simson (Shlomo ben Shimshon of Worms), 21, 303n32
Soloveitchik, Haym, 345n38
Spain. *See* Iberian peninsula
Speyer: rabbinic judicial and arbitrational authority in, 15; thieving, Jewish communal regulations on, 78
Spierenburg, Pieter, 26, 186–87, 190, 369n181
spinning, as respectable female activity, 207–8
stabilitas, medieval concept of, 121
stealing. *See* thieves and thieving
stepmothers, 248
Stow, Kenneth, 15
suburban and rural areas. *See* urban versus suburban/rural environments

suicide, 171, 172, 306n51, 362n138
supercommunal organizations, 16, 30, 55, 58, 158, 169, 216, 259, 317–18n47, 319n53, 375n35, 379n51
synagogues: *beit ha-Elohim* as term for, 342–43n22; circumcision of illegitimate children at, modification of rite for, 239–44; disruption of prayers in, as method of forcing community action, 210, 375n34; Limoges incident (992) and, 124, 274; ostracism of murderers in, 146–47, 148; prayers led by man causing unintentional death of newborn from circumcision, 145–49, 253, 283–84; preaching against theft in, 103–7; Priscus, murdered by Phatir on way to, 115–16, 338n1; punishment of attempted theft from, 28–29, 108–13, 261, 263, 310n84, 347n52; quarrel over leading prayers, murder resulting from, 173–79, 183, 275–76, 364n151; women's involvement in, 253

takanat ha-shuk (Market Stipulation), 14, 46, 57, 95, 98
takanot, 10, 16, 54, 80, 304n35
Takanot Shum, 78
Tamar, accused of harlotry, 208–9, 373n19

taxes: cheating on, 72, 73, 105, 259, 264; English Jews paying taxes directly to king, 357n105; Haim Eliezer Or Zarua' on payment of, 105–6; Jewish attitudes toward tax collectors, 164, 359n116; levied by Jewish communities to meet gentile assessments, 259; plunder economy and, 316n39; on prostitution, 207, 232, 234

Temple, destruction of, 120, 138–39, 271, 340n12, 344n35, 347–48n54, 359n117, 361n129

teshuvah, 32, 237, 238. *See also* punishment and penitential regimes

thieves and thieving, 35–114; actual thief versus others benefiting from theft, different treatment of, 37, 44, 46, 81–82, 262; change and opportunity in 10th-11th century Rhineland, 37–39; Christian religious significance, prohibition of purchase of stolen objects with, 78–79; communal Jewish regulations on, 77–81; fellow Jews, obligation to safeguard assets of, 105–7; gentiles, no obligation to return lost property or correct error of, 46, 62, 108; gentiles, prohibition on stealing from, 46, 62, 73–74, 79–81, 106; gentile victims/perpetrators, rabbinical treatment of, 46; historical insights about, 67–71; Jewish community, theft within and from, 107–13; lost/found property, *halakhah* on, 95–97; magic used to identify thieves and locate stolen goods, 85–90; magic used to steal, 35–36, 90–92; *metzi'ah* (find), goods regarded as, 53, 63; moral concerns, engagement/lack of engagement with, 45–46, 71–77, 80; as most common medieval crime, 36; preaching against, 103–7; riskiness of thieving lifestyle, 49–52, 67–68; "stolen goods privilege," 70

thieves and thieving, cases of: coats, partnership beween Jewish and gentile thieves to steal, 23, 44–45, 307n58; disappearance/death of Jewish merchant of stolen goods and remarriage of wife, 46–52, 265–66; extortion plot against Christian cleric selling stolen gold items to Jew, 58–63, 68, 69–70, 202, 269–70; lamb's wool taken by gentiles and sold to Jews for resale, 63–65; *ma'arufia* rights (exclusive Jew-gentile partnership), 39–46; misleading buyer about value of silver object, 65–67; pit, missing Jew found buried head first by thieves in, 162–63, 358–59n114; plundered goods, financial dispute over

successful attempt to reclaim, 52–54, 267–68; sunken barge, unlawful taking of recovered goods from, 54–58, 92; synagogue, punishment of attempted theft from, 28–29, 108–13, 310n84; "walking dead" stories about stolen land, gentile versus Jewish versions of, 74–77
thieves and thieving, types of, 36–37; armed versus unarmed robbery, 328n116; book theft, 92–103; burglary, 36–37; gentile servants/slaves stealing from Jewish masters, 82–86; highway crimes, 17, 36; petty theft versus grand larceny, 36; trafficking in stolen goods, 37, 46–47, 49–52
Thomas of Monmouth, *The Life and Passion of Saint William the Martyr of Norwich*, 6
Thuringia, books stolen from, 98
"time/hour of rage," murders committed in, 165–70, 260, 291–94, 361n134
Toch, Michael, 312n15, 325n93
Tosafot and Tosafists, 78, 94, 97, 182, 332–33n138, 333n144, 334n146, 352n75, 353n83
Tradition and Crisis (Katz), 151–52
Trent blood libel, 367n160
trial by ordeal: duel, trial by, 43, 124–25; Jewish exemption from, 14, 37, 43; Limoges incident and, 124–25; for thieves and robbers, 314n24

Truce (Peace) of God, 37–38, 69
Tzarfat. *See* France

Ulpian, 202
Urbach, Ephraim E., 332–33n138, 333n144
urban versus suburban/rural environments: concentration of Jews in urban areas, 17, 20; late medieval move of Jews to rural German communities, 19; murder rates and Jews as perpetrators/victims, 17–18; social status of Jews in urban society, 304–5n40; theft, commonness of, in urban environments, 36
Ursul (father-in-law of Milo of York), 160, 161, 289, 290

Via Lemovicensis, 127
Via Touronensis, 344n34
Vienna, prostitution in, 207
vigilantism, 89, 119, 155, 158, 165, 167, 357n104
violence: arson, habitual threats of, 154–55, 354n93; *gazam* and *alam*, 150, 174; in medieval society generally, 117–19, 150–51, 190; as normal social behavior, 116–17; women, as victims of domestic abuse, 93, 191–93, 195, 244–47, 370n4. *See also* anti-Jewish bias/violence; murder and murderers

viticulture, supplying credit to, 313–14n22
Vodola, Elisabeth, 354n88

Weber, Max, 118
Weil, Jacob, 170–73, 185–86, 361–62n137, 365n155, 366n157
weregeld/wergild, 140, 184, 348–49n60
Wilde, Oscar, 345n49
William of Norwich, 6
Willigis of Mainz, 320–21nn60–61
Winchester, England, theft of *etrog* from synagogue in, 113–14
Wissenschaft das Iudentums movement, 22–23, 316–17n43
women and crime: agency of women and, 253–55; *'agunah* (bound woman), 47–48, 163; book theft by woman in troubled marriage, 93, 191–92, 193; emotional responses of women and, 110, 197; fertility, penitential regimes protecting, 252–53, 388n114; gender roles and, 197; lineage insults involving mother/conception, 178, 225–28, 365n154, 366n157; marginalized individuals, women as, 196, 255; masculine construction of records and lack of female voice, 194–96, 197; methodological issues, 194–97; Milo of York, murder of wife of, 158–62, 190, 289–90; murder, males as main perpetrators and victims of, 190; petitioning of medieval Jewish courts by women, 110; pit, missing Jew accused of philandering found buried head first in, 162–63, 358–59n114; pustule-laden man beating wife, 192–93; rape, 17, 193; Sehok ben Astar and Limoges incident, 121, 122, 272; spinning, as respectable female activity, 207–8; twice-widowed women, popular beliefs about, 371n9; violent and abusive spouses, women as victims of, 93, 191–93, 195, 244–47, 370n4; witnesses in Jewish law, women not allowed as, 175. *See also* children; marriage and marital law; prostitution and sexual transgression
World of Our Fathers (Howe), 24
Worms: Jewish presence in, 39; *Memorbuch*, 311n7; rabbinic judicial and arbitrational authority in, 15; thieving, Jewish communal regulations on, 78

Yassif, Eli, 86, 340n9
Yechiel ha-Kohen, 246, 386n101
Yeḥiel of Paris, 227, 333n145
yibbum and *ḥalitzah*: conversion of brother-in-law, 224–26; defined, 380n55; illegitimacy of half-brother-in-law, 221–24

Yitzhak ben Avraham Medro, 108–13
Yohanan, Rabbi, 236–38
Yom-Tov ben Avraham Asevilli/Ishbili. *See* Ritva
Yuval, Israel, 27, 225

zekukim, 98, 333n139
Zimmer, Eric, 258–59
Zionist historiography, 22, 24
Zmora, Hillay, 186
znut and *zonah*, 201–5, 229, 373nn18–19

ABOUT THE AUTHOR

Ephraim Shoham-Steiner is professor of medieval Jewish history at Ben-Gurion University of the Negev in Be'ersheva Israel, where he is the director of the Center for the Study of Conversion and Inter-Religious Encounters (CSOC). He is the author of *On the Margins of a Minority: Leprosy, Madness, and Disability among the Jews of Medieval Europe* (Wayne State University Press, 2014) and the editor of Intricate *Interfaith Networks in the Middle Ages: Quotidian Jewish-Christian Contacts*.

CPSIA information can be obtained
at www.ICGtesting.com
Printed in the USA
LVHW100431200522
719221LV00005B/502